South Asian Perspectives in Mental Health and Psychology

Series Editors

S. M. Yasir Arafat, Bangladesh Specialized Hospital Limited, Dhaka, Bangladesh

Sujita Kumar Kar, Department of Psychiatry, King George's Medical University, Lucknow, India

This series of books is an endeavor to gather and present a comprehensive understanding of the various aspects of mental health that are relevant to people living in South Asia. The books aim to provide in-depth guidance and practical solutions to the mental health challenges that are unique to these areas. The content covers a wide range of topics, including but not limited to, climate change and its impact, prison mental health, perinatal mental health, social psychiatry, mental health and disorder among the elderly population, psychiatry education and training, suicide, SDGs and mental health, trauma, addiction, and social isolation. The books also emphasize the importance of early intervention and provide resources for seeking help. The ultimate goal of this series is to empower individuals and communities to take proactive steps toward enhancing their mental wellbeing. The proposed books will fill the existing unmet need in the region with huge populations in low and middle-income country (LMIC) settings.

South Asia, home to about 2 billion people, is a region of diverse cultures, languages, and religions. It caters to about 25% of the global population. This densely populated region faces a myriad of challenges, both natural and man-made. The frequent occurrence of natural disasters, such as earthquakes, floods, and landslides, threaten the lives and livelihoods of millions of people. War, terrorism, and political instability have caused significant disruptions to the region's socio-political fabric. Poverty, migration, and tropical infectious diseases remain major challenges that hinder progress towards sustainable development. Climate change exacerbates these challenges, causing widespread environmental degradation, food insecurity, and water scarcity. Despite these obstacles, South Asian people have shown remarkable resilience and strength in the face of adversity.

Mental health issues in the South Asian region significantly contribute to the global burden of mental illnesses. However, the region faces plenty of challenges such as high stigma, low mental health literacy, poor budgetary allocation, high out-of-pocket expense for mental health services, lack of adequate infrastructure, and limited human resources are significant barriers in mental healthcare. The majority of research on mental health issues is produced by the western countries which may not fit all in the South Asian culture, albeit evidence is needed to test. There is a paucity of research and evidence-based strategies that are region-specific. This series of books is an attempt to compile the important dimensions of mental health that will benefit the regional people.

Nilamadhab Kar • Sujita Kumar Kar
S. M. Yasir Arafat
Editors

Climate Change, Disaster and Mental Health in South Asia

Springer

Editors
Nilamadhab Kar
Psychiatry
Black Country Healthcare NHS
Foundation Trust
Wolverhampton, UK

Sujita Kumar Kar
Department of Psychiatry
King George's Medical University
Lucknow, India

S. M. Yasir Arafat
Bangladesh Specialized Hospital
Dhaka, Bangladesh

ISSN 3059-3646 ISSN 3059-3522 (electronic)
South Asian Perspectives in Mental Health and Psychology
ISBN 978-981-95-3689-4 ISBN 978-981-95-3690-0 (eBook)
https://doi.org/10.1007/978-981-95-3690-0

This Springer imprint is published by the registered company Springer Nature Singapore Pte Ltd.
The registered company address is: 152 Beach Road, #21-01/04 Gateway East, Singapore 189721, Singapore

Dedicated to our Parents
Harish Chandra Kar and Shantilata Kar
Late Mr. Minaketan Kar and Mrs.
Urmila Kar
Late S M Abdul Khaleq and Amena Begum

Preface

South Asia consists of eight low- and middle-income countries (LMICs). As a region, it is one of the most disaster prone areas of the world. Besides the increased frequency, disasters affect a large number of people in this area, as it is densely populated. The impact of the disasters is also considerably higher considering the scarcity of resources. Recent studies identified that LMICs are more affected by climate change than high-income countries. However, we know little about the mental health impact of frequent disasters like cyclones, river erosions, droughts, floods, and tsunamis and the long-term effects of climate change in South Asian countries. In addition to these natural disasters, human-made disasters are common too in these countries.

The mental health consequences of the disasters are not contained within the immediate post-disaster period; rather, they continue long-term. Ironically, despite the population affected usually being large, the information about the sequelae is scant. In addition, the support systems and resources for the survivors are not as robust as in the developed world. It appears that the enormity of the post-disaster mental health concerns is not adequately appreciated by the authorities in these countries, primarily because of a lack of information and inadequate or ineffective professional suggestions. It is so obvious that while the challenges continue, many survivors with mental health problems secondary to disasters are not recognized, treated, or rehabilitated appropriately. There is an urgent need to emphasize these aspects, especially in the South Asia region, considering its enhanced vulnerabilities.

We did not find any volume discussing disaster psychiatry and the impact of climate change in South Asia. This book will be the first of its kind to discuss the acute and chronic mental health impact of climate change and disasters in South Asia. It also identifies research gaps and gives recommendations for culturally appropriate disaster management in a resource-scarce region of South Asia. It examines the evidence to identify the currently available services for the mental health support of the disaster survivors in the region and suggests methods of their continued and appropriate support.

We started the book with a chapter overviewing the overall vulnerabilities of the South Asian population to disasters and attention to its mental health impact. Then we included the country-wise chapters. For each country, we followed a standard format introduction (introducing the country discussing why the country is prone to disasters), distribution of disasters and changes of climate parameters in the country, existing disaster response system, the mental health impacts of disasters and climate change, preparedness of disasters, lived experiences of people who have gone through climate disasters or some practical case studies, specialized trained human resources, educating materials (education material for public, training materials for disaster responders, material for mental health professionals working in disasters), mental health and disaster management, and preventive measures for mental health impacts due to climate change. We also highlighted country-specific disaster vulnerability, preparedness, research on assessment and interventions done in the countries, status of mental health intervention in their disaster management policy, if any, and suggestions, available research and gaps in it, current challenges in disaster mental health, and ways out. We discussed the public mental health aspects of disaster preparedness and climate change psychiatry in the region. This book will be helpful for clinicians, academics, researchers, health and social care authorities, government agencies, and non-governmental organizations working with climate change, disasters, and mental health. As mental health care needs to be blended with disaster support, disaster responders at all levels need to be aware of the mental health consequences of catastrophic trauma and be sensitive to the needs of the survivors.

Wolverhampton, UK — Nilamadhab Kar
Lucknow, India — Sujita Kumar Kar
Dhaka, Bangladesh — S. M. Yasir Arafat

Contents

About the Editors

Nilamadhab Kar MD, DNB, DPM, FRCPsych, is Consultant Psychiatrist in the Black Country Healthcare NHS Foundation Trust, Wolverhampton, UK. He is the College Tutor for undergraduate and postgraduate psychiatry training and the lead for the International Clinical Fellowship Programme in Psychiatry for the Trust. He is Honorary Professor of Psychiatry at the University of Wolverhampton, UK, and is a visiting Honorary Professor in the Faculty of Contemplative and Behavioural Sciences, Sri Sri University, India. His research contributions have been in the fields of geriatric psychiatry, stress-related mental health disorders, preventive psychiatry, disaster mental health, clinical psychopharmacology, and quality of life. Besides journal articles and book chapters, he has written and edited a few medical books, which include *Handbook of Dementia*, *Comprehensive Textbook of Sexual Medicine*, *Handbook for Disaster Workers*, and *Geriatric Psychiatry in South Asia*. He is the editor of the *Journal of Geriatric Care and Research* and is on the editorial board of several medical and literary journals. He is actively engaged in public education in mental health, regularly writes for newspapers and magazines, and conducts health-related talks and seminars.

Sujita Kumar Kar is currently working as Additional Professor of Psychiatry at King George's Medical University, Lucknow, Uttar Pradesh, India. He is the editor-in-chief of the *Indian Journal of Health, Sexuality and Culture*. He is also the editorial board member and reviewer of various national and international journals. He has written 74 book chapters and more than 500 articles in various national and international journals and made 70 presentations at various national and international conferences. He has been included in the global 2% researcher list released by Stanford University in 2021, 2022, 2023, and 2024. His research interests include brain stimulation, neuropsychiatry, and suicide prevention.

S. M. Yasir Arafat is currently working as Associate Consultant of Psychiatry at Bangladesh Specialized Hospital, Dhaka, Bangladesh. He is affiliated with Frontier University Garowe, Somalia, as Associate Professor; Bangladesh Academy of Sciences as Associated Fellow; and Dnet as Honorary Research Fellow, and he is also affiliated with the Biomedical Research Foundation, Bangladesh, as Senior Research Fellow. He was affiliated with the University of Bristol, UK, as Visiting Senior Research Associate (August 2021–2023). He completed his MD in Psychiatry from Bangabandhu Sheikh Mujib Medical University, Dhaka, and his MBBS from the Dhaka Medical College, Bangladesh. He also did an MPH in Health Economics and an MBA in Marketing. Dr. Arafat has (co)authored more than 350 peer-reviewed articles and more than 50 book chapters, and (co)edited more than 15 books with Springer. He has been included in the global 2% researcher list in 2021, 2022, and 2023. He is an editorial member of more than 10 leading journals in mental health, published by Elsevier, Wiley, Springer, and Taylor & Francis. His research is focused on mental health, suicidal behavior, psychometrics, panic buying, and psycho-sexual disorders.

List of Figures

List of Tables

Chapter 1
Disaster and Mental Health Vulnerabilities of South Asia: An Overview

Nilamadhab Kar, Sujita Kumar Kar, and S. M. Yasir Arafat

1 Introduction

South Asia consists of eight countries, i.e., Afghanistan, Bangladesh, Bhutan, India, Maldives, Nepal, Pakistan, and Sri Lanka, and all of them are low- and middle-income countries (LMICs) (World Bank, 2025; Arafat & Kar, 2024). It is the most populous area of the world, with a quarter of the world's population living here. The countries of the region have many similarities as well as dissimilarities (Arafat & Kar, 2024). One important similarity is disaster proneness.

In the outset it may be prudent to review various definitions of disaster. According to the World Health Organization "a disaster is a severe disruption, ecological and psychological, which greatly exceeds the coping capacity of the affected community." This suggests, disaster for one community may not be perceived as one by another (WHO, 1992). The United Nations International Strategy for Disaster

N. Kar (✉)
Department of Psychiatry, Black Country Healthcare NHS Foundation Trust, Wolverhampton, UK

Research Institute in Health Sciences, University of Wolverhampton, Wolverhampton, UK

Faculty of Contemplative and Behavioural Sciences, Sri Sri University, Cuttack, India
e-mail: n.kar@nhs.net

S. K. Kar
Department of Psychiatry, King George's Medical University, Lucknow, India

S. M. Y. Arafat
Department of Psychiatry, Bangladesh Specialized Hospital, Dhaka, Bangladesh

Department of Public and Community Health, Faculty of Medicine and Health Sciences, Frontier University Garowe, Garowe, Somalia

N. Kar et al. (eds.), *Climate Change, Disaster and Mental Health in South Asia*, South Asian Perspectives in Mental Health and Psychology,
https://doi.org/10.1007/978-981-95-3690-0_1

Reduction (UNDRR) defines it as "A serious disruption of the functioning of a community or a society at any scale due to hazardous events interacting with conditions of exposure, vulnerability and capacity, leading to one or more of the following: human, material, economic and environmental losses and impacts" (UNDRR, 2017). The Disaster Management Act 2005 of Government of India defines disaster as "a catastrophe, mishap, calamity or grave occurrence in any area, arising from natural or manmade causes, or by accident or negligence which results in substantial loss of life or human suffering or damage to, and destruction of, property, or damage to, or degradation of, environment, and is of such a nature or magnitude as to be beyond the coping capacity of the community of the affected area" (Government of India, 2005).

Disaster is a multidimensional construct with ecological, economic, material, psychological, and social components, but not all may be affected in any one event. In the context of a medical disaster, it can be defined as an emergency situation in which the victims are so numerous that the treatment needs far outweigh the resources available (WHO, 1992).

There are frequent disasters of different kinds in the South Asia region due to various reasons, such as geography, climate change, and geopolitical situations. A large proportion of the population in this region is economically compromised due to the socioeconomic status and enduring income disparity persists in the countries. There are issues related to disaster preparedness, inadequate disaster response mechanisms, scarce trauma-care and psychotherapeutic facilities, and social support. So, disasters in these areas affect a large number of people. Additionally, the region pertains to pre-disaster vulnerabilities that intensify the economic and health-related consequences. Similarly, post-disaster readiness of rescue and relief operations and resources for immediate and long-term post-disaster interventions are not optimal. A few specific vulnerabilities for post-disaster mental health problems are depicted below, with suggestions for their management.

2 Disasters in South Asia

The South Asia region stretches from Afghanistan to India and has a varied geography, from deserts to ice-clad mountains, forests, river basins, and long coastal lines. The region is prone to tectonic activities; earthquakes and tsunamis have been commonly reported. Examples of various disasters experienced by the region are given in Table 1.1.

Table 1.1 Notable disasters in South Asia

Type	Examples
Cyclone	1970, Bhola Cyclone, Bangladesh; 1999, Super-cyclone, Odisha; 2007, Sidr, Bangladesh and India; 2009, Aila, Bangladesh; 2020, Amphan; 2024, Dana, India
Drought	1999–2002, Pakistan; 2008–9 Nepal; 2018 Afghanistan; 2014–2015 India; periodically in Bangladesh
Floods	Annual monsoon flooding in India; 1988, 1998, 2024, Bangladesh; 2022, 2025, Pakistan; periodically in Sri Lanka
Tsunami	2004, South Asia tsunami
Landslides	2018, 2024, Kerala; 2024 Nepal
Earthquake	1993, Latur; 2001, Gujarat; 2004, Sumatra, India, Sri Lanka, Maldives; 2015, Nepal, 2025, Afghanistan
Industrial disaster	1984, Bhopal Gas disaster; 2012, Garment Factory fire, Pakistan; 2013, Rana Plaza Collapse, Bangladesh
Rail accidents	1981, Manasi, Bihar; 1995, Firozabad, Uttar Pradesh; 1999, Gaisal, West Bengal; 2023, Balasore, Odisha
Ethnic conflict	Sri Lanka (Sinhalese and Tamil), Pakistan (between Pashtuns, Baluchis, Mohajirs, and Sindhis), North-East India (Nagas, Mizos, Bodos, and Assamese), Kashmir, Bangladesh (Hill tracks); Rohingya, political violence, Bangladesh
Terrorism	1991, Punjab; 1993, 2006, 2008, Mumbai; 2014, Peshawar; 2019, Pulwama; 2025, Pahalgam; periodically in Pakistan; Holey Artisan event, 2016, Bangladesh
Aviation disasters	1996, Charkhi Dadri; 2000, Patna; 2010, Mangalore; 2018, Kathmandu; 2020, Calicut; 2025, Ahmedabad; 2025, Uttara, Dhaka

The list is not exhaustive (Azeem et al., 2023; Kafle et al., 2023; Kumar et al., 2023; Mir & Ahmed, 2020; Murthy, 2014; Wikipedia, 2025)

2.1 Extreme Weather Events

South Asia is home to many large rivers, where floods are almost annual incidences, affecting huge numbers of people, especially in Bangladesh, India, and Pakistan. In fact, the South Asia region is one of the most flood-vulnerable regions of the world (Mirza, 2011). There are instances of other natural events, such as cloud bursts and landslides, which impact life. A large part of the agricultural system depends upon the monsoon, so any changes in weather systems, with more or less rain, lead to droughts or floods, affecting the economy and causing hardships. Floods cause extensive damage to rice crops in the region, threatening food security, especially for poorer sections of the population (Hossain et al., 2021; Mirza, 2011).

Along with these, there are cyclones, which regularly affect the coastal areas of this region. There are usually two to three tropical cyclones that make landfall in India each year. Cyclones are associated with massive damage to properties, and cultivation, increase food insecurity, economic problems, and moderate to severe psychological problems (Hossain et al., 2021).

2.2 Climate Change

Many disasters have their root in climate change (Ansari & Kar, 2024; Padhy et al., 2015). It has been regarded as the cause of more frequent cyclones, floods, glacier melting, and resultant floods (Azeem et al., 2023). Droughts are common too in South Asian regions and are linked to climate change secondary to rising temperatures (Kafle et al., 2023). The impact of climate change is being felt more and more frequently.

Climate change is making the population more vulnerable (Hossain et al., 2020; Wahid et al., 2024). Most of the South Asia region depends upon the climate for cultivation, livelihood, and ultimately socioeconomic status (Jena et al., 2025; Kabir et al., 2016). It is common to see poverty, debt, economic migration, and a decrease in economic status following extreme weather events (Hossain et al., 2020). It is obvious that climate change also affects the health of the population in various ways (Kabir et al., 2016). When the livelihood and social systems are pressured by climate change, it has been predicted that it may increase vulnerability and risk to both human and state security through violence, crime, smuggling, banditry, trafficking, terrorism, and other such activities (Jasparro & Taylor, 2008). In addition, social pathologies, such as increased crime, corruption, gender-based violence, sex crimes, and trafficking, become more prevalent in economically compromised populations (Azad & Khan, 2015).

Climate change has significant adverse psychological effects and is linked to mental health issues, specifically anxiety, depression, and stress-related disorders (Wahid et al., 2024). Evidence suggests the close association of climate change with common mental health issues, such as anxiety, depression, stress, addictive behavior, suicidal behavior, and adjustment disorder (Ansari & Kar, 2024; Padhy et al., 2015).

2.3 Industrial Accidents

Industrial disasters have been reported frequently in this region: commonly fire, industrial accidents, etc. There are many factories, mines, and construction projects running in this region; however, workplace-related safety probably remains a concern in most settings.

A major industrial accident in the region is the Bhopal gas disaster (Murthy, 2014), which is well known, and its impacts are still being felt. The mental health presentations included fatigue, anxiety, irritability, difficulty in concentration, and difficulty in decision-making (Murthy, 2014). There were also reports of neuroses, anxiety states, and adjustment reactions within 6 months, and later, there were neurobehavioral effects of impaired associative learning, motor speed, and precision, besides impacts on other systems (Broughton, 2005). Besides death and disabilities, improper management and inadequate compensation are contributing to the psychological stress of the survivors (Broughton, 2005).

Similarly, road and rail accidents are common and sometimes have devastating consequences, with a huge number of people being affected (Kar, 2023b; Kar et al., 2025; Wikipedia, 2025). There is a series of major rail accidents in the region, and it appears many of them were preventable. Besides human factors, technological upgrades may help prevent many rail accidents in the region.

A large number of people die in road and rail accidents each year, and many have life-changing injuries. As a result, many survivors have not only disabilities but also anxiety, depression, post-traumatic stress disorder (PTSD), phobias, etc. (Arora et al., 2021; Kar et al., 2025). Some of the causes include a lack of a robust system for checking the driving licenses, drunk driving, the state of the roads, etc., or a lack of implementation of the existing systems. There is an urgent need to improve the safety of roads to prevent a lot of deaths and suffering.

Rapid industrialization, poorly regulated work environments, lack of resources, and a lack of knowledge and attitude to improve workplace safety are some of the possible factors behind industrial disasters. Most of these can be addressed with adequate attention to the grave issue of preventable deaths and disabilities.

2.4 *Conflicts and Terrorism*

Politically, most of the regions of South Asia have remained perturbed for a long period. It has seen wars, internal armed conflicts, riots, religious and ethnic conflicts, large-scale displacements, migrations, military rules, increasing terrorism, etc. Geopolitical unrest has become a constant feature in these areas. These human-caused disasters, along with their uncertainties, have affected people over the years, which have been extremely stressful.

The region has experienced major public unrest and riots, which have led to the deaths and disabilities of thousands of people and increased fear and anxiety in the general population. In the last few decades, terrorism has become common, and more frequent incidences have been reported. Some examples are terror attacks such as the 1993 bomb blasts in Mumbai, the 2008 attack in Mumbai, terrorism in Kashmir, ethnic violence in Manipur, Balochistan, and Sri Lanka, political violence in Bangladesh, etc. (Balasinorwala & Shah, 2010; Islam et al., 2025; Joseph & Jaswal, 2014; United Nations, 2025). The psychological impact of these events is massive on the victims; however, there is hardly any literature depicting these or any specific support provided. On a positive note, following conflict resolution, in Northern Sri Lanka, prospects of return migration and optimism in displaced people have been shown to have decreased the prevalence of common mental disorders (Siriwardhana et al., 2015).

2.5 Pandemics and Epidemics

Recently, the mental health vulnerability of the region to disasters was obvious in the face of the COVID-19 pandemic due to the challenges like an inadequate workforce, malfunctioning referral system, and low budget (Arafat et al., 2024; Kabir et al., 2023; Arafat & Kar, 2024). Besides the huge number of deaths directly linked to the COVID-19 infection, a considerable proportion of these were due to inadequate facilities. There were many associated stressors, such as job loss, occupational issues, financial problems, social isolation due to lockdown, etc. In addition, there were stigma, misinformation, and a lack of effective mechanisms to improve awareness of the general population. It was apparent that the psychosocial support system crumbled. This led to many people experiencing diagnosable mental illnesses (Kar et al., 2021a). Although situations were similar the world over, many regions of South Asian countries suffered because of preexisting inadequate resources, improper and lack of coordination by the health and government agencies, and dwindling reliance on the latter by the public (Kar et al., 2023).

Vulnerable groups included economically marginalized people, women, and older adults (Girdhar et al., 2020; Mishra et al., 2020). There were increased reports of domestic abuse and elder abuse (Rina et al., 2020) during the pandemic. Despite learning from previous epidemics and pandemics, even from the first wave of COVID-19, it appears there were continued barriers in managing the second wave, which resulted in multiple deaths and increased trauma for the survivors. The barriers included the limitations of the public health system, and inadequate mobilization or use of available resources (Ransing et al., 2021). This highlighted that effective disaster-related crisis management requires a robust coordinated system that is supported by the appropriate input from the health and social services.

3 Regional Vulnerabilities

3.1 High Density of Population

Around a quarter of the total world population lives in South Asia (Arafat & Kar, 2024). Any major natural event affects a large number of people in these countries, because of the density of the population in many areas. In most of the disasters due to natural events a huge number of people get simultaneously affected, running into millions sometimes. In addition to the number of affected people, a lack of communication to reach these survivors in time, because of disasters such as floods, washed away roads and rail links, and inadequate communication systems pre-disaster, increases the disaster impact in these challenging geographical regions. This affects the timely rescue and relief efforts. The longer people remain in a crisis situation, the greater the risk of negative outcomes.

Besides natural events, there are many human-caused events that are associated with a massive number of people being present. Stampedes at religious congregations and political rallies are a frequent occurrence. This is extremely appalling, considering that these avoidable disastrous incidences keep happening because of a lack of proper infrastructure and crowd management methods. Religious gatherings during the COVID-19 pandemic are an example of how the mass congregation and spread of infection posed a threat and created significant challenges for the government and health systems (Kar et al., 2020, 2021b; Quadri & Padala, 2021).

Any existing support system would get too stretched to meet the demands of post-disaster psychological support. This warrants appropriate pre-disaster preparedness, improvement of existing systems, and a plan how to handle the increased demands during and after a disastrous situation. Establishing and improving local resources, and volunteers as disaster responders and workers, may help.

3.2 Economically Compromised

Although all the countries of the region remain in the LMICs bracket, there is great variation in the economic standards among the South Asian countries (Arafat & Kar, 2024). As disaster preparations and management require a lot of resources, this is a particularly relevant issue for these countries, which experience massive resource loss in each disaster, and building back infrastructures and support systems requires a lot of economic investment.

Pre-disaster economic vulnerability makes it difficult to cope with the trauma of the disasters, with massive destruction to property and livelihood. An economically compromised state in the pre-disaster period jeopardizes appropriate support and recovery of the affected individuals and the region.

The main source of income for a great proportion of the people in this region is agriculture, and most of the region is dependent on monsoon rain for cultivation. Agriculture gets affected by floods, cyclones, and draughts almost every year. This leads to economic hardships, debt, poverty, economic migration, and crimes. Damage to agriculture considerably weakens the prospects of recovery in the post-disaster period. As an example of the impact, farmers' suicide in many parts of India remains a major concern (Kannuri & Jadhav, 2021; Merriott, 2016). It has been suggested that the cause of these suicides is mostly economic rather than psychosocial (Memdani et al., 2024), suggesting state intervention as the primary preventive method (Sathyanarayana Rao et al., 2017).

3.3 Inadequate Infrastructure for Disaster Response

Inadequate infrastructure and connectivity continue to be major issues delaying timely support to disaster-hit areas. There are areas with massive issues of approach even in usual times, in hilly, mountainous areas, areas in river basins, etc. Along with that, there are issues during floods, landslides, or earthquakes when roads are damaged. In the background of an inadequate communication facility for far-flung areas and difficult terrains, earthquake or flood-related disasters lead to communication cutoffs, which make rescue and relief operations extremely difficult.

Rapid disaster response teams are gradually being set up in the South Asian countries. For example, India has enacted the Disaster Management Act and formed the National Disaster Management Authority (NDMA) (Deshpande, 2022). Similar initiatives are also being taken in Bangladesh (Government of Bangladesh, 2020) and other countries. Various strategies to address mental health and psychosocial support following major disasters have been suggested (Nahar et al., 2014; Tasdik Hasan et al., 2020). Regional cooperation in disaster management, in terms of both technical and relief-related support through the established teams, and sharing relevant information by the governments would be really helpful.

3.4 Inadequate Healthcare Resources

Many disasters lead to physical trauma requiring immediate, specific expert-based treatment, which often includes complex surgeries, life-sustaining support, and long-term medical care. Otherwise, these lead to deaths and long-term life-changing disabilities. However, trauma centers and these facilities are scarce in these countries. When these are available, treatment costs become another hurdle for many survivors who have to pay for these treatments themselves. Government support when available is usually limited.

A major part of post-disaster support is psychological care for the affected survivors. There have been many examples of mental health support following disasters (Kar, 2006; Murthy et al., 2003), but these are patchy and short-term, and are hugely inadequate for the population affected. Most of the time, post-disaster support is limited to financial assistance from governments, which is too minuscule in contrast to the degree of resource loss. In essence, the mental health support system for the mass survivors is not appreciably well developed and integrated in South Asian countries, and there is a major scope for development in this area.

Many regions of South Asia have inadequate facilities for mental healthcare, with a lack of appropriately trained personnel and resources, even during the usual, noncrisis period (Arafat & Kar, 2024). Following disasters, the needs go up considerably, and usually available resources cannot match up. Besides the facilities, other factors also hinder psychosocial care. These include lack of awareness, stigma, and the willingness of the affected people to engage in psychological support. These factors make the population more vulnerable. All these suggest the challenges to integrating and providing care in post-disaster situations and developing innovative ways to meet the demands of a large disaster-affected population.

3.5 Scarce Social Care Support

The social care aspects of the communities in South Asian countries are not robust. Disasters lead to many vulnerable survivors with an increasing need for social, occupational, and financial support. Many have lifelong disabilities that need relevant support for independent functioning. It is often seen that after the acute phase of the disaster is over, the plight of the survivors is usually sidetracked, often with other evolving crises. It takes a long time for people who have lost their earning family members or have injury-related disabilities to recover. It would require a lot of support from families, communities, and the state. This kind of support is not adequately coordinated, and there is an acute need for that.

4 Mental Health Impacts

There are many studies in the region following different kinds of disasters that report that a huge proportion of affected people have diagnosable stress-related psychiatric disorders. For example, the proportions of survivors with probable psychiatric disorder were 80.4% following the Odisha super-cyclone (Kar et al., 2004) and 23.2% after a fire in an urban slum (Desai et al., 2004). Even after 4.5 years of the Asian tsunami, 77.6% of survivors had psychiatric morbidity (Kar et al., 2014). In all these presentations, comorbidity was common. Proportions of survivors with specific disorders have been high as well such as PTSD (74%), major depression (89%), generalized anxiety disorder (GAD) (42%), and panic disorder (28%) following the Latur earthquake (Kar, 2000).

Mental health problems usually studied in the post-disaster scenarios include anxiety, depression, and PTSD; however, there are many other kinds of mental health conditions that have been reported as well. Commonly reported psychiatric illnesses among the survivors following disasters in South Asia are provided in Box 1.1, which are similar to other parts of the world. In addition, a large proportion of survivors also suffer from subclinical or subsyndromal mental health problems including subclinical PTSD (Kar et al., 2007; Math et al., 2008).

Box 1.1. Common Post-Disaster Mental Health Conditions
Acute stress reaction
Adjustment disorder
Complicated bereavement
Depressive disorders
Generalized anxiety disorder
Panic disorder
Phobia
Posttraumatic stress disorder
Prolonged grief reaction
Sleep disorders
Somatoform disorders
Substance use disorder
Suicidality

4.1 Mental Health Conditions

Depression as a post-disaster manifestation is common considering multiple traumatic experiences, directly and indirectly, associated with disasters (Desai et al., 2004; Kar et al., 2004; Karim et al., 2024; Mostafizur Rahman et al., 2023). Anxiety disorders are common too following disasters and have been reported by various studies (Kar, 2006; Kar & Bastia, 2006; Karim et al., 2024; Mostafizur Rahman et al., 2023). The most commonly studied one is generalized anxiety disorder. Acute stress reaction has also been reported as an immediate aftermath of disaster (Balasinorwala & Shah, 2010).

PTSD has been culturally validated in this region (Kar et al., 2007) in the post-disaster scenarios. It is a commonly studied condition and has been reported in survivors (Kar, 2000; Kar et al., 2004, 2007; Kar & Bastia, 2006; Karim et al., 2024; Math et al., 2008). The prevalence proportions of PTSD vary considerably, depending upon the nature and degree of trauma and survivor vulnerabilities.

Various other mental health conditions have been reported in post-disaster mental health studies in South Asia, such as phobia, panic disorder, adjustment disorder (Math et al., 2008), prolonged grief reaction (Rajkumar et al., 2015), complicated bereavement, somatoform disorders (Desai et al., 2004), etc. Suicidal behavior is reported to be increased in the community following the disasters (Kar, 2010b; Karim et al., 2024; Mamun et al., 2021), which could be secondary to the traumatic experience, resource loss, inability to cope effectively, and mental health conditions.

Increase in substance use (Kar, 2006) and deterioration in existing substance use disorders are common in the post-disaster period. Sleep problems (Karim et al., 2024), and nightmares (Majumder et al., 2024) have been reported, too, which is understandable considering changes following the disasters, especially those involved with evacuations and displacements, in addition to symptoms of other psychiatric disorders. These psychiatric disorders usually manifest in the acute stage but may evolve later and continue long-term.

Along with mental disorders, there are many psychosocial maladies observed following the stressful experience of disasters and their aftereffects. Gender-based crimes, domestic abuse, and elder abuse (Mostafizur Rahman et al., 2023; Rina et al., 2020) have been reported.

4.2 Mental Health Vulnerability Factors

Studies in South Asia have identified many factors that increase the risk of psychiatric illnesses in survivors in the post-disaster period. The degree of vulnerability in this region is exemplified by the observation that Bangladesh has the highest natural disaster mortality rate in the world (Nahar et al., 2014). A systematic review identified over 50 risk factors for mental health outcomes following extreme weather events in South Asia, which were categorized into demographic, economic, health, disaster exposure, psychological, and community factors (Patwary et al., 2024).

Many sociodemographic risk factors have been repeatedly reported as risk factors contributing to post-disaster psychiatric disorders. Children and adolescents have been observed to be a vulnerable group (Kar et al., 2004; Majumder et al., 2024), alongside older adults (Kar et al., 2004; Suar et al., 2024), in many studies conducted in this region. More than a third (37.9%) of adolescents had psychiatric morbidity around a year after the 1999 super-cyclone (Kar & Bastia, 2006). Women have been reported to have higher risk in most studies (Acharya Pandey et al., 2023; Asim et al., 2019; Fatema et al., 2021; Pyari et al., 2012; Rajkumar et al., 2013), except a few (Mathew et al., 2021).

Lower educational level (Acharya Pandey et al., 2023; Fatema et al., 2021; Kar et al., 2014; Karim et al., 2024; Rajkumar et al., 2015), lower and middle socioeconomic status (Asim et al., 2019; Fatema et al., 2021), and unemployment are also contributing factors for mental illness in the post-disaster period. Similarly, financial crisis after disaster is also associated with mental health problems (Asim et al., 2019; Fatema et al., 2021; Karim et al., 2024).

Various disaster-related factors have been identified as risk factors for psychiatric illnesses. They are the severity of the disaster and degree of exposure (Fatema et al., 2021; Kar et al., 2004, 2014; Silwal et al., 2022) and the need for evacuation and displacement (Kar et al., 2022; Karim et al., 2024). Damage to home (Kar et al., 2022; Kumar et al., 2023), loss of livelihood and livestock (Kar et al., 2014; Karim et al., 2024), and financial losses (Rajkumar et al., 2013) contribute too.

Physical injury during disaster to self or family (Dyster-Aas et al., 2012; Fatema et al., 2021; Karim et al., 2024; Pyari et al., 2012; Rajkumar et al., 2013), death in the family (Fatema et al., 2021; Karim et al., 2024), death of children, and spouse (Rajkumar et al., 2015) are significant risk factors.

Specific observations in the mental state during the disaster have been associated with an increased risk of mental illness later, e.g., fear of death, a feeling of helplessness, seeing dead bodies (Kar et al., 2025), perceiving disaster as stressful, etc. In addition, a lack of adequate post-disaster psychological support may contribute. Several coping measures are used by people to deal with their distress related to disasters. Religious coping is a strategy that is common in this region and is significantly influenced by sociocultural factors. Positive religious coping is found to be an effective measure to deal with stress during large-scale disasters (Fatima et al., 2022).

The preexisting vulnerabilities contribute massively to the mental health impact of the disaster trauma. These include preexisting mental illness (Asim et al., 2019), family conflicts, physical disabilities (Karim et al., 2024), etc. Following the disaster, stressors related to the so-called "second disaster" contribute too toward mental health problems.

In conflict-ridden displaced populations, food insecurity, lower social support availability, and social isolation have been observed to be associated with lower resilience (Siriwardhana et al., 2015). In a study following the tsunami, the absence of fear of recurrence of the tsunami, satisfaction with services received, and receiving counseling services more than three times were found to be protective factors against PTSD (Pyari et al., 2012).

5 Managing Vulnerabilities

5.1 Public Education

Public education is a key intervention that can be provided for various subject areas relevant to disasters. Starting with disaster preparedness, following pre-disaster advice including evacuation, displacement, seeking help, engaging with any crisis management, knowing about stress responses, stress management by self, seeking professional help when required, etc. This can be done by governments, health establishments, and the media channels. Public education can be provided through various means, in the form of booklets in the local language, social media, electronic and print media, etc. The topic can cover disasters, the stress effects, how to prepare for these, and how to take care of oneself in stressful situations.

5.2 Pre-disaster Alarm Systems

As most extreme weather events, such as cyclones, floods, tsunamis, and droughts, can be predicted and there can be some time for preparedness, it is important to improve the pre-disaster alert systems, which will help decrease the impact of trauma through multiple proactive actions by individuals and the authorities. Similarly, regular safety checks in the industries, fire safety, and warnings about troubled areas can be really helpful.

5.3 Pre-disaster Support

Once a disaster is predicted, a lot of measures can be taken to minimize the impact. This may involve evacuation, displacement, protecting the vulnerable individuals appropriately, etc. As an example, pre-cyclone management in Odisha, India, has been successful in decreasing the loss of life and injury risks considerably. Compared to the 1999 super-cyclone, the deaths in subsequent cyclones have been significantly lower. The Odisha model of a coordinated proactive approach to disaster management by the authorities (Mishra, 2023) has been applauded by various agencies. This model can be implemented in all the flood and cyclone-prone areas.

5.4 Robust Immediate Post-Disaster Response

Providing rescue and relief and medical treatment for the injured soon after the disaster is an important activity that can decrease the trauma impact. These can be facilitated by well-trained rescue teams and technological support. For specific situations, there is a need for support from outside technical teams, and for these reasons, regional and international coordination is extremely important to save lives. Besides search and rescue, relief measures must address other urgent post-disaster acute needs. Improving local resources and emboldening healthcare facilities can also be helpful.

5.5 Post-Disaster Trauma Care

Some of the disaster survivors with complicated injuries often have to travel long distances to get appropriate trauma care and support. This delay may increase the chance of disabilities and even fatalities. This is the situation in most areas of South Asian countries. Disabilities impact functionality and working ability and secondarily lead to economic problems and dependency in the long term, which affect mental health. It is essential that post-disaster trauma care facilities are available for needy survivors timely. Local facilities may expedite care and support and improve the chance of survival with a lesser degree of disabilities.

5.6 *Effective Communication*

During and immediately after a disaster crisis, effective communication plays an important role in the response. Often, railroad connectivity is lost, especially following weather-related extreme events, earthquakes, etc. It is important to reach the survivors as quickly as possible. In addition, reestablishing tele-communication and providing information and assurance to survivors are extremely important. In fact, this remains the only lifeline and reassuring source of rescue in extremely disastrous situations.

Besides connecting with the affected population, inter-team communication, and interaction between the central team and the ground-level disaster responders/workers are important to maintain, monitor progress, and support the disaster work. Any communication gap, which is rather frequent, creates problems regarding effective disaster support work. Communication processes and systems should be prioritized and set up early, and any issues should be addressed as soon as possible.

5.7 *Responsible Media*

Supporting public education, timely on-the-ground reports, sharing information, and helpful advice to the public is important. It is important for the media to circulate accurate, verified information. In the day of social media, it is essential that people understand that there is a chance of misinformation in the media, and the need to refrain from reacting to that before verification. Rumors, misinformation, and fake news are additionally stressful during the crisis period of disasters.

It has been seen that during periods of disaster, there is a scarcity of essential things needed in the household due to supply failure, increased demand, or decreased production, which results in panic buying and hoarding behavior (Arafat et al., 2020a, b). Responsible media reporting, adequate disaster preparedness, and educating the public not to worry excessively may prevent panic buying behavior observed during disasters (Arafat et al., 2021).

5.8 Screening for Mental Health Problems

One of the methods of decreasing the secondary impact of the trauma is through screening the affected people and identifying the vulnerable who may develop psychiatric problems (Kumar et al., 2023). This can be done by the initial disaster responders. The intervention for the identified vulnerable groups of people can be prioritized, which may prevent psychiatric consequences from developing later.

5.9 Acute and Long-Term Psychological Support

Psychosocial support for disaster survivors is feasible during the acute post-disaster state as crisis management, psychological first aid (Sathyanarayana Rao, 2004), and later, more specific support for those who have psychiatric illnesses. There have been many examples of support following catastrophic natural events (Kar, 2006; Math et al., 2008; Murthy et al., 2003), railroad accidents (Swain et al., 2025), and industrial disasters (Murthy, 2014).

Psychological support can be provided in various ways. Community outreach clinics, group therapies, and art therapies (Math et al., 2008) have been tried. Telepsychotherapy (Swain et al., 2025) and Internet-based care involving information, counseling, and therapy are other options. There are feasible methods to organize post-disaster psychological intervention and rehabilitation that can be organized, coordinated, and integrated into existing care systems (Kar, 2024a). The interventions must be culture-specific and sensitive, taking into account local belief systems related to the meaning of the disasters.

5.10 Community-Based Care

The psychological support in the post-disaster period should be community-based to address the needs of a huge number of people. It is known that most would cope with the trauma with appropriate support and a smaller proportion would need referral for professional help.

In the community, support through health workers, primary care professionals, and support in schools can be provided. Local volunteers from nongovernmental organizations can be trained to provide care in the form of stress management and counseling (Kar, 2006; Murthy et al., 2003). Training ground-level health and social workers and primary care professionals can be helpful strategies. Establishing a robust referral system and understanding when to refer the survivors for professional help helps manage the complex clinical scenarios with risks.

5.11 Long-Term Follow-Up and Support When Needed

Most people recover from trauma-related mental health problems. However, many do not, without appropriate intervention, and the sequel may continue for long periods. However, this is an area that is not adequately studied in the region. It is essential that those who develop psychiatric problems should be adequately treated and followed up as needed. These survivors should be identified and referred by community-level volunteers and primary-level health and social care professionals. In addition, public education regarding stress symptoms and management might help family caregivers to help and seek appropriate help as required.

Some survivors with disabilities will require long-term support in the form of psychosocial and occupational rehabilitation. There have been only a few reports of psychosocial rehabilitation (Masood et al., 2021).

5.12 National Strategies to Incorporate Post-Disaster Mental Healthcare

It is important to incorporate and prioritize mental health intervention issues in the post-disaster scenarios in the national strategies. In recent years, there has been an appreciable change in the disaster management strategy at the state and national levels, which has led to a decreased impact of the disasters (Jha et al., 2016). However, healthcare infrastructures, especially those for mental health, are already stretched and struggle to cope with increased demands following disasters (Deshpande, 2022; Sharma, 2023). National strategies for disaster management should specify roles and responsibilities of all concerned related to mental healthcare for disaster survivors, provide pathways of care from community to specialized settings, mark out available psychosocial care from crisis support to professional support, and rehabilitation. In addition, these strategies should be adequately funded.

5.13 Regional Cooperation

This is an extremely important area as most disasters affect neighboring regions and information sharing, and sharing technical resources for timely rescue and relief are of great value. Climate change-related extreme weather events affect neighboring countries, so collaboration related to planning, supportive methods, and management is essential. Bangladesh, Bhutan, and India have been proactive in having disaster risk reduction and climate change adaptation policies (Mall et al., 2019). More such regional initiatives are warranted.

6 Research Needs

There is an obvious lack of research on disaster mental health in South Asia, specifically in comparison to the frequency, intensity, and impact of severe weather events, human-caused disasters, and industrial accidents in the region. This is particularly evident in many geopolitical areas. While there are a few studies following severe weather events, there are hardly any on various other types of disasters, especially human-caused disasters, ethnic conflicts, riots, and terrorism. In addition, South Asia has a complex, tumultuous history of invasions, wars, colonization, partitions, and ongoing sociopolitical challenges, which are linked to intergenerational trauma (Shah et al., 2024). Its impact on the population, trauma transmission in biopsychosocial pathways, its influence on trauma vulnerability, and psychosociocultural manifestations are hardly studied.

Most of the disaster mental health studies have been done following the acute post-disaster stage. There is a massive gap in research on long-term consequences and prevalence. In this connection, it is known that many secondary traumas are commonly associated with disasters, which make the post-disaster scenarios more complex for individual survivors. Each of them may have unique challenges, and those need to be understood and supported. There is hardly any study exploring these issues.

Studies on risk factors have mostly reported sociodemographic and disaster-related factors; there is further scope for research on individual and biological risk factors contributing to post-disaster psychiatric disorders.

As most of the survivors in the South Asian region receive hardly any psychological support, it is essential to know about their ways of coping. There are a few observational studies that have reported coping strategies of affected individuals and communities (Kar, 2006, 2022, 2023a, 2024b; Sharma & Kar, 2019). However, there is a need for further research about the cultural ways of coping, what helps and what does not, highlighting their effectiveness.

Psychological interventional studies after disasters are rare in South Asian countries. There is hardly any information about the effectiveness of the interventions provided. In fact, in most scenarios, specific psychological support is not available. There is a need to explore culturally appropriate and acceptable interventions and their effectiveness.

There are many other areas of disaster mental health where the lack of adequate research is obvious. Some of the examples are cultural issues, lack of culturally appropriate assessment tools, biological vulnerabilities, and social concerns following major disasters (Kar, 2010a). There is also inadequate information related to disaster mental healthcare support systems, service delivery, continued support, and rehabilitation (Kar, 2024a, c). These would be immensely helpful to the disaster responders, health authorities, nongovernmental agencies working in disaster situations, and the local governments in arranging disaster support work. It is important to recognize and prevent "the second disasters" related to the distribution of relief and support to the survivors. There should be a greater understanding of the role and behavior of the disaster support workers, their training, and support needs for their work in challenging circumstances.

Major constraints of conducting the disaster mental health research have been the urgency, lack of readiness of the approval systems, funding, etc. There is also a lack of policy indicators for research, poor coordination of services, a lack of trained researchers, and limited resources, which are additional challenges (Padmavati et al., 2020). The disaster-related studies involving assessment and interventions should be an integral part of disaster care and be conducted from the beginning of the rescue and relief efforts and continue long-term. As obvious, these studies need to be multidisciplinary and multilevel, involving local teams collaborating with central, state, or national level institutes for continued support.

7 Conclusion

Disasters, either secondary to catastrophic natural events or human-caused, are becoming more frequent, affecting a larger number of people in the South Asia region. There are massive vulnerabilities in people to disaster trauma, which is multiplying the impact and their mental health consequences. These have short and long-term mental health sequelae. Effective preventive measures for disasters caused or contributed to by humans are a must that needs to be thought through and implemented. Most of the disaster trauma impact can be moderated by adequate disaster preparedness and planning, timely rescue, and relief measures, paired with mental health crisis management. For those affected with mental health problems, additional mental health support is required, which can be integrated with the existing infrastructure of health and social care. There is inadequate research on the impact of disasters, especially in the long term, and the effective intervention methods in this culturally diverse population with multiple vulnerabilities. The growing knowledge base regarding disaster-related support and healthcare management should be shared and efforts should be coordinated for better outcomes.

References

Acharya Pandey, R., Chalise, P., Khadka, S., Chaulagain, B., Maharjan, B., Pandey, J., Nepal, J., & Pandey, C. (2023). Post-traumatic stress disorder and its associated factors among survivors of 2015 earthquake in Nepal. *BMC Psychiatry, 23*, 340. https://doi.org/10.1186/s12888-023-04836-3

Ansari, E., & Kar, S. K. (2024). Mental health amid climate crisis: A narrative review. *Indian Journal of Psychiatry, 66*(11), 987. https://doi.org/10.4103/indianjpsychiatry.indianjpsychiatry_526_24

Arafat, S. M. Y., & Kar, S. K. (2024). Epidemiology of psychiatric disorders and overview of access to mental health care in South Asia. In S. M. Y. Arafat & S. K. Kar (Eds.), *Access to mental health care in South Asia*. Springer. https://doi.org/10.1007/978-981-99-9153-2_1

Arafat, S. M. Y., Kar, S. K., Marthoenis, M., Sharma, P., Hoque Apu, E., & Kabir, R. (2020a). Psychological underpinning of panic buying during pandemic (COVID-19). *Psychiatry Research, 289*, 113061. https://doi.org/10.1016/j.psychres.2020.113061

Arafat, S. M. Y., Kar, S. K., Menon, V., Kaliamoorthy, C., Mukherjee, S., Alradie-Mohamed, A., Sharma, P., Marthoenis, M., & Kabir, R. (2020b). Panic buying: An insight from the content analysis of media reports during COVID-19 pandemic. *Neurology, Psychiatry and Brain Research, 37*, 100–103. https://doi.org/10.1016/j.npbr.2020.07.002

Arafat, S. M. Y., Kar, S. K., & Kabir, R. (2021). Possible controlling measures of panic buying during COVID-19. *International Journal of Mental Health and Addiction, 19*(6), 2289–2291. https://doi.org/10.1007/s11469-020-00320-1

Arafat, S. M. Y., Kar, S. K., Singh, R., & Kabir, R. (2024). Editorial: Assessing and evaluating the psychosocial impact of the Covid-19 pandemic on anxiety and stress: Perspectives from the Indian sub-continent. *Frontiers in Psychiatry, 15*, 1389515. https://doi.org/10.3389/fpsyt.2024.1389515

Arora, D., Belsiyal, C. X., & Rawat, V. S. (2021). Prevalence and determinants of posttraumatic stress disorder and depression among survivors of motor vehicle accidents from a hilly Indian state. *Indian Journal of Psychiatry, 63*(3), 250–257. https://doi.org/10.4103/psychiatry.IndianJPsychiatry_1059_20

Asim, M., Mekkodathil, A., Sathian, B., Elayedath, R., N, R. K., Simkhada, P., & van Teijlingen, E. (2019). Post-traumatic stress disorder among the flood affected population in Indian subcontinent. *Nepal Journal of Epidemiology, 9*(1), 755–758. https://doi.org/10.3126/nje.v9i1.24003

Azad, M. A. K., & Khan, M. M. (2015). Post disasters social pathology in Bangladesh: A case study on AILA affected areas. *Sociology and Anthropology, 3*(2), 85–94. https://doi.org/10.13189/sa.2015.030203

Azeem, S., Cheema, H. A., Shahid, A., Al-Mamun, F., Rackimuthu, S., Ur Rehman, M. E., Essar, M. Y., & Lee, K. Y. (2023). Devastating floods in South Asia: The inequitable repercussions of climate change and an urgent appeal for action. *Public Health in Practice, 5*, 100365. https://doi.org/10.1016/j.puhip.2023.100365

Balasinorwala, V. P., & Shah, N. (2010). Acute stress disorder in hospitalised victims of 26/11-terror attack on Mumbai, India. *Journal of the Indian Medical Association, 108*(11), 757–759–760.

Broughton, E. (2005). The Bhopal disaster and its aftermath: A review. *Environmental Health, 4*, 6. https://doi.org/10.1186/1476-069X-4-6

Desai, N. G., Gupta, D. K., & Srivastava, R. K. (2004). Prevalence, pattern and predictors of mental health morbidity following an intermediate disaster in an urban slum in Delhi: A modified cohort study. *Indian Journal of Psychiatry, 46*(1), 39–51. https://www.ncbi.nlm.nih.gov/pmc/articles/PMC2912676/

Deshpande, R. S. (2022). Disaster management in India: Are we fully equipped? *Journal of Social and Economic Development, 24*(Suppl 1), 242–281. https://doi.org/10.1007/s40847-022-00225-w

Dyster-Aas, J., Arnberg, F. K., Lindam, A., Johannesson, K. B., Lundin, T., & Michel, P.-O. (2012). Impact of physical injury on mental health after the 2004 Southeast Asia tsunami. *Nordic Journal of Psychiatry, 66*(3), 203–208. https://doi.org/10.3109/08039488.2011.621975

Fatema, S. R., East, L., Islam, M. S., & Usher, K. (2021). Health impact and risk factors affecting south and southeast Asian women following natural disasters: A systematic review. *International Journal of Environmental Research and Public Health, 18*(21), 11068. https://doi.org/10.3390/ijerph182111068

Fatima, H., Oyetunji, T. P., Mishra, S., Sinha, K., Olorunsogbon, O. F., Akande, O. S., … & Kar, S. K. (2022). Religious coping in the time of COVID-19 pandemic in India and Nigeria: Finding of a cross-national community survey. *International Journal of Social Psychiatry, 68*(2), 309–315.

Girdhar, R., Srivastava, V., & Sethi, S. (2020). Managing mental health issues among elderly during COVID-19 pandemic. *Journal of Geriatric Care and Research, 7*(1), 29–32.

Government of Bangladesh. (2020). *National Plan for Disaster Management (2021–2025): Action for disaster risk management towards resilient nation*. Ministry of Disaster Management and Relief. https://modmr.portal.gov.bd/sites/default/files/files/modmr.portal.gov.bd/page/a7c2b9e1_6c9d_4ecf_bb53_ec74653e6d05/NPDM2021-25%20DraftVer5_23032020.pdf

Government of India. (2005). The Disaster Management Act, 2005; Act 53.

Hossain, B., Sohel, M. S., & Ryakitimbo, C. M. (2020). Climate change induced extreme flood disaster in Bangladesh: Implications on people's livelihoods in the Char Village and their coping mechanisms. *Progress in Disaster Science, 6*, 100079. https://doi.org/10.1016/j.pdisas.2020.100079

Hossain, A., Ahmed, B., Rahman, T., Sammonds, P., Zaman, S., Benzadid, S., & Jakariya, M. (2021). Household food insecurity, income loss, and symptoms of psychological distress among adults following the Cyclone Amphan in coastal Bangladesh. *PLoS One, 16*(11), e0259098. https://doi.org/10.1371/journal.pone.0259098

Islam, F., Arafat, Y., & Hossain, M. S. (2025). Eye injuries in Bangladesh's 2024 student-led mass uprising: A public health crisis unfolds. *Torture Journal, 35*(1), 1. https://doi.org/10.7146/torture.v35i1.152344

Jasparro, C., & Taylor, J. (2008). Climate change and regional vulnerability to transnational security threats in Southeast Asia. *Geopolitics, 13*(2), 232–256. https://doi.org/10.1080/14650040801991480

Jena, D., Das, S., Mishra, P., Kar, B., Patnaik, S., & Panda, I. (2025). In the shadow of climate change: Exploring livelihood vulnerability in the Juang communities of Keonjhar. *Disaster Advances, 18*(6), 7–17. https://doi.org/10.25303/186da07017

Jha, A., Basu, R., & Basu, A. (2016). Studying policy changes in disaster management in India: A tale of two cyclones. *Disaster Medicine and Public Health Preparedness, 10*(1), 42–46. https://doi.org/10.1017/dmp.2015.116

Joseph, J., & Jaswal, S. (2014). Psychosocial framework for understanding psychological distress among survivors of the November 26, 2008 Mumbai terror attack: Beyond traumatic experiences and emergency medical care. *Prehospital and Disaster Medicine, 29*(3), 330–338. https://doi.org/10.1017/S1049023X14000478

Kabir, R., Khan, H. T. A., Ball, E., & Caldwell, K. (2016). Climate change impact: The experience of the coastal areas of Bangladesh affected by cyclones Sidr and Aila. *Journal of Environmental and Public Health, 2016*(1), 9654753. https://doi.org/10.1155/2016/9654753

Kabir, R., Bai, A. C. M., Syed, H. Z., Hasan, M. R., Vinnakota, D., Kar, S. K., Singh, R., Sathian, B., & Arafat, S. M. Y. (2023). The effect of COVID-19 on the mental health of the people in the Indian subcontinent: A scoping review. *Nepal Journal of Epidemiology, 13*(2), 1268–1284. https://doi.org/10.3126/nje.v13i2.52766

Kafle, H., Khaitu, S., Gyawali, D., Shrestha, D., Koirala, D., Kamaruzzaman, M., Khawas, V., Rasheed, A., Sobue, S., & Yamaguchi, Y. (2023). Historical drought and its trend in South Asia: Spatial and temporal analysis 2000–2020. *APN Science Bulletin*. https://doi.org/10.30852/sb.2022.2022

Kannuri, N. K., & Jadhav, S. (2021). Cultivating distress: Cotton, caste and farmer suicides in India. *Anthropology & Medicine, 28*(4), 558–575. https://doi.org/10.1080/13648470.2021.1993630

Kar, G. C. (2000). Disaster and mental health. *Indian Journal of Psychiatry, 42*(1), 3–13.

Kar, N. (2006). Psychosocial issues following a natural disaster in a developing country: A qualitative longitudinal observational study. *International Journal of Disaster Medicine, 4*, 169–176.

Kar, N. (2010a). Indian research on disaster and mental health. *Indian Journal of Psychiatry, 52*(Suppl 1), S286–S290. https://doi.org/10.4103/0019-5545.69254

Kar, N. (2010b). Suicidality following a natural disaster. *American Journal of Disaster Medicine, 5*(6), 361–368.

Kar, N. (2022). Coping strategies used by adult survivors in the process of recovery from disaster trauma: A narrative review. *Odisha Journal of Psychiatry, 18*(1), 3–10. https://doi.org/10.4103/OJP.OJP_5_22

Kar, N. (2023a). Impact of disasters on the disaster responders: A review of stress, coping, resilience, and supportive methods. *Odisha Journal of Psychiatry, 19*(2), 37. https://doi.org/10.4103/OJP.OJP_23_23
Kar, N. (2023b). Indirect victims of catastrophic events: The case of Odisha train accident. *Journal of Geriatric Care and Research, 10*(2), 33–34.
Kar, N. (2024a). Anatomy of a catastrophe: Managing psychosocial consequence of the 2023 Odisha train accident. *Industrial Psychiatry Journal, 33*(2), 219–225. https://doi.org/10.4103/ipj.ipj_278_24
Kar, N. (2024b). Coping strategies used by children and adolescents following disaster trauma: A review of associated factors and intervention options. *Odisha Journal of Psychiatry, 20*(2), 43–51. https://doi.org/10.4103/OJP.OJP_21_24
Kar, N. (2024c). Research, innovations, and ideas to facilitate mental healthcare delivery in South Asia. In S. M. Y. Arafat & S. K. Kar (Eds.), *Access to mental health care in South Asia: Current status, potential challenges, and ways out* (pp. 197–227). Springer Nature. https://doi.org/10.1007/978-981-99-9153-2_10
Kar, N., & Bastia, B. K. (2006). Post-traumatic stress disorder, depression and generalised anxiety disorder in adolescents after a natural disaster: A study of comorbidity. *Clinical Practice and Epidemiology in Mental Health: CP & EMH, 2*, 17. https://doi.org/10.1186/1745-0179-2-17
Kar, N., Jagadisha, Sharma, P., Murali, N., & Mehrotra, S. (2004). Mental health consequences of the trauma of super-cyclone 1999 in Orissa. *Indian Journal of Psychiatry, 46*(3), 228–237.
Kar, N., Mohapatra, P. K., Nayak, K. C., Pattanaik, P., Swain, S. P., & Kar, H. C. (2007). Post-traumatic stress disorder in children and adolescents one year after a super-cyclone in Orissa, India: Exploring cross-cultural validity and vulnerability factors. *BMC Psychiatry, 7*, 8. https://doi.org/10.1186/1471-244X-7-8
Kar, N., Krishnaraaj, R., & Rameshraj, K. (2014). Long-term mental health outcomes following the 2004 Asian tsunami disaster. *Disaster Health, 2*(1), 35–45. https://doi.org/10.4161/dish.24705
Kar, S. K., Shukla, S., Menon, V., & Arafat, S. M. Y. (2020). Religion and behaviour: Relevance during the current COVID-19 pandemic. *Journal of Geriatric Care and Research, 7*, 140–142.
Kar, N., Kar, B., & Kar, S. (2021a). Stress and coping during COVID-19 pandemic: Result of an online survey. *Psychiatry Research, 295*. https://doi.org/10.1016/j.psychres.2020.113598
Kar, S. K., Ransing, R., Arafat, S. Y., & Menon, V. (2021b). Second wave of COVID-19 pandemic in India: Barriers to effective governmental response. *EClinicalMedicine, 36*, 100915.
Kar, N., Samantaray, N. N., Kar, S., & Kar, B. (2022). Anxiety, depression, and post-traumatic stress a month after 2019 cyclone Fani in Odisha, India. *Disaster Medicine and Public Health Preparedness, 16*(2), 670–677. https://doi.org/10.1017/dmp.2020.368
Kar, B., Kar, N., & Panda, M. C. (2023). Social trust and COVID-appropriate behavior: Learning from the pandemic. *Asian Journal of Social Health and Behavior, 6*(3), 93. https://doi.org/10.4103/shb.shb_183_22
Kar, N., Swain, S. P., Parija, S., Banerjee, S., Mahakul, S., Behura, S. S., Palei, B., & Kar, S. (2025). Posttraumatic stress following the 2023 Odisha train accident: A cross-sectional comparison study of passengers, health professionals, and the local community. *Disaster Medicine and Public Health Preparedness, 19*, e112. https://doi.org/10.1017/dmp.2025.113
Karim, M. Z., Al-Mamun, M., Eva, M. A., Ali, M. H., Kalam, A., Uzzal, N. I., & Das, P. K. (2024). Understanding mental health challenges and associated risk factors of post-natural disasters in Bangladesh: A systematic review. *Frontiers in Psychology, 15*, 1466722. https://doi.org/10.3389/fpsyg.2024.1466722
Kumar, M. T., Kar, N., Namboodiri, V., Joy, A., Sreeenivasan, D., Kumar, S., & Bortel, T. V. (2023). Post-traumatic stress and depression following a landslide linked to the 2018 floods in Kerala, India: Relevance of screening. *Journal of Emergency Management (Weston, Mass.), 21*(1), 85–96. https://doi.org/10.5055/jem.0728
Majumder, J., Saha, I., Bagepally, B. S., Kalita, M., Munikrishnappa, D., Ray, S., Saha, A., & Chakrabarti, A. (2024). Mental health burden following extreme weather events in South-east Asia: A systematic review and meta-analysis. *Indian Journal of Psychiatry, 66*(8), 683–694. https://doi.org/10.4103/indianjpsychiatry.indianjpsychiatry_348_24

Mall, R. K., Srivastava, R. K., Banerjee, T., Mishra, O. P., Bhatt, D., & Sonkar, G. (2019). Disaster risk reduction including climate change adaptation over South Asia: Challenges and ways forward. *International Journal of Disaster Risk Science, 10*(1), 14–27. https://doi.org/10.1007/s13753-018-0210-9

Mamun, M. A., Safiq, M. B., Hosen, I., & Al Mamun, F. (2021). Suicidal behavior and flood effects in Bangladesh: A two-site interview study. *Risk Management and Healthcare Policy, 14*, 129–144. https://doi.org/10.2147/RMHP.S282965

Masood, Z., Moise, I. K., Spika, V., & Ramaprasad, J. (2021). Health interventions implemented in post-disaster South Asia: A scoping review. *International Journal of Disaster Risk Reduction, 63*, 102419. https://doi.org/10.1016/j.ijdrr.2021.102419

Math, S. B., Tandon, S., Girimaji, S. C., Benegal, V., Kumar, U., Hamza, A., Jangam, K., & Nagaraja, D. (2008). Psychological impact of the tsunami on children and adolescents from the Andaman and Nicobar Islands. *Primary Care Companion to the Journal of Clinical Psychiatry, 10*(1), 31–37.

Mathew, G., Varghese, A. D., Sabu, A. M., & Joseph, A. (2021). Screening for post-traumatic stress disorder among adolescents following floods- a comparative study from private and public schools in Kerala, India. *BMC Pediatrics, 21*, 462. https://doi.org/10.1186/s12887-021-02933-4

Memdani, L., Memdani, A., & Memdani, A. (2024). Farmers' suicides in India: A qualitative study of Andhra Pradesh (AP) and Telangana states of India. *Indian Journal of Community Medicine: Official Publication of Indian Association of Preventive & Social Medicine, 49*(4), 629–632. https://doi.org/10.4103/ijcm.ijcm_206_22

Merriott, D. (2016). Factors associated with the farmer suicide crisis in India. *Journal of Epidemiology and Global Health, 6*(4), 217–227. https://doi.org/10.1016/j.jegh.2016.03.003

Mir, M. A., & Ahmed, Z. (2020). Ethnic conflicts in South Asia: Impediments to regional integration. *World Affairs: The Journal of International Issues, 24*(3), 10–19. https://www.jstor.org/stable/48590640

Mirza, M. M. Q. (2011). Climate change, flooding in South Asia and implications. *Regional Environmental Change, 11*(1), 95–107. https://doi.org/10.1007/s10113-010-0184-7

Mishra, O. P. (2023). Creating robust infrastructure and response mechanism: Odisha model of disaster management. In A. Singh (Ed.), *International handbook of disaster research* (pp. 2175–2188). Springer. https://doi.org/10.1007/978-981-19-8388-7_208

Mishra, S., Bhoi, R., Ravan, R., Nath, S., Kar, N., & Padhy, S. (2020). COVID-19 pandemic and care of elderly: Measures and challenges. *Journal of Geriatric Care and Research, 7*(3), 143–146.

Mostafizur Rahman, M., Alam Shobuj, I., Tanvir Hossain, M., & Tasnim, F. (2023). Impact of disaster on mental health of women: A case study on 2022 flash flood in Bangladesh. *International Journal of Disaster Risk Reduction, 96*, 103935. https://doi.org/10.1016/j.ijdrr.2023.103935

Murthy, R. S. (2014). Mental health of survivors of 1984 Bhopal disaster: A continuing challenge. *Industrial Psychiatry Journal, 23*(2), 86–93. https://doi.org/10.4103/0972-6748.151668

Murthy, S., Kar, N., Sekar, K., Swain, S., Mishra, V., & Daniel, U. (2003). *Evaluation report on psychosocial care of survivors of super-cyclone in Orissa*. NIMHANS.

Nahar, N., Blomstedt, Y., Wu, B., Kandarina, I., Trisnantoro, L., & Kinsman, J. (2014). Increasing the provision of mental health care for vulnerable, disaster-affected people in Bangladesh. *BMC Public Health, 14*(1), 708. https://doi.org/10.1186/1471-2458-14-708

Padhy, S. K., Sarkar, S., Panigrahi, M., & Paul, S. (2015). Mental health effects of climate change. *Indian Journal of Occupational and Environmental Medicine, 19*(1), 3–7. https://doi.org/10.4103/0019-5278.156997

Padmavati, R., Raghavan, V., Rera, H., Kearns, M., Rao, K., John, S., & Thara, R. (2020). Learnings from conducting mental health research during 2004 tsunami in Tamil Nadu, India. *BMC Public Health, 20*, 1627. https://doi.org/10.1186/s12889-020-09733-y

Patwary, M. M., Bardhan, M., Haque, M. A., Moniruzzaman, S., Gustavsson, J., Khan, M. M. H., Koivisto, J., Salwa, M., Mashreky, S. R., Rahman, A. K. M. F., Tasnim, A., Islam, M. R., Alam, M. A., Hasan, M., Harun, M. A. Y. A., Nyberg, L., & Islam, M. A. (2024). Impact of extreme weather events on mental health in South and Southeast Asia: A two decades of systematic review of observational studies. *Environmental Research, 250*, 118436. https://doi.org/10.1016/j.envres.2024.118436

Pyari, T. T., Kutty, R. V., & Sarma, P. S. (2012). Risk factors of post-traumatic stress disorder in tsunami survivors of Kanyakumari District, Tamil Nadu, India. *Indian Journal of Psychiatry, 54*(1), 48. https://doi.org/10.4103/0019-5545.94645

Quadri, S. A., & Padala, P. R. (2021). An aspect of Kumbh Mela massive gathering and COVID-19. *Current Tropical Medicine Reports, 8*, 225–230.

Rajkumar, A. P., Mohan, T. S. P., & Tharyan, P. (2013). Lessons from the 2004 Asian tsunami: Epidemiological and nosological debates in the diagnosis of post-traumatic stress disorder in non-Western post-disaster communities. *The International Journal of Social Psychiatry, 59*(2), 123–129. https://doi.org/10.1177/0020764011423468

Rajkumar, A. P., Mohan, T. S., & Tharyan, P. (2015). Lessons from the 2004 Asian tsunami: Nature, prevalence and determinants of prolonged grief disorder among tsunami survivors in South Indian coastal villages. *The International Journal of Social Psychiatry, 61*(7), 645–652. https://doi.org/10.1177/0020764015570713

Ransing, R., Kar, S., & Menon, V. (2021). Potential barriers to handle the second wave of COVID-19 in India. *Journal of Geriatric Care and Research, 8*(1), 36–38.

Rina, K., Maiti, T., Panigrahi, M., Patro, B., Kar, N., & Padhy, S. K. (2020). Impact of COVID-19 pandemic and lockdown on elder abuse. *Journal of Geriatric Care and Research, 7*(3), 103–107.

Sathyanarayana Rao, T. S. (2004). Managing impact of natural disasters: Some mental health issues. *Indian Journal of Psychiatry, 46*(4), 289–292. https://www.ncbi.nlm.nih.gov/pmc/articles/PMC2950945/

Sathyanarayana Rao, T. S., Gowda, M. R., Ramachandran, K., & Andrade, C. (2017). Prevention of farmer suicides: Greater need for state role than for a mental health professional's role. *Indian Journal of Psychiatry, 59*(1), 3–5. https://doi.org/10.4103/psychiatry.IndianJPsychiatry_89_17

Shah, M. H., Roy, S., & Ahluwalia, A. (2024). Intergenerational trauma and mental health disability in the south Asian context. In *The Palgrave encyclopedia of disability* (pp. 1–9). Palgrave Macmillan. https://doi.org/10.1007/978-3-031-40858-8_292-1

Sharma, D. C. (2023). Climate disasters challenge health infrastructures in India. *Lancet (London, England), 402*(10398), 279–280. https://doi.org/10.1016/S0140-6736(23)01512-X

Sharma, A., & Kar, N. (2019). Posttraumatic stress, depression, and coping following the 2015 Nepal earthquake: A study on adolescents. *Disaster Medicine and Public Health Preparedness, 13*(2), 236–242. https://doi.org/10.1017/dmp.2018.37

Silwal, S., Chudal, R., Dybdahl, R., Sillanmäki, L., Lien, L., & Sourander, A. (2022). Post-traumatic stress and depressive symptoms among adolescents after the 2015 earthquake in Nepal: A longitudinal study. *Child Psychiatry and Human Development, 53*(3), 430–439. https://doi.org/10.1007/s10578-021-01136-3

Siriwardhana, C., Adikari, A., Pannala, G., Roberts, B., Siribaddana, S., Abas, M., Sumathipala, A., & Stewart, R. (2015). Changes in mental disorder prevalence among conflict-affected populations: A prospective study in Sri Lanka (COMRAID-R). *BMC Psychiatry, 15*(1), 41. https://doi.org/10.1186/s12888-015-0424-y

Suar, D., Kar, N., & Panigrahi, G. S. (2024). Natural hazards, trauma, and its amelioration: Lessons learned from India. *International Journal of Disaster Risk Reduction, 108*, 104548. https://doi.org/10.1016/j.ijdrr.2024.104548

Swain, S. P., Behura, S. S., Banerjee, S., Mahakul, S., & Kar, N. (2025). A qualitative mixed-method narrative study on psychotherapeutic support needs based on a series of 11 cases of survivors of the 2023 Odisha train accident. *Cureus, 17*(3), e81161. https://doi.org/10.7759/cureus.81161

Tasdik Hasan, M., Adhikary, G., Mahmood, S., Papri, N., Shihab, H. M., Kasujja, R., Ahmed, H. U., Azad, A. K., & Nasreen, M. (2020). Exploring mental health needs and services among affected population in a cyclone affected area in coastal Bangladesh: A qualitative case study. *International Journal of Mental Health Systems, 14*, 12. https://doi.org/10.1186/s13033-020-00351-0

UNDRR (United Nations Office for Disaster Risk Reduction). 2017. The Sendai Framework terminology on disaster risk reduction. "Disaster". https://www.undrr.org/terminology/disaster. Accessed 13 Aug 2025.

United Nations. (2025). Human rights violations and abuses related to the protests of July and August 2024 in Bangladesh. https://www.ohchr.org/sites/default/files/documents/countries/bangladesh/ohchr-fftb-hr-violations-bd.pdf

Wahid, S. S., Islam, M. N., & Raza, W. A. (2024). Climate change and mental health in Bangladesh: Vulnerability, inequality, and the crucial need for intervention on the frontlines of the climate crisis. In S. M. Y. Arafat (Ed.), *Mental health in Bangladesh: From bench to community* (pp. 255–270). Springer Nature. https://doi.org/10.1007/978-981-97-0610-5_15

WHO. (1992). *Psychosocial consequences of disasters: Prevention and management*. Division of Mental Health, Geneva: World Health Organization.

Wikipedia. (2025). List of railway accidents and incidents in India. *Wikipedia*. https://en.wikipedia.org/w/index.php?title=List_of_railway_accidents_and_incidents_in_India&oldid=1281443734

World Bank. (2025). World Bank country and lending groups. Retrieved from June, 09, 2025, https://datahelpdesk.worldbank.org/knowledgebase/articles/906519-world-bank-country-and-lending-groups

Chapter 2
Geological and Climatic Vulnerabilities of South Asia: Mental Health Perspectives of Climate Disasters

Mrutyunjay Mohapatra, Rajib Chattopadhyay, and Gaddale Suresh

1 Introduction

The South-Asian region is home to more than 2 billion people, and it includes the countries of Afghanistan, *Bangladesh*, *Bhutan*, *India*, the Maldives, Nepal, Pakistan, and Sri Lanka. This region of Asia is a climatically and geographically diverse region, influenced by the Great Himalayas, Hindukush, and Karakoram mountains to the north and the Indian Ocean (Arabian Sea and Bay of Bengal) to the south, intersected by glaciers-fed and rain-fed rivers like the Indus, Ganges, Brahmaputra, Narmada, Godavari, etc., resulting in shared climatic and geological risks. South Asia is mainly characterized by four climate zones (Xue & Yanai, 2005). The northern Indian region, as well as the highlands and mountainous regions of Pakistan and Afghanistan, has a dry continental, subtropical climate that is often strongly influenced by midlatitude weather systems. The southern peninsular India and southwest Sri Lanka, as well as the Maldives, are in the zone of equatorial climates. The rest of the areas lie in the tropical zone, with a hot semi-tropical climate in northwest India, a cool-winter hot tropical climate in Bangladesh, and a semiarid tropical climate in the center of the peninsula. Except for the mountainous region, most regions have high humidity, especially along the large coastlines and island countries. There is strong variation in temperature and precipitation in this region. Some places experience extreme cold and snowfall, while some places experience very high temperatures. Similarly, the boreal summer and winter monsoon flow

M. Mohapatra (✉)
India Meteorological Department (IMD), New Delhi, India

R. Chattopadhyay
Indian Institute of Tropical Meteorology (IITM), Pune, India

G. Suresh
National Center for Seismology (NCS), New Delhi, India

N. Kar et al. (eds.), *Climate Change, Disaster and Mental Health in South Asia*, South Asian Perspectives in Mental Health and Psychology,
https://doi.org/10.1007/978-981-95-3690-0_2

shows a distinguished impact on most of these regions. The summer monsoon flow initiates during May, and a dramatic reversal of wind direction, bringing heavy rainfall during the summer months, is noticed, which gives a large amount of rainfall. The summer monsoon rainfall (June–September) and the winter monsoon rainfall (October–December) is crucial for agriculture, water resources, and the livelihoods of millions of people in South Asia. It provides the necessary rainfall for crops and replenishes rivers and reservoirs.

South Asia is highly vulnerable to a range of climate-related hazards, including cyclones, extreme monsoon rainfall and cloud bursts, floods, droughts, and extreme heat waves. A summary of these hazards is given in Table 2.1 (Amarnath et al., 2017; Kafle, 2017). Extreme precipitation events and related flooding occur frequently in the monsoon season in South Asia. Tropical cyclones primarily originating over the warmer Indian Ocean also affect South Asia, bringing out torrential rain, strong winds, and storm surge. Several studies have identified heat wave hotspots over many regions of India. Floods, heat waves, and other weather-related hazards are causing thousands of casualties, and millions of people are affected each year. These hazards are exacerbated by factors like dense coastal populations, reliance on monsoon-fed agriculture, and rapid urbanization. These hazards also cause significant financial loss. For example, the devastating floods in Pakistan during August 2022 impacted over 32 million people and caused damage estimated at around *$30 billion* (Bloomberg, 2022; PTI, 2022). India is estimated to have lost $56 billion during the years 2019–2023, as per an ADB estimate (Prasad, 2024). The National Disaster Management Authority of India (NDMA) estimates that India has lost 2% of its GDP due to disasters. Financial losses in South Asia are projected to reach $160 billion (World Bank, 2021). Similarly, disasters are also responsible for large losses of life in this region. The super cyclones, such as the Odisha Super Cyclone, the Bhola Super Cyclone, the recent floods in Pakistan, intense heat waves, the 2004 Sumatra–Andaman megathrust earthquake and

Table 2.1 Common meteorological and geological hazards and natural disasters over the populated areas of South Asian countries

Regions of South Asia	Hazards
Afghanistan	Earthquakes, floods, cold waves
Bangladesh	Floods, cyclones, sea-level rise, extreme rainfall, droughts
Bhutan	GLOF, flash floods, landslides, earthquakes, forest fires, epidemics
Northwestern India	Droughts, heat waves, earthquakes
Islands and eastern coastal areas of India	Cyclones, floods, sea-level rise, earthquakes, tsunami
Northeastern region	Extreme rainfall, floods, earthquakes, landslides
Central India	Droughts, heat waves, extreme rainfall
Maldives	Sea-level rise, tsunami
Nepal	Floods, extreme rainfall, landslides, GLOF, earthquakes
Pakistan	Floods, droughts, heat waves, earthquakes, tsunami
Sri Lanka	Floods, droughts, sea-level rise, extreme rainfall, tsunami

the resulting Indian Ocean tsunami; significant earthquakes, and numerous landslides triggered by heavy rainfall are all examples of devastation and destruction, collectively claiming hundreds of thousands of lives.

2 Climate Variability and Climate Change Impact on Human Health

The WHO defines health as "a state of complete physical, mental, and social well-being, and not merely the absence of disease or infirmity" (Schramme, 2023; WHO, 1948). It emphasizes that health encompasses more than just the absence of illness or disease; rather, it gives an idea of overall well-being, including physical, mental, and social aspects. The weather and climate have a significant impact on human health in a variety of ways, such as by increasing the frequency of extreme weather events, the emergence and spread of infectious diseases, increasing pollen abundance and allergenicity, and disruptions to agricultural systems, leading to food shortage and malnutrition (Confalonieri et al., 2007). According to the World Bank, the low and middle-income countries are estimated to have severe health consequences (World Bank, 2024). It is anticipated that the already severe health consequences of climate variability and change in South Asia, especially, will continue to deteriorate in the future. The geographical distribution of these diseases will expand, in addition to the rise in the number of diseases and fatalities caused by climate-sensitive health risks. The health risk of climate change is explained in Fig. 2.1 (WHO, 2023). From Fig. 2.1, it is clear that the hazards are related to health outcomes through exposure and vulnerability of the populations. Socioeconomic vulnerability determines the intensity of the risk, while population exposure determines the breadth of the risk in a given geographical region or community.

The South Asian countries face severe health impacts of climate change. The complex topography of the region, including high mountains, plateaus, plains, long coastlines, and low-lying islands, increases its vulnerability to extreme weather events (Sen et al., 2017). For example, flash floods occurred during 2017 in India, Nepal, and Bangladesh, claiming more than 1400 lives, and such disasters are reported to lead to food insecurity (Randell et al., 2021), while catastrophic earthquakes such as the 2015 Nepal event, as documented in the NDMA (India) Earthquake Compendium, caused both mass casualties and long-term psychosocial trauma. Similarly, the 2004 Indian Ocean tsunami had far-reaching mental health impacts across the region.

The physical health consequences of climate variability and change, particularly infections, allergies, and respiratory and cardiovascular diseases, are now widely acknowledged. Nevertheless, the mental health implications of climate change started appearing in literature after the IPCC AR4 report in 2007, which focused on human health and vulnerability as a consequence of climate change. IPCC AR6 report (Intergovernmental Panel on Climate Change (IPCC), 2023) revisits this

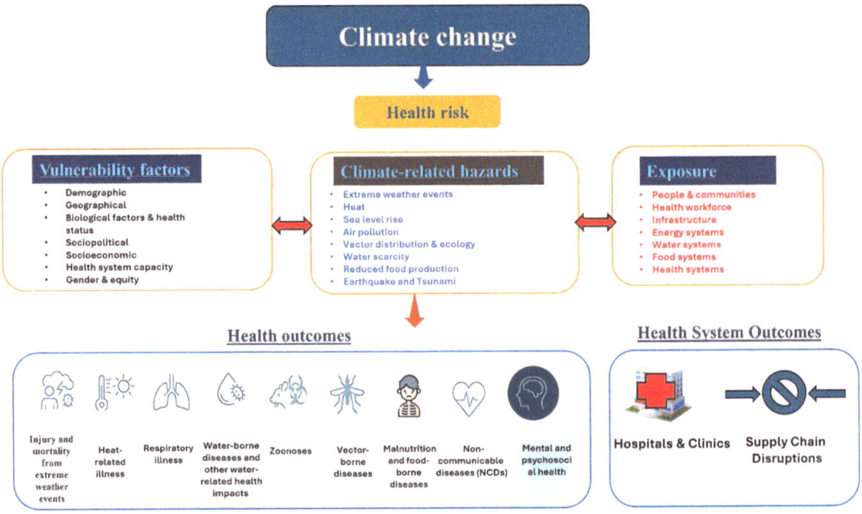

Fig. 2.1 A schematic diagram showing the climate change pathway for different health risks. (Reference: WHO). (Redrawn from source: https://www.who.int/news-room/fact-sheets/detail/climate-change-and-health; https://cdn.who.int/media/images/default-source/health-and-climate-change/risk-pathways-climate-health.jpg?sfvrsn=3ba050b0_6. The above image is redrawn and modified from the WHO website, as referred above)

section (Cissé et al., 2022) and provides some contextual analysis of impacts in this regard. In South Asian countries, mental health issues in the context of natural disasters became a wide topic of discussion after the 2004 Indian Ocean tsunami (Baddam John et al., 2007; Kar et al., 2013). A review study (Patwary et al., 2024) found compelling evidence linking extreme weather events to adverse mental health outcomes in South and Southeast Asia.

The impact of weather and Climate hazards can be quantified through the systematic quantification of health risk. A popular form of the risk equation is given by the United Nations office of Disaster Risk Reduction (Barrett et al., 2021) as (Chap. 2, 11pp):

$$\text{Risk}(\text{R}) = \{\text{Hazard}(\text{H}) \times \text{Exposure}(\text{E})\} \times \text{Vulnerability}(\text{V})$$

Thus, the risk equals zero if one of the three components above is zero. Theoretically, for example, in case of dengue spread, there is no risk if there is no likelihood of a dengue epidemics when vectors are not present and/or the hazard zone is not populated or/and if the population is not vulnerable (e.g., climatic conditions are not favorable) or/and if the resilience of the country to cope and recover is ideal. The risk is often estimated in a geographical domain and is more useful when the domain matches an administrative unit, such as a district, city, ward, village, etc. It can be easily estimated when we have vulnerability maps and socioeconomic data for a particular hazard. It is also clear from the above relations that the health impacts vary according to age, sex, geographical regions, etc. A study by Kazuyuki Uji (2012) indicates that people in the Asia-Pacific are 4 and 25 times more vulnerable to natural disasters when compared with people in Africa and in North America/Europe, respectively. This difference is partly due to a change in the hazard frequency, intensity, or duration of occurrence, or due to increased vulnerability. The health risks associated with climate change are increased due to changes or trends in socioeconomic vulnerability and risk exposure.

Rising temperatures, warmer nights, vanishing green cover with rapid urbanization, increased natural hazards, and diminishing biodiversity have directly threatened ecosystems in recent decades, potentially negatively affecting community and social well-being from a mental health perspective. Environmental psychologists addressed human behavior and the lack of mindful conservation strategies in the context of anthropogenic causes, which threaten human health and well-being and are roadblocks to sustainable development (Clayton et al., 2013). Climate change and geological disasters have forced the migration of communities due to contamination or depletion of natural resources (Almulhim et al., 2024); social and political conflicts have developed over access to diminishing resources (Froese & Schilling, 2019; Minale et al., 2024); an increased incidence of violence and criminal offences is recorded (Mahendran et al., 2021) and individuals may have experienced increased depression, stress, anxiety, and other serious psychotic disorders (Ansari & Kar, 2024; Heinz & Brandt, 2024; Schwartz et al., 2023). These impacts are related to direct or indirect responses to these environmental changes in the short and long term.

3 Short-Term and Long-Term Impact of Climate Hazards in South Asia on Mental Health

The mental health vulnerability in the South Asian regions stems from frequent natural hazards of varying intensity. Some hazards, like drought, evolve slowly. Some hazards, like flash floods or thunderstorms, landslides, or earthquakes, evolve quickly. Regional variation of climate and climatological probability of occurrence of hazard over a region is well known, and the risk impact is minimized based on traditional practices. For example, traditionally, flood management practices are in place in flood-prone areas of India. However, with climate change, regional projections of impact are erratic, and there is a change in hazard probability manifested as a change in the intensity, duration, and frequency. Often, the hazard intensity beats the predicted intensity forecast, and standard disaster preparedness is inadequate. This has necessitated careful reevaluation of hazard impacts in the short and long term based on evidence of climate change. All hazards have short-term and long-lasting impacts. The impact on mental health can be direct, indirect, and intersectional (Heinz & Brandt, 2024). It can also have unequal impacts on the population depending on gender, age, health conditions, etc. Direct impacts occur when a disaster, like a heat wave, affects the mental health of a person, e.g., mood swings and other affective disorders due to a lack of sleep. Indirect impact occurs when, for example, population displacement migration occurs due to a natural calamity like large-scale riverine flooding, storm surge due to a cyclone, or or due to geophysical hazards such as earthquakes, which may result in large-scale mortality, injury, and post-earthquake housing loss, etc. In several parts of South Asia, especially in hilly and mountainous regions, haphazard development and the disruption of ecological balance further increase disaster risk, magnifying both physical and mental health consequences. Such unplanned expansion often involves construction on unstable slopes, deforestation, and inadequate drainage systems, which not only heighten the likelihood of landslides and flash floods but also prolong recovery times. These extended recovery periods can compound psychological distress, leading to prolonged anxiety, depression, and post-traumatic stress among affected populations. Intersectional effects are seen when disasters create social inequality, isolation, exclusion, or discrimination. A 2024 study conducted by the Chintan Environmental Research and Action Group found that an overwhelming 89% of schoolchildren in the Delhi-NCR region reported experiencing anxiety linked to climate change (Agarwal & Tandon, 2025) and, similarly, the post-monsoon mental distress, depression, anxiety, and stress in some districts of Bangladesh, as reported earlier (Kabir et al., 2024). A survey conducted on the doctors/physicians in Nepal highlighted the mental health issues related to climate change and natural disasters (Rai et al., 2025). Similarly, studies conducted in Bhutan (Chhetri et al., 2024) indicate an association of climate hazards with mental health distress. In summary, the mental health issues in South Asia show a strong link with climate variability and change. The mental health distress is much amplified when a disaster strikes a region or community. We briefly review below some studies related to the mental health impact of a few well-known and frequent disasters seen in South Asia:

3.1 Drought

The Indian subcontinent and the South Asian region have seen frequent droughts, some of which are perhaps among the oldest recorded disasters. Droughts mainly due to monsoon failure in South Asia led to famines, and several devastating famines are recorded in Indian history (e.g., the great Bengal famine of 1770, which affected 30 million people with many deaths (Damodaran, 2015). South Asian countries are highly dependent on agriculture, with major rain-fed cropping systems closely linked to the monsoon season (June–September), and droughts lead to large losses in crops in many regions. Future drought projections over South Asia indicate an increase in drought and dryness in different climate change scenarios (Aadhar & Mishra, 2019; Ullah et al., 2022). The severe drought episode frequency is expected to increase under 1.5 °C (40%–75%) and 2 °C (60%–90%) of warming relative to the current climate (Ullah et al., 2022). Studies show droughts have several mental health consequences. A recent study (Narayanan & Suresh, 2024) in India showed that there is an increase in suicide rate by 5.7% in 2022 when compared with 2020, with drought and unseasonal rainfall identified as significant contributing factors. A study from Nepal by Rai et al. (2025) indicated that there is an increased perception of physical and mental harm from drought in the coming years, as per the respondent-based survey. A study by Goudet et al. (2024) highlighted the increased anxiety and depression among women due to droughts and other natural disasters. Similarly, droughts in Pakistan have been studied in the context of mental health, and results indicate increased mental health challenges, including depression, PTSD, and anxiety, especially among women (Daraz et al., 2024). In the desert areas, e.g., Tharparkar district, drought and erratic rainfall have been linked to migration, suicide, and increased mental health challenges (Sheikh Salim & Sughra Tunio, 2019). These mental health issues related to droughts are exacerbated by factors like poverty, food insecurity, and displacement, impacting women and children in rural communities.

3.2 Cyclone

The Indian subcontinent has a huge coastline, which faces the Bay of Bengal to the east, the Arabian Sea to the west, and the Indian Ocean to the south. Also, there are island countries like Sri Lanka and the Maldives, which are in the equatorial region, surrounded by the Indian Ocean. Most of these countries in South Asia face direct and indirect threats from cyclones. Projection studies in South Asia suggest a potential increase in the intensity and frequency of tropical cyclones, with some areas experiencing a decline in frequency while others see an increase. The Bay of Bengal and the Arabian Sea are particularly vulnerable to these changes. Cyclogenesis over the North Indian Ocean, especially the Bay of Bengal, is dependent on several local and remote factors, such as wind shear (or barotropic) instabilities over these regions, remnants of Pacific cyclonic vortices travelling to the Bay of Bengal, and subsequent intensification, moisture convergence, etc. (Sharma et al., 2025). The global warming trend is clearly reflected in the warming of the Bay of Bengal and the Arabian Sea with increased evaporation from warm sea water. Thus, warmer sea-surface temperatures and increased atmospheric moisture create more favorable conditions for cyclogenesis.

A recent study in coastal Bangladesh revealed that 66% of cyclone "Amphan" victims had moderate-to-severe mental health issues, including 10.9% with suicidal ideation (Hossain et al., 2021; Patwary et al., 2024). Sudden unemployment and lack of income led to people living with severe food insecurity, which contributed to mental health risk. These studies also reported gender inequalities in food security after the cyclone. The authors concluded that providing opportunities for jobs to prevent income loss, especially for poor people, can have a positive impact in reducing psychological distress. However, due to the high prevalence of severe psychological symptoms, coherent long-term mental health services are required to deal with such cases. In India, several studies have reported mental health issues in the aftermath of a cyclone landfall. A study by Kar et al. (2004) analyzed the mental health impact of the famous Odisha super-cyclone during 1999. The study observed that 80.4% of the subjects who were selected for the study had probable psychiatric disorders. Post-traumatic stress disorder was found in 44.3%, anxiety disorder in 57.5%, and depression in 52.7% of the respondents. Predisposition to earlier mental health issues and comorbidity had more impact on the people. The study also observed an increase in suicidality. A study over the Sundarbans area reported water-related insecurity and mental distress (e.g., indecisiveness, general anxiety, fear of waterlessness, irritation, loss of self-esteem, etc.) post-cyclone impact (Dasgupta & Basu, 2023). The perceived difficulty in the availability of fresh water with adequate quantity and good quality, alongside the prevalence of waterborne diseases, loss of social relations, and loss of livelihood, are the key determinants of the self-reported emotional stress of the respondents in this area. Another report showed the lingering mental health impact of the "Okhi" cyclone among the fishermen community in Kanyakumari, India, even after 6 years (Subramaniam Gowthami, 2023). The survivors reported recurring flashbacks, insomnia, and negative thought patterns, endure depression, and post-traumatic stress in the long run.

3.3 Heat Waves and Cold Waves: Temperature Extremes

Heat waves and cold waves are extreme temperature fluctuations during the summer and winter seasons. Every year, extreme temperature fluctuation is the norm, and recent heat waves have been deadly in India, Pakistan, and Bangladesh (Tachev, 2025). The cold waves, although they create several health problems, have not had their impacts on mental health well reviewed in the South Asian countries. On the other hand, several studies show an increase in the frequency and intensity of heat waves over South Asia, particularly over India and Pakistan, with high confidence (Shaw et al., 2022). This is consistent with the global picture. According to the IPCC assessment report 6 or AR6 (IPCC, 2023), the frequency and intensity of hot extremes (including heat waves) have increased globally, and those of cold extremes have decreased at the global scale since 1950 (virtually certain). Although there is some uncertainty, this also applies at the regional scale, with more than 80% of AR6 regions showing similar trends assessed to be at least likely. Recently, a variety of heat waves known as humid or moist heat waves, during which increased moisture is available in the atmosphere, leading to strong discomfort, have received significant attention (Ambika et al., 2024; Ha et al., 2022; Lekshmi & Chattopadhyay, 2022).

It is found to have strong health impacts, and not including the moist heat underestimates the mental health impact (Fritz, 2025). There is a clear increasing trend in moist heat waves, as these studies and other studies suggest, which implies increased health risk. Heat-related violence, aggression, and domestic violence are well-documented in India and other countries in South Asia. A study based on three countries in South Asia (India, Pakistan, and Nepal) showed conclusive evidence of domestic violence in low- and middle-income families (Zhu et al., 2023).

3.4 Extreme Rain, Floods, Flash Floods

Hydrological disasters, such as extreme rainfall events and floods, are extremely frequent in South Asian countries. Floods and flash floods pose a significant threat to South Asia, causing substantial damage and loss of life. These disasters are often exacerbated by factors like heavy monsoon rains, highly localized rainfall events (e.g., thunderstorms, mesocyclones, and cloudbursts), climate change, glacial melts, glacial lake outburst floods, etc. Flooding frequency in larger urban areas (urban flooding) is also increasing, with larger losses and damage. Most of the large-scale river floods occur during monsoon times in countries like India, Pakistan, and Bangladesh. Flash floods and mountain floods are common in the foothills of the Himalaya and Nepal. According to some studies, there is no uniform trend (Janizadeh et al., 2024; Trancoso et al., 2024) of flood risk in a warming scenario. In some specific countries, such as Bangladesh, Bhutan, India, and Nepal, the percentage of high flood risk susceptibility is expected to increase under SSP1-2.6 and SSP5-8.5 in the near future (2041–2060) and far future (2081–2100) timeframes. In contrast, Afghanistan and Pakistan may experience a decrease. In Pakistan, recent flooding has caused significant loss and damage, as well as loss of lives (UNICEF, 2023), which is attributed to increased rainfall due to climate change (WMO, 2022). Thus, such projections have uncertainties over South Asia.

Extreme rainfall events are also increasing over the Indian region (Ali et al., 2019; Goswami et al., 2006; Srivastava et al., 2016), including different river basins (Chaubey et al., 2022; Deshpande et al., 2016), which leads to the risk of local flooding and inundations. Similarly, other countries such as Nepal (Shrestha & Sthapit, 2015), Pakistan (Ikram et al., 2017), and Afghanistan (Shokory et al., 2017) show an increase in extreme rainfall events and flood-related hazards, while Bangladesh reports an increase in dry days and a decrease in total precipitation (Imran et al., 2023), and Sri Lanka reported mixed results with certain parts showing a decrease and other regions showing an increase in rainfall in recent years (Nisansala et al., 2020). Urban flooding, such as that which occurred in the city of Bengaluru, India, on 19 May 2025 (Mandyam, 2025), is becoming a common phenomenon. Such flooding of homes in the urban areas, large traffic congestion, public transport coming to a grinding halt, dozens of flooded streets, flooded underpasses, and closed flyovers are becoming common occurrences every year in metropolitan cities in India and other countries in South Asia. Similarly, in many regions of South Asia, landslides occur in the hilly areas of the Eastern Himalayas (Sangi et al., 2025), Western Ghats (Jain et al., 2021, 2024), Nepal (Kc et al., 2024; Petley, 2024), foothills and upper Himalayas (Dikshit et al., 2020), and other places due to extreme rainfall events related to cyclones, monsoon low-pressure systems, swelling rivers, etc. These non-seismic landslides are a major factor of concern, as there is clear evidence that extreme rainfall events are currently increasing over South Asia and are projected to increase under different climate change scenarios (Mondal et al., 2022).

Flooding and extreme rainfall events can significantly impact mental health, leading to conditions like anxiety, depression, and PTSD. These events can cause stress, loss, and disruption, affecting individuals' emotional well-being (Song et al., 2025). Long-term stress is also noticed by some studies. For example, the 2013 Uttarakhand Mountain flooding that devastated vast stretches of the districts in the state of Uttarakhand, India, has caused long-term mental health impacts (Agarwal, 2018). Similarly, other studies have noticed the wide prevalence of PTSD and depression in different parts of India, like Bihar, Ladakh, and Kashmir (Asim et al., 2019; Dar et al., 2018; Ishikawa et al., 2013). A study conducted shortly after the 2022 Bangladesh flash flood found that around 47% of participants reported severe or extremely severe depression, 41% reported severe or extremely severe anxiety, and 36% reported severe or extremely severe stress (Rahman et al., 2025). Post-flood suicidal behavior is also noticed by some studies based on an analysis of Bangladesh (Mamun et al., 2021). Similarly, some studies in Pakistan reported a strong association between floods and mental disorders in Pakistan (Yousuf et al., 2023). The examples, as shown above, are not exhaustive. However, they certainly indicate flooding and extreme rainfall-related disasters trigger several types of mental disorders. With a clear increased rainfall trend and extreme events, mental health impacts are likely to increase.

3.5 Earthquakes and Tsunamis

Earthquakes are sudden disasters that cause large-scale devastation, and the available response time is often very short. Experiencing such sudden events is likely to increase the tendency to develop mental and behavioral disorders. It directly induces fear or causes post-traumatic stress disorder (PTSD) and other depressive symptoms (Bertinelli et al., 2023). Indirectly, adverse impacts, such as the deaths of close ones, physical injuries, destruction of homes, loss of employment, or community displacement following an earthquake, might generate stress and sadness, resulting in "psychological poverty traps" (Ridley et al., 2020) and increasing the risk of suicide (Bertinelli et al., 2023).

The tectonic setting of the South Asian region is characterized by the ongoing collision of the Indian plate with the Eurasian plate along the Himalayan arc, and its interaction with the Indo-Burmese and Makran subduction zones makes it one of the most seismically active regions in the world. Almost the entire SA region experiences tremors, with vast areas vulnerable to damaging earthquakes, both along well-defined plate boundaries (interplate earthquakes) and within tectonic plates (intraplate earthquakes). The Himalayan arc, extending over 2000 km from the Hindukush-Pamir syntaxis in Afghanistan to the Mishmi Hills in Northeast India, is among the world's most seismically active belts, prone not only to earthquakes but also to secondary hazards such as landslides, flash floods, and Glacial Lake Outburst Floods (GLOFs). Four great Himalayan earthquakes exceeding magnitude 8.0 ($M \geq 8.0$) since 1800 include the 1897 Shillong Plateau (M 8.7), 1905 Kangra (M 8.0), 1934 Bihar–Nepal (M 8.3), and 1950 Assam–Tibet (M 8.5). The South Asian region has also experienced several other destructive earthquakes, such as the 1993 Latur–Osmanabad, India (M 6.3); 1997 Jabalpur, India (M 6.0); 1999 Chamoli,

India (M 6.8); 2001 Bhuj, Gujarat, India (M 7.7); 2005 Muzaffarabad, Pakistan (M 7.6); 2009 Bhutan (M 6.3); 2011 Sikkim, India (M 6.9); 2015 Gorkha, Nepal (M 7.9); and 2021 Sonitpur, Assam, India (M 6.4), 2022 Paktika, Afghanistan (M 6.1); and the 2023 Herat earthquake sequence comprising multiple events, Afghanistan (M 6.0-6.3) (https://seismo.gov.in/data-portal; Kayal, 2025)

Among tsunamigenic events, the 1945 Makran coast earthquake in the Arabian Sea (M 8.3) and the 26 December 2004 Indian Ocean earthquake (M 9.3) remain most notable, with the latter ranked among the most catastrophic in history, severely impacting the Andaman and Nicobar Islands, the east coast of India, Sri Lanka, and the Maldives. These disasters, many of which caused tens of thousands of fatalities and large-scale displacement, highlight South Asia's extreme seismic and tsunami vulnerability, further compounded by dense populations, vulnerable infrastructure, unplanned urbanization, and limited preparedness in many areas. Accurate earthquake prediction specifying the exact location, time, and magnitude remains beyond current scientific capability; therefore, priority must be given to earthquake-resilient construction, retrofitting of critical infrastructure, and sustained public awareness and preparedness. Figure 2.2 represents earthquakes of magnitude 5.0 and above recorded across the region.

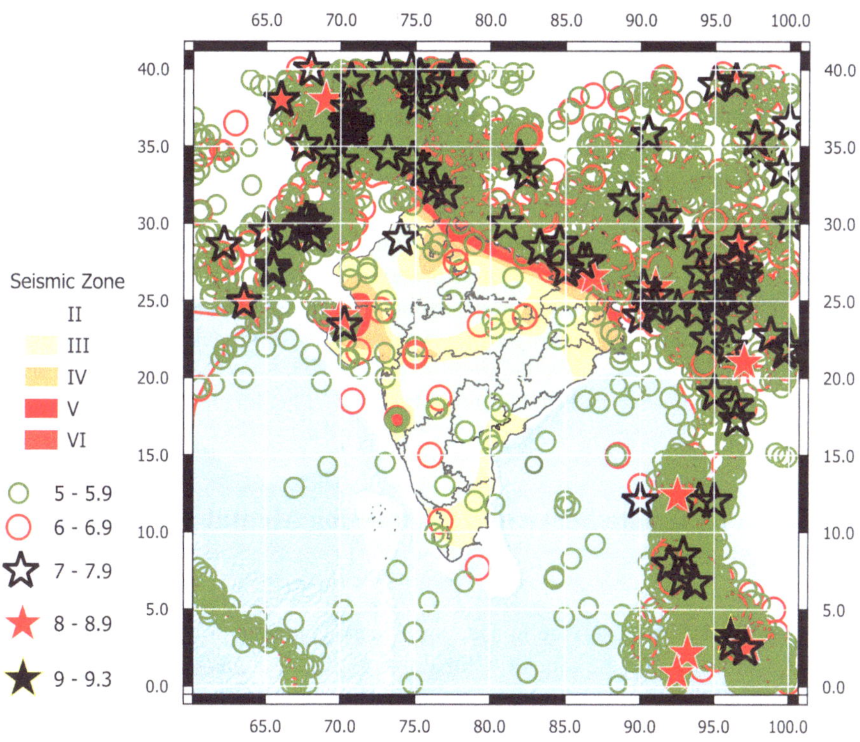

Fig. 2.2 Earthquakes of magnitude 5.0 and above in and around India from the year 1505 to Novemeber 2025; based on earthquake catalogue data obtained from https://seismo.gov.in/data-portal, overlaid with seismic zonation as per BIS Code IS 1893 (Part 1): 2025

Mental distress becomes widespread following major earthquakes, particularly where the collapse of poorly constructed buildings causes mass casualties and severe emotional trauma (Hussaini et al., 2022). These disasters highlight that mental health impacts are a critical, yet often overlooked, consequence of earthquakes, requiring urgent integration of psychosocial care into disaster response and recovery. A study was conducted to estimate the prevalence of PTSD after the 2015 earthquake in Nepal among adult survivors 3 years after the disaster (Acharya Pandey et al., 2023). The study, based on 1076 adult participants, concluded that the prevalence of PTSD among earthquake survivors was 18.9%. These results suggest that enhanced future preparedness is required to handle the impact on mental health of earthquake-related disasters. Climate change can indirectly increase earthquake vulnerability in several ways. Rising sea levels and melting glaciers can alter stress on fault lines, potentially triggering more earthquakes, especially in coastal areas (Irving, 2024). Additionally, changes in precipitation patterns can lead to soil liquefaction and increased landsliding during earthquakes, amplifying their impact.

There are a few studies on the mental health outcomes of the 2004 Indian Ocean tsunami victims. Several studies have noted the high prevalence rates for psychiatric disorders (27.2%) and psychological symptoms (79.7%) in an adult population around 6–9 months following the tsunami in coastal Tamil Nadu (Kar et al., 2013) and other South Asian regions. In Tamil Nadu, the most common psychiatric disorder was depression, followed by alcohol use disorders in males and anxiety disorders in females. Climate change significantly impacts tsunami risks by intensifying coastal hazards, including sea-level rise and extreme weather events. This makes coastal communities more vulnerable to flooding, even from smaller tsunamis. Rising sea levels also mean that tsunamis can travel further inland, increasing the potential for damage.

The above brief review of disasters, both current, and under a warming scenario, suggests that the South Asian region is prone to disasters. The mental health challenges related to climate change issues, which are already recognized in the South Asian region, require further objective connections with regional climate patterns to understand the climate impact, and the climate service has to evolve to provide more practical information to tackle climate-related mental health challenges.

4 Role of Climate Service in Addressing Mental Health Issues

The role of the climate service in shaping risk management policies in the field of mental healthcare may be crucial. Climate services are essential in managing climate risk, as they empower decision-makers with the necessary information to make well-informed choices regarding the mitigation and adaptation to climate-related risks. These tools and methods facilitate the anticipation, avoidance, and management of impacts stemming from extreme weather and gradual changes, thereby playing a crucial role in sustainable development. The climate service is, thus, an essential component of *climate action*, a UN-promoted Sustainable Development Goal (https://sdgs.un.org/goals) aimed at urgently combating climate change and its impacts by strengthening resilience, integrating measures into policies, improving education/awareness, and mobilising resources. A few components of climate service that may be critical for mental health issues related to disaster risk management are:

4.1 Development of Efficient Early Warning Systems for Meteorological and Geophysical Disasters

The risk management of the hazards depends on several factors, including (i) hazard and vulnerability analysis for every disaster, (ii) preparedness and planning at different geographical scales, (iii) continuous early warning systems (EWS), and (iv) prevention and mitigation. The early warning component includes (i) developing realistic skills in monitoring and prediction of disasters, (ii) effective and real-time warning products generation and dissemination, (iii) coordination with disaster response authorities, (iv) capacity building, and (v) public awareness and perception about the credibility of early warning of meteorological and geological hazards. In case of earthquakes that cannot be precisely predicted, rapid earthquake detection and Earthquake Early Warning Systems (EEWS) can issue alerts within seconds of detection, providing valuable time for protective action. When combined with pre-disaster preparedness and strict enforcement of building byelaws, such systems not only enhance physical safety but also help reduce post-event psychological trauma by enabling more controlled emergency responses. This approach allows mental health professionals to design a strategy before a crisis or relapse occurs, allowing for timely intervention and potentially preventing more severe consequences (such as the development of lingering stress, PTSD, etc.). It also allows efficient utilization of manpower resources to deal with such emergency situations. Climate EWS can also help develop mental health EWS, which can help classify individuals into different risk levels based on their observed warning signs and collected data, allowing for targeted intervention. For South Asia, climate forecasts are available through the WMO RA-II regional climate center (RCC) situated at Pune, India (https://rcc.imdpune.gov.in/). The seasonal forecast outlooks are also disseminated through official channels as well as regular stakeholder interaction forums (e.g., SASCOF https://rcc.imdpune.gov.in/sascof.php) with participation from different operational agencies representing the South Asian countries. Weather conditions and probable outlooks for disasters like seasonal droughts, cyclone tracks, heat waves, and cold waves are regularly given. Such forecasts can be used for mental health emergencies like PTSD, poverty-related suicide of farmers, etc.

The new technologies and methodologies include mainly, (i) introduction of modernized observing systems like doppler weather radar, automated weather stations, automated rain gauges, high wind speed recorders; (ii) establishment of digitized forecasting platform and public weather services system; (iii) adoption of global and regional deterministic and ensemble prediction systems and storm surge and coastal inundation models; (iv) high power computing system to run the models and decision support system for forecasting; and (v) implementation of all modern means of communication including dissemination through email, SMS, use of social media, etc. Introduced by India, these have benefitted the entire South Asia in recent decades (Mohapatra & Sharma, 2025; Mohapatra et al., 2025). All the above initiatives led to (i) extension of lead period of warning from 1 day in 2008 to 3 days in 2014 to 5 days in 2018, (ii) extension of cyclone track and intensity forecast from 24 hour in 2008 to 72 hour in 2009 and to 120 hour, in 2013, (iii) introduction of extended range forecast (for next 2 weeks) in 2016 and for cyclogenesis in 2018, (iv) introduction of fishermen warning for entire north Indian Ocean since 2018, (v) district-wise impact based forecast and warning in color coded form in 2018, and (vi) location specific nowcast in the region. During the past 10 years, there has been about a 40–50% improvement in the forecast accuracy of various severe weather events affecting South Asia. The improved warnings with increased accuracy and a high lead time for hazards like cyclones, heavy rainfall, and heat waves have helped the disaster managers and the general public to minimize loss of lives and property.

Another important disaster in the coastal region is the tsunami-related coastal swelling or similar storm surges during cyclones. Tsunami EWS is operated by INCOIS, Hyderabad, India, and provides information on coastal conditions and tsunamis (https://tsunami.incois.gov.in/TEWS/). Although disasters like tsunamis are very fast-onset disasters, the effective communication of such warnings and identification of exact locations in the coastal areas can help in the preparations of health teams for post-disaster response. The tsunami warning system caters to the needs of the whole South Asian region, which has coastlines.

4.2 Development of Long-Term Observation and Climate Monitoring Systems for Proper Health Impact Assessment

The mental health literature discusses various remedial measures to counteract the disease burden related to climate disasters. Human resilience and coping can reduce the effects of mental health stress due to climate change. Climate information plays a crucial role in enhancing human resilience by enabling better preparedness, adaptation, and mitigation of climate-related risks. It helps communities understand potential impacts, develop EWS (as discussed above), and implement effective adaptation strategies. In particular, seismic microzonation studies, which classify regions into different hazard zones based on local geology, soil conditions, and expected ground motion, are critical in densely populated and high-risk urban areas.

These maps provide inputs for earthquake-resistant building codes and can be overlaid with population vulnerability data to produce composite “mental health risk maps” that highlight areas where post-earthquake psychosocial interventions may be most urgently needed.

In India, for example, the Heat Action Plan implemented in Ahmedabad, Nagpur, and several other cities has successfully reduced heat-related mortality by promoting community awareness and establishing heat shelters (Amach, 2019). Such policy actions significantly reduce the impact, including the impact on mental health. Climate information is generated as a part of operational weather and climate services in all South Asian countries. India Meteorological Department (IMD) works with other national and state agencies to provide timely and useful climate information before, during, and after a disaster strikes. In this regard, the cyclone warning system may be mentioned. Starting from the formation of the cyclone to its landfall and dissipation, weather and climate information is shared with the disaster responders. This has created a very positive result due to the generation of specific and operationally useful information (such as affected districts, need for temporary shift of population, etc.) (Mohapatra & Sharma, 2025).

An integral part of climate observation and monitoring systems is the availability of the data for public use. The weather and climate information has to reach people through media, local government agencies, and other nongovernment agencies. In this context, the availability of long-term climate information plays a great role. For example, a hazard atlas is prepared by IMD, which identifies the vulnerability of districts in India related to a specific hazard. An example is shown in Fig. 2.3. The hazard map of drought, heat wave, and floods for the districts of India provides long-term vulnerability information related to a specific hazard. The maps indicate the most severely affected area, based on which a

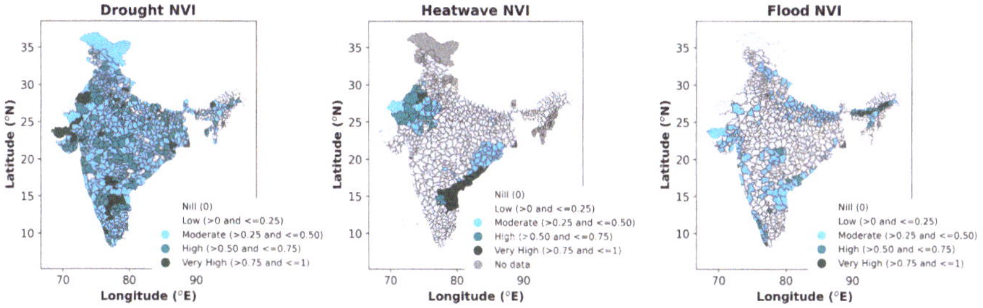

Fig. 2.3 Normalized vulnerability index (NVI) for the districts of India obtained from India Meteorological Department (IMD) Climate Hazard and Vulnerability Atlas. The left panel shows drought, the middle panel shows heat wave, and the right panel shows flood. The districts with darker shades are more vulnerable to the disasters mentioned above. This index is calculated based on data from 1969 to 2019. (Data source: Climate Application and User Interface Group, IMD Pune. For more details refer:https://imdpune.gov.in/hazardatlas/index.html)

mental health risk map can be generated, provided risk-exposure of the population is available (refer to risk equation in Sect. 2). Thus, a mental action plan can be formulated for any district. It is clear from the figure that, since the geo-spatial distributions of districts affected (i.e., vulnerability) are different for different hazards, the risk maps will be different for different types of hazards. In this context, it is important to note that the IMD atlas, as shown here, only considers mortality and meteorological hazard information. There is no mental health information given. Such exposure information generation, including mental health information, is thus extremely necessary for long-term planning and is the need of the hour.

5 Conclusions and Future Scope

Though there have been significant improvement in monitoring and warning system of the hazards in south Asia in recent years, there is still scope for improvement in terms of *(i)* improving meteorological and seismic monitoring networks, especially for the mesoscale hazards (such as thunder storm, hail storm, squall etc.) detection and continuous monitoring, and, in case of seismic, improving earthquake detection and quick dissemination of earthquake report; *(ii)* improving the spatial and temporal scale of forecasts through technological upgradation; *(iii)* applications of early warning to health sector; *(iv)* warning communication to last mile through state of art technology; *(v)* developing synergized standard operation procedure with health agencies; *(vi)* establishing Earthquake Early Warning Systems (EEWS) in high seismic risk zones, *(vii)* institutionalizing training programs for stakeholders, *(viii)* establishing disaster resilient infrastructure supported by detailed city-scale seismic microzonation and risk-informed planning, and *(ix)* establishing a robust third-party audit mechanism for new constructions and retrofitted structures in high-risk areas to ensure compliance with design codes. Ultimately, reducing risk is not just a scientific challenge; it is a societal responsibility. A coordinated strategy that blends innovation, community engagement, and systematic enforcement of preparedness measures, integrating mental health support into risk reduction, will be essential in shaping a safer and multi-hazard resilient South Asia. A 2021 WHO survey of 95 countries found that only nine have thus far included mental health and psychosocial support in their national health and climate change plans. To further popularize the effort, the recent WHO policy brief recommends five important methods for governments to address the mental health impacts of climate change (WHO, 2022). They are as follows: (i) integrate climate and environmental considerations with mental health programs, (ii) integrate mental health support with climate action as a sustainable development goal, (iii) build upon global commitments, (iv) develop community-based approaches to reduce vulnerabilities, and (iv) close the large funding gap that exists currently for development of mental health and psychosocial support system.

In this context, India has a national program, the National Program for Climate Change and Human Health (NPCCHH), which aims to develop a comprehensive climate-information based health system to generate public awareness, capacity-building activities in the healthcare sectors, strengthen health system preparedness to overcome increased risk, and collaborate with climate service providers with respect to the impacts of climate change on mental health (NPCCHH-MoHFW, 2024). A comprehensive mental health action plan has been developed to include climate change and climate information as a part of mental health policy. The main objective of the climate change Program initiated by NPCCHH includes:

- Situational analysis of mental health illness in the context of climate change.
- Awareness generation through Information, Education, and Communication campaigns (IEC).
- Develop a surveillance system on mental health illnesses due to climate change (pilot).
- Capacity building.
- Public health management of mental health problems due to climate change, coordination with different sectors (health and non-health).

Similarly, Bangladesh, Nepal, Pakistan, and many other countries in South Asia have effectively documented the mental health impact of climate change and the policy requirement to improve mental health resilience with a projected increase in the frequency of climate disasters. However, from the review above, it is clear that there is a clear scope for improvement in connecting climate information and mental health policies to improve resilience in the context of climate change. In some countries, such as Sri Lanka and the Maldives, although mental health issues are studied in various contexts, there is further scope for integrating climate change information into the mental health domain.

References

Aadhar, S., & Mishra, V. (2019). A substantial rise in the area and population affected by dryness in South Asia under 1.5 °c, 2.0 °c, and 2.5 °c warmer worlds. *Environmental Research Letters, 14*(11). https://doi.org/10.1088/1748-9326/AB4862

Acharya Pandey, R., Chalise, P., Khadka, S., Chaulagain, B., Maharjan, B., Pandey, J., Nepal, J., & Pandey, C. (2023). Post-traumatic stress disorder and its associated factors among survivors of the 2015 earthquake in Nepal. *BMC Psychiatry, 23*(1), 340. https://doi.org/10.1186/S12888-023-04836-3

Agarwal, M. (2018, July 4). *Waiting to heal: Five years since the Uttarakhand floods, the scars are still fresh.* https://india.mongabay.com/2018/07/waiting-to-heal-five-years-since-the-uttarakhand-floods-the-scars-are-still-fresh/. Last accessed 9 Aug 2025.

Agarwal, N., & Tandon, V. (2025, March 8). *Climate change & the silent storm: India's growing mental health crisis – BW healthcare world.* https://www.bwhealthcareworld.com/article/climate-change-the-silent-storm-indias-growing-mental-health-crisis-553003. Last accessed 9 Aug 2025.

Ali, H., Modi, P., & Mishra, V. (2019). Increased flood risk in Indian sub-continent under the warming climate. *Weather and Climate Extremes, 25*. https://doi.org/10.1016/J.WACE.2019.100212

Almulhim, A. I., Alverio, G. N., Sharifi, A., Shaw, R., Huq, S., Mahmud, M. J., Ahmad, S., & Abubakar, I. R. (2024). Climate-induced migration in the global south: An in depth analysis. *Npj Climate Action, 3*(1), 1–12. https://doi.org/10.1038/s44168-024-00133-1

Amach, O. (2019, July 5). *India: Lessons on dealing with the growing heatwaves | UNDRR*. https://www.undrr.org/quick/77042. Last accessed 9 Aug 2025.

Amarnath G., Alahacoon, N., Smakhtin, V., & Aggarwal, P. (2017). *Mapping multiple climate-related hazards in South Asia*. https://doi.org/10.5337/2017.207.

Ambika, A. K., Rajeev, A., & Huber, M. (2024). Global warming amplifies outdoor extreme moist heat during the Indian summer monsoon. *Earth's Future, 12*(7), e2024EF004673. https://doi.org/10.1029/2024EF004673

Ansari, E., & Kar, S. K. (2024). Mental health amid climate crisis: A narrative review. *Indian Journal of Psychiatry, 66*(11), 987–996. https://doi.org/10.4103/INDIANJPSYCHIATRY.INDIANJPSYCHIATRY_526_24

Asim, M., Mekkodathil, A., Sathian, B., Elayedath, R., N, R. K., Simkhada, P., & van Teijlingen, E. (2019). Post-traumatic stress disorder among the flood affected population in Indian subcontinent. *Nepal Journal of Epidemiology, 9*(1), 755. https://doi.org/10.3126/NJE.V9I1.24003

Baddam John, P., Russell, S., & Russell, P. S. S. (2007). The prevalence of posttraumatic stress disorder among children and adolescents affected by tsunami disaster in Tamil Nadu. *Disaster Management & Response, 5*(1), 3–7. https://doi.org/10.1016/j.dmr.2006.11.001

Barrett, S., Steinbach, D., & Addison, S. (2021). *Assessing vulnerabilities to disaster displacement A good practice review*. http://pubs.iied.org/20671IIED. ISBN: 978-1-78431-935-9. Last accessed 9 Aug 2025.

Bertinelli, L., Mahé, C., & Strobl, E. (2023). Earthquakes and mental health. *World Development, 169*, 106283. https://doi.org/10.1016/J.WORLDDEV.2023.106283

Bloomberg. (2022, September 6). *Damage from Pakistan floods is 'far greater' than $10 Billion, Ahsan Iqbal Says – Bloomberg*. https://www.bloomberg.com/news/articles/2022-09-06/damage-from-pakistan-floods-is-far-greater-than-10-billion?embedded-checkout=true. Last accessed 9 Aug 2025.

Chaubey, P. K., Mall, R. K., Jaiswal, R., & Payra, S. (2022). Spatio-temporal changes in extreme rainfall events over different Indian River Basins. *Earth and Space Science, 9*(3), e2021EA001930. https://doi.org/10.1029/2021EA001930

Chhetri, B., Zangpo, D., & Gyeltshen, D. (2024). Climate change and mental health in Bhutan. *Bhutan Health Journal, 10*(2). https://doi.org/10.47811/bhj.174

Cissé, G., McLeman, R., Adams, H., Aldunce, P., Bowen, K., Campbell-Lendrum, D., Clayton, S., Ebi, K. L., Hess, J., Huang, C., Liu, Q., McGregor, G., Semenza, J., & Tirado, M. C. (2022). Health, wellbeing, and the changing structure of communities. In *Climate change 2022: Impacts, adaptation and vulnerability. Contribution of working group II to the sixth assessment report of the intergovernmental panel on climate change* [H.-O. Pörtner, D.C. Roberts, M. Tignor, E.S. Poloczanska, K. Mintenbeck, A. Alegría, M. Craig, S. Langsdorf, S. Löschke, V. Möller, A. Okem, B. Rama (eds.)] (pp. 1041–1170). Cambridge University Press. doi:https://doi.org/10.1017/9781009325844.009.

Clayton, S., Litchfield, C., & Geller, E. S. (2013). Psychological science, conservation, and environmental sustainability. *Frontiers in Ecology and the Environment, 11*(7), 377–382. https://doi.org/10.1890/120351

Confalonieri, U., Menne, B., Akhtar, R., Ebi, K. L., Hauengue, M., Kovats, R. S., Revich, B., & Woodward, A. (2007). Chapter 8: Human health – AR4 WGII. In M. L. parry, O. F. Canziani, J. P. Palutikof, P. J. van der Linden, & C. E. Hanson (Eds.), (1st ed., pp. 391–431) ISBN 978 0521 70597-4. https://archive.ipcc.ch/publications_and_data/ar4/wg2/en/ch8.html

Damodaran, V. (2015). *The East India company, famine and ecological conditions in eighteenth-century Bengal* (Palgrave Studies in World Environmental History, Part F1874) (pp. 80–101). https://doi.org/10.1057/9781137427274_5

Dar, K. A., Iqbal, N., Prakash, A., & Paul, M. A. (2018). PTSD and depression in adult survivors of flood fury in Kashmir: The payoffs of social support. *Psychiatry Research, 261*, 449–455. https://doi.org/10.1016/J.PSYCHRES.2018.01.023

Daraz, U., Khan, Y., Alsawalqa, R. O., Alrawashdeh, M. N., & Alnajdawi, A. M. (2024). Impact of climate change on women mental health in rural hinterland of Pakistan. *Frontiers in Psychiatry, 15*, 1450943. https://doi.org/10.3389/FPSYT.2024.1450943

Dasgupta, R., & Basu, M. (2023). Mental health and socio-psychological manifestations of cyclone-induced water insecurity in the Indian Sundarban delta. *International Journal of Disaster Risk Reduction, 98*, 104085. https://doi.org/10.1016/J.IJDRR.2023.104085

Deshpande, N. R., Kothawale, D. R., & Kulkarni, A. (2016). Changes in climate extremes over major river basins of India. *International Journal of Climatology, 36*(14), 4548–4559. https://doi.org/10.1002/JOC.4651

Dikshit, A., Sarkar, R., Pradhan, B., Segoni, S., & Alamri, A. M. (2020). Rainfall induced landslide studies in Indian Himalayan region: A critical review. *Applied Sciences, 10*(7), 2466. https://doi.org/10.3390/APP10072466

Fritz, M. (2025). *Beyond the heat: The mental health toll of temperature and humidity in India*. https://arxiv.org/pdf/2503.08761v1

Froese, R., & Schilling, J. (2019). The nexus of climate change, land use, and conflicts. *Current Climate Change Reports, 5*(1), 24–35. https://doi.org/10.1007/S40641-019-00122-1

Goswami, B. N., Venugopal, V., Sangupta, D., Madhusoodanan, M. S., & Xavier, P. K. (2006). Increasing trend of extreme rain events over India in a warming environment. *Science, 314*(5804), 1442–1445. https://doi.org/10.1126/science.1132

Goudet, J. M., Arif, F. B., Owais, H., Ahmed, H. U., & Ridde, V. (2024). Climate change and women's mental health in two vulnerable communities of Bangladesh: An ethnographic study. *PLOS. Global Public Health, 4*(6 June), e0002080. https://doi.org/10.1371/journal.pgph.0002080

Ha, K. J., Seo, Y. W., Yeo, J. H., Timmermann, A., Chung, E. S., Franzke, C. L. E., Chan, J. C. L., Yeh, S. W., & Ting, M. (2022). Dynamics and characteristics of dry and moist heatwaves over East Asia. *npj Climate and Atmospheric Science, 5*(1), 1–11. https://doi.org/10.1038/s41612-022-00272-4

Heinz, A., & Brandt, L. (2024). Climate change and mental health: Direct, indirect, and intersectional effects. *The Lancet Regional Health – Europe, 43*, 100969. https://doi.org/10.1016/J.LANEPE.2024.100969

Hossain, A., Ahmed, B., Rahman, T., Sammonds, P., Zaman, S., Benzadid, S., & Jakariya, M. (2021). Household food insecurity, income loss, and symptoms of psychological distress among adults following the Cyclone Amphan in coastal Bangladesh. *PLoS One, 16*(11), e0259098. https://doi.org/10.1371/JOURNAL.PONE.0259098

Hussaini, S. J., Ali, S. H., Syyeda Rahmat, Z., Islam, Z., & Tharwani, Z. H. (2022). Mental health impacts of earthquake on Afghans amidst humanitarian crisis. *Annals of Medicine and Surgery, 81*, 104521. https://doi.org/10.1016/J.AMSU.2022.104521

Ikram, F., Afzaal, M., Bukhari, S. A. A., & Ahmed, B. (2017). Past and future trends in frequency of heavy rainfall events over Pakistan. *Pakistan Journal of Meteorology, 12*(24), 57.

Imran, H. M., Kala, J., Uddin, S., Saiful Islam, A. K. M., & Acharya, N. (2023). Spatiotemporal analysis of temperature and precipitation extremes over Bangladesh using a novel gridded observational dataset. *Weather and Climate Extremes, 39*, 100544. https://doi.org/10.1016/J.WACE.2022.100544

Intergovernmental Panel on Climate Change (IPCC). (2023). Health, wellbeing and the changing structure of communities. In *Climate change 2022 – Impacts, adaptation and vulnerability* (pp. 1041–1170). Cambridge University Press. https://doi.org/10.1017/9781009325844.009

IPCC. (2023). Weather and climate extreme events in a changing climate. In *Climate change 2021 – The physical science basis* (pp. 1513–1766). Cambridge University Press. https://doi.org/10.1017/9781009157896.013

Irving, K. (2024, July 10). *Will we have more earthquakes because of climate change? | Live Science*. https://www.livescience.com/planet-earth/earthquakes/will-we-have-more-earthquakes-because-of-climate-change

Ishikawa, M., Yamamoto, N., Yamanaka, G., Suwa, K., Nakajima, S., Hozo, R., Norboo, T., Okumiya, K., Matsubayashi, K., & Otsuka, K. (2013). Disaster-related psychiatric disorders among survivors of flooding in Ladakh, India. *International Journal of Social Psychiatry, 59*(5), 468–473. https://doi.org/10.1177/0020764012440677

Jain, N., Martha, T. R., Khanna, K., Roy, P., & Kumar, K. V. (2021). Major landslides in Kerala, India, during 2018–2020 period: An analysis using rainfall data and debris flow model. *Landslides, 18*(11), 3629–3645. https://doi.org/10.1007/s10346-021-01746-x

Jain, N., Roy, P., Jalan, P., Martha, T. R., & Das, I. C. (2024). Irshalwadi landslide in Western Ghats of India: Observations from precursory slope movement, rainfall and soil moisture. *Natural Hazards Research, 4*(4), 579–583. https://doi.org/10.1016/J.NHRES.2024.01.004

Janizadeh, S., Kim, D., Jun, C., Bateni, S. M., Pandey, M., & Mishra, V. N. (2024). Impact of climate change on future flood susceptibility projections under shared socioeconomic pathway scenarios in South Asia using artificial intelligence algorithms. *Journal of Environmental Management, 366*, 121764. https://doi.org/10.1016/J.JENVMAN.2024.121764

Kabir, S., Newnham, E., Dewan, A., Islam, M. M., & Hamamura, T. (2024). Psychological health declined during the post-monsoon season in communities impacted by sea-level rise in Bangladesh. *Communications Earth & Environment, 5*(1), 1–11. https://doi.org/10.1038/s43247-024-01862-1

Kafle, S. K. (2017). Disaster risk management systems in South Asia: Natural hazards, vulnerability, disaster risk and legislative and institutional frameworks. *Journal of Geography & Natural Disasters, 7*(3). https://doi.org/10.4172/2167-0587.1000207

Kar, N., Jagadisha, Sharma, P., Murali, N., & Mehrotra, S. (2004). Mental health consequences of the trauma of super-cyclone 1999 in Orissa. *Indian Journal of Psychiatry, 46*(3), 228. https://pmc.ncbi.nlm.nih.gov/articles/PMC2951648/

Kar, N., Krishnaraaj, R., & Rameshraj, K. (2013). Long-term mental health outcomes following the 2004 Asian tsunami disaster: A comparative study on direct and indirect exposure. *Disaster Health, 2*(1), 35. https://doi.org/10.4161/DISH.24705

Kayal, J. R. (2025). 100 years of Seismology in India: A short review on recent large earthquakes and risk. *Indian Journal of Geosciences, 79*(1), 143–172. ISSN/ISBN 2229 3574 (Print) 2582 3485 (Online) https://www.gsi.gov.in/webcenter/portal/OCBIS/pageQuickLinks/pageIndianJournal

Kazuyuki Uji. (2012). *The health impacts of climate change in Asia-Pacific (Background Paper in One Planet to Share)*. https://cdn.who.int/media/docs/default-source/climate-change/the-health-impacts-of-climate-change-in-asia-pacific65a37137-3449-4936-a711-7fcaa7c1b4ae.pdf?sfvrsn=8358390a_1. Last accessed 9 Aug 2025.

Kc, R., Sharma, K., Dahal, B. K., Aryal, M., & Subedi, M. (2024). Study of the spatial distribution and the temporal trend of landslide disasters that occurred in the Nepal Himalayas from 2011 to 2020. *Environmental Earth Sciences, 83*(1), 1–18. https://doi.org/10.1007/s12665-023-11347-7

Lekshmi, S., & Chattopadhyay, R. (2022). Modes of summer temperature intraseasonal oscillations and heatwaves over the Indian region. *Environmental Research: Climate, 1*(2), 025009. https://doi.org/10.1088/2752-5295/ac9fe7

Mahendran, R., Xu, R., Li, S., & Guo, Y. (2021). Interpersonal violence associated with hot weather. *The Lancet Planetary Health, 5*(9), e571–e572. https://doi.org/10.1016/S2542-5196(21)00210-2

Mamun, M. A., Safiq, M. B., Hosen, I., & Mamun, F. A. (2021). Suicidal behavior and flood effects in Bangladesh: A two-site interview study. *Risk Management and Healthcare Policy, 14*, 129–142. https://doi.org/10.2147/RMHP.S282965

Mandyam, N. (2025, May 20). 3 dead, 500 homes flooded, streets submerged: Marooned Bengaluru braces for 5 more days of heavy rain | Bengaluru News – The Times of India. *Times of India*. https://timesofindia.indiatimes.com/city/bengaluru/3-dead-500-homes-flooded-streets-submerged-marooned-bengaluru-braces-for-5-more-days-of-heavy-rain/articleshow/121281055.cms

Minale, A. S., Alemayehu, Z. Y., & Adam, A. G. (2024). Climate-change-driven conflict: Insights from North Wollo, Northeast Ethiopia. *Sustainable Environment, 10*(1). https://doi.org/10.1080/27658511.2024.2361563

Mohapatra, M., & Sharma, M. (2025). Cyclone warning system in India: A journey of success over 25 years. *Weather and Forecasting, 1*(aop). https://doi.org/10.1175/WAF-D-23-0188.1

Mohapatra, M., Sharma, M., & Pattanaik, D. R. (2025). Evolution of cyclone monitoring and forecasting system in India: A review. *Mausam, 76*(1), 103–124. https://doi.org/10.54302/mausam.v76i1.6940

Mondal, S. K., Huang, J., Wang, Y., Su, B., Kundzewicz, Z. W., Jiang, S., Zhai, J., Chen, Z., Jing, C., & Jiang, T. (2022). Changes in extreme precipitation across South Asia for each 0.5 °C of warming from 1.5 °C to 3.0°C above pre-industrial levels. *Atmospheric Research, 266*, 105961. https://doi.org/10.1016/J.ATMOSRES.2021.105961

Narayanan, S. P., & Suresh, R. (2024). Farmers' suicide in India: "Sociological disaster or unrecognized psychopathology". *Kerala Journal of Psychiatry, 37*(1), 59–65. https://doi.org/10.30834/KJP.37.1.2024.446

Nisansala, W. D. S., Abeysingha, N. S., Islam, A., & Bandara, A. M. K. R. (2020). Recent rainfall trend over Sri Lanka (1987–2017). *International Journal of Climatology, 40*(7), 3417–3435. https://doi.org/10.1002/JOC.6405

NPCCHH (MoHFW). (2024). *National Action plan for climate change and mental health*. https://ncdc.mohfw.gov.in/wp-content/uploads/2024/07/2-National-Action-Plan-on-climate-change-and-Mental-Health.pdf

Patwary, M. M., Bardhan, M., Haque, M. A., Moniruzzaman, S., Gustavsson, J., Khan, M. M. H., Koivisto, J., Salwa, M., Mashreky, S. R., Rahman, A. K. M. F., Tasnim, A., Islam, M. R., Alam, M. A., Hasan, M., Al Harun, M. A. Y., Nyberg, L., & Islam, M. A. (2024). Impact of extreme weather events on mental health in South and Southeast Asia: A two decades of systematic review of observational studies. *Environmental Research, 250*. https://doi.org/10.1016/j.envres.2024.118436

Petley, D. (2024). *The 26 to 28 September 2024 landslide disaster in Nepal*. https://eos.org/thelandslideblog/28-to-28-september-2024-nepal. Last accessed 9 Aug 2025.

Prasad, G. C. (2024). *India hit by a fourth of Asia Pacific's $230 bn economic loss due to weather disasters | Mint*. Mint. https://www.livemint.com/economy/india-hit-by-a-fourth-of-asia-pacifics-230-bn-economic-loss-due-to-weather-disasters-11715768268736.html

PTI. (2022, September 9). *Pakistan floods caused nearly $30 bn economic loss: UN Chief Guterres*. https://www.business-standard.com/article/current-affairs/pakistan-floods-caused-nearly-30-bn-economic-loss-un-chief-guterres-122090901318_1.html. Last accessed 9 Aug 2025.

Rahman, M. M., Shobuj, I. A., Hossain, M. T., Alam, E., Islam, M. K., & Hossain, M. K. (2025). Flood impact on men's mental health: Evidence from flood-prone areas of Bangladesh. *Frontiers in Public Health, 13*. https://doi.org/10.3389/fpubh.2025.1529558

Rai, P., Gauchan, E., Pradhan, R., & Shakya, K. M. (2025). Survey of Nepali doctors on the perception of climate change and health effects. *The Journal of Climate Change and Health, 23*, 100449. https://doi.org/10.1016/J.JOCLIM.2025.100449

Randell, H., Jiang, C., Liang, X. Z., Murtugudde, R., & Sapkota, A. (2021). Food insecurity and compound environmental shocks in Nepal: Implications for a changing climate. *World Development, 145*, 105511. https://doi.org/10.1016/J.WORLDDEV.2021.105511

Ridley, M., Rao, G., Schilbach, F., & Patel, V. (2020). Poverty, depression, and anxiety: Causal evidence and mechanisms. *Science, 370*(6522). https://doi.org/10.1126/science.aay0214

Sangi, L., Ralte, Z., Roluahpuia, B., Dinpuia, L., Lalnunmawia, J., Tlau, L., Sailo, S., Lawmkima, H., Vanthangliana, V., Lalremruatfela, C., & Tluangkima, M. (2025). Preliminary investigation on Cyclone Remal-induced landslides in Aizawl, Mizoram, Northeast India, on the 28th of May 2024. *Landslides, 22*(5), 1563–1575. https://doi.org/10.1007/s10346-025-02477-z

Schramme, T. (2023). Health as complete well-being: The WHO definition and beyond. *Public Health Ethics, 16*(3), 210–218. https://doi.org/10.1093/PHE/PHAD017

Schwartz, S. E. O., Benoit, L., Clayton, S., Parnes, M. K. F., Swenson, L., & Lowe, S. R. (2023). Climate change anxiety and mental health: Environmental activism as buffer. *Current Psychology, 42*(20), 16708–16721. https://doi.org/10.1007/s12144-022-02735-6

Sen, B., Dhimal, M., Latheef, A. T., & Ghosh, U. (2017). Climate change: Health effects and response in South Asia. *BMJ, 359*, j5117. https://doi.org/10.1136/BMJ.J5117

Sharma, M., Mohapatra, M., & Suneetha, P. (2025). Evaluation of operational extended range forecast of cyclogenesis over the north Indian Ocean. *Tropical Cyclone Research and Review, 14*, 82–103. https://doi.org/10.1016/j.tcrr.2025.02.006

Shaw, R., Luo, Y., Cheong, T. S., Abdul Halim, S., Chaturvedi, S., Hashizume, M., Insarov, G. E., Ishikawa, Y., Jafari, M., Kitoh, A., Pulhin, J., Singh, C., Vasant, K., & Zhang, Z. 2022. Asia. In *Climate Change 2022: Impacts, Adaptation and Vulnerability. Contribution of Working Group II to the Sixth Assessment Report of the Intergovernmental Panel on Climate Change* [H.-O. Pörtner, D.C. Roberts, M. Tignor, E.S. Poloczanska, K. Mintenbeck, A. Alegría, M. Craig, S. Langsdorf, S. Löschke, V. Möller, A. Okem, B. Rama (eds.)] (pp. 1457–1579). Cambridge University Press. https://doi.org/10.1017/9781009325844.012.

Sheikh Salim, & Sughra Tunio. (2019, February 6). *The New Humanitarian | In rural Pakistan, 'worst drought in years' drives displacement and hunger.* https://www.thenewhumanitarian.org/news/2019/02/06/rural-pakistan-worst-drought-years-drives-displacement-and-hunger

Shokory, J. A. N., Tsutsumi, J. G., Yamada, H., & Kløve, B. (2017). Intra-seasonal variation of rainfall and climate characteristics in Kabul River basin. *Central Asian Journal of Water Research (CAJWR), 3*(2), 24–40.

Shrestha, R. M., & Sthapit, A. B. (2015). Temporal variation of rainfall in the Bagmati River Basin, Nepal. *Nepal Journal of Science and Technology, 16*(1), 31–40. https://doi.org/10.3126/NJST.V16I1.14355

Song, C., Atun, F., Blanford, J. I., & Anthonj, C. (2025). Impact of flooding on the social and mental health of older adults- A scoping review. *Water Security*, 100190. https://doi.org/10.1016/J.WASEC.2025.100190

Srivastava, A. K., Singh, G. P., & Singh, O. P. (2016). Variability and trends in extreme rainfall over India. *MAUSAM, 67*(4), 745–766. https://doi.org/10.54302/MAUSAM.V67I4.1406

Subramaniam Gowthami. (2023, October). *Six years on, cyclone Ockhi survivors battle lingering mental health impacts.* https://india.mongabay.com/2023/10/six-years-on-cyclone-ockhi-survivors-battle-lingering-mental-health-impacts/

Tachev, V. (2025, March 8). 2025's heatwaves in India, *Pakistan and Bangladesh have arrived.* https://www.climateimpactstracker.com/2025-heatwaves-india-pakistan-bangladesh/

Trancoso, R., Syktus, J., Allan, R. P., Croke, J., Hoegh-Guldberg, O., & Chadwick, R. (2024). Significantly wetter or drier future conditions for one to two thirds of the world's population. *Nature Communications, 15*(1), 1–11. https://doi.org/10.1038/s41467-023-44513-3

Ullah, I., Ma, X., Asfaw, T. G., Yin, J., Iyakaremye, V., Saleem, F., Xing, Y., Azam, K., & Syed, S. (2022). Projected changes in increased drought risks over South Asia under a warmer climate. *Earth's Future, 10*(10), e2022EF002830. https://doi.org/10.1029/2022EF002830

UNICEF. (2023, August). *Devastating floods in Pakistan | UNICEF.* https://www.unicef.org/emergencies/devastating-floods-pakistan-2022. Last accessed 9 Aug 2025.

WHO. (1948). *Summary Reports on Proceedings Minutes and Final Acts of the International Health Conference held in New York from 19 June to 22 July 1946.* World Health Organization.16pp. https://iris.who.int/handle/10665/85573. Last accessed 9 Aug 2025.

WHO. (2022, June 3). *Why mental health is a priority for action on climate change.* https://www.who.int/news/item/03-06-2022-why-mental-health-is-a-priority-for-action-on-climate-change. Last accessed 9 Aug 2025.

WHO. (2023, October 12). *Climate change.* https://www.who.int/news-room/fact-sheets/detail/climate-change-and-health. Last accessed 9 Aug 2025.

WMO. (2022, September 16). *Climate change likely increased intense rainfall in Pakistan: study*. https://wmo.int/media/news/climate-change-likely-increased-intense-rainfall-pakistan-study. Last accessed 9 Aug 2025.

World Bank. (2021, October 28). *South Asia climate roadmap*. https://www.worldbank.org/en/region/sar/publication/south-asia-climate-roadmap. Last accessed 9 Aug 2025.

World Bank. (2024). *The cost of inaction: Quantifying the impact of climate change on health in low- and middle-income countries (English)*. World Bank Group. http://documents.worldbank.org/curated/en/099111324172540265. Last accessed 9 Aug 2025

Xue, Y., & Yanai, M. (2005). Asia, climate of south. In J. E. Oliver (Ed.), *Encyclopedia of world climatology. Encyclopedia of earth sciences series*. Springer. https://doi.org/10.1007/1-4020-3266-8_20

Yousuf, J., Mehmood, H., Aquil, S., Rija, A., Rahmat, Z. S., & Malikzai, A. (2023). Effects of floods on the mental health of Pakistanis: A commentary. *Annals of Medicine and Surgery, 85*(5), 2253. https://doi.org/10.1097/MS9.0000000000000590

Zhu, Y., He, C., Bell, M., Zhang, Y., Fatmi, Z., Zhang, Y., Zaid, M., Bachwenkizi, J., Liu, C., Zhou, L., Chen, R., & Kan, H. (2023). Association of Ambient temperature with the prevalence of intimate partner violence among partnered women in low- and middle-income South Asian Countries. *JAMA Psychiatry, 80*(9), 952–961. https://doi.org/10.1001/JAMAPSYCHIATRY.2023.1958

Chapter 3
Disaster and Mental Health in Bangladesh

Atiqul Haq Mazumder and S. M. Yasir Arafat

1 Introduction

Bangladesh is a densely populated, low-lying nation in South Asia that has long been recognized as one of the world's most vulnerable countries to natural disasters and the adverse effects of climate change. Its unique geographical and climatic conditions, including a vast deltaic floodplain, extensive river networks, and a monsoon climate, make it highly susceptible to recurrent floods, cyclones, storm surges, and riverbank erosion. The country has experienced 75 severe cyclones and floods over the last century, and approximately 1200 kilometers of its riverbanks are subject to active erosion annually. Consequently, an estimated 30 million people are at constant risk (Karim et al., 2024; Wahid et al., 2024; Alam et al., 2021; Hossain et al., 2020; Rahaman et al., 2019).

Bangladesh's climate vulnerability significantly impacts mental health, a topic often overlooked. A systematic review reveals four key themes linking environmental stress to mental ill-health: post-hazard risks, human (im)mobility, social tension, and livelihood loss. Socioeconomic status and gender mediate these impacts, amplifying stress, anxiety, violence, and psychological damage. Integrating mental health into climate action and policy is crucial for a sustainable future (Hayward & Ayeb-Karlsson, 2021).

A. H. Mazumder
Department of Psychiatry, Research Unit of Clinical Medicine, Faculty of Medicine, University of Oulu, Oulu, Finland

S. M. Y. Arafat (✉)
Department of Psychiatry, Bangladesh Specialized Hospital, Dhaka, Bangladesh

Department of Public and Community Health, Faculty of Medicine and Health Sciences, Frontier University, Garowe, Somalia

N. Kar et al. (eds.), *Climate Change, Disaster and Mental Health in South Asia*, South Asian Perspectives in Mental Health and Psychology,
https://doi.org/10.1007/978-981-95-3690-0_3

These geographical vulnerabilities due to its geographical position, low-lying deltaic land crisscrossed by numerous rivers, a monsoon climate, and having a funnel-shaped southern coast are intensified by socioeconomic factors, like poverty, internal displacement, and poor educational attainment. High population density, particularly in coastal regions, coupled with poverty and dependence on climate-sensitive agriculture and fisheries, exacerbates the human impact of disasters. Global climate change is further amplifying these risks, leading to shifts in rainfall patterns, rising sea levels, and an increase in the frequency and intensity of extreme weather events. While Bangladesh is a minor contributor to global greenhouse gas emissions, it disproportionately bears the burden of climate-related death, destruction, and economic loss. This constant struggle against natural and human-induced stressors has profound implications for the mental health and well-being of the Bangladeshi people, a dimension of disaster impact that is critically under-resourced and understudied (Tahsin et al., 2023; Shamsuddoha et al., 2024; Alam et al., 2021; Rahaman et al., 2019).

2 Major Disasters in Bangladesh

Since its war of independence in 1971, which itself left a deep legacy of mental trauma, Bangladesh has been shaped by a history of catastrophic disasters (Cash et al., 2013). A review of the period between 1988 and 1998 shows that fatal natural disasters occurred almost annually, with floods alone costing over 1000 lives within the duration (Alam et al., 2018, 2021). Some of the most significant disaster events are given in Table 3.1.

2.1 *Political Disasters*

The 1971 Liberation War: This foundational conflict resulted in widespread death, injury, and trauma, with over half (51.6%) of injured freedom fighters subsequently developing mental disorders (Alam et al., 2021). The July Mass Uprising (2024) caused at least 1400 deaths and thousands of injuries (United Nations, 2025; Islam et al., 2025).

2.2 *Ethnic Conflicts*

Rohingya crisis in Bangladesh (Jahan et al., 2024)

Table 3.1 Major natural disasters in Bangladesh (1971–2025)

Year	Disaster type	Event name (if applicable)	Key impact/death toll	Affected areas/ notes	Source
1971	Cyclone	November 1971 cyclone	~11,000 deaths	Sunderban coast, Khulna. Low-lying areas inundated	Cyclones—Climate Change Impacts on Health and Population in Bangladesh, n.d.
1972	Drought	Severe drought	Affected 39% of country, half of population	Northwestern regions, widespread crop failure	Droughts—Climate Change Impacts on Health and Population in Bangladesh, n.d.
1974	Flood	1974 flood	Catastrophic, contributed to famine	Widespread, severe impact on lives and properties	Wikipedia contributors, 2025a
1974	Cyclone	August 1974 cyclone	~600 deaths	Khulna coast	Cyclones—Climate Change Impacts on Health and Population in Bangladesh, n.d.
1974	Cyclone	November 1974 cyclone	~200 deaths, 1000 cattle	Cox's Bazar, Chittagong offshore islands	Cyclones—Climate Change Impacts on Health and Population in Bangladesh, n.d.
1975	Drought	Severe drought	Affected 47% of country, 53% of population	Widespread	Droughts—Climate Change Impacts on Health and Population in Bangladesh, n.d.
1979	Drought	Severe drought	Reduced rice production by ~2 million tons; affected 42% cultivated land, 44% population	Widespread crop damage	Droughts—Climate Change Impacts on Health and Population in Bangladesh, n.d.

(continued)

Table 3.1 (continued)

Year	Disaster type	Event name (if applicable)	Key impact/death toll	Affected areas/ notes	Source
1981	Drought	Severe drought	Adversely affected crop production	Widespread	Droughts—Climate Change Impacts on Health and Population in Bangladesh, n.d.
1982	Drought	Drought	~53,000 tons rice production loss	Widespread crop damage	Droughts—Climate Change Impacts on Health and Population in Bangladesh, n.d.
1985	Cyclone	Urir Char Cyclone	~11,069 deaths	Coastal areas, particularly Urir Char	Cyclones—Climate Change Impacts on Health and Population in Bangladesh, n.d.
1987	Flood	1987 flood	1657 deaths	Widespread	Wikipedia contributors, 2025a
1988	Flood	1988 flood	Over 6000 deaths, millions of tons of crops destroyed	Over two-thirds of the country inundated	Wikipedia contributors, 2025a
1988	Cyclone	1988 cyclone/ cyclone 04B	~5704 deaths	Coastal areas	Cyclones—Climate Change Impacts on Health and Population in Bangladesh, n.d.
1989	Drought	1989 drought	~800 deaths	Northwestern districts (e.g., Naogaon, Nawabganj, Nilphamari, Thakurgaon), rivers dried up	Droughts—Climate Change Impacts on Health and Population in Bangladesh, n.d.

(continued)

Table 3.1 (continued)

Year	Disaster type	Event name (if applicable)	Key impact/death toll	Affected areas/ notes	Source
1991	Cyclone	Cyclone Gorky (April 1991)	~138,882–140,000 deaths	Chittagong and Cox's Bazar coasts; material damage ~USD 2.4 billion	Cyclones—Climate Change Impacts on Health and Population in Bangladesh, n.d.
1994–1995	Drought	Persistent drought	Immense damage to crops, especially rice and jute	Northwestern Bangladesh	Droughts—Climate Change Impacts on Health and Population in Bangladesh, n.d.
1996	Tornado	Tangail tornado	~545 deaths	Tangail district	Kunii et al., 1996
1997	Cyclone	May 1997 cyclone	~550 deaths	Coastal areas	Cyclones—Climate Change Impacts on Health and Population in Bangladesh, n.d.
1997	Earthquake	Chittagong earthquake (Mw 6.1)	~23 deaths	Chittagong. Minor damage	Wikipedia contributors, 2024
1998	Flood	1998 flood	~918 deaths	Over two-thirds of the country inundated. Catastrophic, major economic impact	Wikipedia contributors, 2025a
1999	Earthquake	Maheshkhali Island earthquake (Mw 5.2)	~6 deaths	Maheshkhali Island. Moderate damage	Wikipedia contributors, 2024
2003	Earthquake	Khagrachhari earthquake (Mw 5.7)	~2 deaths, 25 injured	Khagrachhari. Moderate damage	Wikipedia contributors, 2024
2004	Flood	2004 flood	~747 deaths	Widespread	Floods—Climate Change Impacts on Health and Population in Bangladesh, n.d.

(continued)

Table 3.1 (continued)

Year	Disaster type	Event name (if applicable)	Key impact/death toll	Affected areas/ notes	Source
2007	Cyclone	Cyclone Sidr (November 2007)	~3363 deaths	Southwestern coastal areas, significant damage to infrastructure and agriculture	Cyclones—Climate Change Impacts on Health and Population in Bangladesh, n.d.
2007	Landslide	Chittagong landslide	Multiple fatalities	Chittagong hilly areas. Triggered by heavy rainfall	Wikipedia contributors, 2025b
2008	Cyclone	2008 (May 8) "Cyclone Nargis"	3500 deaths	Coastal belt of Bangladesh	Cyclones—Climate Change Impacts on Health and Population in Bangladesh, n.d.
2009	Cyclone	Cyclone Aila (May 2009)	~190 deaths	Southwestern coastal areas, severe damage to livelihoods and infrastructure	Cyclones—Climate Change Impacts on Health and Population in Bangladesh, n.d.
2013	Cyclone	2013 (May 16) "Cyclone Mahasen"	17 deaths	Chattogram	Cyclones—Climate Change Impacts on Health and Population in Bangladesh, n.d.
2016	Flood	2016 flood	14 deaths	One of the most devastating floods in recent history, underreported. An estimated 1.9 million people have been affected by flooding across 19 districts of Bangladesh	Floods—Climate Change Impacts on Health and Population in Bangladesh, n.d.

(continued)

Table 3.1 (continued)

Year	Disaster type	Event name (if applicable)	Key impact/death toll	Affected areas/ notes	Source
2016	Cyclone	2016 (May 21) "Cyclone Roanu"	26 deaths	Chattogram. Around 40,000 houses were damaged in the storm	Cyclones—Climate Change Impacts on Health and Population in Bangladesh, n.d.
2017	Flood	2017 flood	Substantial damage to housing, property, and infrastructure	Northeastern regions, particularly Sylhet and Sunamganj	Wikipedia contributors, 2025
2017	Cyclone	2017 (May 28) "Cyclone Mora"	7 deaths	Cox's Bazar	High winds, heavy rain and tidal surges triggered severe floods and landslides
2019	Cyclone	2019 (May 4) "Cyclone Fani"	12 deaths	Coastal belt of Bangladesh (northeastward)	Cyclones—Climate Change Impacts on Health and Population in Bangladesh, n.d.
2020	Cyclone	Cyclone Amphan (May 2020)	~26 deaths, 2.5 million displaced	Southern coast, extensive damage to land and homes	Cyclones—Climate Change Impacts on Health and Population in Bangladesh, n.d.
2021	Earthquake	Chittagong earthquake (Mw 6.2)	~5 injured	Chittagong. Slight damage	Wikipedia contributors, 2024
2023	Earthquake	Chittagong earthquake (Mw 5.5)	Minor damage	Chittagong	Wikipedia contributors, 2024
2024	Flood	2024 flood	71 deaths	Widespread	Communication Department, 2024
2024	Cyclone	Cyclone Remal (May 2024)	Affected ~18 million people	Coastal districts, severe flooding	Tropical Cyclone Remal—May 2024, 2024

(continued)

Table 3.1 (continued)

Year	Disaster type	Event name (if applicable)	Key impact/death toll	Affected areas/ notes	Source
2025	Flood	Mid-May 2025 floods	Loss of lives, displacement of thousands, destruction of homes	Northeastern and southeastern regions (Sylhet, Sunamganj, Moulvibazar, Habiganj, Netrokona, Noakhali, Bhola, Khagrachari, Bandarban, Rangamati). Ongoing	Communication Department, 2025

2.3 *Cyclones*

The nation has been struck by numerous devastating cyclones. The 1991 cyclone claimed an estimated 138,868 lives. More recent cyclones, such as Sidr (2007), Aila (2009), Mahasen (2013), Roanu (2016), Fani (2019), Ramel (2024), and Amphan (2020), have continued to cause significant loss of life and widespread destruction, further compounding community trauma (Karim et al., 2024; Alam et al., 2021; Shume et al., 2025; Response monitoring dashboard: Bangladesh, 2025).

2.4 *Floods*

Severe and recurrent flooding is a defining feature of the Bangladeshi landscape. The 1988, 1998, and 2017 floods and the 2022 and 2024 flash floods are recent examples that have had severe impacts on livelihoods and mental well-being (Islam et al., 2024; Karim et al., 2024; Response monitoring dashboard: Bangladesh, 2025).

2.5 *Tsunami*

2004 South Asia tsunami

2.6 Riverbank Erosion

As a persistent, slow-onset disaster, riverbank erosion displaces countless families annually, leading to loss of homes, land, and social networks (Karim et al., 2024).

2.7 Industrial Disasters

The 2013 Rana Plaza building collapse, which killed over a thousand people, stands as a stark reminder of urban and industrial vulnerabilities, with survivors showing high rates of post-traumatic stress disorder (PTSD) and other stress-related disorders (Alam et al., 2021).

2.8 Aviation Disaster

2018 US Bangla Airlines crash and 2025 Uttara training flight crash at Milestone School and College

2.9 Terrorism

Holey Artisan event 2016, Bangladesh

These events, both sudden and slow onset, create a continuous cycle of loss and stress, forming the backdrop against which the mental health of the population is continuously challenged.

Cyclone Remal, Bangladesh's most powerful storm in over a decade, struck eight southern districts in May 2024, causing significant damage and triggering heavy rains that worsened flooding in the northeast; shortly after, new flash floods hit six northeastern districts for a second time. Monsoon floods intensified in July, affecting five additional northern districts. By mid-August, persistent heavy rains in the northeast and southeast, combined with upstream rainfall from India, led to severe flash floods in the Chattogram region, impacting nine more districts, bringing the total to 29 affected districts nationwide. To address these escalating emergencies, the Humanitarian Coordination Task Team (HCTT) and the government developed and updated a Humanitarian Response Plan (HRP) three times. This plan, concluding in March 2025, sought USD 134 million to provide urgent aid to approximately 2.5 million severely affected people (Response monitoring dashboard: Bangladesh, 2025).

3 Mental Health Impact of Disasters

The psychological consequences of recurring disasters in Bangladesh are severe and pervasive. Survivors often endure not just the loss of homes and livelihoods, but also the trauma of witnessing death, experiencing physical injury, and facing an uncertain future, all of which are significant precursors to mental illness and suicidal behavior (Karim et al., 2024; Mamun et al., 2019, 2021; Hossain et al., 2021; Mahmud et al., 2021; Arobi et al., 2020).

A substantial body of evidence confirms the high prevalence of mental health conditions in post-disaster settings across Bangladesh. Systematic reviews and individual studies have documented alarming rates of depression, anxiety, stress, and PTSD among affected populations. Prevalence rates can be stark, with studies finding depression ranging from 16.3% to as high as 92.7%, and anxiety from 6% to 92.2%, depending on the disaster and population studied. Following floods and cyclones, a majority of affected women have been found to experience moderate to severe depression. For instance, a study in a disaster-prone region found that 63% of women had moderate to severe depressive symptoms (Karim et al., 2024; Moyna et al., 2024).

The mental health impacts are not uniform and are shaped by intersecting vulnerabilities.

3.1 *Gender*

Disasters have a substantial and disproportionate impact on women's mental health, as they are more likely than men to develop psychological difficulties post-calamity (Fatema et al., 2023; Islam, 2010; Akter et al., 2023). These adverse effects include PTSD, depression, anxiety, and stress. A study of 393 women affected by the 2022 Bangladesh flash flood found that 67% experienced severe or extremely severe depression and 65% faced similar levels of anxiety. This mental health burden is severely exacerbated by family violence, which can increase during disasters; women who experienced it reported extremely high rates of severe depression (89%) and anxiety (88%). Greater social and cultural vulnerability, economic instability, and disruptions to daily life contribute to these heightened risks. Women generally experience higher rates of depression, anxiety, and PTSD compared to men. This is often linked to their societal roles, increased caregiving responsibilities post-disaster, economic instability, and heightened risk of gender-based and domestic violence. The burden of collecting potable water in saline-affected areas, for example, increases both physical and mental stress for women. Males mostly experience severe depression (47%), severe anxiety (41%), and severe stress (36%). Factors like age, marital status, housing, occupation, and property loss were linked to these issues. Older, married, illiterate men in temporary housing, and agricultural workers/fishers with low safety ratings were most affected. The findings emphasize the need for targeted psychological interventions and disaster risk reduction strategies for men in flood-prone areas (Shume et al., 2025; Karim et al., 2024; Shamsuddoha et al., 2024; Moyna et al., 2024; Rahman et al., 2023, 2025; Rahaman et al., 2019).

3.2 *Age*

Both the youth and the elderly are particularly vulnerable. Adolescents living in flood shelters exhibit high rates of PTSD and depression. Children who witness the death of loved ones or experience the destruction of their homes can suffer from long-term trauma, manifesting as nightmares, anxiety, and behavioral changes (Al-Mamun et al., 2025; Akhter et al., 2015). The elderly, facing deteriorating physical health and stamina, are also highly susceptible to the psychological stress of disasters (Tasdik Hasan et al., 2020; Karim et al., 2024).

3.3 *Socioeconomic Status*

Poverty is a major determinant of mental health outcomes. Loss of income, damage to crops and property, and food insecurity following a disaster are significant risk factors for psychological distress and suicidal ideation. Those in lower social classes and with less education are more likely to develop suicidal behaviors (Karim et al., 2024; Moyna et al., 2024).

The trauma can be acute, such as the psychotic breakdown experienced by a father upon finding his son's body, or chronic, like the persistent survivor's guilt and nightmares reported by many. The slow-onset impacts of climate change, such as rising temperatures and environmental degradation, also contribute to long-term psychological distress, including anxiety and a sense of hopelessness (Tasdik Hasan et al., 2020; Karim et al., 2024; Wahid et al., 2024; Siddik et al., 2024).

4 Climate Change and Mental Health

Bangladesh's unique geographical and climatic conditions make it exceptionally vulnerable to the impacts of climate change, creating significant threats to the mental well-being of its population. These climate-related risks, including recurrent floods and cyclones, are linked to increased rates of depression, anxiety, PTSD, and substance abuse (Kabir et al., 2016, 2024; Kabir, 2018; Mullick et al., 2014). One nationwide study found that climate-related stressors are associated with the burden of anxiety and depression (Wahid et al., 2023). While the physical health consequences of such disasters are well-documented, the mental health dimensions remain comparatively understudied, complicated by cultural, gender, and linguistic intricacies. Climate change disproportionately harms already disadvantaged populations, including women, the poor, and migrants. A 2024 qualitative study of adolescents displaced by major flooding starkly illustrates this, revealing alarmingly high rates of mental health issues. The study found a severe gender disparity, with 80% of girls experiencing PTSD and 84% suffering from depression, compared to 60.7% and 71.4% for boys, respectively. These outcomes are exacerbated by stressors in temporary shelters, where a lack of privacy is particularly distressing for girls. This evidence highlights a critical need for holistic, gender-sensitive policies and interventions to address the mental health crisis unfolding on the frontlines of climate change (Siddik et al., 2024; Tahsin et al., 2023; Wahid et al., 2024).

5 Current Challenges

Despite the overwhelming evidence of need, the mental health response within Bangladesh's disaster management framework faces profound challenges. A persistent issue is that the mental health of disaster-affected people is consistently neglected and ignored (Tasdik Hasan et al., 2020; Karim et al., 2024).

5.1 Policy and Planning Deficits

Mental health and psychosocial support (MHPSS) has historically been excluded from national disaster management plans. For example, the National Plan for Disaster Management 2010–2015 contained no provision for post-disaster psychosocial care. The primary focus of relief efforts remains on physical health, food, and shelter, while the severe psychological trauma is often left unaddressed (Hossain et al., 2020).

5.2 Resource and Workforce Scarcity

Bangladesh suffers from a critical shortage of mental health professionals, with only around 220 psychiatrists and 50 clinical psychologists for the entire nation. The national budget allocation for mental health is a mere 0.4% of the total health budget. This lack of resources weakens the national capacity to respond effectively to the mental health crises that follow disasters (Choudhury et al., 2006; Alam et al., 2021; Arafat et al., 2024).

5.3 Inadequate Service Delivery

There is a visible gap in the effective delivery of MHPSS to affected populations. Most government and nongovernmental organization (NGO) initiatives lack specific action plans for mental health. Furthermore, there are no dedicated facilities for follow-up care in communities, leaving survivors without long-term support (Alam et al., 2021; Tasdik Hasan et al., 2020).

5.4 Gender Insensitivity in Disaster Risk Reduction

Although women's vulnerability is acknowledged, their leadership potential in disaster management committees is often underutilized. Women frequently feel uncomfortable participating in male-dominated preparedness meetings, hindering the development of truly gender-responsive strategies (Shume et al., 2025).

5.5 Trapped Populations

This concept encompasses climate-induced sociopsychological immobility, which can be exemplified by residents of Dhaka's Bhola Slum. Despite migrating due to environmental pressures, individuals feel psychologically "stuck" due to noneconomic losses like identity, honor, and belonging. Using Q-methodology and discourse analysis, the research reveals that these emotional and psychosocial factors critically influence decisions to stay and overall well-being, underscoring their importance for sustainable climate adaptation policies (Ayeb-Karlsson et al., 2020).

5.6 Cultural and Social Barriers

A cultural fatalistic acceptance of mental health issues and significant social stigma prevent many individuals from seeking help. This can lead to delays in treatment and worsening outcomes, particularly in rural and conservative communities (Tasdik Hasan et al., 2020).

6 Ways Ahead

Addressing the mental health crisis in the context of disasters requires a strategic and multifaceted approach. There are promising signs of a paradigm shift, with the government beginning to move from a purely reactive crisis response to a more comprehensive concept of total management that incorporates primary healthcare (Alam et al., 2021).

6.1 Policy Integration and Governance

It is imperative to formally integrate MHPSS into all phases of the national disaster management cycle—preparedness, response, and recovery. Professionals and advocates are strongly lobbying for the inclusion of post-disaster psychosocial rehabilitation services within the National Plan for Disaster Management. This must be supported by adequate government funding and the creation of multidisciplinary teams to oversee planning and implementation (Hossain et al., 2020).

6.2 Capacity Building and Training

The capacity of the existing healthcare system must be strengthened. This involves providing comprehensive training on disaster psychiatry and psychological first aid to primary healthcare providers, who are the first point of contact for most communities. Furthermore, incentives should be created to encourage young medical graduates to specialize in psychiatry to address the severe workforce shortage (Alam et al., 2021; Hossain et al., 2020).

6.3 Community-Based and Gender-Responsive Interventions

A one-size-fits-all approach is ineffective. Interventions must be community-based, culturally sensitive, and gender-responsive. This includes empowering women and ensuring their active participation and leadership in local disaster management committees. Livelihood and emotional support programs tailored for women can enhance their resilience and mitigate risk factors for depression (Shume et al., 2025; Moyna et al., 2024).

6.4 Strengthening Service Delivery

There is a need to develop resilient, responsive, and self-sustaining health systems that can function during and after disasters. This requires developing adequate infrastructure, ensuring logistical support, and establishing clear pathways for referring individuals with severe mental disorders to specialized care (Alam et al., 2021; Tasdik Hasan et al., 2020).

6.5 Adopting the WHO Framework

Bangladesh's extreme climate disaster vulnerability necessitates urgent mental health interventions, particularly for women and the poor, whose trauma is worsened by social factors like poverty. Current responses are underfunded and poorly integrated. Adapting WHO's post-tsunami framework by training 50,000 Cyclone Preparedness Programme volunteers to deliver community-based clinical/nonclinical support with gender-sensitive outreach, bridging critical service gaps sustainably (Nahar et al., 2014).

6.6 Research and Awareness

To design effective interventions, more robust and calculative measures are needed to create an overall picture of the mental health effects of disasters. Increased public awareness campaigns are also necessary to reduce the stigma associated with mental health issues and encourage help-seeking behavior (Karim et al., 2024).

7 Conclusion

Bangladesh embodies the profound mental health consequences when escalating climate disasters intersect with socioeconomic vulnerability and constrained health systems. Evidence consistently demonstrates that cyclones, floods, and slow-onset environmental changes generate significant psychological burdens—particularly depression, PTSD, anxiety, and suicidality—disproportionately affecting women, children, the poor, and climate-sensitive occupational groups. Current mental health systems, despite progressive policies, remain critically under-resourced to address these challenges, with catastrophic workforce shortages and minimal financing.

The path forward demands integrated approaches that bridge disaster risk reduction, climate adaptation, and mental health systems. Community-based models leveraging existing networks (CPP volunteers, community health workers) offer immediate, scalable solutions when supplemented by task-shifting and digital innovations. Fundamentally, however, sustainable solutions require addressing the socioeconomic drivers of vulnerability: poverty, gender inequality, and livelihood challenges. Without such comprehensive approaches, Bangladesh faces escalating mental health burdens as climate change intensifies. The nation's experience offers crucial lessons for climate-vulnerable countries worldwide: protecting mental well-being is not merely a health sector issue but a core imperative of climate justice and sustainable development.

References

Akhter, S. R., Sarkar, R. K., Dutta, M., Khanom, R., Akter, N., Chowdhury, M. R., & Sultan, M. (2015). Issues with families and children in a disaster context: A qualitative perspective from rural Bangladesh. *International Journal of Disaster Risk Reduction, 13*, 313–323. https://doi.org/10.1016/j.ijdrr.2015.07.011

Akter, R., Roy, T., & Aktar, R. (2023). The challenges of women in post-disaster health management: A study in Khulna District. *International Journal of Disaster Risk Management, 5*(1), 51–66. https://doi.org/10.18485/ijdrm.2023.5.1.5

Alam, M., Halsey, J., Haque, M., Talukdar, M., Moniruzzaman, M., & Crump, A. R. (2021). Effect of natural disasters and their coping strategies in the Kuakata Coastal Belt of Patuakhali Bangladesh. *Computational Water, Energy, and Environmental Engineering, 7*, 161–182. https://doi.org/10.4236/cweee.2018.74011

Alam, F., Hossain, R., Ahmed, H. U., Alam, M. T., Sarkar, M., & Halbreich, U. (2021). Stressors and mental health in Bangladesh: Current situation and future hopes. *BJPsych International, 18*(4), 91–94. https://doi.org/10.1192/bji.2020.57

Al-Mamun, M., Karim, M. Z., & Kalam, A. (2025). The mental health condition of children in flood-affected areas in Bangladesh: Needs urgent attention. *Sage Open Pediatrics, 12*, 30502225251338636. https://doi.org/10.1177/30502225251338636

Arafat, S. M. Y., Giasuddin, N. A., & Mazumder, A. H. (2024). Access to mental health care in Bangladesh—Current status, potential challenges, and ways out. In S. M. Y. Arafat & S. K. Kar (Eds.), *Access to mental health care in South Asia*. Springer. https://doi.org/10.1007/978-981-99-9153-2_3

Arobi, S., Naher, J., & Rashid Soron, T. (2020). Impact of river bank erosion on mental health and coping capacity in Bangladesh. *Global Psychiatry Archives, 2*(2), 195–200.

Ayeb-Karlsson, S., Kniveton, D., & Cannon, T. (2020). Trapped in the prison of the mind: Notions of climate-induced (im) mobility decision-making and wellbeing from an urban informal settlement in Bangladesh. *Palgrave Communications, 6*(1), 1–15. https://doi.org/10.1057/s41599-020-0443-2

Cash, R. A., Halder, S. R., Husain, M., Islam, M. S., Mallick, F. H., May, M. A., Rahman, M., & Rahman, M. A. (2013). Reducing the health effect of natural hazards in Bangladesh. *Lancet (London, England), 382*(9910), 2094–2103. https://doi.org/10.1016/S0140-6736(13)61948-0

Choudhury, W. A., Quraishi, F. A., & Haque, Z. (2006). Mental health and psychosocial aspects of disaster preparedness in Bangladesh. *International Review of Psychiatry, 18*(6), 529–535. https://doi.org/10.1080/09540260601037896

Communication Department. (2024). *BDRCS SITREP-4 SouthEastern flood August 2024 – BDRCS*. BDRCS. https://bdrcs.org/bdrcs-sitrep-4-southeastern-flood-august-2024/

Communication Department. (2025). *Situation report 1- Flood 2025—BDRCS*. BDRCS. https://bdrcs.org/situation-report-1-flood-2025/

Cyclones—Climate change impacts on health and population in Bangladesh. (n.d.). Climate change impacts on health and population in Bangladesh. https://cch.icddrb.org/cyclones#:~:text=The%20deadliest%20cyclone%20ever%20recorded,the%20face%20of%20the%20earth

Droughts—Climate change impacts on health and population in Bangladesh. (n.d.). Climate change impacts on health and population in Bangladesh. https://cch.icddrb.org/droughts

Fatema, S. R., Rice, K., Rock, A., et al. (2023). Physical and mental health status of women in disaster-affected areas in Bangladesh. *Natural Hazards, 117*, 2715–2733. https://doi.org/10.1007/s11069-023-05964-5

Floods—Climate change impacts on health and population in Bangladesh. (n.d.). Climate change impacts on health and population in Bangladesh. https://cch.icddrb.org/floods

Hayward, G., & Ayeb-Karlsson, S. (2021). 'Seeing with Empty Eyes': A systems approach to understand climate change and mental health in Bangladesh. *Climatic Change, 165*(1), 29. https://doi.org/10.1007/s10584-021-03053-9

Hossain, M. M., Sultana, A., & Purohit, N. (2020). Mental health outcomes of quarantine and isolation for infection prevention: A systematic umbrella review of the global evidence. *Epidemiology and Health, 42*, e2020038. https://doi.org/10.4178/epih.e2020038

Hossain, A., Alam, M. J., & Haque, M. R. (2021). Effects of riverbank erosion on mental health of the affected people in Bangladesh. *PLoS One, 16*(7), e0254782. https://doi.org/10.1371/journal.pone.0254782

Islam, M. R. (2010). Vulnerability and coping strategies of women in disaster: A study on coastal areas of Bangladesh. *Arts Faculty Journal, 4*, 147–169.

Islam, M. J., Abdullah, M. S., & Alam, M. (2024). Flooding crisis in Bangladesh: Urgent measures required. *Biodiversity, 25*(2), 95–98. https://doi.org/10.1080/14888386.2024.2330385

Islam, F., Arafat, S. M. Y., & Hossain, M. S. (2025). Eye injuries in Bangladesh's 2024 student-led mass uprising: A public health crisis unfolds. *Torture Journal, 35*(1). https://doi.org/10.7146/torture.v35i1.152344

Jahan, R., Amin, R., & Arafat, S. M. Y. (2024). Practical challenges for mental health services among Rohingya refugee in Bangladesh. *Asian Journal of Psychiatry, 97*, 104069. https://doi.org/10.1016/j.ajp.2024.104069

Kabir, S. M. S. (2018). Psychological health challenges of the hill-tracts region for climate change in Bangladesh. *Asian Journal of Psychiatry, 34*, 74–77. https://doi.org/10.1016/j.ajp.2018.04.001

Kabir, R., Khan, H. T. A., Ball, E., & Caldwell, K. (2016). Climate change impact: The experience of the coastal areas of Bangladesh affected by cyclones Sidr and Aila. *Journal of Environmental and Public Health, 2016*, 9654753. https://doi.org/10.1155/2016/9654753

Kabir, S., Newnham, E., Dewan, A., et al. (2024). Psychological health declined during the post-monsoon season in communities impacted by sea-level rise in Bangladesh. *Communications Earth & Environment, 5*, 687. https://doi.org/10.1038/s43247-024-01862-1

Karim, M. Z., Al-Mamun, M., Eva, M. A., Ali, M. H., Kalam, A., Uzzal, N. I., & Das, P. K. (2024). Understanding mental health challenges and associated risk factors of post-natural disasters in Bangladesh: A systematic review. *Frontiers in Psychology, 15*, 1466722. https://doi.org/10.3389/fpsyg.2024.1466722

Kunii, O., Kunori, T., Takahashi, K., Kaneda, M., & Fuke, N. (1996). Health impact of 1996 tornado in Bangladesh. *Lancet (London, England), 348*(9029), 757. https://doi.org/10.1016/S0140-6736(05)65669-3

Mahmud, K. H., Ahmed, R., & Tuya, J. H. (2021). Geographic variability of post-disaster mental health: Case study after the 2017 flood in Bangladesh. *Geospatial Health, 16*, 1018.

Mamun, M. A., Huq, N., Papia, Z. F., Tasfina, S., & Gozal, D. (2019). Prevalence of depression among Bangladeshi village women subsequent to a natural disaster: A pilot study. *Psychiatry Research, 276*, 124–128. https://doi.org/10.1016/j.psychres.2019.05.007

Mamun, M. A., Safiq, M. B., Hosen, I., & Al Mamun, F. (2021). Suicidal behavior and flood effects in Bangladesh: A two-site interview study. *Risk Management and Healthcare Policy, 14*, 129–142. https://doi.org/10.2147/RMHP.S282965

Moyna, S. A., Hasan, K., Kabir, K. H., Khan, M. A., & Saha, S. K. (2024). Depressive symptoms among women in disaster-prone region in Bangladesh. *Journal of Affective Disorders Reports, 16*, 100762. https://doi.org/10.1016/j.jadr.2024.100762

Mullick, M. S., Nahar, J. S., Chowdhury, N. F., Rahman, W., Islam, M. M., Qusar, M. S., … Shahidullah, M. (2014). Psychiatric disorders among the children of 5 to 18 years old of 'SIDR' affected areas. *Bangabandhu Sheikh Mujib Medical University Journal, 7*(1), 20–26.

Nahar, N., Blomstedt, Y., Wu, B., Kandarina, I., Trisnantoro, L., & Kinsman, J. (2014). Increasing the provision of mental health care for vulnerable, disaster-affected people in Bangladesh. *BMC Public Health, 14*, 708. https://doi.org/10.1186/1471-2458-14-708

Rahaman, M. A., Rahman, M. M., & Rahman, S. H. (2019). Pathways of climate-resilient health systems in Bangladesh. In S. Huq, J. Chow, A. Fenton, C. Stott, J. Taub, & H. Wright (Eds.), *Confronting climate change in Bangladesh. The Anthropocene: Politik—Economics—Society—Science* (Vol. 28). Springer. https://doi.org/10.1007/978-3-030-05237-9_9

Rahman, M. M., Shobuj, I. A., Hossain, M. T., & Tasnim, F. (2023). Impact of disaster on mental health of women: A case study on 2022 flash flood in Bangladesh. *International Journal of Disaster Risk Reduction, 96*, 103935. https://doi.org/10.1016/j.ijdrr.2023.103935

Rahman, M. M., Shobuj, I. A., Hossain, M. T., Alam, E., Islam, M. K., & Hossain, M. K. (2025). Flood impact on men's mental health: Evidence from flood-prone areas of Bangladesh. *Frontiers in Public Health, 13*, 1529558. https://doi.org/10.3389/fpubh.2025.1529558

Response monitoring dashboard: Bangladesh—Cyclone & monsoon floods humanitarian response plan (June 2024 to March 2025)—Bangladesh. ReliefWeb. (2025, July 9). https://reliefweb.int/report/bangladesh/response-monitoring-dashboard-bangladesh-cyclone-monsoon-floods-humanitarian-response-plan-june-2024-march-2025#:~:text=These%20events%20directly%20impacted%2029,plan%20concluded%20in%20March%202025

Shamsuddoha, M., Jabed, M. A., Islam, M. S., Sultana, N., Imran, A., Rabbi, S. N. A., Jenat, T. U., Shams, S., & Sharif, M. M. (2024). Impacts of climate change-induced natural hazards on women and their human rights implications: A study in the southwest coast of Bangladesh. *Journal of Migration and Health, 9*, 100221. https://doi.org/10.1016/j.jmh.2024.100221

Shume, A. Z., Hossain, M. Z., Islam, M. T., Jobaer, M. A., Haque, S. F., & Rahaman, K. R. (2025). Gender-responsive disaster risk reduction strategy at the community level: A qualitative approach to analyze coastal communities in Bangladesh. *Futures, 168*, 103570. https://doi.org/10.1016/j.futures.2025.103570

Siddik, M. A. B., Munmun, M. S., Ahmed, Z., Nabil, K., & Mubin, N. (2024). Climate change, natural disasters, and mental health of adolescents: A qualitative study from Bangladesh. *International Journal of Population Studies, 10*(2), 61–70. https://doi.org/10.36922/ijps.0339

Tahsin, N., Gąsior, W. Z., & Olszewska-Guizzo, A. (2023). Climate change and mental health in Bangladesh: A cultural variability perspective. In *Climate change and health hazards: Addressing hazards to human and environmental health from a changing climate* (pp. 229–249). Springer Nature Switzerland. https://doi.org/10.1007/978-3-031-26592-1_12

Tasdik Hasan, M., Adhikary, G., Mahmood, S., Papri, N., Shihab, H. M., Kasujja, R., Ahmed, H. U., Azad, A. K., & Nasreen, M. (2020). Exploring mental health needs and services among affected population in a cyclone affected area in costal Bangladesh: A qualitative case study. *International Journal of Mental Health Systems, 14*, 12. https://doi.org/10.1186/s13033-020-00351-0

Tropical Cyclone Remal—May 2024. (2024, November 19). ReliefWeb. https://reliefweb.int/disaster/tc-2024-000083-bgd

United Nations. (2025). Human rights violations and abuses related to the protests of July and August 2024 in Bangladesh. https://www.ohchr.org/sites/default/files/documents/countries/bangladesh/ohchr-fftb-hr-violations-bd.pdf. Accessed 21 Feb 2025.

Wahid, S. S., Raza, W. A., Mahmud, I., & Kohrt, B. A. (2023). Climate-related shocks and other stressors associated with depression and anxiety in Bangladesh: A nationally representative panel study. *The Lancet. Planetary Health, 7*(2), e137–e146. https://doi.org/10.1016/S2542-5196(22)00315-1

Wahid, S. S., Islam, M. N., & Raza, W. A. (2024). Climate change and mental health in Bangladesh: Vulnerability, inequality, and the crucial need for intervention on the frontlines of the climate crisis. In S. M. Y. Arafat (Ed.), *Mental health in Bangladesh*. Springer. https://doi.org/10.1007/978-981-97-0610-5_15

Wikipedia contributors. (2024, September 23). List of earthquakes in Bangladesh. *Wikipedia*. https://en.wikipedia.org/wiki/List_of_earthquakes_in_Bangladesh

Wikipedia contributors. (2025a, July 16). Floods in Bangladesh. *Wikipedia*. https://en.wikipedia.org/wiki/Floods_in_Bangladesh

Wikipedia contributors. (2025b, July 20). 2007 Chittagong mudslides. *Wikipedia*. https://en.wikipedia.org/wiki/2007_Chittagong_mudslides#:~:text=The%20death%20toll%20was%20reported,Lebubagan%2C%20the%20worst%20hit%20area

Chapter 4
Disaster, Climate Change, and Mental Health: The Story of Bhutan

Saamdu Chetri and Renitta Sinha

1 Introduction

Climate change is making storms and other weather events worse (Walsh, 2011; Intergovernmental Panel on Climate Change [IPCC], 2011). Bhutan, like its neighbouring countries in South Asian, such as Bangladesh, Nepal, and India, is affected by climate change-related disasters, e.g., floods, landslides, and cyclones. Bhutan is more vulnerable to different types of calamities, as it is highly dependent on agriculture and animal husbandry, and its economy depends on farming (Chogyel & Kumar, 2018). Bhutan aims to be carbon neutral, yet it is especially at risk for calamities related to climate change, such as landslides, erratic monsoons, and glacial lake outburst floods (GLOFs) (Wangchuk & Wangdi, 2018). There is a huge influence on mental health, as shown by the fact that more people in the areas that were damaged are experiencing anxiety, posttraumatic stress disorder (PTSD), and depression (UNDP, 2024). This section will seek to understand how climate change disasters have harmed people's mental health in Bhutan and what needs to be done right soon.

Because of geographical location and conditions, Bhutan is especially likely to be affected by disasters induced by climate change. Many of the country's glacial lakes are at risk of breaking open as the temperature rises (Karma et al., 2019). A GLOF decimated the Punakha Valley in 1994, forcing thousands of people to leave and inflicting long-term mental health concerns (Richards & Reynolds, 2000). Unpredictable monsoons have also generated more landslides and flash floods, which could put people and their farming at risk. These disasters caused people both physical and mental distress for an extended period (UNDP, 2022).

S. Chetri (✉) · R. Sinha
Yogananda School of Spirituality and Happiness, Shoolini University, Solan, Himachal Pradesh, India

N. Kar et al. (eds.), *Climate Change, Disaster and Mental Health in South Asia*, South Asian Perspectives in Mental Health and Psychology,
https://doi.org/10.1007/978-981-95-3690-0_4

Terrible weather can make one feel mentally unwell. Climate-related events have caused PTSD, anxiety, and depression, and are going to increase in Bhutan, especially among women, children, and farmers (Thapa & Acharya, 2017). Research indicates that individuals who endure natural catastrophes face ongoing challenges due to displacement, job loss, and community fragmentation (Norris et al., 2001). The cultural stigma surrounding mental health hinders access to psychological support in Bhutan (Pelzang & Hutchinson, 2018). Traditional Buddhist beliefs may impede persons from obtaining medical care, as they often regard mental distress as karmic retribution.

2 GLOF Impact Story

Bhutan has faced GLOF, like most Himalayan countries. Vividly, the older people in the south narrate stories of the first one that happened in 1968 (B. B. Bhattarai, personal communication, August 7, 2025). B.B. Bhattarai remembers his cousin sister's house being trapped in the flood. He observed, "a few km-long stretches of forest on both banks of the river Sankosh between two villages of Kerabari (now known as Karmaling) and Bijgoan in Nichula, both under Kalikhola subdivision, now known as Lhamoyzingkha, had gone, including all the crops in the fields. In the light of dawn, the other side of the village was visible due to the forest being washed away, the village houses were being swallowed by the water, people on the house rooftop asking for help, and the houses collapsing with them. It was a scene of helplessness."

This flood took many human lives, and especially those of animals. Bhutan then did not have much infrastructure in place. National Centre for Hydrology and Meteorology, Royal Government of Bhutan (NCHM, RGoB, n.d.), noted that the king visited the upper valley in a helicopter and ordered rescue and compensation. Later, he visited the affected houses, consoling people (NCHM, RGoB, n.d.). In southern Bhutan, the government compensated them for the land and provided some grants for them to begin their lives again. In many cases, due to a lack of awareness, people never claimed or asked for compensation. It was believed that the system would take care of their problems, a karma-believing society.

The river is known as Sankosh in the south and Puna Tsang Chu in the north. Most likely, it had a glacier lake outburst due to rains on October 2–5 1968 (Wikipedia, 2025). There was also flooding in Sikkim and Darjeeling at the time. The moraine would have given up due to a heavy increase in water level from rain. There is no record of its extensive damage to ripen rice crops, animals, and humans, as there are no published records to draw information from, except bits of information in Kuensel records recorded by National Centre for Hydrology and Meteorology (NCHM), Royal Government of Bhutan (RGoB), as a compendium, the national newspaper started monthly, to weekly, to daily newspaper today. The news was written, then, mostly from hearing from others, unlike today. It is assumed that the north faced less destruction than the south, as many tributaries on their way added to the volume of the water of the Sankosh river in the 1968 flooding.

Due to the floods, there was a disease spread among animals, and the entire animal stock was wiped out in a matter of a few weeks in the southern river basin settlement of Bhutan, probably making many who lived on animals, poor again (P. L. Bhattrai, personal communication, Aug 8, 2025).

There is no account for anything on this. There could have been massive destruction of material belongings and loss of lives of loved ones. The depression of the people cannot be overruled. However, Bhutanese living with a concept of karma, who accept such things as karmic and let them go, may have helped themselves to stand on their feet again (Landaw & Berzin, n.d.).

The same river again had an outburst in 1994 (Watanabe & Rothacher, 1996), and almost took the famous Punakha Dzong, built by the founding father of Bhutan, Zabdrung Nawang Namgyel, in 1637–1638 (Dzong Administration, Punakha, n.d.). The loss tremendously affected the north (NCHM, RGoB, n.d.), and less so in the south, which may be because the southern river basins had been resettled to safer heights after the 1968 floods.

This large-scale destruction and death could have been avoided in Punakha and Wangdue, where it is reported as the most affected, if the warning system had been functional, if there had been one. It seems to have taken 5 hours for the flood to reach from the outburst lake, before it wiped out the valley, and most were those who were settled along the basin (NCHM, RGoB, n.d.).

Today, the government has established warning signs in the identified places of risk with the support of the World Bank (2024). This is one way to resilience. In the same line, Japan International Cooperation Agency (JICA) made cooperation with the government on disaster and risk reduction through a joint study. The alert comes in the settlement five to 10 hours in advance, according to peasants in Wangdue (north) and Kerabari (south).

3 Flood Damage to Agricultural Land

The 2024 monsoon season was one of the most destructive in recent history, with flash floods and landslides affecting multiple districts, including Thimphu, Bumthang, Paro, and Wangdue (Lhaden, 2025). Furthermore, according to the UNDP climate resilience report, climate-induced floods and landslides have damaged irrigation schemes, market access routes, and crop fields, especially in low-lying and riverine areas. Further, it is reported that the exact hectare loss figures are not fully consolidated. However, the National Centre for Hydrology and Meteorology (NCHM) and the Department of Surface Transport recorded over 30 major flood and landslide events between July and September 2024 (Lhaden, 2025). According to the United Nations Development Programme (2025), the estimated agricultural land affected primarily by floods in 2024 in Dagana, Punakha, Wangdue, and Zhemgang is over 6000 ha.

4 Various Other Disasters

Bhutan had 18 major flood events over 70 years (Hyde, 2025). According to Dhendup (2021), reported in Kuenselonline, 24 glacial lakes in Bhutan have been identified as "potentially dangerous." Similarly, Mool et al. (2001) in the ICIMOD report wrote that 24 of 2674 lakes are dangerous for flooding (United Nations, 2002; Choki Wangmo, 2021).

There were around 61 disasters, mostly from floods, followed by landslides and earthquakes (NCHM, RGoB, n.d.). This figure from 1968 to 2025 does not include road accidents, fires, storms, etc. There is no exact assessment of the human life toll from these disasters. However, in the last 57 years, the count is probably around 2000 human deaths and maybe three times that of domesticated animals.

Most of the destruction happens along the valley where there is a majority of people's settlements. Given regular such events, the government discussed the flooding issues with cross-border neighbours, and how the disaster could be managed with early signs and information. This includes West Bengal and Assam states of India, as well as Bangladesh. There have been several high-level meetings for disaster management with the governments of Bangladesh and India. The discussions also included ways to manage and control the disasters (NCHM, RGoB, n.d.).

For a small country, such disasters have been very expensive. Billions of Ngultrums worth of infrastructural damage has occurred, including roads, government houses, and administration centres, apart from thousands of acres of agricultural and grazing lands lost. As most farming communities are along the valley, there have been substantial crop destructions over the years. No specific studies on the agricultural impact have been conducted yet.

Apart from the natural disasters, Bhutan also experienced the COVID-19 pandemic. A study of students reported the presence of moderate to severe depression in 44.2% and anxiety in 27.3%. Students with family members as frontline workers had significantly higher levels of anxiety (Tshering & Dema, 2022).

5 Disaster Management

Bhutan is served by a road network and the Internet. It has a long-term medical one-stop-consultation system, an adequate number of ambulances, strengthened by two helicopter services to serve people in distress and disasters.

Bhutan has instituted strategies, policies, and plans to mitigate and manage disasters. Different polices for building, settlement, road, and other construction are now in place. Further, disaster management and contingency planning are in place. It considers all kinds of disasters such as flood, windstorm/cyclone, fire, pandemic, snowstorm, hailstone, drought/famine, hazardous waste materials, industrial accidents, landslides, earthquake (Ministry of Home & Cultural Affairs, Royal Government of Bhutan, 2013a; United Nations Office for Disaster Risk Reduction

[UNDRR], 2025; Ministry of Home & Cultural Affairs, Royal Government of Bhutan, 2006; Ministry of Infrastructure & Transport (formerly Works & Human Settlement), Royal Government of Bhutan, 2020).

Given the increasing number of disasters, the government has instituted the Disaster Management Committee, Disaster Management Units, and Rapid Response Team spread down to local levels. Standard operating procedures were created from pre-, during, and post-disasters (NCHM, RGoB, n.d.). The turnaround time is quick and efficient with evacuation to emergency and cluster shelters, first aid, disaster response, and immediate restoration/services continuity until it is resolved.

Apart from the officials engaged in disaster management, the king always employs armed forces for the quick relief of the people. They have helped in rebuilding houses, helping in the feed program, and relocating the suffering victims of natural and human-triggered calamities.

In fact, the King of Bhutan himself is the first to arrive in the places of disaster to comfort people and bring help and support to them. This has been a centuries-old practice of the kings. Presently, the king has developed a plan to convert the entire youth of the country into Desuups (the Guardians of Peace) (Denkar, 2021). There are about 52,000 persons trained as Desuups until mid-2025. Similarly, there is another group of youth with similar plans, and they are called Gyalsups. They are a more technical cadre of national interest servers (Ping, 2021; Herison, 2025). Thus far, close to 6000 people have been trained. Both these groups can be mobilized in a very short period to bring relief to those suffering from any type of disaster, in addition to the set protocols (NCHM, RGoB, n.d.).

Bhutan has installed early warning systems in three river basins (Punatsangchhu, Chamkharchhu, Mangdechhu), but many areas remain uncovered. Bhutan has joined the Global Climate Call to Supercharge Clean Energy Transition (Wangdi, 2025). Further, Bhutan has also joined the global call for glacier protection on the first-ever World Day for Glaciers (Bhutan Broadcasting Service Corporation Limited, 2025). Kuensel (2025) added an opinion piece titled "A call from the mountains: Will we save our glaciers in time?" The report observed that Bhutan faces challenges in expanding the supportive systems due to terrain, cost, and communication limitations. Nevertheless, engineering solutions such as lake drainage have been implemented (e.g., Thorthormi Lake) to reduce flood risks (Hyde, 2025).

5.1 Bhutan's Disaster Risk Management Strategy

Department of Disaster Management, Ministry of Home and Cultural Affairs, Royal Government of Bhutan, 2023, is guided by the Disaster Management Act of 2013 and Bhutan's Five-Year Planning process. It outlines four priority actions:

- *Understanding Disaster Risks* (Hazard and risk identification, public awareness and education, and use of science, technology, and innovation).

- *Strengthening Risk Governance* (Legislative and policy frameworks, mainstreaming disaster risk management into development, and institutional coordination across national and local levels).
- *Investing in Resilience* (Infrastructure upgrades, nonstructural measures (e.g., land-use planning), and risk transfer mechanisms like insurance).
- *Enhancing Disaster Management Capabilities* (Early warning systems, integrated resilience programs, and post-disaster recovery and reconstruction).

5.2 The National Disaster Risk Management Framework

Ministry of Home and Cultural Affairs, Royal Government of Bhutan, 2006, provides a holistic view of Bhutan's disaster landscape and institutional mechanisms, as follows:

- Hazards Identified: Earthquakes, floods, landslides, GLOFs, wildfires
- Institutional Setup: National Disaster Management Authority (NDMA), Dzongkhag and Gewog Disaster Committees, Emergency Operations Centres (NEOC).
- Financial Mechanisms: (His Majesty's Relief Fund, Major Disaster Fund, and Preparedness Budget)

It emphasizes integrating disaster risk management into development sectors, capacity building, and public education (Ministry of Home & Cultural Affairs, Royal Government of Bhutan, 2013b). Disaster management also integrates International Support and Financing (World Bank, 2024).

In 2024, the World Bank approved $40 million in financing to support Bhutan's climate and disaster resilience. This fund was given for strengthening early warning systems for GLOFs and wildfires, enhancing building codes and geo-hazard management, improving financial resilience through disaster risk insurance, and supporting hydropower sector safety and infrastructure resilience. This aligned with Bhutan's 13th Five-Year Plan (July 2024 to June 2029), focusing on safeguarding infrastructure, economy, and communities.

Key challenges identified in a recent policy review were as follows (Devdiscourse, 2025):

(i) Limited technical capacity at local levels
(ii) Inadequate coverage of early warning systems
(iii) Need for better coordination among agencies
(iv) Insufficient data and risk mapping

6 Climate Change

There have been climate changes in Bhutan too, even if the country's land surface is 72% by standing trees and over 80% green. Bhutan has 7.8% of its total land classified as agricultural land. This translates into 0.202 m hectares of agricultural land (United Nations Development Programme, 2005). Further, the report suggests that 75,800 ha, about 2.93% are actively cultivated. Any climate-related disaster affects these.

Bhutan has been witnessing glacier recession (Hyde, 2025). It further says that there has been more formation of lakes with the melting ice over the last two decades. Thus, the danger increases for flood disasters. The receding of glaciers has also posed danger and difficulties for Bhutan's hydropower along the major river basins. Bhutan depends on 99% of its energy from local hydropower. If the global temperature continues to reach 2.5°, 50% of the glacier area and more than 90% of the meltwater supply could be lost (Hyde, 2025).

In the higher altitudes, it was observed in a study by Wangchuk Centennial Park, Bumthang (Rai, 2024), that the snow leopards have been trying to adapt below the snow line and their numbers have been drastically reduced.

Water in many villages has been scarce. In 2008/2009, the government decided to shift four such villages to a better location in Pemagatshel and Sarpang (Namgay, 2011; World Health Organization, 2013). It is always painful to leave one's place where she/he has grown up and go to a new location, and such changes have become necessary.

Due to pouring rains in the south, bringing the dust and factory filth in the air from North Bengal and dumping in the southern foothills of Bhutan, the little chillies called "jerry khorsani" have almost vanished. The very colourful parrots came down from the mountains to feast on them. These varieties of chillies that grew abundantly are no longer growing as wildly, which was the case more than two decades ago (P. L. Bhattarai, personal communication, August 8, 2005).

From the above discussion, Bhutan faces several pressing challenges due to climate change. Many of them are intensified by Bhutan's unique geography and economy. The following gives a clearer understanding:

Glacier Retreat and Water Scarcity

- Bhutan's glaciers are melting rapidly, threatening long-term water availability.
- These affect hydropower generation, agriculture, and drinking water—especially during winter and dry seasons.
- Loss of glacier mass and forming into separate lakes or increasing water in the lake increases the risk of Glacial Lake Outburst Floods (GLOFs).

Erratic Weather and Monsoon Shifts

- Climate change is delaying or intensifying monsoons, causing unpredictable rainfall patterns and extended dry spells.
- This pattern of disruption affects crop cycles and affects food security. It also increases landslide risks.

Natural Disasters Frequency Increase

- Bhutan is experiencing more frequent floods, landslides, and forest fires.
- These events damage infrastructure, displace communities, and strain emergency response systems.

Stress on Forest and Biodiversity

- Rising temperatures and changing precipitation patterns threaten Bhutan's rich biodiversity.
- Forests face increased risk of pests, diseases, and wildfires.
- Species migration and habitat loss are becoming more common.

Vulnerability of Mountain Ecosystems

- The mountainous terrain of Bhutan makes it highly sensitive to soil erosion, land degradation, and ecosystem shifts.
- Climate change accelerates these processes, affecting both natural landscapes and human settlements.

Rural Communities and Impact on Livelihoods

- Over 65% of Bhutanese depend on subsistence farming and natural resources.
- Climate variability affects crop yields, livestock health, and income stability.
- Rural-urban migration is increasing due to climate stress.

Limited Adaptive Capacity

Bhutan's remoteness, small economy, and the terrain limit its ability to invest in climate resilience, including infrastructure, early warning systems, and no banking and insurance companies come forward to provide financial safety nets.

7 Mental Health Issues

Mental health problems are a great challenge in Bhutan, and there is a need to address these. Suicide among youth is high, although it may not be related to disasters. Reportedly, mental health disorders rose from 4200 cases in 2017 to 6858 in 2020. There is also a stigma attached, a lack of awareness, and limited access to care infrastructure (The Borgen Project, n.d.; Pelden, 2021).

7.1 Post-Disaster Mental Health Support

Bhutan is intending to integrate multi-sectoral mental health and psychosocial support (MHPSS) systems. They look at the international models, especially that of Japan, the "Kokoro no Care" system (Watanabe, 2023). There are a few key features. There are emergency mental health teams in different places during crises (e.g., COVID-19). TV awareness campaigns, hotlines, and pamphlets distribution and explanation for public education. Special collaboration between health, education, religious, and community sectors. Emphasis is given on community outreach and long-term care for trauma survivors.

7.2 The Key Organizations Supporting Mental Health

According to the Borgen Project (n.d.), five organizations are actively participating in improving mental health services in Bhutan.

- The Bhutan Canada Foundation, which has been one of the strong partners in the education sector, promotes awareness and education to reduce stigma through symposiums.
- Health Volunteers Overseas (HVO)—They are training professionals at the hospitals on mental health.
- Respect Educate Nurture and Empower Women (RENEW)—It provides counselling for gender-based violence and survivors of domestic abuse.
- United Nations Population Fund-Paro College of Education (UNFPA-PCE) Partnership—They focus on youth resilience and community outreach.
- The Pema Centre—It is a government-funded 60-bed mental health hospital focusing on self-harm, violence, and substance abuse prevention.

7.3 School and Youth-Based Interventions

Pelden (2021) reported the following interventions for young people. Bhutan's Ministry of Education recorded in 3 months 671 counselling cases, of which were 88% youth aged 9–24. Schools are being empowered to address bullying and harassment, create inclusive environments, and offer mental health training.

7.4 Need for Policy and Investment

It is observed that despite growing awareness, mental health receives only 1% of the health budget (Pelden, 2021). The country has only four psychiatrists (The Borgen Project, n.d.). The ongoing national forum to increase and coordinate stakeholders must continue.

8 People and the Government in Bhutan Are Working Together

The mental health consequences of significant catastrophes are often overlooked, despite being a crucial aspect of disaster management. To solve this problem, there needs to be a plan that involves the community, changes the norms, and ensures that mental health care is appropriate for different cultures. Future studies ought to examine the temporal variations in the mental health of catastrophe survivors and the efficacy of treatments within Bhutan's distinct social and cultural context (Department of Disaster Management, Ministry of Home & Cultural Affairs, n.d.).

The government of Bhutan has implemented a range of measures to address climate change. Getting ready for catastrophes is now a primary concern for the National Adaptation Program of Action (NAPA) (National Environment Commission, 2019). Further, this includes technologies that warn people about GLOFs (United Nations Development Programme, 2012). Plans for dealing with disasters do take mental health into account and to aid persons with mental health issues and are being taken. It is essential to incorporate psychological first aid into emergency response plans and to promote mental health awareness through community programs (United Nations Development Programme, 2021). It will also be better if people have access to superior traditional and modern mental health support services (Wangchuk et al., 2020). Climate change is evidently happening in Bhutan, which means that natural disasters may strike more often and with more impact.

The government of Bhutan has worked hard to preserve people's mental health from climate change. For instance, they are building systems that will let people know about GLOFs (UNDP, 2012). But most disaster preparations and interventions don't include mental health. Adding psychological first aid to disaster response plans and increasing participation in community activities are both key steps towards raising awareness of mental health issues (UNDP, 2021). People may also benefit if both old and new mental health support services are improved (Wangchuk et al., 2020).

9 Challenges and Ways Ahead

Bhutan is going through climate change, which makes natural disasters more frequent and have more impact. Disaster management has a number of parts, but the mental repercussions of disasters are often not discussed. Community needs to be involved more rigorously, rules need to be amended, and steps need to be taken to ensure that mental health services are culturally acceptable to fix the issue. Future research must investigate the effectiveness of mental therapies within Bhutan's unique social and cultural environment, as well as the mental health of disaster survivors in temporal variations.

To mitigate the harmful consequences of climate change and natural disasters on mental health, it is vital to integrate mental health issues in all programs for disaster risk reduction and climate adaptation. It should accomplish the Paris Agreement, which suggested governments should include mental health in their Nationally Determined Contributions (NDCs) and their National Adaptation Plans (NAPs) (National Environment Commission, 2019; United Nations Development Programme, 2023).

Following the Disaster Management Act of Bhutan (2013), the health, environment, and disaster management sectors should collaborate to develop regulations about how to overcome the impact of climate change and related disasters on mental health. In vulnerable areas with an increased likelihood of natural catastrophes, it is essential to establish programs that can aid individuals with their mental health resilience and make them stronger mentally. Such projects must consider the culture of the area (World Health Organization, 2024).

It is essential to train volunteers, community, and village health workers on how to support persons with their mental health and provide them with psychological first aid. It will help them respond rapidly and successfully during and after disasters.

The World Health Organization (2024) advises budgeting money into mental health services, including clinics and mobile units in locations that are far away and likely to be hit by catastrophes. Also, adding mental health services to routine healthcare systems enables easier access for people to obtain help, and it may make them feel less uncomfortable about doing so (World Health Organization, 2024).

It is advised to create and use early warning systems for natural catastrophes that include how to get ready for and cope with mental health problems. It can assist people in the community to prepare for the next calamity. To ensure people are ready to deal with the psychological repercussions of catastrophes, they need to obtain regular training in disaster preparedness, including mental health components (World Health Organization, 2024). Furthermore, people who have been injured by natural disasters and climate change should be able to use regulations to develop and enforce legislation that safeguards their mental health rights. This will entail people obtaining support and staying mentally healthy (World Health Organization, 2024).

It is important to reinforce that there must be enough budgets for mental health services and projects that assist people in managing climate change and disasters. The World Health Organization (2024) suggests starting programs to teach people how climate change affects mental health and how crucial it is to receive treatment. It is important to consider the local language in different areas where these plans will be used. It is suggested that individuals be taught about mental health by offering classes in schools and communities. This will help them find and deal with mental health problems early.

Partnerships and cooperation must be encouraged between countries to share resources, useful solutions, and knowledge on how to mitigate the negative effects of climate change on mental health. This entails engaging with organizations from other countries, research institutions, and non-governmental organizations (World Health Organization, 2024). Countries that don't have many resources could provide capacity-building support and technical help. This would help people to design and develop solid strategies for adapting to climate change and improving mental health.

10 Conclusion

These initiatives that are discussed above highlight how crucial it is to fully and appropriately deal with how climate change and natural disasters influence mental health. Bhutan can make its communities stronger and more helpful by considering mental health in its strategies for climate change and disasters. Early warning systems for natural catastrophes can be used by people to prepare well for disasters, which may decrease mental health concerns.

It is crucial to make mental health, cultural practices, and traditional customs a part of climate policy. This will help inclusion and also help across communities, as it is not always spoken about. When one understands the suffering, an appropriate action can be taken. Also, this makes it easier for people in the community to get help with their mental health issues. For example, Bhutan has employed traditional Buddhist methods in programs to help individuals with their mental health. Mindfulness and meditation are two of the strategies that may help people who have been affected by climate-related disasters in different ways, along with modern mental health therapies.

References

Bhutan Broadcasting Service Corporation Limited. (2025, March 24). *Bhutan joins global call for glacier protection on first-ever world day for glaciers*. Bhutan Broadcasting Service. https://www.bbs.bt/226284/

Chogyel, N., & Kumar, L. (2018, November 1). Climate change and potential impacts on agriculture in Bhutan: A discussion of pertinent issues. *Agriculture & Food* Security, 7(79). https://doi.org/10.1186/s40066-018-0229-6. (UNDP – The climate crisis is a health crisis – here's why August 30, 2024).

Choki Wangmo. (2021, April 1). Bhutan records 567 glacial lakes, 17 of which are potentially dangerous. *Kuensel*.

Denkar, T. (2021, February 14). Desuups awarded the "Druk Thuksey" representational pin on the 10th Raising Day. *Daily Bhutan*. https://dailybhutan.com/article/desuups-awarded-the-druk-thuksey-representational-pin-on-the-10th-raising-day

Department of Disaster Management, Ministry of Home & Cultural Affairs. (n.d.). *Acts, rules and publications* [e.g., contingency planning guideline]. Retrieved from https://www.ddm.gov.bt/acts-rules-and-publications/

Department of Disaster Management, Ministry of Home and Cultural Affairs, Royal Government of Bhutan. (2023). *Disaster risk management strategy: "Safe, resilient and happy Bhutan"*. https://www.ddm.gov.bt/publications/disaster-risk-management-strategy-2023

Devdiscourse. (2025, February 13). Bhutan's crisis preparedness: Strengths, gaps, and urgent reforms. *Devdiscourse*. https://www.devdiscourse.com/article/law-order/3262439-bhutans-crisis-preparedness-strengths-gaps-and-urgent-reforms

Dhendup, T. (2021, March 21). 24 glacial lakes in Bhutan identified as "potentially dangerous". *Kuensel*.

Dzong Administration, Punakha. (n.d.). *Punakha Dzong*. https://punakha.gov.bt/tourism/punakha-dzong/#:~:text=The%20Punakha%20Dzong%20(the%20palace,of%20its%20most%20majestic%20structures

Herison, J. (2025, June 12). Gyalsung skilling programme prepares 493 Gyalsups for national service and future careers. *Daily Bhutan*.

Hyde, A. (2025, February 19). Shrinking glaciers in Bhutan. AntarcticGlaciers.org. https://www.antarcticglaciers.org/glaciers-and-climate/glacier-recession/glaciation-in-bhutan-and-its-future-outlook/

Intergovernmental Panel on Climate Change. (2011, November 18). *Summary for policymakers of the special report on managing the risks of extreme events and disasters to advance climate change adaptation (SREX) approved by member governments* [Press note]. https://archive.ipcc.ch/news_and_events/docs/srex/SREX_press_release.pdf

Karma, P., Dorji, L., & Wangmo, S. (2019). Glacial retreat and GLOFs in Bhutan: New dangers. *Bhutan Journal of Environmental Studies, 10*(1), 15–30.

Kuensel. (2025, March 21). A call from the mountains: Will we save our glaciers in time? *Kuensel Online*. https://kuenselonline.com/a-call-from-the-mountains-will-we-save-our-glaciers-in-time

Landaw, J., & Berzin, A. (n.d.). Collective karma and natural disasters. *Study Buddhism*. https://studybuddhism.com/en/advanced-studies/science-of-mind/karma/collective-karma-and-natural-disasters

Lhaden, Y. (2025, March 3). A year of extreme weather in Bhutan. *Kuensel Online*. https://kuenselonline.com/news/a-year-of-extreme-weather

Ministry of Home & Cultural Affairs, Royal Government of Bhutan. (2013a). *Disaster risk management strategy—Bhutan*. Retrieved from https://www.preventionweb.net/publication/disaster-risk-management-strategy-bhutan

Ministry of Home & Cultural Affairs, Royal Government of Bhutan. (2013b). *Disaster Management Act of Bhutan 2013* [Act]. Royal Government of Bhutan. https://lpr.adb.org/sites/default/files/resource/%5Bnid%5D/bhutan-disaster-management-act-2013-english.pdf

Ministry of Home and Cultural Affairs, Royal Government of Bhutan. (2006). *National disaster risk management framework – Reducing disaster risk for a safe and happy Bhutan*. Humanitarian Library. https://www.humanitarianlibrary.org/resource/national-disaster-risk-management-framework-reducing-disaster-risk-safe-and-happy-bhutan-0

Ministry of Infrastructure & Transport (formerly Works & Human Settlement), Royal Government of Bhutan. (2020). National Construction Industry Policy. ESCAP policy documents. Retrieved from https://policy.asiapacificenergy.org/node/4096

Mool, P. K., Wangda, D., Bajracharya, S. R., Joshi, S. P., Kunzang, K., & Gurung, D. R. (2001). *Inventory of glaciers, glacial lakes and glacial lake outburst floods: Monitoring and early warning systems in the Hindu Kush–Himalayan region, Bhutan*. International Centre for Integrated Mountain Development (ICIMOD). Retrieved from https://lib.icimod.org/records/cy6vf-vnc91

Namgay, G. (2011, February 11). Far-flung Pemagatshel villages to be resettled. *Bhutan Observer*. (As cited in *Pemagatshel District*). *Wikipedia*. Retrieved from https://en.wikipedia.org/wiki/Pemagatshel_District

National Centre for Hydrology and Meteorology (NCHM), Royal Government of Bhutan (RGoB). (n.d.). Compendium of climate and hydrological extremes in Bhutan since 1968. *Kuensel*. ISBN 978-99936-721-7-3.

National Environment Commission. (2019). Preparation of a National Adaptation Plan (NAP) for Bhutan, with a focus on the water sector (2019–2023). Project details via the National Environment Commission.

Norris, F. H., Friedman, M. J., & Watson, P. J. (2001). 60,000 disaster victims speak: An empirical review of the 1981–2001 empirical literature. *Psychology, 65*(3), 207–239.

Pelden, S. (2021). *Promoting mental health and well-being deserves our undivided attention and long-term investment: A joint op-ed by UNDP, UNFPA, UNICEF, UNODC, and WHO.* UNICEF Bhutan. https://www.unicef.org/bhutan/stories/promoting-mental-health-and-well-being-deserves-our-undivided-attention-and-long-term

Pelzang, R., & Hutchinson, A. M. (2018a). Patient safety culture in Bhutan's healthcare system: The influence of traditional cultural values. *BMJ Open, 8*(7), e022788. https://doi.org/10.1136/bmjopen-2018-022788

Pelzang, R., & Hutchinson, A. (2018b). Mental health literacy in Bhutan: Problems and approaches. *BMC Public Health, 18*(1), 567.

Ping, C. (2021, July 2). All you need to know about De-suups (Guardians of Peace) in Bhutan. *Daily Bhutan.* https://www.dailybhutan.com/article/all-you-need-to-know-about-de-suups-guardians-of-peace-in-bhutan

Rai, P. (2024, June). *Conservation management plan of Wangchuck Centennial National Park: January 2023–December 2032* [Draft management plan]. Department of Forests and Park Services, Ministry of Energy and Natural Resources, Royal Government of Bhutan. Retrieved from https://www.researchgate.net/publication/381375987_Conservation_Management_Plan_of_Wangchuck_Centennial_National_Park

Richards, S. D., & Reynolds, J. M. (2000). A synopsis of Himalayan glacial hazards. *Quaternary International, 65*(66), 31–47.

Thapa, S. B., & Acharya, L. (2017). Mental health effects in Bhutan of natural disasters. *Disaster Medicine and Public Health Preparedness, 11*(2), 236–242.

The Borgen Project. (n.d.). *5 organizations addressing mental health in Bhutan.* https://borgenproject.org/mental-health-in-bhutan/

Tshering, K., & Dema, K. (2022). Psychological impact during COVID-19 pandemic: A web-based cross-sectional study among students studying at College of Science and Technology (CST), Phuentsholing, Bhutan. *PloS one, 17*(2), e0263999. https://doi.org/10.1371/journal.pone.0263999

United Nations. (2002, June). *Global warming triggers glacial lakes flood threat* [Press release]. UN.

United Nations Development Programme. (2005). *Bhutan human development report 2005: Bringing down barriers—Main report.* UNDP. https://hdr.undp.org/sites/default/files/bhutan_2005_en.pdf

United Nations Development Programme. (2012). *Reducing climate change-induced risks from glacial lake outburst floods in Bhutan* [Project document]. https://www.undp.org/bhutan/publications/reducing-climate-change-induced-risks-glacial-lake-outburst-floods-bhutan

United Nations Development Programme. (2019, June 20). *Bhutan pursues climate resilience with National Adaptation Plan* [Press release]. Retrieved from UNDP Bhutan site. UNDP.

United Nations Development Programme. (2021). *Climate change and mental health: Two new issues confronting South Asia* [Policy brief]. Program for UN Development. https://www.example.com/placeholder-url

United Nations Development Programme. (2022). *Integrating mental health and psychosocial support into peacebuilding* [Policy brief]. https://www.undp.org/publications/integrating-mental-health-and-psychosocial-support-peacebuilding

United Nations Development Programme. (2023, September 16). *Bhutan launches its first National Adaptation Plan* [News release]. Retrieved from UNDP Bhutan.

United Nations Development Programme. (2024, August 30). *The climate crisis is a health crisis – Here's why.* https://climatepromise.undp.org/news-and-stories/climate-crisis-health-crisis-heres-why

United Nations Development Programme. (2025). *Supporting climate resilience and transformational change in the agriculture sector in Bhutan (2020–2025)* [Project webpage]. UNDP. https://adaptation-undp.org/projects/GCF/bhutan/climateresilientagriculture.

Walsh, B. (2011, November 18). IPCC report: Global warming—And changing population—Will worsen the toll of extreme weather. *Time*. https://science.time.com/2011/11/18/ipcc-report-global-warming-and-changing-population-will-worsen-the-toll-of-extreme-weather/

Wangchuk, K., & Wangdi, N. (2018). Carbon neutrality of Bhutan and methods of climate adaptation. *Sustainability, 10*(5), 1653. https://doi.org/10.3390/su10051653

Wangchuk, T., Dema, K., & Jamtsho, S. (2020). Resilience and mental health programs in Bhutan. *International Journal of Social Psychiatry, 66*(4), 387–399. https://doi.org/10.1177/0020764020919475

Wangdi, L. C. (2025, July 23). *Bhutan joins global climate call to supercharge clean energy transition*. United Nations in Bhutan. https://bhutan.un.org/en/298949-bhutan-joins-global-climate-call-supercharge-clean-energy-transition

Watanabe, K. (2023). Multi-sectoral mental health and psychosocial support. *The Druk Journal, 9*(1). https://drukjournal.bt/wp-content/uploads/2023/07/Watanabe-Kozo.pdf

Watanabe, T., & Rothacher, D. (1996). The 1994 Lugge Tsho glacial lake outburst flood, Bhutan Himalaya. *Mountain Research and Development, 16*(1), 77–81. https://doi.org/10.2307/3673894

Wikipedia. (2025). https://en.wikipedia.org/wiki/1968_Sikkim_floods

World Bank. (2024, December 11). *World Bank helps Bhutan enhance climate and disaster resilience* [Press release]. World Bank. https://www.worldbank.org/en/news/press-release/2024/12/11/world-bank-helps-bhutan-enhance-climate-and-disaster-resilience

World Health Organization. (2013). *Bhutan: Water safety planning case study*. World Health Organization. https://cdn.who.int/media/docs/default-source/searo/wsh-och-searo/bhutan-final-wsp.pdf?sfvrsn=17aad559_2

World Health Organization. (2024). *Mental health and climate change: Addressing the psychosocial impacts of environmental change* [Report]. WHO. https://www.who.int/publications/i/item/mental-health-and-climate-change-2024

Chapter 5
Mental Health Consequences of Disasters and Their Management: Current Status in India

Nilamadhab Kar

1 Introduction

India is one of the most disaster-prone countries in the world (World Population Review, 2025). It is among the top countries with natural disaster risk, with a varied geographical region, from deserts to snow-clad mountains, glaciers, rivers, a large coastline, monsoon-based rain, etc. Climate change is contributing to extreme weather events. Besides the extreme weather events, industrial and human-made disasters are common too in India. Disasters are associated with a large number of deaths, disabilities, and massive economic costs. Their impact on the mental health of the survivors, their families, and disaster workers is well-known. Considering frequent disasters of various kinds, a huge number of people in India are affected and have mental health problems both in the short and long term. It is imperative to understand the current state regarding the mental health impact of disasters and their management in India.

N. Kar (✉)
Department of Psychiatry, Black Country Healthcare NHS Foundation Trust, Wolverhampton, UK

Research Institute in Health Sciences, University of Wolverhampton, Wolverhampton, UK

Faculty of Contemplative and Behavioural Sciences, Sri Sri University, Cuttack, India
e-mail: n.kar@nhs.net

N. Kar et al. (eds.), *Climate Change, Disaster and Mental Health in South Asia*, South Asian Perspectives in Mental Health and Psychology,
https://doi.org/10.1007/978-981-95-3690-0_5

1.1 Disaster Vulnerability of India

India is vulnerable to natural disasters on account of its unique geo-climatic conditions. More than 85% of India's geographical area is prone to multiple hazards (Deshpande, 2022). Almost three-fourths of the total Indian states and union territories are disaster-prone. More than 60% of the landmass is predisposed to earthquakes (55% in high seismic zones III–V), about 68% area is susceptible to drought, and 8% to cyclones, and over 40 million hectares are prone to floods (UNDP, 2012).

India is dependent on the monsoon for rain, and changes to the monsoon can lead to drought on one side or floods on the other. The impact of global warming and climate change is also affecting the weather in various ways, from frequent cyclones to cloud bursts, floods, etc. While there are lots of benefits of having a long coastline, this also makes India more vulnerable to cyclones, tsunamis, floods, and coastal hazards (Deshpande, 2022). There are poor housing standards, and infrastructure makes the regions more vulnerable to the impacts of earthquakes and extreme weather events.

Another vulnerability factor is the massive number of people being affected in any major disasters, and the services and support are stretched thin, from crisis management to medium and long-term support. Frequently repeated disasters, for example, floods and cyclones, provide hardly any recovery period.

Most people in India live in rural areas, and survivors in these areas are more vulnerable, probably because the services and supportive infrastructures are scanty there compared to urban areas. However, urban areas are also vulnerable to different kinds of disasters, mostly human-made ones. Rapid urbanization, population density, and poor standards of facilities contribute to vulnerability. Similarly, there is a higher proportion of the economically compromised population in the country, who are impacted more by disasters, sometimes as their work and livelihood are affected in the post-disaster period for various reasons. In addition, there is still a large population with a poor literacy level, who are known to be more vulnerable in disasters.

Along with all these, for various reasons, India suffers from frequent human-made disasters, such as social conflicts, political violence, riots, terrorism, etc. There is a great loss of life and property in all these, and these affect a huge number of people.

1.2 Disaster Categories

Disasters have been categorized into a few broad areas (Deshpande, 2022; Government of India, 2011, 2017). These include the following: (i) water and climate related (e.g., floods, cyclones, tsunami, cloudburst, heat wave, cold wave, avalanches, droughts, sea erosion, thunder and lightning), (ii) land related (e.g., landslides, mudflows, earthquakes, dam failure/bursts, minor fires), (iii) accident related (e.g., forest fires, urban fires, mine flooding, oil spills, major building collapse, electrical disasters and fires, air, road and rail accidents, boat capsizing, village fire, serial bomb blasts, festival related disasters, some of these are deliberate human-induced acts), (iv) industrial (e.g. nuclear leak, industrial chemical leak, operational negligence), and (v) biological (e.g. biological disasters, epidemics, pest attacks, cattle epidemics, food poisoning). The accidental ones can be divided further into human error-related and deliberate human actions, and both kinds of disasters are observed.

2 Recent Major Disasters in India

India is frequently affected by disasters, most commonly extreme weather events and industrial accidents. Examples of recent major disasters of various kinds are given in Box 5.1. This provides the range and type of disastrous events.

3 Disasters and Mental Health Studies

Psychological trauma following disasters is catastrophic, and there is not only an immediate impact, but the deleterious effects continue long term for many survivors. Disasters are associated with various secondary stressors. These are loss of human life, injuries, disabilities, loss of property, loss or damage of houses, short- or long-term displacements, job loss, damaged crops, loss of livestock, etc. These come with a huge economic cost to individuals, the community, and the nation (Deshpande, 2022). Besides personal injury and disabilities, it is sometimes associated with death or injury of the earning member of the family, changes in personal, relational, and social situations, secondary to changed circumstances. There are reports of abuse of more vulnerable survivors.

In addition to all these, there are other issues, such as the problems of getting relief and support from the authorities, and complex community and political issues contributing further to the issue of 'the second disaster' (Kar, 2003). A distinct example of the "second disaster" is the impact of the approaches to manage the COVID-19 pandemic through lockdowns, which raised many secondary stressors (Chhabra et al., 2022; Jain & Dupas, 2022; Kar et al., 2021c). Although instituted to decrease viral transmission, it had many unintended consequences and affected lives in many different ways.

It is known that anyone who experiences disasters, either directly, indirectly, or as disaster responders or workers, is psychologically affected. While most recover from these grossly unusual traumatic experiences, some develop mental health problems. There have been many studies in India regarding the mental health problems following major disasters; some of which are described here, based on the type of disasters. These studies provide the extent and range of mental health problems and associated risk factors.

Box 5.1 Examples of Recent Major Disasters in India

Climate	
1996, Cyclone, Andhra Pradesh	2014, Floods, Kashmir
1999, Super-cyclone, Odisha	2018, Floods and landslides, Kerala
2002, Heat wave, India	2019, Cyclone Fani, Odisha
2004, Tsunami, Andaman and Nicobar, South India	2020, Cyclone Amphan, Odisha, West Bengal
2007, Flood, Bihar	2024, Cyclone Dana, Odisha, West Bengal
2013, Flash floods, Uttarakhand	2024, Landslide, Wayanad, Kerala
2013, Cyclone Phailin, Odisha	2025, Cloud burst, Uttarakhand
Land	
1991, Earthquake, Uttarakhand	2001, Earthquake, Bhuj, Gujarat
1993, Earthquake, Latur, Marathwada	2005, Earthquake, Kashmir
1997, Earthquake, Jabalpur	2015, Earthquake, Nepal, India
Accident	
1995, Train accident, Firozabad	1999, Train accident, West Bengal
1999, Fire, urban slum, Delhi	2023, Train accident, Odisha
Aviation disasters	
1985, Flight 182, Kanishka bombing	2010, Flight 812, crash, Mangalore
1999, Flight 814, hijacking	2020, Flight 1344, crash, Kozhikode
2000, Flight 7412, crash, Patna	2025, Flight 171, crash, Ahmedabad
Terrorism	
1993, Bomb blasts, Mumbai	2008, Terrorist attack, Mumbai
2006, Bomb blasts in trains, Mumbai	2025, Terrorist attack, Pahalgam
Riots	
1984, Delhi	2012, Assam
1992, Bombay	2013, Muzaffarnagar, Uttar Pradesh
2002, Gujarat	2020, Delhi
2008, Kandhamal, Odisha	2023–25, Manipur
Industrial	
1975, Chasnala Mine disaster, Jharkhand	2020, Gas leak, Vizag
1984, Gas tragedy, Bhopal	2022, Factory fire, Delhi
Biological	
2006, Dengue outbreak	2010–11, Dengue and Chikungunya outbreak
2006, H3N1 Avian influenza outbreak	2015, Indian swine flu outbreak
2009, H1N1 Swine flu pandemic	2020, COVID-19 pandemic

Wikipedia (2024, 2025a, b)

Table 5.1 Mental health morbidities following floods and landslides

Observations	Risk factors	Reference
The 2015 floods in Tamil Nadu: overall psychiatric morbidity: 45.1%, 26.9% had PTSD symptoms, 27.4% anxiety, 45.3% depression, and 4.9% had an increase in substance use	Old age. Emphasis on the needs of older persons, better preparedness with basic necessities, and medical and psychological assistance was suggested	Bandla et al. (2019)
The 2018 floods and landslides in Kerala: In adolescents, probable PTSD was present in 34.9%. Deterioration in academic performance was observed in 45.9% who were screen positive for PTSD	Male, higher age, damage during floods, presence of morbidity, camp stay, and loss of pets were significantly associated with PTSD	Mathew et al. (2021)
The 2018 floods and landslides in Kerala: In adults, at 6 weeks post-landslide, 46% had PTSD based on the PTSD checklist. The positive predictive value of PTSD screening on day 3 was 64.3% for PTSD at week 6	Property damage was associated with the risk of PTSD. Early screening was recommended	Kumar et al. (2023)

3.1 Floods and Landslides

Floods are extremely common in India, having annual recurrences affecting various areas. A few studies following floods are given in Table 5.1, along with various risk factors identified for psychiatric morbidity after the floods. Around a month after the 1994 flood in Jagatsinghpur, Odisha, in a community sample of people living in relief camps, 46.7% had adjustment disorder, 33.3% depression, 6.6% posttraumatic stress disorder (PTSD), and 6.6% acute psychosis (Kar et al., 2002). After the 2013 Uttarakhand cloud bursts, floods, and landslides, only 2% had disaster-induced psychiatric diagnoses, characterized by minor mental disorders of depression and anxiety, alongside reported substance use disorder in the community (Channaveerachari et al., 2015). A study on 300 children and adolescents following floods and landslides in Uttarakhand in 2013 reported that 66.7% had psychosocial adversities due to the disaster, distress was present in 18%, and stress-related psychiatric symptoms were present in 13% (Aneelraj et al., 2016). Older adults were more vulnerable to PTSD and depression after the 2008 Bihar floods (Telles et al., 2009).

There were many studies following the 2018 floods and landslides in Kerala. One of the studies highlighted the importance of early screening; on day three of the 2018 Kerala flood and landslide, 70% were screen positive and 30% at week 6 using the primary care PTSD screen (Kumar et al., 2023). Another study after the 2018 floods and landslides in Kerala observed that learned helplessness was found to be high among survivors who were affected by the flood twice rather than once. It was suggested that surviving a moderate amount of risk is perhaps necessary for better psychological well-being, and too many or too few risks in life are detrimental to good psychological health (Joy et al., 2021). A survey 1 year after the 2018 flood affected people in Kerala, found that the vast majority (89.5%) of affected people had subclinical psychiatric symptoms (Asim et al., 2022). Similarly, a study in

Table 5.2 Mental health morbidities following the 1999 Super-cyclone, Odisha

Observations	Risk factors	Reference
Affected people close to the epicenter experienced more anxiety, depression, and posttraumatic stress than the unaffected	The impact of exposure increased, whereas external support decreased anxiety and depression	Suar et al. (2002)
Probable psychiatric disorder: 80.4%, PTSD in 44.3%; anxiety disorder in 57.5%, depression in 52.7%, and comorbidity in 63.4%	Children and adolescents, the elderly, lower socioeconomic status, lower education, unemployment, physical injury, degree of exposure, need for evacuation, death in the family, fear of imminent death during the event, hopelessness, increased stress before disaster, and past psychiatric history	Kar et al. (2004)
In adolescents, around 1 year after the super cyclone, PTSD in 26.9%, depression in 17.6%, anxiety in 12.0%, any diagnosis in 37.9%, and comorbidity in 39.0%	Middle socioeconomic status, prolonged periods of helplessness, lack of adequate post-disaster psychological support, and the severity of the disaster	Kar and Bastia (2006)
In children, PTSD in 30.6% and subsyndromal PTSD in 13.6%. Parents or teachers reported mental health concerns in 7.2%, which was only 12.8% of children with any diagnosis	High exposure, lower educational level, and middle socioeconomic status significantly predicted PTSD. Extreme fear and perceived threat to life during disaster, death in the family, damage to home, and staying in shelters were not significantly associated with PTSD in children. Depression was significantly associated with PTSD	Kar et al. (2007)

Assam reported that flooding is associated with PTSD, depression, and anxiety; and the longer the duration of the flood, the higher the risk of anxiety and depression (Borah & Saikia, 2025).

3.2 *Cyclones*

Cyclones are common in India (Box 5.1), and many of them are in the higher category. One of the most serious cyclones was the 1999 Odisha super-cyclone, which was the most intense tropical cyclone and most destructive in the region. There were many studies following the 1999 super-cyclone. A few examples are presented in Table 5.2.

There have been reports of an increased rate of admission of psychiatric patients to the state hospitals immediately following the disaster, and increased tobacco consumption (Suar & Kar, 2005). Three months after the 1999 super-cyclone, it was reported that increasing age was associated with more anxiety, depression, and posttraumatic stress among survivors (Suar et al., 2007). Around a year after the super-cyclone, death wishes (66.4%), suicidal ideas (38.0%), suicidal plans (18.3%), and attempts (12.6%) were frequently reported by the survivors (Kar, 2010).

One month after the 2019 Fani cyclone in Odisha, the prevalence of probable PTSD was 42.9%, severe anxiety 36.7%, moderately severe depression 16.5%, and severe depression 3.8%. Suicidal cognitions were present in 14% of survivors. Comorbidity was common. The risk factors for PTSD were damage to the house and displacement; the risk for moderate and severe depression were evacuation and displacement; and the risk factor for severe anxiety was displacement (Kar et al., 2021b). A study reported pre-disaster anticipatory clinical level anxiety in 17.3% before the 2024 low intensity Dana cyclone in Odisha; and post-cyclone anxiety was observed in 14.5%, depression in 12.9%, and PTSD in 17.7%; with overall post-cyclone psychiatric morbidity in 24.2%, and comorbidity in 60.0% (Kar & Kar, 2025). The risk factors for psychiatric morbidity were rural background, low socio-economic status, evacuation, perceiving the cyclone as extremely severe, and being stressed just before, during, and after the cyclone (Kar & Kar, 2025).

3.3 The 2004 Asian Tsunami

The 2004 Asian tsunami affected many countries, including India. It was one of the most devastating and deadliest tsunamis in living memory, with over 220,000 deaths, affecting the countries around the Indian Ocean. There were many studies about the mental health of the affected people in India (Table 5.3).

Table 5.3 Mental health morbidities following the 2004 Asian tsunami

Observations	Risk factors	Reference
Children and adolescents in Andaman and Nicobar: adjustment disorder 13.5%, depression 13.5%, panic disorder 10.8%, PTSD 10.8%, schizophrenia 2.7%, other disorders 43.2%. Subclinical syndrome in the majority	Only a few required intensive individual psychiatric interventions; a majority required community-based group interventions	Math et al. (2008b)
Posttraumatic stress symptoms were present in 15.1%	Traumatic grief, female gender, physical injury, death of children, and financial losses but not functional disability	Rajkumar et al. (2013)
4.5 years after the tsunami: psychiatric morbidity 77.6%, anxiety 23.1%, depression 33.6%, PTSD 70.9%, and comorbidity 44.7%	Direct exposure, lack of formal education, perception of disaster as highly stressful, damage to the home, and loss of livelihood and livestock	Kar et al. (2014)
Prolonged grief disorder in 14.2% of tsunami survivors vs. 25.9% of bereaved survivors	Spousal bereavement, extensive damage to homes, fewer years of education, and absence of tsunami-related physical injury were associated with prolonged grief disorder	Rajkumar et al. (2015)

Around 6–9 months after the 2004 Asian tsunami, a study in Tamil Nadu found that 27.2% had psychiatric disorders; 79.7% had psychological symptoms; the commonest disorders were depression, followed by alcohol use disorders in males and anxiety disorders in females; and PTSD was prevalent in 12.5/1000 (Nambi et al., 2007). A study in Kanyakumari reported that psychological distress was clinically significant in 43%, and it was at very high levels in 31% (George et al., 2007). In the Andaman and Nicobar Islands, 5–8% of the population was suffering from significant mental health problems in the early phase of the 2004 tsunami, with a concern that it might increase to 25–30% in the disillusionment phase (Math et al., 2006). It was higher in the displaced population (5.2%) than in the non-displaced (2.8%) (Math et al., 2008a).

A study 14 months after the tsunami found that the post-tsunami trauma of survivors had increased with increasing age, female gender, and more exposure; and widowhood, illiteracy, and lower family income were found to intensify trauma (Suar et al., 2010). It was also reported that indirect effects of tsunami through resource loss were a more potent predictor than the direct effects of exposure on trauma (Suar et al., 2016); similarly, loss of life and property and disaster exposure positively predicted the dimensions of trauma (Suar et al., 2017). In addition to these, bereaved survivors reported more PTSD, depression, anxiety, negative affect, deteriorated mental health, adverse physical health symptoms, alcohol consumption, family conflicts, and fear compared to non-bereaved survivors (Suar et al., 2015).

3.4 *Earthquakes*

There have been many major earthquakes in India in recent years (Box 5.1), and there are a few epidemiological studies. Within a month of the 1993 Latur earthquake in Marathwada, psychiatric morbidity was observed in 59%, PTSD in 23%, and major depression in 21% (Sharan et al., 1996). An ICMR study in the Latur earthquake found 21.46% adult males in the affected group had a psychiatric diagnosis compared to 13.14% in the control; corresponding figures for females were 14.99% and 5.05% (Desai et al., 2004). Another study following this earthquake reported PTSD (74%), major depression (89%), generalized anxiety disorder (42%), and panic disorder (28%) (Kar, 2000).

It has been observed that 1 year after the 2001 earthquake in Gujarat, the mental health problems were increasing and were higher in disabled persons but were "neglected." A study by Oxfam India indicated that 100% of school students and 75% of teachers had psychological problems (R. Sharma, 2002). Following the 2005 earthquake in Kashmir, psychiatric problems observed were adjustment disorders, depression, generalized anxiety disorder, symptoms of PTSD, panic disorder, and insomnia (Chadda & Malhotra, 2006).

3.5 *Fire Disasters*

Fire disasters in urban areas and industries are frequently observed in India. In the 1981 Bangalore fire disaster, 35.8% of the bereaved relatives had psychiatric problems (Narayanan et al., 1987). In the Mandi Dabwali fire disaster, 56% of children had PTSD after 2 months (Sharma et al., 1998).

Survivors of a fire in the 1999 Delhi urban slum area had significantly higher (7.8%) psychiatric disorders compared to 2.2% in the control group (although psychological problems were present in 23.2% vs. 5.0% respectively); the common disorders were depression, substance use disorders, generalized anxiety disorder, and somatoform disorder. Age and participation in relief work were strong predictors, and physical injuries were a weak predictor of mental health morbidity (Desai et al., 2004).

3.6 *Train Accidents*

India has experienced frequent train accidents, and some of them have been extremely severe, with massive loss of lives (Wikipedia, 2025b). Besides the traumatic experience for the passengers and their family members, these also affect the train drivers and the railway staff (Kar, 2024a). Usually, there are fatalities and life-changing injuries among many passengers. There is a dearth of studies on the mental health outcome of the survivors of train accidents in India.

Following the recent 2023 Odisha train accident, 20.7% of passengers had PTSD, compared to 19.0% of health professionals who treated them and 7.7% of local people; seeing dead bodies was a significant contributing factor for PTSD. Passengers also suffered from anxiety (58.3%) and depression (50%) (Kar et al., 2025a). A study on first responders of the 2023 Odisha train accident reported symptoms of probable PTSD in 10.2%, anxiety in 11.6%, and depression in 24.9%. A qualitative analysis suggested the presence of posttraumatic stress symptoms, along with positive factors of increased empathy, resilience, finding a purpose, and the beneficial role of peer support (Ravan et al., 2024).

There is a need for more studies following train accidents to evaluate the extent of the mental health problems, which should include the impact on train drivers and the railway staff. These studies might help to set up an appropriate supportive process for the affected people (Kar, 2024a).

3.7 Aviation Disaster

Aviation disasters are associated with loss, prolonged grief disorder, PTSD, depression, panic, phobia, and other anxiety disorders (Birmes et al., 1999; Catanesi et al., 2013; Gregg et al., 1995; Lenferink et al., 2017; Ornell et al., 2025) in survivors and the indirect victims (Jeronimus et al., 2019). It is reported that the psychological impact of an aviation disaster continues long-term (Davis & Stewart, 2000). Plane hijacking also leads to posttraumatic stress among the hostages (Cremniter et al., 1997). The mental health of the pilots has come under higher scrutiny in recent years. Higher stress and its negative impact on pilots' decision-making ability have been reported, suggesting cognitive flexibility training and stress management interventions (Lakshmana et al., 2025).

There are a few aviation disasters, such as plane crashes and hijackings in India (Box 5.1). However, the mental health aspects of the affected people are hardly available (Kar et al., 2025b). There is a need to study the extent of mental health problems in survivors and their families, support needs, and how these can be provided.

3.8 Riots, Conflicts

There is limited literature on the psychosocial impact of riots, social unrest, and conflicts in India (Bhargava & Gupta, 2020). Unfortunately, these are not uncommon. A study on hospitalized victims following the 1992–1993 Bombay riots reported shock, fear, and helplessness; anger; high posttraumatic stress symptoms; and emotional numbness; specifically 21% had severe anxiety, 41% had paranoid thinking, 36% had suicidal thoughts, and 2% had attempted suicide (Kar, 2000; Shetty & Chhabria, 1997).

In 2002, communal violence in Ahmedabad, women reported posttraumatic stress symptoms, such as reexperiencing, avoidance, and hyperarousal (Mehta et al., 2005). Four years after the communal violence in Ahmedabad, 4.7% of children and adolescents had PTSD, and 9.4% had major depression (Vankar et al., 2007).

Among internally displaced persons residing in different relief camps during the Manipur violence, 65.8% had PTSD, 24.8% had moderate anxiety, and 15.2% had severe anxiety (Rajkumari et al., 2024). Armed conflicts and wars contribute to the traumatic stress and mental health issues of the directly and indirectly affected people. In addition, this has given rise to internal displacements and refugee problems (Sharma et al., 2023), which have impacted mental health. However, there are hardly any in-depth studies about these issues. A systematic review about mental health problems following communal riots in an Indian context suggested that 49% had depression, and PTSD ranged from 4% to 41% (Irshad, 2024).

3.9 Terrorism

India has suffered from terrorism relentlessly, with a long list not just of events but persistent situations over months and years. For example, people in Jammu and Kashmir, Punjab (Trivedi, 2004), Manipur, etc., have been affected by terrorism for a long period. In recent history, there have been many terrorist incidents. The November 26, 2008, Mumbai terror attack (Joseph & Jaswal, 2014) and, recently, the 2025 Pahalgam attacks are stark examples of terroristic activities suffered by the people.

The link between terrorism and mental health is well-known. However, there are only a few studies about the mental health impact or intervention outcome for the survivors of terrorism in India. Following the 1996 bomb blast in a bus as a terrorist activity in Dausa, Rajasthan, 35.5% had psychiatric morbidity on day 3, 19.4% had acute stress reaction, 9.7% had depression, and 6.5% had dissociative amnesia and a range of psychiatric symptoms, such as depersonalization, derealization, sleep disturbances specially generalized sleep loss, loss of appetite, nightmares, situational anxiety, depression, mental irritability, dullness of feelings, self-blame, guilt, loss of interest, suicidal ideas, and worry about finance and family. In the 2nd week after the incident, 12.9% had PTSD, while the depression and dissociative amnesia continued as before (Gautam et al., 1998).

A study in Srinagar reported that the psychiatric outpatient appointment had increased considerably between 1990 and 2001, which was suggested to be linked to the growing impact of terrorism and violence; 2.4% of the patients had PTSD, most (68.2%) having an acute onset (Trivedi, 2004).

3.10 Industrial Disaster

There are many industrial disasters in India, such as fires, chemical leaks, mine disasters, etc. However, studies on the mental health aspects of the survivors are scarce. Most studies are related to the 1984 Bhopal gas tragedy, which is the first industrial disaster in India that has been studied systematically (Murthy, 2014).

Studies suggested that there was poor auditory memory in female and visual memory in male affected persons, and a wide variety of neuropsychiatric symptoms, such as abnormal smell, abnormal taste, faintness, headache, difficulty staying awake, abnormal balance, fatigue, anxiety, and difficulty in concentration, were reported (Murthy, 2014). Within 3 months of the Bhopal gas disaster, 22.6% had mental disorders, which were anxiety neurosis (25%), depression (20%), and adjustment reaction with predominant disturbance of emotions (16%), whereas psychosis was rare (Murthy, 2014; Sethi et al., 1987). One and a half years after the gas disaster, the exposed population had significantly higher psychiatric morbidity than the control (9.4% v 2.5%) (Bhiman, 2001).

3.11 Biological Disasters

Many outbreaks, epidemics, and pandemics have affected India (Box 5.1). Although there are hardly any studies on the mental health aspects of other infection-related disasters, there are many studies following the COVID-19 pandemic (Kabir et al., 2023; Ray, 2022). These have identified issues in the general population and specific groups of people, such as health professionals.

The lockdowns during the COVID-19 pandemic, to control the spread of the virus, became a secondary stressor with considerable psychological impact. It led to isolation, job losses, increased abuse and domestic violence, and mental health issues, such as anxiety and depression, all over the world, including India (Chhabra et al., 2022; Rehman et al., 2021b). People without enough supplies to sustain the lockdown were most affected, and family affluence was found to be negatively correlated with stress, anxiety, and depression (Rehman et al., 2021b).

Various vulnerable groups were identified regarding the mental health problems related to COVID-19 (Patra & Patro, 2020). These included women, children and adolescents, older adults, lower socioeconomic status, and the risk of abuse of vulnerable groups increased (Girdhar et al., 2020; Mishra et al., 2020; Patra & Patro, 2020; Rina et al., 2020). People with previous mental illnesses were more vulnerable too; many experienced relapses of the symptoms, including an increase in suicides (Rangaswamy et al., 2022).

In COVID-19 patients admitted to the hospital, 27% had depression, 67% had anxiety, and 62% had sleep disturbance (Yadav et al., 2021). In another study of inpatients with COVID-19, 40% had depression, 28.8% sleep problems, and suicidal ideas in 5% (Chakrabarti, 2021). In pregnant women, a study reported that 11.1% of them had a moderate or severe level of anxiety (Tikka et al., 2021).

A study on adolescents in rural areas reported anxiety in 35.7% and depression in 30.0% with a higher prevalence in female gender (Mitra et al., 2024). Mental disorders were comparatively less in urban slum dwellers during the COVID-19 pandemic; 3.5% had depression, and 2.5% had anxiety, with half of them believing that it was unnecessary to worry about COVID-19 (Rehman et al., 2021a).

A study of adults with no previous history of mental illness reported mental distress in 35.7% (rural 29.2%, urban 42.2%), depression in 26.3% (rural 19.4%, urban 33.1%), anxiety in 35.7% and stress in 15.6% (Nallapu et al., 2023). Among the COVID survivors, 43.6% had anxiety, 40.6% had depression, and 71.3% had moderate to high stress symptoms (Nongpiur et al., 2023).

A study on healthcare professionals reported that 14.1% had generalized anxiety disorder (Naik et al., 2022). Another study on healthcare professionals reported stress in 33.8%, anxiety in 38.9%, and depression in 43.6%; and the COVID-19-exposed professionals had greater severity in these morbidities (Jakhar et al., 2021). A meta-analysis reported a pooled prevalence of stress at 60.7%, depression in 32.7% anxiety in 34.1%, and sleep disturbance in 26.7%, with higher prevalence in healthcare workers compared to the general population (Singh et al., 2021).

4 Risk Factors for Post-Disaster Psychiatric Disorders

Studies in India on disaster mental health have reported various risk factors. A summary of frequently reported risk factors has been given in Box 5.2. Exposure to disaster itself is the major risk factor, and repeated exposure further increases the risk. A study following the 1999 Odisha super-cyclone on children reported that 43.7% children in high exposure areas had PTSD compared to 11.2% in low exposure areas (Kar et al., 2007).

Excessive, repetitive, and improper media coverage of the disasters and survivors has been observed to be stressful and a contributing factor (Kar et al., 2025a; Ravan et al., 2024). In an interesting study, 3.4% of older adults who reported exposure to natural or human-made disasters in the previous 5 years had a higher prevalence of poor self-rated health, difficulty in activities of daily living, communicable diseases, depressive symptoms, and psychiatric disorders compared to the non-exposed group (Muhammad et al., 2024).

Box 5.2 Examples of Common Risk Factors Identified for Psychiatric Morbidity After Disasters in India

Sociodemographic factors	Disaster factors	Clinical factors
Children and adolescents Female gender Lower education Lower socioeconomic status Older adults Rural background	Being in a shelter Damage to the house Death of family Evacuation Fear of death during a disaster Higher impact Loss of livelihood Repeat exposure Resource loss	Comorbidity History of mental illness

5 Coping and Resilience

Most disaster survivors do not get any external psychosocial support and cope with the traumatic experience themselves. Coping strategies can help support resilience; however, there are many maladaptive strategies (N. Kar, 2022a, 2023a, 2024b). Negative coping styles can lead to adverse psychological outcomes. In the post-disaster scenarios, there is relevance in studying both individual and community coping strategies. There are many Indian studies reflecting on the coping of disaster survivors (Box 5.3).

Box 5.3 Reported Coping Strategies After Major Disasters in India

Individual strategies	
Accepting	Relaxation
Altruistic behavior	Religious activities
Avoidance	Self-help group participation
Belief in God	Singing/listening to devotional songs
Belief in self	Socialization
Distraction	Spirituality
Help seeking	Substance use
Music	Talking to others
Over-the-counter drug use	Venting
Preparedness (pre-disaster)	Viewing trauma from a different angle
Community strategies	
Community or group activities	Social activities
Cultural beliefs	Social groups
Religious ceremonies	Visiting shrines or faith leaders

Understanding the post-disaster coping strategies of individuals, communities, and disaster responders is important, as the beneficial ones can be facilitated (N. Kar, 2022a, 2023a, 2024b). There are many culture-based coping strategies observed in the Indian population. Religious activities, singing and playing devotional songs, were observed as a way of expressing distress and finding hope (Kar, 2006; Murthy et al., 2003) during the 1999 super-cyclone in Odisha.

Specifically, following the 1999 super-cyclone in Odisha these coping strategies were reported by the survivors. While help-seeking, venting, having someone empathetic to talk to, avoiding thinking about the disaster and damages, believing in self and God, hoping that things will be fine, accepting nothing could have been possibly done, and viewing the trauma in a different perspective were reported to be helpful, avoiding thinking about the trauma or venting was not helpful (Kar et al., 2004).

Survivors of the 2004 tsunami valued their unique individual, social, and spiritual coping strategies more than formal mental health services, which suggested that post-disaster interventions should be grounded in ethno-cultural beliefs and practices and should be aimed at strengthening prevailing community coping strategies (Rajkumar et al., 2008). Disasters, suffering, loss, and death are viewed in different angles of *karma* by some survivors; while this helps people to accept and cope, it may hinder taking actions to deal with the trauma (Math et al., 2015).

A study reported dispositional (hope, optimism, striving, grit, and self-efficacy), cognitive (reframing, flexibility, ability to analyze situations and formulate adaptable solutions), and situational (social support, community embeddedness, and collective efficacy) attributes contributing to resilience in the flood survivors in Kerala (Panigrahi & Suar, 2021). Following the 2019 cyclone Fani, higher levels of self-efficacy, hope, cognitive flexibility, collective efficacy, social support, and health were associated with higher levels of resilience among the survivors. Higher resilience supported posttraumatic growth and thriving in terms of meaning, purpose, life satisfaction, sense of accomplishment, and self-worth (Panigrahi & Suar, 2023).

6 Disaster Management

There has been appreciable improvement in disaster management over the years. Pre-disaster warnings, preparedness, evacuations, and a greater presence of supportive agencies in the disaster sites are observed. There are improved communication, coverage, and connectivity. However, there is room for improvement, at least for the mental healthcare of the survivors.

It has been suggested that the impact of disaster trauma can be reduced by facilitating an environment for garnering informational, emotional, and material support, building collective resilience, promoting cross-sector collaboration, preventing corruption and abuses, and executing micro-plans (Suar et al., 2024). These factors might help while designing the psychosocial support for the disaster survivors.

6.1 Community Support

Following major disasters, community support has continued in various forms through local volunteers and nongovernmental organizations. In addition, support from organizations, such as the Red Cross, ActionAid, Oxfam, and the United Nations Development Programme (UNDP), has been available. Local voluntary nongovernmental organizations have provided support for disaster survivors through relief and counseling.

6.2 Local Workforce

Following many disasters in India, local volunteers have been trained to provide counseling, thus disseminating the know-how on mental healthcare for the large mass of disaster survivors. Some of the examples have been *Sneha Karmis* following the Odisha super-cyclone (Murthy et al., 2003; Kar, 2006). Accredited social health activists and female frontline health workers have also been involved in supporting the survivors in different disasters (Krishnan, 2022; Selvaraj et al., 2022; Thomas et al., 2022). These frontline, community-level professionals can be trained in a short period, and they can provide counseling and other mental health-related interventions, alongside other disaster-related support. This assures faster mental healthcare in the communities. Many of the stress-related issues and common mental health problems can be managed this way.

6.3 Supportive Educational Materials

Educational materials relevant for disaster survivors, the counselors, and primary care staff have been prepared in the form of booklets, training manuals, information booklets, or other publications. These are available to support the general public and professionals about disasters, their effects, how to prepare for these, and how to take care of oneself in stressful situations (Diaz et al., 2006; Kar, 2008; Kar & Misra, 2008; Laxminarayan et al., 2004). One of the examples was information manuals on "Disaster Mental Health Care by Medical Officers" from the National Institute of Mental Health and Neurosciences (NIMHANS). It is encouraging to note that many information books are now available in the local languages in different states of India.

6.4 Participation of Mental Health Organizations

Many psychiatric departments in Medical Colleges in India have been involved in supporting the disaster survivors. Following the Bhopal Gas disaster, King George Medical College (KGMC), Lucknow, carried out systematic studies (Murthy, 2014). The NIMHANS has taken many initiatives to support disaster work in India. The work done following the 1999 Odisha super-cyclone was perhaps the major epidemiological work that was undertaken at that time (Kar, 2006; Murthy et al., 2003). The findings provided the ground realities in the post-disaster scenarios (Kar, 2006) and the magnitude of psychiatric concerns in adults (Kar et al., 2004), children, and adolescents (Kar et al., 2007; Kar & Bastia, 2006). In addition, these epidemiological studies highlighted the risk factors for stress-related disorders, self-harm, and suicidality (Kar, 2010) in the post-disaster period in the Indian cultural setup.

A lack of a joined-up approach between various organizations is still evident. Departments of health, psychiatry, psychology, and social care in medical colleges, institutes, universities, and the government should take up the local disaster management responsibilities in a coordinated manner. Large-scale community-based support needs to be instituted.

6.5 Interventional Studies

There are only a few interventional studies involving disaster survivors in India. Considering the enormity of the need, the regular frequency of repeating disasters, and the number of survivors requiring support, interventions have been minuscule. Most survivors are not assessed; their mental health issues remain unidentified and untreated. However, it is useful to discuss the interventions that have taken place following disasters in India. Some of the interventions are mentioned in Box 5.4.

Many studies looked at the feasibility of providing support to the survivors, especially in the community setting. Post-disaster community-based group interventions for psychosocial interventions have been tried and were found to be easy to implement using local resources (Kar, 2006; Vijaykumar et al., 2006). School-based interventions for children and adolescents are relatively easy to set up, and this will encourage the return of the children and adolescents to their routine.

Post-disaster situations are usually stretched for resources and personnel. It has been observed that a range of non-specialist personnel, as well as volunteers from non-governmental organizations, have provided a variety of mental health care, mostly counseling and supportive interventions, following disasters. They have been provided with training by mental health professionals (Murthy, 2014; Murthy et al., 2003). In a study, following the 2004 Asian tsunami, trained volunteers delivered mental health support to the bereaved persons, and there were improvements in psychiatric symptoms and a decrease in suicide attempts (Vijayakumar & Kumar, 2008). Similarly, following the 2005 Kashmir earthquake, local doctors and paramedical staff were trained, and the external team visited villages as an outreach approach (Chadda & Malhotra, 2006).

Box 5.4 Examples of Mental Health Interventions Following Major Disasters in India

Activity therapy	Health information
Art therapy	Normalization of emotional response
Breathing exercises	Problem-solving
Cognitive therapy	Psychoeducation
Counseling	Psychological/emotional first aid,
Crisis intervention	Psychosocial rehabilitation
Facilitation of cultural coping	Relaxation therapy
Facilitation of grieving and re-grieving	Social activity
Facilitation of positive coping	Spirituality
Facilitation of venting/catharsis	Supportive therapies
Grief counseling	Tele-psychiatry
Group therapy	Trauma counseling
Group activity	Yoga and meditation

A study on psychosocial care instituted by NIMHANS for adult, children, and women survivors of the 2004 tsunami showed effectiveness based on the Impact of Event Scale scores (Becker, 2006, 2009). Qualitative studies on group counseling have been reported following the tsunami disaster in Tamil Nadu and the bomb blast in Assam, which highlighted the effectiveness of group interventions in the management of disaster trauma (Maheshwari et al., 2010). There have been studies involving yoga as a post-disaster intervention with positive outcomes (Ransing et al., 2020; Telles et al., 2010).

Post-disaster intervention often needs to deal with the aftermath of a huge number of deaths, grief, and complicated grief. Grief counseling for grieving family members trying to cope with the loss has been suggested and for mainstreaming it with the psychological first aid (Ramamurthy & Juvva, 2024).

An effort for psychotherapeutic support for the passengers of the 2023 train accident suggested that there were many unresolved psychological issues related to the trauma that the survivors could convey comprehensively. A range of interventions were needed, such as psychoeducation, relaxation, supportive and cognitive therapies, and specific trauma-focused cognitive behavioral therapy, and the process of provision of therapies had many challenges (Swain et al., 2025).

A study related to COVID-19 fear and social anxiety disorder suggested that the cognitive-behavioral therapy group had significantly less COVID-related fear than the psychoeducational-supportive therapy group, and the effect of cognitive-behavioral therapy for social anxiety disorder was maintained through lockdown (Samantaray et al., 2022).

There have been a few studies supporting children and adolescent survivors. It has been suggested to start the interventions as early as possible, involving all children and adolescents affected by the disaster (Math et al., 2008b). It was reported in a study 1 year after the 2004 tsunami that the majority of the children were likely to be resilient, and only children with preexisting vulnerability required specific and specialized interventions; hyperactivity came down significantly in the intervention group, which appreciated expression of positive emotions and desisted smoking (Vijayakumar et al., 2006).

There were many challenges in providing psychosocial support during the COVID-19 pandemic. However, greater use of tele-psychiatry (Roy et al., 2021; Singh, 2021) helped to maintain support for individuals with mental health problems. It included both medicinal and psychotherapeutic support. Many initiatives of community participation, support for each other, and support for the health professionals were noteworthy during the pandemic.

It needs to be recognized that conducting interventional studies in the post-disaster situation is difficult even in highly supportive and structured scenarios. There are various concerns and priorities for the survivors (N. Kar, 2003). Survivors are often stressed with real-life issues, which take priority over receiving psychological support. So initial support should address practical issues faced by the survivors, and most of these work needs to be done in the community.

6.6 Administrative Initiatives

There are many actions taken by the national and state governments in India to manage disasters. There is a National Policy on Disaster Management. In 2005, the government of India enacted the Disaster Management Act (Government of India, 2005), The Act defines disaster as "a catastrophe, mishap, calamity or grave occurrence in any area, arising from natural or manmade causes, or by accident or negligence which results in substantial loss of life or human suffering or damage to, and destruction of, property, or damage to, or degradation of, environment, and is of such a nature or magnitude as to be beyond the coping capacity of the community of the affected area" (Government of India, 2005). There have been many administrative changes following this (Chhabra, 2009; Kaur, 2006). The National Disaster Management Authority (NDMA) was founded in 2006. There are the National Disaster Mitigation Fund (NDMF) and State Disaster Mitigation Fund (SDMF) to support these disaster management activities.

The crisis response to disasters and related administrative support has improved in recent years in India. The disaster preparedness, rescue, and relief operations are well conducted following many different kinds of disasters. There are exemplary changes in Odisha, a state frequently affected by cyclones, regarding the management of severe weather-related events (Kumbhar, 2025). However, in all these strategies for the management of disasters, the mental health support system for the disaster survivors is not adequately instituted and coordinated.

6.7 Continuing Challenges

6.7.1 Service Gaps in Psychosocial Support

Despite progress in disaster management in different areas, especially in immediate disaster response, rescue and relief, attention to physical injuries, and financial support, there are still concerns in many areas. Focusing on the mental health of the survivors and their support, a considerable proportion of disaster survivors suffering from diagnosable mental illnesses do not get adequate support. Many of them would require treatment at a secondary level from mental health professionals, and without which their functional capabilities and quality of life remain impaired, besides the continued suffering.

6.7.2 Research Gaps in Disaster Mental Health

There is a gradually increasing knowledge base in India about the disaster mental health. This should help in planning and providing appropriate care and support to the direct and indirect victims. There is still a need for research in various areas of disaster mental health.

Most of the research is focused on PTSD, depression, and anxiety disorders; however, there may be other psychiatric disorders and social aspects that need to be explored. The trends of change in disaster-related mental health problems, especially following improved preparedness, rescue, and relief, with better disaster management, are needed.

More studies on the interventions for post-disaster psychiatric disorders and the effectiveness of those interventions in the short and long term are essential. Intervention approaches involving specific psychotherapies and medicinal treatment, along with their effectiveness, are essential. It needs to be prioritized that the interventions can reach a large number of survivors in a short period of time. The use and effectiveness of tele-psychiatry and tele-psychotherapy need to be explored.

Preventive capabilities of early interventions or psychological first aid to decrease the incidence of post-disaster morbidities are another subject to study. In addition, whether better preparedness, evacuations, and displacement have any influence on psychiatric morbidity needs to be checked. It has been reported that people with high self-esteem and a sense of mastery are more prepared for climate-related disasters such as floods and heat waves (Mishra et al., 2011). More studies about factors that may improve psychological preparedness and the effect of being well-prepared on post-disaster morbidities would be useful.

There is minimal information about the long-term consequences and outcomes of post-disaster psychiatric disorders. This is needed as these would reflect the natural course of these stress-related disorders, the influence of individual or community coping strategies, or the effectiveness of interventions if provided. There is a need for follow-up epidemiological studies among the disaster-affected populations.

Studies on the survivors of specific types of disasters, such as terrorism, riots, conflicts, border problems, and aviation disasters, as well as the disasters involving epidemics and pandemics (Kar et al., 2021a), are scarce. Prevalence and outcome studies following the human-made disasters are needed, too.

Culture-specific stress responses, coping strategies, and resilience factors should be studied extensively (Murthy, 2016; Rajkumar et al., 2008), as these might help inform the community intervention methods following disasters. These can be integrated into the psychosocial support provided to the survivors.

Disaster impact on vulnerable and marginalized populations and their support needs should be studied in depth, so that the support can be streamlined better. These could include children and adolescents (Kar, 2019; Kar & Bastia, 2006; Majumder et al., 2023), older adults (D'cruz & Banerjee, 2020; Kar, 2022b), third genders, and displaced migrants (McGowran et al., 2023; Singh et al., 2020), or refugees. It is also essential to study the mental health problems in the indirect victims, such as family members, relatives, and those who witness the disaster, as there is emerging evidence of stress impacts on these groups of people (Kar, 2023b; Kar et al., 2014).

Another area that lacks research in India is the impact of disasters on first responders, search and rescue teams, relief operators, community counselors, clinicians, and other professionals involved in the care of the disaster survivors (Kar et al., 2025a; Kar & Misra, 2008; Murthy et al., 2003; Ravan et al., 2024). There is evidence that they are also affected psychologically by the traumatic experience (Kar, 2023a). The extent of the problem and the support needs of the disaster responders should be studied as well.

Research should also explore better ways of managing disasters in the limited resource scenarios. The disaster management process should look into how to identify the vulnerable survivors and triage and prioritize their care and support. A process should be put in place categorizing services that are feasible in the community, especially in the rural areas, and the referral process to specialist services when required. There are various constraints and barriers to accessing post-disaster care by the survivors (Kar, 2003). These are pertinent issues to explore and deal with (Padmavati et al., 2020).

Disaster management research may explore how to integrate remote assessments and interventions following disasters when a larger number of people are affected. Tele-psychiatry has been in practice for a long time, and its utility has increased exponentially during the COVID-19 pandemic (Sivakumar et al., 2020). Along with more reliable tele-connectivity, this approach might be more useful in providing post-disaster mental healthcare and support.

7 Future Directions

There has been an improved understanding of the disaster-related mental health issues and supports required in the Indian setting. There should be a clear plan and structured system for psychosocial intervention for the identification, screening and triage, community intervention, referral, and follow-up, following each disaster (Kar, 2025). The supportive measures need to be coordinated (Kar, 2024a), and an individualized care plan for the survivors should be delivered. In essence, a more robust intervention process is required. Interventions should be community-focused; the primary care setups, schools, and other public organizations can be linked up to provide required care, supporting the survivors where they are.

There is a need to increase the disaster workforce, so that counselors, primary care professionals and physicians, clinical psychologists, and social workers are available in the community. The effectiveness of the existing workforce can also be improved by training them with psychological support skills for stress management, counseling, assessing and triaging, etc., while they are involved in the care of the survivors. Multiskilling can be done through cross-training to help meet the increased demands of disaster workers.

Conducting research during or after disasters is extremely difficult to arrange, coordinate, and maintain in challenging situations, especially in remote locations. Integrating research side by side with the disaster work, such as warning, preparedness, rescue, and relief phases, should be considered in the local and national disaster management plan.

8 Conclusions

Evidence base related to disaster mental health in India is growing. There has been much progress in disaster management in the pre-disaster warning, where possible, and the crisis stage, immediately following the disasters. Although mental health concerns related to disasters have been recognized, further actions are required to support the survivors adequately, as it appears many survivors with mental health problems are still not being recognized and receiving intervention. Research to keep track of trends of disaster-related mental health issues, intervention needs, longitudinal outcomes, effectiveness of the interventions, cultural coping and resilience, and the preventative aspect of the early intervention is required. Studies on the specific support required for and the outcome in vulnerable populations, such as affected people from rural backgrounds, lower socioeconomic status, children and adolescents, women, older adults, people with preexisting physical or mental illnesses, and disabilities should be prioritized. As awareness about the mental health issues of the survivors has increased, it is expected that the services and support for them will gradually increase in India, bringing in better outcomes.

References

Aneelraj, D., Kumar, C. N., Somanathan, R., Chandran, D., Joshi, S., Paramita, P., Kasi, S., Bangalore, R. N., & Math, S. B. (2016). Uttarakhand disaster 2013: A report on psychosocial adversities experienced by children and adolescents. *The Indian Journal of Pediatrics, 83*(4), 316–321. https://doi.org/10.1007/s12098-015-1921-1

Asim, M., Sathian, B., van Teijlingen, E., Mekkodathil, A. A., Babu, M. G. R., Rajesh, E., N, R. K., Simkhada, P., & Banerjee, I. (2022). A survey of post-traumatic stress disorder, anxiety and depression among flood affected populations in Kerala, India. *Nepal Journal of Epidemiology, 12*(2), 1203–1214. https://doi.org/10.3126/nje.v12i2.46334

Bandla, S., Nappinnai, N., & Gopalasamy, S. (2019). Psychiatric morbidity in December 2015 flood-affected population in Tamil Nadu, India. *International Journal of Social Psychiatry, 65*(4), 338–344. https://doi.org/10.1177/0020764019846166

Becker, S. M. (2006). Psychosocial care for adult and child survivors of the 2004 tsunami disaster in India. *American Journal of Public Health, 96*(8), 1397–1398. https://doi.org/10.2105/AJPH.2005.064428

Becker, S. M. (2009). Psychosocial care for women survivors of the tsunami disaster in India. *American Journal of Public Health, 99*(4), 654–658. https://doi.org/10.2105/AJPH.2008.146571

Bhargava, R., & Gupta, N. (2020). Social unrest and its impact on mental health. *Indian Journal of Social Psychiatry, 36*(1), 3. https://doi.org/10.4103/ijsp.ijsp_27_20

Bhiman, A. (2001, October 27). Mental health consequences of Bhopal gas tragedy. In *17th world congress of social psychiatry, Agra*.

Birmes, P., Arrieu, A., Payen, A., Warner, B. A., & Schmitt, L. (1999). Traumatic stress and depression in a group of plane crash survivors. *The Journal of Nervous and Mental Disease, 187*(12), 754–755. https://doi.org/10.1097/00005053-199912000-00008

Borah, G., & Saikia, N. (2025). Effect of 'losses' and other secondary stressors on the association between flooding and psychological health outcomes: A cross-sectional study in Bongaigaon District, India. *Journal of Biosocial Science, 57*(3), 400–428. https://doi.org/10.1017/S0021932025000136

Catanesi, R., Martino, V., Candelli, C., Troccoli, G., Grattagliano, I., Vella, G. D., & Carabellese, F. (2013). Posttraumatic stress disorder: Protective and risk factors in 18 survivors of a plane crash. *Journal of Forensic Sciences, 58*(5), 1388–1392. https://doi.org/10.1111/1556-4029.12178

Chadda, R. K., & Malhotra, A. (2006). An experience of provision of psychiatric services in the earthquake-affected area of Kashmir in India. *International Psychiatry, 3*(3), 3–5.

Chakrabarti, S. (2021). Mental health in hospitalised COVID 19 patients in quarantine during second wave in a south Indian private teaching hospital. *Journal of Multidisciplinary Healthcare, 14*, 2777–2789. https://doi.org/10.2147/JMDH.S330812

Channaveerachari, N. K., Raj, A., Joshi, S., Paramita, P., Somanathan, R., Chandran, D., Kasi, S., Bangalore, N. R., & Math, S. B. (2015). Psychiatric and medical disorders in the after math of the Uttarakhand disaster: Assessment, approach, and future challenges. *Indian Journal of Psychological Medicine, 37*(2), 138–143. https://doi.org/10.4103/0253-7176.155610

Chhabra, V. (2009). Connecting care competencies and culture during disasters. *Journal of Emergencies, Trauma and Shock, 2*(2), 95–98. https://doi.org/10.4103/0974-2700.50743

Chhabra, P., Mehta, R., Bansal, H., Kumar, V., & Mittal, R. (2022). The impact of COVID-19 lockdown on mental health: A study from rural population of Haryana, India. *Journal of Family Medicine and Primary Care, 11*(6), 2896–2899. https://doi.org/10.4103/jfmpc.jfmpc_2406_21

Cremniter, D., Crocq, L., Louville, P., Batista, G., Grande, C., Lambert, Y., & Chemtob, C. M. (1997). Posttraumatic reactions of hostages after an aircraft hijacking. *The Journal of Nervous and Mental Disease, 185*(5), 344–346. https://doi.org/10.1097/00005053-199705000-00009

Davis, J., & Stewart, L. (2000). Air flight disaster, posttraumatic stress, and postventive rescue and response: The aftermath of the San Diego PSA 182 plane crash recovery operation, 20 years on. *Accident and Emergency Nursing, 8*(1), 13–19. https://doi.org/10.1054/aaen.1999.0078

Desai, N. G., Gupta, D. K., & Srivastava, R. K. (2004). Prevalence, pattern and predictors of mental health morbidity following an intermediate disaster in an urban slum in Delhi: A modified cohort study. *Indian Journal of Psychiatry, 46*(1), 39–51.

D'cruz, M., & Banerjee, D. (2020). 'An invisible human rights crisis': The marginalization of older adults during the COVID-19 pandemic – an advocacy review. *Psychiatry Research, 292*, 113369. https://doi.org/10.1016/j.psychres.2020.113369

Deshpande, R. S. (2022). Disaster management in India: Are we fully equipped? *Journal of Social and Economic Development, 24*(Suppl 1), 242–281. https://doi.org/10.1007/s40847-022-00225-w

Diaz, J. O. P., Murthy, R. S., & Lakshminarayana, R. (2006). *Advances in disaster mental health and psychological support*. Voluntary Health Association of India Press.

Gautam, S., Gupta, I. D., Batra, L., Sharma, H., Khandelwal, R., & Pant, A. (1998). PSYCHIATRIC MORBIDITY AMONG VICTIMS OF BOMB BLAST. *Indian Journal of Psychiatry, 40*(1), 41–45.

George, C., Sunny, G., & John, J. (2007). Disaster experience, substance abuse, social factors and severe psychological distress in male survivors of the 2004 tsunami in South India. *Indian Journal of Psychiatry, 49*, S47.

Girdhar, R., Srivastava, V., & Sethi, S. (2020). Managing mental health issues among elderly during COVID-19 pandemic. *Journal of Geriatric Care and Research, 7*(1), 29–32.

Government of India. (2005). *The disaster management act, 2005; Act 53*. https://www.indiacode.nic.in/bitstream/123456789/2045/5/A2005-53.pdf

Government of India. (2011). *Disaster mananagement in India*. https://asdma.gov.in/pdf/publication/undp/disaster_management_in_india.pdf

Government of India. (2017). *Disaster management division Ministry of Home Affairs Government of India | NDM India*. https://ndmindia.mha.gov.in/ndmi/Home

Gregg, W., Medley, I., Fowler-Dixon, R., Curran, P., Loughrey, G., Bell, P., Lee, A., & Harrison, G. (1995). Psychological consequences of the Kegworth air disaster. *The British Journal of Psychiatry: the Journal of Mental Science, 167*(6), 812–817. https://doi.org/10.1192/bjp.167.6.812

Irshad, S. (2024). Communal riots and its psychological impact: A systematic review study in Indian context. *Psychology Research and Behavior Management, 17*, 1991–1998. https://doi.org/10.2147/PRBM.S455783

Jain, R., & Dupas, P. (2022). The effects of India's COVID-19 lockdown on critical non-COVID health care and outcomes: Evidence from dialysis patients. *Social Science & Medicine (1982), 296*, 114762. https://doi.org/10.1016/j.socscimed.2022.114762

Jakhar, J., Biswas, P. S., Kapoor, M., Panghal, A., Meena, A., Fani, H., & Kharya, P. (2021). A comparative study of the mental health impact of the COVID-19 pandemic on health care professionals in India. *Future Microbiology, 16*, 1267. https://doi.org/10.2217/fmb-2021-0084

Jeronimus, B. F., Snippe, E., Emerencia, A. C., de Jonge, P., & Bos, E. H. (2019). Acute stress responses after indirect exposure to the MH17 airplane crash. *British Journal of Psychology, 110*(4), 790–813. https://doi.org/10.1111/bjop.12358

Joseph, J., & Jaswal, S. (2014). Psychosocial framework for understanding psychological distress among survivors of the November 26, 2008 Mumbai terror attack: Beyond traumatic experiences and emergency medical care. *Prehospital and Disaster Medicine, 29*(3), 330–338. https://doi.org/10.1017/S1049023X14000478

Joy, J., L. K., Ramachandran, M., & George, S. (2021). Learned helplessness, psychological wellbeing, and proenvironment care behavior among victims of frequent floods in Kerala. *Journal of Neurosciences in Rural Practice, 12*(1), 137–144. https://doi.org/10.1055/s-0040-1721566

Kabir, R., Bai, A. C. M., Syed, H. Z., Hasan, M. R., Vinnakota, D., Kar, S. K., Singh, R., Sathian, B., & Arafat, S. M. Y. (2023). The effect of COVID-19 on the mental health of the people in the Indian subcontinent: A scoping review. *Nepal Journal of Epidemiology, 13*(2), 1268–1284. https://doi.org/10.3126/nje.v13i2.52766

Kar, G. C. (2000). Disaster and mental health. *Indian Journal of Psychiatry, 42*(1), 3–13.

Kar, N. (2003). Mental health in the time of disasters—Management of post-disaster psychiatric problems: A brief overview. *Indian Journal of Psychological Medicine, 26*(2), 5–10.

Kar, N. (2006). Psychosocial issues following a natural disaster in a developing country: A qualitative longitudinal observational study. *International Journal of Disaster Medicine, 4*, 169–176.

Kar, N. (2008). *Preparing for natural disasters: An individual perspective*. Quality of Life Research and Development Foundation.

Kar, N. (2010). Suicidality following a natural disaster. *American Journal of Disaster Medicine, 5*(6), 361–368.

Kar, N. (2019). Depression in youth exposed to disasters, terrorism and political violence. *Current Psychiatry Reports, 21*(8), 73. https://doi.org/10.1007/s11920-019-1061-9

Kar, N. (2022a). Coping strategies used by adult survivors in the process of recovery from disaster trauma: A narrative review. *Odisha Journal of Psychiatry, 18*(1), 3–10. https://doi.org/10.4103/OJP.OJP_5_22

Kar, N. (2022b). War and older adults: Consequences and challenges. *Journal of Geriatric Care and Research, 9*(1), 1–3.

Kar, N. (2023a). Impact of disasters on the disaster responders: A review of stress, coping, resilience, and supportive methods. *Odisha Journal of Psychiatry, 19*(2), 37. https://doi.org/10.4103/OJP.OJP_23_23

Kar, N. (2023b). Indirect victims of catastrophic events: The case of Odisha train accident. *Journal of Geriatric Care and Research, 10*(2), 33–34.

Kar, N. (2024a). Anatomy of a catastrophe: Managing psychosocial consequence of the 2023 Odisha train accident. *Industrial Psychiatry Journal, 33*(2), 219–225. https://doi.org/10.4103/ipj.ipj_278_24

Kar, N. (2024b). Coping strategies used by children and adolescents following disaster trauma: A review of associated factors and intervention options. *Odisha Journal of Psychiatry, 20*(2), 43–51. https://doi.org/10.4103/OJP.OJP_21_24

Kar, N. (2025). Disaster mental health in India: A long journey ahead. In R. Srinivasa Murthy & N. Gupta (Eds.), *Leadership in Indian psychiatry: Converting thoughts into practice 1947–2025* (pp. 187–196). Swaroop Creative Agency.

Kar, N., & Bastia, B. K. (2006). Post-traumatic stress disorder, depression and generalised anxiety disorder in adolescents after a natural disaster: A study of comorbidity. *Clinical Practice and Epidemiology in Mental Health: CP & EMH, 2*, 17. https://doi.org/10.1186/1745-0179-2-17

Kar, N., & Kar, B. (2025). Anticipatory anxiety before the 2024 Dana cyclone in Odisha and subsequent mental health morbidity: A study of preparedness, perceived stress, and risk factors. *Geopsychiary, 2*, 1–8. https://doi.org/10.1016/j.geopsy.2025.100030

Kar, N., & Misra, B. (2008). *Mental health care following disasters—A handbook for disaster workers* (1st ed.). Quality of Life Research and Development Foundation.

Kar, N., Das, I., Misra, B., & Sengupta, J. (2002). Psychiatric morbidity after floods. *Indian Journal of Mental Health and Disabilities, 3*, 3–7.

Kar, N., Jagadisha, Sharma, P., Murali, N., & Mehrotra, S. (2004). Mental health consequences of the trauma of super-cyclone 1999 in orissa. *Indian Journal of Psychiatry, 46*(3), 228–237.

Kar, N., Mohapatra, P. K., Nayak, K. C., Pattanaik, P., Swain, S. P., & Kar, H. C. (2007). Post-traumatic stress disorder in children and adolescents one year after a super-cyclone in Orissa, India: Exploring cross-cultural validity and vulnerability factors. *BMC Psychiatry, 7*, 8. https://doi.org/10.1186/1471-244X-7-8

Kar, N., Krishnaraaj, R., & Rameshraj, K. (2014). Long-term mental health outcomes following the 2004 Asian tsunami disaster. *Disaster Health, 2*(1), 35–45. https://doi.org/10.4161/dish.24705

Kar, N., Kar, B., & Kar, S. (2021a). Stress and coping during COVID-19 pandemic: Result of an online survey. *Psychiatry Research, 295*, 113598. https://doi.org/10.1016/j.psychres.2020.113598

Kar, N., Samantaray, N. N., Kar, S., & Kar, B. (2021b). Anxiety, depression, and post-traumatic stress a month after 2019 Cyclone Fani in Odisha, India. *Disaster Medicine and Public Health Preparedness*, 1–8. https://doi.org/10.1017/dmp.2020.368

Kar, S. K., Ransing, R., Arafat, S. M. Y., & Menon, V. (2021c). Second wave of COVID-19 pandemic in India: Barriers to effective governmental response. *EClinicalMedicine, 36*, 100915. https://doi.org/10.1016/j.eclinm.2021.100915

Kar, N., Swain, S. P., Parija, S., Banerjee, S., Mahakul, S., Behura, S. S., Palei, B., & Kar, S. (2025a). Posttraumatic stress following the 2023 Odisha train accident: A cross-sectional comparison study of passengers, health professionals, and the local community. *Disaster Medicine and Public Health Preparedness, 19*, e112. https://doi.org/10.1017/dmp.2025.113

Kar, S. K., Kar, N., & Arafat, S. M. Y. (2025b) Impact of a plane crash and the unmet psychological needs of affected people: Reflecting on 2025 Ahmedabad disaster. *Indian Journal of Psychiatry 67*(10), 1025–1026. https://doi.org/10.4103/indianjpsychiatry_861_25

Kaur, J. (2006). Administrative issues involved in disaster management in India. *International Review of Psychiatry (Abingdon, England), 18*(6), 553–557. https://doi.org/10.1080/09540260601038449

Krishnan, S. (2022). Exploring female frontline health workers' role and capacities in COVID-19 response in India. *International Journal of Disaster Risk Reduction, 75*, 102962. https://doi.org/10.1016/j.ijdrr.2022.102962

Kumar, M. T., Kar, N., Namboodiri, V., Joy, A., Sreeenivasan, D., Kumar, S., & Bortel, T. V. (2023). Post-traumatic stress and depression following a landslide linked to the 2018 floods in Kerala, India: Relevance of screening. *Journal of Emergency Management (Weston, Mass.), 21*(1), 85–96. https://doi.org/10.5055/jem.0728

Kumbhar, S. (2025). Governing the tides: State capacity and cyclone-caused disaster management in Odisha, India. *Indian Journal of Public Administration, 71*(2), 273–286. https://doi.org/10.1177/00195561251336299
Lakshmana, D., Patangia, B., Antony, J. M., & Rajan, S. K. (2025). Stress and decision-making among civil aviation pilots in India: Mediating role of cognitive flexibility. *Indian Journal Of Occupational And Environmental Medicine, 29*(1), 44–48. https://doi.org/10.4103/ijoem.ijoem_118_24
Laxminarayan, R., Murthy, R. S., & Diaz, J. O. P. (2004). *Disaster mentall health in India.* Indian Red Cross Society.
Lenferink, L. I. M., de Keijser, J., Smid, G. E., Djelantik, A. A. A. M. J., & Boelen, P. A. (2017). Prolonged grief, depression, and posttraumatic stress in disaster-bereaved individuals: Latent class analysis. *European Journal of Psychotraumatology, 8*(1), 1298311. https://doi.org/10.1080/20008198.2017.1298311
Maheshwari, N., Yadav, R., & Singh, N. P. (2010). Group counseling: A silver lining in the psychological management of disaster trauma. *Journal of Pharmacy and Bioallied Sciences, 2*(3), 267–274. https://doi.org/10.4103/0975-7406.68509
Majumder, J., Saha, I., Saha, A., & Chakrabarti, A. (2023). Climate change, disasters, and mental health of adolescents in India. *Indian Journal of Psychological Medicine, 45*(3), 289–291. https://doi.org/10.1177/02537176231164649
Math, S. B., Girimaji, S. C., Benegal, V., Uday Kumar, G. S., Hamza, A., & Nagaraja, D. (2006). Tsunami: Psychosocial aspects of Andaman and Nicobar islands. Assessments and intervention in the early phase. *International Review of Psychiatry (Abingdon, England), 18*(3), 233–239. https://doi.org/10.1080/09540260600656001
Math, S. B., John, J. P., Girimaji, S. C., Benegal, V., Sunny, B., Krishnakanth, K., Kumar, U., Hamza, A., Tandon, S., Jangam, K., Meena, K. S., Chandramukhi, B., & Nagaraja, D. (2008a). Comparative study of psychiatric morbidity among the displaced and non-displaced populations in the Andaman and Nicobar Islands following the tsunami. *Prehospital and Disaster Medicine, 23*(1), 29–34. discussion 35.
Math, S. B., Tandon, S., Girimaji, S. C., Benegal, V., Kumar, U., Hamza, A., Jangam, K., & Nagaraja, D. (2008b). Psychological impact of the tsunami on children and adolescents from the Andaman and Nicobar Islands. *Primary Care Companion to The Journal of Clinical Psychiatry, 10*(1), 31–37.
Math, S. B., Nirmala, M. C., Moirangthem, S., & Kumar, N. C. (2015). Disaster management: Mental health perspective. *Indian Journal of Psychological Medicine, 37*(3), 261–271. https://doi.org/10.4103/0253-7176.162915
Mathew, G., Varghese, A. D., Sabu, A. M., & Joseph, A. (2021). Screening for post-traumatic stress disorder among adolescents following floods- a comparative study from private and public schools in Kerala, India. *BMC Pediatrics, 21*, 462. https://doi.org/10.1186/s12887-021-02933-4
McGowran, P., Mathews, M. A., Johns, H., Harasym, M. C., Raju, E., & Ayeb-Karlsson, S. (2023). Investigating the conditions of vulnerability experienced by migrant workers during the COVID-19 pandemic in Kerala, India. *Disasters*. https://doi.org/10.1111/disa.12614
Mehta, K., Vankar, G., & Patel, V. (2005). Validity of the construct of post-traumatic stress disorder in a low-income country: Interview study of women in Gujarat, India. *The British Journal of Psychiatry: the Journal of Mental Science, 187*, 585–586. https://doi.org/10.1192/bjp.187.6.585
Mishra, S., Suar, D., & Paton, D. (2011). Self-esteem and sense of mastery influencing disaster preparedness behaviour. *Australasian Journal of Disaster and Trauma Studies, 1*. https://trauma.massey.ac.nz/issues/2011-1/mishra.htm
Mishra, S., Bhoi, R., Ravan, R., Nath, S., Kar, N., & Padhy, S. (2020). COVID-19 pandemic and care of elderly: Measures and challenges. *Journal of Geriatric Care and Research, 7*(3), 143–146.

Mitra, A. K., Dutta, S., Mondal, A., & Rashid, M. (2024). COVID-19 pandemic increases the risk of anxiety and depression among adolescents: A cross-sectional study in rural West Bengal, India. *Diseases, 12*(10), 233. https://doi.org/10.3390/diseases12100233

Muhammad, T., Pai, M., Maurya, C., Srivastava, S., & Kumar, M. (2024). Natural and human-made disaster and associated health outcomes among community-dwelling older adults in India: Findings from LASI, 2017–18. *PLoS One, 19*(7), e0307371. https://doi.org/10.1371/journal.pone.0307371

Murthy, R. S. (2014). Mental health of survivors of 1984 Bhopal disaster: A continuing challenge. *Industrial Psychiatry Journal, 23*(2), 86–93. https://doi.org/10.4103/0972-6748.151668

Murthy, R. S. (2016). Psychosocial and behavioral aspects of populations affected by humanitarian emergencies: Recent developments. *Current Opinion in Psychiatry, 29*(5), 280–285. https://doi.org/10.1097/YCO.0000000000000266

Murthy, S., Kar, N., Sekar, K., Swain, S., Mishra, V., & Daniel, U. (2003). *Evaluation report on psychosocial care of survivors of super-cyclone in Orissa*. NIMHANS.

Naik, B. N., Pandey, S., Rao, R., Verma, M., & Singh, P. K. (2022). Generalized anxiety and sleep quality among health care professionals during the COVID-19 pandemic: A cross-sectional study from a tertiary healthcare institution in Eastern India. *Osong Public Health and Research Perspectives, 13*(1), 51–61. https://doi.org/10.24171/j.phrp.2021.0316

Nallapu, S., Ghonge, S., Johnson, S., Vajjala, S. M., & Palal, D. (2023). Impact of COVID-19 pandemic on mental health of general population: A comparison study between rural and urban population. *Industrial Psychiatry Journal, 32*(Suppl 1), S225–S230. https://doi.org/10.4103/ipj.ipj_224_23

Nambi, S., Desai, N., & Shah, S. (2007). Mental health morbidity and service needs in tsunami affected population in coastal Tamil Nadu. *Indian Journal of Psychiatry, 49*, s2–s3.

Narayanan, H., Sathyabati, K., Nardev, G., & Thakar, S. (1987). Grief reaction among bereaved relatives following a fire disaster in a circus. *NIMHANS Journal, 5*, 13–21.

Nongpiur, A., Barman, B., Syiem, K., Mawiong, A. M., Anand, N., & Nune, A. (2023). A cross-sectional study of the mental health burden among COVID-19 survivors. *Indian Journal of Psychiatry, 65*(6), 661–666. https://doi.org/10.4103/indianjpsychiatry.indianjpsychiatry_105_23

Ornell, F., Scherer, J. N., Prates-Baldez, D., Hauck, S., & Kapczinski, F. (2025). Mental health impacts of air disasters: A call for a coordinated response to Brazil's christmas tragedy. *Lancet Regional Health – Americas, 43*, 101016. https://doi.org/10.1016/j.lana.2025.101016

Padmavati, R., Raghavan, V., Rera, H., Kearns, M., Rao, K., John, S., & Thara, R. (2020). Learnings from conducting mental health research during 2004 tsunami in Tamil Nadu, India. *BMC Public Health, 20*, 1627. https://doi.org/10.1186/s12889-020-09733-y

Panigrahi, G. S., & Suar, D. (2021). Resilience among survivors in the aftermath of the 2018 Kerala flood: An avenue toward recovery. *International Journal of Disaster Risk Reduction, 64*, 102477. https://doi.org/10.1016/j.ijdrr.2021.102477

Panigrahi, G. S., & Suar, D. (2023). Antecedents and consequences of resilience among survivors of Cyclone Fani. *Current Psychology: A Journal for Diverse Perspectives on Diverse Psychological Issues, 42*(31), 27203–27216. https://doi.org/10.1007/s12144-022-03835-z

Patra, S., & Patro, B. K. (2020). COVID-19 and adolescent mental health in India. *The Lancet Psychiatry, 7*(12), 1015. https://doi.org/10.1016/S2215-0366(20)30461-2

Rajkumar, A. P., Premkumar, T. S., & Tharyan, P. (2008). Coping with the Asian tsunami: Perspectives from Tamil Nadu, India on the determinants of resilience in the face of adversity. *Social Science & Medicine (1982), 67*(5), 844–853. https://doi.org/10.1016/j.socscimed.2008.05.014

Rajkumar, A. P., Mohan, T. S. P., & Tharyan, P. (2013). Lessons from the 2004 Asian tsunami: Epidemiological and nosological debates in the diagnosis of post-traumatic stress disorder in non-Western post-disaster communities. *The International Journal of Social Psychiatry, 59*(2), 123–129. https://doi.org/10.1177/0020764011423468

Rajkumar, A. P., Mohan, T. S., & Tharyan, P. (2015). Lessons from the 2004 Asian tsunami: Nature, prevalence and determinants of prolonged grief disorder among tsunami survivors in South Indian coastal villages. *The International Journal of Social Psychiatry, 61*(7), 645–652. https://doi.org/10.1177/0020764015570713

Rajkumari, B., Ingudam, D., Yengkokpam, C., Oinam, G., & Yumnam, R. (2024). Psychological effects of Manipur violence among the internally displaced persons residing in relief camps across Imphal valley of Manipur—A cross-sectional study. *Journal of Family Medicine and Primary Care, 13*(10), 4354–4362. https://doi.org/10.4103/jfmpc.jfmpc_341_24

Ramamurthy, C., & Juvva, S. (2024). Integrating grief counseling in responses to disasters and epidemics. *Indian Journal of Social Psychiatry, 40*(3), 206. https://doi.org/10.4103/ijsp.ijsp_78_22

Rangaswamy, T., Grover, S., Tyagi, V., & Bhan, A. (2022). How did the mental health care system in India respond to COVID 19 pandemic? *Schizophrenia Bulletin Open, 3*(1), sgac043. https://doi.org/10.1093/schizbullopen/sgac043

Ransing, R., Pinto da Costa, M., Adiukwu, F., Grandinetti, P., Schuh Teixeira, A. L., Kilic, O., Soler-Vidal, J., & Ramalho, R. (2020). Yoga for COVID-19 and natural disaster related mental health issues: Challenges and perspectives. *Asian Journal of Psychiatry, 53*, 102386. https://doi.org/10.1016/j.ajp.2020.102386

Ravan, J. R., Panda, U. K., Pattnaik, J. I., Banerjee, S., Chaudhuri, T., Patil, S., & Das, R. C. (2024). The psychological impact of disaster on first responders in the aftermath of Bahanaga train tragedy: A mixed methods approach. *Indian Journal of Psychiatry, 66*(11), 1043–1049. https://doi.org/10.4103/indianjpsychiatry.indianjpsychiatry_231_24

Ray, S. (2022). Mental and psychosocial health: A post-COVID concern in India. *Neurology India, 70*(5), 2116–2120. https://doi.org/10.4103/0028-3886.359196

Rehman, T., Singh, T., Sharma, S., Kumar, J., Govindan, D., & Singh, S. M. (2021a). Prevalence of depression and anxiety during the COVID-19 pandemic among the residents of an urban slum in North India. *Journal of Neurosciences in Rural Practice, 12*(1), 153–158. https://doi.org/10.1055/s-0040-1721623

Rehman, U., Shahnawaz, M. G., Khan, N. H., Kharshiing, K. D., Khursheed, M., Gupta, K., Kashyap, D., & Uniyal, R. (2021b). Depression, anxiety and stress among Indians in times of Covid-19 lockdown. *Community Mental Health Journal, 57*(1), 42–48. https://doi.org/10.1007/s10597-020-00664-x

Rina, K., Maiti, T., Panigrahi, M., Patro, B., Kar, N., & Padhy, S. K. (2020). Impact of COVID-19 pandemic and lockdown on elder abuse. *Journal of Geriatric Care and Research, 7*(3), 103–107.

Roy, A., Singh, A. K., Mishra, S., Chinnadurai, A., Mitra, A., & Bakshi, O. (2021). Mental health implications of COVID-19 pandemic and its response in India. *The International Journal of Social Psychiatry, 67*(5), 587–600. https://doi.org/10.1177/0020764020950769

Samantaray, N. N., Kar, N., & Mishra, S. R. (2022). A follow-up study on treatment effects of cognitive-behavioral therapy on social anxiety disorder: Impact of COVID-19 fear during post-lockdown period. *Psychiatry Research, 310*, 114439. https://doi.org/10.1016/j.psychres.2022.114439

Selvaraj, K., Sujiv, A., Banerjee, S., Bandyopadhyay, K., & Deshmukh, P. R. (2022). Expanding roles of accredited social health activists (ASHAs) in the 2019 hepatitis E outbreak in a Peri-urban Slum, Nagpur, India. *Disaster Medicine and Public Health Preparedness, 17*, e270. https://doi.org/10.1017/dmp.2022.232

Sethi, B. B., Sharma, M., Trivedi, J. K., & Singh, H. (1987). Psychiatric morbidity in patients attending clinics in gas affected areas in Bhopal. *The Indian Journal of Medical Research, 86*(Suppl), 45–50.

Sharan, P., Chaudhary, G., Kavathekar, S. A., & Saxena, S. (1996). Preliminary report of psychiatric disorders in survivors of a severe earthquake. *The American Journal of Psychiatry, 153*(4), 556–558.

Sharma, R. (2002). Gujarat earthquake causes major mental health problems. *British Medical Journal, 324*(7332), 259. https://doi.org/10.1136/bmj.324.7332.259c

Sharma, A., Rao, S., & Srinivas, S. (1998). Mandi Dabwali fire disaster. Psychological impact on school children after two months—Preliminary findings. *Indian Journal of Psychiatry, 40*(S), 51–52.

Sharma, V., Sharma, V., Arora, H., Singh, W., Gulati, N., & Sharma, R. (2023). Victims of armed conflict in India: Psychosocial impact and available support. *European Journal of Psychotraumatology, 14*(1), 2178375. https://doi.org/10.1080/20008066.2023.2178375

Shetty, H., & Chhabria. (1997). Bombay riots. In *Proceedings of national workshop on psychosocial consequences of disasters*. NIMHANS.

Singh, G. P. (2021). Telepsychiatry: A game-changer during Covid-19 pandemic and a wave of future psychiatry in India. *Asian Journal of Psychiatry, 64*, 102795. https://doi.org/10.1016/j.ajp.2021.102795

Singh, G. P., Arun, P., & Chavan, B. S. (2020). Migrant workers' needs and perceptions while lodged in a shelter home in India during the COVID-19 pandemic. *The Primary Care Companion for CNS Disorders, 22*(6), 20m02753. https://doi.org/10.4088/PCC.20m02753

Singh, R. K., Bajpai, R., & Kaswan, P. (2021). COVID-19 pandemic and psychological wellbeing among health care workers and general population: A systematic-review and meta-analysis of the current evidence from India. *Clinical Epidemiology and Global Health, 11*, 100737. https://doi.org/10.1016/j.cegh.2021.100737

Sivakumar, P. T., Mukku, S. S. R., Kar, N., Manjunatha, N., Phutane, V. H., Sinha, P., Kumar, C. N., & Math, S. B. (2020). Geriatric telepsychiatry: Promoting access to geriatric mental health care beyond the physical barriers. *Indian Journal of Psychological Medicine, 42*(5_suppl), 41S–46S. https://doi.org/10.1177/0253717620958380

Suar, D., & Kar, S. (2005). Social and Behavioural consequences of the Orissa Supercyclone. *Journal of Health Management, 7*(2), 263–275. https://doi.org/10.1177/097206340500700207

Suar, D., Mandal, M. K., & Khuntia, R. (2002). Supercyclone in Orissa: An assessment of psychological status of survivors. *Journal of Traumatic Stress, 15*(4), 313–319. https://doi.org/10.1023/A:1016203912477

Suar, D., Mishra, S., & Khuntia, R. (2007). Placing age differences in the context of the Orissa supercyclone: Who experiences psychological distress? *Asian Journal of Social Psychology, 10*(2), 117–122. https://doi.org/10.1111/j.1467-839X.2007.00218.x

Suar, D., Das, N., & Hota, L. B. (2010). Social indicators affecting post-tsunami trauma of survivors. *Journal of Health Management, 12*(4), 483–500. https://doi.org/10.1177/097206341001200405

Suar, D., Das, S. S., & Alat, P. (2015). Bereavement, postdisaster trauma, and behavioral changes in tsunami survivors. *Death Studies, 39*(4), 226–233. https://doi.org/10.1080/07481187.2014.979957

Suar, D., Das, S. S., Alat, P., & Suar, J. (2016). Exposure, resource loss, and posttsunami trauma. *Journal of Loss and Trauma, 21*(5), 421–432. https://doi.org/10.1080/15325024.2015.1110457

Suar, D., Sekhar Das, S., Alat, P., & Kumar, R. (2017). Exposure, loss, and support predicting the dimensions of posttsunami trauma. *Journal of Loss and Trauma, 22*(5), 427–439. https://doi.org/10.1080/15325024.2017.1310499

Suar, D., Kar, N., & Panigrahi, G. S. (2024). Natural hazards, trauma, and its amelioration: Lessons learned from India. *International Journal of Disaster Risk Reduction, 108*, 104548. https://doi.org/10.1016/j.ijdrr.2024.104548

Swain, S. P., Behura, S. S., Banerjee, S., Mahakul, S., & Kar, N. (2025). A qualitative mixed-method narrative study on psychotherapeutic support needs based on a series of 11 cases of survivors of the 2023 Odisha train accident. *Cureus, 17*(3), e81161. https://doi.org/10.7759/cureus.81161

Telles, S., Singh, N., & Joshi, M. (2009). Risk of posttraumatic stress disorder and depression in survivors of the floods in Bihar, India. *Indian Journal of Medical Sciences, 63*(8), 330–334.

Telles, S., Singh, N., Joshi, M., & Balkrishna, A. (2010). Post traumatic stress symptoms and heart rate variability in Bihar flood survivors following yoga: A randomized controlled study. *BMC Psychiatry, 10*, 18. https://doi.org/10.1186/1471-244X-10-18

Thomas, J. J., H, C., Kulkarni, P., B, P., & M R, N. M. (2022). Participatory workshop-based intervention for better preparedness and awareness about disaster management among accredited social health activists in India: A brief report. *Disaster Medicine and Public Health Preparedness, 16*(1), 33–35. https://doi.org/10.1017/dmp.2020.256

Tikka, S. K., Parial, S., Pattojoshi, A., Bagadia, A., Prakash, C., Lahiri, D., Jaiswal, J., Puri, M., Kukreti, P., Behera, R. N., Agrawal, S., Garg, S., Dubey, S., Gupta, V., Bajaj, A., Agrawal, A., Singour, C., Patel, G., Maghade, M., … Chandra, P. S. (2021). Anxiety among pregnant women during the COVID-19 pandemic in India—A multicentric study. *Asian Journal of Psychiatry, 66*, 102880. https://doi.org/10.1016/j.ajp.2021.102880.

Trivedi, J. K. (2004). Terrorism and mental health. *Indian Journal of Psychiatry, 46*(1), 7–14.

UNDP. (2012). *Disaster management in India- A status report*. UNDP. https://www.undp.org/india/publications/disaster-management-india-status-report

Vankar, G., Banwari, G., Parikh, V., & Shah. (2007). PTSD in children and adolescents: Four years after the communal violence. *Indian Journal of Psychiatry, 49S*, 4.

Vijayakumar, L., & Kumar, M. S. (2008). Trained volunteer-delivered mental health support to those bereaved by Asian tsunami—An evaluation. *The International Journal of Social Psychiatry, 54*(4), 293–302. https://doi.org/10.1177/0020764008090283

Vijayakumar, L., Kannan, G. K., Ganesh Kumar, B., & Devarajan, P. (2006). Do all children need intervention after exposure to tsunami? *International Review of Psychiatry (Abingdon, England), 18*(6), 515–522. https://doi.org/10.1080/09540260601039876

Vijaykumar, L., Thara, R., John, S., & Chellappa, S. (2006). Psychosocial interventions after tsunami in Tamil Nadu, India. *International Review of Psychiatry (Abingdon, England), 18*(3), 225–231. https://doi.org/10.1080/09540260600655912

Wikipedia. (2024). *COVID-19 pandemic in India*. Wikipedia. https://en.wikipedia.org/w/index.php?title=COVID-19_pandemic_in_India&oldid=1245092051

Wikipedia. (2025a). *List of earthquakes in India*. Wikipedia. https://en.wikipedia.org/w/index.php?title=List_of_earthquakes_in_India&oldid=1298725375

Wikipedia. (2025b). *List of railway accidents and incidents in India*. Wikipedia. https://en.wikipedia.org/w/index.php?title=List_of_railway_accidents_and_incidents_in_India&oldid=1281443734

World Population Review. (2025). *Natural disaster risk by country 2025*. World Population Review. https://worldpopulationreview.com/country-rankings/natural-disaster-risk-by-country

Yadav, R., Yadav, P., Kumar, S. S., & Kumar, R. (2021). Assessment of depression, anxiety, and sleep disturbance in COVID-19 patients at tertiary care center of North India. *Journal of Neurosciences in Rural Practice, 12*(2), 316–322. https://doi.org/10.1055/s-0040-1722811

Chapter 6
Mental Health Effects of Disaster and Climate Change in Nepal

Pawan Sharma, Anup Raj Bhandari, and Ashis Shrestha

1 Introduction

Nepal is a landlocked country between China in the north and India to the south, east, and west. The total area of Nepal is 147,181 square kilometers, and the population of Nepal is approximately 30 million. Nepal has a difficult mountain terrain with roughly 75% of the country covered by mountains. Nepal can be divided into four main physical belts from South to north, each extending east to west across the country. The southernmost region is the Terai, a low-lying, fertile alluvial plain adjacent to the Indian border, above which Terai lies the Churia Range and the Inner Terai valleys, characterized by forested foothills and riverine valleys. Further north, the mid-hill region stretches between the Mahabharat Range and the Great Himalaya. The northernmost Great Himalayan Range includes some of the highest peaks in the world. Nepal was declared a federal republic in 2008. Administratively, Nepal is divided into seven provinces and 77 districts. There are 460 rural municipalities and 293 urban municipalities. Nepal is a low-middle income country (LMIC) with a value of 0.60, which places the country in the medium human development category (United Nations Development Programme, 2024). Approximately one-fifth of the population lives below the poverty line (National Statistics Office, 2024).

Nepal is regarded as one of the most vulnerable countries in the world to disaster. Nepal has faced a wide variety and significant number of natural disasters every year (Aryal, 2014). The major reasons for this vulnerability are rugged topography,

P. Sharma (✉) · A. R. Bhandari
Department of Psychiatry, Patan Academy of Health Sciences, Lalitpur, Nepal
e-mail: Pawansharma@pahs.edu.np

A. Shrestha
Department of General Practice and Emergency Medicine, Patan Academy of Health Sciences, Lalitpur, Nepal

N. Kar et al. (eds.), *Climate Change, Disaster and Mental Health in South Asia*, South Asian Perspectives in Mental Health and Psychology,
https://doi.org/10.1007/978-981-95-3690-0_6

ecological adversity, the prevalence of a number of flood-prone rivers, rapid and unplanned urbanization, poverty, inequality, and uneven development. Nepal is at a higher risk of climate change with major impacts on the underdeveloped regions, where people become more vulnerable to both direct and indirect adverse health events (Tome et al., 2022). It has been estimated that more than 80% of the total population of Nepal is at risk from natural hazards, like floods, landslides, windstorms, hailstorms, fires, earthquakes, and Glacial Lake outbursts. Apart from that, Nepal is in a seismically active zone, making it a high probability area for massive earthquakes. Nepal has been placed among the 20 most disaster-prone countries in the world. The "affect to killed ratio" due to disaster is very high in Nepal among all the South Asian countries. It has been estimated that disaster erodes about 2% of national GDP annually (Ministry of Home Affairs, 2018).

Nepal faced a decade-long civil war in the form of Maoist insurgency from 1996 to 2006, followed by a mega earthquake in 2015. After a few years, the world faced the COVID-19 pandemic in 2019. Between 1971 and 2021, a total of 43,731 disaster events were recorded in Nepal and are growing every year (Karki et al., 2024). One of the many effects of these natural and manmade disasters is the mental health impact. In this chapter, we aim to discuss the effects of disasters and climate change on the mental health of the Nepalese population, disaster management, available research and gaps, challenges, and ways out in the mental health aspects of disasters in Nepal.

2 Impact of Disaster in Nepal

2.1 Impact of Climate Change

The mental health consequences of climate change and disasters in Nepal are increasingly evident, as supported by multiple scientific and grey literature sources. Climate-induced events such as floods, droughts, landslides, and extreme weather patterns have a profound psychological impact on vulnerable populations in Nepal, including women, children, farmers, and individuals with preexisting mental health conditions. A narrative review highlighted that these events lead to a range of mental disorders such as post-traumatic stress disorder (PTSD), depression, anxiety, and substance use, often exacerbated by displacement, resource loss, and social network disruption (Dhimal et al., 2021). Similarly, other studies have identified strong associations between extreme weather and elevated mental health disorders, and introduced emerging concepts such as eco-anxiety, ecological grief, and solastalgia (Rijal, 2023) (Cianconi et al., 2020). Himalayan glacial melt has been estimated to cause 75% loss by 2100, mid-hill landslides, and Terai flooding disproportionately affect agricultural communities (69% of the workforce), with severe psychological impacts on Indigenous groups like the Chepang (Gurubacharya, 2025) in Nepal.

2.2 Impact of Conflict in Nepal

A prospective study done among 298 community participants pre- and post-Maoist insurgency in Nepal showed that the prevalence of depression increased from 30.9% to 40.6%, the prevalence of anxiety increased from 26.2% to 47.7%, and the prevalence of post-conflict PTSD was 14.1%. This suggested conflict exposure to a risk factor for mental disorder (Kohrt et al., 2012). A community-based study among 720 adults in a post-conflict situation showed that the respondents who perceived more negative impact of the conflict, like hampered business/industry and hindrance in getting medical treatment, were more at risk for depression, anxiety, and PTSD (Luitel et al., 2013).

2.3 Impact of the Earthquake of 2015

A systematic literature review of studies from 2015 to 2020 among 2015 earthquake survivors showed that the prevalence rate of post-traumatic stress varied from 4.9% to 51%. The risk of mental health issues among children and adolescents was greater than 23% across studies, which was higher than among adults (Gonzalez et al., 2021). A study done after 4 months of the 2015 earthquake among 513 adults above 16 years using a stratified multistage cluster sampling design in earthquake-affected districts in Nepal showed that 34.3% and 33.8% participants scored above validated cutoff scores for depression and anxiety, respectively. Furthermore, 20.4% participants reported hazardous alcohol use, 10.9% reported suicidal ideation, and 5.2% had elevated rates of PTSD symptoms above a validated cutoff score. The associated factors were female gender, lower caste, and a greater number of perceived needs (Kane et al., 2018). The earthquake also had impacts on other vulnerable populations, such as pregnant mothers, the older age group, children, and adolescents, mainly regarding common mental disorders, PTSD, and stress (Khatri et al., 2018, 2020; Adhikari et al., 2018; Silwal et al., 2018). A systematic review and meta-analysis of 25 studies revealed a pooled incidence of PTSD among the earthquake survivors of Nepal to be 22.6% (ranging from 17.6% to 27.5%) with a high degree of heterogeneity. This incidence varied significantly in terms of the time of assessment, age, sex, ethnicity, marital status, educational level, disease history, injury to the body, bereavement, witnessing death, social support, loss of property, and damage to one's house (Paudel et al., 2025a). A study involving 409 adolescents found that 43.3% exhibited symptoms of post-traumatic stress disorder (PTSD), and 38.1% showed signs of depression. Factors, such as female gender, joint family structures, financial difficulties, displacement, damage to livelihood, and fear of death, were significantly associated with PTSD. Coping strategies, such as talking to others, praying, helping others, hoping for the best, and engaging in certain activities, were common among the affected adolescents (Sharma & Kar, 2019). The 2015 earthquakes caused long-term mental health burdens, with meta-analyses showing 22.6% PTSD prevalence among survivors. Active coping strategies and social support mitigate anxiety and depression (Pandey et al., 2023).

2.4 Impact of COVID-19

The COVID-19 pandemic itself and the measures taken to control it, like lockdown, isolation, and quarantine, have also impacted the mental health of the Nepalese population, as it has the worldwide population (Poudel & Subedi, 2020). An online survey among 142 Nepalese participants showed that about one-fourth of the responders (25.4%) had anxiety, and 7% of them had depressive symptoms, which was higher than the prevalence reported in the National Mental Health Survey (Gupta et al., 2020). The community-level study also reported some levels of psychological distress in the Nepalese people (Shrestha et al., 2020). However, the healthcare workers had more mental health-related problems, especially during the early phase of the pandemic. A web-based study among 475 health workers suggested that 41.9% had symptoms of anxiety, 37.5% had symptoms of depression, and 33.9% had insomnia (Khanal et al., 2020). The symptoms of anxiety and depression were higher among the patients who recovered from COVID-19 as well (Rai et al., 2024). Though all the studies conducted were cross-sectional in nature and based on reporting on a questionnaire, these could be acute reactions to the sudden stress rather than core mental disorders. However, there is no denying the fact that this epidemic had a strong negative impact on the mental health of the Nepalese population.

2.5 Impact of Disaster on Vulnerable Groups in Nepal

Mental health outcomes are more severe among communities already experiencing economic and social vulnerabilities. Youth, especially adolescents, suffer disproportionately, with studies showing high prevalence of PTSD and depression among those residing in flood-prone or disaster-affected areas (Gonzalez et al., 2021). Furthermore, persons with disabilities are among the least protected during disasters and face heightened risk of psychological stress due to barriers in accessing care and shelter (Landry et al., 2016). There was an increase in gender-based violence (GBV) post-disasters in Nepal (Bradley et al., 2023). The level of post-traumatic stress (PTSS) was high among Nepalese adolescents, and trauma exposure was a significant risk factor for PTSS, depressive, and anxiety symptoms (Newnham et al., 2022). Among persons with disabilities, 56% experience disrupted healthcare during extreme weather, and 85% lack early warning access in Nepal (Gurubacharya, 2025). The indigenous communities like Chepang and Tharu faced compounded discrimination and climate risks (Koirala & Ghale, 2024).

3 Policy and Legal Framework Analysis of Nepal for Disaster Management

Nepal's constitution (2015) establishes foundational rights to a healthy environment (Article 30) and healthcare (Article 35) and states that basic healthcare service shall be delivered free of cost to every citizen by the state and emergency healthcare service shall be made accessible to all (Secretariat & Durbar, 2015). Public Health Regulation 2019 further identifies mental health as a component of basic healthcare service, creating a basis for mental health protections. Common mental health problems, including provisional diagnosis, symptomatic treatment, counselling and referral, are under schedule one basic healthcare service in public health regulation (*Nepal Law Commission*, 2018). National Health Policy 2019 Section 6.17 has emphasized the development and expansion of mental health services, while Section 6.11 ensures their delivery during epidemics and disasters (Government of Nepal, 2019). The evolving policy landscape in mental health includes (Singh & Khadka, 2022):

- National Mental Health Policy (1996): First comprehensive policy aiming for minimum mental healthcare by 2000, but ineffective due to implementation gaps and low prioritization.
- Draft Mental Health Policy (2017): Unapproved policy emphasizing rights-based, accessible care and federal budget allocations based on disease burden.
- National Mental Health Strategy and Action Plan of Nepal (2020): This aims to ensure equitable, integrated, rights-based mental health services, but its implementation faces major challenges—including limited workforce, stigma, urban-centric services, and poor digital literacy—requiring strategic solutions like task-shifting, mental health units in all facilities, and improved governance across all government levels.

Despite this critical gap, the Health National Adaptation Plan (HNAP) 2023–2030 recognizes the need for climate-resilient mental health systems (Government of Nepal, 2023a). Moreover, hospital disaster preparedness and response plans of health facilities ensure the delivery of all services, including mental health, during the disaster. To ensure the delivery of the services, health facilities are arranged into a hub and satellite system. There are 25 hub hospitals that coordinate with their satellite hospitals at strategic locations. This is the coordination network used by hospitals during a disaster (Shrestha & Bajracharya, 2022). The "Rapid Response Team Guideline, 2023," by Nepal's Epidemiology and Disease Control Division (EDCD), provides comprehensive protocols for emergency medical teams during public health emergencies. It contains specific arrangements for addressing mental health in disaster response and preparedness, mainly coordinating mental health intervention into the operations of the RRT. It enunciates ways of detecting and then managing mental health concerns among affected populations and providing psychological support as part of interventions for dealing with physical health needs, with an aim to reduce the psychosocial impact of disasters and improve general community resilience (Government of Nepal, 2023). Nepal has established a robust framework of policy and law for disaster management through the Disaster Risk Reduction and Management Act, 2017, which repealed prior laws and established a comprehensive multi-level system for disaster risk reduction, preparedness, response, and recovery across federal, provincial, and local governments (Government of Nepal, 2017). The National Policy on Disaster Risk Reduction (2018), which is in accordance with the Sendai Framework for Disaster Risk Reduction, transparently focuses on community participation, resilience, and a gender-sensitive approach (Government of Nepal, 2018). The institutional framework includes the National Disaster Risk Reduction and Management Authority, provincial disaster management committees, and local disaster management committees, among others, in conjunction with and alongside the Nepal Army and security forces (Government of Nepal, 2017). There are challenges in disaster management in Nepal, including gaps in coordination, limited resources, and uneven enforcement (Nepal et al., 2018). However, the legal and policy instruments developed by Nepal confirm a high degree of commitment to integrating disaster risk reduction into development planning and promoting resilience.

4 Interventions for Disaster Mental Health in Nepal

A study developed and tested a hybrid mental health and disaster preparedness intervention in two earthquake-affected communities in Nepal about 2.5 months after the 2015 earthquake. The three-day intervention was culturally adapted, facilitated by trained Nepalese clinicians, and focused on enhancing disaster preparedness, mental health, and community cohesion. At pre-intervention baseline, greater depression symptoms and lower social cohesion were associated with less disaster preparedness. Depression and PTSD were associated with lower social cohesion. Participation in the intervention increased disaster preparedness, decreased depression- and PTSD-related symptoms, and increased social cohesion. Mediation models indicated that the effect of intervention on depression was partially explained by preparedness. The effect of the intervention on disaster preparedness was partially explained by social cohesion, and the effect of the intervention on depression and PTSD was also partially explained by social cohesion. Data from focus groups illuminate participant perspectives on components of the intervention associated with preparedness, mental health, and social cohesion. This mental health-integrated disaster preparedness intervention is effective in enhancing resilience among earthquake-affected communities in Nepal. This brief, cost-effective group intervention has the potential to be scaled up for use with other communities vulnerable to earthquakes and other natural hazards (Welton-Mitchell et al., 2018).

Another study evaluated the effectiveness of a self-developed brief psychosocial intervention in alleviating psychological symptoms among 380 healthcare workers (HCWs), who had recovered from COVID-19 in a tertiary care hospital of Nepal, by comparing the differences in mean scores of the level of depression, anxiety, stress, and PTSD symptoms before and after the intervention. The study showed a significant reduction in these symptoms (Devkota et al., 2023).

One of the important and impactful interventions post-earthquake of 2015 has been the mhGAP-based integration of mental health into primary healthcare centers in Nepal (Leichner et al., 2021; Upadhaya, 2020). There has been the improvement in the mental health scenario in the post-earthquake context in Nepal, like training of primary healthcare service providers using mhGAP in affected districts and training of psychosocial workers, appointment of mental health focal points in the government and World Health Organization Country Office Nepal, development of a community mental healthcare package, addition of new psychotropic drugs to the government's free drugs list, and development of training curricula for different cadres of health workers (Chase et al., 2018).

5 Research on Disaster Mental Health in Nepal

Disasters provide a limited window of a short time to study their impact and other mental health aspects. Most of the studies conducted in disaster mental health in Nepal are cross-sectional in nature. However, a longitudinal study was conducted that explored the change in prevalence of post-traumatic stress symptoms (PTSS) and depressive symptoms from 18 to 31 months after the 2015 earthquake in Nepal, along with potential risk factors associated with the change in psychiatric symptoms (Silwal et al., 2018). There are some validation studies conducted for the scales of PTSD in Nepal, both for adults and children (TPO Nepal, 2018; Kohrt et al., 2011). There are some qualitative studies conducted in Nepal on mental health during disaster (Kc et al., 2019). Some researchers have also studied human behavior, like sexual behavior and emotional bonding during disasters, especially COVID-19 (Arafat et al., 2020, 2021; Roy et al., 2021). The research related to resilience, both quantitative and qualitative, has studied different aspects of the Nepalese community and healthcare systems (Timalsina et al., 2022; Rawat et al., 2023). In summary, the maximum number of research done in disaster mental health in Nepal are focused on the impact of post-Maoist insurgency, the earthquake of 2015, and COVID-19, and they highlight the critical importance of integrating mental health interventions into disaster response and public health strategies.

6 Challenges and Ways Out

6.1 Human Resource Shortage and Poor Mental Health Services

Nepal has only around 250 to 300 psychiatrists and around 40 clinical psychologists for a population of over 30 million, amounting to an inadequate number of mental health professionals per 100,000 as compared to the global minimum thresholds (Sharma et al., 2024). One of the ways out could be the task shifting approach like training of non-specialized healthcare workers in managing mental health conditions, which has been ongoing in Nepal; however, there are issues that need to be addressed, like proper supervision, availability of psychotropics in community healthcare setups, proper referral, refresher trainings, time-bound projects, lack of proper government ownership, etc. (Paudel et al., 2025b). The urban-rural mismatch of service availability, which becomes more exposed in the vulnerable time of disaster, needs to be addressed.

6.2 Lack of Community-Based Mental Healthcare

During the face of a disaster, there is a critical role of community-based care with a strong focus on engaging the community. The empowerment of lay persons and community health workers in the detection of cases and referral is the key to good mental healthcare, which is lacking in the context of Nepal. The low-intensity approaches, like nonspecialized support, coordination of care between traditional healers, and modern health services, need to be strengthened with the support of a team of specialists (Sherchan et al., 2017).

6.3 Inadequate Infrastructure and Funding

National budget allocations for mental health are minimal in Nepal (Sharma et al., 2024). Emergency preparedness plans mention the mental health needs; however, they are often overlooked in terms of resources and infrastructure. The mental health services run on an ad hoc basis whenever a disaster strikes and is forgotten (Sherchan et al., 2017). The funding for the programs comes in the form of aids and NGO programs; there is always a concern about government ownership and financing to sustain services in disaster-affected areas and scale them up to non-affected parts of the country. There is a need for assurance of continuity of national programs and funding as a disaster can occur at any time.

6.4 Policy Implementation Gap

The 1996 National Mental Health Policy of Nepal was never fully implemented, and the 2017 draft policy is still awaiting approval. Though the mental health strategy and other policy documents of disaster do mention the importance and need for mental health services, the ground-level execution of disaster mental health strategies is weak. This needs to be changed under the leadership of the government with the help of different stakeholders like the private sector, NGOs, INGOs, and formal and informal health and non-health sectors.

6.5 Lack of Research and Surveillance

Most studies conducted on disaster mental health are cross-sectional, with limited longitudinal or intervention-based research. The research is conducted on a wave during the disaster when the funding agencies are active, and no follow-ups are done. Apart from that, no national mental health surveillance with climate vulnerability indicators is available in Nepal. Hence, there is a need for investment in research and surveillance, not only during the time of disaster but also on a regular basis. There is also a dire need for the development of culture-based and contextual interventions for psychosocial support in Nepal to be implemented during and after disasters. The other specific topic that especially needs consideration is longitudinal multidisciplinary research on protective and risk factors of mental health issues during disaster, deeper insight into the PTSD construct, and measurement of the effectiveness of mental health programs and psychosocial support (Tol et al., 2010).

6.6 Vulnerability of the Marginalized Groups

Indigenous groups, persons with disabilities, the elderly, and adolescents are disproportionately affected yet underserved in mental health response systems. Hence, the mental health service during disaster must take these groups into account, and specific strategy must be in place for them.

6.7 Poor Intersectoral Coordination

There is poor intersectoral coordination during disasters in Nepal that severely limits effective mental health response. There are no standard operating procedures (SOPs) guiding collaboration of mental health with other sectors, leading to confusion during emergencies. History has shown that the health and mental health services operate independently, with weak referral systems and untrained primary care workers. Local governments, though empowered under federalism, often lack the capacity and clarity to coordinate mental health efforts effectively during disaster situations (Sherchan et al., 2017). There is definite need for integrated, multidisciplinary approaches that address the mental health dimensions of climate change and disaster.

7 Conclusion

The unique geography and sociopolitical history have made Nepal a vulnerable country to the mental health impacts of disaster and climate change. Many policy-level interventions have laid the groundwork for integrating mental health into disaster response and public health systems, but the implementation remains weak. Vulnerable populations, like women, children, persons with disabilities, and indigenous communities, bear the major psychological stressors. The path forward requires a paradigm shift from reactive to proactive approaches like scaling community-based psychosocial services, embedding mental health in disaster risk reduction and climate policy, and addressing systemic issues like workforce shortages and funding. Nepal must act swiftly to build a resilient mental health system capable of responding to the natural and man-made disasters as well as the global climate change.

References

Adhikari, R. P., Upadhaya, N., Paudel, S., Pokhrel, R., Bhandari, N., Cole, L., & Koirala, S. (2018). Psychosocial and mental health problems of older people in postearthquake Nepal. *Journal of Aging and Health, 30*(6), 945–964. https://doi.org/10.1177/0898264317702056

Arafat, S. M. Y., Alradie-Mohamed, A., Kar, S. K., Sharma, P., & Kabir, R. (2020). Does COVID-19 pandemic affect sexual behaviour? A cross-sectional, cross-national online survey. *Psychiatry Research, 289*, 113050. https://doi.org/10.1016/j.psychres.2020.113050

Arafat, S. M. Y., Kar, S. K., Sharma, P., Alradie-Mohamed, A., & Kabir, R. (2021). Frequency of sexual intercourse among the residents of Bangladesh, India, and Nepal: A cross-sectional web-based pilot study. *Journal of Psychosexual Health, 3*(1), 24–28. https://doi.org/10.1177/2631831820985412

Aryal, K. R. (2014). Disaster vulnerability in Nepal. *International Journal of Disaster Risk Reduction, 9*, 137–146. https://doi.org/10.1016/j.ijdrr.2014.05.009

Bradley, T., Martin, Z., Upreti, B. R., Subedu, B., & Shrestha, S. (2023). Gender and disaster: The impact of natural disasters on violence against women in Nepal. *Journal of Asian and African Studies, 58*(3), 354–371. https://doi.org/10.1177/00219096211062474

Chase, L. E., Marahatta, K., Sidgel, K., Shrestha, S., Gautam, K., Luitel, N. P., Dotel, B. R., & Samuel, R. (2018). Building back better? Taking stock of the post-earthquake mental health and psychosocial response in Nepal. *International Journal of Mental Health Systems, 12*(1), 44. https://doi.org/10.1186/s13033-018-0221-3

Cianconi, P., Betrò, S., & Janiri, L. (2020). The impact of climate change on mental health: A systematic descriptive review. *Frontiers in Psychiatry, 11*. https://doi.org/10.3389/fpsyt.2020.00074
Devkota, N., Gurung, L., Joshi, P., Maharjan, R., Gurung, B., & Karki, U. (2023). Impact of brief psychological intervention on reducing the psychological symptoms after COVID-19 infection among healthcare workers (HCWs) in Nepal. *Journal of Psychiatrists' Association of Nepal, 12*(2), 2. https://doi.org/10.3126/jpan.v12i2.63403
Dhimal, M., Bhandari, D., Dhimal, M. L., Kafle, N., Pyakurel, P., Mahotra, N., Akhtar, S., Ismail, T., Dhiman, R. C., Groneberg, D. A., Shrestha, U. B., & Müller, R. (2021). Impact of climate change on health and Well-being of people in Hindu Kush Himalayan region: A narrative review. *Frontiers in Physiology, 12*. https://doi.org/10.3389/fphys.2021.651189
Gonzalez, R. N., Regmi, P., Aryal, N., & Akudjedu, T. N. (2021). Mental health risk and associated factors in the aftermath of the 2015 earthquake in Nepal: A systematic literature review. *Journal of Manmohan Memorial Institute of Health Sciences, 7*(1), 1.
Government of Nepal. (2018a). Ministry of Home Affairs. *National Policy and Strategic Action Plan for Disaster Risk Reduction and Management 2018–2030*. Retrieved June 14, 2025, from https://www.undp.org/nepal/publications/national-policy-and-strategic-action-plan-disaster-risk-reduction-and-management-2018-2030
Government of Nepal. (2018b). Ministry of Home Affairs. *Nepal Disaster Report 2017. The road to Sendai*. Retrieved June 14, 2025, from.
Government of Nepal. (2019a). Ministry of Home Affairs. *Disaster Risk Reduction and Management Regulation, 2076* (2019). Retrieved June 14, 2025, from https://moha.gov.np/page/disaster-risk-reduction-and-management-regulation-2076
Government of Nepal. (2019b). Ministry of Health and Population. *National Health Policy 2076* (2019). Retrieved June 12, 2025, from https://dohs.gov.np/posts/single/national-health-policy-2076
Government of Nepal. (2023a). *Health National Adaptation Plan climate change health adaptation strategy and action plan*. Ministry of Health and Population. Retrieved June 12, 2025, from http://climate.mohp.gov.np/attachments/article/178/HNAP%20English_2024_FINAL.pdf
Government of Nepal. (2023b). Ministry of Health and Population. *Rapid response team guideline, 2079*. EDCD. Retrieved June 14, 2025, from https://edcd.gov.np/resource-detail/rrt-guideline
Gupta, A. K., Sahoo, S., Mehra, A., & Grover, S. (2020). Psychological impact of 'lockdown' due to COVID-19 pandemic in Nepal: An online survey. *Asian Journal of Psychiatry, 54*, 102243. https://doi.org/10.1016/j.ajp.2020.102243
Gurubacharya, B. (2025, May 16). Nepal hosts environment conference as Himalayan glaciers melt. *AP News*. https://apnews.com/article/nepal-environment-conference-mountains-6a7dc20eb5c74d3f5110fdcc973cd0e4.
http://climate.mohp.gov.np/attachments/article/178/HNAP%20English_2024_FINAL.pdf
https://www.undp.org/nepal/press-releases/rich-countries-attain-record-human-development-half-poorest-have-gone-backwards-finds-un-development-programme
https://www.undp.org/sites/g/files/zskgke326/files/migration/np/Nepal_Disaster_Report_2017.pdf
Kane, J. C., Luitel, N. P., Jordans, M. J. D., Kohrt, B. A., Weissbecker, I., & Tol, W. A. (2018). Mental health and psychosocial problems in the aftermath of the Nepal earthquakes: Findings from a representative cluster sample survey. *Epidemiology and Psychiatric Sciences, 27*(3), 301–310. https://doi.org/10.1017/S2045796016001104
Karki, D., Yadav, R., & Davis, C. (2024). Disaster and social work in Nepal: A discussion. *The British Journal of Social Work, 54*(7), 3199–3220. https://doi.org/10.1093/bjsw/bcae087
Kc, A., Gan, C. C. R., & Dwirahmadi, F. (2019). Breaking through barriers and building disaster mental resilience: A case study in the aftermath of the 2015 Nepal earthquakes. *International Journal of Environmental Research and Public Health, 16*(16), 16. https://doi.org/10.3390/ijerph16162964

Khanal, P., Devkota, N., Dahal, M., Paudel, K., & Joshi, D. (2020). Mental health impacts among health workers during COVID-19 in a low resource setting: A cross-sectional survey from Nepal. *Globalization and Health, 16*(1), 89. https://doi.org/10.1186/s12992-020-00621-z

Khatri, G. K., Tran, T. D., Baral, S., & Fisher, J. (2018). Effect of the 2015 Nepal earthquakes on symptoms of common mental disorders among women who are pregnant. *Journal of Affective Disorders, 228*, 238–247. https://doi.org/10.1016/j.jad.2017.12.016

Khatri, G. K., Tran, T. D., Baral, S., & Fisher, J. (2020). Experiences of an earthquake during pregnancy, antenatal mental health and infants' birthweight in Bhaktapur District, Nepal, 2015: A population-based cohort study. *BMC Pregnancy and Childbirth, 20*(1), 414. https://doi.org/10.1186/s12884-020-03086-5

Kohrt, B. A., Jordans, M. J., Tol, W. A., Luitel, N. P., Maharjan, S. M., & Upadhaya, N. (2011). Validation of cross-cultural child mental health and psychosocial research instruments: Adapting the Depression Self-Rating Scale and Child PTSD Symptom Scale in Nepal. *BMC Psychiatry, 11*(1), 127. https://doi.org/10.1186/1471-244X-11-127

Kohrt, B. A., Hruschka, D. J., Worthman, C. M., Kunz, R. D., Baldwin, J. L., Upadhaya, N., Acharya, N. R., Koirala, S., Thapa, S. B., Tol, W. A., Jordans, M. J. D., Robkin, N., Sharma, V. D., & Nepal, M. K. (2012). Political violence and mental health in Nepal: Prospective study. *The British Journal of Psychiatry, 201*(4), 268–275. https://doi.org/10.1192/bjp.bp.111.096222

Koirala, M., & Ghale, Y. (2024). The environmental impact on livelihood and food security in the Hindu Kush Himalayan region: Current and future challenges for Nepal. In *Sustainable ecological restoration and conservation in the Hindu Kush Himalayan region* (pp. 35–45). https://doi.org/10.1079/9781800622579.0003

Landry, M. D., Sheppard, P. S., Leung, K., Retis, C., Salvador, E. C., & Raman, S. R. (2016). The 2015 Nepal earthquake(s): Lessons learned from the disability and rehabilitation sector's preparation for, and response to, natural disasters. *Physical Therapy, 96*(11), 1714–1723. https://doi.org/10.2522/ptj.20150677

Leichner, A., Akhtar, A., Bhaird, C. N. A., Wener, R., Perera, S. M., & Weissbecker, I. (2021). Mental health integration in primary health services after the earthquake in Nepal: A mixed-methods program evaluation. *Global Mental Health, 8*, e10. https://doi.org/10.1017/gmh.2021.8

Luitel, N. P., Jordans, M. J. D., Sapkota, R. P., Tol, W. A., Kohrt, B. A., Thapa, S. B., Komproe, I. H., & Sharma, B. (2013). Conflict and mental health: A cross-sectional epidemiological study in Nepal. *Social Psychiatry and Psychiatric Epidemiology, 48*(2), 183–193. https://doi.org/10.1007/s00127-012-0539-0

National Statistics Office. (2024). *Nepal in data*. Retrieved June 8, 2025, from https://nepalindata.com/

Nepal Law Commission. (2018). *Public Health Service Regulation, 2077*. Retrieved June 12, 2025, from https://lawcommission.gov.np/content/12609/12609-public-health-service-regulati/

Nepal, P., Khanal, N. R., & Sharma, B. P. P. (2018). Policies and institutions for disaster risk management in Nepal: A review. *Geographical Journal of Nepal, 11*, 1–24. https://doi.org/10.3126/gjn.v11i0.19546

Newnham, E. A., Gao, X., Guragain, B., Jiao, F., Nathan, E., Boyes, M., & Leaning, J. (2022). Daily stressors and mental health following disaster: A school-based assessment of adolescent disaster survivors in China and Nepal. *Journal of Traumatic Stress, 35*(6), 1721–1733. https://doi.org/10.1002/jts.22876

Pandey, R., Chalise, P., Khadka, S., Chaulagain, B., Maharjan, B., Pandey, J., Nepal, J., & Pandey, C. (2023). Post-traumatic stress disorder and its associated factors among survivors of 2015 earthquake in Nepal. *BMC Psychiatry, 23*(1), 340. https://doi.org/10.1186/s12888-023-04836-3

Paudel, P., Sah, A., & Khanal, A. (2025a). Posttraumatic stress disorder and associated factors in the aftermath of the 2015 earthquake in Nepal: A systematic review and meta-analysis. *PLoS One, 20*(2), e0310233. https://doi.org/10.1371/journal.pone.0310233

Paudel, S., Chalise, A., Khatri, D., Poudel, S., & Khanal, A. (2025b). Nepal's mental health system from public health perspective: A thematic synthesis based on health system building blocks. *The Lancet Regional Health – Southeast Asia, 36*. https://doi.org/10.1016/j.lansea.2025.100588

Poudel, K., & Subedi, P. (2020). Impact of COVID-19 pandemic on socioeconomic and mental health aspects in Nepal. *International Journal of Social Psychiatry, 66*(8), 748–755. https://doi.org/10.1177/0020764020942247

Rai, P., Karmacharya, B. M., Gautam, K., Dhital, S. R., Shrestha, S., Paneru, B., Chaudhary, K., & Shrestha, A. (2024). Prevalence and factors associated with depression and anxiety among patients recovered from COVID-19: A cross-sectional study in a tertiary care hospital in Nepal. *BMJ Public Health, 2*(1). https://doi.org/10.1136/bmjph-2024-001112

Rawat, A., Pun, A., Ashish, K., Tamang, I. K., Karlström, J., Hsu, K., & Rasanathan, K. (2023). The contribution of community health systems to resilience: Case study of the response to the 2015 earthquake in Nepal. *Journal of Global Health, 13*, 04048. https://doi.org/10.7189/jogh.13.04048

Rijal, R. (2023). Climate change and mental illness: Another pandemic post coronavirus disease 2019? *Journal of Kathmandu Medical College, 12*(3), 3.

Roy, D., Kar, S. K., Arafat, S. M. Y., Sharma, P., & Kabir, R. (2021). Emotional bonding and sexual activity during COVID-19 lockdown: A cross-national pilot study. *Journal of Psychosexual Health, 3*(3), 236–241. https://doi.org/10.1177/26318318211027482

Secretariat, C. A., & Durbar, S. (2015). Constitution of Nepal 2015 Kathmandu: *Constituent Assembly Secretariat, 19*, 505.

Sharma, A., & Kar, N. (2019). Posttraumatic stress, depression, and coping following the 2015 Nepal earthquake: A study on adolescents. *Disaster Medicine and Public Health Preparedness, 13*(2), 236–242. https://doi.org/10.1017/dmp.2018.37

Sharma, P., Gautam, K., & Marahatta, K. (2024). Access to mental health care in Nepal: Current status, potential challenges, and ways out. In S. M. Y. Arafat & S. K. Kar (Eds.), *Access to mental health care in South Asia: Current status, potential challenges, and ways out* (pp. 91–111). Springer Nature. https://doi.org/10.1007/978-981-99-9153-2_6

Sherchan, S., Samuel, R., Marahatta, K., Anwar, N., Van Ommeren, M. H., & Ofrin, R. (2017). Post-disaster mental health and psychosocial support: Experience from the 2015 Nepal earthquake. *WHO South-East Asia Journal of Public Health, 6*(1), 22. https://doi.org/10.4103/2224-3151.206160

Shrestha, A., & Bajracharya, S. (2022). Full-scale simulation exercise-a preparedness for trauma mass casualty incident: Nepal. *American Journal of Disaster Medicine, 17*(2), 131–142. https://doi.org/10.5055/ajdm.2022.0427

Shrestha, D. B., Thapa, B. B., Katuwal, N., Shrestha, B., Pant, C., Basnet, B., Mandal, P., Gurung, A., Agrawal, A., & Rouniyar, R. (2020). Psychological distress in Nepalese residents during COVID-19 pandemic: A community level survey. *BMC Psychiatry, 20*(1), 491. https://doi.org/10.1186/s12888-020-02904-6

Silwal, S., Dybdahl, R., Chudal, R., Sourander, A., & Lien, L. (2018). Psychiatric symptoms experienced by adolescents in Nepal following the 2015 earthquakes. *Journal of Affective Disorders, 234*, 239–246. https://doi.org/10.1016/j.jad.2018.03.002

Singh, R., & Khadka, S. (2022). Mental health law in Nepal. *BJPsych International, 19*(1), 24–26. https://doi.org/10.1192/bji.2021.52

Timalsina, R., Songwathana, P., & Sae-Sia, W. (2022). Factors explaining resilience among Nepalese older adults experiencing disasters: A cross-sectional study. *International Journal of Disaster Risk Reduction, 69*, 102756. https://doi.org/10.1016/j.ijdrr.2021.102756

Tol, W. A., Kohrt, B. A., Jordans, M. J. D., Thapa, S. B., Pettigrew, J., Upadhaya, N., & de Jong, J. T. V. M. (2010). Political violence and mental health: A multi-disciplinary review of the literature on Nepal. *Social Science & Medicine, 70*(1), 35–44. https://doi.org/10.1016/j.socscimed.2009.09.037

Tome, J., Richmond, H. L., Rahman, M., Karmacharya, D., & Schwind, J. S. (2022). Climate change and health vulnerability in Nepal: A systematic review of the literature since 2010. *Global Public Health, 17*(7), 1406–1419. https://doi.org/10.1080/17441692.2021.1924824

TPO Nepal. (2018). A translation and validation study of the post traumatic growth inventory among Nepali children and adults—TPO Nepal. Retrieved June 13, 2025, from https://www.

tponepal.org/a-translation-and-validation-study-of-the-post-traumatic-growth-inventory-among-nepali-children-and-adults-2/

United Nations Development Programme. (2024). *Rich countries attain record human development, but half of the poorest have gone backwards, finds UN Development Programme*. UNDP. Retrieved June 8, 2025, from

Upadhaya, N. (2020). *Strengthening mental health systems in fragile setting: Opportunities and challenges for strengthening mental health systems in low and middle income countries: A case example from Nepal* [Doctoral thesis 1 (Research UU/Graduation UU), Utrecht University]. https://research-portal.uu.nl/ws/portalfiles/portal/74820954/thesis_rotatie_fc_5f09d58581285.pdf

Welton-Mitchell, C., James, L. E., Khanal, S. N., & James, A. S. (2018). An integrated approach to mental health and disaster preparedness: A cluster comparison with earthquake affected communities in Nepal. *BMC Psychiatry, 18*(1), 296. https://doi.org/10.1186/s12888-018-1863-z

Chapter 7
Climate Change, Disaster, and Mental Health in Pakistan

Anila Sadaf Mubashir, Saad Ullah Adnan Abbasi, and Rida Kainaat

1 Introduction

n. Pakistan has a long history of natural disasters and is particularly susceptible to frequent earthquakes and floods. Moreover, the impacts of climate change are increasingly affecting the country's environment, contributing to more frequent and severe extreme weather events(ENVPK, 2021). ts geographical location, climate, and socioeconomic factors contribute to its vulnerability. Climate change has exacerbated these risks, leading to increased frequency and severity of disasters (IPCC, 2021). The country's unique geography, with the Himalayan Mountain range and the Indus River system, makes it susceptible to floods and landslides. Additionally, its location in a seismically active region increases the risk of earthquakes (Bilham, 2019). The impact of disasters on Pakistan's population is further compounded by factors such as poverty, lack of infrastructure, and limited access to healthcare (WHO, 2020). The country's socioeconomic conditions make it challenging to respond to and recover from disasters, leading to significant human and economic losses. For instance, widespread poverty, low adaptive capacity, and the concentration of vulnerable populations in hazard-prone districts amplify the impact of disasters such as floods, droughts, and glacial lake outbursts. (Malik et al., 2012).

A. S. Mubashir (✉) · S. U. A. Abbasi · R. Kainaat
Department of Applied Psychology, National University of Modern Languages Rawalpindi, Rawalpindi, Pakistan
e-mail: anilasadaf@numl.edu.pk

N. Kar et al. (eds.), *Climate Change, Disaster and Mental Health in South Asia*, South Asian Perspectives in Mental Health and Psychology,
https://doi.org/10.1007/978-981-95-3690-0_7

1.1 Distribution of Disasters and Changes of Climate Parameters in the Country

Pakistan experiences a range of disasters, including floods, earthquakes, landslides, and droughts. Floods are one of the most common disasters in Pakistan, with the country experiencing major floods in 2010, 2011, and 2022 (FFC, 2022). These floods have caused significant damage to infrastructure, agriculture, and human settlements, leading to substantial economic losses and the displacement of people. Earthquakes pose another significant threat to Pakistan, as the country is situated in a seismically active region (Bilham, 2019). The 2005 Kashmir earthquake, which killed over 80,000 people, is a stark reminder of the devastating impact of earthquakes in Pakistan (WHO, 2005). Climate change has led to changes in temperature and precipitation patterns in Pakistan, exacerbating disaster risks. The country has experienced a rise in average temperature, with increased frequency of heatwaves (IPCC, 2021). These changes have significant implications for disaster risk management and mental health in Pakistan (WHO, 2020). Understanding these changes is crucial for developing effective adaptation and mitigation strategies to reduce the impact of disasters on communities.

1.2 Existing Disaster Response System

Pakistan's disaster response system has undergone significant changes over the years, with a shift from a reactive to a proactive approach. The National Disaster Management Authority (NDMA) is the primary agency responsible for disaster management in Pakistan. The NDMA works closely with provincial disaster management authorities, district administrations, and other stakeholders to respond to disasters. The NDMA has developed a National Disaster Management Plan (NDMP) that outlines the country's disaster management framework. The plan emphasizes preparedness, response, and recovery, and provides guidelines for disaster risk reduction and management (NDMA, 2012). The NDMA also has a Standard Operating Procedure (SOP) for disaster response, outlining the roles and responsibilities of various agencies and stakeholders. Despite these efforts, Pakistan's disaster response system continues to face significant challenges. The country's disaster management infrastructure is often overwhelmed by the scale of disasters, leading to delays and inefficiencies in response efforts (Malik et al., 2012).

1.3 Impact of Disaster and Climate Change on Mental Health

Disasters and climate change can have a significant impact on mental health in Pakistan. The country's vulnerability to disasters, combined with the psychological trauma caused by these events, can lead to a range of mental health issues (WHO, 2020). Survivors of disasters may experience anxiety, depression, post-traumatic stress disorder (PTSD), and other mental health problems (Khalily, 2011). Climate change can also have a significant impact on mental health in Pakistan. Rising temperatures, changing precipitation patterns, and increased frequency of extreme weather events can lead to stress, anxiety, and trauma (IPCC, 2021).

The impact of disasters and climate change on mental health in Pakistan is further compounded by the country's limited mental health resources. There is a shortage of mental health professionals, including psychologists, psychiatrists, and counselors, which can make it difficult for survivors of disasters to access the support they need (WHO, 2020). Studies have shown that disasters and climate change can have a disproportionate impact on vulnerable populations, including women, children, and older adults (WHO, 2020).

To address the mental health impacts of disasters and climate change, Pakistan needs to prioritize mental health support and services. This can include training mental health professionals, increasing access to mental health services, and promoting mental health awareness and education (Khalily, 2011). Additionally, disaster response efforts should prioritize the mental health needs of survivors, including providing psychological support and counseling services (WHO, 2020).

In Pakistan, the conflicts and disasters caused by climate change have profoundly impacted mental health across different ages, genders, and professions. The existing literature outlines both the dire need and the insufficient response from the systems in place. Commentaries and reviews highlight that the recurrent floods, earthquakes, and large-scale displacement create long-lasting psychosocial stressors that overtax the system's already limited resources. There have been calls for the MHPSS to be part of the disaster response framework (Abidi, 2024; Riaz et al., 2023; Alvi et al., 2023). Studies focused on displaced populations find that inner displacement severely disrupts education for younger children and is linked to greater mental health challenges in adolescence (Ahmad et al., 2020). Other studies focusing on flood-affected communities highlight that children show the greatest need for targeted mental health support (Cheema et al., 2023; Yousuf et al., 2023).

Numerous studies highlight the specific mental health impacts of climate disasters: women's psychology of recovery and coping strategies after floods in the Punjab region were found to be highly local and culturally specific (Ahmad et al., 2025), while mental health investigations in the rural climate sticks of the region accentuated the burdens of climate–impacted women's health (Daraz et al., 2024). More generally, the literature on displacement contends that forcibly relocated and disrupted livelihoods are associated with chronic anxiety, depression, and complex grief (Akram & Mushtaq, 2024; Iqbal et al., 2023) oe. Children's distress is a significant contributing factor toward climate-change anxiety and fuels the decline in psychosocial well-being (Soomro et al., 2024). Longitudinal and event-based studies conducted after large-scale disasters have found that both survivors and responders experience high rates of post-traumatic stress disorder (PTSD) and other psychiatric conditions comorbid with post-traumatic stress disorder; for instance, studies conducted after the 2010 floods and the 2005 earthquake showed affected communities and recovery workers suffered from PTSD and chronic psychosocial and emotional consequences (Chung et al., 2014; Ehring et al., 2011).

As explored in commentaries and empirical papers, the migration and social disruption that follow certain floods might increase the neurodevelopmental risks for children and worsen service provision shortfalls (Rehan et al., 2023). In addition, man-made disasters, like suicide bombings, add layers of trauma that worsen the existing mental health burden for the population (Shoib et al., 2024; Ishtiaq et al., 2025). The economic and system burden of mental illness after disasters is also addressed by other authors, pointing to the direct and indirect costs mental illness contributes to economic productivity, drawing attention to the need for financing MHPSS in the framework of disaster preparedness (Alvi et al., 2023; Yousuf et al., 2023). At the service-delivery level, there is debate among healthcare innovators and commentators regarding the need for scalable telepsychiatry and digital forms of psychosocial care to overcome geographic and resource barriers after disasters (Qadir et al., 2016; Riaz et al., 2023). As outlined in the literature, a multisectoral response is needed that (1) considers children, women, refugees, and first-responders as the primary vulnerable populations (Cheema et al., 2023; Ahmad et al., 2025; Daraz et al., 2024; Ehring et al., 2011); (2) incorporates MHPSS into the emergency response in health and education (Riaz et al., 2023; Abidi, 2024); (3) integrates mental health burden assessment and economic forecasting with post-disaster surveillance and planning (Alvi et al., 2023; Iqbal et al., 2023); and (4) implements remote and displaced community access interventions to scale, designed contextually and using relevant technology (Qadir et al., 2016; Soomro et al., 2024).

Disasters and climate change often expose individuals to trauma, leading to increased risks of anxiety, depression, and post-traumatic stress disorder. Evidence highlights the importance of timely psychosocial interventions in mitigating these effects. Psychological First Aid (PFA), for example, has been shown to be an effective approach in supporting individuals after traumatic events, enhancing coping, and promoting recovery (Wang et al., 2024).

1.4 Disaster and Climate Change, Mental Health Impacts, Preparedness, and Response

To enhance mental health preparedness for disasters in Pakistan, a multipronged and culturally grounded strategy is required. Pakistan faces a severe shortage of trained mental health professionals, with fewer than 500 psychiatrists serving over 230 million people, most of whom are concentrated in urban areas (Gadit, 2011;

World Health Organization [WHO], 2022). Expanding the training and availability of psychologists, psychiatrists, counselors, and community health workers is therefore critical, particularly in rural and disaster-prone regions, where access to care is limited (Khalily, 2011).

Preparedness also requires the development of culturally adapted assessment tools and interventions. For instance, after the 2005 Kashmir earthquake, studies documented high rates of post-traumatic stress disorder (PTSD), depression, and anxiety among survivors (Naeem et al., 2011). Interventions such as culturally adapted cognitive-behavioral therapy and community-based psychosocial programs have shown promise in addressing trauma symptoms in Pakistan's disaster-affected populations (Rahman et al., 2016). Tailoring such tools to local idioms of distress and cultural values enhances their acceptability and effectiveness.

Mental health must be fully integrated into Pakistan's national disaster response frameworks. Current policies often prioritize physical infrastructure and relief but neglect psychosocial care (Mirza & Jenkins, 2004). Finally, advancing research on the mental health impacts of disasters is essential to inform evidence-based programming. Longitudinal studies following the 2010 floods and 2005 earthquake underscore the persistence of psychiatric morbidity years after the events (Naeem et al., 2011). Investing in research that evaluates interventions, integrates technology for outreach, and strengthens monitoring and evaluation can guide the development of sustainable and scalable mental health strategies. By prioritizing these initiatives, Pakistan can reduce the psychological burden of disasters and strengthen national resilience in the face of climate change.

1.5 Cases from People Who Have Lived Through Climate Disasters

The impact of climate disasters on individuals and communities in Pakistan can be profound. Climate disasters, such as floods, heat waves, and landslides, can cause significant damage to infrastructure, livelihoods, and human life. Here are some stories from people who have lived through climate disasters:

- *Floods in Sindh:* "I lost my home and livelihood due to the floods. I had to relocate to a temporary shelter with my family. It was a difficult time, but the community came together to support each other. We received some assistance from the government and NGOs, but it was not enough to rebuild our lives. The experience was traumatic, and it took us a long time to recover."—*Rohan, Sindh*
- *Heat wave in Karachi:* "The heat wave was unbearable. I had to stay indoors with my family to avoid the heat. We had to rely on charity for food and water. It was a challenging time, but we managed to cope. The heat wave also had a significant impact on my family's health, especially the elderly and children."—*Amna, Karachi*

- *Landslide in Khyber Pakhtunkhwa:* "The landslide destroyed our village. We had to evacuate immediately. It was a traumatic experience, but we are rebuilding our lives. The government and NGOs provided some assistance, but we still face many challenges. The landslide also had a significant impact on our livelihoods, and it will take us a long time to recover."—*Ali, Khyber Pakhtunkhwa*

These stories highlight the human impact of climate disasters in Pakistan. They also demonstrate the resilience and solidarity of communities in the face of adversity. Climate disasters can have a significant impact on mental health, livelihoods, and infrastructure. It is essential to provide support and assistance to individuals and communities affected by climate disasters.

2 Community-Based Disaster Risk Reduction and Management (CBDRRM)

Community-Based Disaster Risk Reduction and Response Management involves the use of the community and its resources to respond to disasters. In CBDRRMP, a community is self-sufficient and knows its weaknesses and strengths. Therefore, the community is recognized for its adaptability and maintenance of local control, safety, and well-being for CBDRRM, along with the minimization of external dependency.

Some of the leading principles include participation, ownership, inclusiveness, and sustainability. Ownership encourages long-term responsibilities, while active participation ensures that the entire community works toward implementing the strategies. Access for vulnerable groups, including women, children, and the disabled, is provided through inclusiveness. Sustainability ensures that there is continuous action on the responsive strategies, which override the immediate responsive action gaps. Adoption of these principles enables the community to recover quickly from a crisis.

CBDRRM is implemented through multi-village risk assessments, planning, capacity building, and active community involvement. While these approaches empower people with skills and materials, the absence of proper funding and adequate technical and community-level capacity, as well as public understanding, tends to interfere with more efficient deployment of available resources. There is, however, room to grow in the domains of partnerships, as well as in the application of novel resources and the deployment of tested frameworks. There is abundant proof in the case studies of Pakistan and Nepal, where people-centered frameworks for disaster planning reduced impacts and enhanced recovery, which underscores the need for more focused and tailored application of CBDRRM.

3 Monitoring and Evaluation of Community-Based Disaster Risk Reduction and Management

The assessment and monitoring (A&M) processes and systems, most important as a part of CBDRRM A&M, maintain effectiveness, improve accountability, and aid strategic guidance. To have a strong A&M framework, there should be logical objectives accompanied by definitive parameters, routine data assembling, thorough analysis, and clear dissemination. Despite prevalent resource and data quality limitations, poor engagement, and constrained systems, new participatory techniques and e-tools have opened new pathways. Community-centered evaluations, accountability, and systems accountability have seen the best outcomes. Pakistan and Nepal projects show evidence that effective A&M systems improve planning for disasters and enhance the ability to reproduce successful systems in other places.

Looking ahead, CBDRRM requires greater integration into national and local policies, supported by training, resources, and sustained partnerships. Scaling up efforts, applying innovative technologies, and strengthening collaboration among governments, organizations, and communities will make disaster responses more inclusive and effective. Similarly, advancing M&E through clear frameworks, capacity building, and impact evaluations will help refine strategies and ensure long-term sustainability. Together, these measures can make CBDRRM a cornerstone of disaster resilience and sustainable development.

4 Holistic Recommendations for Addressing Climate Change, Disasters, and Mental Health in Pakistan

4.1 Policy and Government-Level Interventions

To effectively address the psychological consequences of climate-induced disasters, mental health must be mainstreamed within Pakistan's national disaster and climate frameworks. This includes incorporating mental health as a core component of the National Disaster Risk Reduction (DRR) Strategy, the National Climate Change Policy, and all emergency preparedness protocols. Moreover, every district-level disaster plan should feature a dedicated Mental Health Response Component, complete with trained personnel, logistical systems, and allocated funding.

In parallel, there is a need for the establishment of Climate and Disaster Mental Health Task Forces across federal, provincial, and district levels. These interdisciplinary bodies should integrate psychologists, psychiatrists, social workers, climate experts, and emergency responders. Their primary roles would encompass conducting rapid psychological assessments, coordinating immediate response mechanisms, and guiding long-term mental health rehabilitation strategies. Legal and institutional reforms are also essential. This involves introducing legislative amendments to recognize disaster-induced mental health conditions under Pakistan's

Mental Health Acts and institutionalizing mental health preparedness as a mandatory function of agencies such as the National Disaster Management Authority (NDMA), Provincial Disaster Management Authorities (PDMAs), and health departments.

Finally, investment in resilient and inclusive infrastructure is critical. Climate-resilient shelters should be designed using trauma-informed principles, incorporating features such as appropriate ventilation, color schemes, spatial planning, and lighting to foster psychological recovery. Additionally, temporary housing and health camps must ensure universal accessibility—particularly for the elderly, people with disabilities, and women—in order to minimize psychological distress during displacement.

4.2 National-Scale Psychosocial Surveillance and Policy Integration

A population-level understanding of disaster-related psychological distress is essential to guide resource allocation and policy priorities. In their commentary, Yousuf et al. (2023) synthesize health-system reports and humanitarian agency data following the 2022 monsoon floods, estimating that over five million Pakistanis experienced moderate to severe psychological distress in the disaster's aftermath. By triangulating quantitative indicators—such as rates of new psychiatric consultations and self-reported distress in relief camps—with qualitative accounts from field workers, they spotlight a critical blind spot: although physical health surveillance is routinely embedded in national emergency protocols, psychosocial metrics remain marginal or entirely absent. This disparity not only obscures the true scale of mental health needs but also undermines the ability of decision-makers to deploy targeted interventions where they are most needed.

Yousuf and colleagues argue that integrating mental health indicators into Pakistan's National Disaster Risk Assessment (NDRA) frameworks must become a policy imperative. Drawing on global best practices—such as the World Health Organization's Mental Health Gap Action Programme (mhGAP) and the Sendai Framework's call for "people-centered" resilience metrics—they propose a tiered surveillance model. At the community level, trained volunteers and lady health workers would conduct rapid psychosocial assessments using brief, culturally validated tools, reporting data via mobile platforms to district disaster management authorities. At the provincial and national levels, these data streams would feed into an integrated dashboard, enabling real-time mapping of psychosocial hotspots and informing both short-term relief efforts and long-term capacity-building investments.

To operationalize this vision, Yousuf et al. (2023) recommend three strategic actions. First, NDMA and Provincial Disaster Management Authorities (PDMAs) should formally adopt psychosocial indicators—such as the Psychological Distress Scale and referrals to mental health services—into their standardized after-action reports. Second, the Ministry of National Health Services must allocate dedicated funding for training a nationwide cadre of "Psychosocial Surveillance Officers," who bridge disaster response and community outreach. Third, partnerships with academic institutions and NGOs are needed to pilot, evaluate, and refine data collection instruments, ensuring cultural relevance and logistical feasibility in Pakistan's diverse contexts. Embedding these measures within existing emergency response architectures will transform mental health from an afterthought into a core component of Pakistan's disaster resilience strategy.

4.3 Culturally Adapted Psychological Therapies and Interventions

Culturally adapted psychological interventions offer vital support in disaster-affected regions of Pakistan. Culturally adapted cognitive behavioral therapy (CBT) involves tailoring sessions with examples and metaphors relevant to Pakistani life, such as flooding, loss of cattle, or distress within joint family systems. Delivery should be bilingual—using Urdu or regional languages—and integrated with spiritual practices, like dua, zikr, and community prayer, to support emotional regulation. Acceptance and commitment therapy (ACT) can also be locally grounded by framing its core concept of acceptance through Islamic values, such as Taqdeer or divine destiny. Value-based commitment exercises can center on rebuilding family bonds, contributing to community reconstruction, and drawing on spiritual resilience. For trauma survivors, narrative exposure therapy (NET) is effective in helping individuals, particularly those affected by floods or earthquakes, reconstruct their trauma timeline. Incorporating family and religious storytelling into these sessions enhances emotional catharsis and meaning-making. Psychological first aid (PFA) should be expanded through community-level training programs aimed at teachers, lady health workers, religious leaders, and volunteers. This can provide immediate psychological support, reduce the risk of chronic PTSD, and encourage culturally appropriate help-seeking behavior. Finally, group-based therapies and communal healing should take place in culturally meaningful settings such as community halls, madrassas, or bethaks. Peer-led sessions—whether for women, farmers, or youth groups—can help reduce stigma and strengthen collective coping mechanisms.

4.4 Capacity Building and Training

To strengthen the nation's capacity for disaster-responsive mental health care, a comprehensive training and education framework should be established. Curriculum development is a foundational step, involving the integration of climate-disaster mental health modules into psychology, psychiatry, social work, and nursing syllabi. These modules should cover critical topics such as trauma-informed care, culturally adapted therapy, grief processing, and community psychosocial mobilization. In parallel, national certification programs should be introduced in the form of short courses—ranging from 3 to 6 months—focusing on disaster mental health intervention for frontline responders, NGO personnel, and community mobilizers. A cascade training model, using a "train-the-trainer" methodology, can further amplify reach by empowering master trainers in each province to equip local teams in delivering therapy and psychological first aid. To complement these efforts, simulation-based disaster response exercises should be conducted, replicating mass trauma scenarios and integrating both physical rescue operations and psychological triage protocols. Lastly, cross-sector collaboration is essential: partnerships between the National Disaster Management Authority (NDMA), academic institutions, psychiatric hospitals, and nongovernmental organizations can facilitate joint workshops and field-based training, ensuring an integrated, resilient, and contextually grounded mental health response system.

4.5 Community Mobilization and Public Engagement

To foster culturally resonant and community-driven mental health support in disaster-affected areas, a range of strategies must be implemented. First, religious and cultural framing of mental health can play a transformative role. Collaborating with religious scholars to develop sermons (khutbas) that address mental health from an Islamic perspective can help normalize psychological well-being as part of spiritual care. Religious gatherings provide a powerful platform for disseminating psychological first aid (PFA) techniques and self-care tools in ways that are both accessible and contextually meaningful.

Building strong community support networks is equally essential. Initiating youth and women's community groups that meet regularly for emotional sharing and collective problem-solving can foster resilience, peer support, and localized recovery. To broaden impact, media and awareness campaigns should be launched through diverse platforms—TV, radio, TikTok, and YouTube—to share survivor stories and reduce stigma while encouraging help-seeking behaviors. Engagement with trusted local influencers, including teachers, village elders, and tribal leaders, can further strengthen outreach by positioning them as mental health champions within their communities.

Finally, establishing robust feedback loops and accountability systems is vital to ensure that interventions are effective and culturally appropriate. Community-led monitoring mechanisms can play a key role in evaluating psychological support initiatives and reinforcing respectful, inclusive program delivery. Together, these strategies can cultivate a mental health response that is both empowering and sustainable in the face of climate-related adversity.

5 Conclusion

As Pakistan grapples with the escalating frequency and intensity of climate-related disasters, it is not only the physical landscapes that are being altered, but also the psychological and emotional fabric of its people. The country's vulnerability lies in its geographic location, fragile infrastructure, high population density, and limited resources for disaster preparedness and response, all of which make it disproportionately exposed to floods, earthquakes, heatwaves, and landslides. The mental health concerns arising from these disasters are profound. Survivors often endure waves of anxiety, depression, and post-traumatic stress that remain unspoken, untreated, and deeply stigmatized. The burden is particularly heavy on women, children, the elderly, and marginalized groups, whose access to mental healthcare is further constrained by poverty, cultural stigma, and inadequate health systems.

Some efforts have been made to address these challenges. Pakistan has integrated psychosocial support into certain humanitarian responses, established mental health policies, and initiated training programs for health professionals. Civil society organizations and international partners have also contributed by providing psychosocial first aid and community-based support after disasters. However, these initiatives remain limited in scope, under-resourced, and fragmented. Moving forward, a more coordinated and sustainable approach is needed. This includes strengthening assessment protocols, expanding professional training, embedding culturally adapted therapies, and mobilizing communities as active partners in resilience-building. Policymakers must prioritize mental health in disaster planning, leverage technology for outreach, and foster partnerships across government, academia, and civil society. By weaving psychological well-being into the heart of climate resilience, Pakistan can ensure that disaster recovery is not only about rebuilding homes and cities but also about restoring hope, dignity, and emotional strength among its people.

References

Abidi, S. M. A. (2024). Beyond the tragedy: Illuminating challenges in disaster management and mental health support in resource-constrained environments. *Prehospital and Disaster Medicine, 39*(6), 442–444. https://doi.org/10.1017/S1049023X24000657

Ahmad, N., Hussain, S., & Shaheen, N. (2020). Internal displacement: Relationship of mental health and education of children in Swat, Pakistan. *Pakistan Journal of Medical Sciences, 36*(5), 909–913. https://doi.org/10.12669/pjms.36.5.1847

Ahmad, M. S., Shah, R., Khan, S., et al. (2025). Exploring psychological recovery and coping mechanisms: Post-flood mental health and resilience of women in Punjab, Pakistan. *Discover Sustainability, 6*, 107. https://doi.org/10.1007/s43621-025-00799-5

Akram, S., & Mushtaq, S. (2024). Environmental change and floods: The long-ignored effects of displacement on mental health. *Frontiers in Public Health, 12*, 1434123. https://doi.org/10.3389/fpubh.2024.1434123

Alvi, M. H., Ashraf, T., Kiran, T., Iqbal, N., Gumber, A., Patel, A., & Husain, N. (2023). Economic burden of mental illness in Pakistan: An estimation for the year 2020 from existing evidence. *BJPsych International, 20*(3), 54–56. https://doi.org/10.1192/bji.2023.4

Bilham, R. (2019). Himalayan earthquakes: A review of historical seismicity and early 21st century slip potential. *Geological Society, London, Special Publications, 483*, 423–482. https://doi.org/10.1144/SP483.16

Cheema, H. A., Rehan, S. T., Shahid, A., Head, M. G., Jawad, M. Y., & Shah, J. (2023). The mental health of children in flood-affected areas in Pakistan needs urgent attention. *The lancet. Psychiatry, 10*(1), 7. https://doi.org/10.1016/S2215-0366(22)00381-9

Chung, M. C., Jalal, S., & Khan, N. U. (2014). Posttraumatic stress disorder and psychiatric comorbidity following the 2010 flood in Pakistan: Exposure characteristics, cognitive distortions, and emotional suppression. *Psychiatry, 77*(3), 289–304. https://doi.org/10.1521/psyc.2014.77.3.289

Daraz, U., Khan, Y., Alsawalqa, R. O., Alrawashdeh, M. N., & Alnajdawi, A. M. (2024). Impact of climate change on women mental health in rural hinterland of Pakistan. *Frontiers in Psychiatry, 15*, 1450943. https://doi.org/10.3389/fpsyt.2024.1450943

Ehring, T., Razik, S., & Emmelkamp, P. M. G. (2011). Prevalence and predictors of posttraumatic stress disorder, anxiety, depression, and burnout in Pakistani earthquake recovery workers. *Psychiatry Research, 185*(1–2), 161–166. https://doi.org/10.1016/j.psychres.2009.10.018

Federal Flood Commission (FFC). (2022). *Flood report 2022*. Government of Pakistan.

Gadit, A. A. M. (2011). Psychiatry in Pakistan: 1947–2006: A new balance sheet. *Journal of the Pakistan Medical Association, 57*(9), 453–463.

Intergovernmental Panel on Climate Change. (2021). *Climate change 2021: The physical science basis. Contribution of Working Group I to the Sixth Assessment Report of the Intergovernmental Panel on Climate Change* (V. Masson-Delmotte, P. Zhai, A. Pirani, S. L. Connors, C. Péan, S. Berger,... B. Zhou, Eds.). Cambridge University Press. https://doi.org/10.1017/9781009157896.

Iqbal, A., Sheikh, A., Ali, E., & Islam, Z. (2023). Impact of prolonged flooding in Pakistan: In the middle of unexpected health emergency. *The International Journal of Health Planning and Management, 38*(2), 536–540. https://doi.org/10.1002/hpm.3604

Ishtiaq, H., Batool, T. E., Mamoon, B., Majeed, A. I., Atta, M., Atta, A., & Masood, S. (2025). Mental health problems in Pakistani society as a consequence of violence and trauma: A case for better integration of care. *Cureus, 17*(5), e83486. https://doi.org/10.7759/cureus.83486

Khalily, M. T. (2011). Mental health problems in Pakistani society as a consequence of violence and trauma: A case for better integration of care. *International Journal of Integrated Care, 11*, e128. https://doi.org/10.5334/ijic.662

Malik, S. M., Awan, H., & Khan, N. (2012). Mapping vulnerability to climate change and its repercussions on human health in Pakistan. *Globalization and Health, 8*(31). https://doi.org/10.1186/1744-8603-8-31

Mirza, I., & Jenkins, R. (2004). Risk factors, prevalence, and treatment of anxiety and depressive disorders in Pakistan: Systematic review. *BMJ, 328*(7443), 794. https://doi.org/10.1136/bmj.328.7443.794

Naeem, F., Ayub, M., Masood, K., Gul, H., Khalid, M., Farrukh, A.,... Kingdon, D. (2011). Prevalence and psychosocial risk factors of PTSD: 18 months after Kashmir earthquake in Pakistan. *Journal of Affective Disorders, 130*(1–2), 268–274. https://doi.org/10.1016/j.jad.2010.10.035.

National Disaster Management Authority (NDMA). (2012). National disaster management plan. Government of Pakistan.

Qadir, T. F., Fatima, H., Usmani, M. H., & Hussain, S. A. (2016). Telepsychiatry in Pakistan after natural disasters. *Lancet Psychiatry, 3*(11), 1016. https://doi.org/10.1016/S2215-0366(16)30323-6

Rahman, A., Hamdani, S. U., Awan, N. R., Bryant, R. A., Dawson, K. S., Khan, M. F.,... van Ommeren, M. (2016). Effect of a multicomponent behavioral intervention in adults impaired by psychological distress in a conflict-affected area of Pakistan: A randomized clinical trial. JAMA, *316*(24), 2609–2617. https://doi.org/10.1001/jama.2016.17165

Rehan, S. T., Ahmed, M., Bukhsh, A. N., Bari, K., Hussain, H. U., Ullah, I., & Asghar, M. S. (2023). Heavy migration of flood affectees in Pakistan and increased risk of autism spectrum disorder in children: A call to action. *International Journal of Surgery, 109*(3), 313–315. https://doi.org/10.1097/JS9.0000000000000136

Riaz, M. M. A., Nayyer, B., Lal, A., Nawaz, F. A., & Zil-E-Ali, A. (2023). Climate change and mental health: A call to action to include mental health and psychosocial support services in the Pakistan flood crisis. *BJPsych International, 20*(3), 56–58. https://doi.org/10.1192/bji.2023.13.(1), 14–23.

Shoib, S., Tayyeb, M., Armiya'u, A. Y., Shah, J., Swed, S., & Chandradasa, M. (2024). Suicide bombing and impending mental health disaster in Pakistan. *International Journal of Surgery: Global Health, 7*(1), e0096. https://doi.org/10.1097/GH9.0000000000000096

Soomro, S., Zhou, D., & Charan, I. A. (2024). Investigating associations between climate change anxiety and children's mental health in Pakistan: Impacts and priority actions. *Disaster Medicine and Public Health Preparedness, 18*, e277. https://doi.org/10.1017/dmp.2024.267

Wang, L., Norman, I., Edleston, V., Oyo, C., & Leamy, M. (2024). The effectiveness and implementation of psychological first aid as a therapeutic intervention after trauma: An integrative review. *Trauma, Violence & Abuse, 25*(4), 2638–2656. https://doi.org/10.1177/15248380231221492

World Health Organization (WHO). (2005). *Earthquake in Pakistan: WHO's response*. World Health Organization.

World Health Organization (WHO). (2020). *Mental health and psychosocial support in emergencies*. World Health Organization.

World Health Organization (WHO). (2022). *WHO mental health atlas 2020: Country profiles – Pakistan*. WHO.

Yousuf, J., Mehmood, H., Aquil, S., Rija, A., Syyeda Rahmat, Z., & Malikzai, A. (2023). Effects of floods on the mental health of Pakistanis: A commentary. *Annals of Medicine and Surgery (London), 85*(5), 2253–2255. https://doi.org/10.1097/MS9.0000000000000590

Chapter 8
Mental Health Effects of Disaster and Climate Change in Afghanistan, the Maldives, and Sri Lanka

Sujita Kumar Kar, S. M. Yasir Arafat, and Nilamadhab Kar

1 Introduction

The South Asian region, which includes countries like Afghanistan, Sri Lanka, and the Maldives, faces numerous challenges that make its population particularly vulnerable. Natural disasters, climate change impacts, sociopolitical conflicts, war, and the ongoing threat of terrorism all contribute to a complex landscape of hardship. As South Asia is one of the most densely populated regions in the world, these issues significantly affect the well-being of millions. Mental healthcare needs in this area are tremendous, as many individuals struggle with the psychological effects of these hardships. Unfortunately, there is a major gap in the availability and provision of mental health services. Both Afghanistan and the Maldives find it difficult to offer adequate mental healthcare to their people, leaving many without the support they urgently require. This persistent challenge emphasizes the pressing need for better mental health resources and services across South Asia (Mohamed & Mansoor, 2025; Arafat & Kar, 2024; Cameron et al., 2021; Kar et al., 2025; Kar & Arafat,

S. K. Kar (✉)
Department of Psychiatry, King George's Medical University, Lucknow, India

S. M. Y. Arafat
Department of Psychiatry, Bangladesh Specialized Hospital, Dhaka, Bangladesh

Faculty of Medicine and Health Sciences, Department of Public and Community Health, Frontier University Garowe, Garowe, Somalia

N. Kar
Department of Psychiatry, Black Country Healthcare NHS Foundation Trust, Wolverhampton, UK

Research Institute in Health Sciences, University of Wolverhampton, Wolverhampton, UK

Faculty of Contemplative and Behavioural Sciences, Sri Sri University, Cuttack, India

N. Kar et al. (eds.), *Climate Change, Disaster and Mental Health in South Asia*, South Asian Perspectives in Mental Health and Psychology,
https://doi.org/10.1007/978-981-95-3690-0_8

2025; Mohd Saleem et al., 2021; Shoib et al., 2024). Sri Lanka is also affected by disasters, climate change, and political unrest continuously; as a result, the care services are affected from time to time.

The latest evidence supports that the burden of mental illnesses in South Asia is significant. However, the data from Afghanistan, Bhutan, and the Maldives are scarce (Arafat & Kar, 2024; Hossain et al., 2020). Disasters and climate change are important risk factors of mental illnesses and are likely to add to the burden of mental illnesses in these countries. This chapter aims to highlight the mental health issues associated with disasters and climate change in Afghanistan, Sri Lanka, and the Maldives.

2 Country Overview of Afghanistan, the Maldives, and Sri Lanka

2.1 *Afghanistan*

Afghanistan is a country of South Asia, with a population of more than 41 million (by 2023), and a rapid growth of population in the country, expecting the population to nearly double by 2050 (WHO, 2024a). Nearly three-fourths of Afghans are between 15 and 64 years of age. The life expectancy at birth is 59.1 years in 2021. The most common cause of death among females is ischemic heart disease, whereas among males, the most common cause of death is collective violence and legal intervention (WHO, 2024a). The healthcare sector in Afghanistan has been adversely affected over the past two decades due to the American invasion, war, and political conflicts (WHO, 2025a).

2.2 *Maldives*

The Maldives is the smallest country in Asia, comprised of a group of islands in the Indian Ocean. The current population of the Maldives is 0.53 million (by 2023) and is projected to increase to 0.59 million by 2050 (WHO, 2024b). The majority of the population (approximately 85%) in the Maldives belongs to the age group of 15–64 years, and the life expectancy at birth is 75.4 years (WHO, 2024b). The leading causes of death in the Maldives are stroke and ischemic heart disease (WHO, 2024b, 2025b). A significant healthcare challenges exist in the Maldives regarding the management of noncommunicable diseases. Even the allocated funds are not adequately utilized for the management of noncommunicable diseases (WHO, 2025b).

2.3 *Sri Lanka*

Sri Lanka is a South Asian Island country in the Indian Ocean. It is a low- and middle-income country and famous for its tourist destinations. The current population of Sri Lanka is about 23 million (by 2023) and is projected to increase to about 25 million by 2050 (WHO, 2024c). The majority of the population (approximately 76%) in Sri Lanka belongs to the age group of 15–64 years, and the life expectancy at birth is 77.2 years (WHO, 2024c). The leading causes of death in Sri Lanka are stroke and ischemic heart disease (WHO, 2024b, 2025b). Significant healthcare challenges exist in the country regarding the management of noncommunicable diseases. The country has more than 4% gross domestic product allocation in health (WHO, 2024c).

3 Disasters and Climate Change-Related Incidents in Afghanistan, Maldives, and Sri Lanka

3.1 *Afghanistan*

Afghanistan is undergoing severe turmoil due to war, terrorism, invasion, political conflicts, addiction-related issues, crimes, and financial crisis, which ultimately led to a humanitarian crisis in the country (Rajmil et al., 2022). After the recent Taliban rule, several international agencies had withdrawn the financial support from Afghanistan, further worsening the crisis (Rajmil et al., 2022; Safi et al., 2024).

Several disasters have hit Afghanistan in recent times, adversely. The notable disasters in the recent past happened in the years 2022 and 2023, killing more than one thousand people and injuring many more, with extreme damage in the country (Essar et al., 2022; Mahase, 2023; Mallapaty, 2022; Shepherd, 2023). Withdrawal of support by the international agencies, after the Taliban government took charge in Afghanistan, resulted in several difficulties in dealing with the recent disaster-related care in Afghanistan (Ramozi et al., 2023). It affected the vulnerable populations, like women and children, the most in Afghanistan (Ramozi et al., 2023). Serial earthquakes in the Herat region of Afghanistan also resulted in extensive damage to the healthcare system, intensifying the humanitarian crisis (Ramozi et al., 2024). Afghanistan is located at the edge of the Eurasian tectonic plate (Akhundzadah, 2025). Many of the tectonic activities of the Eurasian, Indian, and Arabian tectonic plates converge around the region of Afghanistan, making it highly vulnerable to earthquakes (Akhundzadah, 2025).

Several occasions of flash floods also affected the lives of Afghans frequently. Such incidents used to happen in the months of July and August (Essar et al., 2024). Approximately one million Afghans are affected by floods every year, resulting in significant loss of finances, jobs, and mortality (Yolchi et al., 2024). Flood is an important contributing factor to food insecurity in Afghanistan (Yolchi et al., 2024).

Afghanistan is a vulnerable country that is adversely affected by climate change (Masudi et al., 2025). Over several decades, there has been a rise in temperature, destruction of environmental resources, food insecurity, depletion of water resources, and drought; the climatic changes are associated with migration, displacement, social instability, and insecurity (Safi et al., 2024). Climate change challenges are attributed to poverty, hunger, malnutrition, and diarrheal diseases (Safi et al., 2024). In the year 2018–2019, drought caused significant displacement of population and financial losses in the country. Rapid climate change is adversely affecting water resources in Afghanistan (Shokory et al., 2023). Dietary diversity at the household level is also affected by climate change (Yolchi & Wang, 2025). Climate change is often associated with the displacement and migration of people. It, in return, may lead to conflict. Climate change-related displacement directly and indirectly leads to conflict in Afghanistan (Přívara & Přívarová, 2019). Environmental changes compelled locally affected inhabitants to leave their native places and migrate to other places (within the country and outside the country). These displaced populations live in refugee camps or seek asylum. Their invasion to other places often results in conflicts and violence (Přívara & Přívarová, 2019). Conflict on the other hand increases the risk of disaster by weakening the disaster response capacities of the system (Mena & Hilhorst, 2021).

Afghanistan has signed international agreements to mitigate the climate change-related effects and developed institutional policies to regulate the clinical change change-related effects (Masudi et al., 2025). Afghanistan has developed the Climate Change Strategy and Action Plan, the National Environmental Action Plan, and the National Environment Strategy to consolidate the policies and programs aiming at mitigating climate change hazards (Masudi et al., 2025). To deal with the disaster-related issues, several collaborative care models have been proposed, and initiatives have been taken in recent years by the government of Afghanistan (Kaneda et al., 2023). Community participation is a helpful strategy to mitigate the post-disaster damage. Lack of adequate female participation in the post-disaster management program might be responsible for accurately obtaining gender-sensitive information and gender-sensitive risk assessment (Mushwani et al., 2025). Several national regulating bodies in Afghanistan regulate the national level programs, policies, and other initiatives with respect to disaster management. To name the important agencies are (Mushwani & Ahmad, 2025):

- Afghanistan National Disasters Management Authority (ANDMA)
- Afghanistan National Water Affairs Regulation Authority (NWARA)
- Afghanistan Hydrometeorological Department (AHMD)

Research in Afghanistan found several hurdles in community participation following a disaster (Sadiqi et al., 2017). They are:

- Inadequate community reserve
- Insufficient competent human resources
- Gender issues
- Scarcity of nongovernmental organization involvement

- Lack of policies, programs, and practices
- Security concerns

Addressing these issues by the Afghan government effectively is expected to improve the disaster management plan in the country. The flood situation and effect are not uniform across the country; hence, the action plans and policies should target the particularly vulnerable zones (Yolchi et al., 2024).

3.2 Maldives

The Maldives is affected by climate change. The major climate change-related events that pose concerns in the Maldives are (Stojanov et al., 2017):

- Sea water rise
- Coastal erosion
- Saline water intrusion
- Change in monsoon pattern
- Change in rainfall

As a result of climate change, people migrate and plan settlement in other countries (Stojanov et al., 2017).

As per a report, the deaths due to air pollution in the Maldives were 31.8 per 100,000 population by 2019 (WHO, 2024b).

The typical geographical location of the Maldives makes it highly vulnerable to disasters. It is a country consisting of multiple tiny islands, which are on the verge of submersion under the sea due to rising water levels in the sea associated with climate change (Herrera-Cano (MIB) & Herrera-Cano, 2016; Sakamoto et al., 2022). The increasing population in Maldives and expectations to meet the needs of the people of the country resulted in coral mining and filling of the underlying areas to increase the land surface for accommodation of more people, which is ultimately damaging the natural defense of the coastline, increasing the risk of disasters (Naylor, 2015).

Disaster produces devastation and destruction. Reconstruction is an important measure of repair that requires community involvement (Lawther, 2009). There is a need for capacity building at the community level to enhance community participation in the post-disaster reconstruction. Another unique issue in the Maldives is related to communication, as the country consists of multiple mini islands with poor land connectivity, which may stand as a major obstacle in carrying out the post-disaster reconstruction and evacuation of people to safe places during/before the disaster (Ibrahim & Hameed, 2006).

To deal with the climate change-related issues, the Maldives has designed a program in the name of "Integrating Climate Change Risks into Resilient Island Planning in the Maldives" with support from the United Nations Development

Program and the Least Developed Countries Fund (Sovacool, 2012a, b). This aims at achieving:

- Infrastructure development
- Sensitization of the policymakers
- Improving the health system
- Addressing food insecurity
- Maintaining the coral reef biodiversity
- Human settlement
- Maintaining tourism and fisheries

Since the 2004 tsunami, the government of the Maldives has taken several initiatives to deal with the disaster risk management in collaboration with private organizations, and the public (Herrera-Cano (MIB) & Herrera-Cano, 2016; Pardasani, 2006; Suppasri et al., 2015). As disaster management deals with significant mobilities (displacement and replacement) and settlement (both temporary and long-term), there is a need for structured planning to deal with such issues in the Maldives (Kothari et al., 2023).

The Maldives has a Disaster Management Act 2015, which makes the state responsible for protecting its people, their health, well-being, property, and the natural and built-up environment from natural and man-made disasters and hazards including public health emergencies (Sattar et al., 2022). During the COVID-19 pandemic, the Maldives set up the National Emergency Operations Center (NEOC) to deal with the disaster (Sattar et al., 2022).

3.3 Sri Lanka

Sri Lanka is prone to disasters due to its geographic, climatic, and sociopolitical factors. It has experienced a civil war of more than two and a half decades (1983–2009), two leftist insurrections (1971, 1987–89), Easter Sunday bombings of 2019, and a political mass uprising (2022). There are several natural disasters, like floods, landslides, cyclones, earthquakes, forest fires, tornadoes, droughts, and tsunamis (2004) (Somasundaram, 2013). Disasters incur a huge financial toll. One study found that Sri Lanka spends at least 19 million USD in a year for direct healthcare expense due to floods and droughts (De Alwis & Noy, 2019).

4 Mental Health Effects of Disasters and Climate Change-Related Incidents in Afghanistan, the Maldives, and Sri Lanka

4.1 Afghanistan

The collective trauma resulting from disaster, climate change, war, political instability, and conflicts resulted in significant disruption of social integrity and several mental health issues, such as depression, anxiety, substance use disorder, and post-traumatic stress disorder in people in Afghanistan (Mohd Saleem et al., 2021). The climate change-related events and disasters in Afghanistan resulted in the forced displacement of the population, particularly the vulnerable populations, resulting in several physical and mental health-related issues (Mohammadi et al., 2023). In addition to the above, intergenerational trauma is one of the most important psychosocial issues affecting the mental health of Afghan people who are in multiple disastrous situations, both natural and human-made (Ullah et al., 2023).

The common mental health issues encountered following forced displacement following disasters include (Dhimal et al., 2021; Mohammadi et al., 2023):

- Anxiety
- Depression
- Loneliness
- Post-traumatic stress disorder
- Premigration and postmigration trauma
- Psychosomatic disorder
- Substance use disorder
- Stress-related disorders
- Suicidal behavior
- Behavioral problems

Climate change and disaster increase the risk of violence and disruption of healthcare facilities and increase the burden on caregivers of people with health issues (Vig, 2025). Despite several incidents of disaster in Afghanistan, the research estimating the mental health impact of disasters on the Afghan population is scarce (Mohammadi et al., 2023).

4.1.1 General Population

People of Afghanistan have remained under the constant turmoil of political changes, internal armed conflicts, and war. The impact of these on the mental health of the population has been huge. A cross-sectional survey of the three key regions of Afghanistan reported the prevalence of depression at 72.05%, anxiety at 71.94%, and stress at 66.49% (Neyazi et al., 2024). This highlighted the mental health crisis of the general population in Afghanistan, facing multiple traumas over the years.

Another survey in eight areas reported that 47.1% of the general population reported a high level of distress in the previous month, and 39.4% felt poor mental health was affecting their lives (Schwartz et al., 2023).

A national survey of the general population found 12-month PTSD prevalence of 5.34%, as major depressive episode 11,71%, generalized anxiety disorder 2.78%, suicidal thoughts 2.26%, and lifetime suicidal attempts 3.50% which are close to those reported in other countries. The point prevalence of psychological distress was 47.1%, and substantial impairment due to mental health was 39.4%. Described as a highly traumatized population, 80% lived in very dangerous areas. Also, 64.7% of the Afghan population had personal experience of at least one traumatic event, 78.5% had witnessed one such event, 60.8% of the sample experienced collective violence in relation to war, and 48.8% reported four or more events (Kovess-Masfety et al., 2021).

4.1.2 Children and Adolescents

A study of high school students reported that poor mental health, specifically anxiety and depression, was significantly associated with higher exposure to war, and the major concerns were security situation (56%), air pollution (41%), and not having anyone to talk to (28.8%) (Razjouyan et al., 2022).

4.1.3 Specific Professional Groups

Mental health challenges of healthcare workers during the COVID-19 pandemic have been highlighted; decades of multiple traumatic experiences, insecurity, instability, poor economy, and scarce resources contributed to the deteriorating situation (Islam et al., 2022). A survey of healthcare workers in Afghanistan found 52.3% had symptoms of depression, 48.8% anxiety, and 46.9% stress (Samsoor & Stanikzai, 2024).

Among the combat soldiers deployed to Afghanistan, a comparison between those with or without critical military incidence showed the prevalence of PTSD was 6.4% vs. 1.1%; depression was 7.0% vs. 1.1%; anxiety disorders were 15.9% vs. 2.8%; and multimorbidity was 4.8% vs. 0.4% (Wesemann et al., 2024).

4.1.4 Mental Health of Afghan Refugees

A huge number of Afghan people are displaced within and outside the country because of the situation, specifically decades of war and armed conflict, economic hardships, and uncertainty. The refugees have immense mental health issues, which are also contributed to by a factor of separation from their families, traumatic memories in Afghanistan, and isolation and lack of control in a new country. A considerable proportion of them have anxiety, depression, and PTSD symptoms (Nylen et al., 2025). There is a dearth of information about their mental health and support. The refugees in other countries present with a range of common mental disorders related to traumatic stress, loss, and grief, with a resultant increased need for mental health assistance and support (Silove & Ventevogel, 2022).

4.1.5 Challenges in the Provision of Mental Healthcare

There are many concerns related to the provision of mental healthcare in war and armed conflict-ridden Afghanistan. Living in dangerous areas of Afghanistan decreases access to mental healthcare (Kovess-Masfety et al., 2022). In addition, there is a lack of trained mental health professionals, when the crisis of mental health due to human-made situations continues (Rahimi & Azimi, 2012).

While the mental health support for the general public is not a priority, the concerns of vulnerable groups, such as pregnant and postnatal women, LGBTQ individuals, older adults, ethnic minority groups, and Afghan refugees living overseas, remain neglected, and these groups have heightened risks of mental health issues and suicide (Tay, 2024).

It has been recognized that following earthquakes, the mental conditions of the victims deteriorate. Absence of local psychiatric facilities and proper roads delays the early response and makes the follow-up difficult. There have been efforts to support victims and train local healthcare workers through external mental health professionals; however, local sociocultural beliefs and stigma make it difficult (Hussaini et al., 2022).

Mental health remains a hugely stigmatized topic in Afghanistan, which is contributed by cultural, religious, socioeconomic, and environmental factors. In the current situation, mental health services are not a priority in Afghanistan (Schwartz et al., 2023).

4.2 Maldives

As disasters and climate change-related incidents often hit the Maldives, the health infrastructure and psychosocial support systems are frequently disrupted, adversely affecting the mental health (Ibrahim & Hameed, 2006). Despite having a high risk of climate change-related disasters, such as tsunamis and rising sea level, there is inadequate information about how these are affecting the mental health of the islanders.

Disasters and climate change in the Maldives have resulted in mass displacements, homelessness, and disrupted livelihoods (Ibrahim & Hameed, 2006; Kelman et al., 2021), which is a significant cause of stress among the population. The hardships produced by the disasters often affected the self-esteem, maladjustment, and increased risk of psychiatric disorders (Kelman et al., 2021). Uncertainty, poor livelihood, insufficient social support, discrimination, and financial challenges add to the stress in the community (Eweida et al., 2024; Kelman et al., 2021).

During the COVID-19 pandemic lockdown period, financial problems and job loss increased, so also the abuse and violence, which led to higher stress in the families (Sattar et al., 2022). This had a massive impact on the mental well-being of vulnerable people.

A cross-sectional study of adult COVID-19 inpatients admitted to isolation facilities in Maldivian nations found that 9% had depression, 23% had anxiety, and 12% had stress. Symptomatic patients had higher stress than the non-symptomatic ones (Dey et al., 2022).

After the 2004 tsunami disaster, a lot of initiatives were taken to strengthen the disaster preparedness program in the country and build the psychosocial support system (Ibrahim & Hameed, 2006). Following the 2004 tsunami, a community outreach program was arranged to provide psychosocial support, which was provided by local people after receiving training, so the program was culturally appropriate (Ibrahim & Hameed, 2006).

4.3 Sri Lanka

The prevalence of psychiatric disorders among disaster survivors in Sri Lanka is higher than in the general population (Rodrigo & Liyanage, 2017). Along with the immediate psychological symptoms and disorders, disasters cause enduring effects (Wickrama et al., 2024).

4.3.1 Armed Conflict

Sri Lanka experienced a 26 year-long armed conflict in the Northen part, which led to death, internal displacement, and external migration of a large number of people. This was associated with a huge impact on the mental health of the population. There were increased psychosocial problems in the families and communities, as a collective sense, and war-related complex psychosocial issues were preventing recovery (Siriwardhana & Wickramage, 2014). There was also psychological distress among half of the disabled soldiers, and 41.7% soldiers with lower limb amputations and spinal injuries had PTSD and poorer mental health (Siriwardhana & Wickramage, 2014). A study found the rates of symptoms of depression, anxiety, and PTSD were 22.2%, 32.6%, and 7%, respectively, among internally displaced persons due to war (Husain et al., 2011). Factors associated with poor mental health were unresolved grief, self-harm, suicidal ideations, insecurity, poverty, teenage pregnancies, gender-based and domestic violence, neglect of the elderly, etc. (Siriwardhana & Wickramage, 2014).

Humanitarian workers providing relief in conflict zones also had mental health problems, such as 19.0% had symptoms of PTSD, 58.0% reported depressive symptoms, and 53.0% anxiety symptoms (Siriwardhana & Wickramage, 2014). There is limited information about the mental health of the rebels in the conflict.

During the trauma of the internal war between rebels and state forces from January to May 2009, there were displacements, deaths, injuries, deprivation of basic necessities, and medical care; it was reported that family and community relationships, networks, were destroyed; and there were not only collective symptoms of despair, passivity, silence, loss of values and ethical mores, and amotivation but also resilience and post-traumatic growth (Somasundaram, 2010).

4.3.2 Children and Adolescents

More than half the children were exposed to armed conflict and experienced direct violence, loss of family, and displacement. There is some suggestion that the child combatants and suicide bombers had numerous psychological issues, such as somatization, PTSD, depression, anxiety, and behavioral and conduct disorders. Associations between exposure to conflict and poorer psychological outcomes and school absenteeism have been established in a national sample of children and adolescents (Siriwardhana et al., 2013).

In the post-conflict Sri Lanka, a study on adolescents reported that 15.6% had war related exposure, and in them, 93.4% were internally displaced, 8.9% had dropped out of school, 3.9% had depression, and 7% had substance use (Dissanayake et al., 2023).

4.3.3 The 2004 Asian Tsunami

One study identified the impact after 8 years of the tsunami reflected by the symptoms of depression and post-traumatic stress disorder (PTSD) (Ranasinghe et al., 2023). After the tsunami, it was noted that the rate of PTSD was low in comparison to Western countries, while somatic symptoms appeared and were presented to physicians other than mental health professionals (Hollifield et al., 2008; D'Souza & Singh, 2005). One study found that the rates of depression, anxiety, and PTSD were 16%, 30%, and 21% respectively, among the adults after the 2004 tsunami (Hollifield et al., 2008; Neuner et al., 2006). The prevalence of PTSD was double among females than among males (Ranasinghe & Levy, 2007).

PTSD was significantly higher among children who were exposed to tsunami (Neuner et al., 2006). After the same disaster, the prevalence of PTSD among the children ranged from 19 to 53.6% (Gunaratne et al., 2013). One study reported that 41% of adolescents, along with 19.6% of their mothers, had PTSD after 4 months of the event (Wickrama & Kaspar, 2007).

Armed conflict and natural disasters could be attributed for common prevalence of psychotic disorders in Sri Lanka (Keraite et al., 2016). One study found that 82.4% of the children were exposed to at least one war-related event, about 71% were directly affected by the tsunami, about 20% of the children had met the criteria of major depressive disorder (MDD), and 22.6% had past suicidal behavior (Catani et al., 2008). PTSD symptoms were significantly higher among older adults who experienced disasters severely in comparison to those who were not experienced so (Nomura et al., 2010). Mass trauma and violence within the family were significantly associated with the development of childhood mental disorders (Sriskandarajah et al., 2015).

4.3.4 National Plan and Actions

The mental health impact of armed conflict was acknowledged early in Sri Lanka. To raise awareness and to deal with the psychosocial effects of armed conflict on children, the Health Reach Sri Lanka project (1993–1996) was undertaken based on the "health initiative as peace initiative." It was based on creative play and trauma-healing (Chase et al., 1999).

After the 2004 tsunami, a national plan for action was formulated in collaboration with the WHO Regional Office and local authorities (Mahoney et al., 2006). Several psychological measures were utilized for the survivors, such as not forcing individuals to vent their experiences, active listening, and not labelling survivors with psychiatric disorders like PTSD (Mahoney et al., 2006). In the early phase of rescue, surgical and medical supplies were ensured, followed by ensuring safe accommodation, pure water, and nutrition. After that, mental health supports, such as psychological first aid, were ensured.

The country has passed Disaster Preparedness Plans and Disaster Management Act (Sri Lanka Disaster Management Act No.13 of 2005, Mahoney et al., 2006). It prioritized some additional aspects, like pluralism, building resilience, and utilization of digital mental health services, to combat the sociopolitical disasters (Jayawickreme et al., 2025). For children, Happy/Sad Letter Box (HSLB) Project was tested and found effective (Commers et al., 2014). Individuals' inner positivity, spirituality, sharing thoughts, being engaged, and external support were identified as resilient factors after the tsunami (Ekanayake et al., 2013). Another study noted that utilization of enduring cultural practice and inner positivity is a resilient factor, while low spirituality is a risk factor for post-traumatic stress (Wickrama et al., 2017).

5 Conclusion

This chapter discusses the disaster, climate change, and their impact on mental health in three South Asian countries (Afghanistan, the Maldives, and Sri Lanka). Depending on their geographic locations and sociocultural milieu, these countries have their unique challenges related to disasters. Although both natural and human-made disasters are frequent in these countries, there is a scarcity of information on the mental health impact of disasters and culturally appropriate intervention measures. There is a need for further extensive research, and the international, regional, and local agencies of mental health, disaster, and climate change should prioritize addressing the mental health needs of disaster survivors in these low- and middle-income countries.

References

Akhundzadah, N. A. (2025). Earthquake risk severity and urgent need for disaster management in Afghanistan. *GeoHazards, 6*(1), 9. https://doi.org/10.3390/geohazards6010009

Arafat, S. M. Y., & Kar, S. K. (Eds.). (2024). *Access to mental health care in South Asia: Current status, potential challenges, and ways out*. Springer Nature. https://doi.org/10.1007/978-981-99-9153-2

Cameron, C. M., O'Leary, P. J., Lakhani, A., Osborne, J. M., de Souza, L., Hope, K., Naimi, M. S., Khan, H., Jawad, Q. S., & Majidi, S. (2021). Violence against children in Afghanistan: Community perspectives. *Journal of Interpersonal Violence, 36*(5–6), 2521–2540. https://doi.org/10.1177/0886260518760610

Catani, C., Jacob, N., Schauer, E., Kohila, M., & Neuner, F. (2008). Family violence, war, and natural disasters: A study of the effect of extreme stress on children's mental health in Sri Lanka. *BMC Psychiatry, 8*, 33. https://doi.org/10.1186/1471-244X-8-33

Chase, R., Doney, A., Sivayogan, S., Ariyaratne, V., Satkunanayagam, P., & Swaminathan, A. (1999). Mental health initiatives as peace initiatives in Sri Lankan schoolchildren affected by armed conflict. *Medicine, Conflict, and Survival, 15*(4), 379–393. https://doi.org/10.1080/13623699908409479

Commers, M. J., Morival, M., & Devries, M. W. (2014). Toward best-practice post-disaster mental health promotion for children: Sri Lanka. *Health Promotion International, 29*(1), 165–170. https://doi.org/10.1093/heapro/das047

D'Souza, R., & Singh, B. (2005). The mental health challenge in Sri Lanka from working within the disaster area. *World Psychiatry: Official Journal of the World Psychiatric Association (WPA), 4*(2), 68.

De Alwis, D., & Noy, I. (2019). The cost of being under the weather: Droughts, floods, and health-care costs in Sri Lanka. *Asian Development Review, 36*(2), 185–214.

Dey, R. K., Mansoor, S., Hilmy, A. I., et al. (2022). Emotional distress in COVID-19 patients in Maldives. *BMC Psychiatry, 22*, 184. https://doi.org/10.1186/s12888-022-03826-1

Dhimal, M., Bhandari, D., Dhimal, M. L., Kafle, N., Pyakurel, P., Mahotra, N., Akhtar, S., Ismail, T., Dhiman, R. C., Groneberg, D. A., Shrestha, U. B., & Müller, R. (2021). Impact of climate change on health and well-being of people in Hindu Kush Himalayan region: A narrative review. *Frontiers in Physiology, 12*. https://doi.org/10.3389/fphys.2021.651189

Dissanayake, L., Jabir, S., Shepherd, T., Helliwell, T., Selvaratnam, L., Jayaweera, K., Abeysinghe, N., Mallen, C., & Sumathipala, A. (2023). The aftermath of war; mental health, substance use and their correlates with social support and resilience among adolescents in a post-conflict region of Sri Lanka. *Child and Adolescent Psychiatry and Mental Health, 17*(1), 101. https://doi.org/10.1186/s13034-023-00648-1

Ekanayake, S., Prince, M., Sumathipala, A., Siribaddana, S., & Morgan, C. (2013). "We lost all we had in a second": Coping with grief and loss after a natural disaster. *World Psychiatry: Official Journal of the World Psychiatric Association (WPA), 12*(1), 69–75. https://doi.org/10.1002/wps.20018

Essar, M. Y., Nemat, A., Islam, Z., Ahmad, S., & Shah, J. (2022). Devastating earthquake in Afghanistan amid a humanitarian crisis: A call for action. *The Lancet. Global Health, 10*(9), e1244–e1245. https://doi.org/10.1016/S2214-109X(22)00318-7

Essar, M. Y., Wahdati, S., O'Sullivan, B., Nemat, A., & Blanchet, K. (2024). Cycles of disasters in Afghanistan: The urgent call for global solidarity. *PLOS Global Public Health, 4*(1), e0002751. https://doi.org/10.1371/journal.pgph.0002751

Eweida, R. S., Najeeb, F., Khonji, L. M., Bin Shalhoub, A. A., Ahmed El-Sayed Mohamed, M., & Ibrahim, N. (2024). Looking back and moving forward: A spatial-based pilot study of psychological security and social cohesion among Maldivian academics amid climate change. *Sustainability and Climate Change, 17*(4), 267–280. https://doi.org/10.1089/scc.2024.0092

Gunaratne, C., Kremer, P. J., Lewis, A. J., & Clarke, V. (2013). Trauma symptoms in children after the tsunami. *Sri Lanka Journal of Child Health, 42*(4), 192–199.

Herrera-Cano (MIB), C., & Herrera-Cano, A. (2016). Maldivian disaster risk management and climate change action in tourism sector: Lessons for the sustainable development agenda. In *Climate change and the 2030 corporate agenda for sustainable development* (Vol. 19, p. 0). Emerald Group Publishing Limited. doi:https://doi.org/10.1108/S2051-503020160000019006.

Hollifield, M., Hewage, C., Gunawardena, C. N., Kodituwakku, P., Bopagoda, K., & Weerarathnege, K. (2008). Symptoms and coping in Sri Lanka 20-21 months after the 2004 tsunami. *The British Journal of Psychiatry: The Journal of Mental Science, 192*(1), 39–44. https://doi.org/10.1192/bjp.bp.107.038422

Hossain, M. M., Purohit, N., Sultana, A., Ma, P., McKyer, E. L. J., & Ahmed, H. U. (2020). Prevalence of mental disorders in South Asia: An umbrella review of systematic reviews and meta-analyses. *Asian Journal of Psychiatry, 51*, 102041.

Husain, F., Anderson, M., Lopes Cardozo, B., Becknell, K., Blanton, C., Araki, D., & Vithana, E. K. (2011). Prevalence of war-related mental health conditions and association with displacement status in postwar Jaffna District, Sri Lanka. *JAMA, 306*(5), 522–531. https://doi.org/10.1001/jama.2011.1052

Hussaini, S. J., Ali, S. H., Syyeda Rahmat, Z., Islam, Z., & Tharwani, Z. H. (2022). Mental health impacts of earthquake on Afghans amidst humanitarian crisis. *Annals of Medicine and Surgery (2012), 81*, 104521. https://doi.org/10.1016/j.amsu.2022.104521

Ibrahim, A., & Hameed, A. (2006). Mental health and psychosocial response after the worst natural disaster in the history of the Maldives. *International Review of Psychiatry, 18*(6), 567–572. https://doi.org/10.1080/09540260601038431

Islam, Z., Rija, A., Mohanan, P., Qamar, K., Jahangir, K., Nawaz, F. A., & Essar, M. Y. (2022). Afghanistan's humanitarian crisis and its impacts on the mental health of healthcare workers during COVID-19. *Global Mental Health (Cambridge, England), 9*, 61–64. https://doi.org/10.1017/gmh.2022.3

Jayawickreme, N., Jayawickreme, E., McCaffrey, A. Z., & Thiruvarangan, M. (2025). Mental health futures in post-war Sri Lanka: Resilience, relational pluralism, and implementation pathways. *SSM-Mental Health*, 100465. https://doi.org/10.1016/j.ssmmh.2025.100465

Kaneda, Y., Ozaki, A., Hashemy, T., Shrestha, R., & Madadi, S. (2023). The importance of the Taliban and the International Community Collaboration in Building Support systems for experts working in earthquake-affected areas in Afghanistan-perspectives from a triple disaster experience in Fukushima. *Disaster Medicine and Public Health Preparedness, 17*, e265. https://doi.org/10.1017/dmp.2022.260

Kar, S. K., & Arafat, S. M. Y. (2025). Geriatric psychiatry in other south Asian countries: Afghanistan, Bhutan, the Maldives. In N. Kar, S. K. Kar, & S. M. Y. Arafat (Eds.), *Geriatric psychiatry in South Asia* (pp. 113–123). Springer Nature Singapore. https://doi.org/10.1007/978-981-96-7469 5_7

Kar, S. K., Parmar, A., & Arafat, S. M. Y. (2025). Forensic psychiatry and prison mental health in other south Asian countries (Afghanistan, Bhutan, and the Maldives). In A. Parmar, S. K. Kar, & S. M. Y. Arafat (Eds.), *Forensic psychiatry and prison mental health in South Asia* (pp. 97–106). Springer Nature Singapore. https://doi.org/10.1007/978-981-96-7206-6_7

Kelman, I., Ayeb-Karlsson, S., Rose-Clarke, K., Prost, A., Ronneberg, E., Wheeler, N., & Watts, N. (2021). A review of mental health and wellbeing under climate change in small

Island developing states (SIDS). *Environmental Research Letters, 16*(3), 033007. https://doi.org/10.1088/1748-9326/abe57d
Keraite, A., Sumathipala, A., Siriwardhana, C., Morgan, C., & Reininghaus, U. (2016). Exposure to conflict and disaster: A national survey on the prevalence of psychotic experiences in Sri Lanka. *Schizophrenia Research, 171*(1–3), 79–85. https://doi.org/10.1016/j.schres.2016.01.026
Kothari, U., Arnall, A., & Azfa, A. (2023). Disaster mobilities, temporalities, and recovery: Experiences of the tsunami in the Maldives. *Disasters, 47*(4), 1069–1089. https://doi.org/10.1111/disa.12578
Kovess-Masfety, V., Keyes, K., Karam, E., et al. (2021). A national survey on depressive and anxiety disorders in Afghanistan: A highly traumatized population. *BMC Psychiatry, 21*, 314. https://doi.org/10.1186/s12888-021-03273-4
Kovess-Masfety, V., Karam, E., Keyes, K., Sabawoon, A., & Sarwari, B. A. (2022). Access to care for mental health problems in Afghanistan: A national challenge. *International Journal of Health Policy and Management, 11*(8), 1442–1450. https://doi.org/10.34172/ijhpm.2021.46
Lawther, P. M. (2009). Community involvement in post disaster re-construction – case study of the British red cross Maldives recovery program. *International Journal of Strategic Property Management, 13*(2), 153–169. https://doi.org/10.3846/1648-715X.2009.13.153-169
Mahase, E. (2023). Afghanistan: 114 000 people need lifesaving healthcare after earthquakes, says WHO. *BMJ (Clinical Research Ed.), 383*, 2452. https://doi.org/10.1136/bmj.p2452
Mahoney, J., Chandra, V., Gambheera, H., De Silva, T., & Suveendran, T. (2006). Responding to the mental health and psychosocial needs of the people of Sri Lanka in disasters. *International Review of Psychiatry (Abingdon, England), 18*(6), 593–597. https://doi.org/10.1080/09540260601129206
Mallapaty, S. (2022). Deadly Afghanistan quake challenges scientists trying to study it. *Nature, 607*(7919), 433. https://doi.org/10.1038/d41586-022-01858-x
Masudi, M., Rahimi, A., Ejaz, E., Kargar, A. A., Hasin, B. A., & Shayan, N. A. (2025). Evaluating the effectiveness and challenges of climate change policies in Afghanistan. *Environmental Quality Management, 34*(4), e70086. https://doi.org/10.1002/tqem.70086
Mena, R., & Hilhorst, D. (2021). The (im)possibilities of disaster risk reduction in the context of high-intensity conflict: The case of Afghanistan. *Environmental Hazards, 20*(2), 188–208. https://doi.org/10.1080/17477891.2020.1771250
Mohamed, A., & Mansoor, S. (2025). Challenges and opportunities in the mental health landscape of the Maldives. *Australasian Psychiatry: Bulletin of Royal Australian and New Zealand College of Psychiatrists, 33*(2), 195–196. https://doi.org/10.1177/10398562241289879
Mohammadi, M., Jafari, H., Etemadi, M., Dalugoda, Y., Ali, H. M., Phung, H., Ahmadvand, A., Dwirahmadi, F., Barnes, P., & Chu, C. (2023). Health problems of increasing man-made and climate-related disasters on forcibly displaced populations: A scoping review on global evidence. *Disaster Medicine and Public Health Preparedness, 17*, e537. https://doi.org/10.1017/dmp.2023.159
Mohd Saleem, S., Shoib, S., Dazhamyar, A. R., & Chandradasa, M. (2021). Afghanistan: Decades of collective trauma, ongoing humanitarian crises, Taliban rulers, and mental health of the displaced population. *Asian Journal of Psychiatry, 65*, 102854. https://doi.org/10.1016/j.ajp.2021.102854
Mushwani, H., & Ahmad, M. M. (2025). Disaster management in Afghanistan. In *Routledge handbook of public policy in the global south*. Routledge.
Mushwani, H., Arabzai, A., Safi, L., Chaiya, C., & Sahak, K. (2025). Evaluation of gender-based challenges during natural disasters in the central region of Afghanistan: A case study of Parwan Province. *World Development Perspectives, 37*, 100646. https://doi.org/10.1016/j.wdp.2024.100646
Naylor, A. K. (2015). Island morphology, reef resources, and development paths in the Maldives. *Progress in Physical Geography: Earth and Environment, 39*(6), 728–749. https://doi.org/10.1177/0309133315598269

Neuner, F., Schauer, E., Catani, C., Ruf, M., & Elbert, T. (2006). Post-tsunami stress: A study of posttraumatic stress disorder in children living in three severely affected regions in Sri Lanka. *Journal of Traumatic Stress, 19*(3), 339–347. https://doi.org/10.1002/jts.20121

Neyazi, A., Mohammadi, A. Q., Razaqi, N., Rahimi, B. A., Sifat, S., Rahimy, N., Tareen, Z., Mehmood, Q., Satapathy, P., & Griffiths, M. D. (2024). Health survey on anxiety, depression, and stress in Afghanistan: A large-scale cross-sectional study amid ongoing challenges. *Discover Mental Health, 4*(1), 38. https://doi.org/10.1007/s44192-024-00090-5

Nomura, A., Honda, S., Hayakawa, H., Amarasinghe, S., & Aoyagi, K. (2010). Post-traumatic stress disorder among senior victims of tsunami-affected areas in southern Sri Lanka. *Acta Medica Nagasakiensia, 55*(1), 41–46. https://doi.org/10.11343/amn.55.41

Nylen, A. J., Deluca, G., Bala, B., Charvis, J. S., Tanzer, J. R., Bah, O., & Levine, A. C. (2025). Then, we lost everything: Afghan refugee mental health challenges post-2021 evacuation. *Journal of Immigrant and Minority Health, 27*(2), 251–257. https://doi.org/10.1007/s10903-024-01640-3

Pardasani, M. (2006). Tsunami reconstruction and redevelopment in the Maldives: A case study of community participation and social action. *Disaster Prevention and Management, 15*(1), 79–91. https://doi.org/10.1108/09653560610654257

Přívara, A., & Přívarová, M. (2019). Nexus between climate change, displacement and conflict: Afghanistan case. *Sustainability, 11*(20), 5586.

Rahimi, Y. A., & Azimi, S. (2012). War and the crisis of mental health in Afghanistan. *International Psychiatry: Bulletin of the Board of International Affairs of the Royal College of Psychiatrists, 9*(3), 55–57.

Rajmil, D., Morales, L., Aira, T., & Cardona Valles, M. (2022). Afghanistan: A multidimensional crisis. *Peace Review, 34*(1), 41–50. https://doi.org/10.1080/10402659.2022.2023428

Ramozi, M., Kaneda, Y., Barati, H., Ozaki, A., & Mousavi, S. H. (2023). Earthquakes and Taliban decrees: The plight of afghan women and children. *Cureus, 15*(11), e48663. https://doi.org/10.7759/cureus.48663

Ramozi, M., Barati, H., Kaneda, Y., Ozaki, A., & Kotera, Y. (2024). Herat's catastrophe: Earthquakes deepen Afghanistan's healthcare crisis. *JMA Journal, 7*(4), 603–604. https://doi.org/10.31662/jmaj.2024-0002

Ranasinghe, P. D., & Levy, B. R. (2007). Prevalence of and sex disparities in posttraumatic stress disorder in an internally displaced Sri Lankan population 6 months after the 2004 tsunami. *Disaster Medicine and Public Health Preparedness, 1*(1), 34–41. https://doi.org/10.1097/DMP.0b013e318068fbb7

Ranasinghe, P. D., Zhang, X., Hwang, J., Ranasinghe, P. M., Karunathilake, I. M., & Everly, G. S. (2023). PTSD and depression 8 years after the 2004 tsunami in Sri Lanka. *Disaster Medicine and Public Health Preparedness, 17*, e183. https://doi.org/10.1017/dmp.2022.73

Razjouyan, K., Farokhi, H., Qaderi, F., Qaderi, P., Masoumi, S. J., Shah, A., Pourhoseingholi, M. A., Ahmadi, A., Lucero-Prisno, D. E. I., Ozaki, A., Kotera, Y., Shah, J., Negin, F., & Qaderi, S. (2022). War experience, daily stressors and mental health among the inter-Taliban generation young adults in northern Afghanistan: A cross-sectional school-based study. *Frontiers in Psychiatry, 13*, 877934. https://doi.org/10.3389/fpsyt.2022.877934

Rodrigo, A., & Liyanage, N. (2017). Disaster and mental health: The role of Sri Lankan psychiatrists. *Sri Lanka Journal of Psychiatry, 8*(1), 1–2. https://doi.org/10.4038/sljpsyc.v8i1.8131

Sadiqi, Z., Trigunarsyah, B., & Coffey, V. (2017). A framework for community participation in post-disaster housing reconstruction projects: A case of Afghanistan. *International Journal of Project Management, 35*(5), 900–912. https://doi.org/10.1016/j.ijproman.2016.11.008

Safi, L., Mujeeb, M., Sahak, K., Mushwani, H., & Hashmi, S. K. (2024). Climate change impacts and threats on basic livelihood resources, food security and social stability in Afghanistan. *GeoJournal, 89*(2), 85. https://doi.org/10.1007/s10708-024-11077-8

Sakamoto, A., Nishiya, K., Guo, X., Sugimoto, A., Nagasaki, W., & Doi, K. (2022). Mitigating impacts of climate change Induced Sea level rise by infrastructure development: Case of the Maldives. *Journal of Disaster Research, 17*(3), 327–334. https://doi.org/10.20965/jdr.2022.p0327

Samsoor, A. A., & Stanikzai, M. H. (2024). Depression, anxiety and stress symptoms among afghan healthcare workers: A cross-sectional analytical study. *Indian Journal Of Occupational And Environmental Medicine, 28*(2), 154–158. https://doi.org/10.4103/ijoem.ijoem_34_24

Sattar, S. A., Musthafa, M., Rushdhy, I., & Pal, I. (2022). National perspectives of COVID-19 in the Maldives. In *Pandemic risk, response, and resilience* (pp. 157–172). https://doi.org/10.1016/B978-0-323-99277-0.00013-9

Schwartz, L., Lane, H., & Hassanpoor, Z. (2023). Overview and understanding of mental health and psychosocial support in Afghanistan. *International Health, 15*(5), 601–607. https://doi.org/10.1093/inthealth/ihad055

Shepherd, A. (2023). Thousands killed in Afghanistan quake. *BMJ (Clinical Research ed.), 383*, 2333. https://doi.org/10.1136/bmj.p2333

Shoib, S., Hussaini, S. S., Nazari, S. K., & Saeed, F. (2024). Mental healthcare in Afghanistan. In S. M. Y. Arafat & S. K. Kar (Eds.), *Access to mental health care in South Asia* (pp. 17–27). Springer Nature Singapore. https://doi.org/10.1007/978-981-99-9153-2_2

Shokory, J. A. N., Schaefli, B., & Lane, S. N. (2023). Water resources of Afghanistan and related hazards under rapid climate warming: A review. *Hydrological Sciences Journal, 68*(3), 507–525. https://doi.org/10.1080/02626667.2022.2159411

Silove, D., & Ventevogel, P. (2022). Living through interminable adversity: The mental health of the afghan people. *World Psychiatry: Official Journal of the World Psychiatric Association (WPA), 21*(1), 55–56. https://doi.org/10.1002/wps.20955

Siriwardhana, C., & Wickramage, K. (2014). Conflict, forced displacement and health in Sri Lanka: A review of the research landscape. *Conflict and Health, 8*(1), 22. https://doi.org/10.1186/1752-1505-8-22

Siriwardhana, C., Pannala, G., Siribaddana, S., Sumathipala, A., & Stewart, R. (2013). Impact of exposure to conflict, tsunami and mental disorders on school absenteeism: Findings from a national sample of Sri Lankan children aged 12-17 years. *BMC Public Health, 13*, 560. https://doi.org/10.1186/1471-2458-13-560

Somasundaram, D. (2010). Collective trauma in the Vanni- a qualitative inquiry into the mental health of the internally displaced due to the civil war in Sri Lanka. *International Journal of Mental Health Systems, 4*, 22. https://doi.org/10.1186/1752-4458-4-22

Somasundaram, D. (2013). Recent disasters in Sri Lanka: Lessons learned. *The Psychiatric Clinics of North America, 36*(3), 321–338. https://doi.org/10.1016/j.psc.2013.05.001

Sovacool, B. K. (2012a). Expert views of climate change adaptation in the Maldives. *Climatic Change, 114*(2), 295–300. https://doi.org/10.1007/s10584-011-0392-2

Sovacool, B. K. (2012b). Perceptions of climate change risks and resilient Island planning in the Maldives. *Mitigation and Adaptation Strategies for Global Change, 17*(7), 731–752. https://doi.org/10.1007/s11027-011-9341-7

Sriskandarajah, V., Neuner, F., & Catani, C. (2015). Parental care protects traumatized Sri Lankan children from internalizing behavior problems. *BMC Psychiatry, 15*, 203. https://doi.org/10.1186/s12888-015-0583-x

Stojanov, R., Duží, B., Kelman, I., Němec, D., & Procházka, D. (2017). Local perceptions of climate change impacts and migration patterns in Malé, Maldives. *The Geographical Journal, 183*(4), 370–385. https://doi.org/10.1111/geoj.12177

Suppasri, A., Goto, K., Muhari, A., Ranasinghe, P., Riyaz, M., Affan, M., Mas, E., Yasuda, M., & Imamura, F. (2015). A decade after the 2004 Indian Ocean Tsunami: The progress in disaster preparedness and future challenges in Indonesia, Sri Lanka, Thailand and the Maldives. *Pure and Applied Geophysics, 172*(12), 3313–3341. https://doi.org/10.1007/s00024-015-1134-6

Tay, A. K. (2024). Hope in hardship: Charting a new course for mental health in Afghanistan. *BJPsych Open, 10*(3), e102. https://doi.org/10.1192/bjo.2024.66

Ullah, H., Ahmad, H., Tharwani, Z. H., Shaeen, S. K., Rahmat, Z. S., & Essar, M. Y. (2023). Intergenerational trauma: A silent contributor to mental health deterioration in Afghanistan. *Brain and Behavior, 13*(4), e2905. https://doi.org/10.1002/brb3.2905

Vig, S. (2025). Climate change and mental health of women in developing countries. *Climatic Change, 178*(6), 118. https://doi.org/10.1007/s10584-025-03960-1

Wesemann, U., Renner, K. H., Rowlands, K., Köhler, K., Hüttermann, N., & Himmerich, H. (2024). Incidence of mental disorders in soldiers deployed to Afghanistan who have or have not experienced a life-threatening military incident-a quasi-experimental cohort study. *Frontiers in Public Health, 12*, 1357836. https://doi.org/10.3389/fpubh.2024.1357836

WHO. (2024a). Afghanistan. Datadot. https://data.who.int/countries/004

WHO. (2024b). *Maldives*. Datadot. https://data.who.int/countries/462

WHO. (2024c). *Sri Lanka*. Datadot. https://data.who.int/countries/144

WHO. (2025a). *Afghanistan*. https://www.who.int/about/accountability/results/who-results-report-2024-2025/region-EMRO/2024/afghanistan

WHO. (2025b). *Country profile: Maldives South East Asia Region*. https://www.who.int/about/accountability/results/who-results-report-2024-2025/region-SEARO/2024/maldives

Wickrama, K. A., & Kaspar, V. (2007). Family context of mental health risk in Tsunami-exposed adolescents: Findings from a pilot study in Sri Lanka. *Social Science & Medicine (1982), 64*(3), 713–723. https://doi.org/10.1016/j.socscimed.2006.09.031

Wickrama, T., Wickrama, K. A. S., Banford, A., & Lambert, J. (2017). PTSD symptoms among tsunami exposed mothers in Sri Lanka: The role of disaster exposure, culturally specific coping strategies, and recovery efforts. *Anxiety, Stress, & Coping, 30*(4), 415–427. https://doi.org/10.1080/10615806.2016.1271121

Wickrama, T., Merten, M. J., Wickrama, K. A. S., & Terrell, A. (2024). Adolescents' tsunami exposure and mental health consequences: Protective role of cultural coping strategies. *International Journal of Environmental Research and Public Health, 21*(6), 756. https://doi.org/10.3390/ijerph21060756

Yolchi, J., & Wang, H. (2025). The impact of climate change on household dietary diversity in Afghanistan. *Climate Risk Management, 47*, 100687. https://doi.org/10.1016/j.crm.2025.100687

Yolchi, J., Wang, H., & Pede, V. (2024). Impact of floods on food security in rural Afghanistan. *International Journal of Disaster Risk Reduction, 112*, 104746. https://doi.org/10.1016/j.ijdrr.2024.104746

Chapter 9
Mental Health Aspects of Famine, Flood and Cyclones

Joydeep Majumder, Indranil Saha, Writama Guha, and Neha Dahiya

1 South Asia and Vulnerability to Famine, Flood and Cyclones

The South Asian region, comprising Afghanistan, Bangladesh, Bhutan, India, Maldives, Nepal, Pakistan and Sri Lanka, is uniquely bounded from north to south by the Himalayan range, the Thar Desert, the Indo-Gangetic Plain, the Indian Ocean, the Bay of Bengal and the Arabian Sea. The distinct geographical features in South Asia limit the lateral exchange of oceanic and continental air masses and modify the climate to create highly variable and often extreme climatic conditions across South Asia. The region is thus marked by considerable spatial and temporal variation in temperature, rainfall and humidity, leading to climatic challenges, such as floods, droughts and heatwaves, impacting agriculture, infrastructure and human livelihoods.

J. Majumder (✉)
Scientist E, ICMR-Regional Medical Research Centre, Bhubaneswar, India
e-mail: majumder.j@gov.in

I. Saha
Scientist E, ICMR-National Institute for Research in Bacterial Infections, and Associate Professor, Faculty of Medical Research, Academy of Scientific and Innovative Research (AcSIR), Kolkata, India

W. Guha
Project Technical Support III, ICMR-Centre for Ageing and Mental Health, Kolkata, India

N. Dahiya
Scientist D, Indian Council of Medical Research, New Delhi, India

N. Kar et al. (eds.), *Climate Change, Disaster and Mental Health in South Asia*, South Asian Perspectives in Mental Health and Psychology,
https://doi.org/10.1007/978-981-95-3690-0_9

1.1 Famines

Climate-related famine, until the last century, posed a serious risk to South Asia, primarily due to the region's geographical susceptibility and reliance on agriculture that depends on monsoon rains. While traditional famine is rare in South Asia today, food insecurity and crises still arise due to climate variability and extreme weather events. In the history of South Asia, the most notable famines are the Great Bengal Famine of 1770, the Bengal Famine of 1943 and the 1974 Bangladesh Famine. Although these famines had socioeconomic underpinnings beyond direct climatic causes, major famines in India between 1870 and 2016 have also been linked to soil moisture drought (Mishra et al., 2019), rising population, low crop yields and inadequate irrigation (FAO, 2010). Droughts are common across South Asia, especially across Afghanistan, Pakistan, Nepal, Sri Lanka and India, and are commonly associated with famines (Kafle, 2017).

1.2 Floods and Cyclones

South Asia has been the epicentre of weather-related hazards, frequently experiencing floods, cyclones, glacial lake outbursts and river overflows. Over the last three decades, these countries have experienced an upsurge in the frequency and intensity of such events, particularly during monsoon and snowmelt seasons. These events are intensified by climate change, deforestation and inadequate infrastructure, affecting millions across the region. Most townships and urban cities in the developing countries of South Asia are regarded as flood risk areas (Shah et al., 2020). India, Nepal and Bangladesh reeled under massive flooding during the last decade. The extensive coastlines of India, Bangladesh and Sri Lanka are particularly vulnerable to cyclones. Even though cyclones cause acute devastation on their own, the events are often accompanied by flooding, exacerbating the ill impact on regional residents. Cyclone-induced storm surges originate in the southern and central parts of the Bay of Bengal and crash down on the low-lying coastal areas of these countries, affecting thousands of lives. Meanwhile, the Maldives faces severe threats from climate change, particularly sea level rise and coastal erosion, due to its low elevation, compounded by extreme weather events and tidal interactions (Kafle, 2017; Wadey et al., 2017).

Although not the most frequently occurring, Glacial Lake Outburst Floods (GLOFs) are a significant cause of floods in the Himalayan areas of India, Pakistan and Bhutan, especially endangering the Hindu-Kush Himalayan Region. Similar outbursts have caused massive impacts in Pakistan (Barsuwat Glacier in 2016; Shishper Glacier in 2020), Nepal (Pokhara in 2012; Lower Barun Glacial Lake in 2020) and Bhutan (Thorthormi Glacier in 2018). These events threaten mountain communities while having cascading impacts on surrounding low-lying regions. The drainage of water from elevated glacial lakes inundates valleys, damages transport networks and displaces populations, compounding socioeconomic vulnerabilities.

To the extent of disaster management, all South Asian nations have formal disaster management frameworks, often led by the national disaster management authorities (Kafle, 2017). These systems operate under the broader guidance of the Sendai Framework for Disaster Risk Reduction (2015–2030) (UNDRR, 2015). For the Global South, building a resilient disaster management structure is a critical challenge with its lack of socioeconomic resources and heightened climatic vulnerability.

2 Effects of Extreme Weather Events in South Asia

2.1 Vulnerable Population and Predisposing Factors

All inhabitants experiencing extreme weather events can be termed as vulnerable populations. However, the effects of climatic events are not distributed equally across the population. Children, women, older adults, neglected communities, homeless individuals and those with pre-existing mental health conditions (Majumder et al., 2024) are disproportionately affected as some of the most vulnerable to the erratic occurrences of weather events, in terms of mental health effects.

Although disaster vulnerability is a multifaceted concept, the risk factors are linked to subsequent psychological impairment (Deglon et al., 2023). Vulnerability to adverse mental health effects is often intensified by pre-existing conditions, such as exposure to family adversities, chronic stress or violence prior to extreme weather events. Among survivors, post-event factors such as loss of livelihood, limited social support, spiritual struggle and declining physical health increase dependence on others. These serve as key mediators in the development of psychological distress following such events. In certain cases, gendered vulnerability during disasters is exacerbated by cultural norms that expect women to prioritize the care of family members over their own safety. This responsibility makes it harder for women to reach safe places during extreme events, as they are expected to evacuate children and older family members first (Fatema et al., 2021).

Among others, evidence shows that children are disproportionately affected by extreme weather events, facing physical issues like injuries and malnutrition. Equally, mental health challenges such as trauma and anxiety, disruptions to education due to displacement, school destruction and poverty-driven opportunistic earning are outcomes in them (Edwards et al., 2021). These recurrent events significantly hinder their physical, cognitive and social growth. Older adults experiencing physical decline face additional challenges during weather events, including limited mobility that hinders evacuation to safer areas. Lack of essential resources such as medications and transportation, combined with social isolation and limited support networks, exacerbates their challenges. These factors contribute to heightened mental health issues, including anxiety, depression, post-traumatic stress disorder (PTSD) and sleep disturbances, underscoring the need for age-sensitive disaster preparedness and response strategies (Song et al., 2025).

Disaster-induced food insecurity arises when extreme weather events disrupt livelihoods, limiting access to sufficient, safe and nutritious food, thereby threatening health, well-being and long-term recovery of affected communities. As global scientific literature underscores a significant negative correlation between food insecurity and mental health outcomes (Ae-Ngibise et al., 2021), the psychosocial lived experience of food insecurity is nuanced and warrants focussed attention and evaluation. Research found that women from severely food-insecure households in Nepal are at a significantly higher risk of generalized anxiety disorder (GAD) and panic attacks (Southard & Randell, 2024). Likewise, socioeconomic instability, increased violence and aggression due to economic stress, disrupted schooling, limited access to healthcare and post-disaster migration tend to affect entire communities, with certain groups being disproportionately impacted.

2.2 *Psychological Impact*

Research on mental health effects of extreme events highlights two key areas: peritraumatic distress, associated with acute reactions and PTSD, and later onset and enduring distress, disrupting survivors' everyday functioning (Cianconi et al., 2020). Catastrophic occurrences like floods and cyclones thus expose survivors to states of helplessness, leaving them highly vulnerable to lasting somatic symptoms and psychosocial sequelae and mental injuries (Suar et al., 2024). The experience of extreme weather events is so severely traumatic that not only are residents scarred psychologically, socially and economically, but even tourists who experienced such disasters are left with a sustained impact, reporting fear, fear of recurrence, nightmares and a sense of helplessness (Majumder et al., 2024). It is often observed that extreme weather events lead to inaccessibility to food and often trigger panic buying and hoarding, driven by perceived scarcity, fear, insecurity and social influence (Arafat et al., 2020). While storing dry food is a practical approach, excessive hoarding exacerbates existing shortages during such events. Therefore, in the recent flood crisis in Manipur, India, authorities took steps to restrict hoarding to prevent artificial scarcity and price inflation.

2.2.1 Famine

Droughts and famines are historically interlinked, often resulting in widespread food insecurity and long-lasting psychological trauma. Prenatal exposure to famine has been associated with increased risks of developing mental disorders such as schizophrenia and depression in adulthood (Eichenauer & Ehlert, 2023). Interestingly, individuals who experienced the Great Chinese Famine during adolescence were found to be at heightened risk for late-life depression (Guo et al., 2024). These outcomes illustrate how the psychosocial repercussions of such crises are embedded in the socioeconomic and psychological fabric of communities. Literature also reports a range of mental health outcomes and elevated suicide risk among older populations facing famines (Sena et al., 2018).

Farmers in drought-prone regions like Marathwada, India, face severe mental health challenges. Prolonged droughts heighten the risk of depression and anxiety, often leading to forced migration and community displacement (Cianconi et al., 2020). Crop failure, mounting debt and economic insecurity contribute to high rates of farmer suicides. Survivors often suffer from substantial psychological distress, manifested through headaches, sadness, fatigue and mental fog, which hinders their economic recovery (Bhise et al., 2019). Needless to say, these make the path to economic survival even more challenging for the struggling families, intensifying the vicious cycles of poverty. While climate-related famines have largely been controlled in the twenty-first century, millions of children in Afghanistan still suffer from malnutrition due to severe food shortages. A study in Kabul found that 90% of food-insecure women showed signs of depression, anxiety or high stress (Zahidi et al., 2022). These figures underscore the gendered and intergenerational burden of food-related crises.

2.2.2 Flood and Cyclones

The severity of mental health impacts resulting from extreme weather events such as floods and cyclones has been well documented (Majumder et al., 2024; Patwary et al., 2024), with evidence linking these events to a wide range of psychopathological outcomes, including anxiety, depression, post-traumatic stress disorder, substance abuse and suicidal ideation (Cianconi et al., 2020).

Coastal regions of Bangladesh and India are highly susceptible to floods and cyclones. Kar et al. found that the fear of death experienced during 2019 Cyclone Fani was a significant factor linked to the potential development of PTSD in its aftermath (Kar et al., 2022). Similarly, following 2020 Cyclone Amphan, cyclone-induced moderate-to-severe mental health symptoms, including over 10% rate of suicidal ideation, were reported (Hossain et al., 2021). Literature reveals strong links between economic loss, food insecurity and poor mental health outcomes, with income loss and lack of food significantly worsening psychological distress after extreme weather events. It is noteworthy that significant income loss can exacerbate household food insecurity, thereby compounding the impact of both factors on deteriorating mental health outcomes. The low-lying coastal areas are particularly affected by flooding, which leads to saline water intrusion into agricultural fields, degrading soil fertility and disrupting cultivation for extended periods. As a direct consequence, floods lead to grief, displacement and psychological stress due to the loss of lives and possessions (Cianconi et al., 2020).

In addition to people experiencing mental health challenges after disasters, children often retain disaster memories more deeply, potentially leading to long-term psychological consequences. Older adults' restrictive mobility hinders free movement and limits access to essential resources, including medications, transportation and aid. These vulnerabilities, coupled with social isolation, limited support networks and inadequate information, lead to increased rates of common mental disorders among older adults.

While grief is a natural response to loss, survivors of extreme weather events often experience it with varying intensity and duration. Psychosocial support must consider factors such as survivor's guilt, substance use, mental illness and suicidal ideation when addressing mental health needs (Math et al., 2015). Beyond materialistic losses, the emotional toll of losing loved ones can be overwhelming, making it even harder for individuals to cope with other forms of loss. A systematic review found multiple cyclone and flood studies reporting deaths of kin (Majumder et al., 2024). Such bereavement raises risks for psychiatric disorders like mood, anxiety and substance use (Keyes et al., 2014).

While scientific research has focussed much more on the immediate impact of extreme events, especially in terms of classical mental disorders like PTSD, anxiety and mood disorders, the psychosocial impact of these events is felt for longer periods. Besides, emerging climate-related emotional responses such as 'eco-anxiety' (apprehension and stress about anticipated threats to salient ecosystems) and 'ecological grief' (grief in relation to ecological loss) are being documented. These phenomena reflect a deeper, enduring psychological burden associated with the growing frequency and severity of climate events globally (Patwary et al., 2024). Research shows that ecological anxiety and grief affect groups unequally, with those reliant on land-based livelihoods being most vulnerable (Cunsolo et al., 2020). In South Asia, where agrarian economies dominate, this vulnerability is heightened. Particularly, women and children are at increased violence and risks of abuse in emergency housing, among families facing food and shelter insecurity (Seddighi et al., 2021; Thurston et al., 2021), emphasizing the effective monitoring and support systems to safeguard mental health and overall well-being.

Meanwhile, in the Maldives, despite being highly vulnerable to sea level rise due to its low elevation, it was the 2004 tsunami that triggered the establishment of a formal disaster management system. However, mental health remains an underexplored area in the disaster context. Key challenges include governance issues, limited access to services, a shortage of trained professionals, weak preventive strategies and a lack of research in this domain (Mohamed & Mansoor, 2025).

2.3 Case Studies

This section explores key case studies of extreme weather events, highlighting their multifaceted impacts on affected populations, with a particular focus on psychosocial consequences, community resilience and gaps in disaster preparedness and post-disaster management.

2.3.1 Kedarnath, India 2013 Flash Flood

The Glacial Lake Outburst Flood (GLOF) that triggered the 2013 Kedarnath flash flood in Uttarakhand, India, remains one of the most catastrophic and unexpected climatic disasters in the region's history. The disaster was precipitated by a combination of unprecedented rainfall, sudden glacial lake bursts and terrain instability. Entire villages were washed away, especially in and around the Kedarnath Valley, resulting in over 5000 deaths, thousands missing and more than 100,000 people stranded. Infrastructural losses included roads, bridges and homes, alongside irreversible damage to the region's ecological balance. Beyond the physical destruction, the disaster deeply impacted the psychological well-being of survivors. A study revealed increased prevalence of anxiety, depression and PTSD among residents, particularly those who lost family members or witnessed traumatic events. Many survivors struggled with survivor's guilt, disrupted livelihoods and persistent fear of future disasters. The study emphasized that while rescue and rehabilitation efforts were mobilized, mental health support needs to be structured, integrating psychosocial care into disaster response policies and ensuring long-term psychological services (Parmar & Shanker, 2016). The Kedarnath disaster highlighted the critical need for community-based mental health preparedness in future climate and disaster response strategies.

2.3.2 Southern Sri Lanka 2017 Flood

In May 2017, the southern regions of Sri Lanka faced a devastating flood, exacerbated by the arrival of a precursor weather system linked to Cyclone Mora and torrential monsoon rains. The resulting flash floods and landslides wreaked havoc across several southern districts. The disaster affected over 700,000 inhabitants, displacing thousands and leaving hundreds either dead or missing. Critical infrastructure, including roads, bridges and electricity lines, was damaged, and widespread farming and property losses further strained the affected communities. Beyond the physical toll, it had long-lasting psychosocial effects on the survivors, particularly among children and families who lost their homes and loved ones. Research on the survivors in the relief camps revealed various psychosocial challenges such as interpersonal conflicts, stress and anxiety, exacerbated by overcrowded conditions and lack of privacy (Amarakoon et al., 2024). An editorial in the *Sri Lanka Journal of Psychiatry* emphasized the crucial role of mental health professionals in disaster scenarios (Rodrigo & Liyanage, 2017). These findings underscore the importance of incorporating mental health support into disaster preparedness and response strategies to address the psychological well-being of affected populations.

2.3.3 Northwest Pakistan 2022 Flood

In South Asia, Pakistan is highly flood-prone, with vulnerability intensified by sudden rainfall from the Suleman Mountains and recurring floods along the Indus River. The catastrophic 2022 flood affected nearly one million people; claimed over 1400 lives; injured 12,700 individuals; and damaged over 1.17 million homes, exposing deeply rooted structural vulnerabilities and gendered risks. Research reported a profound mental health impact on affected populations, particularly women, underscoring a gendered dimension of vulnerability. The study attributes this disparity to multiple intersecting factors, including limited mobility, neglect in rehabilitation efforts, heightened susceptibility to disease and food insecurity. These findings highlight the urgent need for gender-sensitive disaster response frameworks and underscore how socioeconomic and structural inequalities amplify the psychological and physical toll of climate-induced adversities (Ahmad et al., 2025).

Two poignant references from flood survivors in Pakistan reflect the psychosocial toll of disaster and the underlying systemic gaps in post-disaster response. One survivor shared, 'the flood disaster was a catastrophic situation and the social expectations had created a situation of trials and tribulations. I felt my life was not worth living and I tried to rely on myself to come out of this catastrophic situation because I was neglected at every step of rehabilitation'. Another echoed, 'Self-done is well done. No one cares about you unless you stand up for yourself'. These testimonies highlight the deep vulnerabilities of communities to disaster risk in the region, as well as pervasive inadequacies in the post-disaster management system. This sentiment shows growing self-reliance, with spiritual beliefs, religious coping and past disaster experiences helping people adjust emotionally after floods.

2.4 Resilience Strategies and Adaptive Behaviours

In the face of increasing devastation caused by climate change, the global community has prioritized action plans, checking and controlling the emission of harmful agents into the environment (e.g. Kyoto Protocol, 1997; Paris Agreement, 2015). These efforts at mitigation are sustained efforts with long-term goals, while communities and policymakers exposed to chronic recurrences of these disasters are learning how to respond to such events (Haque et al., 2022). Community efforts are closely linked to individual resilience, as seen in the 2004 Andaman and Nicobar Tsunami, where strong family ties, social support, altruism and spirituality helped survivors cope (Math et al., 2008). Even though climatically vulnerable communities require critical external support (socioeconomic, political, structural) and are even seen relying on individual resilience, community support forms the backbone of shaping disaster management strategies from both disaster survivors and policymakers in South Asia. Resilience as an individual characteristic is an important factor in determining adaptation and recovery post-disaster.

In South Asian nations, where collectivist societal cultures are deeply ingrained (Gilmoor et al., 2019), coping mechanisms and resilience strategies in the face of devastating extreme weather events, be it cyclones, floods or famines, are shaped by a synergistic blend of cultural norms, community-based practices and institutional support systems. These collective approaches foster solidarity, shared recovery and adaptive responses that are both immediate and long-term. Religious and spiritual beliefs often serve as important sources of psychological support before, during and in the aftermath of extreme weather events. Reliance on prayer, rituals and faith often serves as a sense of emotional support amid uncertainty and loss. It fosters inner resilience while strengthening the communal bonds through shared beliefs and collective rituals. Pre-existing religious beliefs and spirituality among Pakistani women played a crucial role in recovery after the 2022 flood (Ahmad et al., 2025).

The role of social support or social connections is crucial to mitigate the harmful effects and benefit post-disaster recovery among communities (Dinh et al., 2021; Sadri et al., 2018). Informal care, such as food sharing, arrangements of alternative housing and emotional encouragement, is provided by the community members, thereby raising social cohesion and an easier return to normalcy. Lived experiences of disasters provide lessons for the future, which are transmitted through generations and sustained as part of indigenous knowledge in the community. Thus, despite topographical hardships in South Asia, social cohesiveness is nurtured across generations as an inherent strength within the community. Community's traditional and indigenous adaptive architecture, for example, raised homes, food storage methods, weather pattern observation and embankment maintenance, equip them to anticipate potential hazards and strengthen their resilience against recurring extreme weather events in the region. Local administrations and nongovernmental organizations (NGOs) play vital roles in disaster response by coordinating aid, issuing early warnings and supporting resilience-building. Their efforts, ranging from trauma counselling to livelihood training, help reduce stigma around mental health and foster sustainable recovery in disaster-affected South Asian communities, especially among vulnerable and marginalized populations.

Disaster management frameworks across South Asia have structured collaborative coordination between federal, state and local administration, NGOs and community members. The countries have separate bodies specifically created to focus on disaster management that play the leading role in disaster management efforts (e.g. Department of Disaster Management and Cyclone Preparedness Programme in Bangladesh, Department of Disaster Management in Bhutan, National Disaster Management Council in Maldives and National Disaster Management Authority in India). While we deliberate on resource development and training, literature reports the availability of disaster management training manuals across most South Asian nations. However, structured training in organizational practices facilitating systematic learning in disaster management needs to be more cohesive. In Bangladesh, participation in training initiatives on disaster preparedness was limited, and coherence among community members would boost their participation (Paul et al., 2022). Thus, a cohesive plan actively involving the local communities, stakeholders and the local administration is essential. Such inclusive collaboration can effectively implement disaster management plans which would be inclusive, adaptive and sustainable over time.

It is well recognized that in the aftermath of disasters, providing immediate physical relief and support takes precedence; thus, mental health often becomes a secondary concern. Beyond this, persistent stigma, limited mental health awareness and societal reluctance to seek professional help hamper timely psychological support. Moreover, many developing nations grapple with an unequal distribution of trained mental health resources and fragmented implementation of mental health policies, which hinder equitable access to mental healthcare (Munikrishnappa et al., 2024). Addressing mental health in post-disaster contexts, thus, requires a paradigm shift that elevates psychological well-being as an explicit component of disaster response.

3 Current Challenges

3.1 Disaster Vulnerability, Preparedness and Interventions

For the Global South, building a resilient disaster management structure is a critical challenge with its socio-spatial, as well as socio-economic, configuration and heightened climatic vulnerability. In the context of the Sendai Framework, South Asia's disaster management prioritizes hydrometeorological hazards like floods, salinity intrusion and glacial melt, due to the region's high mountain ranges and extensive coastlines. The model uses a mix of structural (e.g. embankments) and nonstructural (e.g. community guidelines) measures. Nonstructural measures such as timely, reliable information are especially crucial for minimizing agricultural losses, which are the most common impacts following disasters (Uchiyama et al., 2021).

While robust disaster management is essential, community-level adaptation strategies equally contribute to strengthening climate resilience in South Asia. Literature emphasizes that programmes engaging local communities at the grassroots level are cost-effective and efficient. Building climate resilience also helps mitigate economic losses, which are a major cause of post-disaster distress. Their poignant reminder captures this reality: 'Even if they survive the violent wind or water, they still face gradual loss of livelihood; gram by gram of grain and inch by inch of land; slowly, but surely.' (Haque et al., 2022).

Another prominent example comes from Sri Lanka, wherein the willingness of farmers to adopt soil and water conservation measures is influenced by their perception of soil erosion, access to training and guidance from extension officers (Udayakumara, 2022). In Bhutan, farmers' adoption of traditional rice varieties exemplifies a sustainable climate-resilient strategy in securing their livelihoods amid climate change (Tshotsho, 2022), highlighting how indigenous practices support community adaptation to climatic adversities. These nonstructural measures can control financial losses by investing in community-level engagement and information sharing. Over time, such practices would not only boost agricultural climate resilience but also control economic losses and food insecurity, being major factors driving poor mental health among disaster-affected communities.

Another grassroots-level activity fostering community engagement is the conservation of the mangrove ecosystem on the Indo-Bangladesh east coast, which serves as a natural barrier to cyclonic storms in coastal areas like Sundarbans and Odisha (Das, 2022) and Bangladesh. Early warning systems (EWSs) are widely recognized as effective preparedness tools for extreme events. Prior to 2009 Cyclone Aila, EWS and emergency preparedness in the Indian Sundarbans were largely inadequate, exposing critical gaps in disaster readiness (Sahana et al., 2023). Since then, improvisations augmented the establishment of block-level committees with defined responsibilities. However, many families still rely on local kin and community for early warnings due to economic hardship and limited administrative outreach. This highlights the importance of integrating institutions, task teams and local communities into EWS frameworks. As demonstrated by India's post-Aila efforts, such systems are critical for disaster risk reduction (DRR). However, significant gaps remain in delivering timely, clear and actionable warnings to the last-mile vulnerable populations (Wadhawan, 2023). Another pressing concern in the aftermath of extreme weather events is the immediate relief that often overshadows mental health interventions and research. Implementing structured psychological support or conducting rigorous research during such times becomes a challenge. Moreover, post-disaster research efforts frequently encounter ethical constraints, limiting the scope, while multiple similar studies get initiated in isolation.

3.2 *Mental Health Intervention in Disaster Management*

While economic losses form a major chunk of post-disaster devastation, health is an aspect that closely follows. In the aftermath of the disaster, accessibility of healthcare resources poses a big challenge, especially in low-income countries. While climatic events may pose a risk of damage to health infrastructure, healthcare systems are disrupted following communication interruption, damaged roads and disruption in electricity supply. Thus, in disaster management, providing adequate and critical healthcare is a crucial task (Salam et al., 2023). Stagnant water and saline water intrusion can cause vector-borne diseases and spread water-borne infections. Maintaining personal hygiene becomes especially difficult in this scenario, even more so if people have been displaced to shelter houses.

In the deluge of events following a disaster, establishing a centralized system with strong interagency coordination can streamline mental health responses and research, ensuring timely, effective support for affected communities in post-disaster scenarios. Special care needs to be provided to the most vulnerable populations, like women and children, marginalized communities, who are at increased risk of hostility post-disasters. Although early warnings and evacuation to shelters are essential during climate disasters, emergency accommodations can also heighten the vulnerability of women and children to some forms of abuse. Thus, shelter houses should be monitored effectively to eliminate such risks.

3.3 Disaster Management: Innovative Models

Despite facing challenges like limited resources, weak infrastructure and economic constraints, South Asia has produced exemplary disaster management efforts that have drawn global recognition and inspiration. In the context of cyclone disaster management by Odisha in 2013, the state pioneered an early warning dissemination system, ensuring that critical alerts reach even the most remote villages through sirens and mass messaging, when disaster management infrastructure was sparse. In another display of innovative responses to the climate change–related severe drought of 2016 in the Marathwada region, Indian Railways launched the innovative ‘Jaldoot’ or ‘water train’ service, delivering approximately 2.5 million litres of water to the drought-stricken Latur region in Maharashtra.

One of the recognized disaster management models in South Asia is from Bangladesh, where over 70,000 volunteers were trained to issue early warnings, manage evacuations and provide first aid. This community-based approach drastically reduced cyclone-related fatalities. At the institutional level, Bangladesh’s Standing Orders on Disaster (SOD) provide a comprehensive framework for disaster management, effectively coordinating preparedness, response and recovery efforts across various agencies (Shammin et al., 2022).

Similarly, following the 2004 tsunami, Sri Lanka enhanced disaster preparedness through early warning systems, public education and evacuation drills, led by the Disaster Management Centre to strengthen coastal hazard response. After the 2015 Nepal earthquake, women’s groups and youth networks led local recovery. School-based disaster risk reduction (DRR) education and safer building codes were introduced, boosting community awareness and resilience through seismic-resistant reconstruction and engagement.

4 Way Forward: Future Directions and Recommendations

In addressing the complex mental health and psychosocial challenges arising from climate-induced extreme weather events in South Asia, a comprehensive, integrated approach, rooted in preventive medicine, should prioritize long-term resilience and community-based care over short-term relief. Mental healthcare should prioritize natural emotional responses and be delivered by trained community workers to ensure accessibility and cultural sensitivity. Integrating mental health components into relief packages can foster spontaneous community participation and help reduce the stigma traditionally associated with mental health issues. However, rehabilitation should respect local cultural norms and focus on empowering communities, enhancing their solidarity and resilience to better handle future weather events. Active involvement of the local community not only helps in capacity building but also in sustained community participation (Math et al., 2015) (Fig. 9.1).

Firstly, a series of reorientation training modules needs to be prepared with tailored content for different groups of responders. These modules must address the specific tasks to combat challenges and psychosocial dynamics relevant to each group, e.g. emergency responders, local individuals, students, farming community and healthcare professionals in primary healthcare settings. They must be trained in basic psychological first aid to provide immediate relief in high-stress situations. These reorientation modules would decentralize psychosocial support, making it more accessible and contextually relevant across all levels of disaster response.

Additionally, investing in climate-resilient housing and agricultural practices is crucial for mitigating the long-term impacts of climate change. It can reduce economic shocks and recurrence of displacement, protect livelihoods and build community resilience. Strengthening infrastructure and sustainable farming would help vulnerable populations better withstand the ill effects of extreme weather events.

Further, shelter homes must be monitored and structured as safe spaces, particularly to prevent violence and abuse against women and children. Structured psychosocial interventions in shelter homes can also aid in restoring routine and emotional stability for students, helping reduce academic demotivation and isolation caused by disrupted education during climate-related disasters.

Fig. 9.1 A comprehensive model for effective extreme weather event management in South Asia

Lastly, long-term resilience-building programmes should be implemented to provide sustained recovery pathways. Remote mental health services, such as India's Tele-MANAS, can expand access to care, especially in underserved regions. Mental health and psychosocial support (MHPSS) should be integrated into all relevant health and community-based programmes.

5 Conclusion

The surge in extreme weather events in South Asia underscores the urgent need to address their profound mental health consequences. This chapter illustrated that climate-induced extreme events do not merely result in immediate physical and economic losses but leave enduring psychological scars, particularly among children, women, older adults and farmers. The mental health impacts, from trauma, anxiety, depression and PTSD, are further exacerbated by poverty, displacement, food insecurity and lack of access to care.

Despite these challenges, the region demonstrates significant resilience through community-based coping strategies, religious faith, support of stakeholders and local administration. However, fragmented mental health responses, limited trained personnel and the absence of integrated services present important challenges that inspire a critical need for a paradigm shift, from reactive, relief-based responses to proactive, preventive and inclusive disaster mental health systems.

A holistic approach needs to be adopted, one that embeds mental health and psychosocial support within disaster preparedness and response frameworks. Emphasizing local capacity-building, culturally sensitive interventions and coordinated research efforts would build a resilient, responsive and sustainable mental health infrastructure for extreme weather-prone South Asian communities.

References

Ae-Ngibise, K. A., Asare-Doku, W., Peprah, J., Mujtaba, M. N., Nifasha, D., & Donnir, G. M. (2021). The mental health outcomes of food insecurity and insufficiency in West Africa: A systematic narrative review. *Behavioral Sciences, 11*(11), 146. https://doi.org/10.3390/bs11110146

Ahmad, M. S., Shah, R., Khan, S., Kizi, J. S. M., Fatima, T., & Malik, A. (2025). Exploring psychological recovery and coping mechanisms: Post-flood mental health and resilience of women in Punjab, Pakistan. *Discover Sustainability, 6*(1), 107. https://doi.org/10.1007/s43621-025-00799-5

Amarakoon, V., Trafford, J., Udeshika, T., Amarasekara, D. S., & Wickramasinghe, D. (2024). Towards happy relief campers: Surfacing psycho-social issues, conflicts and other problems for flood-affected residents and officials in Kuruwita, Sri Lanka. *International Journal of Disaster Risk Reduction, 101*, 104259. https://doi.org/10.1016/j.ijdrr.2024.104259

Arafat, S. M. Y., Kar, S. K., Marthoenis, M., Sharma, P., Hoque Apu, E., & Kabir, R. (2020). Psychological underpinning of panic buying during pandemic (COVID-19). *Psychiatry Research, 289*, 113061. https://doi.org/10.1016/j.psychres.2020.113061

Bhise, M. C., Marwale, A. V., Mohide, A. C., Jadhav, S. S., & Murambikar, G. P. (2019). Psychological distress in survivors of farmers' suicides in drought prone Aurangabad and Jalna Districts of Marathwada region in Maharashtra, India. *Annals of Indian Psychiatry, 3*(2), 143. https://doi.org/10.4103/aip.aip_29_19

Cianconi, P., Betrò, S., & Janiri, L. (2020). The impact of climate change on mental health: A systematic descriptive review. *Frontiers in Psychiatry, 11*. https://doi.org/10.3389/fpsyt.2020.00074

Cunsolo, A., Harper, S. L., Minor, K., Hayes, K., Williams, K. G., & Howard, C. (2020). Ecological grief and anxiety: The start of a healthy response to climate change? *The Lancet Planetary Health, 4*(7), e261–e263. https://doi.org/10.1016/S2542-5196(20)30144-3

Das, S. (2022). Valuing the role of mangroves in storm damage reduction in coastal areas of Odisha. In *Climate change and community resilience* (pp. 257–273). Springer Nature Singapore. https://doi.org/10.1007/978-981-16-0680-9_17

Deglon, M., Dalvie, M. A., & Abrams, A. (2023). The impact of extreme weather events on mental health in Africa: A scoping review of the evidence. *Science of the Total Environment, 881*, 163420. https://doi.org/10.1016/j.scitotenv.2023.163420

Dinh, N. C., Ubukata, F., Tan, N. Q., & Ha, V. H. (2021). How do social connections accelerate post-flood recovery? Insights from a survey of rural households in central Vietnam. *International Journal of Disaster Risk Reduction, 61*, 102342. https://doi.org/10.1016/j.ijdrr.2021.102342

Edwards, B., Gray, M., & Borja, J. (2021). The influence of natural disasters on violence, mental health, food insecurity, and stunting in The Philippines: Findings from a nationally representative cohort. *SSM – Population Health, 15*, 100825. https://doi.org/10.1016/j.ssmph.2021.100825

Eichenauer, H., & Ehlert, U. (2023). The association between prenatal famine, DNA methylation and mental disorders: A systematic review and meta-analysis. *Clinical Epigenetics, 15*(1), 152. https://doi.org/10.1186/s13148-023-01557-y

FAO. (2010). *The state of world fisheries and aquaculture*. https://www.fao.org/4/I1820e/I1820e00.htm

Fatema, S. R., East, L., Islam, M. S., & Usher, K. (2021). Health impact and risk factors affecting south and southeast asian women following natural disasters: A systematic review. *International Journal of Environmental Research and Public Health, 18*(21). https://doi.org/10.3390/ijerph182111068

Gilmoor, A. R., Adithy, A., & Regeer, B. (2019). The cross-cultural validity of post-traumatic stress disorder and post-traumatic stress symptoms in the Indian context: A systematic search and review. *Frontiers in Psychiatry, 10*. https://doi.org/10.3389/fpsyt.2019.00439

Guo, L., Sang, B., Li, S., Xia, Z., Li, M., Yang, M., Yin, W., & Liu, Y. (2024). From starvation to depression: Unveiling the link between the great famine and late-life depression. *BMC Public Health, 24*(1), 3096. https://doi.org/10.1186/s12889-024-20604-8

Haque, A. K., Mukhopadhyay, P., Nepal, M., & Shammin, R. (2022). Climate change and community resilience: Insights from South Asia. In *Climate Change and Community Resilience: Insights from South Asia*. Springer Nature. https://doi.org/10.1007/978-981-16-0680-9

Hossain, A., Ahmed, B., Rahman, T., Sammonds, P., Zaman, S., Benzadid, S., & Jakariya, M. (2021). Household food insecurity, income loss, and symptoms of psychological distress among adults following the cyclone Amphan in coastal Bangladesh. *PLoS One, 16*(11), e0259098. https://doi.org/10.1371/journal.pone.0259098

Kafle, S. K. (2017). Disaster risk management systems in South Asia: Natural hazards, vulnerability, disaster risk and legislative and institutional frameworks. *Journal of Geography & Natural Disasters, 7*(3). https://doi.org/10.4172/2167-0587.1000207

Kar, N., Samantaray, N. N., Kar, S., & Kar, B. (2022). Anxiety, depression, and post-traumatic stress a month after 2019 Cyclone Fani in Odisha, India. *Disaster Medicine and Public Health Preparedness, 16*(2), 670–677. https://doi.org/10.1017/dmp.2020.368

Keyes, K. M., Pratt, C., Galea, S., McLaughlin, K. A., Koenen, K. C., & Shear, M. K. (2014). The burden of loss: Unexpected death of a loved one and psychiatric disorders across the life course in a national study. *American Journal of Psychiatry, 171*(8), 864–871. https://doi.org/10.1176/appi.ajp.2014.13081132

Majumder, J., Saha, I., Bagepally, B. S., Kalita, M., Munikrishnappa, D., Ray, S., Saha, A., & Chakrabarti, A. (2024). Mental health burden following extreme weather events in South-east Asia: A systematic review and meta-analysis. *Indian Journal of Psychiatry, 66*(8), 683–694. https://doi.org/10.4103/indianjpsychiatry.indianjpsychiatry_348_24

Math, S. B., John, J. P., Girimaji, S. C., Benegal, V., Sunny, B., Krishnakanth, K., GS, U. K., Hamza, A., Tandon, S., Jangam, K., Meena, K. S., Chandramukhi, B., & Nagaraja, D. (2008). Comparative study of psychiatric morbidity among the displaced and non-displaced populations in the Andaman and Nicobar Islands following the tsunami. *Prehospital and Disaster Medicine, 23*(1), 29–34. https://doi.org/10.1017/S1049023X00005513

Math, S. B., Nirmala, M. C., Moirangthem, S., & Kumar, N. C. (2015). Disaster management: Mental health perspective. *Indian Journal of Psychological Medicine, 37*(3), 261–271. https://doi.org/10.4103/0253-7176.162915

Mishra, V., Tiwari, A. D., Aadhar, S., Shah, R., Xiao, M., Pai, D. S., & Lettenmaier, D. (2019). Drought and famine in India, 1870–2016. *Geophysical Research Letters, 46*(4), 2075–2083. https://doi.org/10.1029/2018GL081477

Mohamed, A., & Mansoor, S. (2025). Challenges and opportunities in the mental health landscape of the Maldives. *Australasian Psychiatry, 33*(2), 195–196. https://doi.org/10.1177/10398562241289879

Munikrishnappa, D., Majumder, J., Kalita, M., Shivarudraiah, M., Saha, I., & Chakrabarti, A. (2024). Bridging the mental health treatment gap in India: Opportunities and challenges: A narrative review. *Journal of Mental Health and Human Behaviour, 29*(2), 55–61. https://doi.org/10.4103/jmhhb.jmhhb_167_24

Parmar, M. K., & Shanker, S. (2016). A descriptive cross-sectional survey to understand the health status of people after 2013 Kedarnath Flood in Srinagar, Pauri Garhwal, Uttrakhand. *International Journal of Engineering and Techniques, 2*(5), 164–174. http://www.ijet-journal.org

Patwary, M. M., Bardhan, M., Haque, M. A., Moniruzzaman, S., Gustavsson, J., Khan, M. M. H., et al. (2024). Impact of extreme weather events on mental health in South and Southeast Asia: A two decades of systematic review of observational studies. *Environmental Research, 250*, 118436. https://doi.org/10.1016/j.envres.2024.118436

Paul, S. K., Naim, J., & Mou, M. A. (2022). Assessing efficiency of disaster management institutions at local level in the coastal region of Bangladesh. *Nature-Based Solutions, 2*, 100024. https://doi.org/10.1016/j.nbsj.2022.100024

Rodrigo, A., & Liyanage, N. (2017). Disaster and mental health: The role of Sri Lankan psychiatrists. *Sri Lanka Journal of Psychiatry, 8*(1), 1. https://doi.org/10.4038/sljpsyc.v8i1.8131

Sadri, A. M., Ukkusuri, S. V., Lee, S., Clawson, R., Aldrich, D., Nelson, M. S., Seipel, J., & Kelly, D. (2018). The role of social capital, personal networks, and emergency responders in post-disaster recovery and resilience: A study of rural communities in Indiana. *Natural Hazards, 90*(3), 1377–1406. https://doi.org/10.1007/s11069-017-3103-0

Sahana, M., Patel, P. P., Rehman, S., Rahaman, M. H., Masroor, M., Imdad, K., & Sajjad, H. (2023). Assessing the effectiveness of existing early warning systems and emergency preparedness towards reducing cyclone-induced losses in the Sundarban Biosphere Region, India. *International Journal of Disaster Risk Reduction, 90*, 103645. https://doi.org/10.1016/j.ijdrr.2023.103645

Salam, A., Wireko, A. A., Jiffry, R., Ng, J. C., Patel, H., Zahid, M. J., Mehta, A., Huang, H., Abdul-Rahman, T., & Isik, A. (2023). The impact of natural disasters on healthcare and surgical services in low- and middle-income countries. *Annals of Medicine & Surgery, 85*(8), 3774–3777. https://doi.org/10.1097/MS9.0000000000001041

Seddighi, H., Salmani, I., Javadi, M. H., & Seddighi, S. (2021). Child abuse in natural disasters and conflicts: A systematic review. *Trauma, Violence, & Abuse, 22*(1), 176–185. https://doi.org/10.1177/1524838019835973

Sena, A., Freitas, C., Feitosa Souza, P., Alpino, T., Pedroso, M., Corvalan, C., Barcellos, C., & Carneiro, F. (2018). Drought in the Semiarid Region of Brazil: Exposure, vulnerabilities and health impacts from the perspectives of local actors. *PLoS Currents*. https://doi.org/10.1371/currents.dis.c226851ebd64290e619a4d1ed79c8639

Shah, S. M. H., Mustaffa, Z., Teo, F. Y., Imam, M. A. H., Yusof, K. W., & Al-Qadami, E. H. H. (2020). A review of the flood hazard and risk management in the South Asian Region, particularly Pakistan. *Scientific African, 10*, e00651. https://doi.org/10.1016/j.sciaf.2020.e00651

Shammin, M. R., Firoz, R., & Hasan, R. (2022). Frameworks, stories and learnings from disaster management in Bangladesh. In *Climate change and community resilience* (pp. 239–256). Springer Nature Singapore. https://doi.org/10.1007/978-981-16-0680-9_16

Song, C., Atun, F., Blanford, J. I., & Anthonj, C. (2025). Impact of flooding on the social and mental health of older adults- A scoping review. *Water Security*, 100190. https://doi.org/10.1016/j.wasec.2025.100190

Southard, E. M. L., & Randell, H. (2024). Food insecurity and women's mental health in the Chitwan Valley of Nepal. *SSM – Mental Health, 6*, 100337. https://doi.org/10.1016/j.ssmmh.2024.100337

Suar, D., Kar, N., & Panigrahi, G. S. (2024). Natural hazards, trauma, and its amelioration: Lessons learned from India. *International Journal of Disaster Risk Reduction, 108*, 104548. https://doi.org/10.1016/j.ijdrr.2024.104548

Thurston, A. M., Stöckl, H., & Ranganathan, M. (2021). Natural hazards, disasters and violence against women and girls: A global mixed-methods systematic review. *BMJ Global Health, 6*(4), e004377. https://doi.org/10.1136/bmjgh-2020-004377

Tshotsho. (2022). Indigenous practices of paddy growers in Bhutan: A safety net against climate change. In *Climate change and community resilience* (pp. 87–100). Springer Nature Singapore. https://doi.org/10.1007/978-981-16-0680-9_6

Uchiyama, C., Ismail, N., & Stevenson, L. A. (2021). Assessing contribution to the Sendai framework: Case study of climate adaptation and disaster risk reduction projects across sectors in Asia-Pacific (2015–2020). *Progress in Disaster Science, 12*, 100195. https://doi.org/10.1016/j.pdisas.2021.100195

Udayakumara, E. P. N. (2022). Farmer adaptation to climate variability and soil erosion in Samanalawewa catchment in Sri Lanka. In *Climate change and community resilience* (pp. 291–307). Springer Nature Singapore. https://doi.org/10.1007/978-981-16-0680-9_19

UNDRR. (2015). *Sendai framework for disaster risk reduction 2015–2030*. https://www.undrr.org/quick/11409

Wadey, M., Brown, S., Nicholls, R. J., & Haigh, I. (2017). Coastal flooding in the Maldives: An assessment of historic events and their implications. *Natural Hazards, 89*(1), 131–159. https://doi.org/10.1007/s11069-017-2957-5

Wadhawan, S. (2023). *Strengthening India's disaster preparedness with technology*. https://www.ceew.in/publications/how-can-india-strengthen-climate-disaster-preparedness-with-multi-hazard-effective-early-warning-systems

Zahidi, F., Khalid, M., Surkan, P. J., & Azadbakht, L. (2022). Associations between food insecurity and common mental health problems among reproductive-aged women in Kabul-Afghanistan. *Frontiers in Nutrition, 8*. https://doi.org/10.3389/fnut.2021.794607

Chapter 10
Earthquakes and Mental Health in South Asia

Ravi Philip Rajkumar

1 Earthquakes: Definition and Impact

An earthquake can be defined as "a violent and abrupt shaking of the ground, caused by movement between tectonic plates along a fault line in the earth's crust" (World Health Organization, 2025). Earthquakes vary in magnitude from minor, imperceptible events to large-scale catastrophes that can devastate human habitations and cause massive fatalities (Kato & Ben-Zion, 2021; Zhu et al., 2021). The latter are referred to as "large" or "major" earthquakes and constitute one of the most important types of natural disasters. A large earthquake can be formally defined as one with a moment magnitude (Mw) of 7 or above. Large earthquakes are characterized by prior weakening or deformation of vulnerable crustal zones or fault lines, followed by smaller and then larger "slips" leading to large-scale damage (Wu et al., 2016; Kato & Ben-Zion, 2021). The direct damage caused by an earthquake can be compounded by subsequent "chains of geological hazards", such as landslides and floods, triggered by the initial seismic event (Fan et al., 2019; Arrell et al., 2024).

Certain geographical regions are more prone to earthquakes than others, and these are referred to as seismic zones. Larger regions of this sort, often encompassing several seismic zones, are known as seismic belts. While a knowledge of these zones is useful in devising earthquake preparedness plans, it is not possible to predict when exactly an earthquake—or a large earthquake—will occur, even in a vulnerable zone (Mishra, 2020; Petrillo & Zhuang, 2022). With advances in technology, it may be possible to predict an impending earthquake and issue early warnings. However, even with such methods, known as "earthquake early warning" (EEW) systems, instructions to evacuate or take other safety measures can be issued only a

R. P. Rajkumar (✉)
Department of Psychiatry, Jawaharlal Institute of Postgraduate Medical Education and Research (JIPMER), Puducherry, India

N. Kar et al. (eds.), *Climate Change, Disaster and Mental Health in South Asia*, South Asian Perspectives in Mental Health and Psychology,
https://doi.org/10.1007/978-981-95-3690-0_10

few seconds in advance. This is unlike the scenario with other forms of natural disaster, such as extreme weather events, where early warnings are possible several hours ahead of a catastrophic event (Kumar et al., 2022).

Based on these facts, it can be deduced that the human cost of large earthquakes is substantial and is likely to remain so in the immediate future. It is estimated that at least 700,000 people lost their lives to earthquakes in the decade 2000–2010, and this number is expected to rise to 2.5 to 3 million over the course of the twenty-first century (Holzer & Savage, 2013). Earthquake-related deaths account for more than half of global deaths caused by natural disasters (World Health Organization, 2025). The structural damage and economic loss caused by large earthquakes can affect food and water security, employment, trade, social stability, and civil liberties. Recovery from these effects is often prolonged and incomplete (Aksoy et al., 2024). The socioeconomic impact of earthquakes is often experienced most severely by groups with pre-existing psychosocial or economic vulnerabilities (Atreya et al., 2022; Hussaini et al., 2022; Wang & Wang, 2023).

An earthquake that occurs beneath a large water body may produce large, powerful waves that can devastate coastal regions. Such waves are referred to as tsunamis. About 80% of tsunamis are caused by earthquakes; the remainder are related to other geological processes such as underwater volcanic eruptions or landslides. The extent of damage caused by a tsunami is positively correlated with the height of its waves: water heights of 1 metre or more cause the greatest damage. Over the past century, large tsunamis have been associated with fatalities that range from hundreds of thousands to millions (Reid & Mooney, 2023). Tsunamis and earthquakes are discussed together in this chapter for several reasons: (a) the close mechanistic link between them, particularly in South Asia; (b) the sudden, unpredictable, and potentially devastating impact of both these disaster types; and (c) their similar effects on mental health (Oe et al., 2021).

1.1 The Effect of Earthquakes on Mental Health

Earthquakes also have profound effects on health, and these vary over time. In the period immediately after an earthquake, health care systems must cope with a high load of acute injuries and related medical complications, such as shock, crush syndrome, or hypothermia. This often overwhelms existing resources, necessitating the institution of strict triage protocols (Peng & Hu, 2021; Yilmaz et al., 2024). Following this, a second wave of ill health arises due to a lack of access to essential health care or medications. This leads to the exacerbation of pre-existing disorders, particularly noncommunicable diseases (Hassan et al., 2020; Aydin et al., 2025). Alongside this, increases in the incidence of infectious diseases may also occur, particularly in low- and middle-income countries (Najafi et al., 2022). In the longer term, acute injuries may leave people with enduring disabilities or deformities (Chishtie et al., 2019), and the psychological and socioeconomic stresses of earthquake-induced damage can increase the likelihood of chronic cardiovascular and gastrointestinal disorders (Kusević et al., 2021).

These effects on physical health are paralleled by temporally similar changes in mental health. In the acute phase, symptoms of acute stress disorder or adjustment disorder are common (Efendi et al., 2023). These are followed by the exacerbation of pre-existing mental illnesses (Aydin et al., 2025) and the emergence and persistence of post-traumatic stress disorder (PTSD) and depression. Though PTSD symptoms may improve over time, depression tends to persist (Ando et al., 2017; Liang et al., 2019). A total of 10–35% of those affected by an earthquake experience suicidal ideation, though the frequency of such ideas tends to return to pre-earthquake levels after four or more years (Jahangiri et al., 2020). The approximate prevalence of mental health problems in different populations following an earthquake, based on recent systematic reviews and meta-analyses, is presented in Table 10.1 (Ando et al., 2017; Dube et al., 2018; Cénat et al., 2020; Futterman et al., 2023; Olk et al., 2025; Peng et al., 2025). Apart from directly affected populations, persons involved in relief work or health care during an earthquake can also experience psychological distress. A recent systematic review found that 11–21% of medical workers experience PTSD following an earthquake (Tahernejad et al., 2023). Apart from these well-defined syndromes, some earthquake survivors experience symptoms that appear to be highly specific to this form of disaster. These include "earthquake obsession", which is characterized by intrusive and maladaptive thoughts about past or future earthquakes (Kartol et al., 2025), and "post-earthquake dizziness syndrome" (PEDS), a psychosomatic condition that may arise from a combination of vestibular dysfunction, autonomic imbalance, and psychosocial stress (Miwa et al., 2025).

This table reveals that the mental health impacts of an earthquake are both substantial and highly variable. Some of this variability may be due to differences in study methodology, such as the screening instruments or diagnostic criteria used, or the time elapsed between the earthquake and interviews with participants (Kar & Sharma, 2021). Setting this aside, there are several risk factors for adverse mental health outcomes following an earthquake, and these should be considered when

Table 10.1 Prevalence of mental disorders following earthquakes

Population	Depression (%)	Anxiety (%)	Post-traumatic stress disorder (%)
General adult population	6–54	20–35	10–54
Children and adolescents	26–39	Data not available[a]	22–31
Elderly adults	14–33	7–15	16–23
Pregnant and postpartum women	29–41	29[b]	12–29

[a]No meta-analytic estimate of prevalence exists. Indirect estimates suggest that 60–80% of children and adolescents experience significant anxiety after an earthquake

[b]This estimate was based on a single study

Table 10.2 Risk factors for mental health problems after an earthquake

Category	Risk factors
Demographic	• Female gender • Age[a] • Family structure or size[b] • Widowhood[c]
Pre-earthquake	• Past or family history of mental illness • Exposure to previous trauma • Chronic medical illness[c] • Neuroticism • Locus of control—external or attributed to "chance"/"fate" • Maladaptive cognitive style
Earthquake-related	• Being trapped or injured during the event • Witnessing injuries or damage • Injury of a family member • Bereavement • Loss of home or other material/financial resources • Involvement in rescue work[d]
Post-earthquake	• Poor social support • Lack of insurance coverage • Lack of access to mental health care

[a]Older age is a risk factor for PTSD in adolescents and the elderly
[b]Having siblings (for children and adolescents only) or living in a nuclear family may be associated with PTSD
[c]This risk factor is relevant mainly in elderly adults
[d]Some, but not all, rescue workers may have elevated rates of PTSD, depending on the other vulnerability factors listed in this table

planning mental health services (Sirotich & Camisasca, 2024; Peng et al., 2025). These are listed in Table 10.2.

The mental health burden of an earthquake is aggravated by difficulties in providing adequate health care—and particularly mental health care—to survivors, their families, and others affected either directly or indirectly. Moreover, as the mental health sequelae of an earthquake often persist over time, emergency care does not suffice: many survivors will require long-term care, with a focus on psychosocial interventions, to achieve symptom remission and functional recovery (Raviola et al., 2020; Ramezankhani & Sabouri, 2023; Hoang et al., 2025). Establishing and maintaining such services is especially difficult if mental health infrastructure and manpower are lacking—for example, due to economic underdevelopment—or if they are overloaded by other disasters or health crises (Patwary et al., 2023). In such scenarios, specific services for vulnerable populations, such as children and the elderly, may be non-existent or rudimentary and may need to be developed "from the ground up" during recovery from an earthquake (Legha & Solages, 2015; Balikuddembe et al., 2024).

2 Earthquake Vulnerability and Preparedness in South Asia

The geographical region of South Asia includes eight countries: Afghanistan, Bangladesh, Bhutan, India, the Maldives, Nepal, Pakistan, and Sri Lanka. Seismological data and research have revealed that several regions in North and West India, Afghanistan, Pakistan, and Nepal are vulnerable to large earthquakes (Walling & Mohanty, 2009; Rehman & Burton, 2020; Sreejaya et al., 2022; Malik et al., 2024; Raghukanth et al., 2024; Akhundzadah, 2025). Recent large earthquakes in this region include the 2015 Nepal earthquake (Giri et al., 2024) and the 2019 Kashmir earthquake (Sreejith et al., 2021). The coastal regions of South India, along with the Maldives and Sri Lanka, are vulnerable to the effects of tsunamis in the Indian Ocean, as seen most recently in 2004 (Sonak et al., 2008). Figure 10.1 illustrates the earthquake and tsunami vulnerability zones in South Asia.

Progress in earthquake preparedness in South Asia over the past two decades has been uneven. During the 2001 earthquake in Gujarat, India, it was observed that emergency medical care was being provided by temporary military hospitals in rudimentary conditions, due to extensive damage to civilian hospitals. General

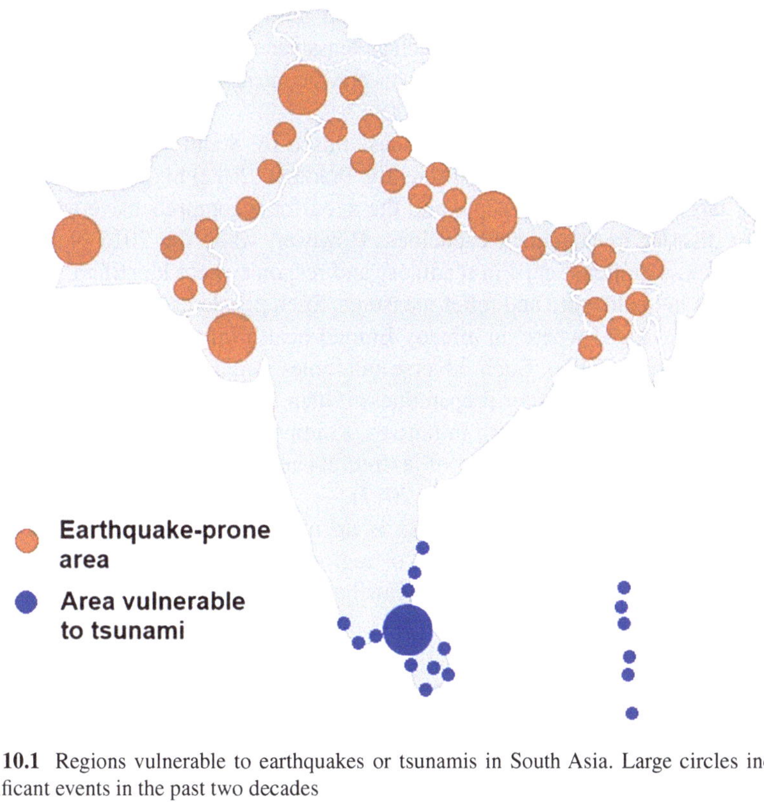

Fig. 10.1 Regions vulnerable to earthquakes or tsunamis in South Asia. Large circles indicate significant events in the past two decades

disaster relief measures were found to be inadequate, and this was attributed to several factors:

- The absence of a clear disaster readiness policy
- Poor coordination between different sectors or agencies involved in relief work
- Shortages and misallocations of specific resources
- Delays due to bureaucratic procedures

The aftermath of this earthquake highlighted the need for a more systematic approach to earthquake preparedness policies and relief efforts, not just in India, but in the South Asian region (Sharma, 2002; Bremer, 2003). Very similar observations were made during the 2005 earthquake in northern Pakistan. Immediately after this disaster, emergency medical care—including major surgeries—could be provided in a military hospital (Yasin et al., 2009). However, interviews with survivors revealed that relief and recovery efforts were often inadequate, and basic amenities such as a safe supply of potable water were lacking. This underlined the need for better preparedness and infrastructure for earthquake relief (Halvorson & Hamilton, 2010; Magan et al., 2010).

A significant improvement in this regard was noted in India during the 2004 Indian Ocean tsunami, where attempts were made to follow the World Health Organization (WHO)'s guidelines on natural disasters. This led to a more rapid resumption of health care, rapid recovery and return of victims' bodies, and an avoidance of unnecessary measures such as mass vaccinations or burials. The resilience of the affected population during this crisis contributed significantly to a positive and cost-effective response (Roy, 2006).

In other cases, concerns about readiness raised by South Asian experts do not seem to influence policymakers sufficiently. Pradhan (2012) highlighted the risk of a future large earthquake in Nepal and the need for a comprehensive approach to building disaster management capacities. However, when the 2015 Nepal earthquake struck, significant gaps in readiness and response were identified, leading to deficiencies in health care and relief measures. Such problems were more severe in remote or rural areas where an already limited health infrastructure was severely damaged (Sharma, 2015). Such adverse outcomes could be prevented through a proactive approach to disaster preparedness (Ofrin & Landry, 2015). The need for community participation in such initiatives, to improve public awareness, engagement, and resilience in the face of a future earthquake, was also highlighted (Adhikari et al., 2016; Fredricks et al., 2017).

Public awareness of earthquake risk is an important component of readiness plans, particularly in vulnerable cities or regions. A survey of urban residents in Bangladesh revealed that most respondents had low awareness of seismic risk and of key preparedness or safety measures. Lower education was associated with a lower level of readiness (Paul & Bhuiyan, 2010).

From the available literature, it can be concluded that there are significant deficits in awareness, risk perception, readiness, and resources for earthquake management in South Asian countries. It is likely that such deficits could exacerbate the effects of earthquakes on mental health. This situation is likely to improve in the coming decades, particularly as each country formulates and implements a more comprehensive disaster management policy, and moves from a "reactive" to a "pro-active" approach to earthquake preparedness (Jha et al., 2016; Choudhury & Haque, 2024). For such policies to be effective, they should be implemented effectively at the local level (Ogra et al., 2021).

3 Earthquakes and Mental Health in South Asia

Several researchers have examined the mental health impact of earthquakes in individual South Asian countries, both in the general population and in vulnerable groups. Most of this work has focussed on the presence of specific disorders, such as depression, PTSD, or anxiety disorders, in affected individuals. Due to the challenges in conducting in-depth interviews in traumatized populations, most individual studies have relied on screening instruments, using predefined cut-off values to identify symptoms of these disorders. A certain degree of psychological distress is "normal" after an earthquake: for example, a person who has experienced earthquake-related bereavement may go through the process of grieving but would not require a diagnosis of depression. On the other hand, because of the stigma attached to mental illness or cultural values which dictate the "acceptable" forms of expressing psychological distress, some patients may under-report symptoms even when these are considerable. For these reasons, the estimates of the prevalence of each disorder following an earthquake presented in the studies reviewed should be considered approximate and provisional. Nevertheless, they can be considered useful "guideline values" when designing the mental health components of earthquake readiness plans.

3.1 Effects on the General Population

South Asian research on the psychological sequelae of earthquakes in affected communities is over two decades old. A pilot study conducted after the 1993 Latur earthquake in Maharashtra, India, found that 59% of 56 affected adults developed a mental disorder. The most common diagnoses were PTSD (23%) and depression (21%) (Sharan et al., 1996). The first systematic work in this area was published after the 2001 Bhuj earthquake in Gujarat, which resulted in over 20,000 deaths and 165,000 survivors with significant injuries (Roy et al., 2002). Following this disaster, unofficial estimates suggested that about 30% of survivors were experiencing symptoms of psychological distress, with even higher estimates in specific vulnerable groups (Sharma, 2002). Subsequently, it has been found that a significant number of persons affected by earthquakes develop depression, anxiety, or PTSD. In a survey of patients seeking out-patient psychiatric treatment for trauma-related disorders in Nepal, 67.8% reported that the earthquake was the most traumatic event they had experienced (Koirala et al., 2020).

Community-based research on mental health in South Asian populations affected by earthquakes is summarized in Table 10.3.

There is considerable variability in these results: for example, the estimated prevalence of PTSD in the above studies ranges from 3% to nearly 65%. Some of this variability may result from methodological issues, but a more relevant explanation is that PTSD evolves over weeks or months following exposure to an earthquake. In fact, formal diagnostic criteria for PTSD require that symptoms last for at least 1 month, and patients may develop PTSD as late as 6 months after trauma exposure. If studies assessing patients 6 or more months after the event are examined separately, then a prevalence of 19–65% is obtained, with most results in the range of 30–45%. A single study from Nepal has examined whether the prevalence of PTSD declines over time. In this study, the estimated prevalence fell from 33% at 3 months to 28.5% at 11 months, but this change was not statistically significant. It is likely that at least a quarter to a third of directly affected individuals experience significant PTSD symptoms in South Asian countries.

Estimates of the prevalence of significant depression or anxiety in survivors are less variable. Between 8% and 34% of affected persons have significant depressive symptoms, with a tendency towards a higher prevalence over time, from around 11% in the month after the earthquake to 18–33% after 1–6 years. There is relatively less data on anxiety, but about 15–34% of patients have either significant anxiety symptoms or an anxiety disorder.

Though most research in this area has focussed on anxiety, depression, and PTSD, other forms of psychopathology may also arise in adults after an earthquake. Of the 1291 individuals affected by the 2005 North Pakistan earthquake, 17–30% reported psychotic symptoms of one form or the other, even if they did not qualify for a diagnosis of psychotic disorder. Lower education, female gender, prior trauma exposure, involvement in rescue work, and the presence of anxiety, depression, or PTSD were all associated with the presence of these symptoms (Ayub et al., 2015). Another condition commonly seen after an earthquake is adjustment disorder, often related to the death of a family member. In such cases, it is important for clinicians to distinguish between "normal" grief—which often resolves over time, with the help of community support and traditional rituals—and "abnormal" grief, characterized by exaggerated or atypical symptoms and a subsequent risk of PTSD or depression (Shah, 2013).

The variables associated with psychopathology after earthquakes in South Asian populations are similar to those described in the global literature (Table 10.2). Risk factors for PTSD or depression in survivors from these countries are female gender, lower education, prior social disadvantage, and—most significantly—the direct and indirect impacts of the earthquake. These include both immediate losses, such as bereavement, loss of housing, or damage to property, and long-term outcomes such as homelessness and food insecurity. Individuals experiencing direct physical injury or threat during an earthquake may be at a particularly high risk of PTSD.

Table 10.3 Prevalence of mental disorders in earthquake-affected communities in South Asia

Study	Study characteristics	Time between earthquake and assessment	Prevalence of mental disorders	Risk factors identified, if any
2001 Gujarat earthquake				
Roy et al., 2005	133 patients treated for earthquake-related injuries (mean age 32 years, 62.4% female) from 11 affected villages	3 months	9–45% PTSD symptoms	Not assessed
2005 Kashmir earthquake[a]				
Chadda et al., 2007	303 adolescents and adults (mean age 40.2 years, 46% female) visiting emergency mental health clinics in affected regions	≥2 weeks	Depression 22.6% Adjustment disorder 39.6% PTSD 3.3% Other stress-related disorder 21.8% Suicidality 10%	Not assessed
Humayun, 2008	141 adults (mean age 25.2 years, 68.86% female) identified as "vulnerable" after assessment in the emergency department of a teaching hospital[b]	4 weeks	Adjustment disorder 35.5%[c] Depression 11.4% PTSD 6.4% Dissociative disorder 2.8%	Not assessed, but see footnote[b]
PACTT, 2008	112 adults (median age 34 years, 50% female) living in relief camps	8 months	PTSD 46.8% Depression 27.9%	Female gender
Naeem et al., 2011	1291 adults (mean age 32.9 years, 60.3% female) from an affected city	18 months	PTSD 46.6%	Female gender, lower education, nuclear family, lower income, past trauma exposure, presence in a vehicle or building during the earthquake, death of a relative, damage to housing or property

(continued)

Table 10.3 (continued)

Study	Study characteristics	Time between earthquake and assessment	Prevalence of mental disorders	Risk factors identified, if any
Ali et al., 2012	300 adults (mean age 37.7 years, 39.3% female) from three affected districts	30 months	PTSD 41.3%	Female gender, older age, single marital status, being the family head, unemployment, lower income, living in temporary housing
Aziz & Aslam, 2012	40 adults (mean age 37.7 years, 50% female) rescued from rubble in an affected district	6 years	PTSD 32.5% Depression 17.5% Dysthymia 15% Panic disorder 20% Social phobia 20% Generalized anxiety disorder 15% Psychosis 10% Suicidality 17.5%	Not assessed
Feder et al., 2013	200 adults (mean age 37.7 years, 19.5% female) from an affected area in northwest Pakistan	3 years	PTSD 64.6%	Female gender, lower education
2015 Nepal earthquake				
Jha et al., 2017	*Wave 1:* 159 adults (age 18–65 years, 61.6% female) from three villages with mild to moderate exposure	*Wave 1:* 3 months	PTSD 33%	Not assessed
	Wave 2: 203 adults (age 18 years and above, 79% female) from a village with high exposure	*Wave 2:* 11 months	PTSD 28.5%	

(continued)

Table 10.3 (continued)

Study	Study characteristics	Time between earthquake and assessment	Prevalence of mental disorders	Risk factors identified, if any
Kane et al., 2018	513 adults (mean age 42.1 years, 58.5% female) from three affected districts	4 months	Anxiety 33.8% Depression 34.3% PTSD 5.2% Suicidality 10.9% Harmful use of alcohol 20.4%	Female gender, lower caste, higher perceived needs (e.g. for shelter or food)
Thapa et al., 2018	198 adults (mean age 35.1 years, 62.6% female) from an affected district	14 months	PTSD 26.8% Anxiety 20.2% Depression 8.1%	Female gender, younger age (<30 years), single marital status
Baral & Bhagwati, 2019	291 adults (mean age 43.6 years, 43.1% female) from an affected village	10 months	PTSD 24.1%	Female gender, older age, lack of formal education, physical injury to self
Schwind et al., 2019	223 adults (mean age 45.1 years, 65% female) from an affected district	1 year	PTSD 9% Depression 33.2%	Female gender, older age, belonging to disadvantaged castes or ethnic groups, lower education, physical injury, damage to housing or property
Acharya Pandey et al., 2023	1076 adults (mean age 40.5, 56.3% female) from four affected districts	3 years	PTSD 18.9%	Female gender, lack of formal education, employment as a farmer, damage to personal property

Abbreviations: PACTT, Pakistan-Aberdeen Collaborative Trauma Team; PTSD, post-traumatic stress disorder

[a]This earthquake affected communities in both India and Pakistan

[b]Patients were considered "vulnerable" if they had suffered significant earthquake-related losses or injuries, had no caregiver, appeared distressed, had decreased sleep or appetite, and/or were not adherent to medical treatment

[c]Most of these cases were grief-related reactions

Suicidal behaviour is a serious, but relatively less studied, after-effect of exposure to an earthquake. Based on the available data, about 10% of survivors, either in the community or seeking care at emergency mental health facilities, report significant suicidal ideas or plans in the weeks or months immediately after an earthquake. Even less is known about long-term suicide risk in survivors. A paper from Pakistan reported that almost 19% of survivors reported suicidal ideas 6 years after the earthquake. Participants in this study had experienced severe earthquake-related trauma and needed to be rescued from collapsed buildings or rubble and may not be representative of survivors in general. Nevertheless, those involved in providing mental health care for South Asian earthquake survivors should be aware of the possibility of an increased risk of suicide, even after several years or months have passed.

3.2 Effects on Children and Adolescents

During and after an earthquake, children and adolescents may experience the loss of their parents, relatives, or friends; they may witness scenes of death or devastation, be injured themselves, or be separated from their families during relief efforts. Their homes and schools may be destroyed, preventing them from returning to familiar places and routines. To put it briefly, an earthquake can destroy a child's "secure base", both materially and psychologically. This places children at a high risk of a wide range of adverse mental health outcomes.

Some of the psychiatric syndromes seen in children or adolescents after an earthquake, such as PTSD, depression, anxiety disorders, and adjustment disorders, are similar to those experienced by adults. However, children's psychological responses vary significantly according to their developmental stage. Typical "adult" presentations may be seen in older adolescents, but at a younger age, psychological distress may manifest itself more in behavioural or biological changes. These include separation anxiety or "clinginess", temper tantrums, enacting violent themes while playing, nightmares, disturbances in sleep or appetite, temporary regression (e.g. nocturnal enuresis in a young child who was previously dry by night), academic difficulties, a preoccupation with their own traumatic experience, or excessive guilt. Adolescents may also resort to substance use or exhibit conduct symptoms following an earthquake. To a certain extent, such responses are temporary and normal and may even be adaptive—they represent the child's attempt to "work through" his or her own trauma. Thus, not all children with such symptoms require treatment, and a careful evaluation by a trained professional is required to separate developmentally normal and abnormal psychological responses in children affected by an earthquake (Becker, 2007; Margolin et al., 2010). South Asian research in this field is summarized in Table 10.4.

Apart from a single study examining the 2005 Pakistan earthquake, all this work is based on children and adolescents affected by the 2015 Nepal earthquake and may not be directly applicable to other South Asian countries. These results show that anywhere from 4.8% to 64.8% of individuals experience significant levels of PTSD symptoms in such a situation, with most studies yielding estimates of 15–30%. Significant depressive symptoms have been observed in 3.2% to 43.2% of children and adolescents after an earthquake, and studies measuring both conditions in the same sample have generally found depression to be slightly more common than PTSD. Diagnostic criteria and screening instruments can significantly influence these values, particularly in the case of PTSD, and should be considered when

Table 10.4 Prevalence of mental disorders in children and adolescents affected by earthquakes in South Asia

Study	Study characteristics	Time between earthquake and assessment	Prevalence of mental disorders	Risk factors identified, if any
2005 Kashmir earthquake				
Ayub et al., 2012	1154 children and adolescents (age 7–16 years, 51.3% female) from an affected city	18 months	PTSD 64.8% Emotional or behavioural disorder 34.6%[a]	*PTSD:* younger age, living in temporary accommodation *Emotional or behavioural disorder:* gender (hyperactivity ↑ in boys, emotional disorder ↑ in girls)
2015 Nepal earthquake				
Schwind et al., 2018	62 children and adolescents (age 8–17 years, 56.5% female) from an affected village	1 year	PTSD 4.8% Depression 3.2%	Higher levels of earthquake exposure
Silwal et al., 2018	893 adolescents (age 11–17 years, 48.7% female) from two affected districts	1 year	PTSD 25.3% Depression 31.9%	Female gender, prior trauma exposure, living in a district more severely affected by the earthquake
Adhikari et al., 2019	200 adolescents (age 13–17 years, 45% female) attending schools in two affected districts	1 year	Psychological distress 10–40% Symptom scores:[b] Depression 11% Anxiety 28% Phobic anxiety 40% Somatization 36% Paranoid ideation 10%	Female gender, living in a district more severely affected by the earthquake
Kar & Sharma, 2021	360 adolescents (mean age 15.2 years, 53.3% female) attending schools in two affected districts	1 year	PTSD 14.7%–31.7%[c]	Female gender
Sharma et al., 2021	125 adolescents (mean age 18.3 years, 47.2% female) attending college in an affected district	4 years	PTSD 19.2% Depression 43.2%	Higher levels of earthquake exposure, difficulty in romantic relationships

(continued)

Table 10.4 (continued)

Study	Study characteristics	Time between earthquake and assessment	Prevalence of mental disorders	Risk factors identified, if any
Silwal et al., 2022	515 adolescents (age 11–17 years, 58.1% female) from two affected districts	*Baseline:* 18 months *Follow-up:* 31 months	PTSD 26% Depression 37.5% PTSD 20.4% Depression 33.2%	Living in areas with a more severe impact, exposure to post-earthquake traumatic incidents
Llach et al., 2025	941 children and adolescents (age 8–18 years) from three affected districts	3–4 months	PTSD 48.3%	Younger age, female gender

Abbreviations: PTSD, post-traumatic stress disorder

[a]Assessed using a general screening instrument: symptom types were assessed, but not specific diagnoses

[b]The instrument used in this study measured different symptom dimensions but could not be used to make specific diagnoses

[c]This study compared the prevalence of PTSD using four different sets of diagnostic criteria based on the American Psychiatric Association and World Health Organization manuals. Results were 14.7%, 15.6%, 22.2%, and 31%, respectively

comparing results (Kar & Sharma, 2021). A single longitudinal study from Nepal found a decrease of 4–5% in the prevalence of both symptom sets over time, though this was not statistically significant (Silwal et al., 2022). Interestingly, a similar change in PTSD over time was reported in adults from the same country. Non-specific symptoms of emotional distress are also common but have been less frequently studied. Following the 2005 Pakistan earthquake, almost 35% of affected children exhibited one or more of these symptoms. There was some gender variation observed in symptom type, with boys exhibiting more hyperactivity and girls experiencing more emotional distress (Ayub et al., 2012).

Risk factors for adverse mental health outcomes were reasonably consistent across studies. Female gender was significantly associated with a greater risk of PTSD and depression, as was younger age (Ayub et al., 2012; Silwal et al., 2018; Adhikari et al., 2019; Kar & Sharma, 2021; Llach et al., 2025). Earthquake-related factors, such as living in a region with a more severe impact, loss of housing, or higher personal exposure, were crucial determinants of PTSD in this population (Ayub et al., 2012; Schwind et al., 2018; Adhikari et al., 2019; Sharma et al., 2021; Silwal et al., 2022). Pre- and post-earthquake exposure to traumatic situations was also associated with worse mental health outcomes in adolescents (Silwal et al., 2018, 2022).

3.3 Other Vulnerable Populations

Apart from children and adolescents, certain other populations may be more likely to develop a mental illness following an earthquake. This may be due to either a pre-existing psychosocial vulnerability or higher levels of exposure to traumatic stress following the incident. The first of these groups is exemplified by

- *The elderly*, who have higher rates of physical illness, disability, depression, and economic disadvantage than younger adults. In a sample of 362 elderly adults (mean age 70 years) exposed to the 2015 Nepal earthquake, interviewed 18–24 months after exposure, 32% screened positive for PTSD and 16% for depression. A further 35% had PTSD symptoms that did not qualify for a diagnosis. PTSD was significantly associated with lower health-related quality of life in this group (Wagle et al. 2021).
- *Pregnant or postpartum women*, in whom the effects of an earthquake can amplify the physical and mental health risks associated with pregnancy and childbirth, as well as any pre-existing vulnerabilities, such as family discord or domestic violence. In a study of 469 women exposed to the 2015 Nepal earthquake during pregnancy, 38.4% screened positive for depression. Earthquake-associated depressive symptoms were associated with a slight reduction in infant birth weight (Khatri et al., 2018, 2020).
- *Persons with pre-existing medical illnesses*, in which an earthquake can disrupt access to necessary health care and exacerbate illness-related stressors. Among 305 persons with HIV/AIDS affected by the 2015 Nepal earthquake, 44% had symptoms of PTSD. These symptoms improved over 6 months along with access to and adherence to antiretroviral treatment (Negi et al., 2018).
- *Persons with earthquake-induced major injuries resulting in disability,* such as traumatic brain or spinal cord injuries or limb injuries requiring amputation. In a hospital-based study of 187 persons with spinal injuries related to the 2005 Pakistan earthquake, 5.8% screened positive for depression (Rathore et al., 2007). In 82 patients receiving rehabilitation for spinal injuries 18–20 months after the 2015 Nepal earthquake, depression was associated with lower social support, lower resilience, and reduced self-efficacy (Bhattarai et al., 2018).

The second group consists of relief, rehabilitation, and health care workers who are involved in providing either acute or long-term care to earthquake victims. In a survey of medical personnel conducted 2 months after the 2015 Nepal earthquake, 17–22% were diagnosed with PTSD. This was more common in female staff and in those exposed to a higher patient load, longer working hours, or more frequent witnessing of patients' suffering (Shrestha, 2015). A qualitative study of Korean relief workers who provided emergency aid during the same earthquake identified five domains that led to stress: (i) conflicts in communication with local authorities; (ii) issues related to team coordination, manpower, and workload; (iii) personal concerns; (iv) issues related to local culture, language, and dietary patterns; and (v) disaster-related stressors (Lee et al., 2017). These findings suggest that work-related stressors are an important contributor to the mental health of first responders.

Personnel involved in long-term rehabilitation and repair work may also experience psychological distress. Two years after the 2005 Kashmir earthquake, a survey of 267 workers involved in these efforts found that 43% screened positive for PTSD and19% for anxiety or depression. A relatively smaller number (8%) showed features of burnout. Female gender, past trauma exposure, severe earthquake exposure, low social support, and work-related stress were associated with PTSD (Ehring et al., 2011).

3.4 Coping and Resilience

How individuals cope with the trauma of an earthquake and its aftermath is an important determinant of long-term mental health. Conversely, maladaptive coping, such as substance use or avoidance, can exacerbate mental disorders precipitated by an earthquake. Overall, it has been seen that South Asian communities exhibit considerable resilience in the face of this type of disaster. This may be related to existing community resources or specific cultural, religious, or spiritual practices (Hall et al., 2017).

Baral and Bhagwati (2019) examined the relationship between coping and PTSD in survivors of the 2015 Nepal earthquake. Those without PTSD had higher levels of active and distraction coping, while those with PTSD were more likely to use passive or religious coping or to use substances. In contrast to this finding, survivors of the 2005 Pakistan earthquake who described themselves as religious or prayed regularly had a lower risk of PTSD (Ali et al., 2012). One reason for this discrepancy is that both positive and negative forms of religious coping exist and have distinct effects on mental well-being. In a separate study of survivors of the 2005 earthquake, negative religious coping—characterized by a belief that God was punishing them—was associated with higher negative affect and more severe PTSD symptoms (Feder et al., 2013). A sense of meaning or purpose in life can also contribute to individuals' resilience and self-efficacy in the wake of a disaster. Three years after the 2005 earthquake, Pakistani survivors who reported a sense of purpose had fewer PTSD symptoms and more positive emotions (Feder et al., 2013).

Levels of social support among a community significantly influence recovery and resilience after an earthquake. Two and a half years after the 2005 earthquake in Pakistan, survivors' ratings of social capital were inversely correlated with the likelihood of suffering from PTSD (Ali et al., 2012), and perceived social support was associated with higher levels of positive affect (Feder et al., 2013). In a survey of 295 rural residents affected by the 2015 Nepal earthquake, giving and receiving emotional support were associated with lower depression scores. On the other hand, giving instrumental support while receiving little or none in return was associated with higher depression. These findings suggest that the beneficial effects of social support are strongest when they are reciprocal—when there is "give and take" in a community (Pandit & Nakagawa, 2021). In another study conducted 3 years after this earthquake, self-rated social support was associated with a 60% reduction in the risk of PTSD (Acharya Pandey et al., 2023).

4 Mental Health After the 2004 Asian Tsunami

The South Asian countries affected by the 2004 tsunami were Sri Lanka, the Maldives, and the southern coastal regions of India (Fig. 10.1). Researchers from these countries have examined the mental health impact of this catastrophic event on adults from affected communities, on children and adolescents, and on other vulnerable populations. This work is summarized in Table 10.5.

This research reveals that PTSD and depression were common outcomes in adults affected by the tsunami. The estimated prevalence of PTSD was 13–56% in the first 6 months after the tsunami and 13–71% over the next 8 years. However, there was no evidence of a clear time trend. Depression affected 16–34% of survivors, while anxiety was seen in 23–30%. The study with the longest-term follow-up (8 years) found relatively low rates of psychopathology (PTSD 13%, depression 19%), suggesting that some of these symptoms may decrease with time, but not in all survivors. Risk factors for these outcomes were analogous to those seen in earthquakes. They include female gender, low education or income, and tsunami-related loss or injury—particularly bereavement, injury to oneself or one's family, loss of home or property, and internal displacement (Procter, 2005). Exposure to past traumatic events was predictive of post-tsunami PTSD in a study from Sri Lanka, perhaps reflecting the ongoing civil unrest in the period preceding this disaster. Individual perception of the tsunami as more threatening or dangerous was associated with PTSD in three independent samples. This finding is important because it highlights the role of individual cognitive processes in post-tsunami mental health, and these can be targeted in tsunami preparedness programmes.

Among children and adolescents affected by the tsunami, the estimated prevalence of PTSD ranged from 11% to 82%. Higher rates of PTSD (39–82%) were seen in the first 6 months after exposure and dropped to 14–25% over 3 years. Only one study from India examined the prevalence of depression (13.5%) and anxiety disorders (10.8%) in this population. General symptoms of psychological distress, not fitting into any of the above categories, were seen in 32% of affected adolescents 8 months post-tsunami. Most of the predictors of PTSD in youth (bereavement, loss of property or housing, more severe exposure, homelessness, or displacement) were akin to those observed in adults. However, children or adolescents with prior trauma, paternal alcohol abuse, maternal depression, or ongoing stressors at school or in the home were more likely to experience PTSD. This suggests that such "background" factors may be particularly important in this age group and should be assessed carefully in children experiencing psychological distress after a disaster.

Bereavement is an important determinant of mental well-being in tsunami survivors. Among adult survivors from South India, interviewed 14 months after this

Table 10.5 Prevalence of mental disorders in populations affected by the 2004 Asian tsunami

Study	Study characteristics	Time between tsunami and assessment	Prevalence of mental disorders	Risk factors identified, if any
General population				
Kumar et al., 2007	314 adults (mean age 35.8 years, 51.3% female) from an affected village, India	2 months	PTSD 12.7%	Female gender, no regular source of income, personal injury, bereavement
Ranasinghe & Levy, 2007	267 adults (age ≥ 16 years) in temporary shelters, Sri Lanka	6 months	PTSD 56%	Female gender, comorbid depression
Hollifield et al., 2008	89 adults (mean age 44.5 years, 53% female) in a severely affected region, Sri Lanka	20–21 months	PTSD 21% Depression 16% Anxiety 30%	Perception of threat to one's life, injury to or death of a family member
Math, John, et al., 2008a	12,784 survivors (88–97% adults) in relief camps on an affected island, India	>1 month	3.7% psychiatric morbidity overall Adjustment disorder 37.5% Depression 21.5% Anxiety disorders 17.5% PTSD 11.2%[a]	Displacement due to the tsunami
Lommen et al., 2009	113 adults (mean age 35.9 years, 71.7% female) from villages for displaced persons, Sri Lanka	15 months	PTSD 52.2%	Female gender, loss of work-related equipment, negative interpretation of tsunami-related memories
Kar et al., 2013	666 adults (mean age 42.7 years, 55.4% female) with either direct ($n = 353$) or indirect ($n = 313$) exposure, India	4.5 years	PTSD 70.9% Depression 33.6% Anxiety 23.1% Suicidal ideation 17.3% Suicide attempt 6.5%	No formal education, perception of disaster as stressful, damage to one's home, loss of livelihood or livestock

(continued)

Table 10.5 (continued)

Study	Study characteristics	Time between tsunami and assessment	Prevalence of mental disorders	Risk factors identified, if any
Pyari et al., 2012; Pyari & Ravindran, 2016[b]	299 adults (mean age 38.6 years, 59.5% female) from a highly affected district, India	6 months	PTSD 52.8%	Female gender, urban residence, injury to self or family members, bereavement
Ranasinghe et al., 2022	325 adults (age $\geq$ 18 years) directly affected, 5 coastal districts, Sri Lanka	8 years	PTSD 10.5–13.3% Depression 18.8%	Female gender, subjective health, prior trauma, depression, severity of tsunami exposure
Children and adolescents				
Neuner et al., 2006	264 children (age 8 to 14 years, 50.8% female) from three severely affected coastal regions, Sri Lanka	3–4 weeks	PTSD 13.9–38.8%[c]	Severity of tsunami exposure, bereavement, past trauma exposure
Vijayakumar, Kannan, & Daniel, 2006a	230 children and adolescents (mean age 12.4 years, 50.9% female) from an affected village, India	1 year	Not directly measured[d]	Tsunami exposure associated with anxiety and PTSD, family history of mental illness associated with depression
John et al., 2007	502 children and adolescents (mean age 12.9 years, 60.4% female) from three affected villages, India	*Wave 1:* 2 months *Wave 2:* 6 months	*Wave 1:* PTSD 70.7% *Wave 2:* PTSD 81.6%	Female gender, older age, bereavement, loss of life or property
Wickrama & Kaspar, 2007	325 adolescents (age 12–19 years) from two affected villages, Sri Lanka	4 months	PTSD 40.9%	Prolonged displacement, family or socioeconomic losses, maternal mental illness
Math et al., 2008b	37 children and adolescents (age < 18 years, 48.6% female) with direct or familial tsunami exposure from an affected island, India	3 months	Adjustment disorder 13.5% Depression 13.5% Panic disorder 10.8% PTSD 10.8%	Not assessed

(continued)

Table 10.5 (continued)

Study	Study characteristics	Time between tsunami and assessment	Prevalence of mental disorders	Risk factors identified, if any
Agampodi et al., 2011	593 adolescents (mean age 14.8 years, 57.3% female) from an affected city, Sri Lanka	8 months	Probable mental disorder 32.2%	Direct exposure to tsunami, perception of being affected by tsunami or tsunami-related rumours, living in a temporary shelter, paternal alcohol use disorder, academic pressure, school-related stressors
Ponnamperuma & Nicolson, 2016	414 adolescents (age 12–16 years, 54.3% female) from an affected district, Sri Lanka	3 years	PTSD 9% Partial PTSD 16%	Female gender, severity of tsunami exposure, prior trauma or abuse, negative trauma appraisals
Ponnamperuma & Nicolson, 2018	753 adolescents (age 12–16 years, 53.9% female) from an affected district, Sri Lanka	3 years	PTSD 4.8% Partial PTSD 9.3%	Female gender, prior trauma, current stressors
Other vulnerable groups				
Wickrama & Kaspar, 2007	325 mothers of adolescent children from two affected villages, Sri Lanka	4 months	PTSD 19.6% Depression 37.8%	Not assessed
Viswanath et al., 2012	Elderly survivors ($n = 75$, mean age 67.6 years, 50.5% female) attending emergency mental health clinics at an affected island, India	>1 month	Adjustment disorder 40% Depression 22.5% Anxiety disorders 18% PTSD 11%	Not assessed
Banford et al., 2016	Mothers of adolescent children ($n = 163$, mean age 43.6 years), Sri Lanka	4 years	Depression 46%	Not assessed

Abbreviations: PTSD, post-traumatic stress disorder

[a]475 of the 12,784 persons screened fulfilled criteria for a psychiatric diagnosis; the relative frequencies within this group are provided in the paper

[b]The results of this study were presented in two papers

[c]In this study, children fulfilled all the diagnostic criteria for PTSD except the duration criterion

[d]This study examined associations between risk factors and dimensional measures of psychopathology. No prevalence estimates were given

disaster, those who experienced bereavement had higher levels of PTSD, depressive and anxiety symptoms, and general psychological distress. Such symptoms extended beyond the period of 6–12 months, usually considered to represent "normal" grief, and are associated with poorer physical health (Suar et al., 2015).

There is little data on the risk of suicidal ideation or attempts following tsunami exposure. In a survey of adults conducted 4 ½ years after exposure, suicidal ideation over this period was reported by 17.3%, and 6.5% had made a suicide attempt. Individuals with a more direct exposure to the tsunami were at a higher risk of both outcomes.

4.1 Coping and Resilience After the Tsunami

Not all individuals exposed to the tsunami experienced significant psychological harm. On the contrary, in one study of over 12,000 affected persons in relief camps, less than 4% fulfilled criteria for a psychiatric diagnosis (Math et al., 2008a). As is the case with earthquakes (Sect. 3.4), individual and social factors can contribute to psychological resilience and to recovery from acute, tsunami-induced stress disorders. In the study just quoted, factors contributing to resilience included family and community support, altruistic behaviour, and engagement in religious or spiritual practices.

Such protective factors retain their importance even over longer periods of time. In Sri Lankan adults interviewed 20–21 months after the tsunami, factors cited as helpful in adapting to post-tsunami life included self-perceived strength, support from relatives or friends, religious practices, and access to adequate health care (Hollifield et al., 2008). In a survey of mothers from the same country, conducted 3 years after the tsunami, factors contributing to lower levels of PTSD and depression included self-perception of resilience, support from family or community, and involvement in specific cultural or religious rituals and practices. On the other hand, passive religious coping was positively associated with PTSD (Wickrama & Wickrama, 2008; Wickrama et al., 2017).

Similar factors operate in children and adolescents. Experts involved in relief work in South India found that most children exhibited remarkable levels of resilience immediately after the tsunami. Only a minority required psychological intervention, and these children often had psychosocial vulnerabilities predating their exposure to this event (Vijayakumar et al., 2006b). Among Sri Lankan adolescents in affected villages, the practice of certain culturally sanctioned rituals, good mother-child relationships, and family support were associated with lower levels of depression and PTSD (Wickrama & Kaspar, 2007; Wickrama et al., 2024). Perceived social support has also been associated with less severe PTSD symptoms in tsunami-exposed adolescents (Ponnamperuma & Nicolson, 2018).

5 Improving Mental Health Care and Preparedness for Earthquakes and Tsunamis in South Asia

Prompt and efficient psychosocial interventions are an essential component of recovery from an earthquake or tsunami. These are more likely to be accepted by survivors if there is sufficient engagement with and participation of local communities. For example, when community mental health clinics were set up in relief camps at the Andaman and Nicobar Islands after the 2004 tsunami, they were used by large numbers of survivors (Viswanath et al., 2012). Receiving appropriate counselling or psychological support after a disaster can prevent adverse mental health outcomes. This was observed in women in Kanyakumari, South India, surveyed 6 months after the tsunami. In this sample, women who had received more than three such sessions were 67% less likely to experience persistent symptoms of PTSD (Pyari & Ravindran, 2016).

Mental health care is also an important aspect of earthquake preparedness. This is supported by several findings from the literature:

- Individual perceptions of disaster risk, threat, or stress are an important predictor of post-tsunami PTSD (Hollifield et al., 2008; Lommen et al., 2009; Kar et al., 2013). These can be targeted through educational or cognitive interventions, allowing for more realistic threat appraisals and the adoption of safety measures.
- Maladaptive coping strategies such as alcohol use may be adopted by up to 20% of tsunami survivors, leading to worse mental health outcomes (Kane et al., 2018); paternal alcohol use disorder was also associated with PTSD in adolescents affected by the tsunami (Agampodi et al., 2011). Thus, the prevention and treatment of alcohol use disorders can improve individual resilience in the face of a disaster.
- Prior trauma or abuse is a predictor of poor mental health following an earthquake or tsunami in adolescents as well as in adults (Neuner et al., 2006; Naeem et al., 2011; Ponnamperuma & Nicolson, 2016; Silwal et al., 2018; Ranasinghe et al., 2022). Addressing pre-earthquake traumatic stress can reduce the likelihood of PTSD after exposure to these disasters.

The conclusion to be drawn from these findings is straightforward: mental health interventions can have both preventive and therapeutic roles in South Asian communities at risk of or already exposed to earthquakes or tsunamis. However, setting up and maintaining effective mental health services either after such a disaster or in anticipation of it is by no means easy. Before discussing effective or potentially effective strategies in this area, it is important to understand the challenges that are likely to be encountered in providing mental health care to an earthquake-affected community.

5.1 Barriers and Challenges

Several experts have examined the main factors impeding effective mental health care after earthquakes or tsunamis in South Asia, both in general and in relation to specific events or their aftermath. These challenges, which are summarized in Table 10.6, underline the need for sustained improvements in both mental health care systems and disaster preparedness.

From this table, it is evident that some of these challenges predate the earthquake itself and reflect long-lasting societal problems (Fernando, 2005; Hussaini et al., 2022). Mental health care in most South Asian countries remains a low priority both conceptually and in terms of funding. This results in a lack of personnel, treatment facilities, and training opportunities, particularly in disaster mental health and trauma-focussed therapies (Khan, 2006; Komesaroff & Sundram, 2006; Hall et al., 2017; Abdul-Hamid et al., 2021). In some cases, poor funding for mental health may reflect general poverty and a lack of basic infrastructure, as in the case of Afghanistan (Hussaini et al., 2022; Akram et al., 2024). In others, general socioeconomic development may be good, but there is a disproportionate deficit in the mental health care budget and a lack of training facilities, as in the Maldives (Ibrahim & Hameed, 2006a). Another important challenge faced by some countries is a prior ongoing crisis that burdens an already weak mental health care system. This was observed in Sri Lanka, where the tsunami compounded the effects of an ongoing civil war (Cheng, 2006), and in Nepal, where a civil war occurring a decade before the earthquake led to mistrust of the government and poor disaster readiness (Welton-Mitchell et al., 2018). A more severe instance of this phenomenon was seen in the 2022 Afghanistan earthquake, which occurred in the background of both civil unrest and the COVID-19 pandemic (Hussaini et al., 2022; Akram et al., 2024). These problems may be worsened by the lack of a comprehensive earthquake management policy, either in general or in relation to mental health (Pradhan, 2012; Chase et al., 2018).

Immediately after an earthquake, affected communities—including health care workers—are likely to experience high levels of negative emotions and cognitions. These include feelings of sadness, fear, anger, being "overwhelmed", and a sense of helplessness or lack of agency (Mahoney et al., 2006; Somasundaram, 2013). Against this backdrop, there may be a poor implementation of existing plans (Chase et al., 2018) and a general atmosphere of "chaos" characterized by bureaucratic inefficiency and poor coordination between government agencies, between the government and nongovernmental agencies, and between relief workers (state or non-state) and communities. This problem may be compounded by linguistic and cultural barriers in the case of aid offered by overseas workers or agencies, leading to miscommunication, mistrust, and the ineffective use of resources (Ganesan, 2006; Welton-Mitchell et al., 2018; Hussaini et al., 2022). In such an atmosphere, rumours and even outright misinformation (e.g. about the extent of damage or death tolls) may circulate by word of mouth or through the media. This leads to higher levels of anxiety and depression (Powell et al., 2019).

Table 10.6 Barriers to the provision of mental health care after earthquakes and related disasters in South Asia

Time period	Barriers
Pre-earthquake	• General socioeconomic vulnerability (e.g. high levels of poverty or lack of access to basic amenities) • Low priority or funding for mental health • Lack of mental health manpower and infrastructure • Lack of training in disaster mental health • Lack of training in trauma-related therapy techniques • Lack of integration of mental health care with primary/community health care • Lack of a comprehensive earthquake management policy • Low population awareness or preparedness • Effect of other ongoing crises, such as civil unrest or infectious disease epidemics • Pre-existing societal "fault lines" related to caste, religion, or ethnicity
Acute (immediately after the event)	• Damage to existing infrastructure • Weak implementation of existing earthquake management policies • "Overloading" of existing mental health care facilities • Stigma against help-seeking for mental disorders • Supply chain problems (e.g. for medications) • Feelings of helplessness, powerlessness, or being "overwhelmed" at the community level • Poor coordination between the government, non-state aid workers, and affected communities • Underutilization of existing personnel • Misinformation • Mistrust of "foreign" aid efforts • Possible harm from unnecessary or culturally inappropriate interventions
Post-earthquake	• Assumption that acute needs have been met and no long-term mental health care is required • Insufficient funding or government support for long-term mental health care growth • Insufficient rehabilitation of affected persons in terms of housing, education, or work • Chronic stress due to bereavement, homelessness, or loss of income/livelihood • Stigma against help-seeking for long-term mental health concerns • Maladaptive coping by affected individuals (e.g. substance use)

Sources: Khan, 2006; Cheng, 2006; Ganesan, 2006; Komesaroff & Sundram, 2006; Mahoney et al., 2006; Math et al., 2006; Somasundaram, 2013; Thapa, 2015; Hall et al., 2017; Chase et al., 2018; Leichner et al., 2018; Welton-Mitchell et al., 2018; Alisha et al., 2019; Powell et al., 2019; Bhardwaj et al., 2020; Abdul-Hamid et al., 2021; Hussaini et al., 2022; Akram et al., 2024

If mental health care is offered in isolation, without attention to physical health, information about the status of loved ones, or provision of other essentials (e.g. food or financial assistance), it may be rejected by communities. This is likely to happen when there is a shortage of trained personnel, such as social workers, who can help survivors with such concerns (Ganesan, 2006; Powell et al., 2019). Though these concerns have been raised by some experts, the opposite scenario is far more common in South Asia: relief efforts often focus on a limited number of resources, such as food, clothing, or short-term financial aid, with less attention to equally important concerns such as housing and mental health (Ogra et al., 2021). Even when mental health care is provided, it may be suboptimal due to a lack of familiarity with trauma-centred therapies or cultural insensitivity (Ganesan, 2006; Abdul-Hamid et al., 2021). Patients requiring pharmacotherapy may not be able to access it due to supply chain disruptions caused by the earthquake (Hall et al., 2017).

Barriers to mental health care also exist in the rebuilding phase, lasting for weeks or months. Often, an initial offer of treatment or psychological first aid leads to the assumption that mental health needs have been met and that nothing further is required (Bhardwaj et al., 2020). This results in a scenario of "one-off efforts" where there is little lasting commitment to improving mental health care or to treating the long-term mental health effects of an earthquake, such as chronic depression or PTSD (Khan 2006). This results in mental health initiatives that peak immediately after an earthquake but cannot be sustained due to a lack of funding or political will (Chase et al., 2018). In fact, the mental health needs of an affected community may be higher at this stage. This is both because some conditions, such as PTSD, evolve gradually over weeks or months (Math et al., 2006) and because the earthquake leaves a trail of poverty, unemployment, bereavement, and homelessness in its wake, all of which are ongoing stressors that are not easily resolved (Mahoney et al., 2006; Somasundaram, 2013). This is aggravated by deficiencies in rehabilitative measures, leaving people reliant on temporary housing or uncertain financial assistance, and by maladaptive forms of coping such as substance misuse. As a result, this "second wave" of mental morbidity is often treated insufficiently or not at all (Komesaroff & Sundram, 2006; WHO India, 2006).

5.2 *Effective Interventions and Strategies for Mental Health Care*

Despite these barriers, the mental health scenario in South Asian communities affected by earthquakes or by the 2004 tsunami is by no means entirely negative. The "shock to the system" caused by these disasters led to a "boost" or "acceleration" in mental health care in several affected countries, characterized by greater awareness of mental health issues among policymakers, a slight increase in the mental health care budget, and increases in manpower, training, and community involvement. Such positive changes have been observed in India (WHO India, 2006), Sri Lanka (Cheng, 2006), the Maldives (Ibrahim & Hameed, 2006a), and Nepal (Chase et al., 2018; Alisha et al., 2019). Alongside these salutary changes, a number of cost-effective, community-based interventions or approaches, aimed at improving mental health, have been designed and tested in South Asian populations affected by these disasters (Chatterjee, 2005; Shah, 2013; Welton-Mitchell et al., 2018). These interventions are summarized in Table 10.7.

A careful reading of the literature summarized above suggests that the most successful interventions, regardless of their specifics, have four features in common:

- They involve members of the local community in volunteer or leadership roles through appropriate training. This empowers the community, restores a sense of agency to its members, and ensures sustainable mental health care even after a specific programme is concluded.

Table 10.7 Potentially effective interventions or strategies to improve mental health after an earthquake or tsunami in South Asian populations

Intervention	Level of evidence
Teacher-assisted interventions to improve child and adolescent mental health (Becker, 2007)	++
Volunteer-led group interventions to improve adult mental health (Vijayakumar & Kumar, 2008)	++
Community-based group therapy for women with trauma exposure (Becker, 2009)	++
A combination of psychiatric care with traditional practices (e.g. yoga, reading religious verses) aimed at promoting mental health (Shah, 2013)	++
"Hybrid" group intervention addressing both mental health and disaster preparedness (Welton-Mitchell et al., 2018)	++
Use of telemedicine and mobile health (mHealth) technology to provide psychological interventions to affected communities (Bhardwaj et al., 2020)	++
Group problem-solving therapy for affected communities (Sangraula et al., 2020)	++
Integration of mental health into primary health by training community health workers (Leichner et al., 2018)	++
Long-term (>6 months) psychological support for victims (WHO India, 2006)	+
Counselling regarding avoidance or reduction of substance use after a disaster (WHO India, 2006)	+
Short films, audiovisual aids, and educational material about disaster mental health and readiness in the local language (Vijayakumar et al., 2006c; Somasundaram, 2013)	+
Grief counselling or therapy for those bereaved (Sumathipala et al., 2006; Somasundaram, 2013)	+
Provision of separate services for vulnerable populations, such as the elderly (Viswanath et al., 2012)	+
Income generation and employment opportunities for survivors (Somasundaram, 2013)	+
Training and sensitization on disaster mental health for community health workers (Jha & Shakya, 2015; Chadda & Malhotra, 2006)	+/−
Improving coordination between national, regional, and international agencies providing mental health support (Somasundaram, 2013)	+/−
Training therapists in trauma-focussed therapies (Abdul-Hamid et al., 2021)	+/−

++, good evidence of efficacy based on a pre-/post-intervention study design in affected populations; +, anecdotal or qualitative evidence of benefit in affected population; +/−, expert or professional recommendation but no reports of direct effectiveness

- They are adapted to the victim's language and culture and sometimes make use of traditional practices and customs in synergy with psychological interventions. This improves acceptability and reduces the stigma associated with seeking "mental" or "psychiatric" care (Greene et al., 2017).
- They address concerns that are relevant to the concerned community and disaster type (such as material losses or bereavement), rather than focusing on general issues or concepts (such as "trauma" or "depression"). In other words, they are "psychosocial" and not merely "psychological" (Fernando, 2005).
- They are cost-effective, making use of locally available human and material resources, maximizing benefit to affected communities or authorities without placing an undue financial burden on any of the stakeholders.

Other approaches, such as making use of mobile phones to coordinate mental health care, provide safety information or raise awareness, also show promise; however, their relative recency means that they have not been systematically evaluated in South Asian earthquake or tsunami scenarios.

Another key aspect of successful mental health interventions after an earthquake is proper coordination and assignment of responsibilities among state authorities, external non-state relief workers, and communities (Vijayakumar et al., 2006b). If such coordination is lacking, available manpower and resources are not used efficiently, relief workers experience higher levels of stress, and the perceived needs of affected communities are not met, leading to apathy or even resistance. Such coordination and cooperation may be difficult in countries where there is political instability or civil unrest, as observed during the 2022 Afghanistan earthquake (Akram et al., 2024).

Finally, it should be remembered that mental health care is only one component of earthquake or tsunami readiness and relief. Survivors of these disasters experience personal, material, and economic losses that are difficult or even impossible to replace. For best results, mental health interventions should go hand in hand not just with immediate relief measures, but with long-term efforts at rehabilitation and reconstruction in affected regions and communities and with preparedness measures for future disasters of the same kind. In other words, mental health care should be seen as part of a broader vision of "building back better" after an earthquake or related event (Sherchan et al., 2017; Chase et al., 2018).

5.3 Fostering Psychological Resilience and "Psychological Preparedness" in Affected or At-Risk Communities

To "build back better" implies addressing all components of disaster vulnerability, including the psychosocial dimension (Chase et al., 2018). This includes not just mental health but developing appropriate and adaptive levels of knowledge, attitudes, and practices regarding a possible earthquake or tsunami in vulnerable zones, without exaggerating risks or causing undue anxiety. Even if levels of awareness in communities are low, this can be remedied through educational interventions. In a study of urban residents located in a seismic zone in India, it was found that the distribution of informational material, demonstrations of safety behaviours, and education regarding the maintenance of a "disaster kit" resulted in a significant increase in awareness and household preparedness post-intervention (Agarwalla et al., 2020).

Such interventions could be expanded to include information and advice on the psychological after-effects of earthquakes or general mental health literacy (Shakya, 2016; Hall et al., 2017). A study conducted in affected communities about 10 weeks after the 2015 Nepal earthquake demonstrated the feasibility of this approach. The intervention developed in this case involved manual-based group sessions based on international guidelines but modified to reflect the local culture. Topics covered in the manual included awareness of common mental and physical health problems after an earthquake, coping strategies, reducing the stigma surrounding mental health issues, the link between disaster readiness and mental health, household- and community-level preparedness, helping others, and building resilience (Welton-Mitchell et al., 2018).

Despite the hardships they have endured, disaster-affected communities in South Asia exhibit high levels of resilience and cohesiveness, and this can be leveraged to support post-earthquake recovery (Chadda & Malhotra, 2006; Vijayakumar et al., 2006b; Shah, 2013; Somasundaram, 2013; Hall et al., 2017). A year after the 2015 Nepal earthquake, community dwellers felt that their participation in relief efforts was successful and felt that their ties to their families and neighbours and their ability to mobilize local resources could prove valuable in the event of a future disaster (Rawat et al., 2023). In South Asia, these resources include the initiatives and efforts of community leaders, teachers, and faith-based leaders and organizations (Makhdum & Javed, 2006; Ibrahim & Hameed, 2006b; Hall et al., 2017). More generally, existing social structures and cultural practices can also contribute to resilience and recovery earthquake or a tsunami, and it is important that these are strengthened, not disrupted, during relief and rehabilitation work (Somasundaram, 2013; Welton-Mitchell et al., 2018). In certain cases, resilience can be fostered by encouraging participation in traditional rituals or practices, often with a spiritual or religious basis: this has been observed following the 2001 Gujarat earthquake in India (Shah, 2013) and following the 2004 tsunami in Sri Lanka (Wickrama et al., 2017, 2024). Another approach that may aid collective recovery and build resilience is to involve affected communities in "normalizing" acts, such as sports or cultural festivals (Vijayakumar et al., 2006b) or recreational activities in general (Ibrahim & Hameed, 2006b). The net effect of drawing on such resources and promoting such activities is to increase social cohesion and encourage communities to gradually move beyond the collective trauma of an earthquake.

Improving earthquake preparedness is another essential component of building psychosocial resilience. This can include

- The formulation of better earthquake readiness plans, which should be disseminated among vulnerable communities through appropriate information,

education, and communication (IEC) approaches in the local language (Hetenyi & Subedi, 2023).
- Improving existing communication systems for the provision of warnings, instructions related to safety, and information on available aid and health care, both by strengthening existing mechanisms and by making use of technological advances (Hall et al., 2017).
- Improving coordination between the relevant government departments, local nongovernmental organizations, and at-risk communities, in order to ensure effective cooperation and synergy between them if an earthquake should occur in the future (Vijayakumar et al., 2006b).

Such strategies must be accompanied by concerted efforts to develop remedies for concerns related to public health, food security, housing, education, employment, and reconstruction of infrastructure in affected communities (Komesaroff & Sundram, 2006; Somasundaram, 2013; Chase et al., 2018). Reconstruction efforts should ideally be based on "green" principles that foster sustainable development (Sonak et al., 2008). Doing so would allow affected communities to grow in resilience across all domains—physical, psychological, social, economic, and environmental—and to be better equipped to face further disasters of this sort.

6 Conclusion

Earthquakes and tsunamis are among the most devastating types of natural disasters, whether considered in terms of mortality or of material and economic loss. This devastation is frequently accompanied by symptoms of mental disorder, which can often be chronic and disabling. The events of the past two decades have shown that South Asian populations exposed to these disasters often develop symptoms of depression or PTSD, particularly when they have experienced significant personal loss or injury. The mental health impact of these disasters in South Asia is exacerbated by a lack of disaster preparedness, shortages of mental health manpower and infrastructure, and the atmosphere of chaos and powerlessness that follows these events. These difficulties notwithstanding, it is possible to address post-earthquake or post-tsunami mental health problems through community-based psychosocial interventions. Such interventions should not be purely "psychotherapeutic": they must be tailored to the needs of affected communities and combined with relief measures which address issues of physical health, housing, food security, and personal and family safety. In the months following an earthquake, efforts should be made to draw on community resources, customs, and practices to facilitate a return to pre-disaster patterns of life. Continued mental care should remain available for those survivors requiring it. These psychosocial approaches must be integrated with broader efforts to "build back better": rebuilding homes and infrastructure in an environmentally sustainable manner, facilitating returns to education and employment, and developing earthquake readiness plans with the participation of affected or at-risk South Asian communities.

References

Abdul-Hamid, W., Karki, C. B., Hughes, J. H., & Morgan, S. (2021). The need for trauma therapy for victims of man-made trauma compared to those of natural disaster, a survey of health professionals. *Psychiatria Danubina, 33*(Suppl 1), 13–17.

Acharya Pandey, R., Chalise, P., Khadka, S., Chaulagain, B., Maharjan, B., Pandey, J., Nepal, J., & Pandey, C. (2023). Post-traumatic stress disorder and its associated factors among survivors of 2015 earthquake in Nepal. *BMC Psychiatry, 23*(1), 340. https://doi.org/10.1186/s12888-023-04836-3

Adhikari, B., Mishra, S. R., & Raut, S. (2016). Rebuilding earthquake struck Nepal through community engagement. *Frontiers in Public Health, 4*, 121. https://doi.org/10.3389/fpubh.2016.00121

Adhikari, S., Thakur, A., Pratt, C., Feinn, R., Sewack, W., & Hill, D. (2019). Psychological distress among adolescent students following the April 25, 2015 massive earthquake in Nepal. *Cureus, 11*(6), e4809. https://doi.org/10.7759/cureus.4809

Agampodi, T. C., Agampodi, S. B., & Fonseka, P. (2011). Prevalence of mental health problems in adolescent schoolchildren in Galle District, Sri Lanka: Eight months after tsunami. *Asia-Pacific Journal of Public Health, 23*(4), 588–600. https://doi.org/10.1177/1010539509349866

Agarwalla, R., Pathak, R., Siddiqui, A., Panda, M., Gupta, E., & Islam, F. (2020). A community-based intervention study to assess the effectiveness of awareness imparted on earthquake preparedness among the residents of South Delhi, India. *Indian Journal of Community Medicine: Official Publication of Indian Association of Preventive & Social Medicine, 45*(3), 375–378. https://doi.org/10.4103/ijcm.IJCM_404_19

Akhundzadah, N. A. (2025). Earthquake risk severity and urgent need for disaster management in Afghanistan. *GeoHazards, 6*(1), 9. https://doi.org/10.3390/geohazards6010009

Akram, S., Baloch, M. Y. J., Alrefaei, A. F., Almutairi, M. H., Idrees, M., & Al-Kubaisi, H. A. R. A. (2024). Interface between mental health and the earthquake: Considering humanitarian endeavor. *Frontiers in Public Health, 12*, 1326407. https://doi.org/10.3389/fpubh.2024.1326407

Aksoy, C. G., Chupilkin, M., Koczan, Z., & Plekhanov, A. (2024). Unearthing the impact of earthquakes: A review of economic and social consequences. *Journal of Policy Analysis and Management*, 1–24. https://doi.org/10.1002/pam.22642

Ali, M., Farooq, N., Bhatti, M. A., & Kuroiwa, C. (2012). Assessment of prevalence and determinants of posttraumatic stress disorder in survivors of earthquake in Pakistan using Davidson Trauma Scale. *Journal of Affective Disorders, 136*(3), 238–243. https://doi.org/10.1016/j.jad.2011.12.023

Alisha, K. C., Gan, C. C. R., & Dwirahmadi, F. (2019). Breaking through barriers and building disaster mental resilience: A case study in the aftermath of the 2015 Nepal earthquakes. *International Journal of Environmental Research and Public Health, 16*(16), 2964. https://doi.org/10.3390/ijerph16162964

Ando, S., Kuwabara, H., Araki, T., Kanehara, A., Tanaka, S., Morishima, R., Kondo, S., & Kasai, K. (2017). Mental health problems in a community after the Great East Japan Earthquake in 2011: A systematic review. *Harvard Review of Psychiatry, 25*(1), 15–28. https://doi.org/10.1097/HRP.0000000000000124

Arrell, K., Rosser, N. J., Kincey, M. E., Robinson, T. R., Horton, P., Densmore, A. L., Oven, K.J., Shrestha, R., & Pujara, D. S. (2024). The dynamic threat from landslides following large continentalearthquakes. *PloS one, 19*(8), e0308444. https://doi.org/10.1371/journal.pone.0308444

Atreya, K., Rimal, N. S., Makai, P., Baidya, M., Karki, J., Pohl, G., & Bhattarai, S. (2022). Dalit's livelihoods in Nepal: Income sources and determinants. *Environment, Development and Sustainability*, 1–29. Advance online publication. https://doi.org/10.1007/s10668-022-02582-2

Aydin, Ö. F., Yilmaz, S., Ulusoy, M., & Polat, M. (2025). Analyzing emergency department presentations linked to secondary earthquake effects. *The American Journal of Emergency Medicine, 89*, 61–66. https://doi.org/10.1016/j.ajem.2024.12.037

Ayub, M., Poongan, I., Masood, K., Gul, H., Ali, M., Farrukh, A., Shaheen, A., Chaudhry, H. R., & Naeem, F. (2012). Psychological morbidity in children 18 months after Kashmir earthquake of 2005. *Child Psychiatry and Human Development, 43*(3), 323–336. https://doi.org/10.1007/s10578-011-0267-9

Ayub, M., Saeed, K., Kingdon, D., & Naeem, F. (2015). Rate and predictors of psychotic symptoms after Kashmir earthquake. *European Archives of Psychiatry and Clinical Neuroscience, 265*(6), 471–481. https://doi.org/10.1007/s00406-014-0561-1

Aziz, S., & Aslam, N. (2012). Psychiatric Morbidity and Work and Social AdjustmentAmong Earthquake Survivors Extricated from under the Rubble. *Indian Journal of Psychological Medicine, 34*(4), 346–349. https://doi.org/10.4103/0253-7176.108215

Balikuddembe, J. K., Reinhardt, J. D., Vahid, G., & Di, B. (2024). A scoping review of post-earthquake healthcare for vulnerable groups of the 2023 Turkey-Syria earthquakes. *BMC Public Health, 24*(1), 945. https://doi.org/10.1186/s12889-024-18395-z

Banford, A., Ivey, D. C., Wickrama, T., Fischer, J., Prouty, A., & Smith, D. (2016). The role of natural disaster in individual and relational adjustment in Sri Lankan mothers following the 2004 tsunami. *Disasters, 40*(1), 134–157. https://doi.org/10.1111/disa.12137

Baral, I. A., & Bhagwati, K. C. (2019). Post traumatic stress disorder and coping strategies among adult survivors of earthquake, Nepal. *BMC Psychiatry, 19*, 118. https://doi.org/10.1186/s12888-019-2090-y

Becker, S. M. (2007). Psychosocial care for adult and child survivors of the tsunami disaster in India. *Journal of Child and Adolescent Psychiatric Nursing: Official Publication of the Association of Child and Adolescent Psychiatric Nurses, Inc, 20*(3), 148–155. https://doi.org/10.1111/j.1744-6171.2007.00105.x

Becker, S. M. (2009). Psychosocial care for women survivors of the tsunami disaster in India. *American Journal of Public Health, 99*(4), 654–658. https://doi.org/10.2105/AJPH.2008.146571

Bhardwaj, A., Subba, P., Rai, S., Bhat, C., Ghimire, R., Jordans, M. J. D., Green, E., Vasudevan, L., & Kohrt, B. A. (2020). Lessons learned through piloting a community-based SMS referral system for common mental health disorders used by female community health volunteers in rural Nepal. *BMC Research Notes, 13*(1), 309. https://doi.org/10.1186/s13104-020-05148-5

Bhattarai, M., Maneewat, K., & Sae-Sia, W. (2018). Psychosocial factors affecting resilience in Nepalese individuals with earthquake-related spinal cord injury: A cross-sectional study. *BMC Psychiatry, 18*(1), 60. https://doi.org/10.1186/s12888-018-1640-z

Bremer, R. (2003). Policy development in disaster preparedness and management: Lessons learned from the January 2001 earthquake in Gujarat, India. *Prehospital and Disaster Medicine, 18*(4), 372–384. https://doi.org/10.1017/s1049023x00001345

Cénat, J. M., McIntee, S. E., & Blais-Rochette, C. (2020). Symptoms of posttraumatic stress disorder, depression, anxiety and other mental health problems following the 2010 earthquake in Haiti: A systematic review and meta-analysis. *Journal of Affective Disorders, 273*, 55–85. https://doi.org/10.1016/j.jad.2020.04.046

Chadda, R. K., & Malhotra, A. (2006). An experience of provision of psychiatric services in the earthquake-affected area of Kashmir in India. *International Psychiatry: Bulletin of the Board of International Affairs of the Royal College of Psychiatrists, 3*(3), 3–5.

Chadda, R. K., Malhotra, A., Kaw, N., Singh, J., & Sethi, H. (2007). Mental health problems following the 2005 earthquake in Kashmir: Findings of community-run clinics. *Prehospital and Disaster Medicine, 22*(6), 541–546. https://doi.org/10.1017/s1049023x00005409

Chase, L. E., Marahatta, K., Sidgel, K., Shrestha, S., Gautam, K., Luitel, N. P., Dotel, B. R., & Samuel, R. (2018). Building back better? Taking stock of the post-earthquake mental health and psychosocial response in Nepal. *International Journal of Mental Health Systems, 12*, 44. https://doi.org/10.1186/s13033-018-0221-3

Chatterjee, P. (2005). Mental health care for India's tsunami survivors. *The Lancet, 365*(9462), 833–834. https://doi.org/10.1016/S0140-6736(05)71023-0

Cheng, M. H. (2006). Post-tsunami boost to southeast Asia's mental health care. *The Lancet, 367*(9504), 15–17. https://doi.org/10.1016/S0140-6736(06)67904-X

Chishtie, J., Chishtie, F., Yoshida, K., & Balogh, R. (2019). Spinal cord injury rehabilitation and pressure ulcer prevention after the 2005 South Asian Earthquake: A CBR case study from Pakistan. *Disability and Rehabilitation, 41*(14), 1655–1663. https://doi.org/10.1080/09638288.2018.1445783

Choudhury, M., & Haque, C. E. (2024). Disaster management policy changes in Bangladesh: Drivers and factors of a shift from reactive to proactive approach. *Environmental Policy and Governance, 34*, 445–462. https://doi.org/10.1002/eet.2094

Dube, A., Moffatt, M., Davison, C., & Bartels, S. (2018). Health outcomes for children in Haiti since the 2010 earthquake: A systematic review. *Prehospital and Disaster Medicine, 33*(1), 77–88. https://doi.org/10.1017/S1049023X17007105

Efendi, G. Y., Temeltürk, R. D., Çakmak, I. B., & Dinçer, M. (2023). Surviving the immediate aftermath of a disaster: A preliminary investigation of adolescents' acute stress reactions and mental health needs after the 2023 Turkey earthquakes. *Children (Basel, Switzerland), 10*(9), 1485. https://doi.org/10.3390/children10091485

Ehring, T., Razik, S., & Emmelkamp, P. M. (2011). Prevalence and predictors of posttraumatic stress disorder, anxiety, depression, and burnout in Pakistani earthquake recovery workers. *Psychiatry Research, 185*(1–2), 161–166. https://doi.org/10.1016/j.psychres.2009.10.018

Fan, X., Scaringi, G., Korup, O., West, A. J., van Westen, C. J., Tanyas, H., … & Huang, R. (2019). Earthquake-induced chains of geologic hazards: Patterns, mechanisms, and impacts. *Reviews of Geophysics, 57*(2), 421–503. https://doi.org/10.1029/2018RG000626

Feder, A., Ahmad, S., Lee, E. J., Morgan, J. E., Singh, R., Smith, B. W., Southwick, S. M., & Charney, D. S. (2013). Coping and PTSD symptoms in Pakistani earthquake survivors: Purpose in life, religious coping and social support. *Journal of Affective Disorders, 147*(1–3), 156–163. https://doi.org/10.1016/j.jad.2012.10.027

Fernando, G. A. (2005). Interventions for survivors of the tsunami disaster: Report from Sri Lanka. *Journal of Traumatic Stress, 18*(3), 267–268. https://doi.org/10.1002/jts.20042

Fredricks, K., Dinh, H., Kusi, M., Yogal, C., Karmacharya, B. M., Burke, T. F., & Nelson, B. D. (2017). Community health workers and disasters: Lessons learned from the 2015 earthquake in Nepal. *Prehospital and Disaster Medicine, 32*(6), 604–609. https://doi.org/10.1017/S1049023X1700680X

Futterman, I. D., Grace, H., Weingarten, S., Borjian, A., & Clare, C. A. (2023). Maternal anxiety, depression and posttraumatic stress disorder (PTSD) after natural disasters: A systematic review. *The Journal of Maternal-Fetal & Neonatal Medicine, 36*(1), 2199345. https://doi.org/10.1080/14767058.2023.2199345

Ganesan, M. (2006). Psychosocial response to disasters--some concerns. *International Review of Psychiatry (Abingdon, England), 18*(3), 241–247. https://doi.org/10.1080/09540260600656035

Giri, B., Malla, A., & Chattu, V. K. (2024). The recent 2023 earthquake in Nepal: A global health perspective. *Journal of Nepal Medical Association, 62*(275), 478–482. https://doi.org/10.31729/jnma.8642

Greene, M. C., Jordans, M. J. D., Kohrt, B. A., Ventevogel, P., Kirmayer, L. J., Hassan, G., Chiumento, A., van Ommeren, M., & Tol, W. A. (2017). Addressing culture and context in humanitarian response: Preparing desk reviews to inform mental health and psychosocial support. *Conflict and Health, 11*, 21. https://doi.org/10.1186/s13031-017-0123-z

Hall, M. L., Lee, A. C., Cartwright, C., Marahatta, S., Karki, J., & Simkhada, P. (2017). The 2015 Nepal earthquake disaster: Lessons learned one year on. *Public Health, 145*, 39–44. https://doi.org/10.1016/j.puhe.2016.12.031

Halvorson, S. J., & Hamilton, J. P. (2010). In the aftermath of the Qa'yamat: The Kashmir earthquake disaster in northern Pakistan. *Disasters, 34*(1), 184–204. https://doi.org/10.1111/j.1467-7717.2009.01124.x

Hassan, S., Nguyen, M., Buchanan, M., Grimshaw, A., Adams, O. P., Hassell, T., Ragster, L., & Nunez-Smith, M. (2020). Management of chronic noncommunicable diseases after natural disasters in the Caribbean: A scoping review. *Health affairs (Project Hope), 39*(12), 2136–2143. https://doi.org/10.1377/hlthaff.2020.01119

Hetenyi, G., & Subedi, S. (2023). A call to action for a comprehensive earthquake education policy in Nepal. *Seismica, 2*(2), 1–10. https://doi.org/10.26443/seismica.v212.242

Hoang, T., Noy, I., & Van, T. L. (2025). Heterogenous mental health impacts of a forced relocation: The red zone in Christchurch (New Zealand). *Health Economics*. Advance online publication. https://doi.org/10.1002/hec.70004

Hollifield, M., Hewage, C., Gunawardena, C. N., Kodituwakku, P., Bopagoda, K., & Weerarathnege, K. (2008). Symptoms and coping in Sri Lanka 20–21 months after the 2004 tsunami. *The British Journal of Psychiatry: The Journal of Mental Science, 192*(1), 39–44. https://doi.org/10.1192/bjp.bp.107.038422

Holzer, T. L., & Savage, J. C. (2013). Global earthquake fatalities and population. *Earthquake Spectra, 29*(1), 155–175. https://doi.org/10.1193/1.4000106

Humayun, A. (2008). South Asian earthquake: psychiatric experience in a tertiary hospital. *Eastern Mediterranean Health Journal = La Revue de Sante De La Mediterranee Orientale = Al-Majallah Al-Sihhiyah Li-Sharq Al-Mutawassit, 14*(5), 1205–1216.

Hussaini, S. J., Ali, S. H., Syyeda Rahmat, Z., Islam, Z., & Tharwani, Z. H. (2022). Mental health impacts of earthquake on Afghans amidst humanitarian crisis. *Annals of Medicine and Surgery (2012), 81*, 104521. https://doi.org/10.1016/j.amsu.2022.104521

Ibrahim, A., & Hameed, A. (2006a). Mental health and psychosocial support aspects of disaster preparedness in the Maldives. *International Review of Psychiatry (Abingdon, England), 18*(6), 573–578. https://doi.org/10.1080/09540260601129784

Ibrahim, A., & Hameed, A. (2006b). Mental health and psychosocial response after the worst natural disaster in the history of the Maldives. *International Review of Psychiatry (Abingdon, England), 18*(6), 567–572. https://doi.org/10.1080/09540260601038431

Jahangiri, K., Yousefi, K., Mozafari, A., & Sahebi, A. (2020). The prevalence of suicidal ideation after the earthquake: A systematic review and meta-analysis. *Iranian Journal of Public Health, 49*(12), 2330–2338. https://doi.org/10.18502/ijph.v49i12.4815

Jha, A., & Shakya, S. (2015). Rational for conducting PTSD research and challenges of recruiting and training volunteers to screen and treat PTSD among the Nepal 2015 earthquake survivors. *JNMA; Journal of the Nepal Medical Association, 53*(199), 202–207.

Jha, A., Basu, R., & Basu, A. (2016). Studying policy changes in disaster management in India: A tale of two cyclones. *Disaster Medicine and Public Health Preparedness, 10*(1), 42–46. https://doi.org/10.1017/dmp.2015.116

Jha, A., Shakya, S., Zang, Y., Pathak, N., Pradhan, P. K., Bhatta, K. R., Sthapit, S., Niraula, S., & Nehete, R. (2017). Identification and treatment of Nepal 2015 earthquake survivors with posttraumatic stress disorder by nonspecialist volunteers: An exploratory cross-sectional study. *Indian Journal of Psychiatry, 59*(3), 320–327. https://doi.org/10.4103/psychiatry.IndianJPsychiatry_236_16

John, P. B., Russell, S., & Russell, P. S. (2007). The prevalence of posttraumatic stress disorder among children and adolescents affected by tsunami disaster in Tamil Nadu. *Disaster Management & Response: DMR: An Official Publication of the Emergency Nurses Association, 5*(1), 3–7. https://doi.org/10.1016/j.dmr.2006.11.001

Kane, J. C., Luitel, N. P., Jordans, M. J. D., Kohrt, B. A., Weissbecker, I., & Tol, W. A. (2018). Mental health and psychosocial problems in the aftermath of the Nepal earthquakes: Findings from a representative cluster sample survey. *Epidemiology and Psychiatric Sciences, 27*(3), 301–310. https://doi.org/10.1017/S2045796016001104

Kar, N., & Sharma, A. (2021). Matching the symptom profile of adolescent disaster survivors with changing diagnostic criteria of posttraumatic stress disorder: Focus on ICD-11. *Indian Journal of Psychological Medicine, 43*(2), 100–105. https://doi.org/10.1177/0253717620926848

Kar, N., Krishnaraaj, R., & Rameshraj, K. (2013). Long-term mental health outcomes following the 2004 Asian tsunami disaster: A comparative study on direct and indirect exposure. *Disaster Health, 2*(1), 35–45. https://doi.org/10.4161/dish.24705

Kartol, A., Üztemur, S., & Gökalp, A. (2025). Exploring the complex relationships between earthquake obsession and mental well-being among earthquake survivors: Serial mediation and moderated mediation analysis. *Journal of Health Psychology*, 13591053251341189. Advance online publication. https://doi.org/10.1177/13591053251341189

Kato, A., & Ben-Zion, Y. (2021). The generation of large earthquakes. *Nature Reviews, 2*, 26–39. https://doi.org/10.1038/s43017-020-00108-w

Khan, M. M. (2006). Earthquake 2005: Challenges for Pakistani psychiatry. *International Psychiatry: Bulletin of the Board of International Affairs of the Royal College of Psychiatrists, 3*(3), 21–23.

Khatri, G. K., Tran, T. D., Baral, S., & Fisher, J. (2018). Effect of the 2015 Nepal earthquakes on symptoms of common mental disorders among women who are pregnant. *Journal of Affective Disorders, 228*, 238–247. https://doi.org/10.1016/j.jad.2017.12.016

Khatri, G. K., Tran, T. D., Baral, S., & Fisher, J. (2020). Experiences of an earthquake during pregnancy, antenatal mental health and infants' birthweight in Bhaktapur District, Nepal, 2015: A population-based cohort study. *BMC Pregnancy and Childbirth, 20*(1), 414. https://doi.org/10.1186/s12884-020-03086-5

Koirala, R., Søegaard, E. G. I., Ojha, S. P., Hauff, E., & Thapa, S. B. (2020). Trauma related psychiatric disorders and their correlates in a clinical sample: A cross-sectional study in trauma affected patients visiting a psychiatric clinic in Nepal. *PLoS One, 15*(6), e0234203. https://doi.org/10.1371/journal.pone.0234203

Komesaroff, P. A., & Sundram, S. (2006). Challenges of post-tsunami reconstruction in Sri Lanka: Health care aid and the Health Alliance. *The Medical Journal of Australia, 184*(1), 23–26. https://doi.org/10.5694/j.1326-5377.2006.tb00091.x

Kumar, M. S., Murhekar, M. V., Hutin, Y., Subramanian, T., Ramachandran, V., & Gupte, M. D. (2007). Prevalence of posttraumatic stress disorder in a coastal fishing village in Tamil Nadu, India, after the December 2004 tsunami. *American Journal of Public Health, 97*(1), 99–101. https://doi.org/10.2105/AJPH.2005.071167

Kumar, R., Mittal, H., Sandeep, S., & Sharma, B. (2022). Earthquake genesis and earthquake early warning systems: Challenges and a way forward. *Surveys in Geophysics, 43*, 1143–1168. https://doi.org/10.1007/s10712-022-09710-7

Kusević, Z., Krstanović, K., & Kroflin, K. (2021). Some psychological, gastrointestinal and cardiovascular consequences of earthquakes. *Psychiatria Danubina, 33*(Suppl 4), 1248–1253.

Lee, K., Lee, S. H., Park, T., & Lee, J. Y. (2017). Stressors of Korean disaster relief team members during the Nepal earthquake dispatch: A consensual qualitative research analysis. *Journal of Korean Medical Science, 32*(3), 507–513. https://doi.org/10.3346/jkms.2017.32.3.507

Legha, R. K., & Solages, M. (2015). Child and adolescent mental health in Haiti: Developing long-term mental health services after the 2010 earthquake. *Child and Adolescent Psychiatric Clinics of North America, 24*(4), 731–749. https://doi.org/10.1016/j.chc.2015.06.004

Leichner, A., Akhtar, A., Nic A Bhaird, C., Wener, R., Perera, S. M., & Weissbecker, I.(2018). Mental health integration in primary health services after the earthquake in Nepal: a mixed-methodsprogram evaluation. *Global Mental Health (Cambridge, England), 8*, e10. https://doi.org/10.1017/gmh.2021.8

Liang, Y., Cheng, J., Ruzek, J. I., & Liu, Z. (2019). Posttraumatic stress disorder following the 2008 Wenchuan earthquake: A 10-year systematic review among highly exposed populations in China. *Journal of Affective Disorders, 243*, 327–339. https://doi.org/10.1016/j.jad.2018.09.047

Llach, C. D., Pailhez, G., Conejo-Gonzalez, C., Singh, P. M., & Bulbena, A. (2025). Post-traumatic stress and joint hypermobility in children and adolescents of Nepal after exposure to an earthquake. *European Child & Adolescent Psychiatry, 34*(4), 1353–1363. https://doi.org/10.1007/s00787-024-02559-8

Lommen, M. J., Sanders, A. J., Buck, N., & Arntz, A. (2009). Psychosocial predictors of chronic Post-Traumatic Stress Disorder in Sri Lankan tsunami survivors. *Behaviour Research and Therapy, 47*(1), 60–65. https://doi.org/10.1016/j.brat.2008.10.009

Magan, M., Bile, K. M., Kazi, B. M., & Gardezi, Z. (2010). Safe water supply in emergencies and the need for an exit strategy to sustain health gains: Lessons learned from the 2005 earthquake in Pakistan. *Eastern Mediterranean Health Journal = La Revue De Sante De La Mediterranee Orientale = Al-Majallah Al-Sihhiyah Li-Sharq Al-Mutawassit, 16*(*Suppl*), S91–S97.

Mahoney, J., Chandra, V., Gambheera, H., De Silva, T., & Suveendran, T. (2006). Responding to the mental health and psychosocial needs of the people of Sri Lanka in disasters. *International Review of Psychiatry (Abingdon, England), 18*(6), 593–597. https://doi.org/10.1080/09540260601129206

Makhdum, M. A., & Javed, A. (2006). Earthquake in Pakistan and Kashmir: Suggested plan for psychological trauma relief work. *International Psychiatry: Bulletin of the Board of International Affairs of the Royal College of Psychiatrists, 3*(1), 16–18.

Malik, J. N., Srivastava, E., Gadhavi, M. S., Livio, F., Sharma, N., Arora, S., Parrino, N., Burrato, P., & Sulli, A. (2024). Holocene surface-rupturing paleo-earthquakes along the Kachchh Mainland Fault: Shaping the seismic landscape of Kachchh, Western India. *Scientific Reports, 14*(1), 11612. https://doi.org/10.1038/s41598-024-62086-z

Margolin, G., Ramos, M. C., & Guran, E. L. (2010). Earthquakes and children: The role of psychologists with families and communities. *Professional Psychology, Research and Practice, 41*(1), 1–9. https://doi.org/10.1037/a0018103

Math, S. B., Girimaji, S. C., Benegal, V., Uday Kumar, G. S., Hamza, A., & Nagaraja, D. (2006). Tsunami: Psychosocial aspects of Andaman and Nicobar Islands. Assessments and intervention in the early phase. *International Review of Psychiatry (Abingdon, England), 18*(3), 233–239. https://doi.org/10.1080/09540260600656001

Math, S. B., John, J. P., Girimaji, S. C., Benegal, V., Sunny, B., Krishnakanth, K., Kumar, U., Hamza, A., Tandon, S., Jangam, K., Meena, K. S., Chandramukhi, B., & Nagaraja, D. (2008a). Comparative study of psychiatric morbidity among the displaced and non-displaced populations in the Andaman and Nicobar Islands following the tsunami. *Prehospital and Disaster Medicine, 23*(1), 29–35. https://doi.org/10.1017/s1049023x00005513

Math, S. B., Tandon, S., Girimaji, S. C., Benegal, V., Kumar, U., Hamza, A., Jangam, K., & Nagaraja, D. (2008b). Psychological impact of the tsunami on children and adolescents from the Andaman and Nicobar Islands. *Primary Care Companion to the Journal of Clinical Psychiatry, 10*(1), 31–37. https://doi.org/10.4088/pcc.v10n0106

Mishra, O. P. (2020). Seismic microzonation study of south Asian cities and its implications to urban risk resiliency under climate change scenario. *International Journal of Geosciences, 11*, 197–237. https://doi.org/10.4236/ijg.2020.114012

Miwa, T., Fujiwara, K., Matsuyoshi, H., & Nomura, Y. (2025). Post-earthquake dizziness syndrome (PEDS): A comprehensive review of recent advances. *Auris, Nasus, Larynx, 52*(3), 253–257. https://doi.org/10.1016/j.anl.2025.04.003

Naeem, F., Ayub, M., Masood, K., Gul, H., Khalid, M., Farrukh, A., Shaheen, A., Waheed, W., & Chaudhry, H. R. (2011). Prevalence and psychosocial risk factors of PTSD: 18 months after Kashmir earthquake in Pakistan. *Journal of Affective Disorders, 130*, 268–274. https://doi.org/10.1016/j.jad.2010.10.035

Najafi, S., Akahavan Rezayat, A., Beyzaei, S. F., Shahriari, Z., Taheri Tabar, M., GhasemiNour, M., Mosaed, R., Khadem-Rezaiyan, M., & Hamidi Farahani, R. (2022). Incidence of infectious diseases afterearthquakes: a systematic review and meta-analysis. *Public health, 202*, 131–138. https://doi.org/10.1016/j.puhe.2021.11.005

Negi, B. S., Joshi, S. K., Nakazawa, M., Kotaki, T., Bastola, A., & Kameoka, M. (2018). Impact of a massive earthquake on adherence to antiretroviral therapy, mental health, and treatment

failure among people living with HIV in Nepal. *PLoS One, 13*(6), e0198071. https://doi.org/10.1371/journal.pone.0198071
Neuner, F., Schauer, E., Catani, C., Ruf, M., & Elbert, T. (2006). Post-tsunami stress: A study of posttraumatic stress disorder in children living in three severely affected regions in Sri Lanka. *Journal of Traumatic Stress, 19*(3), 339–347. https://doi.org/10.1002/jts.20121
Oe, M., Takebayashi, Y., Sato, H., & Maeda, M. (2021). Mental health consequences of the Three Mile Island, Chernobyl, and Fukushima nuclear disasters: A scoping review. *International Journal of Environmental Research and Public Health, 18*(14), 7478. https://doi.org/10.3390/ijerph18147478
Ofrin, R. H., & Landry, M. D. (2015). Making "prevention and preparedness" a recovery priority: Lessons from the response to the 2015 Nepal earthquake. *WHO South-East Asia Journal of Public Health, 4*(2), 107–109. https://doi.org/10.4103/2224-3151.206679
Ogra, A., Donovan, A., Adamson, G., Viswanathan, K. R., & Budimir, M. (2021). Exploring the gap between policy and action in Disaster Risk Reduction: A case study from India. *International Journal of Disaster Risk Reduction, 63*, 102428. https://doi.org/10.1016/j.ijdrr.2021.102428
Olk, K., Osmani, V., & Klug, S. J. (2025). Post-traumatic stress disorder and depression among children and adolescents after earthquake disasters: A systematic review and meta-analysis. *Journal of Affective Disorders*, 119750. Advance online publication. https://doi.org/10.1016/j.jad.2025.119750
PACTT: Pakistan–Aberdeen Collaborative Trauma Team*, Rana, B. M. H., Ali, S., Yusufi, B., Alexander, D. A., Klein, S., Lee, A. J., Jones, G. T., & Macfarlane, G. (2008). The psychological and psychosocial impact of the Pakistan Kashmir earthquake after 8 months: A preliminary evaluation by PACTT. *International Psychiatry: Bulletin of the Board of International Affairs of the Royal College of Psychiatrists, 5*(2), 43–46.
Pandit, A., & Nakagawa, Y. (2021). How does reciprocal exchange of social support alleviate individuals' depression in an earthquake-damaged community? *International Journal of Environmental Research and Public Health, 18*(4), 1585. https://doi.org/10.3390/ijerph18041585
Patwary, M. M., Ashraf, S., Swed, S., & Shoib, S. (2023). The impact of the devastating Turkey-Syria earthquake on the fragile health care system in war-torn Syria. *Prehospital and Disaster Medicine, 38*(4), 537–538. https://doi.org/10.1017/S1049023X23005903
Paul, B. K., & Bhuiyan, R. H. (2010). Urban earthquake hazard: Perceived seismic risk and preparedness in Dhaka City, Bangladesh. *Disasters, 34*(2), 337–359. https://doi.org/10.1111/j.1467-7717.2009.01132.x
Peng, Y., & Hu, H. (2021). Assessment of earthquake casualties and comparison of accuracy of five injury triage methods: Evidence from a retrospective study. *BMJ Open, 11*(10), e051802. https://doi.org/10.1136/bmjopen-2021-051802
Peng, Y., Chen, Q., Xu, H., Shi, M., Li, L., & Wu, X. V. (2025). The prevalence and risk factors for post-traumatic stress disorder, depression and anxiety among older survivors post-earthquake: A systematic review and meta-analysis. *Journal of Affective Disorders, 370*, 168–180. https://doi.org/10.1016/j.jad.2024.10.113
Petrillo, G., & Zhuang, J. (2022). The debate on the earthquake magnitude correlations: A meta-analysis. *Scientific Reports, 12*(1), 20683. https://doi.org/10.1038/s41598-022-25276-1
Ponnamperuma, T., & Nicolson, N. A. (2016). Negative trauma appraisals and PTSD symptoms in Sri Lankan adolescents. *Journal of Abnormal Child Psychology, 44*(2), 245–255. https://doi.org/10.1007/s10802-015-9985-y
Ponnamperuma, T., & Nicolson, N. A. (2018). The relative impact of traumatic experiences and daily stressors on mental health outcomes in Sri Lankan adolescents. *Journal of Traumatic Stress, 31*(4), 487–498. https://doi.org/10.1002/jts.22311
Powell, T., Li, S. J., Hsiao, Y., Ettari, C., Bhandari, A., Peterson, A., & Shakya, N. (2019). Investigating the aftershock of a disaster: A study of health service utilization and mental health symptoms in post-earthquake Nepal. *International Journal of Environmental Research and Public Health, 16*(8), 1369. https://doi.org/10.3390/ijerph16081369

Pradhan, R. L. (2012). Earthquake preparedness plans – Building up capacity and readiness. *JNMA; Journal of the Nepal Medical Association, 52*(185), I–II.
Procter, N. G. (2005). Tsunami waves of mental trauma. *Contemporary Nurse, 18*(3), 215–218. https://doi.org/10.5172/conu.18.3.215
Pyari, T. T., & Ravindran, T. K. S. (2016). Sex differentials in the risk factors of post traumatic stress disorder among tsunami survivors in Tamil Nadu, India. *Asian Journal of Psychiatry, 23*, 46–50. https://doi.org/10.1016/j.ajp.2016.07.006
Pyari, T. T., Kutty, R. V., & Sarma, P. S. (2012). Risk factors of post-traumatic stress disorder in tsunami survivors of Kanyakumari district, Tamil Nadu, India. *Indian Journal of Psychiatry, 54*(1), 48–53. https://doi.org/10.4103/0019-5545.94645
Raghukanth, S. T. G., Podili, B., Sreejaya, K. P., Gupta, I. D., Roshan, A. D., Sinha, R., … & Murty, C. V. R. (2024). Draft earthquake zone map of India. *Journal of Earth System Science, 133*(3), 158. https://doi.org/10.1007/s12040-024-02368-2
Ramezankhani, A., & Sabouri, M. (2023). Assessing the method of providing health services to at-risk groups during natural events (earthquake): A systematic review. *Journal of Education and Health Promotion, 12*, 367. https://doi.org/10.4103/jehp.jehp_1624_22
Ranasinghe, P. D., & Levy, B. R. (2007). Prevalence of and sex disparities in posttraumatic stress disorder in an internally displaced Sri Lankan population 6 months after the 2004 tsunami. *Disaster Medicine and Public Health Preparedness, 1*(1), 34–43. https://doi.org/10.1097/DMP.0b013e318068fbb7
Ranasinghe, P. D., Zhang, X., Hwang, J., Ranasinghe, P. M., Karunathilake, I. M., & Everly, G. S. (2022). PTSD and depression 8 years after the 2004 tsunami in Sri Lanka. *Disaster Medicine and Public Health Preparedness, 17*, e183. https://doi.org/10.1017/dmp.2022.73
Rathore, M. F., Rashid, P., Butt, A. W., Malik, A. A., Gill, Z. A., & Haig, A. J. (2007). Epidemiology of spinal cord injuries in the 2005 Pakistan earthquake. *Spinal Cord, 45*(10), 658–663. https://doi.org/10.1038/sj.sc.3102023
Raviola, G., Rose, A., Fils-Aimé, J. R., Thérosmé, T., Affricot, E., Valentin, C., Daimyo, S., Coleman, S., Dubuisson, W., Wilson, J., Verdeli, H., Belkin, G., Jerome, G., & Eustache, E. (2020). Development of a comprehensive, sustained community mental health system in post-earthquake Haiti, 2010–2019. *Global Mental Health (Cambridge, England), 7*, e6. https://doi.org/10.1017/gmh.2019.33
Rawat, A., Pun, A., Ashish, K. C., Tamang, I. K., Karlström, J., Hsu, K., & Rasanathan, K. (2023). The contribution of community health systems to resilience: Case study of the response to the 2015 earthquake in Nepal. *Journal of Global Health, 13*, 04048. https://doi.org/10.7189/jogh.13.04048
Rehman, K., & Burton, P. W. (2020). Seismicity and seismic hazard parameters in and around Pakistan. *Journal of Seismology, 24*, 635–653. https://doi.org/10.1007/s10950-020-09917-4
Reid, J. A., & Mooney, W. D. (2023). Tsunami occurrence 1900–2020: A global review, with examples from Indonesia. *Pure and Applied Geophysics, 180*, 1549–1571. https://doi.org/10.1007/s00024-022-03057-1
Roy, N. (2006). The Asian tsunami: PAHO disaster guidelines in action in India. *Prehospital and Disaster Medicine, 21*(5), 310–315. https://doi.org/10.1017/s1049023x00003939
Roy, N., Shah, H., Patel, V., & Coughlin, R. R. (2002). The Gujarat earthquake (2001) experience in a seismically unprepared area: Community hospital medical response. *Prehospital and Disaster Medicine, 17*(4), 186–195. https://doi.org/10.1017/s1049023x00000480
Roy, N., Shah, H., Patel, V., & Bagalkote, H. (2005). Surgical and psychosocial outcomes in the rural injured – A follow-up study of the 2001 earthquake victims. *Injury, 36*(8), 927–934. https://doi.org/10.1016/j.injury.2005.02.017
Sangraula, M., Turner, E. L., Luitel, N. P., van 't Hof, E., Shrestha, P., Ghimire, R., Bryant, R., Marahatta, K., van Ommeren, M., Kohrt, B. A., & Jordans, M. J. D. (2020). Feasibility of Group Problem Management Plus (PM+) to improve mental health and functioning of adults in earthquake-affected communities in Nepal. *Epidemiology and Psychiatric Sciences, 29*, e130. https://doi.org/10.1017/S2045796020000414

Schwind, J. S., Formby, C. B., Santangelo, S. L., Norman, S. A., Brown, R., Hoffman Frances, R., Koss, E., & Karmacharya, D. (2018). Earthquake exposures and mental health outcomes in children and adolescents from Phulpingdanda village, Nepal: A cross-sectional study. *Child and Adolescent Psychiatry and Mental Health, 12*, 54. https://doi.org/10.1186/s13034-018-0257-9

Schwind, J. S., Norman, S. A., Brown, R., Frances, R. H., Koss, E., Karmacharya, D., & Santangelo, S. L. (2019). Association between earthquake exposures and mental health outcomes in Phulpingdanda village after the 2015 Nepal earthquakes. *Community Mental Health Journal, 55*, 1103–1113. https://doi.org/10.1007/s10597-019-00404-w

Shah, S. (2013). Holistic approach to community in crisis. *The Psychiatric Clinics of North America, 36*(3), 403–416. https://doi.org/10.1016/j.psc.2013.05.010

Shakya, D. R. (2016). The Nepal earthquake: Use of a disaster to improve mental health literacy. *BJPsych International, 13*(1), 8–9. https://doi.org/10.1192/s205647400000088x

Sharan, P., Chaudhary, G., Kavathekar, S. A., & Saxena, S. (1996). Preliminary report ofpsychiatric disorders in survivors of a severe earthquake. *The American Journal of Psychiatry, 153*(4), 556–558. https://doi.org/10.1176/ajp.153.4.556

Sharma, R. (2002). Gujarat earthquake causes major mental health problems. *BMJ (Clinical research ed.), 324*(7332), 259. https://doi.org/10.1136/bmj.324.7332.259c

Sharma, D. C. (2015). Nepal earthquake exposes gaps in disaster preparedness. *Lancet (London, England), 385*(9980), 1819–1820. https://doi.org/10.1016/S0140-6736(15)60913-8

Sharma, V., Levin, B. L., Rahill, G. J., Baldwin, J. A., Luitel, A., & Marhefka, S. L. (2021). Post-earthquake self-reported depressive symptoms and post-traumatic stress disorder and their correlates among college-youths in Kathmandu, Nepal. *The Psychiatric Quarterly, 92*(4), 1595–1609. https://doi.org/10.1007/s11126-021-09928-5

Sherchan, S., Samuel, R., Marahatta, K., Anwar, N., Van Ommeren, M. H., & Ofrin, R. (2017). Post-disaster mental health and psychosocial support: Experience from the 2015 Nepal earthquake. *WHO South-East Asia Journal of Public Health, 6*(1), 22–29. https://doi.org/10.4103/2224-3151.206160

Shrestha, R. (2015). Post-traumatic stress disorder among medical personnel after Nepal earthquake, 2015. *Journal of Nepal Health Research Council, 13*(30), 144–148.

Silwal, S., Dybdahl, R., Chudal, R., Sourander, A., & Lien, L. (2018). Psychiatric symptoms experienced by adolescents in Nepal following the 2015 earthquakes. *Journal of Affective Disorders, 234*, 239–246. https://doi.org/10.1016/j.jad.2018.03.002

Silwal, S., Chudal, R., Dybdahl, R., Sillanmäki, L., Lien, L., & Sourander, A. (2022). Post-traumatic stress and depressive symptoms among adolescents after the 2015 earthquake in Nepal: A longitudinal study. *Child Psychiatry and Human Development, 53*(3), 430–439. https://doi.org/10.1007/s10578-021-01136-3

Sirotich, A. C., & Camisasca, E. (2024). PTSD risk factors in earthquake survivors and their families: A systematic review. *European Journal of Psychotraumatology, 15*(1), 2365477. https://doi.org/10.1080/20008066.2024.2365477

Somasundaram, D. (2013). Recent disasters in Sri Lanka: Lessons learned. *The Psychiatric Clinics of North America, 36*(3), 321–338. https://doi.org/10.1016/j.psc.2013.05.001

Sonak, S., Pangam, P., & Giriyan, A. (2008). Green reconstruction of the tsunami-affected areas in India using the integrated coastal zone management concept. *Journal of Environmental Management, 89*, 14–23. https://doi.org/10.1016/j.jenvman.2007.01.052

Sreejaya, K. P., Raghukanth, S. T. G., Gupta, I. D., Murty, C. V. R., & Srinagesh, D. (2022). Seismic hazard map of India and neighbouring regions. *Soil Dynamics and Earthquake Engineering, 163*, 107505. https://doi.org/10.1016/j.soildyn.2022.107505

Sreejith, K. M., Jasir, M. C. M., Agarwal, R., & Rajawat, A. S. (2021). The 2019 September 24, Mw = 6, Mirpur earthquake, NW Himalaya: Geodetic evidence for shallow, near-horizontal decollement rupture of the Main Himalayan Thrust. *Tectonophysics, 816*, 229013. https://doi.org/10.1016/j.tecto.2021.229013

Suar, D., Das, S. S., & Alat, P. (2015). Bereavement, postdisaster trauma, and behavioral changes in tsunami survivors. *Death Studies, 39*(1–5), 226–233. https://doi.org/10.1080/07481187.2014.979957

Sumathipala, A., Siribaddana, S., & Perera, C. (2006). Management of dead bodies as a component of psychosocial interventions after the tsunami: A view from Sri Lanka. *International Review of Psychiatry (Abingdon, England), 18*(3), 249–257. https://doi.org/10.1080/09540260600656100

Tahernejad, S., Ghaffari, S., Ariza-Montes, A., Wesemann, U., Farahmandnia, H., & Sahebi, A. (2023). Post-traumatic stress disorder in medical workers involved in earthquake response: A systematic review and meta-analysis. *Heliyon, 9*(1), e12794. https://doi.org/10.1016/j.heliyon.2023.e12794

Thapa, K. (2015). Mental health in post-earthquake Nepal. *Nepal Journal of Epidemiology, 5*(4), 520–521. https://doi.org/10.3126/nje.v5i4.14261

Thapa, P., Acharya, L., Bhatta, B. D., Paneru, S. B., Khattri, J. B., Chakraborty, P. K., & Sharma, R. (2018). Anxiety, depression and post-traumatic stress disorder after earthquake. *Journal of the Nepal Health Research Council, 16*(38), 53–57.

Vijayakumar, L., & Kumar, M. S. (2008). Trained volunteer-delivered mental health support to those bereaved by Asian tsunami – An evaluation. *The International Journal of Social Psychiatry, 54*(4), 293–302. https://doi.org/10.1177/0020764008090283

Vijayakumar, L., Kannan, G. K., & Daniel, S. J. (2006a). Mental health status in children exposed to tsunami. *International Review of Psychiatry (Abingdon, England), 18*(6), 507–513. https://doi.org/10.1080/09540260601037581

Vijayakumar, L., Kannan, G. K., Ganesh Kumar, B., & Devarajan, P. (2006b). Do all children need intervention after exposure to tsunami? *International Review of Psychiatry (Abingdon, England), 18*(6), 515–522. https://doi.org/10.1080/09540260601039876

Vijaykumar, L., Thara, R., John, S., & Chellappa, S. (2006c). Psychosocial interventions after tsunami in Tamil Nadu, India. *International Review of Psychiatry (Abingdon, England), 18*(3), 225–231. https://doi.org/10.1080/09540260600655912

Viswanath, B., Maroky, A. S., Math, S. B., John, J. P., Benegal, V., Hamza, A., & Chaturvedi, S. K. (2012). Psychological impact of the tsunami on elderly survivors. *The American Journal of Geriatric Psychiatry: Official Journal of the American Association for Geriatric Psychiatry, 20*(5), 402–407. https://doi.org/10.1097/JGP.0b013e318246b7e9

Wagle, S., Amnatsatsue, K., Adhikari, B., Kerdmongkol, P., Van der Putten, M., & Silpasuwan, P. (2021). Health-related quality of life after the 2015 Gorkha earthquakes, among older adults living in Lalitpur District of Central Nepal. *Disaster Medicine and Public Health Preparedness, 15*(3), 298–307. https://doi.org/10.1017/dmp.2019.154

Walling, M. Y., & Mohanty, W. K. (2009). An overview on the seismic zonation and microzonation studies in India. *Earth-Science Reviews, 96*, 67–91. https://doi.org/10.1016/j.earscirev.2009.05.002

Wang, Z., & Wang, F. (2023). Well-being effects of natural disasters: Evidence from China's Wenchuan earthquake. *Journal of Happiness Studies, 24*(2), 563–587. https://doi.org/10.1007/s10902-022-00609-z

Welton-Mitchell, C., James, L. E., Khanal, S. N., & James, A. S. (2018). An integrated approach to mental health and disaster preparedness: A cluster comparison with earthquake affected communities in Nepal. *BMC Psychiatry, 18*(1), 296. https://doi.org/10.1186/s12888-018-1863-z

WHO India of the UN Team for Recovery Support. (2006). Report of the psychosocial support programme in tsunami-affected populations in India. *International Review of Psychiatry (Abingdon, England), 18*(3), 299–308. https://doi.org/10.1080/09540260600658304

Wickrama, K. A., & Kaspar, V. (2007). Family context of mental health risk in Tsunami-exposed adolescents: Findings from a pilot study in Sri Lanka. *Social Science & Medicine (1982), 64*(3), 713–723. https://doi.org/10.1016/j.socscimed.2006.09.031

Wickrama, K. A., & Wickrama, K. A. (2008). Family context of mental health risk in Tsunami affected mothers: Findings from a pilot study in Sri Lanka. *Social Science & Medicine (1982), 66*(4), 994–1007. https://doi.org/10.1016/j.socscimed.2007.11.012

Wickrama, T., Wickrama, K. A. S., Banford, A., & Lambert, J. (2017). PTSD symptoms among tsunami exposed mothers in Sri Lanka: The role of disaster exposure, culturally specific coping strategies, and recovery efforts. *Anxiety, Stress, and Coping, 30*(4), 415–427. https://doi.org/10.1080/10615806.2016.1271121

Wickrama, T., Merten, M. J., Wickrama, K. A. S., & Terrell, A. (2024). Adolescents' tsunami exposure and mental health consequences: Protective role of cultural coping strategies. *International Journal of Environmental Research and Public Health, 21*(6), 756. https://doi.org/10.3390/ijerph21060756

World Health Organization. (2025). Earthquakes. https://www.who.int/health-topics/earthquakes#tab=tab_1

Wu, X.-W., Qin, S.-Q., Xue, L., Yang, B.-C., Li, P., & Zhang, K. (2016). Physical mechanism of major earthquakes by earthquake cases analysis. *Chinese Journal of Geophysics, 59*(6), 658–675. https://doi.org/10.1002/cjg2.30015

Yasin, M. A., Malik, S. A., Nasreen, G., & Safdar, C. A. (2009). Experience with mass casualties in a subcontinent earthquake. *Ulusal Travma Ve Acil Cerrahi Dergisi = Turkish Journal of Trauma & Emergency Surgery: Tjtes, 15*(5), 487–492.

Yilmaz, S., Tatliparmak, A. C., & Ak, R. (2024). The pathophysiology of injuries and deaths managed in emergency departments after earthquake disasters: A narrative review. *Disaster Medicine and Public Health Preparedness, 18*, e252. https://doi.org/10.1017/dmp.2024.253

Zhu, J., Li, S., Song, J., & Wang, Y. (2021). Magnitude estimation for earthquake early warning using a deep convolutional neural network. *Frontiers in Earth Science, 9*, 653226. https://doi.org/10.3389/feart.2021.653226

Chapter 11
Epidemic, Pandemic and Mental Health

Sujita Kumar Kar, Khirod Chandra Moharana, and Mohita Joshi

1 Introduction

Epidemics and pandemics are forms of disasters and are not uncommon. Following several disasters such as floods, earthquakes, cyclones or wars, epidemics or pandemics may emerge, thereby extending the impact of the disaster (Kessler & Wittchen, 2008). Epidemics and pandemics produce significant psychological distress (Dalal et al., 2020; Roy et al., 2020; Taylor et al., 2008). The psychological impacts of epidemics or pandemics extend beyond the period of the epidemic/pandemic. Psychological distress during the post-disaster period is a matter of serious concern (Chatterjee & Kar, 2022; Kessler & Wittchen, 2008). The psychological distress may persist in the population even for a long time after the epidemic/pandemic is over (Greenhalgh et al., 2024; Kessler & Wittchen, 2008; Koc et al., 2022). Inclusion of psychological distress mitigating components in the disaster management plan helps in providing psychological support to individuals during the epidemic or pandemic (Maunder et al., 2008). Bioterrorism is a threat to mankind, and it may result in an outbreak of an epidemic. Hence, inclusion of psychological interventions in the disaster preparedness plan is expected to mitigate the mental health impacts of bioterrorism (Terhakopian & Benedek, 2007).

This chapter discusses the various mental health challenges that arise during epidemics and pandemics. It examines how these public health crises can lead to increased anxiety, depression and stress among individuals and communities. It also discusses the psychological impact of social isolation, uncertainty and fear and

S. K. Kar (✉) · M. Joshi
Department of Psychiatry, King George's Medical University, Lucknow, India
e-mail: sujitakumarkar@kgmcindia.edu

K. C. Moharana
Department of Anthropology, University of Allahabad, Prayagraj, Uttar Pradesh, India

N. Kar et al. (eds.), *Climate Change, Disaster and Mental Health in South Asia*, South Asian Perspectives in Mental Health and Psychology,
https://doi.org/10.1007/978-981-95-3690-0_11

highlights the importance of providing mental health support and resources during such times. Through this discussion, we aim to better understand the complex relationship between infectious disease outbreaks and mental health outcomes, shedding light on the need for comprehensive care that addresses both physical and psychological well-being. The COVID-19 pandemic is one of the devastating pandemics that the planet has witnessed in the twenty-first century. This chapter also puts some emphasis on the mental health issues associated with the COVID-19 pandemic.

2 Landmark Epidemics and Pandemics of the Last Century

The last century has witnessed several epidemics and pandemics worldwide, resulting in significant mortality, morbidity and socioeconomic chaos. Table 11.1 summarizes the impact of epidemics and pandemics.

3 Impact of Epidemic and Pandemic on Mental Health

Epidemics and pandemics are serious threats to mankind. The impact of an epidemic or pandemic is not limited to mortality and morbidity; it also produces several social and financial challenges. The psychological footprint of an epidemic or pandemic is larger than the footprint of physical morbidities (Cabarkapa et al., 2020; Preti et al., 2020; Stuijfzand et al., 2020; Taylor, 2022).

As pandemics have widespread and global impact, the mental health consequences are expected to be more voluminous and global, whereas the mental health impact of an epidemic is expected to be more regional (Taylor, 2022). The mental health impact of the pandemic depends on the severity of the pandemic as well as the extent of social disruption due to the pandemic (Taylor, 2022). No one is spared from the impact of an epidemic or pandemic in the affected geographical zones. Vulnerable populations include those with medical or mental illnesses, extremes of ages, pregnant women, the underprivileged population, ethnic and gender minorities, the migrant population and healthcare workers (Cabarkapa et al., 2020; Chatterjee et al., 2020; Dalal et al., 2020; Prakash et al., 2023; Preti et al., 2020; Stuijfzand et al., 2020).

The influenza pandemic is one of the frequently occurring large-scale pandemics globally (Medina, 2016; Taubenberger & Morens, 2010; Threats et al., 2005; WHO, 2025e). Every year, more than a billion cases of influenza are detected globally, which are mostly seasonal and commonly affect the pediatric population (WHO, 2025e). It has been documented that the pandemics of influenza used to occur at approximate intervals of 40 years (Taubenberger & Morens, 2010). A serious pandemic occurred in 1918, which is well known as "Spanish Flu," and affected mental health significantly (Alpert et al., 2023; Khan & Huremović, 2019). A lot of

Table 11.1 The landmark epidemics and pandemics in the world

Serial No.	Time frame	Landmark epidemics and pandemics of the last century	Causative agent	Geographical areas affected	Total mortality reported
1.	Early 1900s to mid-1950s	Poliomyelitis (Polio) epidemic	Poliovirus	**Initial major epidemic foci:** **Scandinavia:** saw some of the earliest recognized large outbreaks (late 1800s, early 1900s) **The United States** experienced increasingly large epidemics from the early 1900s, often starting in urban centres **Spread within and between these initial regions (Europe, North America):** The virus spread extensively within and between European countries and the USA and Canada This was driven by the movement of people (travel, migration) and facilitated by urbanization **Spread to other parts of the world:** Subsequently, through mechanisms like colonialism, global trade and travel (including post-World War II movements), the epidemic pattern of polio spread to • Asia • Africa • South America • Oceania (Noori et al., 2017; WHO, 2025c)	The critical factor for its historical designation as a major epidemic/pandemic-level threat was the portion (around 0.5% to 1% of all infections) that led to paralytic disease. In the early 1980s, an estimated 300,000 to 400,000 people suffered from paralytic polio cases every year. In 2020, there were 1873 paralytic polio cases (Dattani et al., 2022)

(continued)

Table 11.1 (continued)

Serial No.	Time frame	Landmark epidemics and pandemics of the last century	Causative agent	Geographical areas affected	Total mortality reported
2.	1918–1920	Spanish flu pandemic	H1N1 strain of the influenza virus	It affected the following geographical areas: **North America:** • United States (origin of the first wave in Kansas, Boston and other camps in the second wave, isolated outbreaks in the third wave) • Canada (labourers passed through) • Mexico • Central America • Caribbean region **Europe:** • France (reached first from the USA, origin of the second wave in Brest; affected in the third wave) • Western front countries (Germany, Belgium, Luxembourg, Switzerland) • Eastern Europe • Great Britain (affected in the third wave) • Russia (Arkhangelsk, then spread southwest to northeast) • Serbia (affected in the third wave) **Asia:** • Japan (and its colonies, Taiwan and Korea) • British India (Bombay/Mumbai as an epicentre) • China (suggested origin, affected in the second wave) • Iran **Africa:** • North Africa • Sierra Leone (Freetown) • Spread through the rest of the African Continent (along coasts, rivers, railways) • South Africa (another outbreak source) • Ethiopia (via the Zambezi River from South Africa) • Liberia (suggested origin for the second wave) **Oceania:** • Australia (overseas servicemen returning; origin of the third wave) (Mulheren, 2020)	It sparked a devastating global health crisis that infected approximately 500 million people worldwide—about one-third of the global population at the time—and resulted in an estimated 50 to 100 million deaths, accounting for roughly 3% to 5% of the world's population (Np & J, 2002)

3.	1957–1958	Asian flu pandemic	Influenza A virus subtype H2N2	It affected the following geographical areas: **Asia:** • China (origin in Guizhou in Southern China) • Hong Kong Japan • The Philippines • Malaysia • Indonesia **North America:** **United States:** • Entered via San Diego, California, and Newport, Rhode Island • Epicentres in Montana, Arizona and Florida • Spread inland from the West, East, and Gulf coasts, particularly affecting heavily populated urban areas • Experienced a second wave in early 1958 • While some areas, like parts of Appalachia, interior Texas and the northern plains, escaped the worst, the flu was present in the broader USA **Canada:** • Full pandemic exploded from September through November • Maritime provinces were hardest hit • Ontario (including Montreal, which was hit by a second wave) and British Columbia were also affected, though they fared better • Other provinces fell in between • While lightly populated expanses escaped the worst, the flu was present in broader Canada (Mc Donald, 2025)	It is estimated that the pandemic resulted in approximately 2 million deaths globally, including 80,000 in the United States (Mc Donald, 2025)

(continued)

Table 11.1 (continued)

Serial No.	Time frame	Landmark epidemics and pandemics of the last century	Causative agent	Geographical areas affected	Total mortality reported
4.	1968–1969	Hong Kong flu pandemic	Influenza A virus subtype H3N2	The following geographical areas were affected by the Hong Kong Flu (1968): **Asia:** • Hong Kong (origin) • Vietnam • Singapore • India • Philippines • Japan • Other unspecified parts of Asia **Oceania:** • Australia (specifically northern Australia, mentioned as an early point of spread) **Europe:** • Europe (general) **The Americas:** • United States (entered via California, became widespread) • South America **Africa:** • Africa (general) (Sino Biological, 2025; Staff, 2024)	The Hong Kong Flu caused an estimated 1–4 million deaths worldwide, with 500,000 infections in Hong Kong and approximately 33,800 deaths in the United States (Sino Biological, 2025; Staff, 2024)

5.	1972	Smallpox	Variola virus	The following geographical areas were affected by Variola (Smallpox): **Africa:** • Northeast Africa (believed origin) • Egypt (ancient evidence) • North Africa (source of spread to Europe) • Mecca (Saudi Arabia—sixth-century epidemic and source for Yugoslav outbreak via a pilgrim from Iraq) **Asia:** • Far East (early spread) • India (early spread) • China (early spread) • Asia Minor (possible route to Europe) • Iraq (Basra, Baghdad—where the pilgrim contracted it before the Yugoslav outbreak) **Europe:** General introduction between the fifth and seventh centuries, frequent outbreaks in the Middle/New Ages Specifically mentioned for outbreaks between 1950 and 1971: • Belgium • Czechoslovakia • Denmark • France • East Germany • West Germany • Spain • England • Italy • Holland (Netherlands) • Poland • Switzerland • Sweden • USSR Yugoslavia (post-war outbreak in 1972, specifically affecting Serbia (Central Serbia, Kosovo, Vojvodina) and Montenegro) **The Americas ("New World"):** • Cuba (fifteenth century) • Mexico (fifteenth century, affecting the Aztecs) • Other parts of the New World, affecting the Incas and many Indian tribes • Canada (outbreaks between 1950 and 1971) **Oceania:** • Australia (Sydney, nineteenth century) (Ristanovic, 2016)	Among people known to be infected with the variola major virus, around 30% are estimated to have died. During that century, smallpox caused an estimated 300–500 million deaths worldwide (Berche, 2022; Ochmann, 2024)

(continued)

Table 11.1 (continued)

Serial No.	Time frame	Landmark epidemics and pandemics of the last century	Causative agent	Geographical areas affected	Total mortality reported
6.	Identified in the early 1980s (ongoing)	HIV/AIDS pandemic	Human immunodeficiency virus 1 and 2	The following geographical areas were affected: **Africa:** • Central Africa (DRC/Cameroon region): believed to have originated from SIV (primates) and early human epicentre (e.g. Kinshasa) • Sub-Saharan Africa: later became the most heavily affected region globally (East, Southern, West Africa) **The Americas:** • Caribbean (e.g. Haiti): important early node • North America (e.g. USA—major cities): spread from the Caribbean/Africa/Europe • South America (e.g. Brazil): significant early epidemics **Europe:** • Western Europe (e.g. France, UK): introduced from Africa/Americas • Eastern Europe & Central Asia (e.g. Russia, Ukraine): epidemics emerged, often later **Asia:** • Southeast Asia (e.g. Thailand): major epicentre • South Asia (e.g. India): significant epidemic • East Asia (e.g. China): spread through various routes **Oceania:** • Australia & New Zealand: patterns similar to other Western nations • Pacific Islands (e.g. Papua New Guinea): varying impact (WHO, 2025b)	An estimated 80 million people had been infected worldwide since the start of an epidemic that has turned into a pandemic, and around 36 million are believed to have died from AIDS-related illnesses (UNAIDS, 2020) Of the estimated 40.0 million (confidence bounds: 36.0–44.8 million) people living with HIV worldwide in 2023, 2.38 million (1.83–2.97 million) were children aged 0–19 (WHO, 2025b)

7.	2002–2004	Severe acute respiratory syndrome (SARS)	SARS-CoV-1	The 2002–2004 SARS outbreak originated in Foshan, Guangdong, China. It spread to 29–30 countries and territories worldwide The highest concentration of cases was in • Mainland China • Hong Kong • Taiwan • Other significantly affected countries included Canada and Singapore. Many other countries reported a smaller number of cases (Cherry, 2004; WHO, 2025d)	As of December 2003, the WHO reported 8096 probable SARS cases from 29 countries and regions, leading to 774 deaths (a 9.6% case fatality rate) (WHO, 2025d)
8.	1998–ongoing sporadic	Nipah virus epidemic	Nipah virus	**Initial Outbreak (1998–1999):** • **Malaysia:** first isolated during an epidemic among pig farmers **Subsequent outbreaks (since 1999):** **South Asia (general region)** **Bangladesh:** specifically in the western and northwestern regions **India:** • West Bengal (over the Bangladesh-India border) • Kerala (Sun et al., 2024)	Nipah virus remains a considerable public health concern due to its ability to infect a wide range of animals and cause severe disease in humans with an extremely high case fatality rate (43% to 100%) (Sun et al., 2024)

(continued)

Table 11.1 (continued)

Serial No.	Time frame	Landmark epidemics and pandemics of the last century	Causative agent	Geographical areas affected	Total mortality reported
9.	2009–2010	Swine flu pandemic	Human flu virus, H1N1 influenza	**Origin (Feb–March 2009):** first evidence appeared in La Gloria, Veracruz, Mexico, and then emerged in **Mexico City** **Spread within North America (April 2009):** spread to the United States (Texas, New York, California and other places), suspected to be carried by travellers from Mexico Affected several provinces in Canada (Nova Scotia, Alberta, Ontario, British Columbia) **Initial international spread (late April 2009):** reached Spain via air travel from Mexico. Confirmed cases in Germany, Austria, the United Kingdom, Israel and New Zealand. Suspected cases in Australia, Chile, Colombia and France **Wider global spread leading to pandemic declaration (by June 2009):** continued spread across multiple regions of the world Upsurges in cases were noted in Chile, Japan, Australia and the United Kingdom prior to the pandemic declaration on 11 June 2009 **Continued global and internal spread (post-June 2009):** by late August 2009, cases were reported globally By late October 2009, 48 states in the United States reported widespread illness, indicating extensive internal spread (Rogers, 2009)	In the United States, from 12 April 2009 to 10 April 2010, the CDC estimated that the (H1N1)pdm09 virus caused approximately 60.8 million cases and 12,469 deaths (CDC, 2019)

10.	2014–2016	Ebola epidemic	Ebola virus	**Origin and initial epicentre:** started in **Guinea** **Rapid regional spread:** quickly spread to the neighbouring countries of **Sierra Leone and Liberia**, reaching the capital cities of these three nations **Further international spread:** the disease subsequently spread to seven additional countries: • Italy • Mali • Nigeria • Senegal • Spain • The United Kingdom • The United States of America (USA) **Secondary local transmission:** secondary infections (local spread after importation) occurred in Italy, Mali, Nigeria and the USA (WHO, 2025a)	By its conclusion in June 2016, the Ebola outbreak had resulted in over 28,600 infections and 11,325 deaths (WHO, 2025a)
11.	2015–2016	Zika virus epidemic	Zika virus	**Origin (April 2015):** began in **Brazil** **Primary spread:** affected other countries in the Americas Specifically impacted other parts of South and North America To date, a total of 86 countries and territories have reported evidence of mosquito-transmitted Zika infection **Additional spread:** reached several islands in the Pacific (WHO, 2016)	Mortality from the Zika virus is rare; the virus continued to circulate: Brazil reported 18,941 cases in 2020, accounting for 83% of all reported cases in the Region of the Americas The overall cumulative incidence of ZIKV disease in the region of the Americas in 2020 was 2.34 per 100,000 population (WHO, 2022a)

(continued)

Table 11.1 (continued)

Serial No.	Time frame	Landmark epidemics and pandemics of the last century	Causative agent	Geographical areas affected	Total mortality reported
12.	2019–present	COVID-19 pandemic	SARS-CoV-2	Global spread of SARS-CoV-2 (COVID-19): **China:** • Wuhan (initial outbreak and epicentre) • Spread from Wuhan to all provinces in mainland China Initial intercontinental spread (largely from China): • Asia (various destinations) • Europe (e.g. early cases in France; Italy then became a major hotspot) • North America (early importations) **Second phase of global spread (Europe became a major secondary source):** Further spread within Europe (e.g. Spain, UK became significant hotspots) • **North America (USA):** became a global epicentre (largely from European strains) • **Latin America (e.g. Brazil):** significantly affected, becoming a major hotspot • **South Asia (e.g. India):** became a major hotspot • **Africa:** spread across the continent, with most early imported cases from Europe and the USA • **Oceania:** affected as part of the global spread to "hundreds of destinations across the world," though not detailed as a primary early epicentre in this text (Li et al., 2021)	Globally, an estimated 14.83 million excess deaths occurred during the COVID-19 period, which is 2.74 times higher than the 5.42 million deaths officially reported as due to COVID-19 (William, 2022)

similarities exist between the "Spanish Flu" pandemic in 2018 and the COVID-19 pandemic spanning between 2020 and 2022 (Alpert et al., 2023). Similarly, outbreaks of Ebola, Zika and SARS (severe acute respiratory syndrome) have been reported in epidemic form from time to time (Medina, 2016).

Quarantine and isolation are common safety measures during any epidemic or pandemic. These processes break the chain of infection. However, the restrictions associated with quarantine and isolation are psychologically distressing (Chatterjee & Chauhan, 2020; Huremović, 2019). The major psychological concerns during the quarantine and isolation period are lifestyle restrictions, boredom and a sense of uncertainty (Chatterjee & Chauhan, 2020). The majority of disaster preparedness plans emphasize critical components such as controlling the spread of epidemics or pandemics, implementing safety measures, managing various medical conditions and facilitating vaccination efforts. While these aspects are undeniably important for public health, a significant gap often exists regarding the mental health needs that arise during such crises. The psychological impact of epidemics or pandemics can be profound, leading to increased anxiety, depression and other mental health issues among the population. Unfortunately, mental health support and resources are frequently overlooked in these plans, highlighting the need for a more comprehensive approach that incorporates mental well-being as a fundamental element of disaster preparedness and response strategies (Terhakopian & Benedek, 2007). Addressing these needs can play a crucial role in fostering resilience and ensuring a holistic recovery for individuals and communities affected by such events.

4 Epidemic and Pandemic and Mental Health: Explanatory Models

Explanatory models have emerged as a critique of the traditional reliance on purely bio-psychiatric explanations for the diagnosis, aetiology and treatment of mental illness. The need to recognize culture as a determinant of mental illness was institutionally accepted in 1987 when the *Diagnostic and Statistical Manual (DSM)-III R* was published with a cautionary note about the cross-cultural applicability of the diagnostic categories (American Psychiatric Association, 1987). In subsequent versions of DSM, more and more provisions were incorporated to recognize the role of culture in diagnosis and experience of mental illness (American Psychiatric Association, 1994).

Arthur Kleinman coined the term "Explanatory Model" in 1978 to use cultural data in diagnosis, aetiology and treatment of mental illness (Kleinman et al., 1978). For him, an explanatory model is a complex, culturally determined process of making sense of one's illness, ascribing meanings to symptoms, evolving causal attributions and expressing suitable expectations of treatment and related outcomes (Kleinman et al., 1978). He questioned the claim for cross-cultural validity of psychiatric categories included in the DSM and stressed the need to recognize the role of multiple factors in the origin, diagnosis and treatment of mental illness (Kleinman et al., 1978). In our previous sections, we have already discussed mental health problems which are observed during pandemics and epidemics. In this section, let us examine the role of explanatory models during pandemics and epidemics and their consequences on mental health.

4.1 Explanatory Models During Pandemics and Epidemics

Pandemics and epidemics are great periods of crisis and upheaval. The recent COVID-19 pandemic has refreshed human memory of the vulnerability of the human species to death, fear, uncertainty and chaos before the fury of nature. We have already discussed how epidemics and pandemics have been responsible for the rise in mental health problems. However, the crucial task of this paper is also to examine how the suffering and experience of mental illness during pandemics and epidemics are mediated through how human beings interpret illness. We hold culturally determined beliefs about misfortune, suffering, illness and health, which determine our response to suffering and illness. Many studies have shown that the explanatory models of illness shape individual response to mental health problems in the form of treatment-seeking behaviour, compliance with treatment and the process of recovery (Bhugra et al., 2024; Dinos et al., 2017; Kirmayer & Bhugra, 2009). There are various types of explanatory models, such as the biomedical model, the religious model and the psychosocial model.

4.2 Biomedical Explanatory Model

The biomedical model is based on the idea that mental illness is a disease of the brain. It assumes that mental disorders such as schizophrenia, major depressive disorder, attention deficit/hyperactivity disorder (ADHD) and substance use disorders are considered biologically originated malfunctions of the brain (Andreasen, 1985). The model argues that specific biological factors are responsible for the origin of mental disorders, and the treatment includes inventing drugs and other related interventions which can specifically target underlying biological dysfunction (Moncrieff, 2008). People who hold a biomedical explanatory model assume that pandemics and epidemics disturb the chemical processes in the brain, resulting in mental illness.

The biomedical explanatory model is a dominant model worldwide today. Individuals, communities and countries around the world subscribed to the biomedical model during COVID-19, and as a result, most countries could implement measures such as quarantine, social distancing and vaccination. Vaccines were developed, viruses with their new variants were tracked, and required healthcare facilities at the hospitals were organized, thanks to the biomedical model of illness.

Increased acceptance of the biomedical explanatory model is a result of the spread of modern education and a belief in the advancement of science and technology (Wainwright, 2008).

Individuals who believe in the biomedical explanatory model assume that a particular epidemic or pandemic is a result of a certain microorganism, for example, a virus. It is believed that strategies to check the spread of disease-causing microorganisms are the best method to contain an epidemic or pandemic (Zamora-Ledezma et al., 2020). The fundamental idea behind this model is that the disease-causing microorganisms have specific roles in creating an imbalance in the neurological functions. Consequently, the treatment-seeking behaviour and compliance with treatment are highly observed among individuals who subscribe to the biomedical explanatory model. Recovery from an illness depends upon whether there is any compatibility between the explanatory models of the patient and the caregivers. Vaccine hesitancy during COVID-19 was also observed to be more prevalent among those individuals or communities who do not subscribe to the biomedical explanatory model (Dror et al., 2020; Sallam, 2021).

4.3 Religious Explanatory Model

Biomedical explanatory models can help in solving many aspects of human health and illness. However, the question of "why me" is not answered by any biological knowledge. Existential issues such as this are well tackled by religious explanatory models. Human beings often try to find meaning in the sufferings that they undergo. Meaningless suffering is unbearable and often leads to mental health problems (Glaw et al., 2017; Pihlström, 2019). Religious explanatory models contain meanings to human suffering and illness and help in answering various existential questions. Concepts such as karma (Anand, 2009; Narayanan et al., 1986) and theodicy are used in religious explanatory models. Religious explanatory models consider epidemics as a form of punishment for injustice or wrongs done at the community or societal level. Nature is considered a greater force which punishes any wrongs done at societal level. Thus, suffering is seen as a punishment and is accepted with humility (Das, 2010). People who subscribed to religious explanatory models believed that COVID-19 was a punishment to the people for some injustice done to certain communities, animals or plants. People who suffered from mental illness during pandemics believed in the karma theory to get a meaning to their suffering (Keshavan, 2020). It is also believed in religious explanations that suffering and illness create resilience among individuals and need to be taken positively.

Religious explanatory models can quench our thirst-related existential questions but can derange our behaviour at the biomedical level. Individuals accepting religious explanatory models may not adhere to the treatment regime and other strategies such as quarantine and social distancing. Recovery from an illness, too, is a problem due to the lack of congruity between the explanatory models of the patients and the caregivers (Gopalkrishnan, 2018). The cultural competency of the practitioners increases when there is a congruity between the explanatory models of the patient and the practitioners (Bassey & Melluish, 2013).

The negative side of the religious model is that it usually promotes discrimination and stigma (Mathison et al., 2022; Rosen et al., 2008) against the mentally ill. As illness is seen as a punishment for sin or bad karma, the patient is usually stigmatized for being a sinner. Epidemics and pandemics are considered to happen due to divine will, and thus, attempts towards mitigation are rarely encouraged. Mentally ill persons are seen as left by God to suffer as a form of punishment, and thus, it is argued that this explanatory model contributes very little towards patients' care and recovery (Meyer, 2001; Sheikh & Furnham, 2000). Thus, it is argued that religious explanatory models are linked to fatalism and guilty feelings among the patients. Some religious explanations are different. They allow the patients to stay positive during the illness in spite of chronic and terminally ill conditions (Fatima et al., 2022). There are possibilities in some religious traditions to condition one's mind and body towards healing and recovery, not through biological processes but through mind-body medicine and mindfulness. For example, the karma theory is also used by many individuals to transform suffering through ethical living and mindfulness (Kaufman, 2005; Narayanan et al., 1986; Omprakash, 1989; Potter, 1980).

4.4 Psychosocial Explanatory Model

Arthur Kleinman and Sung (1979) contend that the attribution of illness to psychosocial factors is a universal phenomenon among patients, including those in industrialized societies (Kleinman & Sung, 1979). The psychosocial explanatory model attributes illness to psychological aspects, which usually result from social factors. Anthropologists have shown that this is the dominant model of illness among non-industrialized communities (Murdock, 1980; Murdock et al., 1980). The recent pandemic of COVID-19 witnessed the use of psychosocial explanatory models across cultures.

A psychosocial explanatory model is based on the idea that mental health problems during pandemics are a reasonable reaction to extraordinary environmental stressors (Schluter et al., 2022; Serafini et al., 2020). A large section of the population holds to this explanatory model of mental illness during pandemics. They assume that stressors such as loss of biodiversity, destruction of pathogens' habitat due to consumerism and globalization are the real factors behind pandemics and epidemics. Resulting fear, isolation and social upheaval during pandemics are the root cause of mental health problems according to the psychosocial explanatory model. People having the above explanatory model need proper counselling rather than drugs. This explanatory model is linked to a higher level of stress as the individuals feel helpless before macro forces like political economy, societal factors, globalization and market. Regarding the cause of mental illness, these people hold that widespread uncertainty, isolation, economic instability, fear of infection and fear of death (Kuljancic et al., 2023; Menzies & Menzies, 2020; Roy et al., 2020) are the causes of mental illness. Thus, counselling and community intervention and state support are the major factors in addressing mental health issues according to this explanatory model.

5 COVID-19 and Mental Health: The Recent Experiences

The COVID-19 pandemic affected the psychological well-being from the very beginning of the pandemic. The threat of COVID-19 was so severe that it created panic among the general public and increased the perceived mental healthcare needs among them (Chen et al., 2021; Roy et al., 2020). Stigma, unawareness and infodemic also affected the mental well-being of the public during COVID-19 (Kar et al., 2020d).

Broadly, the mental health impact of the COVID-19 pandemic was due to the social integrity disruption and consequence of being infected with COVID-19 (Penninx et al., 2022). Survivors of COVID-19 infection reported cognitive impairment, fatigue and mood changes for a longer time, even after recovering from COVID-19 infection (Penninx et al., 2022) (Fig. 11.1). A spectrum of behavioural changes ranging from alteration of sexual behaviour, panic buying, addictive behaviour, sleeping behaviour and binge-watching behaviour has been reported during the COVID-19 pandemic (Arafat et al., 2020a, b, c, 2022; Arafat & Kar, 2021a, b; Dixit et al., 2020; Grover et al., 2020; Gupta et al., 2020; Kar et al., 2020b; Lehmiller

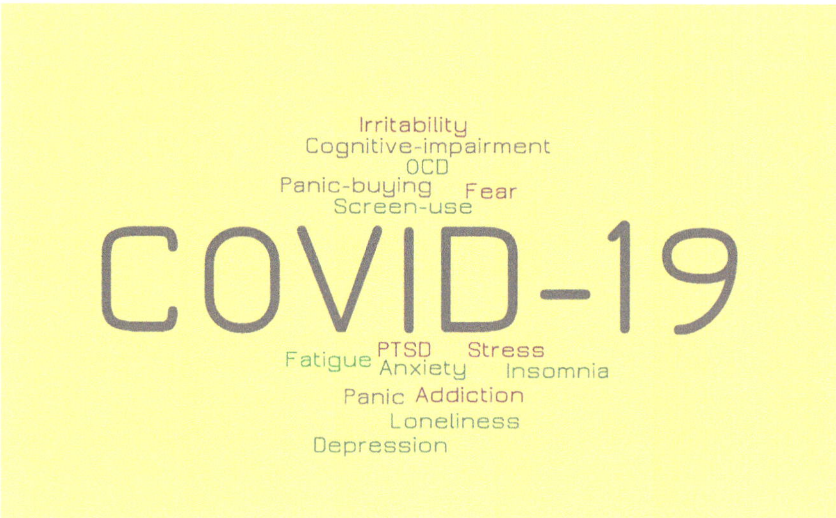

Fig. 11.1 Word cloud showing common mental health issues associated with COVID-19 infection

et al., 2021; Rajkumar, 2020). The psychological impact of COVID-19 infection may persist long (classically known as long-COVID) and may manifest in the form of fatigue, blunting of cognition, sleep disturbances, anxiety and depression (Greenhalgh et al., 2024; Koc et al., 2022; Monje & Iwasaki, 2022; Scholkmann & May, 2023). Vaccination against COVID-19 was found to be effective in reducing the neuropsychiatric manifestations associated with COVID-19 infection (Elmazny et al., 2023).

The mental health of people engaged in providing healthcare during COVID-19 was significantly affected (Dalal et al., 2020; Dua, 2021; Kar & Singh, 2020; Prakash et al., 2023; Sharma et al., 2023; Singh et al., 2021). Anxiety, depression, burnout, fear, guilt, somatic symptoms, sleep disturbances, nightmares and stress are commonly reported psychological issues among healthcare workers during COVID-19 (Kar et al., 2020c, 2021a; Prakash et al., 2023; Sharma et al., 2023; Singh et al., 2021; Thakkar, 2021). The pandemic severity was so serious that in the initial phase (2020–2021), there was significant chaos in healthcare management due to a lack of preparedness, inadequate infrastructure, excessive workload and several administrative reasons (Kar et al., 2020c, 2021a). Violence against doctors, hesitancy to use the COVID-19 vaccine and uncooperativeness of the public during COVID-19 were also attributed to the healthcare challenges and psychological distress of healthcare workers (Kar et al., 2021b; Tripathy & Ogunmola, 2021). Academics are significantly affected during the COVID-19 pandemic. It adversely affected the mental health of children and adolescents, as well as those pursuing higher education (Aristovnik et al., 2021; Kar et al., 2020e, g; Keržič et al., 2021). The shift to online teaching and training, the postponement of examinations and the closure of schools have significantly hampered students' education, thereby increasing their psychological distress.

As COVID-19 affected the elderly population more seriously due to several age-related factors, significant mortality in elderly people happened due to COVID-19 infection (Arevalillo-Gozalo, 2021; Dalal et al., 2020; Sharma et al., 2021). During the lockdown phase of the COVID-19 pandemic, several restrictions in lifestyle due to lack of opportunities for the same, closure of schools and offices and limited availability of essential resources produced severe chaos globally, and it significantly attributed to the mental health issues in public (Chatterjee et al., 2020; Dalal et al., 2020; Kar et al., 2020g, h; Sharma et al., 2021). The marginalized population, like the migrant population, prisoners and homeless people, faced more mental health challenges during the COVID-19 pandemic (Chatterjee et al., 2020; Dalal et al., 2020; González-Riera et al., 2024; Himani & Pandya, 2021; Johnson et al., 2021; Kar et al., 2020a, h; Tsai & Wilson, 2020). People with pre-existing mental illnesses or physical illnesses and those from ethnic minorities were affected adversely during the COVID-19 pandemic (Weich, 2022).

Several social challenges may have contributed to mental health issues during the COVID-19 pandemic (Chatterjee et al., 2020; Dalal et al., 2020; Kar et al., 2020g, h; Penninx et al., 2022). The common social challenges are listed in Fig. 11.2.

Fig. 11.2 COVID-19-related social challenges that contribute to mental health issues

The mental health issues associated with COVID-19 have significantly reduced, and the mental well-being has been substantially improved following the pandemic (Reutter et al., 2024). The emergence of mental health issues and the worsening of pre-existing mental health states during the COVID-19 pandemic, alongside the subsequent improvement in global mental well-being as the pandemic came under control, indicate a potential causal and/or moderating role of the pandemic in psychological issues.

However, some beneficial effects of the pandemic are also reported, which have a bearing on mental well-being. The COVID-19 pandemic acted as a positive buffer for work-life balance for many people. It also helped in improving closeness and family dynamics (Penninx et al., 2022). Several climatic benefits were also reported during the pandemic, which might have beneficial health effects (Arafat et al., 2020d; Kar et al., 2020f; Ponce et al., 2024; Tripathy et al., 2020). The COVID-19 pandemic has been an eye-opener for everyone. It has generated insights into the lacunae and gaps in existing healthcare systems, approaches and preparedness to face a pandemic.

6 Future Directions

Epidemics and pandemics result in the disruption of healthcare delivery. As a result of this, patients with mental health issues face difficulty in reaching healthcare facilities. During the recent COVID-19 pandemic, to bridge the gap in healthcare delivery, teleconsultation services were used effectively to deliver mental healthcare (Agarwal et al., 2023; Blandford et al., 2020; Padhy et al., 2022). The recent COVID-19 pandemic resulted in a surge of common mental illnesses like depression and anxiety by 25% globally (WHO, 2022b). It indicates that any future pandemic is likely to cause an increase in the number of mental health issues, and the disaster preparedness plan needs to take this into account. Persons on quarantine and isolation, vulnerable populations and marginalized populations face more mental health issues, so additional emphasis should be given to these populations (Chatterjee et al., 2020; Costa et al., 2022; Dalal et al., 2020; Rajkumar, 2020). The pandemic resulted in panic buying and hoarding of essential household items at home, producing social chaos and panic in public (Arafat et al., 2020b, c; Arafat & Kar, 2021a; Costa et al., 2022). Adequate measures at the administrative level need to be taken to prevent infodemic, sensitize the public and ensure the availability of essential things to the general public during future pandemics and epidemics. Early intervention using an evidence-based approach is a key measure to control psychological distress associated with the pandemic (Morganstein, 2022). Hence, appropriate measures need to be taken for early identification and effective intervention to counter the mental health issues associated with epidemics and pandemics in future.

7 Conclusion

Epidemics and pandemics produce significant impairment in mental health. As epidemics and pandemics are frequently occurring phenomena globally, it is important to give importance to mental health in the disaster preparedness plan for future disasters. The pandemic can have a long-lasting impact on mental health, as evident from the recent COVID-19 pandemic (e.g. long-COVID); hence, it is important to look for the evolving mental health issues even after the epidemic or pandemic is over.

References

Agarwal, A., Gupta, P. K., Singh, A., & Kar, S. K. (2023). Conceptual model of Remotely Accessed Mobile Application for Psychiatric disorder Screening (RoAdMAPS): A self-screening and referral aid for mental health in India. *The Lancet Regional Health – Southeast Asia, 8*. https://doi.org/10.1016/j.lansea.2022.100100

Alpert, J. L., Steinberg, A. (Lu), & Laddis, B. A. (2023). Lessons learned from the 1918 "forgotten flu". In C. R. Figley, L. E. A. Walker, & I. A. Serlin (Eds.), *Pandemic providers: Psychologists respond to Covid* (pp. 19–32). Springer International Publishing. https://doi.org/10.1007/978-3-031-27580-7_2

American Psychiatric Association. (1987). *Diagnostic and statistical manual of mental disorders (3rd edn revised) (DSM-III-R).* American Psychiatric. https://psychiatryonline.org/doi/book/10.1176/appi.books.9780890420188.dsm-iii-r

American Psychiatric Association. (1994). *Diagnostic and statistical manual of mental disorders: DSM-IV* (Vol. 4). American Psychiatric Association. https://smartnet.niua.org/sites/default/files/webform/ai-strategy/pdf-diagnostic-and-statistical-manual-of-mental-disorders-dsm-iv-american-psychiatric-association-pdf-download-free-book-3ae44d1.pdf

Anand, J. (2009). Psychological healing and faith in the doctrine of Karma. *Mental Health, Religion & Culture, 12*(8), 817–832.

Andreasen, N. C. (1985). *The broken brain: The biological revolution in psychiatry.* Harper & Row Publishers. https://psycnet.apa.org/record/1985-98165-000

Arafat, S. M. Y., & Kar, S. K. (2021a). Prevention of panic buying during public health emergency. *Asia-Pacific Journal of Public Health.* journals.sagepub.com. https://doi.org/10.1177/10105395211014699

Arafat, S. M. Y., & Kar, S. K. (2021b). Sex during pandemic: Panic buying of sex toys during COVID-19 lockdown. *Journal of Psychosexual Health.* https://doi.org/10.1177/26318318211013347

Arafat, S. M. Y., Alradie-Mohamed, A., Kar, S. K., & … (2020a). Does COVID-19 pandemic affect sexual behaviour? A cross-sectional, cross-national online survey. *Psychiatry ….* ncbi.nlm.nih.gov. https://www.ncbi.nlm.nih.gov/pmc/articles/PMC7190529/

Arafat, S. M. Y., Kar, S. K., Marthoenis, M., Sharma, P., Hoque Apu, E., & Kabir, R. (2020b). Psychological underpinning of panic buying during pandemic (COVID-19). *Psychiatry Research, 289*, 113061. https://doi.org/10.1016/j.psychres.2020.113061

Arafat, S. M. Y., Kar, S. K., Menon, V., Kaliamoorthy, C., Mukherjee, S., Alradie-Mohamed, A., Sharma, P., Marthoenis, M., & Kabir, R. (2020c). Panic buying: An insight from the content analysis of media reports during COVID-19 pandemic. *Neurology, Psychiatry and Brain Research, 37*, 100–103. https://doi.org/10.1016/j.npbr.2020.07.002

Arafat, S. M. Y., Tripathy, S., Kar, S. K., & Kabir, R. (2020d). Climate and clean air responses to COVID-19: A comment. *International Journal of Public Health, 65*(6), 715–716. https://doi.org/10.1007/s00038-020-01415-1

Arafat, S. M. Y., Menon, V., Vinnakota, D., & … (2022). Studies on sexual behavior during COVID-19 pandemic: A bibliometric analysis. *Journal of Psychosexual Health.* https://doi.org/10.1177/26318318211067070

Arevalillo-Gozalo, E. (2021). Potential determinants of age-related severity in COVID-19. *Indian Journal of Health, Sexuality and Culture*, 7(Spcl), Article Spcl.

Aristovnik, A., Keržič, D., Ravšelj, D., Tomaževič, N., & Umek, L. (2021). Impacts of the Covid-19 pandemic on life of higher education students: Global survey dataset from the first wave. *Data in Brief, 39*, 107659. https://doi.org/10.1016/j.dib.2021.107659

Bassey, S., & Melluish, S. (2013). Cultural competency for mental health practitioners: A selective narrative review. *Counselling Psychology Quarterly, 26*(2), 151–173. https://doi.org/10.1080/09515070.2013.792995

Berche, P. (2022). Life and death of smallpox. *Presse Medicale (Paris, France: 1983), 51*(3), 104117. https://doi.org/10.1016/j.lpm.2022.104117

Bhugra, D., Pemberton, M., Gnanapragasam, S., & Poulter, D. (2024). Culture, mental health and mental illnesses. In D. Kingdon, G. Stein, & P. Rowlands (Eds.), *Seminars in general adult psychiatry* (3rd ed., pp. 699–725). Cambridge University Press. https://doi.org/10.1017/9781911623861.032

Blandford, A., Wesson, J., Amalberti, R., AlHazme, R., & Allwihan, R. (2020). Opportunities and challenges for telehealth within, and beyond, a pandemic. *The Lancet Global Health, 8*(11), e1364–e1365. https://doi.org/10.1016/S2214-109X(20)30362-4

Cabarkapa, S., Nadjidai, S. E., Murgier, J., & Ng, C. H. (2020). The psychological impact of COVID-19 and other viral epidemics on frontline healthcare workers and ways to address it: A rapid systematic review. *Brain, Behavior, & Immunity - Health, 8*, 100144. https://doi.org/10.1016/j.bbih.2020.100144

CDC. (2019, June 11). *2009 H1N1 pandemic*. Centers for Disease Control and Prevention. https://archive.cdc.gov/flu/pandemic-resources/2009-h1n1-pandemic.html

Chatterjee, K., & Chauhan, V. S. (2020). Epidemics, quarantine and mental health. *Medical Journal Armed Forces India, 76*(2), 125–127. https://doi.org/10.1016/j.mjafi.2020.03.017

Chatterjee, S., & Kar, S. K. (2022). COVID 19 in pregnancy and neurodevelopmental disorder: The four-fold levels of prevention. *Asian Journal of Psychiatry, 70*, 103046. https://doi.org/10.1016/j.ajp.2022.103046

Chatterjee, S., Basu, S., Bhardwaj, Y. A., Arafat, S. M., Roy, D., & Kar, S. K. (2020). The health crisis of marginalized populations during COVID-19 pandemic: Challenges and recommendations. *International Journal of Social Sciences, 9*(3), 185–191.

Chen, P. J., Pusica, Y., Sohaei, D., Prassas, I., & Diamandis, E. P. (2021). An overview of mental health during the COVID-19 pandemic. *Diagnosis (Berlin, Germany), 8*(4), 403–412. https://doi.org/10.1515/dx-2021-0046

Cherry, J. D. (2004). The chronology of the 2002–2003 SARS mini pandemic. *Paediatric Respiratory Reviews, 5*(4), 262–269. https://doi.org/10.1016/j.prrv.2004.07.009

Costa, A. C. d. S., Menon, V., Phadke, R., Dapke, K., Miranda, A. V., Ahmad, S., Essar, M. Y., & Hashim, H. T. (2022). Mental health in the post COVID-19 era: Future perspectives. *Einstein, 20*, eCE6760. https://doi.org/10.31744/einstein_journal/2022CE6760

Dalal, P. K., Roy, D., Choudhary, P., Kar, S. K., & Tripathi, A. (2020). Emerging mental health issues during the COVID-19 pandemic: An Indian perspective. *Indian Journal of Psychiatry, 62*(Suppl 3), S354–S364. https://doi.org/10.4103/psychiatry.IndianJPsychiatry_372_20

Das, G. (2010). *The difficulty of being good: On the subtle art of dharma*. Oxford University Press. https://books.google.com/books?hl=en&lr=&id=UXIvUFR3P74C&oi=fnd&pg=PR11&dq=(Das+2009%3B+humility&ots=A6j9k1fKwg&sig=ypCPHhY0TASWwCacd2o9gfy6Gj8.

Dattani, S., Spooner, F., Ochmann, S., & Roser, M. (2022). Polio. *Our World in Data*. https://ourworldindata.org/polio

Dinos, S., Ascoli, M., Owiti, J. A., & Bhui, K. (2017). Assessing explanatory models and health beliefs: An essential but overlooked competency for clinicians. *BJPsych Advances, 23*(2), 106–114. https://doi.org/10.1192/apt.bp.114.013680

Dixit, A., Marthoenis, M., Arafat, S. M. Y., Sharma, P., & Kar, S. K. (2020). Binge watching behavior during COVID 19 pandemic: A cross-sectional, cross-national online survey. *Psychiatry Research, 289*, 113089. https://doi.org/10.1016/j.psychres.2020.113089

Dror, A. A., Eisenbach, N., Taiber, S., Morozov, N. G., Mizrachi, M., Zigron, A., Srouji, S., & Sela, E. (2020). Vaccine hesitancy: The next challenge in the fight against COVID-19. *European Journal of Epidemiology, 35*(8), 775–779. https://doi.org/10.1007/s10654-020-00671-y

Dua, M. (2021). Mental health concerns of healthcare workers during the COVID-19 pandemic. *Indian Journal of Health, Sexuality and Culture, 7*(Spcl), Article Spcl.

Elmazny, A., Magdy, R., Hussein, M., Elsebaie, E. H., Ali, S. H., Abdel Fattah, A. M., Hassan, M., Yassin, A., Mahfouz, N. A., Elsayed, R. M., Fathy, W., Abdel-Hamid, H. M., Abdelbadie, M., & Soliman, S. H. (2023). Neuropsychiatric post-acute sequelae of COVID-19: Prevalence, severity, and impact of vaccination. *European Archives of Psychiatry and Clinical Neuroscience, 273*(6), 1349–1358. https://doi.org/10.1007/s00406-023-01557-2

Fatima, H., Oyetunji, T. P., Mishra, S., & … (2022). Religious coping in the time of COVID-19 pandemic in India and Nigeria: Finding of a cross-national community survey. *International Journal of Social Psychiatry, 68*(2), 309–315. https://doi.org/10.1177/0020764020984511

Glaw, X., Kable, A., Hazelton, M., & Inder, K. (2017). Meaning in life and meaning of life in mental health care: An integrative literature review. *Issues in Mental Health Nursing, 38*(3), 243–252. https://doi.org/10.1080/01612840.2016.1253804

González-Riera, F. J., García-Iglesias, J. J., Allande-Cussó, R., Ruiz-Frutos, C., Rodríguez-Diaz, L., Vázquez-Lara, J. M., Fernández-Carrasco, F. J., Fagundo-Rivera, J., & Gómez-Salgado,

J. (2024). Mental health of prison inmates during the COVID-19 pandemic: A systematic review. *International Journal of Public Health, 69*, 1607166. https://doi.org/10.3389/ijph.2024.1607166

Gopalkrishnan, N. (2018). Cultural diversity and mental health: Considerations for policy and practice. *Frontiers in Public Health, 6*, 179.

Greenhalgh, T., Sivan, M., Perlowski, A., & Nikolich, J. Ž. (2024). Long COVID: A clinical update. *Lancet (London, England), 404*(10453), 707–724. https://doi.org/10.1016/S0140-6736(24)01136-X

Grover, S., Sahoo, S., Mehra, A., Avasthi, A., Tripathi, A., Subramanyan, A., Pattojoshi, A., Rao, G. P., Saha, G., Mishra, K. K., Chakraborty, K., Rao, N. P., Vaishnav, M., Singh, O. P., Dalal, P. K., Chadda, R. K., Gupta, R., Gautam, S., Sarkar, S., … Janardran Reddy, Y. C. (2020). Psychological impact of COVID-19 lockdown: An online survey from India. *Indian Journal of Psychiatry, 62*(4), 354. https://doi.org/10.4103/psychiatry.IndianJPsychiatry_427_20

Gupta, R., Grover, S., Basu, A., Krishnan, V., Tripathi, A., Subramanyam, A., Nischal, A., Hussain, A., Mehra, A., Ambekar, A., Saha, G., Mishra, K. K., Bathla, M., Jagiwala, M., Manjunatha, N., Nebhinani, N., Gaur, N., Kumar, N., Dalal, P. K., … Avasthi, A. (2020). Changes in sleep pattern and sleep quality during COVID-19 lockdown. *Indian Journal of Psychiatry, 62*(4), 370. https://doi.org/10.4103/psychiatry.IndianJPsychiatry_523_20

Himani, H., & Pandya, A. (2021). COVID-19 and prisoners in India: Most neglected population and their mental health needs. *Indian Journal of Health, Sexuality and Culture, 7*(Spcl), Article Spcl.

Huremović, D. (2019). Mental health of quarantine and isolation. In D. Huremović (Ed.), *Psychiatry of pandemics: A mental health response to infection outbreak* (pp. 95–118). Springer International Publishing. https://doi.org/10.1007/978-3-030-15346-5_9

Johnson, L., Gutridge, K., Parkes, J., Roy, A., & Plugge, E. (2021). Scoping review of mental health in prisons through the COVID-19 pandemic. *BMJ Open*. https://doi.org/10.1136/bmjopen-2020-046547

Kar, S. K., & Singh, A. (2020). Mental health of mental health professionals during COVID-19 pandemic: Who cares for it? *Asian Journal of Psychiatry, 53*, 102385.

Kar, S. K., Arafat, S. M. Y., Marthoenis, M., & Kabir, R. (2020a). Homeless mentally ill people and COVID-19 pandemic: The two-way sword for LMICs. *Asian Journal of Psychiatry, 51*, 102067. https://doi.org/10.1016/j.ajp.2020.102067

Kar, S. K., Arafat, S. M. Y., Sharma, P., Dixit, A., Marthoenis, M., & Kabir, R. (2020b). COVID-19 pandemic and addiction: Current problems and future concerns. *Asian Journal of Psychiatry, 51*, 102064. https://doi.org/10.1016/j.ajp.2020.102064

Kar, S. K., Dwivedi, S., Maurya, A. K., Singh, M., Kumar, R., Kumar, P., Chaubey, A., Singh, N., Singh, G., M, N., Kumar, R., Gupta, N., & Mallick, A. (2020c). Enhancing preparedness among frontline doctors during COVID-19 pandemic: Learning from experience. *Indian Journal of Psychological Medicine, 42*(5), 489–491. https://doi.org/10.1177/0253717620952052

Kar, S. K., Oyetunji, T. P., Prakash, A. J., Ogunmola, O. A., Tripathy, S., Lawal, M. M., Sanusi, Z. K., & Arafat, S. M. Y. (2020d). Mental health research in the lower-middle-income countries of Africa and Asia during the COVID-19 pandemic: A scoping review. *Neurology, Psychiatry and Brain Research, 38*, 54–64. https://doi.org/10.1016/j.npbr.2020.10.003

Kar, S. K., Rai, S., Sharma, N., & Singh, A. (2020e). Student suicide linked to NEET examination in India: A media report analysis study. *Indian Journal of Psychological Medicine*, 0253717620978585. https://doi.org/10.1177/0253717620978585

Kar, S. K., Tripathy, S., Roy, D., & Yasir Arafat, S. M. (2020f). Cherished serendipitous effects of disastrous COVID-19 pandemic: The desired side effects of an undesired event. *Indian Journal of Psychiatric Nursing, 17*(2), 114. https://doi.org/10.4103/IOPN.IOPN_32_20

Kar, S. K., Verma, N., & Saxena, S. K. (2020g). Coronavirus infection among children and adolescents. In *Coronavirus disease 2019 (COVID-19)*. Springer. https://doi.org/10.1007/978-981-15-4814-7_7

Kar, S. K., Yasir Arafat, S. M., Kabir, R., Sharma, P., & Saxena, S. K. (2020h). Coping with mental health challenges during COVID-19. In S. K. Saxena (Ed.), *Coronavirus disease*

2019 (COVID-19): Epidemiology, pathogenesis, diagnosis, and therapeutics (pp. 199–213). Springer. https://doi.org/10.1007/978-981-15-4814-7_16

Kar, S. K., Shankar, A., Verma, S. K., Verma, P., Kumar, R., Dwivedi, S., Maurya, A. K., & Kumar, R. (2021a). Attributes of distress among healthcare workers infected with COVID-19. *Indian Journal of Clinical Psychiatry, 1*(1), 51–53.

Kar, S. K., Singh, A., Tripathy, S., & Sharma, D. (2021b). Violence against doctors: Mental health repercussions and remedies. *Indian Journal of Health, Sexuality and Culture, 7*(Spcl), Article Spcl.

Kaufman, W. R. (2005). Karma, rebirth, and the problem of evil. *Philosophy East and West, 55*(1), 15–32.

Keržič, D., Alex, J. K., Alvarado, R. P. B., Bezerra, D. da S., Cheraghi, M., Dobrowolska, B., Fagbamigbe, A. F., Faris, M. E., França, T., González-Fernández, B., Gonzalez-Robledo, L. M., Inasius, F., Kar, S. K., Lazányi, K., Lazăr, F., Machin-Mastromatteo, J. D., Marôco, J., Marques, B. P., Mejía-Rodríguez, O., … Aristovnik, A. (2021). Academic student satisfaction and perceived performance in the e-learning environment during the COVID-19 pandemic: Evidence across ten countries. *PLoS One, 16*(10), e0258807. https://doi.org/10.1371/journal.pone.0258807.

Keshavan, M. S. (2020). Building resilience in the COVID-19 era: Three paths in the: Bhagavad Gita. *Indian Journal of Psychiatry, 62*(5), 459–461.

Kessler, R. C., & Wittchen, H.-U. (2008). Post-disaster mental health need assessment surveys—The challenge of improved future research. *International Journal of Methods in Psychiatric Research, 17*(Suppl 2), S1–S5. https://doi.org/10.1002/mpr.266

Khan, S., & Huremović, D. (2019). Psychology of the pandemic. In D. Huremović (Ed.), *Psychiatry of pandemics: A mental health response to infection outbreak* (pp. 37–44). Springer International Publishing. https://doi.org/10.1007/978-3-030-15346-5_3

Kirmayer, L. J., & Bhugra, D. (2009). Culture and mental illness: Social context and explanatory models. In *Psychiatric Diagnosis* (pp. 29–40). Wiley. https://doi.org/10.1002/9780470743485.ch3

Kleinman, A., & Sung, L. H. (1979). Why do indigenous practitioners successfully heal? *Social Science & Medicine. Part B: Medical Anthropology, 13*(1), 7–26.

Kleinman, A., Eisenberg, L., & Good, B. (1978). Culture, illness, and care: Clinical lessons from anthropologic and cross-cultural research. *Annals of Internal Medicine, 88*(2), 251–258. https://doi.org/10.7326/0003-4819-88-2-251

Koc, H. C., Xiao, J., Liu, W., Li, Y., & Chen, G. (2022). Long COVID and its management. *International Journal of Biological Sciences, 18*(12), 4768–4780. https://doi.org/10.7150/ijbs.75056

Kuljancic, D., Cvjetkovic Bosnjak, M., Siladji, D., Hinic, D., Veskovic, D., Janjic, N., Ratkovic, D., Zivanovic, O., Vasic, V., & Sakic, B. (2023). The role of COVID-19-associated fear, stress and level of social support in development of suicidality in patients diagnosed with affective and stress-induced psychiatric disorders during the COVID-19 pandemic—A comparative analysis. *Brain Sciences, 13*(5), 812. https://doi.org/10.3390/brainsci13050812

Lehmiller, J. J., Garcia, J. R., Gesselman, A. N., & Mark, K. P. (2021). Less Sex, but More Sexual Diversity: Changes in Sexual Behavior during the COVID-19 Coronavirus Pandemic. *Leisure Sciences, 43*(1–2), 295–304. https://doi.org/10.1080/01490400.2020.1774016.

Li, J., Lai, S., Gao, G. F., & Shi, W. (2021). The emergence, genomic diversity and global spread of SARS-CoV-2. *Nature, 600*(7889), 7889. https://doi.org/10.1038/s41586-021-04188-6

Mathison, L. A., Jackson, R., & Wade, N. G. (2022). Stigma and mental health in the Abrahamic religious traditions. In D. L. Vogel & N. G. Wade (Eds.), *The Cambridge handbook of stigma and mental health* (pp. 347–366). Cambridge University Press. https://doi.org/10.1017/9781108920995.020

Maunder, R. G., Leszcz, M., Savage, D., Adam, M. A., Peladeau, N., Romano, D., Rose, M., & Schulman, B. (2008). Applying the lessons of SARS to pandemic influenza: An evidence-based approach to mitigating the stress experienced by healthcare workers. *Canadian Journal of Public Health = Revue Canadienne De Santé Publique, 99*(6), 486–488. https://doi.org/10.1007/BF03403782

Mc Donald, P. (2025). *Asian flu epidemic of the 1950s | EBSCO Research Starters*. https://www.ebsco.com/research-starters/history/asian-flu-epidemic-1950s

Medina, M.-J. (2016). Pandemic influenza planning for the mental health security of survivors of mass deaths. In A. J. Masys (Ed.), *Exploring the security landscape: Non-traditional security challenges* (pp. 79–100). Springer International Publishing. https://doi.org/10.1007/978-3-319-27914-5_5

Menzies, R. E., & Menzies, R. G. (2020). Death anxiety in the time of COVID-19: Theoretical explanations and clinical implications. *Cognitive Behaviour Therapist, 13*, e19. https://doi.org/10.1017/S1754470X20000215

Meyer, B. (2001). 4 'You devil, go away from me!' Pentecostalist African Christianity and the powers of good and evil. In P. Clough & J. P. Mitchell (Eds.), *Powers of good and evil: Social transformation and popular belief* (pp. 104–134). Berghahn Books. https://www.degruyter-brill.com/document/doi/10.1515/9781782387565-007/pdf?licenseType=restricted&srsltid=AfmBOopCRGAOE56R4XgBaab_v5xuZE2QFfxDYLXy2ennlOdv5rcUzCGw

Moncrieff, J. (2008). The disease-Centred model of drug action in psychiatry. In J. Moncrieff (Ed.), *The myth of the chemical cure: A critique of psychiatric drug treatment* (pp. 1–13). Palgrave Macmillan UK. https://doi.org/10.1007/978-0-230-58944-5_1

Monje, M., & Iwasaki, A. (2022). The neurobiology of long COVID. *Neuron, 110*(21), 3484–3496. https://doi.org/10.1016/j.neuron.2022.10.006

Morganstein, J. C. (2022). Preparing for the next pandemic to protect public mental health. *The Psychiatric Clinics of North America, 45*(1), 191–210. https://doi.org/10.1016/j.psc.2021.11.012

Mulheren. (2020). Mapping the Spanish flu pandemic. *Earth.Org*. https://earth.org/data_visualization/pandemic-map-the-spanish-flu/

Murdock, G. P. (1980). *Theories of illness: A world survey*. University of Pittsburgh Press. https://books.google.com/books?hl=en&lr=&id=1OYZDDVEzEQC&oi=fnd&pg=PR7&dq=Theories+of+illness:+A+world+survey.+Pittsburgh&ots=9mpJNiiJTa&sig=ogbxDsvgPDpmoiyL6bD1b3G1K5Q

Murdock, G. P., Wilson, S. F., & Frederick, V. (1980). World distribution of theories of illness. *Transcultural Psychiatric Research Review, 17*(1–2), 37–64. https://doi.org/10.1177/136346158001700102

Narayanan, H. S., Mohan, K. S., & Radhakrishnan, V. K. (1986). The Karma theory of mental illness. *Nimhans Journal, 4*(1), 61–63.

Noori, N., Drake, J. M., & Rohani, P. (2017). Comparative epidemiology of poliovirus transmission. *Scientific Reports, 7*(1), 17362.

Np, J., & J, M. (2002). Updating the accounts: Global mortality of the 1918–1920 'Spanish' influenza pandemic. *Bulletin of the History of Medicine, 76*(1). https://doi.org/10.1353/bhm.2002.0022

Ochmann. (2024). *Smallpox—Our world in data*. https://ourworldindata.org/smallpox

Omprakash, S. (1989). The doctrine of Karma: Its psychosocial consequences. *American Journal of Community Psychology, 17*(1), 133.

Padhy, S. K., Menon, V., & Kar, S. K. (2022). Covid-19 and tele-health: Time to move from practice to policy. *Indian Journal of Psychological Medicine, 44*(1), 100–101. https://doi.org/10.1177/02537176211056789

Penninx, B. W. J. H., Benros, M. E., Klein, R. S., & Vinkers, C. H. (2022). How COVID-19 shaped mental health: From infection to pandemic effects. *Nature Medicine, 28*(10), 2027–2037. https://doi.org/10.1038/s41591-022-02028-2

Pihlström, S. (2019). Meaningful and meaningless suffering. *Human Affairs, 29*(4), 415–424. https://doi.org/10.1515/humaff-2019-0036

Ponce, S. A., Green, A., Strassle, P. D., & Nápoles, A. M. (2024). Positive and negative aspects of the COVID-19 pandemic among a diverse sample of US adults: An exploratory mixed-methods analysis of online survey data. *BMC Public Health, 24*, 22. https://doi.org/10.1186/s12889-023-17491-w

Potter, K. H. (1980). 10. The Karma theory and its interpretation in some Indian philosophical systems. In W. Doniger O'Flaherty (Ed.), *Karma and rebirth in classical Indian traditions* (pp. 241–267). University of California Press. https://doi.org/10.1525/9780520377967-012

Prakash, A. J., Agarwal, V., Kar, S. K., & Dalal, P. K. (2023). The psychological impact of COVID-19 duty among resident doctors working in a COVID-hospital: A short-term follow-up study. *Indian Journal of Psychiatry, 65*(1), 107–112. https://doi.org/10.4103/indianjpsychiatry.indianjpsychiatry_159_22

Preti, E., Di Mattei, V., Perego, G., Ferrari, F., Mazzetti, M., Taranto, P., Di Pierro, R., Madeddu, F., & Calati, R. (2020). The psychological impact of epidemic and pandemic outbreaks on health-care workers: Rapid review of the evidence. *Current Psychiatry Reports, 22*(8), 43. https://doi.org/10.1007/s11920-020-01166-z

Rajkumar, R. P. (2020). COVID-19 and mental health: A review of the existing literature. *Asian Journal of Psychiatry, 52*, 102066. https://doi.org/10.1016/j.ajp.2020.102066

Reutter, M., Hutterer, K., Gründahl, M., Gall, D., Dannlowski, U., Domschke, K., Leehr, E. J., Lonsdorf, T. B., Lueken, U., Reif, A., Schiele, M. A., Zwanzger, P., Pauli, P., Hein, G., & Gamer, M. (2024). Mental health improvement after the COVID-19 pandemic in individuals with psychological distress. *Scientific Reports, 14*(1), 5685. https://doi.org/10.1038/s41598-024-55839-3

Ristanovic. (2016). *Smallpox as an actual biothreat: Lessons learned from its outbreak in ex-Yugoslavia in 1972*. ResearchGate. https://www.researchgate.net/publication/311620038_Smallpox_as_an_actual_biothreat_lessons_learned_from_its_outbreak_in_ex-Yugoslavia_in_1972

Rogers. (2009). *Influenza pandemic (H1N1) of 2009 | Causes, Symptoms & Treatment | Britannica*. https://www.britannica.com/event/influenza-pandemic-H1N1-of-2009

Rosen, D. D., Greenberg, D., Schmeidler, J., & Shefler, G. (2008). Stigma of mental illness, religious change, and explanatory models of mental illness among Jewish patients at a mental-health clinic in North Jerusalem. *Mental Health, Religion and Culture, 11*(2), 193–209.

Roy, D., Tripathy, S., Kar, S. K., Sharma, N., Verma, S. K., & Kaushal, V. (2020). Study of knowledge, attitude, anxiety & perceived mental healthcare need in Indian population during COVID-19 pandemic. *Asian Journal of Psychiatry, 51*, 102083. https://doi.org/10.1016/j.ajp.2020.102083

Sallam, M. (2021). COVID-19 vaccine hesitancy worldwide: A concise systematic review of vaccine acceptance rates. *Vaccines, 9*(2), 160. https://doi.org/10.3390/vaccines9020160

Schluter, P. J., Généreux, M., Landaverde, E., Chan, E. Y. Y., Hung, K. K. C., Law, R., Mok, C. P. Y., Murray, V., O'Sullivan, T., Qadar, Z., & Roy, M. (2022). An eight country cross-sectional study of the psychosocial effects of COVID-19 induced quarantine and/or isolation during the pandemic. *Scientific Reports, 12*(1), 13175. https://doi.org/10.1038/s41598-022-16254-8

Scholkmann, F., & May, C.-A. (2023). COVID-19, post-acute COVID-19 syndrome (PACS, 'long COVID') and post-COVID-19 vaccination syndrome (PCVS, 'post-COVIDvac-syndrome'): Similarities and differences. *Pathology, Research and Practice, 246*, 154497. https://doi.org/10.1016/j.prp.2023.154497

Serafini, G., Parmigiani, B., Amerio, A., Aguglia, A., Sher, L., & Amore, M. (2020). The psychological impact of COVID-19 on the mental health in the general population. *QJM: Monthly Journal of the Association of Physicians, 113*(8), 531–537. https://doi.org/10.1093/qjmed/hcaa201

Sharma, S., Mehra, M., & Dayal, S. (2021). Mental health implications of COVID-19 and lockdown among general and special populations: An Indian perspective. *Indian Journal of Health, Sexuality and Culture, 7*(Spcl), Article Spcl.

Sharma, S. K., Joseph, J., Dhandapani, M., Varghese, A., Radha, K., Das, K., Jangra, N., Rozha, P., Varkey, B. P., & Rachel, R. (2023). The psychological morbidity among health care workers during the early phase of Covid-19 pandemic in India: A systematic review and meta-analysis. *Indian Journal of Community Medicine: Official Publication of Indian Association of Preventive & Social Medicine, 48*(1), 12–23. https://doi.org/10.4103/ijcm.ijcm_159_22

Sheikh, S., & Furnham, A. (2000). A cross-cultural study of mental health beliefs and attitudes towards seeking professional help. *Social Psychiatry and Psychiatric Epidemiology, 35*(7), 326–334. https://doi.org/10.1007/s001270050246

Singh, J., Sood, M., Chadda, R. K., Singh, V., & Kattula, D. (2021). Mental health issues and coping among health care workers during COVID19 pandemic: Indian perspective. *Asian Journal of Psychiatry, 61*, 102685. https://doi.org/10.1016/j.ajp.2021.102685

Sino Biological. (2025). *Hong Kong Flu (1968 Influenza Pandemic) | Sino Biological*. https://www.sinobiological.com/research/virus/1968-influenza-pandemic-hong-kong-flu

Staff. (2024, June 29). Hong Kong Flu. *World of History*. https://worldofhistorycheatsheet.com/hong-kong-flu/

Stuijfzand, S., Deforges, C., Sandoz, V., Sajin, C.-T., Jaques, C., Elmers, J., & Horsch, A. (2020). Psychological impact of an epidemic/pandemic on the mental health of healthcare professionals: A rapid review. *BMC Public Health, 20*, 1230. https://doi.org/10.1186/s12889-020-09322-z

Sun, Y.-Q., Zhang, Y.-Y., Liu, M.-C., Chen, J.-J., Li, T.-T., Liu, Y.-N., Zhang, L.-Y., Wang, T., Yu, L.-J., Che, T.-L., Tang, T., Xu, Q., Lv, C.-L., Jiang, B.-G., Golding, N., Mehlman, M. L., Hay, S. I., Fang, L.-Q., & Liu, W. (2024). Mapping the distribution of Nipah virus infections: A geospatial modelling analysis. *The Lancet Planetary Health, 8*(7), e463–e475. https://doi.org/10.1016/S2542-5196(24)00119-0

Taubenberger, J. K., & Morens, D. M. (2010). Influenza: The once and future pandemic. *Public Health Reports, 125*(Suppl 3), 16–26.

Taylor, S. (2022). The psychology of pandemics. *Annual Review of Clinical Psychology, 18*, 581–609. https://doi.org/10.1146/annurev-clinpsy-072720-020131

Taylor, M. R., Agho, K. E., Stevens, G. J., & Raphael, B. (2008). Factors influencing psychological distress during a disease epidemic: Data from Australia's first outbreak of equine influenza. *BMC Public Health, 8*, 347. https://doi.org/10.1186/1471-2458-8-347

Terhakopian, A., & Benedek, D. M. (2007). Hospital disaster preparedness: Mental and behavioral health interventions for infectious disease outbreaks and bioterrorism incidents. *American Journal of Disaster Medicine, 2*(1), 43–50.

Thakkar, A. (2021). Burnout in mental health professionals during the COVID-19 pandemic. *Indian Journal of Health, Sexuality and Culture, 7*(Spcl), Article Spcl.

Threats, I. of M. (US) F. on M., Knobler, S. L., Mack, A., Mahmoud, A., & Lemon, S. M. (2005). The story of influenza. In *The threat of pandemic influenza: Are we ready? Workshop summary*. National Academies Press (US). https://www.ncbi.nlm.nih.gov/books/NBK22148/

Tripathy, S., & Ogunmola, O. A. (2021). COVID vaccination: Myths and hesitancy, and impact on vaccine drive worldwide. *Indian Journal of Health, Sexuality and Culture, 7*(Spcl), Article Spcl.

Tripathy, S., Kar, S. K., Roy, D., Mishra, S., & Arafat, S. M. (2020). Community perception of the environmental and wellness impact of COVID-19 and its possible implications for elderly population. *Journal of Geriatric Care and Research, 7*(2), 68.

Tsai, J., & Wilson, M. (2020). COVID-19: A potential public health problem for homeless populations. *The Lancet Public Health, 5*(4), e186–e187. https://doi.org/10.1016/S2468-2667(20)30053-0

UNAIDS. (2020). *UNAIDS data 2020 | UNAIDS*. https://www.unaids.org/en/resources/documents/2020/unaids-data

Wainwright, D. (2008). Illness behaviour and discourse of health. In D. Wainwright (Ed.), *A sociology of health* (pp. 76–96). Sage. http://www.sagepub.com/books/Book229076#tabview=toc

Weich, S. (2022). *Mental health after covid-19*. https://doi.org/10.1136/bmj.o326

WHO. (2016). *Zika virus disease outbreak 2015–2016*. https://www.who.int/emergencies/situations/zika-virus-outbreak

WHO. (2022a). *Zika epidemiology update—February 2022*. https://www.who.int/publications/m/item/zika-epidemiology-update%2D%2D-february-2022

WHO. (2022b, March 2). *COVID-19 pandemic triggers 25% increase in prevalence of anxiety and depression worldwide*. https://www.who.int/news/item/02-03-2022-covid-19-pandemic-triggers-25-increase-in-prevalence-of-anxiety-and-depression-worldwide

WHO. (2025a). *Ebola outbreak 2014–2016—West Africa*. https://www.who.int/emergencies/situations/ebola-outbreak-2014-2016-West-Africa

WHO. (2025b). *HIV statistics—Global and regional trends*. UNICEF DATA. https://data.unicef.org/topic/hivaids/global-regional-trends/

WHO. (2025c). *Poliomyelitis*. https://www.who.int/news-room/fact-sheets/detail/poliomyelitis

WHO. (2025d). *Severe Acute Respiratory Syndrome (SARS)*. https://www.who.int/health-topics/severe-acute-respiratory-syndrome

WHO. (2025e, February 28). *Influenza (seasonal)*. https://www.who.int/news-room/fact-sheets/detail/influenza-(seasonal)

William, W. (2022). The WHO estimates of excess mortality associated with the COVID-19 pandemic. *Nature*. https://www.nature.com/articles/s41586-022-05522-2

Zamora-Ledezma, C., Clavijo C, D. F., Medina, E., Sinche, F., Santiago Vispo, N., Dahoumane, S. A., & Alexis, F. (2020). Biomedical science to tackle the COVID-19 pandemic: Current status and future perspectives. *Molecules, 25*(20), 4620. https://doi.org/10.3390/molecules25204620

Chapter 12
Mental Health and Industrial Disasters in South Asia

R. Srinivasa Murthy

1 Introduction

1.1 Mental Health and Disasters: International Experiences

The emotional health of populations exposed to disasters is a well-recognized public health priority. World Health Report, 2001 (WHO, 2001) observed

> Conflicts, including wars and civil strife, and disasters affect a large number of people and result in mental problems. It is estimated that globally, about 50 million people are refugees or are internally displaced. In addition, millions are affected by natural disasters, including earthquakes, floods, typhoons, hurricanes, and similar large-scale calamities. Such situations take a heavy toll on the mental health of the people involved, most of whom live in developing countries, where the capacity to take care of these problems is extremely limited. Between a third and a half of all the affected persons suffer from mental distress. The most frequent diagnosis made is posttraumatic stress disorder (PTSD), often along with depressive or anxiety disorders. In addition, most individuals report psychological symptoms that do not amount to disorders. PTSD arises after a stressful event of an exceptionally threatening or catastrophic nature and is characterized by intrusive memories, avoidance of circumstances associated with the stressor, sleep disturbances, irritability and anger, lack of concentration, and excessive vigilance. The point prevalence of PTSD in the general population, according to GBD 2000, is 0.37%. The specific diagnosis of PTSD has been questioned as being culture-specific and also as being made too often. Indeed, PTSD has been called a diagnostic category that has been invented based on socio-political needs. Even if the suitability of this specific diagnosis is uncertain, the overall significance of mental morbidity among individuals exposed to severe trauma is generally accepted. Studies on victims of natural disasters have also shown a high rate of mental disorders. A recent study from China found a high rate of psychological symptoms and a poor quality of life among earthquake survivors. The study also showed that post-disaster support was effective in the improvement of well-being.

R. Srinivasa Murthy (✉)
National Institute of Mental Health and Neurosciences, Bengaluru, India

N. Kar et al. (eds.), *Climate Change, Disaster and Mental Health in South Asia*, South Asian Perspectives in Mental Health and Psychology,
https://doi.org/10.1007/978-981-95-3690-0_12

Mental health and disasters are very much in the news. It is 80 years since the bombing of Hiroshima (Farago, 2025). It is also the marking of 80 years of the Auschwitz Concentration camp. At the time of writing this book chapter, *The New York Times* referred to this time as 'Eighty years after the city's destruction, we seem to be blundering into a new age of nuclear perils. It is time for culture to rediscover the courage to be afraid' (*New York Times*, Aug 1, 2025).

It is significant to recall that, though the two atom bombs were dropped in August 1945, it took nearly two decades for scientists to study the aftereffects of the bombing, as noted by Lifton (1968), the first scientist to study the Japanese population in 1962: 'Overall, people resisted knowing- and especially feeling- the full truth of Hiroshima because that truth was too threatening, too unfamiliar in its dimensions, and for Americans, a potential accusation'.

Humanity has moved on, and today, study and response to mental health aspects of disasters are well established. A few examples illustrate the international situations.

The inaugural issue of *The Lancet-Primary Health Care*, July 2025, presents the current scenario of conflicts as follows (Pfeiffern & Martsenkovskyi, 2025):

> As of 2023, a record fifty-nine active military conflicts were documented worldwide, which is the highest number since the post-World War II era. The majority of these conflicts were characterised by unprecedented and escalating violence against civilians and essential infrastructure, disproportionately affecting women and children, and resulting in the forced displacement of over 117.3 million people, including refugees and internally displaced people.....*Recent armed conflicts have been accompanied by a rapid decline in population mental health, placing enormous strain on already fragile national mental health systems. These challenges highlight the crucial need for rapid, effective, and easily scalable mental health interventions that can reach displaced and conflict-affected populations where traditional care infrastructure is unavailable. (emphasis added).* Although international initiatives have prioritised the training of highly specialised professionals in trauma-focused treatments, the availability of such services is likely to remain limited for years to come.

Another report of 9 August 2025, in *The Lancet*, observed (Osendarp et al., 2025)

> As scientists and members of the Standing Together for Nutrition Consortium (ST4N) who have been "Standing Together For Nutrition" during recent crises, we use evidence of the impact of crises on nutrition to advocate for the people most affected. Now, in the face of the world's indifference, we are compelled to speak out about the horrifying human-made famine unfolding in Gaza and other conflict areas, including Sudan, South Sudan, and Yemen. Widespread starvation is deliberately used as a weapon of war, at a scale that we never thought possible. It is a moral failure that in 2025, more than 12 million people are living in Integrated Food Security Phase Classification (IPC) phase 5 (catastrophe) famine conditions - the most extreme food insecurity level according to the gold-standard IPC. These famines are not only claiming lives today, but they are also inflicting irreversible intergenerational trauma and damage.

Two other recent reports from Sri Lanka and Sudan present the continuing human cost of conflicts. The impact of conflicts on mental health keeps emerging from recent studies. A recent report from Sudan (Hussein et al., 2025) reported PTSD in 56.9% of participants and poor well-being in 40% of participants; proportions among health care workers were 60.5% and 27.5%, respectively, and both had a significant negative correlation. PTSD was predicted by male gender, urban residence, nonmedical profession, insufficient income, living with two to ten households or more than 20 households, living in conflict zones, and refugee resettlement.

A 10-year follow-up study from Sri Lanka on the impact of the conflicts in the country (Thamotharampillai et al., 2025) reported a high degree of continuing emotional impact. Levels of PTSD (46.8%), depression (57.1%), anxiety (60.7%), stress (50%), and somatization (40.2%) were high, and functional disability (36.4%) was common. Individual-level consequences were significantly higher in districts with high trauma as compared to those with low trauma burdens. Coping intensity was correlated with anxiety, stress, PTSD, and somatization. At the family level, dysfunctional families had a higher proportion of members with suicidal thoughts, mental health issues, alcohol and drug abuse, poor income, lack of essential facilities, and dissatisfaction with family life. At the community level, common problems reported were use of illicit drugs (86.2%) and alcohol (84.5%), family problems (36.4%), unemployment (32%), and financial problems (26.3%). Study villages scored very low in structural social capital. Authors concluded, 'collective trauma deeply affects communities by disrupting individual mental health, family and community dynamics, leading to persistent dysfunction'. Effective post-war recovery requires reversing the war atmosphere with integrated psychosocial interventions targeting individual, family, and community dynamics simultaneously.

A recent review provides a comprehensive account of the psychological foundations of PTSD, involving disturbances to memory as well as to identity. A broader focus on identity may be able to accommodate group and communal influences on the experience of trauma and PTSD, as well as the impact of resource loss. Authors summarize current evidence concerning the biological foundations of PTSD, with a particular focus on genetic and neuroimaging studies. They observe that progress in prevention has been disappointing, and there is now extensive evidence supporting the efficacy of a variety of psychological treatments for established PTSD, including trauma-focused interventions, such as trauma-focused cognitive behaviour therapy (TF-CBT), eye movement desensitization and reprocessing (EMDR), and non-trauma-focused therapies, which also include some emerging identity-based approaches, such as present-centred and compassion-focused therapies. Additionally, there are promising interventions that are neither psychological nor pharmacological, or that combine a pharmacological and a psychological approach, such as 3,4-methylenedioxymethamphetamine (MDMA)–assisted psychotherapy. They also review advances in the priority areas of adapting interventions in resource-limited settings and across cultural contexts and of community-based approaches. They conclude by identifying future directions for work on trauma and mental health (Brewin et al., 2025).

2 Disaster Mental Health Studies in India

It was a little over 4 years back when the Andhra Cyclone resulted in the first examination of the emotional impact of the disaster (Rao & Zubair, 1979). Prof H.S. Narayan of the National Institute of Mental Health and Neurosciences (NIMHANS), Bengaluru, is the pioneer in this field, through his 1980 study of understanding the emotional aspects of disasters and community-level interventions following the Bangalore circus tragedy (Narayana, 1986). However, it was the 1984 Bhopal disaster that took disaster mental health to a public health priority (Srinivasa Murthy & Isaac, 1987; Srinivasa Murthy, 2014). Since that horrific disaster, India has experienced a large number of disasters such as the Latur earthquake of 1993 (Sharan et al., 1996; Acharya, 2000; Pande et al., 2000a, b), the 1999 supercyclone in Orissa (Srikala et al., 2000; Kishore Kumar et al., 2000), the Bhuj earthquake of 2001, Gujarat riots of 2002 (Lakshminarayana et al., 2004), tsunami of 2004 (Math et al., 2006; WHO, 2005), Kashmir floods in 2014, forest fires in Uttarakhand in 2018, and the Kerala floods of August 2018 (Parasuraman & Unnikrishnan, 2000). In the last 40 years, the Environmental Protection Act was enacted in 1986 (Government of India, 1986), and the formation of the National Disaster Management Agency (NDMA) and the National Disaster Response Force (NDRF) is another important development (Srinivasa Murthy, 2018; NDMA, 2009).

3 Industrial Disasters in India

The mental health impact of industrial disasters is as important as that due to conflicts and natural disasters. The human elements of poor planning, lax regulations, faulty designs, inadequate training, and supervision contributing to the industrial disaster, following the disaster, lack of awareness of the mental health impact, limited availability of mental health interventions, and inadequacy of legal remedies, all add to the suffering of the survivors.

This chapter covers in detail (i) three Indian industrial accidents (Bhopal disaster and Odisha train accident, Telangana factory blasts), (ii) the administrative and structural changes that have occurred in the last 40 years, and (iii) the areas for future action by the general public, politicians, planners, press, professionals, non-governmental organizations, and the governments.

In India, industrial disasters were in the news in 2025 for a number of reasons. The Bhopal disaster continues to occupy the attention of the public, professionals, politicians, courts, and voluntary organizations (Box 1). The 2023 Odisha train accident provides new insights about the needs and challenges of providing care (Box 2). There have been many industrial disasters, e.g. in Telangana/Andhra Pradesh, the most recent one on 30 June, 2025 (Box 3).

4 Bhopal Industrial Disaster

The Bhopal disaster is the most studied disaster event in India. It is still in the news (Box 1), after 40+ years, which illustrates the issues of industrial safety and mental health consequences and the challenges of providing care and compensation. At a personal level, it has been three decades of learning and scientific contribution (Srinivasa Murthy & Isaac, 1987; Srinivasa Murthy et al., 1987; Srinivasa Murthy, 1990, 2000a, b, 2001, 2002, 2004, 2006, 2014, 2016; Basu & Srinivasa Murthy, 2003).

Box 1 Bhopal Disaster—Recent Developments (from The Hindu)

1. 3 Dec 2024: *The toxins of the Bhopal disaster*
2. 9 Jan 2025: *HC asks Centre, MP govt to digitise medical records of Bhopal gas tragedy survivors*
3. 13 Jan 2025: *Bhopal's 40-year-old past is Pithampur's paranoid future*
4. 19 Jan 2025: *The trouble with disposing of Bhopal's Union Carbide waste*
5. 27 Jan 2025: *Torch rally in Pithampur to oppose Bhopal gas waste disposal*
6. 27 Feb 2025: *Bhopal gas tragedy: Supreme Court says critics of Bhopal toxic waste disposal adopting 'not-in-my-backyard' principle, refuses to intervene*
7. 3 July 2025: *The incineration of toxic waste from the Bhopal tragedy took time and effort*
8. 30 June 2025: *All 337 Tons of Union Carbide Waste were burnt to ashes in Madhya Pradesh*
9. 3 July 2025: *Away from the edge: On waste disposal from the 1984 Bhopal plant accident; the incineration of toxic waste from the Bhopal tragedy took time and effort*
10. 18 July 2025: *Plea in Supreme Court says Bhopal gas victims have been misclassified*

This subject, which is of international interest, is reflected in the recent article in *The Times* (London), 4 July 2025, titled *The toxic legacy of Bhopal, India's chemical 'volcano'; decades on from the world's worst industrial disaster, chemical waste has finally been cleared. But victims' sons and daughters still pay the price* (Dhillon, 2025).

4.1 The Disaster

The gas disaster happened in the Union Carbide India Limited (UCIL) factory located in Bhopal, a city in Central India, on the night of 2 December 1984. About 40 tonnes of methyl isocyanate (MIC), an 'extremely hazardous chemical', leaked into the environment, forming a cloud of poisonous gas. Considering the immediate and long-term effects, it is considered the biggest industrial disaster in human history.

The leaked chemical covered an area about 7 km in radius of the plant, affecting about 200,000 people. More than 2000 (about 1% of those directly exposed) died on the night of the disaster. It is reported that multiple factors contributed to the disaster, such as the entry of water into the tank with MIC, dysfunctional gauges measuring the temperature and pressures, the refrigeration unit, the gas scrubber, and the flare tower, which burns off the escaping MIC. Negligence and poor operational procedures were also associated (Jayaraman, 1984, 1985). Besides 2000 people who died immediately, in the following 40 years, more than 25,000 people died, as a consequence of exposure to MIC and its impact on health. In addition, 200,000 survivors continued to experience a wide variety of ill health and disabilities.

In this connection, the Bhopal Gas Relief Act was passed in 1985. There was an out-of-court compensation settlement between UCIL and the Government of India for $470 million in 1989. Many years after that, in August 2012, the Supreme Court of India recognized the continuing needs and the rights of the survivors and ordered the implementation of appropriate measures for health care.

4.2 Bhopal Disaster: Mental Health Research

The Indian Council of Medical Research (ICMR), New Delhi, focused on the health impacts of the survivors. The ICMR arranged to explore the health issues, such as immediate effects on various systems (specifically, vision, lungs, gastrointestinal, and gynaecological issues), and mental health problems. The following section focuses on the mental health initiatives from 1984 to 2025.

4.3 First Period (Dec 1984–Feb 1985)

The Advisory Committee on Mental Health of ICMR recognized and focused on the mental health needs of the affected population since the beginning, from 1984. The service needs and research were viewed both in the short-term and long-term perspectives. The acute needs were the understanding and provision of care for confusional states, reactive psychoses, anxiety-depression reactions, and grief reactions. Long-term needs were based on the psychological reactions to the acute and chronic disabilities; psychological problems of the exposed subjects, who were not affected then, to the uncertainties of the future; effects of broken social units on children and adults; and psychological problems related to rehabilitation (Srinivasa Murthy et al., 1987). The involvement of the psychiatrists/neurologists at the field level did not occur till about 8 weeks after the disaster.

4.4 Second Period (March 1985–1994)

During the first decade of the disaster, a large number of studies reported high physical morbidity especially the eyes and lungs, along with several other physical symptoms (Mackenzie, 1985; Tachakra 1987; Andersson et al., 1988; Misra, 1986; Misra et al., 1988; Gupta et al., 1988; ICMR, 1989; Cullinan et al., 1996; Medico-Friend Circle, 1996, 1997; Menon, 1999; Editorial, 2000; Lapierre & Moro, 2001; The Statesman, 2014; Srinivasa Murthy, 2014).

The first team of mental health professionals studied the magnitude and nature of the psychiatric problems. They interacted with the local medical staff, studied patients attending the health centres, and also assessed mental health problems in the general population. The initial observations suggested that around 50% of the community and 20–30% of people attending medical facilities had mental health needs (Sethi et al., 1987; Srinivasa Murthy & Isaac, 1987).

Due to the lack of local resources and the enormity of the needs, a mental health team from King George Medical College, Lucknow, was located in Bhopal, from February–May 1985. Based on the self-rating questionnaire (SRQ), 30.3% patients were identified to have a probable psychiatric disorder. Following further evaluation by present state evaluation (PSE) (Wing et al., 1975), a prevalence rate was confirmed at 22.6%. Major diagnoses were anxiety (25%), depression (37%), adjustment disorder with prolonged depressive reaction (20%), and adjustment disorder with predominant disturbance of emotions (16%); it was observed that there were hardly any patients with psychosis related to the disaster (Sethi et al., 1987).

Neurological studies (Bharucha & Bharucha, 1987) involving 129 adults and 47 children reported stroke, encephalopathy, cerebellar ataxia, vertigo, and hearing loss in a few patients. There were transitory symptoms such as loss of consciousness, muscle weakness, tremors, ataxia, and easy fatigability. Among children, loss of consciousness was reported in half, whereas fits, generalized hypotonia, weakness, and mental regression were rarely observed. Several publications addressed many dimensions of the mental health aspects of disaster (Basu & Srinivasa Murthy, 2003; Srinivasa Murthy, 1990, 2000a, b, 2001, 2004, 2006, 2014, 2016).

4.5 Longitudinal Studies

Following the initial studies, the ICMR identified mental health as an important aspect of all research efforts with the general population, which led to the longitudinal study of mental health effects under the newly formed Bhopal Gas Disaster Research Centre. Two mental health studies and one training event were conducted during the 1985–1994 period. An initial screening (Verghese et al., 1973) was followed by PSE (Wing et al., 1975) for diagnosis, involving a random sample of 700 families from severely exposed, mildly exposed, and nonexposed areas. The results of the studies were striking. The prevalence rates were 139.2/1000 in the severely exposed area, 80.8/1000 in the mildly exposed area, and 26.8/1000 in the nonexposed area. On the disaster night, people who were sleeping outside their houses had a higher prevalence rate (145.8/1000) compared to those inside (108.5/1000). The exposure to MIC gas was a contributing factor to the incident psychiatric disorders. Among the demographic variables, the lower-income group had the highest prevalence (269.2/1000), compared to the middle-income group (122.9/1000) (ICMR, 2012). Psychiatric disorders were more prevalent in women than in men survivors.

All mentally ill survivors were followed up yearly. During the first to fourth follow-up, the proportions of patients with continuing illness were 89.6%, 66.8%, 56.8%, and 47.4%, respectively, suggestive of gradual improvements. More than half of the patients (58.3%) received psychiatric treatment from the local doctors during the first follow-up. Importantly, 37.4% patients did not accept any intervention. The rate of recovery increased gradually, from 7.6% to 44.4% in the mildly exposed area and from 14.3% to 36.6% in the nonexposed area. It was a concern that nearly half of the patients were still symptomatic after 5 years of follow-up (ICMR, 1989, 2012). In children (0–15 years), the prevalence of mental illness was 12.7% in the exposed area compared to 2.4% in the control area. To address the urgent need for mental health support, local medical officers were trained in Bhopal City (Srinivasa Murthy & Isaac, 1987). It was a 6-day manual-based training with positive feedback regarding its usefulness.

4.6 Third Period (1995–2010)

The ICMR decided to withdraw from direct involvement and transferred the responsibility to the state. Initially, there were limited mental health care facilities in Bhopal; however, there were developments such as the creation of departments of psychiatry in all five medical colleges at that time. One qualitative study in 2003 through interviews of 26 survivors found that despite the continuing suffering of the affected population, no systematic effort was made to tackle the mental health problems secondary to the gas disaster (Basu & Srinivasa Murthy, 2003).

4.7 Fourth Period (2010–2014)

Health care of the survivors and research were again under focus following the Bhopal court judgement of June 2010. The National Institute for Research in Environmental Health (NIREH) was set up in Bhopal (NIREH, 2012, 2013). Continuing mental health needs of the survivors were studied. It also led to developing a training programme and manual for the doctors in Bhopal (Srinivasa Murthy, 2016). Studies around 2014 reported anxiety, depression, posttraumatic stress disorder, and adjustment disorders among survivors. Besides, there were mental health problems directly and indirectly related to the disaster, the latter from secondary stressors. In addition, there were psychiatric disorders, unrelated to the disaster, in people with chronic physical conditions.

4.8 Fifth Period (2014–2024)

During this period, the mental health manual for the doctors was revised, considering the mental health needs of the survivors (Srinivasa Murthy, 2016). Further, all the doctors working at the peripheral health services, on a day-to-day basis, were trained utilising the mental health manual. They were supported by the well-developed psychiatry departments in the city medical colleges by that time and the mental health team of the Bhopal Gas Memorial Research Centre.

4.9 Sixth Period (2025–)

The human needs, health, finances, social needs, rehabilitative needs, etc., continue to be experienced by the survivors. There is much that needs to be addressed even after four decades (Box 1). The removal and burning of some of the toxic waste material are positive steps.

4.10 Lessons of the Bhopal Disaster

There are many lessons to learn from the largest man-made disasters in a developing country. The disaster effects were a combination of both the substances inhaled and the psychological effects of living through a disaster experience. No formal mental health infrastructure was available to provide immediate post-disaster mental health care. A number of innovative approaches were developed to provide mental health care, especially suitable for use in developing countries. This disaster was the subject of intensive health research prospectively for the first 5 years, including mental health aspects. There have been improper assessments of disability, which are linked to inadequate compensation. There was a lack of rehabilitation activities and facilities. There is no longitudinal research to explore changing morbidity, the effectiveness of the care, and interventions. There was no connecting process with the primary health care for continuing mental health care, public mental health education, self-care suggestions, and psychosocial interventions. In addition, there was poor coordination with voluntary organizations, leading to mistrust.

5 Odisha Train Accident

Train accidents are common in India. However, there is a lack of a process to evaluate the needs and to provide psychosocial support to the survivors. Most often, the support provided to survivors is in the form of monetary compensation and/or physical care. In the case of train accidents, there are special challenges, such as limited awareness about the impact of the accident on the survivors, lack of awareness regarding the requirement for emotional support, survivors belonging to geographically highly dispersed areas, and lack of availability of psychological support or personnel in most places. It is against this background that systematic studies of the 2023 Odisha accident provided information about the mental health impact and the variety of needs of the survivors of the train accident (Box 2). The team studied in depth a group of survivors and carried out a systematic study with comparison groups for the different types of mental health conditions (Kar, 2024; Kar et al., 2025; Swain et al., 2025).

Box 2 Psychiatric Studies Following the 2023 Odisha Train Accident

1. Anatomy of a catastrophe: Managing psychosocial consequence of the 2023 Odisha train accident (Kar, 2024)
2. Posttraumatic Stress Following the 2023 Odisha Train Accident: A Cross-sectional Comparison Study of Passengers, Health Professionals, and the Local Community (Kar et al., 2025)
3. A Qualitative Mixed-Method Narrative Study on Psychotherapeutic Support Needs Based on a Series of 11 Cases of Survivors of the 2023 Odisha Train Accident (Swain et al., 2025)

The 2023 Odisha train accident in India is one of the deadliest train accidents in recent history. On 2 June 2023, three trains collided in Balasore District in Odisha State of eastern India. The Coromandel Express entered the passing loop instead of the main line near Bahanaga Bazar railway station at full speed and collided with a goods train. Due to the high speed of the Coromandel Express, its 21 coaches derailed, and three of those collided with the oncoming SMVT Bengaluru Howrah Superfast Express on the adjacent track. A total of 296 people were killed in the crash, and more than 1200 others were injured. Many of these injuries required hospital admission, emergency operations, and treatment in intensive care units. The lack of appropriate and adequate medical facilities locally meant that most seriously injured victims were transported to hospitals far away in different cities. The hospitals were overburdened with patients with complicated injuries. For some of the passengers, the injuries meant lifelong physical and functional disability.

The mental health team studied posttraumatic stress symptoms (PTSS) and posttraumatic stress disorder (PTSD), associated factors, and quality of life (QOL) of a group of passengers ($n = 58$) affected by the 2023 Odisha train accident, comparing it with health professionals ($n = 42$) such as doctors and nurses who treated them and individuals from the local community ($n = 65$). The team also checked for anxiety and depression in passengers. It was a cross-sectional study that assessed accident experience and used the PTSD checklist, WHOQOL-BREF, General Anxiety Disorder, and Patient Health Questionnaire scales. The PTSS were common, specifically, intrusive memories (36.4%), feeling upset while reminded of the experience (33.9%), and avoidance of memories (30.9%). Strong negative feelings, loss of interest, feeling distant, and irritability or anger outbursts were significantly more common among passengers than others. PTSD was present in 20.7% of passengers, 19.0% of health professionals, and 7.7% of local participants. Seeing dead bodies significantly contributed to PTSD. Clinical levels of anxiety (58.3%) and depression (50%) were present in passengers, which were significantly associated with PTSD, along with fear of death. Passengers had the worst QOL and health satisfaction among the groups.

In addition to the affected passengers, their family members and other people were indirect victims of the accident with psychological concerns (Kar, 2023). Another study, using a qualitative, mixed-method, narrative design, reported interview outcomes of the affected passengers. The passengers and their family members had many trauma-related psychological concerns. In summary, the psychotherapeutic needs of the survivors, their families, and indirect victims were unmet. The psychological interventions that were considered to be appropriate were psychoeducation, relaxation therapies, and cognitive therapies. There is a specific role for trauma-focused cognitive behavioural therapy. All these could be provided in-person, group, or online methods. However, considering the geographically dispersed survivor population, tele-psychotherapy could be considered. In addition, training other health care personnel to provide psychological support locally might be possible.

6 Industrial Disasters in Telangana and Andhra Pradesh

On the morning of 30 June at 9.10 a.m., an explosion tore through Sigachi Industries, a pharmaceutical factory, and flattened a three-storeyed building in Pashamylaram on the outskirts of Hyderabad. The stock market–listed entity estimated the death toll at 39 of the 143 workers who were on-site during the explosion (Box 3).

Box 3 Industrial Accidents in Telangana and Andhra Pradesh
Recent Accidents

1. 30 June 2025: *Sigachi industrial accident kills 40 people*
2. 1 July 2025: *Telangana factory blast: CM announces ₹1 crore to families of deceased workers, ₹10 lakhs to severely injured*
3. 2 July 2025: *Telangana factory blast: Sigachi Industries continued to operate with old machinery despite warnings, claims victim's son*

4. 2 July 2025: *Telengana factory blast: loopholes and apathy exposed as death toll rises to 40* (*India Today*)
5. 2 July 2025: *Before the Telangana factory blast that killed 36, suspected malfunctions and red flags—mandatory inspections are being ignored on the pretext of Ease of Doing Business and Speed of Doing Business, alleges Narasinga Rao*
6. 3 July 2025: *CITU blames lack of safety audits for recurrent accidents at pharma units*
7. 5 July 2025: *How poor workers are paying the price*
8. 6 July 2025: *What are the lessons from the Telangana blast?*

Earlier Accidents in Telangana and Andhra Pradesh

9. The blast at pharma company Escientia's plant in the Atchutapuram Special Economic Zone (SEZ) in Anakapalli district, Andhra Pradesh, is the worst industrial accident, with seventeen workers killed and many injured
10. 30 June 2024: A massive explosion rocked a pharma plant at the same SEZ, leading to deaths and injuries. The Atchutapuram SEZ, among the State's largest SEZs, is home to the factories of more than 100 companies
11. 7 May 2020: 12 people died after a styrene monomer vapour leak from a polymers unit at Venkatapuram village on the outskirts of Visakhapatnam (Barnagarwala, 2025; Nanisetti, 2025; First Post, 2025)

The industrial accidents of Telangana and Andhra Pradesh have drawn attention to the lapses and needed changes. Nanisetti (2025) raises the following questions and presents some of the corrective actions. What are the lessons from the Telangana blast? What are the safety and quality concerns, particularly in smaller pharmaceutical firms? Are regulatory checks not being carried out? What are the protocols to be followed? Are pollution norms being adhered to? How big is the pharma market?

The laxity of the regulatory framework was stark on the day of the explosion. When the fire department and emergency personnel rushed to the site, they did not have any information about what they were up against. The state and central pollution control boards mandate a board outside factory premises listing details about the pollution potential of the institution and factory operations. The firefighting and disaster rescue operations are guided by this information. The green board or environmental display boards outside the Sigachi Industries did not have proforma environmental data, leaving fire and disaster rescue workers clueless about the nature of the material involved and how to douse the fire. A tough regulatory framework with periodic check-ups would have ensured that information was available for a faster emergency response.

Hyderabad and Telangana's pharmaceutical industry growth has been aided by lax zoning and regulatory norms. Industrial areas have to be necessarily away from residential areas. The initially isolated industrial area is now surrounded by residential areas. In the absence of robust and reliable public transport, worker colonies have cropped up close to the factories and industrial areas. This affects the livelihood and health of people in the industrial cluster and surrounding areas. Environmentalists have documented how tonnes of toxic chemicals and effluents have been released into the ground and water bodies around the region. The Musi River remains highly polluted, with a study on 'Pharmaceutical pollution of the world's rivers' placing it in the 22nd position worldwide in terms of concentration of active pharmaceutical ingredients. The author concludes, 'the pharmaceutical sector holds the potential to attract investments and create high employment opportunities in Hyderabad and other places in India. To capitalise on this potential, India must establish a robust regulatory framework. The explosions and accidents are loud warning signs for the industry and the country'.

7 National Developments in Disaster Care

7.1 Environment Protection Act (EPA), 1986

One of the positive outcomes of the Bhopal disaster is the enactment of the Environment Protection Act (EPA) in 1986 to provide for the protection and improvement of the environment. It empowers the central government to establish authorities charged with the mandate of preventing environmental pollution in all its forms and to tackle specific environmental problems that are peculiar to different parts of the country. The act was last amended in 1991.

7.2 National Disaster Management Authority (NDMA)

The establishment of the National Disaster Management Authority (NDMA) in 2005 and the National Disaster Response Force (NDRF) is a major advance in disaster care in India (Government of India, 2005; NDMA, 2009). This would help the mental health care of the affected population as well. The NDMA, 2005, has outlined psychosocial care as follows:

> Psycho-social support in the context of disasters refers to comprehensive interventions aimed at addressing a wide range of psycho-social problems arising in the aftermath of a disaster. Psycho-social support and mental health services should be considered as a continuum of interventions in disaster situations. Psycho-social support will comprise general interventions related to the larger issues of relief work needs, social relationships, and harmony to promote or protect the psycho-social well-being of the survivors. Mental health services will comprise interventions aimed at the prevention or treatment of psychological

symptoms or disorders. These interventions help individuals, families, and groups to restore social cohesion and infrastructure, along with maintaining their independence and dignity.

The National Disaster Response Force (NDRF) is a specialized force in India, tasked with the responsibility of responding to natural and man-made disasters. It operates under the National Disaster Management Authority of the Ministry of Home Affairs and was established in 2006 with the aim of strengthening disaster management capabilities in the country.

Awareness and preparedness campaigns are key components of a proactive approach to disaster management. In case of any disaster, the local population is the actual first responder. It may take some time for the district or state administration to mobilize rescue teams, including police and fire personnel. If the local people are properly sensitized about the precautions and preventive actions to be taken in case of any calamity, the loss of life and damage to property can be drastically reduced. Thus, one of the most important tasks of NDRF is to continuously engage themselves in community capacity building and public awareness programmes, which include training of people (the first-responders) and concerned government officials at different levels in the areas with high vulnerability. Along with community capacity building and public awareness exercises, NDRF is also actively engaged in area familiarization exercises. Such exercises provide first-hand knowledge about the topography, access route to various disaster-prone areas, and the availability of local infrastructure/logistics, which can be used in disaster response operations. The force has trained almost four million volunteers (Wikipedia, 2025).

8 Industrial Accidents in Asian Countries

Industrial accidents are common in all Asian countries. Some examples are given below. These are associated with deaths, injuries, and disabilities and have a huge mental health impact.

8.1 Bangladesh

2005—A fire at a garment factory outside Dhaka kills 22 people and injures more than 50; at least 64 people are killed and about 100 are injured when a garment factory building collapsed in Dhaka.

2006—A garment factory building collapses in Dhaka, killing 21 workers and injuring dozens; a fire at a textile factory in the port city of Chittagong kills 65 workers and injures dozens.

2010—A fire at a garment factory in a Dhaka suburb kills 21 workers and injures about 50; a fire at a factory supplying global retailers kills 26 people and injures about 100 near Dhaka.

2012—A fire at the Tazreen Fashions factory supplying western brands in Dhaka kills 112 workers and injures more than 150.

2013—At least 1136 people were killed and hundreds were injured when an eight-storey building housing five garment factories supplying global brands collapsed on the outskirts of Dhaka. The collapse of the Rana Plaza was the worst industrial accident in Bangladesh.

2016—More than 100 people fell ill in Bangladesh after inhaling gas that leaked from a fertilizer factory in the town of Chittagong; a fire at Tampaco Foils, a food and cigarette packaging factory, north of Dhaka, killed at least 34 people and injured dozens.

2017—At least 13 people have been killed and over 50 others injured in a boiler explosion in a Gazipur factory, and the survivors blame the lack of safety measures for the accident.

2021—A massive fire in a food processing factory of Hashem Food Ltd., Narayanganj, left at least 52 people killed (DHAKA Tribune Desk, 2022).

8.2 Bhutan

Bhutan's country strategic plan (2024–2028) identifies enhancing resilience to natural disasters and the climate crisis as a key focus area (World Food Programme, 2024).

8.3 Pakistan

The accident rate in the mining sector is increasing and becoming far too common in all provinces of Pakistan. About 318 coal mine workers lost their lives in 45 fatal accidents between 2010 and 2018 (Iqbal, 2018).

8.4 Sri Lanka

Gunasekara and Alwis (2008) reported on the accidents in the process industry that have occurred in the past 10 years, from 1997 to 2006, in Sri Lanka. Fire incidents observed in 38 accidents were analyzed. The results show that the highest number of accidents has occurred during processing operations, followed by accidents during maintenance and repair work. The cause analysis shows that many accidents have occurred due to technical and human failures.

One of the worst industrial disasters occurred in 2021. On 20 May 2021, X-Press Pearl caught fire off the coast of Colombo, Sri Lanka. The vessel was engulfed in flames on 27 May and declared a total loss. After burning for 12 days, the vessel sank on 2 June as it was being towed to deeper waters. The incident was deemed the worst marine ecological disaster in Sri Lankan history due to the chemical products that were spilled (Wikipedia, 2025).

9 Challenges and Way Forward

Based on the last four decades of research on the mental health aspects of industrial disasters, challenges remain; however, some conclusions can be drawn.

9.1 Industrial Safety

Despite information, rules, regulations, and laws, industrial safety norms are not followed adequately. There is an urgent need for regulatory norms and their adherence. Greater emphasis on control of industrial pollution is paramount. The training of all levels of industrial personnel regarding the safety norms and preventive actions is vital. There is a need for periodic checking and review of the functioning of both the factories and the safety mechanisms.

9.2 Mental Health Perspectives

The mental health perspectives of industrial disasters can be summarised as follows:

Industrial disaster exposure is a risk to mental health, as affected populations have a higher prevalence of psychiatric problems. It is essential to identify the increased mental health needs of the affected population and to provide appropriate care. There is a need for both community and hospital-based psychiatric intervention, with a seamless process appropriate for the individual patient, along with integrating general medical and specialist care. Survivors can also be helped through the use of 'self-care' techniques.

Multiple complex needs of the industrial disaster survivors require support from social welfare, labour, and law so that the concerns can be addressed holistically. This can be achieved through continuous evaluation and discussion with the survivors regarding their needs. Disaster survivors require support to rebuild their community and specific support for the vulnerable groups, such as the disabled, chronically ill persons, and the elderly. There is a need for further research exploring long-term continuing psychosocial issues of the survivors and the effectiveness of various interventions.

10 Conclusion

Industrial disasters pose a grave challenge for the resource-scarce South Asian countries. There is a massive need for the affected populations, and managing their mental health issues remains inadequate. Industrial disasters offer both challenges and opportunities for innovations in mental health assessment and interventions. Prioritising industrial safety, monitoring risks, adequate and timely risk management, readiness to deal with emergencies, identifying effective interventions, skill training of the personnel, and supporting and utilizing the community resources are some of the suggestions that might address the concerns. Both individual and community needs must be looked into simultaneously. Exploring appropriate interventions and service provision methods in the disaster-affected industrial communities, which could benefit the survivors, remains a priority area.

References

Acharya, N. (2000). Double victims of Latur earthquake. *The Indian Journal of Social Work, 61*, 558–564.

Andersson, N., Kerr Muir, M., Mehra, V., & Salmon, A. G. (1988). Exposure and response to methyl isocyanate: Results of a community based survey in Bhopal. *British Journal of Industrial Medicine, 45*, 469–475. https://doi.org/10.1136/oem.45.7.469

Barnagarwala, T. (2025, July 6). How poor workers are paying the price. *Scroll.in*.

Basu, A. R., & Srinivasa Murthy, R. (2003). Disaster and mental health. *Economic and Political Weekly, 38*, 1074–1082.

Bharucha, E. P., & Bharucha, N. E. (1987). Neurological manifestations among those exposed to toxic gas at Bhopal. *The Indian Journal of Medical Research, 86*(Suppl), 59–62.

Brewin, C. R., Atwoli, L., Bisson, J. I., Galea, S., Koenen, K., & Lewis-Fernández, R. (2025). Post-traumatic stress disorder: Evolving conceptualization and evidence, and future research directions. *World Psychiatry, 24*, 52–80.

Cullinan, P., Acquilla, S. D., & Dhara, V. R. (1996). Long term morbidity in survivors of the 1984 Bhopal gas leak. *National Medical Journal of India, 9*, 5–10.

DHAKA Tribune Desk. 05 June 2022. https://www.dhakatribune.com/271825

Dhillon, A. (2025, July 04). The toxic legacy of Bhopal, India's chemical 'volcano'. *The Times (London)*.

Editorial. (2000). Has the world forgotten Bhopal? *The Lancet, 2*(356), 1863.

Farago, J. (2025, August 1). 80 years after Hiroshima bombing, art needs 'courage to be afraid'. *New York Times*.

First Post. (2025). Telengana pharma factory blast: What caused the explosion that killed 42 people? June 30, 2025.

Government of India. (1986). *Environment Protection Act, 1986*. Ministry of Environment, Forests and Climate Change.

Government of India. (2005). *The Disaster Management Act*. Ministry of Enviornment, Government of India, New Delhi.

Gunasekera, M. Y., & de Alwis, A. A. P. (2008). Process industry accidents in Sri Lanka: Analysis and basic lessons learnt. *Process Safety and Environmental Protection, 86*(6), 421–426. https://doi.org/10.1016/j.psep.2008.05.002

Gupta, B. N., Rastogi, S. K., Chandra, H., Mathur, A. K., Mathur, N., Mahendra, P. N., et al. (1988). Effect of exposure to toxic gas on the population of Bhopal: Part I – Epidemiological, clinical, radiological and behavioral studies. *Indian Journal of Experimental Biology, 26*, 149–160.

Hussein, M. F., Saleeb, M., Tolba, B., Mohamed, Y. Y., Gebreal, A., & Mohamed, A. O. A. (2025). Assessment of post-traumatic stress disorder and well-being among Sudanese during the ongoing war: A cross-sectional study. *BMC Psychology, 13*, 181. https://doi.org/10.1186/s40359-025-02542-1

ICMR. (1989). *The health problems of Bhopal gas victims: Assessment and management-working manual-2*. ICMR.

ICMR. (2012). *Health effects of the toxic gas leak from the union carbide methyl isocyanate plant in Bhopal, technical report on population based long-term clinical studies (1985–1994)*. ICMR.

Iqbal, N. (2018). SC urged to order inquiry into deaths of 318 coal miners in eight years. *Dawn*. https://www.dawn.com/news/1431825

Jayaraman, K. S. (1984). Toxic gas: Pesticide plant leak wreaks disaster in India. *Nature, 312*, 581. https://doi.org/10.1038/312581a0

Jayaraman, K. S. (1985). Bhopal disaster: Technical inquiry underway. *Nature, 313*, 89.

Kar, N. (2023). Indirect victims of catastrophic events: The case of Odishatrain accident. *Journal of Geriatric Care and Research, 10*(2), 33–34.

Kar, N. (2024). Anatomy of a catastrophe: Managing psychosocial consequence of the 2023 Odisha train accident. *Industrial Psychiatry Journal, 33*, 219–225.

Kar, N., Swain, S. P., Parija, S., Banerjee, S., Mahakul, S., Behura, S. S., Palei, B., & Kar, S. (2025). Posttraumatic stress following the 2023 Odisha train accident: A cross sectional comparison study of passengers, health professionals, and the local community. *Disaster Medicine and Public Health Preparedness, 19*, e112. https://doi.org/10.1017/dmp.2025.113

Kishore Kumar, K. V., Chandrashekar, C. R., Chowdhury, P., Parthasarathy, R., Girimaji, S., Sekar, K., & Srinivasa Murthy, R. (2000). *Supercyclone: Psychosocial care for community level helpers. Information manual 2*. Books for Change.

Lakshminarayana, R., Srinivasa Murthy, R., & Diaz, J. O. (2004). *Disaster mental health in India*. Indian Red Cross Society.

Lapierre, D., & Moro, J. (2001). *It was five past midnight in Bhopal*. Full Circle.

Lifton, R. J. (1968). *Death in life: Survivors of Hiroshima*. Random House.

Mackenzie, D. (1985). Design failings that caused Bhopal disaster. *New Scientist*, 3–4.

Math, S. B., Girimaji, S. C., Benegal, V., Uday Kumar, G. S., Hamza, A., & Nagaraja, D. (2006). Tsunami: Psychosocial aspects of Andaman and Nicobar islands. Assessments and intervention in the early phase. *International Review of Psychiatry, 18*, 233–239. https://doi.org/10.1080/09540260600656001

Medico-Friend Circle (MFC). (1996). Health effects of the Bhopal gas leak disaster-part I, MFC Bulletin; November–December.

Medico-Friend Circle (MFC). (1997). Health effects of the Bhopal gas leak disaster-part II, MFC Bulletin; January–February.

Menon, M. N. (1999, September 2). Law according to injustice. *The Telegraph*, 199.

Misra, N. P. (1986). Bhopal tragedy – A year later. *The Journal of the Association of Physicians of India, 34*, 307.

Misra, U. K., Nag, D., Nath, P., Khan, W. A., Gupta, B. N., & Ray, P. K. (1988). A clinical study of toxic gas poisoning in Bhopal, India. *Indian Journal of Experimental Biology, 26*, 201–204.

Nanisetti, S. (2025, July 6). What are the lessons from Telangana blast? *The Hindu*.

Narayana, H. S. (1986). Grief reaction among bereaved relatives following a fire disaster in circus. *NIMHANS Journal, 5*, 13–22.

National Disaster Management Authority (NDMA). (2009). *National Disaster Management guidelines: Psychosocial support and mental health services in disasters*. National Disaster Management Authority, Government of India.

NIREH Annual Report. (2012–2013). Bhopal: National Institute for Research in Environmental Health (ICMR).

NIREH Annual Report. (2013–2014). Bhopal: National Institute for Research in Environmental Health (ICMR).

Osendarp, S., Haddad, L., Fabrizio, C., Andridge, C., et al. (2025). The famines in Gaza and other conflict areas are a moral failure. *The Lancet, 406*, 572–573.

Pande, N. R., Phadke, S. S., Dalal, M. S., & Agashe, M. M. (2000a). Mental health care in Marathwada earthquake disaster-1: Organisation of services. *The Indian Journal of Social Work, 61*, 640–651.

Pande, N. R., Phadke, S. S., Dalal, M. S., Gadkari, P. J., Nagapurkar, U. S., & Agashe, M. (2000b). Mental health care in Marathwada earthquake disaster-2: Short-term outreach counselling. *The Indian Journal of Social Work, 61*, 640–651.

Parasuraman, S., & Unnikrishnan, P. V. (2000). *India disasters report: Towards a policy initiative*. Oxford University Press.

Pfeiffern, E., & Martsenkovskyi, D. (2025). Urgent need for mental health care for Ukrainian children affected by war. *Lancet Primary Care, 1*, 100005. https://doi.org/10.1016/j.lanprc.2025.100005. Published Online July 17, 2025.

Rao, B. K., & Zubair, M. (1979). Cyclonic stress-psychiatric morbidity in Andhra Pradesh. *Indian Journal of Psychiatry, 21*, 84–85.

Sethi, B. B., Sharma, M., Trivedi, J. K., & Singh, H. (1987). Psychiatric morbidity in patients attending clinics in gas affected areas in Bhopal. *The Indian Journal of Medical Research, 86*(Suppl), 45–50.

Sharan, P., Chaudhary, G., Kavathekar, S. A., & Saxena, S. (1996). Preliminary report of psychiatric disorders in survivors of a severe earthquake. *The American Journal of Psychiatry, 153*, 556–558. https://doi.org/10.1176/ajp.153.4.556

Srikala, B., Chandrashekar, C. R., Kishore Kumar, K. V., Chowdhury, P., Parthasarathy, R., Girimaji, S., et al. (2000). *Supercyclone: Psychosocial care for individuals. Information manual 1*. Books for Change.

Srinivasa Murthy, R. (1990). Bhopal. *International Journal of Mental Health, 19*, 30–35.

Srinivasa Murthy, R. (2000a). Disaster and mental health: Responses of mental health professionals. *The Indian Journal of Social Work, 61*, 675–692.

Srinivasa Murthy, R. (2000b). Psychosocial consequences. In S. Parasuraman & P. V. Unnikrishnan (Eds.), *India disasters report*. Oxford University Press.

Srinivasa Murthy, R. (2001). Has the world forgotten Bhopal? *Lancet, 10*(357), 810. https://doi.org/10.1016/s0140-6736(05)71245-9

Srinivasa Murthy, R. (2002). Bhopal gas leak: Impact on mental health. In J. M. Havenaar, J. G. Cwikel, & E. J. Bromet (Eds.), *Toxic turmoil: Psychological and societal consequences of ecological disasters* (pp. 129–148). Kluwer Academic.

Srinivasa Murthy, R. (2004). Bhopal gas disaster. In R. Lakshminarayana, R. Srinivasa Murthy, & J. O. Diaz (Eds.), *Disaster mental health in India* (pp. 91–101). Indian Red Cross Society.

Srinivasa Murthy, R. (2006). The experience of the Bhopal disaster. In J. J. Lopez-Ibor, G. Christodolou, M. Maj, N. Sartorius, & A. Okasha (Eds.), *Disasters and mental health* (pp. 193–200). Wiley.

Srinivasa Murthy, R. (2014). Mental health of survivors of 1984 Bhopal disaster: A continuing challenge. *Industrial Psychiatry Journal, 23*, 86–93.

Srinivasa Murthy, R. (2016). Psychosocial and behavioral aspects of populations affected by humanitarian emergencies: Recent developments. *Current Opinion in Psychiatry, 29*(5), 280–285. https://doi.org/10.1097/YCO.0000000000000266

Srinivasa Murthy, R. (2018). Disaster mental health and social psychiatry: Challenges and opportunities. *Indian Journal of Social Psychiatry, 34*, 323–327.

Srinivasa Murthy, R., & Isaac, M. K. (1987). Mental health needs of Bhopal disaster victims and training of medical officers in mental health aspects. *The Indian Journal of Medical Research, 86*(Suppl), 51–58.

Srinivasa Murthy, R., Isaac, M. K., Chandrashekar, C. R., & Bhide, A. S. (1987). *Manual of mental health for medical officers – Bhopal disaster*. ICMR.

Swain, S. P., Behura, S. S., Banerjee, S., et al. (2025). A qualitative mixed-method narrative study on psychotherapeutic support needs based on a series of 11 cases of survivors of the 2023 Odisha train accident. *Cureus, 17*(3), e81161. https://doi.org/10.7759/cureus.81161

Tachakra, S. S. (1987). The Bhopal disaster. *Journal of the Royal Society of Health, 107*, 1–2. https://doi.org/10.1177/146642408710700101

Thamotharampillai, P., Perera, R., Vijayasangar, T., et al. (2025). Collective trauma- psychosocial consequences of war in northern Sri Lanka 10 years on, a mixed methods study. *SSM – Mental Health, 8*, 100457.

The New York Times. (2025). Hiroshima anniversary. https://www.nytimes.com/interactive/2025/08/03/arts/hiroshima-anniversary.html

The Statesman. (2014). 30 years after Bhopal. 2014 Dec 1–13.

Verghese, A., Beig, A., Senseman, L. A., Rao, S. S., & Benjamin, V. (1973). A social and psychiatric study of a representative group of families in Vellore town. *The Indian Journal of Medical Research, 61*, 608–620.

Wikipedia. (2025). National Disaster Response Force. https://en.wikipedia.org/wiki/National_Disaster_Response_Force. Accessed 18 Aug 2025.

Wing, J. K., Sartorius, N., & Cooper, J. E. (1975). *Present state examination*. Wiley.

World Food Programme. (2024). Emergency preparedness and response in Bhutan. March 2024.

World Health Organisation-Regional Office of South East Asia. (2005). *WHO-SEARO. Mental health and psychosocial relief efforts after the tsunami in South East Asia.*

World Health Organization. (2001). *World Health Report 2001. Mental health: New understanding, new hope*. World Health Organisation.

Chapter 13
Mental Health Aspects of War and Violent Extremism in South Asia

Darya Rostam Ahmed, Rania H. Al-Taie, and Sheraz Ibrahim

1 Introduction

1.1 War, Terrorism, and Ethnic Violence in South Asia

South Asia faces complex security challenges shaped by interstate rivalries, internal insurgencies, terrorist networks, and communal violence. South Asia, which encompasses Afghanistan, Pakistan, India, Nepal, Bhutan, Bangladesh, Sri Lanka, and the Maldives, is home to over 25% of the global population (World Bank, 2024). Among them, seven nations are classified as low- and middle-income countries (LMICs), except the Maldives, which is now considered an upper-middle-income country (World Bank, 2025). Interstate and intrastate conflicts, the India-Pakistan conflict over Kashmir, exemplify how geopolitical tensions can prolong violence and displacement. Despite multiple wars (1947–1948, 1965, 1971, 1999, 2025) and numerous ceasefires, the region remains unstable, with nonstate actors like those involved in the Pulwama attack often escalating tensions (Center for Strategic and International Studies, 2025; Schofield, 2010; Ganguly, 2002; Bukhari, 2019).

D. R. Ahmed (✉)
Faculty of Science and Health, Department of Clinical Psychology, Koya University, Koya, Kurdistan Region, Iraq

Department of Medical Laboratory Science, College of Science, Knowledge University, Erbil, Iraq
e-mail: darya.rostam@koyauniversity.org

R. H. Al-Taie
Mustansiryia University, College of Medicine, Baghdad, Iraq

S. Ibrahim
British International University, Erbil, Iraq
e-mail: ham3126@uomustansiriyah.edu.iq

N. Kar et al. (eds.), *Climate Change, Disaster and Mental Health in South Asia*, South Asian Perspectives in Mental Health and Psychology,
https://doi.org/10.1007/978-981-95-3690-0_13

Civilians face cross-border shelling and displacement, leading to chronic stress and psychological trauma (Staniland, 2015). Afghanistan represents a complex context shaped by decades of internal conflict and international involvement. Historical events, from the Soviet intervention to the political shifts following the Taliban's return in 2021, have contributed to prolonged instability. This environment has significantly impacted the population's mental health, with ongoing challenges related to violence, displacement, and disrupted access to psychosocial care. Regional incidents, including the 2014 Peshawar school attack, underscore how cross-border dynamics may influence security and mental health outcomes beyond Afghanistan's borders (Tinnes, 2023). In mid-2024, large-scale protests in Bangladesh were followed by a forceful response from security forces. A UN fact-finding report noted serious human rights concerns, including reports of excessive force and due process violations. The events underscore the importance of upholding human rights standards and ensuring institutional accountability (Office of the United Nations High Commissioner for Human Rights, 2024). South Asia continues to experience some of the world's highest rates of terrorism and conflict-related violence. Between 2007 and 2022, the region experienced 17,854 terrorist attacks, ranking second globally after the Middle East and North Africa (Statista, 2023).

1.2 Terrorism and Extremism: Religious and Ideological Extremism, Ethnic, Community, and Communal Violence

Terrorist threats in South Asia come from both global jihadist groups, such as Al Qaeda and the Islamic State of Khorasan Province (ISIS-K), and local groups, such as Lashkar-e-Taiba and Jaish-e-Mohammed. These organizations exploit regional conflicts to spread fear, as seen in attacks like the 2008 Mumbai siege and the 2021 Kabul airport bombing (Tankel, 2014; Mir, 2020). Their actions worsen public anxiety, post-traumatic stress disorder (PTSD), and intergenerational trauma among affected populations. Other insurgent movements in the northeast of India, such as the National Socialist Council of Nagaland (NSCN-IM) and the United Liberation Front of Asom (ULFA), are rooted in ethno-political grievances. Although distinct in ideology, these groups contribute to a pervasive culture of fear and distress (Baruah, 2020). Extremism is not confined to one religion. Hindu nationalism has triggered repeated anti-Muslim violence in India, including the Gujarat pogrom (2002) and the Delhi riots (2020) (Jaffrelot, 2024). In Sri Lanka, Buddhist nationalist groups have targeted Muslims after the conflict (Haniffa, 2021). These patterns of violence fuel community-wide trauma and mistrust, obstructing reconciliation and mental health recovery. Unlike organized insurgencies, ethnic riots are often politically motivated and erupt suddenly. In India, violence tends to spike in electorally competitive areas (Wilkinson, 2004). Sri Lanka, despite ending the civil war in 2009, continues to witness anti-Tamil and anti-Muslim riots (Gunasekara, 2018). Myanmar's military violence against the Rohingya displaced nearly a million people and exacerbated religious tensions in neighboring Bangladesh (Human Rights Watch, 2016). These events cause mass displacement, chronic stress, and long-term psychological damage. The interconnectedness of conflicts between states, insurgents, and communal groups is evident. Intelligence agencies in South Asia have been implicated in supporting proxies, while diaspora networks fund ideological groups across borders (Nair & Sambanis, 2019).

The April 2025 Pahalgam attack in Kashmir, in which The Resistance Front killed unarmed tourists, represents a disturbing continuation of religion-linked violence in South Asia. While the immediate incident targeted civilians, its implications were geopolitical, exposing persistent fractures between India and Pakistan and raising concerns over China's muted response (Pandey & Mishra, 2025). Analysts argue that such violence, although framed within religious narratives, is frequently weaponized during politically sensitive periods, contributing to cycles of mistrust and psychological trauma across communities (Khan et al., 2025).

2 Humanitarian Consequences of War and Terrorism in South Asia

South Asia's conflicts inflict humanitarian crises that last beyond battlefield events, erode health systems, displace communities, and deepen gender and generational inequities. The displacement crisis has forced millions of people in South Asia to leave their homes due to ongoing violence. Afghanistan alone represents 2.6 million registered refugees and 3.5 million internally displaced persons (IDPs); many live in informal settlements with limited access to portable water or formal schooling (UNHCR, 2023). The Rohingya crisis led to the creation of the world's largest refugee settlement in Cox's Bazar, Bangladesh, where more than 1 million Rohingya refugees face significant challenges in accessing necessities such as clean water, sanitation, and health care (Oxfam International, 2024).

One of the lesser-known but deeply complex internal displacements in South Asia involves the Kashmiri Pandits, a Hindu minority who fled the Kashmir Valley during the insurgency of 1989–1990. There was escalating violence against them and targeted killings (Wikipedia, 2025). While the causes of their migration are debated, ranging from targeted threats to the broader collapse of governance, it remains clear that tens of thousands were uprooted from their ancestral homes, with many still living in camps or resettled areas across India (Sarkaria, 2009). On a more localized scale, Datta (2016) explores how displacement and communal violence affected Kashmiri Pandits, revealing how forced migration and nostalgia intertwine with ruptured inter-religious relationships, further reflecting the long-standing fractures in religious coexistence (Datta, 2016). Collectively, these studies illuminate the complex and often volatile interface between religion, identity, and violence in the region.

In areas of Afghanistan under Taliban control, local nongovernmental organizations (NGOs) reported a rise in child marriage between 2016 and 2020 and attributed this trend to economic hardship and the breakdown of protective institutions (UNICEF, 2021). In Sri Lanka's former war zone, widows face systematic harassment at military checkpoints (Perera et al., 2009). Legal responses to war crimes, terrorism, and ethnic violence, although covered by core international humanitarian law treaties ratified by South Asian states, face patchy enforcement. India's Armed Forces (Special Powers) Act grants de facto immunity to soldiers in conflict zones, complicating prosecutions for civilian killings in Kashmir and Manipur (Human Rights Watch, 2008). Bangladesh established the International Crimes Tribunals to address atrocities committed during the 1971 war; however, critics like Rahman and Methab (2016) have raised concerns about selective justice and political interference in these trials. Sri Lanka's Office on Missing Persons and its promised hybrid court system remain under-resourced, illustrating how legal mechanisms often lag behind rhetorical commitments to accountability (Amnesty International, 2017).

Case studies of humanitarian responses and challenges in Afghanistan show mobile health teams funded by the International Committee of the Red Cross (ICRC) providing basic trauma care in provinces where public clinics have closed, but insecurity forces frequently change routes and service suspensions (ICRC, 2021). In Bangladesh's Cox's Bazar refugee camps, the World Food Programme (WFP) has experienced reduced per capita food rations since 2023 due to funding shortages, increasing malnutrition risks for the Rohingya population (Li, 2023). Indian civil society groups such as the Citizens for Justice and Peace provide legal aid to riot victims, but slow court calendars and witness intimidation prolong cases for years (Jaffrelot, 2024). Gaps and prospects in regional humanitarian programming reveal that mental health and psychosocial support services remain the missing cornerstone. Less than 2% of South Asian health budgets focus on mental health, leaving PTSD, depression, and substance misuse largely untreated (Maramis et al., 2011). A sustainable response requires that national governments eliminate bureaucratic barriers to aid delivery, donors commit multiyear funding streams, and peace processes incorporate community-based rehabilitation and reparations into their design (Petersen et al., 2017). Without such measures, the silent suffering of survivors threatens to perpetuate cycles of violence, undermining fragile ceasefires and economic recovery.

3 Mental Health Consequences of War and Terrorism in South Asia

War and violence are among the most critical factors affecting mental health. Among the many consequences of armed conflict, the mental health of civilian populations is particularly severe (Murthy & Lakshminarayana, 2006). At present, there are numerous ongoing global conflicts and wars, some of them including South

Asian countries, such as the tensions between India and Pakistan, as well as the Rohingya crisis and instances of ethnic cleansing in Myanmar and Bangladesh, further exacerbating these threats (Ahmed et al., 2024). The proportion of civilian casualties in armed conflicts has escalated dramatically over time, accounting for one in seven deaths during World War I. This figure rose to two-thirds in World War II and reached approximately 90% in conflicts by the late twentieth century (Guha-Sapir & van Panhuis, 2002; Gordon et al., 2010). In South Asia, a recent study revealed that experiences of violence, displacement, and trauma are strongly correlated with the development of anxiety, depression, and PTSD (Mudunna et al., 2025). War and terrorism leave behind more than physical destruction; they inflict deep and lasting psychological scars (Murthy & Lakshminarayana, 2006). A national study in Afghanistan revealed that more than 60% of the respondents had experienced multiple traumatic events, with depression, anxiety, and PTSD affecting 67.7%, 72.2%, and 42% of the population, respectively (Murthy & Lakshminarayana, 2006). Sri Lanka demonstrated similarly alarming statistics, with 64% of individuals exhibiting psychosocial impairments, including somatization and functional disability, primarily due to prolonged exposure to conflict-related stressors (Somasundaram & Sivayokan, 1994). In war-torn areas of Sri Lanka, the study assessed individuals aged over 15 years and found that nearly 50% had experienced between five and nine war-related stressors, while a mere 6% reported no exposure.

In India, a study by Gautam et al. (1998) investigating psychiatric outcomes among survivors of a bus bombing revealed a psychiatric morbidity rate of 35.4% just 3 days post-event. Two weeks later, this figure remained high at 29.3%, with PTSD identified as the most prevalent diagnosis (12.9%), followed by depression (9.6%) and dissociative amnesia (6.4%). Years of conflict in Kashmir have badly affected mental health, with the number of people needing psychological help rising sharply since the 1980s (Margoob & Dutta, 1991; Margoob & Ahmad, 2006). The significant impact of war, terrorism, violence, and conflict confirmed from other examples, such as in Syria and Iraq, that civilians exposed to displacement and suffering from PTSD and depression conflict met the criteria for PTSD (Kakaje et al., 2021; Levy & Sidel, 2013). However, during war and conflicts, many factors that deteriorate the mental health of people, such as the duration of the conflict (acute, prolonged, or recurrent), geographical setting (rural or urban), the patterns of displacement, and vulnerable groups, all shape psychological outcomes (David et al., 2017).

During ongoing conflicts, women and elderly populations face particularly severe and unique mental health burdens. In South Asia, women and elderly populations face severe and unique mental health burdens during ongoing conflicts. Women, traditionally associated with nurturing and peacebuilding roles, often endure profound psychological distress in war zones. In Afghanistan under Taliban rule (1996–2001), gender-based restrictions, such as banning women from employment, enforcing male guardianship, and compulsory veiling, deepened psychological suffering, with many women exhibiting somatic symptoms like fainting as a socially acceptable expression of emotional pain (Amowitz et al., 2003; Cardozo

Table 13.1 Examples of psychological consequences of war and violent extremism in South Asian countries

Country	Context	Key psychological impacts
Afghanistan (Khalily, 2009, 2011)	The psychological aftermath of decades of war and instability	High prevalence of depression and anxiety Substance dependence as a significant public health crisis Minimal treatment access
Nepal (Tol et al., 2009; Kienzler & Sapkota, 2020)	Long-term impact of Maoist conflict (1996–2006), historical structural violence, and discrimination	Persistent emotional and cognitive effects Influence of caste, gender, and ethnic disparities Cultural stigma and silence
Pakistan (Khalily, 2011)	Youth exposure to conflict in the Swat Valley	Over 80% of youth report PTSD symptoms High levels of hypervigilance, sleep disturbance, and intrusive memories

et al., 2005). Similarly, the elderly in conflict-affected areas are particularly vulnerable due to limited mobility, scarce resources, and social isolation, which heighten their exposure to trauma. Studies show that dependent elderly individuals are significantly more likely to experience serious psychological distress than their independent counterparts (Jain et al., 2022; Summers et al., 2019). These effects are compounded by the rising elderly population in South Asia, projected to reach 334 million by 2050 (Center, 2002). Moreover, the psychological consequences of violence often span generations; intergenerational trauma in South Asia manifests in disrupted family dynamics and increased rates of PTSD, anxiety, and depression among descendants of conflict survivors (Shah et al., 2024). Examples are shown in Table 13.1.

4 Mental Health Interventions in Conflict-Affected South Asia: Availability, Gaps, and Future Directions

Despite having national mental health policies, South Asian countries face major implementation challenges. According to *The Lancet* report in 2011, on average, South Asian countries allocated approximately 2% of their total government health budgets to mental health (Maramis et al., 2011). Sri Lanka successfully scaled up nonspecialist primary care capacity using the WHO Mental Health Gap Action Program (mhGAP) model, improving the detection and referral of mental disorders among displaced populations (Siriwardhana et al., 2013). Pakistan established a mental health clinic in Timergara to manage psychosocial problems among women, using brief, culturally adapted interventions. Despite early success, only 34% of new patients returned for follow-up, mainly due to the centralization of services, barriers to gender mobility, stigma, and insecurity (Shah et al., 2014). Community-based mental health interventions (CBMHI) have been implemented across South Asia. These programs utilized laypersons, teachers, and parents to deliver basic psychological care within community settings. According to Willmot et al.'s (2023) review, this approach broadened the accessibility of services and helped reduce stigma. However, it also encountered several limitations, including insufficient regional data on depression, challenges in reaching marginalized rural populations, and concerns over the quality of care due to limited supervision (Willmot et al., 2023). Improving mental health systems in conflict-affected areas requires a multi-faceted approach that focuses on policy, service delivery, equity, and accountability. Key governance strategies include elevating the public health priority of mental health through national advocacy and establishing mental health units (Petersen et al., 2017). The key recommendations for strengthening mental health and psychosocial support (MHPSS) assistance in conflict zones are presented in Table 13.2.

Table 13.2 Strategies to strengthen mental health support in conflict zones

Strategy	Description
Capacity building for mental health professionals and finance allocation	Focuses on training, supervision, and quality assurance. Strategies include task sharing to nonspecialists, context-specific training, sustained supervision with feedback, integrating mental health into health and education systems, allocating dedicated mental health budgets, ensuring supply of psychotropic medications, and upgrading infrastructure for counseling and inpatient care (Endale et al., 2020; Petersen et al., 2017)
Community engagement	Strengthens participation by defining intersectoral roles and involving communities in planning and policymaking. Equity strategies include anti-stigma campaigns, improved detection of mental disorders at the community level, integration of mental health into primary care, and addressing geographic, financial, and cultural barriers (Petersen et al., 2017)
Documentation and accountability	Improve data collection at the primary care level, promote routine monitoring, empower service users to provide feedback, and adopt the WHO Quality Rights program. Investment in feasible monitoring indicators ensures ethical and quality service delivery in fragile contexts (Petersen et al., 2017)
Professional interventions	Implements stepped care models, peer-led counseling, behavioral activation, and life skills training, with evidence from India, Pakistan, and Nepal. Mind–body interventions have also shown promise in managing depression and anxiety (Maddock et al., 2021)
Electronic mental health and psychosocial support (eMHPSS)	Expand access to care through video conferencing, self-help apps, and online counseling platforms. eMHPSS addresses barriers such as stigma, insecurity, and logistical challenges by providing evidence-based mental health services remotely to underserved populations (Ahmed et al., 2024)

5 Recommendation

Drawing from the synthesis of current research and contextual realities in South Asia, we propose a set of urgent and actionable recommendations. First, there is a critical need to improve the systematic recording of short- and long-term mental health conditions among populations exposed to trauma. This includes capturing the full spectrum of psychiatric disorders, psychosocial challenges, and comorbidities and identifying context-specific risk factors, protective factors, and treatment outcomes. Without such data, interventions risk being fragmented, poorly targeted, and unsustainable. Second, we advocate for the integration of community engagement at every stage of mental health program development and implementation of all layers of the MHPSS pyramid of interventions, including specialized and nonspecialized services. However, consider involving community leaders, caregivers, teachers, and survivors themselves, not only to increase trust and accessibility, but also to ensure that services are culturally acceptable and grounded in local realities. Special attention must be paid to the developmental needs of children and adolescents. We recommend comprehensive evaluations of cognitive development in youth affected by conflict, with interventions tailored to mitigate long-term impairments. Equally important is the need to challenge and transform harmful cultural narratives around mental illness. Due to the sociocultural context of South Asian countries, awareness campaigns should emphasize that mental disorders are health conditions, not moral failings, and that seeking care is a sign of strength, not weakness, regardless of gender. Finally, mental health must be elevated as a core component of the humanitarian response and national health policy.

6 Conclusion

The conflicts of South Asia do not merely ring in headlines but reside in minds, mutate across generations, and whisper through villages long after the last bomb has fallen. Behind the figures are shattered families, muzzled women, scarred children, and older people left in the ruins of memory. This chapter has not merely chronicled pain but revealed the systemic fissures that allow psychological injuries to rot in obscurity. And yet, in all of this shadow, there is radiance. Communities, empowered, are vessels of healing. Technology, trusted, has the power to extend the care that borders deny. Moreover, culture, compassionately addressed, has the power to turn silence into a voice and shame into strength. Healing from war requires more than medicine; it takes justice, narratives, and unyielding compassion. In survivors' minds, war does not end; it mutates. However, with unflinching reform, grounded research, and care that is centered in the whole self, we can recast that aftermath. Not as a legacy of despair, but as a movement of healing, dignity, and renewal. For peace is not the negation of conflict, but the realization of mental integrity.

References

Ahmed, D. R., & Al Diab Al Azzawi, M. (2024). The current global threat of weapons of mass destruction to humanity and public health. *Discover Public Health, 21*(1), 37. https://doi.org/10.1186/s12982-024-00161-6

Ahmed, D. R., & Heun, R. (2024). Standard guidelines on electronic mental health and psychosocial support for humanitarian assistance. *The Lancet Psychiatry, 11*(6), 403–404. https://doi.org/10.1016/S2215-0366(24)00070-1

Amnesty International. (2017). *Only justice can heal our wounds. Listening to the demands of families of the disappeared in Sri Lanka.* Amnesty International.

Amowitz, L. L., Heisler, M., & Iacopino, V. (2003). A population-based assessment of women's mental health and attitudes toward women's human rights in Afghanistan. *Journal of Women's Health, 12*(6), 577–587. https://doi.org/10.1089/154099903768248285

Baruah, S. (2020). *In the name of the nation: India and its northeast.* Stanford University Press.

Bukhari, F. (2019). *Kashmir car bomb kills 44; India demands Pakistan act against militants.* Reuters. https://www.reuters.com/article/world/kashmir-car-bomb-kills-44-india-demands-pakistan-act-against-militants-idUSKCN1Q31QP/

Cardozo, B. L., Bilukha, O. O., Gotway, C. A., Wolfe, M. I., Gerber, M. L., & Anderson, M. (2005). Report from the CDC: Mental health of women in postwar Afghanistan. *Journal of Women's Health, 14*(4), 285–293. https://doi.org/10.1089/jwh.2005.14.285

Center, E. W. (2002). *The future of population in Asia.*

Center for Strategic and International Studies. (2025). *What led to the recent crisis between India and Pakistan?* https://www.csis.org/analysis/what-led-recent-crisis-between-india-and-pakistan

Datta, A. (2016). Dealing with dislocation: Migration, place and home among displaced Kashmiri Pandits in Jammu and Kashmir. *Contributions to Indian Sociology, 50*(1), 52–79. https://doi.org/10.1177/0069966715615021

David, S., Gazi, R., Mirzazada, M. S., Siriwardhana, C., Soofi, S., & Roy, N. (2017). Conflict in South Asia and its impact on health. *BMJ, 357.* https://doi.org/10.1136/bmj.j1537

East-West Center. (2002). The future of population in Asia. East-West Center. ISBN: 0-866338-199-6. Available at: http://hdl.handle.net/10125/3403

Endale, T., Qureshi, O., Ryan, G. K., Esponda, G. M., Verhey, R., Eaton, J., … Murphy, J. (2020). Barriers and drivers to capacity-building in global mental health projects. International Journal of Mental Health Systems, 14, 1–12. https://doi.org/10.1186/s13033-020-00420-4.

Ganguly, S. (2002). *Conflict unending: India-Pakistan tensions since 1947.* Columbia University Press.

Gautam, S., Gupta, I. D., Batra, L., Sharma, H., Khandelwal, R., & Pant, A. (1998). Psychiatric morbidity among victims of bomb blast. *Indian Journal of Psychiatry, 40*(1), 41–45.

Gordon, S., Baker, A., Duten, A., & Garner, P. (2010). *Study exploring the evidence relating health and conflict interventions and outcomes.* http://webarchive.nationalarchives.gov.uk/20111210182747/http://www.stabilisationunit.gov.uk/attachments/article/523/ExploringtheevidencerelatingHealthandConflictinterventionsandoutcome.pdf

Guha-Sapir, D., & van Panhuis, W. G. (2002). *Armed conflict and public health: A report on knowledge and knowledge gaps* (No. UCL-Université Catholique de Louvain). CRED.

Gunasekara, T. (2018). The history and politics of "Muslimphobia" and anti-Muslim violence in Sri Lanka. *DBS Jeyaraj.* https://dbsjeyaraj.com/dbsj/?p=58938

Haniffa, F. (2021). Reconciliation' problems in post-war Sri Lanka: The anti-muslim movement and Ulema Council responses. In J. E. Dağyeli, C. Ghrawi, & U. Freitag (Eds.), *Claiming and making muslim worlds: Religion and society in the context of the global.* De Gruyter. https://doi.org/10.1515/9783110726534-010

Human Rights Watch. (2008). *India: Repeal armed forces special powers act.* Human Rights Watch. https://www.hrw.org/news/2008/08/18/india-repeal-armed-forces-special-powers-act.

Human Rights Watch. (2016). *Burma Events of 2016.* Human Rights Watch. https://www.hrw.org/world-report/2017/country-chapters/burma

International Committee of the Red Cross. (2021). *Asia and the Pacific: Annual report 2021*. ICRC.
Islam, M. R. (2019). National trials of international crimes in Bangladesh: Transitional justice as reflected in judgments. Brill | Nijhoff. https://doi.org/10.1163/9789004389380
Jaffrelot, C. (2024). *Gujarat under Modi*. Hurst.
Jain, N., Prasad, S., Czárth, Z. C., Chodnekar, S. Y., Mohan, S., Savchenko, E., et al. (2022). War psychiatry: Identifying and managing the neuropsychiatric consequences of armed conflicts. *Journal of Primary Care & Community Health*. https://doi.org/10.1177/21501319221106625
Kakaje, A., Al Zohbi, R., Hosam Aldeen, O., Makki, L., Alyousbashi, A., & Alhaffar, M. B. A. (2021). Mental disorder and PTSD in Syria during wartime: A nationwide crisis. *BMC Psychiatry, 21*, 1–16. https://doi.org/10.1186/s12888-020-03002-3
Khalily, M. T. (2009). Personality characteristics of addicts and non-addicts determined through Rorschach findings. *Pakistan Journal of Psychology, 40*(1).
Khalily, M. T. (2011). Mental health problems in Pakistani society as a consequence of violence and trauma: A case for better integration of care. *International Journal of Integrated Care, 11*, e128. https://doi.org/10.5334/ijic.662
Khan, Z., Ali, F., & Khan, S. (2025). Beyond the border: How political rhetoric disrupts trade, CSR, and livelihoods in Pakistan. *CSR, and Livelihoods in Pakistan (April 27, 2025)*. https://doi.org/10.2139/ssrn.5232272.
Kienzler, H., & Sapkota, R. P. (2020). The long-term mental health consequences of torture, loss, and insecurity: A qualitative study among survivors of armed conflict in the Dang District of Nepal. *Frontiers in Psychiatry, 10*, 941. https://doi.org/10.3389/fpsyt.2019.00941
Levy, B. S., & Sidel, V. W. (2013). Adverse health consequences of the Iraq War. *The Lancet, 381*(9870), 949–958. https://doi.org/10.1016/S0140-6736(13)60254-8
Li, K. (2023). *WFP's Rohingya refugee operation in Bangladesh receives major funding boost of US$ 87 million from the United States*. World Food Programme. https://www.wfp.org/news/wfps-rohingya-refugee-operation-bangladesh-receives-major-funding-boost-us-87-million-united
Maddock, A., Blair, C., Ean, N., & Best, P. (2021). Psychological and social interventions for mental health issues and disorders in Southeast Asia: A systematic review. *International Journal of Mental Health Systems, 15*(1), 56. https://doi.org/10.1186/s13033-021-00482-y
Maramis, A., Van Tuan, N., & Minas, H. (2011). Mental health in Southeast Asia. *The Lancet, 377*(9767), 700–702. https://doi.org/10.1016/S0140-6736(10)62181-2
Margoob, A. M., & Ahmad, S. A. (2006). Community prevalence of adult post traumatic stress disorder in south Asia: Experience from Kashmir. *Jammu Kashmir Practitioner, 13*(1), S18–S25.
Margoob, M. A., & Dutta, K. S. (1991). Mental disorders in Kashmir: A socio-demographic study of 4601 cases. *Health Administ, 2*(2), 53–58.
Mir, A. A. (2020). Is Al-Qaeda in Afghanistan still a threat? For whom? *Middle East Institute*, 4–8.
Mudunna, C., Weerasinghe, M., Tran, T., Antoniades, J., Romero, L., Chandradasa, M., & Fisher, J. (2025). Nature, prevalence and determinants of mental health problems experienced by adolescents in south Asia: A systematic review. *The Lancet Regional Health-Southeast Asia, 33*. https://doi.org/10.1016/j.lansea.2025.100532
Murthy, R. S., & Lakshminarayana, R. (2006). Mental health consequences of war: A brief review of research findings. *World Psychiatry, 5*(1), 25.
Nair, G., & Sambanis, N. (2019). Violence exposure and ethnic identification: Evidence from Kashmir. *International Organization., 73*(2), 329–363.
Office of the United Nations High Commissioner for Human Rights. (2024). *Report of the United Nations Fact-Finding Mission on human rights violations in the context of the 2024 Bangladesh protests*. https://www.ohchr.org
Oxfam International. (2024). *Bangladesh*. https://www.oxfam.org.nz/what-we-do/our-work/bangladesh/
Pandey, G., & Mishra, A. K. (2025). The silk route and the sword: China's shadow in the indo-Pak conflict post-Pahalgam attack. *RESEARCH REVIEW International Journal of Multidisciplinary, 10*(4), 118–127. https://doi.org/10.31305/rrijm.2025.v10.n4.013

Perera, J., Gunawardane, N. S., & Jayasuriya, V. (2009). *Evidence on gender based violence (GBV) in Sri Lanka*. https://www.semanticscholar.org/paper/Evidence-on-Gender-Based-Violence-(-GBV-)-in-Sri-Perera-Gunawardane/1d7291ee7ffc47842ab0cdac7a5c468c82134f34

Petersen, I., Marais, D., Abdulmalik, J., Ahuja, S., Alem, A., Chisholm, D., Egbe, C., Gureje, O., Hanlon, C., Lund, C., Shidhaye, R., Jordans, M., Kigozi, F., Mugisha, J., Upadhaya, N., & Thornicroft, G. (2017). Strengthening mental health system governance in six low- and middle-income countries in Africa and South Asia: Challenges, needs and potential strategies. *Health Policy Planning, 32*(5), 699–709. https://doi.org/10.1093/heapol/czx014

Sarkaria, M. K. (2009). Powerful pawns of the Kashmir conflict: Kashmiri pandit migrants. *Asian and Pacific Migration Journal, 18*(2), 197–230. https://doi.org/10.1177/011719680901800202

Schofield, V. (2010). *Kashmir in conflict: India, Pakistan and the unending War*. I.B. Tauris.

Shah, S., Van den Bergh, R., Van Bellinghen, B., Severy, N., Sadiq, S., Afridi, S. A., … Zachariah, R. (2014). Offering mental health services in a conflict affected region of Pakistan: Who comes, and why?. *PLoS One, 9*(6), e97939. https://doi.org/10.1371/journal.pone.0097939

Shah, M. H., Roy, S., & Ahluwalia, A. (2024). Intergenerational trauma and mental health disability in the south Asian context. In *The Palgrave encyclopedia of disability* (pp. 1–9). Springer Nature Switzerland. https://doi.org/10.1007/978-3-031-40858-8_292-1

Siriwardhana, C., Adikari, A., Van Bortel, T., McCrone, P., & Sumathipala, A. (2013). An intervention to improve mental health care for conflict-affected forced migrants in low-resource primary care settings: A WHO MhGAP-based pilot study in Sri Lanka (COM-GAP study). *Trials, 14*, 1–7. https://doi.org/10.1186/1745-6215-14-423

Somasundaram, D. J., & Sivayokan, S. (1994). War trauma in a civilian population. *The British Journal of Psychiatry, 165*(4), 524–552. https://doi.org/10.1192/bjp.165.4.524

Staniland, P. (2015). Militias, ideology, and the state. *Journal of Conflict Resolution, 59*(5), 770–793.

Statista. (2023, March). *Terrorist attacks from 2007 to 2022, by region*. Statista. https://www.statista.com/statistics/489581/terrorist-attacks-by-region/

Summers, A., Leidman, E., Pereira Figueira Periquito, I. M., & Bilukha, O. O. (2019). Serious psychological distress and disability among older persons living in conflict affected areas in eastern Ukraine: A cluster-randomized cross-sectional household survey. *Conflict and Health, 13*, 1–10. https://doi.org/10.1186/s13031-019-0194-0

Tankel, S. (2014). *Storming the world stage: The story of Lashkar-e-Taiba*. Oxford University Press.

Tinnes, J. (2023). The Taliban. *Perspectives on Terrorism, 17*(3), 83–127.

Tol, W., Kohrt, B., Jordans, M., Thapa, S., Pettigrew, J., Upadhaya, N., & de Jong, J. T. V. M. (2009). Political violence and mental health: A systematic multi-disciplinary review of findings From Nepal. https://doi.org/10.1016/j.socscimed.2009.09.037

UNHCR. (2023). *Global trends report 2022*. UNHCR. https://www.unhcr.org/global-trends-report-2022

UNICEF. (2021). *Situation analysis of children and women in Afghanistan*. UNICEF.

Wikipedia. (2025). *Exodus of Kashmiri Hindus*. https://en.wikipedia.org/wiki/Exodus_of_Kashmiri_Hindus

Wilkinson, S. I. (2004). *Votes and violence: Electoral competition and ethnic riots in India*. Cambridge University Press.

Willmot, R. A., Sharp, R. A., Kassim, A. A., & Parkinson, J. A. (2023). A scoping review of community-based mental health intervention for children and adolescents in South Asia. *Cambridge Prisms: Global Mental Health, 10*, e1. https://doi.org/10.1017/gmh.2022.49

World Bank. (2024). *Population, total – South Asia*. Retrieved from https://data.worldbank.org/region/south-asia

World Bank. (2025, March 27). *Maldives overview*. https://www.worldbank.org/en/country/maldives/overview

Chapter 14
Disaster and Disability

Akshaya B. Raj, Preethy Kathiresan, and Naresh Nebhinani

1 Introduction

Disasters, whether natural or human-made, pose a persistent threat to human life, well-being, and ecosystems. As per the United Nations Office for Disaster Risk Reduction (UNDRR), a disaster is a serious disruption of the functioning of a community or a society involving widespread human, material, economic, or environmental losses and impacts, which exceeds the ability of the affected community or society to cope using its own resources (UNDRR, 2017).

The Emergency Events Database (EM-DAT) reported 393 natural hazard-related disasters globally in 2024 alone, signifying a steady increase over the past decade. These events resulted in 16,753 deaths and affected approximately 167 million individuals, with estimated economic losses reaching USD 242 billion (EM-DAT, 2024). The proportion of people affected by disasters has risen dramatically by nearly 71% from 1187 per 100,000 population (2005–2014) to 2032 per 100,000 population (2014–2023), according to UNDRR (2024).

South Asia, home to nearly two billion people, is among the most disaster-prone regions globally. Its unique geographical, climatic, and socioeconomic features contribute to frequent and devastating disruptions. Countries such as India, Bangladesh, Nepal, Pakistan, and Sri Lanka are regularly affected by earthquakes, floods, cyclones, landslides, droughts, tsunamis, and, increasingly, climate-related hazards such as heatwaves and glacial lake outburst floods. Notable catastrophic events include the 2004 Indian Ocean tsunami, the 2005 Kashmir earthquake, the

A. B. Raj · N. Nebhinani (✉)
Department of Psychiatry, All India Institute of Medical Science, Jodhpur, Rajasthan, India

P. Kathiresan
Department of Psychiatry, All India Institute of Medical Science, Delhi, India

N. Kar et al. (eds.), *Climate Change, Disaster and Mental Health in South Asia*, South Asian Perspectives in Mental Health and Psychology,
https://doi.org/10.1007/978-981-95-3690-0_14

2015 Nepal earthquake, and the 2022 Pakistan floods, each causing large-scale mortality, displacement, trauma, and disabilities (Kanta Kafle, 2017).

The World Health Organization (WHO) defines disability as "an umbrella term covering impairments, activity limitations, and participation restrictions," emphasizing the interaction between health conditions and contextual (environmental and personal) factors (WHO, 2001). Disability is a dynamic and multifaceted condition that includes visible and invisible physical, sensory, intellectual, and psychosocial impairments. Disasters can create new disabilities through trauma and injury, worsen pre-existing impairments by disrupting services, or induce psychological conditions such as depression, anxiety, and post-traumatic stress disorder (PTSD) (Subramaniam & Villeneuve, 2020).

The United Nations Convention on the Rights of Persons with Disabilities (UNCRPD) reinforces a rights-based perspective, asserting that disability results from the interaction between individuals with impairments and the barriers that hinder full participation in society. During disasters, these barriers are often magnified, manifesting as inaccessible infrastructure, inadequate communication systems, and the exclusion of persons with disabilities (PwDs) from preparedness and emergency planning (UNCRPD, 2006). Disasters frequently interrupt access to healthcare services, mobility aids, and caregiver support systems, thereby aggravating pre-existing impairments and generating new disabilities.

The Sendai Framework for Disaster Risk Reduction (2015–2030), adopted by all South Asian nations, marked a global shift in disaster governance by mandating the inclusion of persons with disabilities in all phases of disaster risk management. It calls for accessible early warning systems, PwD participation in decision-making, and universal design in infrastructure (UNDRR, 2015). However, the national disaster management strategies in South Asia often fall short. The focus remains predominantly on infrastructure and economic recovery, with limited attention to inclusive planning.

This chapter examines the intersection between disaster and disability in the South Asian context. It begins by examining how disasters contribute to both physical and psychological impairments. It then highlights the specific barriers faced by persons with disabilities during emergencies, including evacuation, rescue, and relief. The discussion extends to mental health impacts, policy responses, and the comparative gap between South Asia and developed nations. The chapter concludes with actionable recommendations for a more inclusive, rights-based, and resilient disaster management system.

2 Disasters Causing Disabilities

Disasters have both direct and indirect impacts on human health, often resulting in temporary or permanent disabilities. These may be physical, sensory, cognitive, or psychosocial in nature, arising from trauma, structural collapse, disrupted healthcare systems, or long-term psychological stress (Morales, 2025). In South Asia, the risk and burden of such disaster-induced disabilities are particularly high due to high population density, fragile health infrastructure, and limited access to rehabilitative care (Nguyen-Trung et al., 2025).

2.1 Physical Trauma–Related and Secondary Disabilities

Natural disasters such as earthquakes, landslides, and floods commonly result in traumatic injuries. Collapsing buildings, debris, and fires cause blunt trauma, crush injuries, fractures, amputations, and spinal cord injuries. For example, during the 2015 Nepal earthquake, over 22,000 people were injured. Many developed long-term locomotor disabilities due to spinal injuries or limb loss. Inadequate rehabilitation facilities and the absence of assistive devices led to long-term dependency and functional decline (Disasters Emergency Committee Nepal, 2016). The 2005 Kashmir earthquake caused thousands of severe injuries, including sensory impairments like loss of vision or hearing. Limited access to emergency care in remote mountainous regions led to preventable complications such as gangrene, infection, and permanent disability (Mulvey et al., 2008).

2.2 Psychosocial Disabilities and Mental Health Impacts

Psychosocial and mental health consequences represent a substantial but frequently overlooked category of disaster-induced disability. Psychological distress, if unaddressed, can evolve into chronic psychiatric conditions such as post-traumatic stress disorder (PTSD), generalized anxiety disorder (GAD), depression, insomnia, panic attacks, and adjustment disorders. After the 1993 Latur earthquake, psychiatric morbidity affected nearly 59% of survivors, with PTSD and depression being most prevalent (Kar, 2010). The 1999 Odisha super cyclone left over half the assessed population with symptoms of anxiety and depression. Adolescents were particularly vulnerable, with 26% showing PTSD and 17% experiencing depression (Fanchiotti et al., 2020). Following the 2004 Indian Ocean tsunami, displaced populations in India and Sri Lanka experienced high levels of psychological trauma (Wachtendorf et al., 2006).

3 Persons with Disabilities in Disasters

Disasters disproportionately affect PwDs, threatening both their immediate survival and long-term well-being. Global and regional evidence consistently demonstrates that PwDs face substantially higher risks during disasters, including increased rates of mortality, injury, displacement, and neglect. For example, following the 2011

Great East Japan earthquake and tsunami, the mortality rate among persons with disabilities was more than twice that of the general population (Fujii, 2015). In South Asia, these challenges are further intensified by the frequent occurrence of large-scale natural hazards such as floods, earthquakes, and cyclones, compounded by systemic deficiencies in accessibility and inclusion.

3.1 Disruption of Healthcare and Essential Services

Disasters frequently exacerbate disabilities by disrupting healthcare services and essential support systems. For individuals with chronic illnesses or functional impairments, such service disruptions can have life-altering consequences (Morales, 2025). Individuals with diabetes or hypertension may suffer strokes or cognitive decline due to a lack of medications. Children with epilepsy or autism may experience behavioral regression when deprived of medications or structured routines (Mann et al., 2021).

The loss or damage of assistive devices such as wheelchairs or hearing aids during displacement further increases mobility restrictions and dependency (Stough et al., 2010). The absence of these devices can result in secondary complications such as pressure ulcers, contractures, and chronic musculoskeletal pain (Subramaniam & Villeneuve, 2020). Disruptions in access to rehabilitation, physiotherapy, medications, and mental healthcare compound these problems (Murthy, 2022). Additionally, supply chain breakdowns affect both medical supplies and assistive technology, while healthcare workers may lack the necessary training to address complex impairments. Schools serving children with disabilities may be damaged or repurposed as relief shelters, and social isolation becomes a serious concern, particularly for individuals with cognitive or psychosocial disabilities (Stough et al., 2017).

3.2 Gendered and Age-Specific Impacts

Women and girls with disabilities face compounded risks due to gender-based discrimination, inaccessible environments, and heightened safety concerns. They often bear a dual burden: increased vulnerability during evacuation and caregiving responsibilities in shelters despite their own impairments (Engelman et al., 2022; Stough et al., 2017). Older adults with visual, hearing, or cognitive impairments may refuse evacuation due to mobility limitations, attachment to familiar environments, or fear of unfamiliar shelter conditions (Priestley & Hemingway, 2006). Data from the Longitudinal Aging Study in India (LASI) indicate that older persons affected by floods or heatwaves experienced functional decline in activities such as cooking, toileting, and financial management (Yadav et al., 2024).

Children with disabilities are particularly vulnerable in disaster settings. Disruption in schooling, separation from specialized educators, and loss of structured routines can cause regression in developmental milestones (Mann et al., 2021). In Bangladesh, children with autism and Down syndrome were observed to lose critical developmental gains during floods due to the absence of rehabilitation services (Jang & Ha, 2021).

3.3 Barriers to Rescue and Evacuation

Evacuation during disasters is often rapid, chaotic, and poorly adapted to the needs of persons with disabilities. In South Asia, emergency response systems frequently overlook the specific requirements of PwDs. Many individuals are physically unable to move, struggle to understand emergency alerts, or refuse to evacuate without their caregivers, assistive devices, or emotional supports (Bakhshian & Martinez-Pastor, 2023). During the 2005 Kashmir earthquake, individuals with mobility impairments were left behind in multistorey buildings as rescue teams lacked both training and appropriate equipment (Mulvey et al., 2008). Persons with hearing impairments may not receive auditory alerts, while those with visual impairments may miss visual-only signals. Emergency vehicles often lack ramps, lifts, or wheelchair-secure spaces. Medical evacuations frequently fail to accommodate portable oxygen, seizure medications, or communication aids for individuals with complex conditions. In the absence of inclusive protocols, responders prioritize speed over safety, sometimes resulting in the abandonment or unsafe evacuation of PwDs (Subramaniam & Villeneuve, 2020; Engelman et al., 2022; McDermott et al., 2016).

3.4 Communication and Information Gaps

Effective disaster response requires multi-sectoral coordination across health, law enforcement, transportation, social welfare, and local governance, all of which must be trained in disability inclusion. Inclusive communication is fundamental to disaster risk reduction, yet PwDs are often excluded from information dissemination efforts. Most South Asian countries fail to utilize multimodal platforms combining audio, visual, tactile, and simplified formats to ensure information accessibility. Even when alerts are sent via SMS or radio, they often fail to account for individuals with low literacy or cognitive disabilities. Rescue personnel may be untrained in communicating with persons who are deaf, autistic, or experiencing psychological distress, leading to mismanagement of evacuation or care (Nguyen-Trung et al., 2025; Engelman et al., 2022).

During the Nepal earthquake, many rural PwDs lacked access to mobile phones, radios, or community-based early warning mechanisms, resulting in delayed evacuations and increased harm. Disaster management committees rarely include PwDs or their representatives, leading to policy gaps that fail to address their needs (Nguyen-Trung et al., 2025).

In Kerala, a state in India, the State Disaster Management Authority (KSDMA) has made important progress by training over 2600 PwDs and caregivers in evacuation techniques and first aid, as well as developing Braille booklets and sign language videos on disaster response (KSDMA, 2019b). In contrast, countries like Japan and Australia have incorporated personalized emergency preparedness plans into community response systems, registering PwDs in advance and ensuring their prioritization during evacuation (Subramaniam & Villeneuve, 2020).

3.5 Inadequate Relief Infrastructure and Relief Inaccessibility

Disaster relief shelters across South Asia often lack even the most basic accessibility features. The Indian National Building Code, for example, does not mandate universal design standards for temporary shelters, resulting in widespread inaccessibility (Murthy, 2022; NDMA, 2019). Shelters frequently lack ramps, handrails, wide entrances, or adapted sanitation facilities. PwDs who reach shelters may become fully dependent on caregivers and deprived of dignity and autonomy.

During Cyclone Amphan in West Bengal, shelters were located several kilometers from affected communities and accessible only on foot through flooded terrain, rendering them inaccessible to individuals with visual or mobility impairments. Post-disaster assessments in Sri Lanka and Pakistan found that PwDs were often relegated to peripheral areas of relief camps, living in unhygienic conditions with limited privacy and heightened exposure to abuse, infection, and psychological harm (Kanta Kafle, 2017; Priestley & Hemingway, 2006).

Standardized relief supplies—including food, water, and hygiene kits—are rarely adapted to meet diverse disability needs. Water containers may be too heavy for some, and distributed food may be difficult to chew or swallow without assistive devices. Following the tsunami in Tamil Nadu, many PwDs lacked access to suitable diets, medications, or feeding support as caregivers struggled to stand in long relief queues. Women with disabilities, in particular, face serious risks related to privacy, safety, and abuse in overcrowded, mixed-gender shelters. Most emergency shelters across South Asia remain designed for the general population, lacking critical features such as ramps, grab bars, adapted toilets, or private areas for women and girls with disabilities (Kruger et al., 2018).

However, several promising practices have emerged across South Asia:

Odisha, India: The Inclusive Vulnerability and Capacity Assessment (IVCA) model involves PwDs in shelter planning, mock drills, and community-based needs assessments (NDMA, 2019).

Bangladesh: NGOs such as BRAC and the Centre for Disability in Development (CDD) have piloted disability-inclusive disaster teams that map PwDs in communities and assign "evacuation buddies" prior to cyclone season (Jang & Ha, 2021).

Sri Lanka: Post-tsunami, community-based rehabilitation workers identified PwDs and connected them to prosthetic services, targeted aid, and psychosocial support (Priestley & Hemingway, 2006).

4 Disaster and Mental Health

Mental health remains a critically important yet often neglected component of disaster response, particularly for PwDs. While disasters impact the psychological well-being of entire populations, PwDs face unique and intensified challenges owing to physical limitations, social exclusion, dependency, and disruptions in caregiving or support systems. These factors elevate their vulnerability to a wide spectrum of mental health concerns, ranging from acute stress reactions to chronic psychiatric disorders—problems often exacerbated by barriers to care, pervasive stigma, and systemic neglect (Kar, 2010; Engelman et al., 2022).

Many PwDs rely on structured routines and consistent caregiving for emotional regulation and daily functioning. Disasters disrupt this fragile stability, triggering emotional dysregulation and behavioral difficulties. Children with autism spectrum disorder or intellectual disabilities may exhibit regression, increased aggression, sleep disturbances, and sensory overload during and after disasters. Separation from caregivers due to injury, death, or evacuation further amplifies anxiety and trauma, especially for those who are nonverbal or unable to navigate unfamiliar environments independently (Mann et al., 2021; Stough et al., 2010).

4.1 Heightened Risk of Psychological Distress

Evidence from both global and South Asian contexts indicates that PwDs experience significantly elevated levels of psychological distress following disasters (Nguyen-Trung et al., 2025). For instance, following the 1999 Odisha super cyclone, 44.3% of survivors exhibited post-traumatic stress disorder (PTSD), while 52.7% experienced depression—rates even higher among those with physical and sensory disabilities (Kar, 2010). Similar findings were reported after the 2004 Indian Ocean tsunami in Tamil Nadu and Sri Lanka, where PwDs reported heightened levels of anxiety, grief, survivor's guilt, and anticipatory fear of future disasters (Murthy, 2022; Priestley & Hemingway, 2006). For individuals with pre-existing psychosocial disabilities such as schizophrenia or bipolar disorder, disasters frequently disrupt medication adherence and continuity of therapeutic care. In the absence of crisis intervention services, such disruptions can lead to relapse, hospitalization, or even suicide (Murthy, 2022).

4.2 Mental Health Issues After Disaster

The evacuation process itself can be highly traumatic for PwDs, especially when it involves forced physical handling, loss of autonomy, or chaotic and overstimulating environments. Overcrowded shelters often lack personal space, privacy, or accommodations for sensory and emotional needs, compounding psychological distress (Subramaniam & Villeneuve, 2020; Bakhshian & Martinez-Pastor, 2023). Women with disabilities are particularly vulnerable to harassment, verbal abuse, and neglect in these settings—risks that often go unaddressed due to a lack of trained staff, accessible grievance mechanisms, and trauma-informed care protocols. These experiences frequently go unreported, leading to untreated psychological harm and long-term distress.

Post-traumatic stress disorder (PTSD) is among the most prevalent mental health outcomes, presenting with symptoms such as nightmares, flashbacks, avoidance behaviors, and emotional numbing. For PwDs, PTSD often compounds the challenges of managing pre-existing impairments, creating additional functional limitations (Neria et al., 2008).

Chronic grief and survivor's guilt are also frequent, particularly among PwDs who have lost caregivers or witnessed deaths during disasters. These unresolved emotions may lead to social withdrawal, loss of purpose, and suicidal ideation in the absence of structured psychosocial support services.

4.3 Barriers to Mental Health Services

Services for PwDs during and after disasters remain severely limited across South Asia. Disaster response frameworks tend to focus on physical rescue and immediate relief, with minimal integration of mental health or psychosocial support. Existing services are often urban-centric, poorly resourced, and rarely designed to meet the specific needs of PwDs.

Multiple barriers prevent PwDs from accessing mental healthcare, including communication obstacles, including a lack of sign language interpreters or simplified communication formats; physical inaccessibility of healthcare facilities; stigma and discrimination, particularly toward intellectual and psychosocial disabilities; and neglect of rural and marginalized populations in outreach and service delivery.

While digital mental health tools and tele-psychiatry platforms offer scalable solutions, adoption among PwDs remains limited. Barriers such as digital illiteracy, inaccessible technology design, and unreliable connectivity in disaster-prone regions continue to restrict the reach of these innovative services.

5 Disability Inclusion in Disaster Risk Reduction: Existing Disaster Response System

Incorporating disability inclusion into disaster risk reduction (DRR) is both a moral imperative and a practical necessity. From a rights-based perspective, frameworks such as the UN Convention on the Rights of Persons with Disabilities (UNCRPD), the Sendai Framework for Disaster Risk Reduction (2015–2030), and the Sustainable Development Goals (SDGs) mandate the development of inclusive, equitable, and participatory approaches to disaster management. These instruments assert that persons with disabilities must not be passive recipients of aid but active participants in the design, implementation, and monitoring of DRR strategies (UNCRPD, 2006; UNDRR, 2015; Wilkins et al., 2021).

Universal design in infrastructure, accessible communication systems, and participatory planning benefit a wide range of vulnerable groups—not only persons with disabilities, but also older adults, children, and pregnant women. Such inclusive practices help minimize the long-term economic and social costs of disasters by preventing the perpetuation of pre-existing inequalities during recovery efforts.

5.1 The Sendai Framework and Disability Inclusion

Adopted at the Third UN World Conference on Disaster Risk Reduction in 2015, the Sendai Framework for Disaster Risk Reduction (2015–2030) is a landmark agreement that centers inclusion, equity, and human rights in managing disaster risk. Notably, the framework explicitly recognizes persons with disabilities as key stakeholders in all stages of DRR. The Sendai Framework outlines four priorities for action, ensuring disability-inclusive DRR.

Understanding Disaster Risk
The framework calls for disaggregated data collection, including disability status, to enhance understanding of risk exposure. It also recognizes the value of local knowledge and lived experience, encouraging the integration of insights from persons with disabilities.

Strengthening Disaster Risk Governance
Inclusive governance structures are essential for representing the needs of persons with disabilities in national and local DRR policies, strategies, and institutional mechanisms.

Investing in Disaster Risk Reduction for Resilience
The framework promotes the development of accessible infrastructure, early warning systems, and shelter facilities. Investments that address systemic barriers contribute to long-term resilience for all.

Enhancing Disaster Preparedness
The framework encourages inclusive preparedness planning and recognizes the critical role of persons with disabilities in recovery and reconstruction efforts to avoid reinforcing pre-disaster vulnerabilities (UNDRR, 2015).

The Sendai Framework reflects a significant shift in disaster policy from viewing persons with disabilities to recognizing them as agents of change and contributors to resilience-building.

The framework reinforces key principles of the UNCRPD, including nondiscrimination, accessibility, and meaningful participation, and aligns with the SDGs, particularly **SDG 11** (sustainable cities and communities) and **SDG 13** (climate action).

These link disability inclusion with broader goals of resilience and sustainable development.

Despite its progressive vision, the implementation of disability-inclusive DRR under the Sendai Framework remains uneven.

The Sendai Framework has led to policy shifts in several countries, including in South Asia, where national DRR strategies are beginning to reflect disability inclusion principles.

5.2 Challenges in Disability-Inclusive DRR

While the Sendai Framework offers a robust foundation, its practical application faces persistent obstacles, particularly in low- and middle-income settings. A major barrier to inclusive DRR is the lack of disability-disaggregated data. Without accurate information on the number, location, and needs of PwDs, governments struggle to design targeted interventions. Many national disaster plans fail to mention disability at all, and the absence of relevant indicators makes progress difficult to measure or fund (Wilkins et al., 2021).

Moreover, PwDs are often excluded from DRR committees, simulations, and strategic planning. This lack of representation perpetuates the design of policies that fail to account for the lived realities and contributions of persons with disabilities. Cultural attitudes that view disability as helplessness or shame hinder inclusive planning and response (Arbeiter-Samariter-Bund Deutschland et al., 2021).

Effective disability-inclusive DRR demands coordination across sectors, including health, infrastructure, education, and emergency services. However, fragmented institutional responsibilities, untrained personnel, and limited budgets result in ineffective implementation. Disaster management authorities and disability services frequently operate in parallel, rather than in coordination.

6 Disability-Inclusive DRR: South Asia vs. Developed Countries

Although global frameworks advocate for inclusive DRR, the extent and effectiveness of implementation vary widely between developed and developing nations. In South Asia, despite growing recognition of the rights of persons with disabilities (PwDs), critical gaps remain in planning, infrastructure, training, data systems, and accountability, especially when compared to countries like Japan, the United States, and Australia.

6.1 Early Warning Systems and Communication

Developed countries invest heavily in multimodal early warning systems. The US Integrated Public Alert and Warning System (IPAWS) disseminates alerts across visual, auditory, and vibration platforms to reach individuals with sensory disabilities (Federal Emergency Management Agency, 2025).

In South Asia, by contrast, early warning systems often rely on loudspeakers or SMS messages, which are inaccessible to many PwDs. Critical alerts are frequently issued without subtitles, sign language interpretation, or simplified messaging, leaving people with hearing, visual, or cognitive impairments uninformed during emergencies.

6.2 Infrastructure and Shelter Accessibility

Emergency shelters and public buildings in high-income countries are generally compliant with accessibility standards such as the Americans with Disabilities Act (ADA) or Australia's Disability Discrimination Act. Features like accessible entrances, adapted toilets, tactile flooring, and auditory cues are standard (Know-the-ADA, 2024).

In contrast, temporary shelters in South Asia often established in schools or public halls rarely include any accessibility adaptations. Even hospitals and rehabilitation centers in rural or peri-urban areas frequently lack essential features such as ramps, wide doors, or accessible toilets (Farid et al., 2024).

6.3 Training and Capacity of Emergency Personnel

In developed countries, emergency responders, healthcare workers, and public servants receive mandatory training in disability inclusion. Standard operating procedures guide communication with individuals with intellectual or sensory disabilities, handling of individuals with spinal injuries, and provision of psychological first aid for persons with psychosocial disabilities (Almukhlifi et al., 2021).

In South Asia, however, emergency personnel, including volunteers, health workers, and police, often lack basic disability awareness. Disability-sensitive training modules are rarely integrated into national curricula or operational guidelines, leaving responders ill-equipped to support PwDs during crises (Farid et al., 2024).

6.4 Data Systems and Information Infrastructure

Robust data systems in developed countries allow for real-time, disaggregated information on disability status, health needs, and geographic location. In the United States, agencies like the Census Bureau and the Department of Health and Human Services provide critical datasets that inform emergency planning and targeted interventions.

In South Asia, disability data remain fragmented, outdated, and poorly integrated into disaster planning. South Asian countries rarely maintain real-time disability registries or personalized preparedness plans. Assessments often reduce disability to a checkbox category, failing to distinguish between types of impairments or the specific support needs of individuals. This results in generalized, inadequate responses during emergencies (Farid et al., 2024).

7 South Asia: Disability-Inclusive DRR in Practice

Although the Sendai Framework for Disaster Risk Reduction (2015–2030) has influenced regional DRR policies, the scale and quality of disability inclusion differ widely. This section examines national-level progress, promising practices, and persisting gaps in selected South Asian countries.

7.1 Nepal

Nepal is highly vulnerable to multiple natural hazards such as earthquakes, floods, landslides, and forest fires, with over 80% of the population exposed to disaster risks. Persons with disabilities (PwDs) in Nepal face compounded risks due to both environmental hazards and systemic exclusion. Legislative frameworks like the Disaster Risk Reduction and Management (DRRM) Act 2017, the National Policy for Disaster Risk Reduction 2018, and the Act Relating to Rights of Persons with Disabilities (2017) provide a legal basis for inclusion. However, significant gaps persist in translating these policies into effective practice at the local level. While some progress has been made through partnerships with government agencies, OPDs (Organizations of Persons with Disabilities), and development partners such as CBM, Handicap International, and Atullya Foundation in training, accessible communication, and localized preparedness, PwDs are often excluded from decision-making and risk assessments. Persistent challenges include a lack of disability data, inaccessible shelters, disruptions to services, and limited participation in early warning systems (CBM Global Disability Inclusion-NFDN et al., 2024).

7.2 Bangladesh

Bangladesh has made important strides in piloting disability-inclusive disaster risk reduction (DiDRR), particularly through initiatives such as the National Resilience Programme (NRP) implemented by the Centre for Disability in Development (CDD). The pilot project, conducted in Kurigram district—a highly flood-prone region—focused on building resilience among persons with disabilities (PwDs) through capacity building, accessible infrastructure, inclusive early warning systems, and community-based approaches. The project applied a community-based inclusive development (CBID) model, forming self-help groups (SHGs), mapping PwDs, and actively involving organizations of persons with disabilities (OPDs) in disaster management structures like Ward Disaster Management Committees (WDMCs). Practical measures included accessible flood-resilient housing, installation of ramps in clinics, disability-inclusive search and rescue training, and development of inclusive early warning dissemination methods (e.g., flags, loudspeakers, and door-to-door alerts). The project also strengthened linkages between PwDs and government service providers to ensure inclusion in livelihood support, healthcare, and relief distribution. Despite challenges such as COVID-19 disruptions and resource limitations, the project demonstrated the feasibility of integrating disability inclusion into disaster risk management at the local level (Centre for Disability in Development [CDD], 2022).

7.3 India

According to the National Family Health Survey (NFHS-5, 2019–21), the prevalence of disability in India stands at 0.93%, with locomotor and mental disabilities being the most commonly reported. Given India's vast and diverse geography, coupled with a population exceeding 1.4 billion, the country remains acutely vulnerable to both natural and human-induced disasters (Pattnaik et al., 2023).

The National Disaster Management Authority (NDMA) has taken significant steps to promote DiDRR. The National Disaster Management Plan 2019 specifically highlights the need to address the vulnerabilities of PwDs distinctly. In 2019, NDMA also issued National Guidelines on Disability Inclusive Disaster Risk Reduction, providing a framework for departments and states to integrate disability considerations into disaster risk management. States like Odisha, Tamil Nadu, and Kerala have piloted inclusive community preparedness initiatives, including simulation exercises with the participation of persons with disabilities (NDMA, 2019).

Kerala serves as a model for DiDRR implementation through its extensive capacity-building programs. In collaboration with the Inter University Centre for Disability Studies, Kerala State Disaster Management Authority (KSDMA) conducted state-wide training to empower PwDs in disaster preparedness. Between 2016 and 2018, 2667 PwDs and caregivers participated in specialized training sessions, using disability-friendly materials such as Braille books and sign language videos. During the 2018 Kerala floods, trained volunteers, including persons with disabilities, actively participated in rescue operations, demonstrating the effectiveness of inclusive training in real disaster contexts (KSDMA, 2019a).

7.4 *Sri Lanka*

Sri Lanka has experienced multiple natural disasters, including the 2004 Indian Ocean tsunami, floods, droughts, and landslides, which have revealed significant gaps in addressing the needs of PwDs in disaster response and recovery. Post-disaster rebuilding efforts, guided by the Build Back Better (BBB) framework, have increasingly recognized the importance of including marginalized groups such as women and PwDs. The Sendai Framework for Disaster Risk Reduction and national policies such as the Disaster Management Act (2005) and the National Policy on Disaster Management (2010) have provided a policy foundation for inclusion. However, practical implementation remains limited, with ongoing challenges such as inaccessible shelters, a lack of disability data, insufficient assistive infrastructure, and the absence of trained personnel to support PwDs during emergencies. While there have been efforts by agencies like UNDP, NBRO, and UNICEF to incorporate accessibility into reconstruction—especially in health, education, and social care facilities—many public spaces still lack basic accessibility features like ramps, handrails, tactile indicators, and braille signage. The inclusion of disability perspectives in disaster risk reduction in Sri Lanka remains a work in progress, requiring stronger coordination, data systems, and enforcement of inclusive design standards (De Silva & Jayathilaka, 2020).

7.5 Pakistan

Pakistan faces multiple natural and human-induced disasters, which disproportionately affect PwDs, estimated to be over 27 million in the country. Despite high vulnerability, PwDs remain largely excluded from disaster preparedness and response efforts. Social stigma, lack of accessibility, and absence of inclusive policies further aggravate their risks during disasters. Over time, Pakistan has made legal and policy advancements. The journey began with the Employment and Rehabilitation Ordinance (1981), followed by the National Policy for Persons with Disabilities (2002) and its National Plan of Action (2006). More comprehensive provincial laws were enacted between 2018 and 2022, including the Sindh Empowerment of Persons with Disabilities Act (2018), the Punjab Empowerment of Persons with Disabilities Act (2022), and similar laws in Balochistan, Gilgit-Baltistan, and Islamabad Capital Territory (ICT). The ICT Rights of Persons with Disabilities Act (2020) notably mandates disability inclusion in disaster risk reduction (DRR). Pakistan has also ratified the UN Convention on the Rights of Persons with Disabilities (International disability alliance, 2011) and endorsed the Sendai Framework for Disaster Risk Reduction. The National Disaster Management Authority (NDMA), while leading disaster management, has only partially integrated disability inclusion in its plans, such as the National Disaster Management Plan 2024. Although initiatives by civil society and the Ageing, Disability and Diversity Taskforce (ADDTF) have promoted awareness, significant gaps remain. To ensure effective disability-inclusive DRR, Pakistan must strengthen legal enforcement, build institutional capacity, improve data collection, and ensure the active participation of PwDs at all stages of disaster management (Sheikh, 2014).

7.6 Bhutan

Bhutan, a small Himalayan nation highly vulnerable to earthquakes, landslides, glacial lake outburst floods (GLOFs), and climate-induced disasters, recognizes the importance of inclusive disaster risk reduction. PwDs in Bhutan face unique challenges during disasters due to barriers in accessibility, limited inclusive early warning systems, and gaps in preparedness planning. The Constitution of Bhutan guarantees equality and protection for all citizens, including PwDs, and Bhutan is a State Party to the UN Convention on the Rights of Persons with Disabilities (UNCRPD), ratified in 2010. The Disaster Management Act of Bhutan (2013) provides the legal foundation for disaster preparedness, response, and recovery, though explicit provisions for PwDs remain limited. Bhutan's National Disaster Risk Management Strategy (2013) and subsequent policies have increasingly emphasized the need for vulnerability assessments and inclusive approaches. The Gross National Happiness Commission also integrates disability and disaster resilience as part of Bhutan's broader development goals. While disability-inclusive DRR is still evolving, ongoing capacity-building, awareness programs, and the involvement of organizations such as Disabled People's Organizations (DPOs) are helping to advance inclusive practices (Royal Government of Bhutan, 2013).

7.7 *Maldives*

The Maldives, vulnerable to hazards like tsunamis, storms, and sea-level rise, has made significant strides in ensuring disaster risk reduction is inclusive of PwDs. Central to this effort is the Protection of the Rights of Persons with Disabilities and Provision of Financial Assistance Act (Disability Act 2010), which mandates accessibility and safeguards for PwDs during disasters, including integration of disability councils in disaster planning. Complementing this, the Disaster Risk Reduction Strategy 2024–2030 explicitly recognizes the Disability Act's role, highlighting accessibility standards (Article 18), inclusion in disaster plans (Article 28), and prioritized protection during emergencies (Article 29A). The Maldives also ratified the UN Convention on the Rights of Persons with Disabilities (UNCRPD) in 2010 and endorsed the Sendai Framework for Disaster Risk Reduction (2015–2030), promising inclusive DRR approaches. National progress has been supported by the National Disability Registry, Disability Council, and key agencies like the Ministry of Social and Family Development and the National Social Protection Agency, which coordinate inclusion across disaster management and recovery (Government of Maldives, 2024).

7.8 *Afghanistan*

Afghanistan faces recurring disasters—earthquakes, floods, and landslides—on top of decades of conflict and instability. These crises disproportionately impact PwDs. The Afghanistan National Disaster Management Authority (ANDMA), established under the National Disaster Management Law (2012) and later reinforced by strategic plans like the 2010 Strategic National Action Plan for DRR, leads national disaster efforts. ANDMA implements the Sendai Framework priorities, but on-the-ground inclusion of PwDs remains limited due to institutional weakness and fragmented community-level coordination. Afghanistan ratified the UN Convention on the Rights of Persons with Disabilities (UNCRPD) in 2012 and enacted the 2013 Law on Rights and Privileges of Persons with Disabilities, which outlaws discrimination and reserves jobs for PwDs. However, DRR policies still predominantly view disability as a generic vulnerability category, rather than engaging PwDs as active stakeholders in planning or execution. Although civil society and some humanitarian actors—such as Handicap International—have worked to include PwDs in resilience building, overall progress is uneven (Ministry of Disaster Management and Humanitarian Affairs, Afghanistan, 2024).

8 Recommendations: Advancing Disability-Inclusive Disaster Risk Reduction

Building a disaster-resilient society demands a deliberate, rights-based, and inclusive approach, one that positions persons with disabilities not as passive recipients of aid but as active contributors to disaster preparedness, response, and recovery.

8.1 Integrate Disability Across All DRR Policies and Plans

Embed disability-specific provisions in national, state, and local DRR policies, ensuring alignment with the Sendai Framework for Disaster Risk Reduction and the UN Convention on the Rights of Persons with Disabilities (UNCRPD). Mandate inclusive planning within District Disaster Management Authorities (DDMAs), supported by dedicated budget allocations and accountability frameworks.

8.2 Strengthen Disability Data Collection and Utilization

Develop and maintain disability-disaggregated data systems using standardized tools and conduct participatory risk mapping to identify households with persons with disabilities. Promote inclusive early warning systems that disseminate alerts through accessible formats such as SMS, audio messages, sign language, and pictograms.

8.3 Build Institutional and Community Capacities

Train frontline responders, healthcare workers, and local administrators on disability awareness, inclusive communication strategies, and universal design principles. Regularly conduct mock drills and simulation exercises with active participation from persons with disabilities.

8.4 Ensure Accessible Infrastructure and Relief Services

Enforce accessibility standards for all critical infrastructure, including shelters, hospitals, schools, and public transportation hubs. Develop accessible evacuation protocols, including the pre-positioning of assistive devices and transport options that accommodate diverse impairments.

8.5 Promote Leadership and Participation of Persons with Disabilities

Ensure the representation of persons with disabilities and their representative organizations in DRR governance bodies at all administrative levels. Invest in leadership development, training, and participation pathways for persons with disabilities within the disaster management ecosystem.

8.6 Secure Sustainable Financing and Cross-Sectoral Collaboration

Allocate dedicated funding for disability-inclusive DRR within national disaster preparedness and climate adaptation budgets. Promote intersectoral collaboration across health, education, housing, social welfare, and emergency services to ensure a coordinated response.

9 Conclusion

The intersection of disaster risk and disability is no longer a peripheral issue; it is now central to the design and implementation of inclusive and effective DRR strategies. The Sendai Framework for Disaster Risk Reduction 2015–2030 marks a critical turning point in global DRR policy, explicitly recognizing the rights, agency, and resilience of persons with disabilities. However, the translation of policy into practice remains inconsistent, particularly in regions such as South Asia, where high levels of vulnerability are compounded by limited resources, infrastructural challenges, and deeply rooted social inequalities.

This chapter has examined the disproportionate risks faced by persons with disabilities in disaster contexts, the structural and systemic barriers that contribute to their exclusion, and the emerging examples of promising practices in countries such as Nepal, Bangladesh, India, and Sri Lanka. These cases illustrate that progress is both possible and achievable, especially when persons with disabilities are engaged as active agents of resilience rather than passive recipients of aid. Nonetheless, achieving genuine inclusion requires more than policy declarations. It demands the deliberate design of inclusive systems and infrastructure, effective cross-sectoral coordination between government and civil society, and sustained investments in accessibility, data systems, and capacity building.

References

Almukhlifi, Y., Crowfoot, G., Wilson, A., & Hutton, A. (2021). Emergency healthcare workers' preparedness for disaster management: An integrative review. *Journal of Clinical Nursing, 34*(12), 4958–4973. https://doi.org/10.1111/jocn.15965

Arbeiter-Samariter-Bund Deutschland, Christian Blind Mission, International Disability Alliance, Centre for Disability in Development, & Malteser International. (2021). *Including persons with disabilities in disaster risk reduction: Global study snapshot [PDF]*. DiDRRN. https://www.malteser-international.org/fileadmin/Files_sites/malteser-international/A-About_us/E--Service/C-Publications/Specialized_Publications/DiDRR_Study_in_English.pdf

Bakhshian, E., & Martinez-Pastor, B. (2023). Evaluating human behaviour during a disaster evacuation process: A literature review. *Journal of Traffic and Transportation Engineering (English Edition), 10*(4), 485–507.

CBM Global Disability Inclusion, National Federation of the Disabled–Nepal (NFDN), Handicap International, & Atullya Foundation. (2024, January 29). Disability-inclusive disaster risk reduction (DiDRR) country brief: Nepal [Country brief]. https://www.maketherightreal.net/files/documents/learning/DiDRR-country-brief-Nepal-20240129.pdf

Centre for Disability in Development (CDD). (2022). *Piloting community-based inclusive disaster risk reduction (DiDRR) in Kurigram, Bangladesh: Experience from the National Resilience Programme (NRP)*. CDD.

De Silva, C., & Jayathilaka, R. (2020). Disaster risk reduction and resilience of persons with disabilities in Sri Lanka. *FARU Journal, 1*(1), 270–278. Retrieved from https://faru.sjp.ac.lk

Disasters Emergency Committee. (2016). *Nepal earthquake: Final report*. DEC. https://www.dec.org.uk/sites/default/files/PDFS/dec_nepal_final_report_lr_singles.pdf

EM-DAT. (2024). *Emergency events database: The international disaster database*. Centre for Research on the Epidemiology of Disasters (CRED), Université catholique de Louvain. Retrieved from https://www.emdat.be

Engelman, A., Craig, L., & Iles, A. (2022). Global disability justice in climate disasters: Mobilizing people with disabilities as change agents. *Health Affairs, 41*(10), 1496–1504. https://doi.org/10.1377/hlthaff.2022.00474

Fanchiotti, M., Dash, J., Tompkins, E. L., & Hutton, C. W. (2020). The 1999 super cyclone in Odisha, India: A systematic review of documented losses. *International Journal of Disaster Risk Reduction, 51*, 101790.

Farid, Z. I., Islam, M. A., Roberts, P. S., & Glick, J. (2024). *Disability inclusive disaster risk reduction (DiDRR) in South Asia: Status, prospects, and challenges*. Mavs Open Press.

Federal Emergency Management Agency. (2025). *Integrated Public Alert & Warning System (IPAWS)*. U.S. Department of Homeland Security. https://www.fema.gov/emergency-managers/practitioners/integrated-public-alert-warning-system

Fujii, K. (2015). *The Great East Japan Earthquake and persons with disabilities affected by the earthquake: Why is the mortality rate so high? Interim report on JDF support activities and proposals*. Japan Disability Forum. https://www.dinf.ne.jp/doc/english/resource/JDF_201503/1-1-1.html Sources.

Government of Maldives. (2024). *Disaster Risk Reduction Strategy 2024–2030. National Disaster Management Authority, Government of the Republic of Maldives*. https://ndma.gov.mv/storage/uploads/9kobKXw8/gxyiyu5x.pdf

Jang, J. H., & Ha, K. M. (2021). Inclusion of children with disabilities in disaster management. *Children (Basel), 8*(7), 581. https://doi.org/10.3390/children8070581

Kanta Kafle, S. (2017). Disaster risk management systems in South Asia: Natural hazards, vulnerability, disaster risk and legislative and institutional frameworks. *Journal of Geography & Natural Disasters, 7*(3) https://www.omicsonline.org/open-access/disaster-risk-management-systems-in-south-asia-natural-hazards-vulnerability-disaster-risk-and-legislative-and-institutional-frame-2167-0587-1000207-95107.html

Kar, N. (2010). Indian research on disaster and mental health. *Indian Journal of Psychiatry, 52*(Suppl 1), S286–S290.
Kerala State Disaster Management Authority (KSDMA). (2019a). *Write-up on disability inclusive disaster risk reduction*. KSDMA.
Kerala State Disaster Management Authority (KSDMA). (2019b). *State initiative on disability inclusive disaster risk reduction (DiDRR): Kerala model*. KSDMA.
Know-the-ADA. (2024). Global comparison of ADA and international disability laws. https://know-the-ada.com/global-comparison-of-ada-and-international-disability-laws/
Kruger, J., Hinton, C. F., Sinclair, L. B., & Silverman, B. (2018). Enhancing individual and community disaster preparedness: Individuals with disabilities and others with access and functional needs. *Disability and Health Journal, 11*(2), 170–173. https://doi.org/10.1016/j.dhjo.2017.12.005
Mann, M., McMillan, J. E., Silver, E. J., & Stein, R. E. K. (2021). Children and adolescents with disabilities and exposure to disasters, terrorism, and the COVID-19 pandemic: A scoping review. *Current Psychiatry Reports, 23*(12), 80.
McDermott, S., Martin, K., & Gardner, J. D. (2016). Disaster response for people with disability. *Disability and Health Journal, 9*(2), 183–185. https://doi.org/10.1016/j.dhjo.2015.12.005
Ministry of Disaster Management and Humanitarian Affairs, Afghanistan. (2024, February). *Current state of early warning system in Afghanistan* [PDF]. Humanitarian Library. https://www.humanitarianlibrary.org/sites/default/files/2024/02/early_warning_Afghanistan.pdf.
Morales, D. X. (2025). Natural disaster vulnerability among people with disabilities: Insights from the 2024 Household Pulse Survey. *Disability and Health Journal, 18*(2), 101763. https://doi.org/10.1016/j.dhjo.2024.101763
Mulvey, J. M., Awan, S. U., Qadri, A. A., & Maqsood, M. A. (2008). Profile of injuries arising from the 2005 Kashmir earthquake: The first 72h. *Injury, 39*(5), 554–560.
Murthy, R. S. (2022). Disaster mental health in India. In *DisasterMentalHealthV2CA*. National Institute of Mental Health and Neurosciences (NIMHANS).
National Disaster Management Authority. (2019). *National disaster management guidelines on disability-inclusive disaster risk reduction*. NDMA.
Neria, Y., Nandi, A., & Galea, S. (2008). Post-traumatic stress disorder following disasters: A systematic review. *Psychological Medicine, 38*(4), 467–480.
Nguyen-Trung, K., Thuy, T. T. T., Anh, N. P., Cong-Lem, N., Huyen, D. T., Diu, L. T., Giang, N. H., & Simon, M. (2025). Vulnerabilities of people with different types of disabilities in disasters: A rapid evidence review and qualitative research. *Disasters, 49*(3), e12686. https://doi.org/10.1111/disa.12686
Pattnaik, S., Murmu, J., Agrawal, R., Rehman, T., Kanungo, S., & Pati, S. (2023). Prevalence, pattern and determinants of disabilities in India: Insights from NFHS-5 (2019–21). *Frontiers in Public Health, 11*, 1036499. https://doi.org/10.3389/fpubh.2023.1036499
Priestley, M., & Hemingway, L. (2006). Disability and disaster recovery: A tale of two cities? *Journal of Social Work in Disability & Rehabilitation, 5*(3–4), 23–42. https://doi.org/10.1300/J198v05n03_02
Royal Government of Bhutan. (2013). *National disaster risk management strategy of Bhutan*. Department of Disaster Management.
Sheikh, M. A. (2014). *Disability-inclusive disaster risk reduction: Status brief on Pakistan* (STEP-DiDRR Project). Special Talent Exchange Program (STEP), South Asian Disability Forum (SADF).
Stough, L. M., Sharp, A. N., Decker, C., & Wilker, N. (2010). Disaster case management and individuals with disabilities. *Rehabilitation Psychology, 55*(3), 211–220.
Stough, L. M., Ducy, E. M., & Kang, D. (2017). Addressing the needs of children with disabilities experiencing disaster or terrorism. *Current Psychiatry Reports, 19*(4), 24.
Subramaniam, P., & Villeneuve, M. (2020). Advancing emergency preparedness for people with disabilities and chronic health conditions in the community: A scoping review. *Disability and Rehabilitation, 42*(22), 3256–3264.

UNDRR. (2024). *Global assessment report on disaster risk reduction 2024*. United Nations Office for Disaster Risk Reduction.

United Nations. (2006). *Convention on the Rights of Persons with Disabilities*. https://www.un.org/development/desa/disabilities/convention-on-the-rights-of-persons-with-disabilities.html

United Nations Office for Disaster Risk Reduction (UNDRR). (2015). Sendai framework for disaster risk reduction 2015–2030. Retrieved from https://www.undrr.org/publication/sendai-framework-disaster-risk-reduction-2015-2030

United Nations Office for Disaster Risk Reduction (UNDRR). (2017). The Sendai framework terminology on disaster risk reduction. "Disaster". https://www.undrr.org/terminology/disaster

Wachtendorf, T., Kendra, J. M., Rodríguez, H., & Trainor, J. (2006). The social impacts and consequences of the December 2004 Indian Ocean tsunami: Observations from India and Sri Lanka. *Earthquake Spectra, 22*(3_suppl), 693–714.

WHO. (2001). *International classification of functioning, disability and health (ICF)*. World Health Organization.

Wilkins, A., Pennaz, A., Dix, M., Smith, A., Vawter, J., Karlson, D., et al. (2021). Challenges and opportunities for Sendai framework disaster loss reporting in the United States. *Progress in Disaster Science, 10*, 100167.

Yadav, J., Ranjan, R., & Peden, A. E. (2024). The self-reported human health impacts of disaster on people in India: A cross-sectional analysis of the Longitudinal Aging Study India. *Prehospital and Disaster Medicine, 39*(6), 402–414. https://doi.org/10.1017/S1049023X25000020

International Disability Alliance. International Disability Alliance. (2011, September 21). Pakistan ratifies the CRPD. *online*, https://www.internationaldisabilityalliance.org/blog/pakistan-ratifies-crpdInternational Disability Alliance (2011).

Chapter 15
Disaster and Mass Behavior

Sandesh Venu, Deepta Subramanian, Natarajan Varadharajan, and Vikas Menon

1 Introduction

Disasters in general pose significant challenges to individuals, communities, and governments. People's responses to disasters are shaped by a variety of sociocultural, psychological, and geographical factors that influence collective behavior. Reactions can oscillate between cooperation and resilience or veer into chaos, which frequently stems from anxiety, uncertainty, and misinformation circulating on social media (Beaglehole et al., 2018; Srivastava, 2010).

A comprehensive understanding of how individuals collectively behave during disasters is essential for effective planning, policymaking, preparedness, and response strategies (Chartoff et al., 2025). Disaster psychiatry, an emerging field, seeks to explore the psychosocial impact of disasters, the role of risk perception, and the formulation of preventive and management strategies (Christodoulou, 2024).

In the South Asian context, where high population density, variable literacy rates, and socioeconomic disparity coexist, mass behavior takes on distinctive forms during disaster. Cultural values, religious beliefs, and traditional knowledge systems significantly influence collective coping and adaptation strategies, sometimes enhancing resilience while other times fostering stigma, denial, or misinformation. For instance, panic buying (PB) has emerged as a recurring phenomenon during disasters such as the COVID-19 pandemic or cyclones, ranging from food hoarding to stockpiling medicines (Arafat et al., 2020a).

S. Venu · D. Subramanian
Department of Psychiatry, Pondicherry Institute of Medical Sciences (PIMS), Kalapet, Puducherry, India

N. Varadharajan · V. Menon (✉)
Department of Psychiatry, Jawaharlal Institute of Postgraduate Medical Education and Research (JIPMER), Puducherry, India

N. Kar et al. (eds.), *Climate Change, Disaster and Mental Health in South Asia*, South Asian Perspectives in Mental Health and Psychology,
https://doi.org/10.1007/978-981-95-3690-0_15

This chapter explores the complex relationship between disaster events and human behavior. It focuses on contemporary challenges, such as PB, and examines its mental health implications within the South Asian context. It aims to provide practitioners, researchers, and policymakers with a deeper understanding of how communities respond to crises. It highlights empirical patterns and theoretical frameworks, appropriate management strategies, and the importance of local communities in these situations.

2 Disaster Patterns, Climate Change, and Response System

2.1 Disaster Terminology

Disaster has been conceptualized in diverse ways due to interdisciplinary and geographical variations and is defined as an ecological event of significant magnitude exceeding the intrinsic coping ability of the community, thereby disrupting the normal functioning with detrimental effects to human life, the economy, and the environment, warranting external assistance (Keller & Al-Madhari, 1996; Noji, 2000; Pan American Health Organization, 2000; Shrivastava et al., 1988; United Nations Environment Programme, 2004; United Nations International Strategy for Disaster Reduction, 2009; United Nations Office for Disaster Risk Reduction, 2007). Even though catastrophe is used interchangeably with disaster, the latter surpasses a higher threshold of impact severity (Braga et al., 2008; Nestrovski & Seligmann-Silva, 2000). Disasters are often broadly categorized into three types based on their origin and causative factors: natural, manmade, and hybrid. They may also be classified based on contextual parameters surrounding the event's occurrence and its effects (Table 15.1).

2.2 Disaster Trends and Climatic Parameters: Global and South Asian Perspectives

The incidence of disasters has markedly increased globally, both in terms of frequency and impact. A decadal comparative analysis revealed a doubling of climate-related disasters between 2000 and 2019. Between 1994 and 2013, approximately 91% of all recorded natural disasters were attributed to climate-related events, with floods and storms accounting for nearly three-quarters of them (Centre for Research on the Epidemiology of Disasters (CRED), 2024; The Human Cost of Disasters, 2020). There has also been an increase in droughts, earthquakes, tsunamis, and temperature events.

The South Asian subcontinent represents one of the most disaster-prone regions globally, with heightened vulnerability to climatic extremes. A commonly observed

Table 15.1 Classification of disasters by type, origin, and contextual parameters

Category	Subtype/ parameter	Examples	Definition/context
Natural disasters	Beneath the earth's surface	Tsunami, earthquake	Arise from geophysical processes beyond human control
	On the surface	Landslides, avalanches	
	Meteorological	Cyclones	
	Biological	Communicable diseases	
Manmade disasters	Warfare-related	Nuclear, chemical attacks	Result from intentional human actions, especially in conflict
	Accidental	Fires, explosions	Arise unintentionally due to human activity or error
Hybrid disasters	Natural–human interaction	Deforestation-induced landslides, soil erosion	Occur when anthropogenic activity intensifies the impact of natural forces (e.g., land misuse leading to increased disaster vulnerability)
Contextual parameters	Scale of impact	Small-scale: local floods Large-scale: earthquakes	Degree to which the disaster affects populations—localized events vs. those requiring national or international intervention
	Frequency	Episodic: explosions, earthquakes chronic droughts	Describes the temporal pattern—sudden, short-term events vs. slow-building, long-lasting phenomena
	Onset	Sudden: volcanic eruptions Slow: sea level rise	Refers to the speed at which the disaster unfolds
	Nature of event	Abrupt: building collapse; gradual: international conflict	Describes whether the event emerges suddenly or evolves through complex, escalating processes over time

(Centre for Research on the Epidemiology of Disasters (CRED), 2024; Fowlkes & Miller, 1983; International Committee of the Red Cross (ICRC), 1994; Mohamed Shaluf, 2007; Sendai Framework for Disaster Risk Reduction 2015–2030, 2015; Turner & Pidgeon, 1997; United Nations Environment Programme, 2004)

climatic change across South Asia (SA) is the rise in surface temperatures, alongside regional variations in precipitation, contributing to a complex and recurrent pattern of floods, droughts, earthquakes, tropical cyclones, torrential rainfall, droughts, and heat waves (Centre for Research on the Epidemiology of Disasters (CRED), 2024; *Global Risks 2014*, 2014; *Intergovernmental Panel on Climate Change*, 2012; Hock et al., 2019; Krishnan et al., 2019; World Bank, 2023). Table 15.2 provides an overview of major disasters that have occurred in South Asian countries in recent decades.

Table 15.2 Major disasters reported in South Asian countries in recent decades (Kanta Kafle, 2017; Memon, 2013)

Country	Disaster type	Disaster event	Year(s)	People affected/deaths
Bangladesh	Natural	Flood Cyclone	1974, 1988, 2004 1970, 1991	150 million affected 35 million affected
	Manmade	Nimtoli electrical accident Rana Plaza Collapse	2010 2013	122 deaths 1100 deaths
Bhutan	Natural	Windstorm Flood	1994 1994, 2000	65,000 affected 1600 affected
	Manmade	Chamkhar fire	2010	267 deaths
India	Natural	Flood Cyclone Earthquake Drought	1993 1999 2001 2002	128 million affected 15 million affected 1.8 million affected 300 million affected
	Manmade	Mining disaster Bhopal gas leak Mumbai terror attacks	1975 1984 2008	372 deaths 50,000 deaths 160 deaths
Maldives, Sri Lanka, India	Natural	Tsunami	2004	4.62 million affected
Nepal	Natural	Earthquake Flood Landslide	1934, 1988, 2015 1993 2002	17 million affected 5.5 million affected 2.6 million affected
Pakistan	Natural	Earthquake Flood	1974, 2005 1992, 1998, 2010	5.23 million affected 41 million affected
	Manmade	Hunza Lake disaster Karachi factory fire	2010 2012	20,000 affected 289 deaths
Sri Lanka	Natural	Cyclone Flood	1978 1989, 2003	1 million affected 1.8 million affected
	Manmade	Colombo collapse X-Press Pearl incident Civil war	2017 2021 1983–2009	Long-term environmental impact, large-scale casualties

2.3 Country-Specific Disaster Vulnerabilities in South Asia

Each country in the region faces unique disaster challenges, influenced by various factors. Common contributions to the region's vulnerability include high emission rates of greenhouse gases, rapid population growth, dense urban areas compounded by degradation of nature, lack of strong governance, poverty and unstable political situations (2014 Annual Report | Pages | WWF, 2014; Global Assessment Report on Disaster Risk Reduction (2009) | UNDRR, 2009). Among South Asian countries, Bangladesh is considered the most vulnerable, with India and Pakistan also facing significant risks (World Disasters Report 2010, 2017). A trend toward a rise in sea level by 3.1 mm per year has been observed in the Himalayan region and parts of India, contributing to increased drought risk (Panthi et al., 2017).

Afghanistan suffers vastly due to earthquakes, sandstorms, and avalanches, as well as war and civil unrest. Bhutan frequently experiences landslides, flash floods, and forest fires. Major seismic disasters in SA include the Gorkha earthquake in Nepal (2015), the Gujarat earthquake in India (2001), and the Kashmir earthquake in Pakistan (2005), each causing extensive damage and loss of life (United Nations International Strategy for Disaster Reduction (UNISDR), 2005).

India experiences variable disasters like landslides in the Himalayas, floods and cyclones in coastal areas, and droughts in the northeast. Coastal erosion and salinity intrusion are growing concerns in the Maldives, Bangladesh, and Sri Lanka. In Sri Lanka, tsunamis, along with cyclones, deforestation, mining, and prolonged political and ethnic conflicts, have significantly contributed to its complex disaster landscape (Asian Disaster Reduction Center (ADRC), 2023; Centre for Excellence in Disaster Management and Humanitarian Assistance, 2024; Hettiarachchi, 2024).

Table 15.3 outlines the country-specific disaster management authorities and related policies across South Asian nations.

3 Mental Health Outcomes of Disasters in South Asia

3.1 Natural Disasters

Natural disasters across SA have been associated with elevated rates of psychiatric morbidity, with post-traumatic stress disorder (PTSD), depression, and anxiety representing the most frequently observed outcomes.

Most flood-related studies focused on post-monsoon flooding in India, except for one on flash floods in Ladakh, North India (Ishikawa et al., 2013), and two from Bangladesh (Mostafizur Rahman et al., 2023; Rahman et al., 2025). The reported prevalence of PTSD symptoms ranged from 0.6% to 82%, followed by depressive symptoms (1.6%–65.2%) and anxiety symptoms (1.1%–44.3%) (Asim et al., 2022; Bandla et al., 2019; Ishikawa et al., 2013; Mamun et al., 2021). Subclinical symptoms of PTSD were observed in up to 90% of adults 1 year post-flood (Asim et al., 2022), highlighting the long-term psychological impacts of floods. General psychiatric symptoms were reported in up to two-thirds of affected survivors, with psychological distress more commonly observed among women and children (Aneelraj et al., 2016; Mostafizur Rahman et al., 2023; Thomas et al., 2021). There are limited studies on suicide and substance use disorders in flood survivors. In a flood-affected

Table 15.3 Disaster response systems and preparedness strategies in South Asian countries

Country	Disaster management authorities and policies	Key functions and roles
Bangladesh	Ministry of Disaster Management and Relief—the National Emergency Operation Centre (NEOC) National Disaster Response Coordination Group (NDRCG) Cyclone Preparedness Programme (CPP)	Response coordination, information dissemination, and resource mobilization Mobilizes resources, coordinates inter-agency efforts, and supervises response operations, including urban search and rescue missions Engage local volunteers in early warning dissemination, evacuation assistance, and first-response activities
Bhutan	National Emergency Operation Centre (NEOC)—Emergency Operation Centres (EOCs) National Centre for Hydrology and Meteorology (NCHM)	Coordinates disaster response efforts Conduct training programs for disaster management representatives across all Dzongkhags and Thromdes Specialized training for Search and Rescue (SAR) teams, public education campaigns, and community-based programs to raise awareness and enhance local preparedness Dedicated budget allocation and emergency funds Development of early warning systems for various natural hazards, including floods and glacial lake outburst floods (GLOFs)
India	Disaster Management Act, 2005—National Disaster Management Agency (NDMA)	Holistic, proactive, multi-disaster, and technology-driven strategy for risk reduction and management Formulating policies and coordinating resources, as well as overseeing the implementation Prevention, mitigation, preparedness, response, recovery, and rehabilitation are the core areas of focus The national disaster response fund and disaster mitigation fund cover the immediate and recurring expenses
Maldives	Maldives Disaster Risk Reduction Strategy 2024–2030—National Disaster Management Council (NDMC)	Aligned with the Sendai Framework and the Paris Agreement Focuses on safeguarding the nation's natural and built environments against climate hazards, aiming for disaster preparedness and building resilient communities

(continued)

Table 15.3 (continued)

Country	Disaster management authorities and policies	Key functions and roles
Nepal	National Policy and Strategic Action Plan for Disaster Risk Reduction and Management (2018–2030)—Nepal National Disaster Risk Reduction Policy (2018)	Building a safer, adaptive, and resilient nation by reducing disaster risks and losses in lives, livelihoods, and infrastructure by coordinating with provincial and local governments Emphasis is on community-based disaster risk management Targets integrating disaster risk reduction into development planning
Sri Lanka	Disaster Management Act, 2005	Focus on institutional arrangements, hazard assessment, early warning systems, and community-based risk reduction
Pakistan	Disaster Management Act, 2010	Aims to develop early warning systems, build a stronger local coordinating system, provide immediate risk assessment and response, and build back resilient communities

(Global Forum on Migration and Development (GFMD), 2024; Government of India, 2005; Government of Nepal, 2017; Government of the Islamic Republic of Pakistan, 2010; Government of the People's Republic of Bangladesh, 2012; Kanta Kafle, 2017; Mall et al., 2019; National Disaster Management Authority (NDMA), 2025; Parliament of the Democratic Socialist Republic of Sri Lanka, 2005; Parliament of the Kingdom of Bhutan, 2013)

population in Bangladesh, more than half of the survivors reported suicidal ideation during the early post-disaster phase (Mamun et al., 2021). However, studies from India reported lower rates, possibly due to differences in assessment methods. Increased substance use after flooding was observed in up to 15.8% of Indian samples (Thomas et al., 2021), which warrants more comprehensive evaluation in future research.

In the aftermath of the 2004 Indian Ocean tsunami, studies from Sri Lanka and India consistently reported elevated rates of PTSD, depression, and psychological distress in both adults and children. In the initial post-tsunami phase (3–6 months), the prevalence of PTSD among adults varied from 12% to 56%, with higher rates observed in women and those who suffered significant loss or injury (Kumar et al., 2007; Ranasinghe & Levy, 2007). Among children and adolescents, PTSD symptoms were highest immediately following the event, affecting up to 80% of the survivors, with nearly one-fourth continuing to experience persistent symptoms for many years (John et al., 2007; Ponnamperuma et al., 2020). Depressive symptoms were also common (10%–16%) in the first year post-disaster, often co-occurring with PTSD (Hollifield et al., 2008; Math et al., 2008). Suicidal ideations were reported by 25% of survivors up to 5 years post-disaster, reflecting the chronicity of mental health impact (Kar et al., 2014).

Studies related to earthquakes are from high-seismic-prone areas of Nepal and Pakistan. High rates of post-traumatic stress, depression, anxiety, and psychosocial dysfunction among adults and children have been reported following the 2005 Kashmir and 2015 Nepal earthquakes. Among adults, higher rates of post-traumatic stress (24%–46.6%) were observed in females and injured individuals (Ali et al., 2012; Baral & Bhagawati, 2019; Naeem et al., 2011). Depressive and anxiety symptoms were also prominent, affecting about one-third of survivors, including pregnant women (Kane et al., 2018; Khatri et al., 2018). In children and adolescents, post-traumatic symptoms were more prevalent compared to adults (40%–65%), with significantly higher emotional distress observed among girls, whereas boys showed higher hyperactivity, suggesting gender-specific response patterns (Ayub et al., 2012; Sharma & Kar, 2019; Silwal et al., 2018). Longitudinal data suggest symptoms of PTSD and depression persist up to 4 years after the earthquake in one-third of adolescents (Silwal et al., 2022). Among recovery workers, PTSD affected over 40%, with the earthquake intensity, occupational stressors, and limited social support being contributory (Ehring et al., 2011). One unique finding from Pakistan was the high rate (30.4%) of subclinical psychotic symptoms among earthquake survivors (Ayub et al., 2015), highlighting the extended spectrum of trauma-related mental health outcomes. Studies related to other natural disasters are given in Table 15.4.

3.2 *Manmade Disasters*

Although less frequently studied than natural disasters, manmade disasters in SA have been associated with significant and long-lasting psychiatric consequences. The 1984 Bhopal gas leak remains the region's most extensively studied industrial disaster. Within 3 months, 22.6% of survivors reported predominantly anxiety, depression, and adjustment disorders. Long-term data showed 4% higher morbidity among the exposed population starting within 5 years and lasting for decades (Kar, 2010; Murthy, 2014). The 2013 Rana Plaza factory collapse in Bangladesh, another catastrophic industrial event, resulted in 60.2% of injured workers reporting post-traumatic symptoms 1 year later (Fitch et al., 2015).

Following the 1992 Mumbai riots and the 1996 terrorist bombing in Rajasthan, survivors reported psychological and behavioral symptoms, including severe stress, anger, suicidal ideation, helplessness, fear, and persistent worry about the future (Kar, 2010). Similarly, after the 2023 terrorist attacks and fire incidents in Lahore, half of the children and adolescents reported PTSD symptoms, and 15% showed depressive symptoms within two months, with greater severity among those exposed to terrorism compared to fire (Abbas et al., 2024). Manmade disasters also affect first responders and occupationally entrapped individuals, such as in the 2023 Uttarkashi tunnel collapse. Although formal psychiatric morbidity rates were relatively low, one-third of workers experienced disorientation and circadian rhythm disturbances due to prolonged entrapment in an artificially lit and confined space (Kundu et al., 2025).

Studies related to psychiatric morbidity after disasters and associated risk factors are given in Tables 15.4 and 15.5.

Table 15.4 Major studies related to psychiatric morbidity after disaster in South Asia

Author and year	Region and year of disaster	Study design	Study population and sample size	Timepoint measured	Assessment tools	Prevalence	Key findings
Studies related to flood							
Aneelraj et al., 2016	Uttarakhand, India—2013 Himalayan floods	Cross-sectional community-based	Children and adolescents aged 5–19 years; $N = 300$	Within 1 month post-disaster	IES	Psychological adversity: 66.7% Psychological distress: 18% Subsyndromal PTSD: 13%	Loss of shelter and loss of playing space were associated with psychological distress in children
Mamun et al., 2021	Bangladesh—2019 floods	Cross-sectional community-based	Adult flood survivors from two districts; $N = 348$	4–5 months post-flood	PHQ-9, GAD-7, TSQ-10	PTSD: 82.8% Depression: 65.2% Anxiety: 44.3% Suicidal ideation: 57.5% Suicide plan: 5.7%	High prevalence of suicidal ideation among survivors
Mathew et al., 2024	Kerala, India—2018 floods	Cross-sectional community-based	Adults (≥18 years) from three districts; $N = 600$	3 months post-flood	TSQ	PTSD: 49.7%	No prior flood exposure, higher family income, education, flood-related injury, and death of a family member were risk factors

(continued)

Table 15.4 (continued)

Studies related to flood

Author and year	Region and year of disaster	Study design	Study population and sample size	Timepoint measured	Assessment tools	Prevalence	Key findings
Telles et al., 2009	Bihar, India—2008 Kosi River floods	Cross-sectional camp-based	Adults (≥15 years), $N = 1289$	1 month post-flood	SQD	Higher PTSD and depression scores among elderly (≥60 years)	Older age, displacement, and poor socioeconomic status were risk factors
Thomas et al., 2021	Karnataka, India—2018 floods	Cross-sectional community-based	Adults aged 18–65 years; $N = 171$	4–6 months post-flood	DSM-5 self-rated level 1 cross-cutting symptom measure	66.7% had at least one psychiatric symptom; sleep problems: 35.7%; depression: 33%; anxiety: 31%; substance abuse: 15.8%; suicidal ideations: 1.2%	Leaving the house during the disaster and damage to the house were found to be significant factors
Wind et al., 2013	Uttar Pradesh, India—2008 recurrent floods	Cross-sectional, community-based (flood-affected vs. non-affected)	Adult affected ($N = 318$) and non-affected ($N = 308$)	1 month post-second flood	HSCL-25	The affected group had significantly higher anxiety (Cohen's $d = 0.92$) and depression (Cohen's $d = 1.22$) compared to non-affected group	Recurrent exposure, poverty, and social and environmental erosion were predictors

Studies related to earthquakes							
Baral & Bhagawati, 2019	Nepal—2015 earthquake	Cross-sectional community-based	Adults aged ≥20 years; *N* = 291	10 months	PCL-5	PTSD: 24.1%	Female gender, older age, and injury during earthquake were predictors
Ayub et al., 2015	Pakistan—2005 Kashmir earthquake	Cross-sectional community-based	Adults aged ≥18 years; *N* = 1291	18 months	PSQ	Psychotic symptoms: 20%–30%	High prevalence of self-reported subclinical psychotic symptoms
Chadda et al., 2007	Jammu & Kashmir, India—2005 earthquake	Cross-sectional community-based	Adults and adolescents = 303	5–6 weeks	Clinical interview (ICD-10 criteria)	Adjustment disorders: 39.6%; depression: 21.8%; PTSD: 3.3%; suicidal ideation in 10.2%	Possible psychological resilience attributed to prior conflict exposure in the region
Ehring et al., 2011	Pakistan—2005 Kashmir earthquake	Cross-sectional survey of rehabilitation workers	Earthquake recovery workers aged ≥18 years; *N* = 267	24 months	IES-R, PADQ,	PTSD: 42.6%; depression: 23.3%; anxiety: 18.8%	Recovery workers reported long-term psychiatric symptoms
Khatri et al., 2018	Nepal—2015 earthquake	Cross-sectional community-based	Pregnant women aged ≥15 years; *N* = 497	6 months	EPDS-N	Depression: 21.9% (EPDS >12)	Earthquake experience and intimate partner violence were risk factors

(continued)

Table 15.4 (continued)

Author and year	Region and year of disaster	Study design	Study population and sample size	Timepoint measured	Assessment tools	Prevalence	Key findings
Studies related to flood							
Kumar & Fonagy, 2013	Gujarat, India—2001 earthquake	Cross-sectional community-based	Children aged 8–15 years; $N = 128$	3.4 years	UCLA PTSD-RI	Probable PTSD: 24.3%	Higher trauma exposure, loss of family members, material destruction, and post-disaster adversities were risk factors
Sharma & Kar, 2019	Nepal—2015 earthquake	School-based cross-sectional survey	Adolescents aged 12–19 years; $N = 409$	1 year	CPSS	PTSD: 43.3%; depression: 38.1%	Female gender, joint family, financial problems, displacement, and injury were associated
Studies related to tsunami							
John et al., 2007	Tamil Nadu, India—2004 tsunami	Two-wave cross-sectional survey	Children and adolescents aged 5–18 years; $N = 502$	2 and 6 months post-tsunami	CBCL-PTSD-TR	Acute PTSD: 70.7%; delayed PTSD: 10.9%; overall prevalence of PTSD: 81.6%	Adolescents exposed to loss of life or property, female gender, and early or middle adolescence period had higher prevalence

Kar et al., 2014	Tamil Nadu, India—2004 tsunami	Cross-sectional community-based	Adults aged ≥18 years; $N = 666$	4.5 years post-disaster	SRQ, SDS, SAS, SRS-PTSD	Psychiatric morbidity (SRQ): 77.6%; PTSD: 70.9%; depression: 33.6%; anxiety: 23.1%; suicidal ideation: 24.6%; suicide attempt: 6.5%	Low education, low socio economic status (SES), perceived severity, home damage, injury, and loss of livelihood or livestock were significantly associated with SRQ positive status
Neuner et al., 2006	Sri Lanka—2004 tsunami	Cross-sectional community-based	Children aged 8–14; $N = 264$	3–4 weeks post-tsunami	UCLA PTSD-RI	PTSD: 13.9%–38.8%	Death of family members, severity of trauma exposure, and previous trauma predicted PTSD symptoms
Ponnamperuma et al., 2020	Sri Lanka—2004 tsunami	School-based cross-sectional with prospective sub-study	Adolescents aged 12–16; $N = 729$ (T1), $N = 90$ (T2)	4 years post-tsunami (T1); 16 months later (T2)	UCLA PTSD-RI, CIDI	PTSD: 23.7% EBP: 13.7	PTSD in adolescents amplified emotional and behavioral problems, leading to greater functional impairment
Rajkumar et al., 2015	Tamil Nadu, India—2004 tsunami	Cross-sectional community-based	Adults ≥12 years; $N = 643$	9 months post-tsunami	DSM-5 PGD criteria, IES-R	PGD in bereaved: 25.9%	Spousal bereavement, home destruction, and low education were risk factors for PGD

(continued)

Table 15.4 (continued)

Author and year	Region and year of disaster	Study design	Study population and sample size	Timepoint measured	Assessment tools	Prevalence	Key findings
Studies related to flood							
Ranasinghe et al., 2022	Sri Lanka—2004 tsunami	Cross-sectional community-based	Adults aged ≥16 years; $N = 430$	8 years post-disaster	PSS-I	PTSD: 2.8%; partial PTSD: 10.5%; depression: 18.8%	PTSD prevalence declined over time
Studies related to cyclone							
Hanć et al., 2022	West Bengal, India—Cyclone Aila, 2009	Cross-sectional	Children aged 8–11; $N = 837$ (336 prenatal exposure, 216 postnatal exposure, 285 controls)	Assessed at 8–11 years	CTRS-R:S	Higher Attention Deficit Hyperactivity Disorder scores in Aila-exposed vs. controls; highest effect for hyperactivity (OR = 1.23)	Postnatal exposure, males, maternal stress, and low SES were predictors
Kar & Bastia, 2006	Orissa, India—1999 super-cyclone	Cross-sectional, school-based	Adolescents; $N = 108$	14 months post-disaster	MINI-KID	PTSD: 26.9%, MDD: 17.6%, GAD: 12%	Comorbid PTSD+MDD (14.6%) was associated with academic decline, middle socioeconomic status, prolonged helplessness, and lack of post-disaster psychological support

Kar et al., 2022	Odisha, India—Cyclone Fani, 2019	Cross-sectional community-based	Adults from three rural villages; $N = 80$	1 month post-cyclone	PC-PTSD-5 GAD-7 PHQ-9	Probable PTSD: 42.9%; severe anxiety: 36.7%; moderate to severe depression: 65.9%; suicidal ideation in 14%	Damage to house, evacuation, and displacement were risk factors
Studies related to manmade disasters							
Abbas et al., 2024	Lahore, Pakistan—2023 terrorist attack and fire incident	Cross-sectional, community-based	Children and adolescents aged 8–17 years; $N = 80$	2 months post-disaster	CTSQ, DSRS-C	PTSD: 50%; depression: 15%	Children exposed to terrorism had more severe PTSD than those exposed to fire
Fitch et al., 2015	Bangladesh—2013 Rana Plaza collapse	Cross-sectional	Injured garment workers aged ≥18 years; $N = 181$	1 year	PCL-S	PTSD: 60.2%	Being married, high job position, and concussion injury were risk factors
Kundu et al., 2025	Uttarakhand, India—2023 tunnel collapse	Mixed-method observational study	Male tunnel workers; $N = 33$	Within 1 week post-rescue (17 days after incident)	GAD-7, PHQ-9, ISI	Clinically significant anxiety: 6%; depression: 12%; insomnia: 15%	Disorientation, lack of light–dark cycle, and delayed sleep–wake routines were risk factors

(continued)

Table 15.4 (continued)

Author and year	Region and year of disaster	Study design	Study population and sample size	Timepoint measured	Assessment tools	Prevalence	Key findings
Studies related to flood							
Ravan et al., 2024	Odisha, India—2023 train tragedy	Mixed-methods study	First responders; $N = 225$	1 month post-disaster	PCL-5, PHQ-9, GAD-7	PTSD: 10.2%; depression: 24.9%; anxiety: 11.6; sleep difficulties: 35.1%; increased alcohol use: 18.1%	Untrained volunteers were the most affected; peer support emerged as a protective factor

CBCL-PTSD-TR: Child Behaviour Checklist Post-Traumatic Stress Disorder Scale—Tamil Revised, CIDI: Composite International Diagnostic Interview, CPSS: Child PTSD Symptom Scale, CTRS-R:S: Conner's Teacher Rating Scale—Revised (Short Version), CTSQ: Child Trauma Screening Questionnaire, DSM-5: Diagnostic and Statistical Manual of Mental Disorders—Fifth Edition, DSRS-C: Depression Self-Rating Scale for Children, EPDS-N: Edinburgh Postnatal Depression Scale—Nepali version, GAD-7: Generalized Anxiety Disorder—7, HSCL-25: Hopkins Symptom Checklist—25, ICD-10: International Classification of Diseases—10th Edition, IES: Impact of Event Scale, IES-R: Impact of Event Scale—Revised, ISI: Insomnia Severity Index, MINI-KID: Mini International Neuropsychiatric Interview for Children and Adolescents, PCL-5: PTSD Checklist for DSM-5, PCL-S: PTSD Checklist—Specific Version, PC-PTSD-5: Primary Care PTSD Screen for DSM-5, PADQ: Pakistan Anxiety and Depression Questionnaire, PHQ-9: Patient Health Questionnaire—9, PGD: Prolonged Grief Disorder, PSQ: Psychosis Screening Questionnaire, PSS-I: PTSD Symptom Scale—Interview Version, SAS: Zung Self-Rating Anxiety Scale, SDS: Zung Self-Rating Depression Scale, SQD: Screening Questionnaire for Disaster Mental Health, SRQ: Self-Reporting Questionnaire, SRS-PTSD: Self-Rating Scale for PTSD, TSQ: Trauma Screening Questionnaire, UCLA PTSD-RI: University of California at Los Angeles PTSD Reaction Index

Table 15.5 Risk factors for psychiatric morbidity after disasters in South Asia

Domains	Risk factors
Demographic factors	Female gender (Aseem et al., 2022; Kane et al., 2018; Silwal et al., 2022) Older age (Ali et al., 2012; Pyari et al., 2012) Adolescents and children (Ayub et al., 2012; John et al., 2007; Silwal et al., 2022) Lower education (Ahmad et al., 2010; Baral & Bhagawati, 2019) Unmarried/widowed (Ali et al., 2012; Rajkumar et al., 2015)
Disaster exposure and severity	Direct trauma exposure (Neuner et al., 2006; Sharma & Kar, 2019) Injury to self or family (Kumar et al., 2007; Pyari et al., 2012) Bereavement/loss of family (Rajkumar et al., 2015; Suar et al., 2015) Loss of home/property/displacement (Kar et al., 2014; Rajkumar et al., 2015; Telles et al., 2009; Thomas et al., 2021)
Health-related factors	Pre-existing illness (Murthy, 2014) Physical disability (Fitch et al., 2015; Mathew et al., 2021)
Psychological factors	Low resilience and optimism (Ahmad et al., 2010) Maladaptive coping (Baral & Bhagawati, 2019) Negative trauma appraisal (Lommen et al., 2009)
Economic factors	Poverty/low income (Ali et al., 2012; Mamun et al., 2021) Loss of livelihood (Kar et al., 2014) Financial loss and unemployment (Fitch et al., 2015; Patwary et al., 2024)

4 Mass Behavior

4.1 Understanding the Concept of Mass Behavior

Mass behavior is a broad term that is often used synonymously with crowd behavior, collective behavior, swarm behavior, mob psychology, herding, and crowd psychology. It pertains to the actions or conduct exhibited by large groups of people, often in contexts like social movements, public gatherings, or collective responses to events. It is an impromptu behavior by a group of people outside conventional frameworks following a major societal event, causing quick, disorganized, and emotionally motivated changes.

It can be either an impulse-generated or fear-based response that may exacerbate, mitigate, prevent, or operate independently of harm (Bonner, 1953; Cantril, 1941; Espinola, 2016; Freud, 1921). Within the framework of constructive versus destructive responses, these behaviors have been categorized into value-oriented movements, hostile outbursts, panics, and craze behaviors. Examples of mass behavior include altruism, rumors, looting, PB, riots, social anarchy, and compassion satisfaction (McPhail, 1989; Smelser, 1962).

4.2 Factors Influencing Mass Behavior

4.2.1 Psychological Factors

The classical theories proposed that people become suggestible and unreasonable in a crowd, having a "collective mind," losing their sense of self and reason (Le Bon, 1895). Increased emotional reactivity and anonymity allow people to be easily influenced, where emotions spread quickly and personal accountability fails, leading to a lowering of behavioral standards (Bonner, 1953; Hatfield et al., 1994; Zimbardo, 1969). Freud suggested that community participation lowers personal responsibility by accessing the unconscious mind. Whereas it has also been theorized that individuals in a mass gathering experience a regression to earlier psychological states, leading to a diminished capacity for reality testing (Nitzgen, 2022). However, these ideas have drawn criticism for pathologizing social activity and being unduly deterministic.

In contrast, more recent theories conceptualize crowd behavior as dynamic and shaped by interaction rather than pre-existing norms or irrationality (Turner & Killian, 1987). Social Identity Theory posits that individuals define themselves through group memberships (Tajfel Turner, 1979). The Social Identity Model of Leadership (SIMOL) builds on this by proposing that leadership influence in crowds depends on identity alignment, with leaders perceived as prototypical representatives of the group (Drury, 2020; Hogg, 2001; Reicher et al., 2004).

4.2.2 Societal Factors

Persuasive communication, simple language, and charismatic leadership are considered essential for influencing group behavior and collective sentiment (Weber, 1947). Some argue that effective leadership is grounded in shared social identity between leaders and followers. However, existing models like SIMOL insufficiently address the role of social control within this leader–follower dynamic (Drury, 2020). The threshold model of collective behavior argues that individual behavior is heavily influenced by the actions of others (Granovetter, 1978).

4.3 Cultural and Religious Influences on Mass Behavior

Culture is viewed as a set of values, traditions, and skillsets built over time and generation among a group of people, which aid them in coping with and shaping their responses to various threats, including disasters (Rahmani et al., 2022). The behavior of the community during a disaster is determined more by culture than threat, according to anthropologists (Oliver-Smith, 1996). Various aspects of culture determine the way people perceive, communicate, and respond during disasters (Kulatunga, 2010; Arunotai, 2008). A subdomain of value orientation theory decides on the approach people take, namely submissive, dominant, or co-existent, which in turn guides their psychological and analytical skills (Kluckhohn & Strodtbeck, 1961). However, the degree to which they follow also depends on acculturation and assimilation. Similarly, cultural beliefs influence the explanations people offer as the reason for the event, the expressions of distress, both immediate and delayed, and the coping styles during recovery (Rahmani et al., 2022).

4.3.1 Religious and Traditional Beliefs Shaping Mass Behavior in South Asia

Cultural factors contribute to the vast differences in causality attributions to disasters. Despite the wide media coverage and awareness campaigns, there exists a state of neglect and indifference in many regions, specifically the Middle East and low-income countries, due to a fatalistic attitude that drives people to take risks as opposed to taking precautions. They believe disasters as "Will of God" or as a retribution to their sins, which affects their immediate behaviors and acceptance of help as well as future planning and adopting to precautions (Baytiyeh & Naja, 2014; Gaillard & Texier, 2010; Gianisa & Le De, 2018; O'Connell et al., 2017; Wickrama et al., 2017).

Similarly, communities respond differently to potential threats based on value systems. For example, during the eruption of the Merapi volcano in 2006, numerous communities refused to evacuate disaster-prone areas, believing that their ancestors who lived there were angry and they should not abandon them (Lavigne et al., 2008). In catholic regions of Mount Vesuvius and Etna, communities accept risk as they interpret it as God's will and trust divine protection (Chester et al., 2008). In some settings, both Christian (Catholic) and pre-Christian animist beliefs frame disasters as divine punishment, moral tests, or cosmic balancing acts, which shape attitudes toward preparedness and fatalism (Bankoff et al., 2013).

Certain tribal communities exhibit collective behavioral adaptations based on their traditional ecological knowledge. Living in close connection with nature, they observe animal behaviors and predict disasters, thereby moving to safer places. This was evident when the Moken community, who believed in tsunamis based on ancient stories, moved away from the sea after seeing low tide (Arunotai, 2008). Such examples reflect how mass behavior can be guided by culturally transmitted knowledge systems. Region-specific cultural frameworks also shape mass coping patterns. Tsunami survivors of the Matara district in Sri Lanka reported better coping due to cultural values they uphold (Ekanayake et al., 2013). Collective mourning practices also vary widely across religious and regional contexts, and during disasters, and the disruption of these rituals may result in widespread psychological distress. Studies have shown an increase in depression and complicated grief among survivors when they have not mourned properly (Suwalowska et al., 2021). Rituals such as chanting, recitals, dance, and communal music serve not only as individual coping strategies but also as culturally sanctioned mass behaviors that facilitate emotional processing and collective healing. In some communities, prayer is collectively preferred over formal medical or psychiatric help, reflecting a shared belief system; however, such practices have not been extensively studied in disaster contexts (Goodwin et al., 2016; Wickrama et al., 2017).

Similarly, rebuilding cultural monuments in the post-disaster phase has a greater impact on community cohesion (Krüger et al., 2015). In Bangladesh, Islamic beliefs shape risk perception and collective coping. In the United States and Caribbean, religious leaders can become key actors in disaster recovery (Hoffman & Oliver-Smith, 2002). Sometimes, these beliefs lead to collective behaviors like ritualistic or organized responses, mass prayers, pilgrimages, or repentance movements, which may be mislabeled as panic (Clarke, 2002). Religious institutions (churches, mosques, temples) often become trusted social hubs as they have pre-existing communication networks and a deep reach into marginalized groups. These networks can mobilize large groups for awareness campaigns, relief efforts, early warnings, and collective action. Thus, religious beliefs can both help fill the institutional gaps as well as hinder disaster response with fatalistic beliefs and religious politics. Hence, including religious leaders in planning as well as respecting local belief systems can aid in better disaster management (Schipper, 2010).

4.3.2 Gender, Sexuality, and Cultural Norms During Disasters

Studies have shown that pre-existing cultural beliefs about gender and sexuality become particularly evident during disasters. For instance, women are often prioritized for aid, with financial assistance being more readily provided to households without male members (Arsenijević et al., 2018; Zaidi et al., 2010). Disaster planners often ignore women's roles, treating them as passive victims rather than active responders (Bradshaw & Fordham, 2013). Cultural norms related to modesty, clothing, gender segregation, and mobility significantly shape women's exposure to risk and access to support. Marginalized gender groups face even greater challenges; for example, interviews with hijra individuals after Cyclone Fani in Odisha (2019) revealed that many were denied access to shelters (Sharan & Gaillard, 2025; Trieb, 2015). These examples highlight how gender-based cultural beliefs can both facilitate and hinder disaster response, depending on the underlying value systems.

4.3.3 Cultural Patterns in Mass Help Seeking During Disasters

Cultural customs can affect mass help-seeking behavior during disasters. In some regions, including Pakistan, ambulances are culturally perceived as vehicles for the critically ill or deceased, leading to their avoidance even in emergencies. At a collective level, populations in many regions tend to rely on folk medicine and traditional healing systems rather than allopathic care, reflecting culturally sanctioned group behaviors. In many settings, magico-religious interpretations such as spirit possession continue to influence communal responses to mental health needs, often taking precedence over psychiatric explanations even in disaster contexts (Tran et al., 2019). In some regions, mass behavioral responses are guided by religious institutions and traditional leaders, who act as trusted sources of support. Churches often become emergency shelters, counseling centers, and rapid response facilitators (Fletcher et al., 2013). Cultural differences also play a role in preventive health care, where lower literacy, lack of information, and mistrust toward the healthcare system contribute to collective avoidance of preventive measures and formal interventions (Rahmani et al., 2022).

4.4 Phases of Mass Community Reactions After a Disaster (Math et al., 2015; Young et al., 1998)

These phases are commonly used to describe the emotional reactions, psychological responses, and adaptation of communities affected by a disaster, offering insights into how to provide the necessary support and resources at each stage.

1. Heroic phase (1 week): Encompasses the immediate aftermath, where the focus is on unity and collective action. Actions are directed at saving lives and providing basic needs.
2. Honeymoon phase (2–8 weeks): The early recovery period thrives on a sense of optimism that the crisis is over. People begin rebuilding their lives with assistance from governments and various aid organizations.
3. Disillusionment phase (2–8 months): Marked feelings of frustration, disappointment, and realization come into play as people realize that recovery is more difficult than anticipated. Depression, anxiety, and PTSD often rise during this time.
4. Restoration phase: The long-term recovery and rebuilding phase, which marks the return of stability and a new normal life.

4.5 Thematic Patterns of Mass Behavior

4.5.1 Looting

This refers to stealing others' goods, which happens in the post-disaster phase along with other violent crimes. Owing to the questionable availability of necessities, delayed aid, and logistical issues, people take things from others for survival, more so from evacuated homes and areas of civil unrest (Sheikhi et al., 2025).

4.5.2 Social Anarchy

Refers to the philosophy that promotes collective well-being, social equality, and cooperative economics, focusing on community and solidarity (Venkatesh, 2024). Anarchist principles like mutual aid and horizontal organization offer effective alternatives to traditional disaster response by prioritizing community response, enacting relations they wish to see, and building alternative structures within (Disaster Anarchy – Mutual Aid and Radical Action, 2022).

4.5.3 Community Resilience

When many people are affected by the same incident, they form a temporary community, which may sometimes grow and last as long as circumstantial communities. They resonate with solidarity and cohesion, exhibiting a strong will and equal participation with emergency responders despite panic, which is community resilience (Drury et al., 2013).

4.5.4 Altruism

A phenomenon in which an individual performs a seemingly selfless act for another person or a group, irrespective of a threat to self (Nagel, 1978). This behavior boosts happiness and positive emotions (Aknin & Whillans, 2021). Disasters often evoke spontaneous acts of altruism and solidarity among affected populations, often leading to widespread acts of generosity among survivors (Ultramari & Szuchman, 2017; Zaki, 2020). Various actions like volunteering (Hui et al., 1991), giving to charity (Liu & Aaker, 2008), spending money on others (Dunn et al., 2008), and small gestures such as being kind have all demonstrated an increase in community bonding (Rudd et al., 2014). Studies have shown that such strong social ties are known to influence collective behavior during disaster (Carey & Markus, 2016; Weiss-Sidi & Riemer, 2023).

Empathy, cohesion, group selection and positive experiences derived from helping others are the reasons for widespread acts of altruism during disasters (Li et al., 2023). Donations following disasters are influenced significantly by increased media exposure (Zagefka & James, 2015). On the other hand, such spontaneous acts of voluntary help can also lead to an overwhelming aid burden, incoordination, redundancy, and victim dependency (Dynes, 1994).

4.5.5 Compassion Satisfaction and Catastrophe Compassion

Both are distinctly similar yet different terms. Compassion satisfaction is the pleasure of helping others. Catastrophe compassion is a widespread and beneficial prosocial behavior observed during disasters that fosters social connection, solidarity, and shared resilience while reducing stress and loneliness (Figley, 1995; Stamm, 2010; Zaki, 2020). Higher compassion satisfaction was associated with greater resilience among disaster responders (Kınık et al., 2024). It can act as a psychological buffer, reducing the negative impact of trauma exposure and enhancing professional motivation in humanitarian aid contexts (Adwi et al., 2025). The most widely observed act of cooperation in history is social distancing, where people showed more interest in following distancing when it was framed as a way to help others than themselves (Jordan et al., 2021).

4.5.6 Compassion Fatigue

People with high levels of compassion could also develop burnout, especially the frontline workers, which becomes detrimental to the role they play, causing underutilization of resources, poor and inefficient delivery of care (Adwi et al., 2025; Dehlin & Lundh, 2018; Figley, 1995).

4.5.7 Mass Panic and Fear-Driven Behaviors

Fear-driven behaviors are actions triggered by perceived or real threat affecting an individual or a group, commonly seen in the face of a traumatic event, which modulate future harm. These behaviors can increase, decrease, act independently, or prevent harm. The level of fear depends on the magnitude and destructive potential of the threat (Espinola, 2016). Mass panic is a type of fear-related behavior; others include disaster syndrome (collective helplessness), normalcy bias, fear avoidance, panic contagion, anticipatory anxiety, and moral panic. While some collective responses, such as seeking safety and complying with official guidance, are considered constructive, others, such as uncontrolled panic, fleeing into unsafe areas, or widespread avoidance, are viewed as maladaptive behaviors (Drury et al., 2019; Kinateder et al., 2015; Zhang et al., 2022).

Mass panic is defined as an episodic irrational fear response involving loss of control that spreads among a group of people caught in serious threatening circumstances. There are three components, namely, external threat, individual perception, and observational learning. According to the social attachment model, humans seek familiar people and places during crises. The presence or absence of these attachment figures significantly influences the perceived severity of the crisis. Mass panic is more likely to arise in unfamiliar environments (e.g., tourists in a fire), where the lack of social attachment, heightened fear, and perceived entrapment collectively escalate distress and maladaptive behaviors. Common panic behaviors, such as fleeing, hoarding, or withdrawing, worsen crises by stressing supply systems, triggering financial instability, or obstructing orderly evacuations. Public safety messages and safety drills could reduce the risk of such situations (Fletcher & Aunger, 2024; Mawson, 2005).

4.5.8 Collective Coping and Help Seeking

Collective or communal coping is defined as when a group perceives a disaster as "our problem" and tackles it through shared thinking and action. The focus shifts to coping together rather than getting help. It is based on resource pooling, solidarity, and emotional buffering (Wlodarczyk et al., 2016b). Collective efficacy is the shared belief in their ability to work as a group among individuals affected by disaster, thereby fostering resilience and reducing psychological distress (Benight, 2004). Collective coping strategies such as group reflection, regulated emotional sharing, distraction, and seeking social support contribute to post-traumatic growth and social well-being. Spiritual rituals (e.g., praying, religious gatherings) and secular rituals (e.g., group vigils) were linked to communal reappraisal and well-being (Wlodarczyk et al., 2016a). Relying solely on individual coping during disasters can lead to exhaustion and hinder recovery, whereas tangible assistance (such as shelter and food) and emotional support play a critical role in buffering stress and facilitating resilience. Collective coping can be materialistic, such as rebuilding homes; based on communal sharing, morality, and wisdom; or religious. However, collective coping poses challenges such as potential dependency, social stigma, or exacerbation of inequalities (Zaumseil & Schwarz, 2014).

4.5.9 Collective Behavior During Mass Events

Mass mobilization requires the coordinated attention and collective engagement of group members. Political crowds are driven by shared identity, purpose, and emotional dynamics, which can be explained by models of social contagion. The crowd contains pre-screened ideologically aligned people whose emotions escalate easily (Petersen, 2020). Supporters act in defense of the group, and violence is framed as protecting the group rather than personal aggression. The feedback loop between enthusiastic followers and an assertive leader amplifies energy, reducing critical judgment and heightening polarization. Protester presence and confrontational chants serve to reinforce group cohesion and justify defensive aggression in real time (Taub, 2016). After events like the Grenfell Tower fire and COVID-19, shared traumatic experiences foster strong group identity, amplify perceptions of injustice, and inspire collective action through protests and mutual aid. Media amplification and official messaging can coordinate public perception, causing either solidarity rallies or triggering protests depending on perceived government performance and fairness (Kırseven & Işıklı, 2020; Vestergren et al., 2022).

In religious events like the Kumbh mela, high crowd density combined with emotional fervor leads to "serpentine" flows, group clustering, and competition for limited space. These dynamics often precede dangerous crowd pressures and potential crushes. Hajj Pilgrims who felt a strong shared identity reported higher perceived safety even in dense crowds, owing to expectations of mutual support. 79% of the stampedes in India between 1954 and 2012 occurred at religious events, claiming over 7000 lives in that period. High density, blocked exits, and poor communication create major hazards. A fatal stampede (>120 deaths) in Hathras, India, notes that crowd accidents are especially common at religious events in developing countries and calls for regulated planning, monitoring, and public education like road safety campaigns (Alnabulsi & Drury, 2014; Gayathri et al., 2020; Haghani & Feliciani, 2024; Illiyas et al., 2013; Parameswaran Kunjukrishnan & Krishnakumariamma, 2024).

4.5.10 Mass Evacuation

A mass evacuation refers to the organized removal of large populations from areas at risk due to disasters. While logistical aspects are often prioritized, evacuation planning frequently overlooks psychological and behavioral factors, which significantly influence evacuation outcomes (Leonard, 1985). Real-world evacuation data reveal that in panic situations, individuals tend to follow congested exits instead of rationally choosing less crowded ones. While moderate panic can aid evacuation flow, full-blown panic causes crowd stampedes and compressive asphyxia. Balanced panic levels, with visible alternatives and voice alerts, lead to optimal evacuation outcomes (Pecio, 2025). Evacuation behavior is often shaped by intentional cooperation, reinforcing the impact of leadership and group identity (von Sivers et al., 2016). Interviews tracking post-disaster mobility and livelihood patterns in earthquake-impacted villages of Nepal and narratives from tsunami and landslide-affected households of Srilanka identified that displacement is often semi-permanent, reshaping community structures and urbanization patterns. Evacuation is often hindered not only by the unavailable shelters or warning but also by factors such as fear of burglary, religious practices, and perceived sense of safety at home (Ahsan et al., 2016; Islam, 2023). During Cyclone Amphan in Bangladesh (2020), many coastal households faced a difficult choice between the risk of COVID-19 infection and the safety offered by cyclone shelters. Similar dilemmas were observed in Odisha and West Bengal, India, necessitating dynamic and adaptive shelter deployment strategies. These instances show that evacuation behavior is highly nuanced, shaped by both the physical threat and concerns about health safety (Alam et al., 2023). Social supports, prior disaster experience, and trust in warnings facilitate better evacuation, whereas strong social ties can both support and delay evacuation (Collins et al., 2018).

4.6 Panic Buying as Collective Behavior in Disasters

Panic buying, driven by perceived scarcity and fear, has been observed during the COVID-19 lockdown and pre-cyclone warnings, leading to surges in food, medicine, and essential supply purchases. PB is a sudden rush of shopping spree by crowds, buying more than necessary for their immediate needs (Billore & Anisimova, 2021; Brindal et al., 2022). It can be conceptualized as "the phenomenon of a sudden increase in buying of one or more essential goods in excess of regular need provoked by adversity, usually a disaster or an outbreak resulting in an imbalance between supply and demand" (Arafat et al., 2020a, c, d, e; Yasir Arafat et al., 2020).

This behavior results from complex interactions between biological, psychological, and social elements, with major factors including fear of shortage, loss of control, insecurity, distrust, and media influence (Arafat et al., 2020b; Rajkumar, 2021). Some view it as a normal reaction to an impending shortage, while others argue that shopping is an outlet for internal turmoil (Yuen et al., 2020; Zeng et al., 2020). In most instances, the behavior occurs in a collective form rather than as isolated individual acts, where the fear and urgency are influenced by various factors, resulting in a chain reaction of buying that spreads rapidly within the crowd or broader community.

4.6.1 Pathways to Panic Buying as Mass Behavior

PB often begins as an individual response but quickly evolves into a collective pattern during disasters. It is shaped by shared fears, social cues, and media influence. This section outlines how PB becomes a mass behavior through mechanisms like perceived scarcity, emotional contagion, and herd dynamics.

Scarcity as a Mass Cue

Perceived scarcity has been identified as one of the important triggers for PB after disasters. It often begins as a sudden increase in purchases, followed by a supply chain shortage. Usually, the sense of scarcity, created by uncertainty and insecurity, turns to a collective buying behavior. There is fear of loss of access to goods and anticipated regret for not purchasing in time. People imitate others' behavior, believing that if many are buying, it signals an impending shortage, thus amplifying PB collectively (Arafat et al., 2020c, 2020d; Motamed-Jahromi et al., 2021; Yuen et al., 2020). This shared sense of fear and urgency, reinforced by observing others, turns PB into a widespread, mass-level response.

Role of Media in Collective Panic

The media have an important role in triggering panic among the public by showing images of empty shelves and reporting shortages. Such coverage of stockpiling and scarcity triggers further demands for products, creating a feedback loop that causes PB. Additionally, the spread of rumors through the media contributes to misinformation and irrational consumer behavior. Acting as an information system, media interact with psychological factors such as fear, uncertainty, and perceived scarcity, influencing collective behavior at the population level. News of rising prices or product shortages can reinforce the belief that others are stockpiling, leading to herd behavior. Responsible media reporting that reassures the public is essential for managing PB as a mass behavioral response (Arafat et al., 2020c, 2020d, 2020e; Yasir Arafat et al., 2020).

Contagion Theory

Contagion theory explains PB as a mass behavior that can influence the emotions of a crowd. People are driven by collective emotions such as fear and anxiety. The behavior is often triggered and reinforced by observing others' actions, and individuals tend to imitate what others are doing, even if they initially had no intention to do so. Crowds may temporarily lose rational judgment, and the decision to buy comes from a collective emotional wave rather than individual reasoning. In this context, PB is understood as a crowd-driven mass emotional response, caused by shared fear and urgency (Putri et al., 2021; Yuen et al., 2020).

4.6.2 Implication of Panic Buying as Mass Behavior

PB was mostly observed during the early phases of the COVID-19 pandemic and had a direct impact on healthcare systems and supply chains. Media-based content analysis of PB during the COVID-19 pandemic revealed consequences such as commodity shortages, price inflation, heightened public fear, and the emergence of black markets (Arafat et al., 2020c, 2020d). It led to sudden shortages of essential items such as hand sanitizers, gloves, masks, tissue papers, and COVID-related medications (PTI, 2020; Sharma, 2020). The increased demand and resulting shortage of personal protective equipment during this period placed healthcare workers at considerable risk to their safety (World Health Organization, 2020). Apart from healthcare items, people also bought large amounts of everyday essentials like rice, oil, salt, sugar, flour, spices, soap, baby products, and packaged food (Arafat et al., 2020a, 2020c, 2020d, 2020e; Yasir Arafat et al., 2020). PB is not limited to health crises, but can also emerge as a collective response to the perceived threat of disasters such as cyclones, flood, earthquake, armed conflict, or war in South Asian context (Arafat et al., 2020c; Times News Network, 2025). Since PB occurs on a large scale and spreads quickly through communities, its impact is usually felt at the population level, as a form of collective behavior. However, there is a dearth of studies that explicitly examine PB as a mass behavior phenomenon, with most available findings extrapolated from general social observations.

4.6.3 Managing Panic Buying Within a Mass Behavior Framework

Managing PB requires understanding it not as isolated consumer acts but as a dynamic mass behavioral phenomenon influenced by collective emotions, social learning, and contextual triggers. One of the most widely discussed and emphasized preventive strategies for PB is responsible media reporting. Media coverage has the potential to either aggravate or mitigate PB, depending on how the situation is portrayed to the public (Arafat et al., 2020b; Yasir Arafat et al., 2020). Negative presentation of the reports is commonly seen in media, such as using the term "panic buying" and showing empty shelves, which could potentially increase the behavior.

Media in low- and middle-income countries are more likely to discuss rumors, impacts, and causes, but often lack balance, with fewer reports offering expert opinions or remedial measures (Yasir Arafat et al., 2020). Implementing media reporting guidelines is essential as a population-level strategy to prevent PB. Irresponsible reporting, such as showing empty shelves, long queues in front of supermarkets, and spreading unverified information, should be strictly avoided. Monitoring media content, sharing accurate information, and building public trust in the supply system are essential to break the feedback loop that keeps PB as mass behavior during disasters (Arafat et al., 2021).

The second major area is the role of government and other stakeholders. A lack of trust in authorities during disasters can trigger mass panic and collective buying behavior. The government should regularly assure the public of the uninterrupted supply of essential goods and communicate the status of stock availability. They should develop a detailed plan in advance to anticipate PB and outline measures for its regulation during disasters or health crises. Authorities need to correct false information spread through social media and other platforms. In the post-disaster phase, ensuring the smooth functioning of supply chains and visible availability of essential goods is important to reduce public fear and restore confidence among the population (Arafat et al., 2021; Arafat & Kar, 2021; Menon & Varadharajan, 2021). Raising public awareness, subsidized sales of essential goods, reducing import duties, monitoring markets, and enforcing penalties for hoarding are some of the key measures proposed for authorities to prevent PB during disasters (Arafat et al., 2022b).

Psychological measures have also been suggested to address PB, including group therapy that focuses on limiting discussions about scarcity to reduce collective anxiety. Promoting a sense of kinship and social connectedness is also recommended to foster mutual support within the community (Arafat et al., 2021; Arafat & Kar, 2021). In addition, online group cognitive behavioral therapy (CBT), when delivered in group settings such as through telepsychiatry, has been proposed as a structured intervention to address PB at a collective level by modifying shared thought patterns and behaviors, particularly during disasters and public health emergencies (Kar et al., 2020).

4.7 Case Studies on Mass Behavior from South Asia

Compared to Western countries, mass behavior in disaster settings has been less systematically studied in SA, with available literature comprising media reports, anecdotal observations, and limited epidemiological investigations, most of them demonstrating timely support even before formal aid was activated.

4.7.1 Community Response During the 2015 Nepal Earthquake

Following the 2015 deadly Nepal earthquake, with 8800 fatalities, the initial critical response came from local communities, where they rescued one another from debris, shared limited food and shelter, and organized informal support work as mutual aid, alleviating distress. Youth groups played a key role, helping in the transport of relief goods across difficult terrain, while local non-governmental agencies, in coordination with the military, the United Nations, the Government of Nepal, and 450 humanitarian agencies, deployed thousands of volunteers delivering critical aid. These efforts reflect positive collective behaviors such as altruism, compassion satisfaction, catastrophe compassion, and elements of social anarchy expressed through spontaneous community-led actions (Ovesen & Heiselberg, 2016).

4.7.2 Collective Behaviors During the 2018 Kerala Floods in India

The 2018 Kerala floods showed collective mass behavior, including rapid evacuation, mutual aid, and spontaneous rescue. Among 364 households surveyed, 93.4% evacuated quickly; 62% assisted others, 30% provided food, 2.5% offered shelter, and 56.6% helped protect animals or valuables. Only 4.4% received government aid, while many were supported by NGOs and volunteers, highlighting community resilience (Thomas et al., 2023). Fishermen also played a crucial role in rescue efforts. Of 418 surveyed, 98.6% participated in group missions, 99% driven by humanitarian motives. Despite limited training and mostly primary education, they used personal boats for rescues. Only a third had prior experience, yet 94.7% reported high satisfaction and 85.6% gained confidence (Joseph et al., 2020). These efforts reflect how community-based disaster resilience and compassion compensated for institutional gaps.

4.7.3 Case Studies of Panic Buying in South Asia

Most of the research on PB has been conducted after the COVID-19 pandemic, with more studies from India and Bangladesh (Arafat et al., 2022a). Episodes of PB have been reported in many countries worldwide after the COVID-19 pandemic (Sim et al., 2020). A study on the analysis of media reports revealed that the 1998 pre-flood rumors, the 2007 student riot curfews, and the COVID-19 pandemic in 2020 precipitated episodes of PB in Bangladesh. Each event triggered collective fears regarding the scarcity of essential goods, leading large sections of the population to stockpile food items, hygiene products, and medicines beyond regular needs (Arafat et al., 2020e). In Odisha, India, the 2024 cyclone warning led to PB as people rushed to stock up on essentials amid fears of supply disruption (PTI, 2024). A similar pattern was observed in Tamil Nadu, where past flood experiences contributed to public anxiety and prompted bulk purchasing ahead of the cyclone (The Statesman News Service, 2024). The most frequently reported triggers were perceived scarcity, increased demand, the essential nature of goods, anticipation of price hikes, and uncertainty (Arafat et al., 2020c; Motamed-Jahromi et al., 2021).

4.7.4 Patterns and Triggers of Looting After Disasters

After Cyclone Aila (2009), displaced populations in Bangladesh engaged in mass theft and violence due to economic collapse and weak governance (Azad & Khan, 2015). During the 2007 floods in Bihar and Orissa, communities looted supplies and assaulted officials (Reuters, 2007). Comparable incidents were reported during the 2015 Chennai floods, wherein flood-affected villagers forcibly intercepted relief trucks, seized supplies, and vandalized vehicles belonging to volunteers (The News Minute, 2015). The 2010 Pakistan floods saw extensive looting in Sindh and Punjab amid severe displacement (CNN, 2010). Pre-existing socioeconomic disparities, weakened state capacity, and lack of social trust amplify antisocial behaviors after disasters (Sheikhi et al., 2025).

4.7.5 Violence and Civil Unrest in Post-Disaster Contexts

Violence following natural disasters has been reported in SA, though systematic studies on civil unrest remain scarce. Available evidence largely comes from media accounts. During the 2014 Bihar floods, people protested delays in relief by attacking officials and blocking roads (Gupta, 2014). A similar response followed Cyclone Yemyin in 2007, when flood-affected residents in Turbat, Pakistan, vandalized the mayor's office and clashed with police over the lack of aid (CBC News, 2007). In the aftermath of the 2015 Nepal earthquake, frustration over the slow government response led to clashes in Kathmandu, where survivors rioted and damaged public property (NDTV, 2015).

Such maladaptive behaviors are context-specific, often arising in settings of inequality, weak governance, and social tension, and may be triggered by sensationalized media narratives. On the ground, however, collective behaviors such as cooperation, mutual aid, and altruism are more common among disaster survivors (Milsten et al., 2024).

4.7.6 COVID-19 and Mass Behavior

The COVID-19 pandemic prompted significant mass behavioral shifts, largely driven by fear of infection, self-motivation, health promotion efforts, and government regulations. The population actively adopted preventive measures such as hand hygiene, mask use, physical distancing, and cough etiquette. Practices like avoiding handshakes, public gatherings, and spitting in public became widely observed. The crisis also reshaped aspects of daily life, encouraging home-cooked food, using community kitchens, work-from-home arrangements, and increased use of digital platforms, including telemedicine. These behaviors were not adopted in isolation, but rather emerged as a collective phenomenon influenced by shared perceptions and social norms (Gupta et al., 2021). During the pandemic, people across various parts of India clapped and applauded together from their homes at a government-designated time to express gratitude toward healthcare workers, a gesture that was also observed in other countries (Manthorpe et al., 2022; Tiwari, 2020). Another major form of mass behavior observed during the pandemic in India was the mass migration of urban migrant workers to rural areas following the nationwide lockdown. Without transport or support, thousands moved together on foot, by bicycle, and in trucks, demonstrating how shared distress and uncertainty can lead to spontaneous collective action (Pillai, 2024; Sahoo et al., 2022). These examples during the pandemic show how people responded not just as individuals, but as a collective shaped by common fears, needs, and the urge to support one another.

5 Management of Mass Behaviors During Disasters

The definition of disaster management as per the Disaster Management Act, 2005, is "*a continuous and integrated process of planning, organising, coordinating and implementing measures which are necessary or expedient*" which broadly includes mitigation, prevention, response/rescue, and the recovery phases. Mental health professionals (MHPs, which include psychiatrists, psychologists, and psychiatric social workers) are crucial in providing care, advocacy, training, and rehabilitation activities (Government of India, 2005; National Disaster Management Authority (NDMA), 2025).

Disasters, whether natural or manmade, have a cascading effect on mental illness. They undermine the fundamental sense of safety and stability expected by any community, overwhelming coping mechanisms, and leading to widespread emotional and social disruption.

Community's reaction after a disaster follows four psychological phases: heroic phase (days to weeks—survivors display altruism, collective resilience, cooperation), honeymoon phase (2–4 weeks—relief efforts and media/VIP attention fostering hope and trust), disillusionment phase (3–36 months—administrative delays, limited resources, disappointment due to broken promises), and restoration phase (marks gradual recovery).

Mental health interventions regarding mass behaviors can be categorized into primary (preventive/before disaster), secondary (heroic, honeymoon, and disillusionment phase), and tertiary interventions (restoration phase) (Math et al., 2015) (Fig. 15.1).

Effective disaster management starts before a disaster strikes, especially in areas prone to natural disasters or war-torn regions. The physical and economic impacts of disasters often precede their psychological and social effects. The most common disorders that arise in the aftermath of a disaster include adjustment disorder,

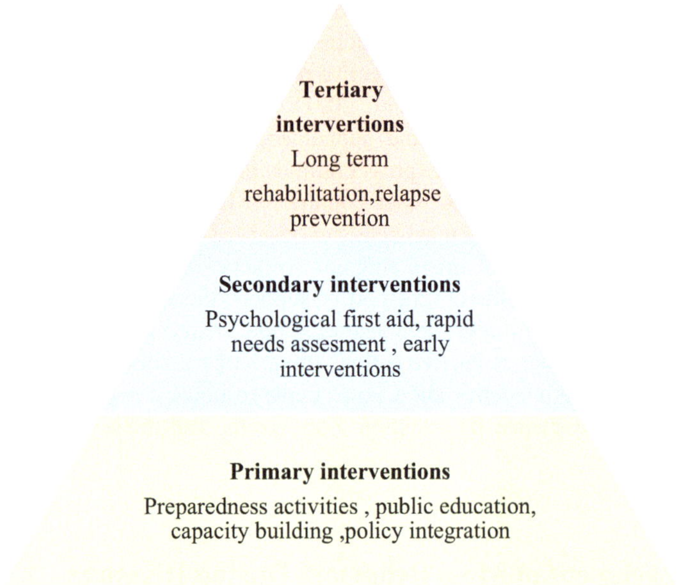

Fig. 15.1 Three-tiered mental health intervention model in disaster settings

anxiety and depressive disorders, PTSD, substance use disorders, and the exacerbation of pre-existing conditions.

Vulnerable groups include women, children, the elderly (particularly those who are medically ill), marginalized communities like LGBTQ+ individuals, and impoverished populations. These disorders frequently arise in a collective manner, shaped by shared emotional responses, disrupted community dynamics, and social contagion. As such, they are best understood through the lens of mass behavior, including collective panic, grief, displacement, and institutional distrust, rather than solely as individual psychopathology.

Several psychosocial factors contribute to its vulnerability, including loss of family members, disruption of social networks, resources, and mistrust in the government (Murthy, 2018). Mass behavior usually involves psychological responses shared by large groups who may not be present together. It is shaped by collective experience, media influence, and social contagion and is more relevant in the disillusionment and restoration phase.

A closely related yet distinct concept is crowd behavior, which refers to actions of individuals physically gathered in a shared place and acting under a heightened collective emotion (Drury, 2020). This becomes relevant in the heroic and the honeymoon phase when people gather for rescue, support, or resource distribution. Managing crowd behaviors during disasters is primarily the responsibility of local or district authorities, guided by protocols and support from state and national authorities. Hence, crowd behavior and its management are not discussed here as they fall outside the scope of this chapter.

Also, there is limited literature specifically addressing disaster-related management of mass behavior; therefore, this chapter extrapolates from general disaster mental health principles to contextualize mass behaviors (World Health Organization & UNHCR, 2015).

5.1 Primary Interventions

Primary interventions serve as universal preventive strategies that occur well before a disaster strikes, particularly in high-risk areas during the preparedness phase. These interventions include governmental strategies, policy-level initiatives, capacity building, and trauma-informed approaches.

5.1.1 Government and Policy-Level Interventions

Governments play a critical role across all phases of a disaster—from preparedness and prevention to response and recovery. Their actions directly influence relief measures and the long-term resilience of affected populations. Additionally, the past experiences of communities in disaster-prone areas significantly shape their perception, preparedness, and behavior during future crises.

Well-designed policies and frameworks need to be in place, which, apart from enhancing preparedness, will foster a sense of hope and trust within communities. For instance, during the COVID-19 pandemic, mass behaviors such as panic buying emerged and were driven by uncertainty, fear, and eroding trust in authorities (Yuen et al., 2020). A few broad strategies that governments can adopt include:

Transparent Communication

Timely and accurate information dissemination via appropriate government channels or ministries is vital. It must include information on

- Local preparedness efforts
- Designated contact personnel
- Availability of adequate essential goods
- Assurance of supply chain continuity

Community Awareness

These aim to shape public behavior during crises through mass communication. Social media and news channels can be utilized by involving trusted local leaders or celebrities to address responsible practices such as avoiding PB, and counter misinformation. It involves interactive, localized efforts to engage the community in disaster preparedness. The community's helplessness can be reduced by offering suitable warnings and directing resources toward creating protocols that train individuals to respond, triage, and recognize various roles among them. Implementing regular awareness and outreach initiatives about typical responses to threats or disasters is essential to lessen the anxiety that may occur. Unlike broader education campaigns, these efforts are hands-on and aim to empower communities through knowledge and participation.

Capacity Building

Disaster management is analogous to democracy in that it is conducted by the people, for the people, and of the people. Consequently, it is imperative to enhance the capacity of non-governmental organizations (NGOs) and community health workers in regions prone to disasters. Such capacity building ensures that these stakeholders are adequately prepared to respond effectively to emergencies.

This can be achieved through various strategies:

1. **Regular mock drills:** These exercises should simulate both logistical and psychological scenarios, including PB and the dissemination of misinformation.
2. **Information, education, and communication initiatives:** It is beneficial to employ visual aids, posters, and mobile outreach vans equipped with videos that address emotional preparedness in the local languages.
3. **Basic disaster communication and psychological first aid training:** Providing training in these areas is essential to enable individuals to support those affected during disasters.
4. **Promotion of mutual assistance through peer support systems:** Fostering a culture of community support enhances overall resilience.

Currently, there exists a significant gap in efforts aimed at mental health preparedness in the context of disasters, which warrants immediate attention (Sutar et al., 2022).

5.1.2 Trauma-Informed Approaches

A trauma-informed approach (TIA) is an organizational and clinical framework that acknowledges the long-term impact of trauma and integrates this understanding into the management of disaster survivors. The approach aims at fostering resilience, promoting psychological safety, and empowerment in communities that experience disaster. It is achieved by the following components: realizing and recognizing the trauma and related responses, resisting re-traumatization by promoting peer and community supports, ensuring physical and emotional safety, and empowering people based on the gender, cultural, and historical contexts of the community (Murthy, 2018).

TIA has been specifically advocated for children, as one of the most vulnerable groups, who frequently experience disruptions in attachment, behavior, cognitive functioning, emotions, and sleep patterns. These disruptions can present as nightmares, social withdrawal, declining academic performance, and developmental regression. Experiencing disasters in childhood is classified as an adverse childhood experience (ACE), which has a strong connection to mental health issues in adulthood (Kar, 2009; Sasaki et al., 2024).

In the context of management of mass behaviors, this approach enables service providers, especially those involved in health, education, and social services, to create spaces that promote recovery rather than retraumatize. Although the components of TIA are broadly similar to the psychological first aid (PFA) described under secondary interventions described below, TIA represents a more comprehensive system-wide approach that extends beyond immediate crisis to reshape how services can be effectively delivered across the community.

5.1.3 Use of Creative Arts

The use of creative arts as a valuable non-verbal tool in a trauma-informed approach has been advocated, as it promotes self-expression, helps externalize feelings, enhances sensory processing, and builds trust with the service provider.

5.2 Secondary Interventions

This section addresses the essential interventions that must be implemented immediately following a disaster (heroic and honeymoon phase). Vulnerable groups, including children, the elderly, individuals with medical conditions, pregnant women, impoverished populations, and refugees, are primarily the focus of these secondary interventions. The MHP is required to perform a rapid needs assessment, which encompasses evaluating the psychological impacts, identifying available mental health resources, understanding the sociocultural and religious perspectives of the community, recognizing high-risk populations, facilitating community grieving processes, collaborating with administrative officials, and establishing referral and outreach programs for stress management. A critical resource in the immediate aftermath of a disaster is psychological first aid (PFA).

5.2.1 Psychological First Aid

Psychological first aid (PFA) is a compassionate and non-intrusive method designed to assist individuals experiencing distress, particularly during or immediately following a crisis. It is widely recognized as one of the most evidence-based practices in mental health support and was first articulated by Rapheal in 1986. The primary objective of PFA is to alleviate immediate suffering and to prevent the development of potential psychological issues in the future.

The fundamental principles of PFA encompass the following:

1. Providing practical care and support.
2. Identifying urgent needs, such as food, water, and shelter.
3. Listening attentively without exerting pressure on individuals to communicate.
4. Offering comfort to facilitate relaxation.
5. Connecting individuals with relevant information and support groups to enhance their sense of control.
6. Making appropriate referrals and ensuring the safety of those in distress.

In particular, for children, it is crucial to reunite them with family members as soon as possible. PFA is not confined to mental health professionals; any member of the community, such as school teachers, lay counselors, or local leaders, can be taught to provide it. It's important to distinguish PFA from psychological debriefing, which involves individuals expressing their emotions, perceptions, and thoughts related to trauma and is not the same as PFA (Ali & Weltgesundheitsorganisation, 2011).

5.2.2 Strengths-Based Approach

The strength-based approach emphasizes the MHP's focus on the existing capabilities, coping skills, and resilience of children affected by trauma, rather than solely on the psychological problems or symptoms.

Community engagement is a central aspect of this approach. In many South Asian countries, strong social networks and shared cultural identities exist, which serve as a buffer against distress. This can be utilized by MHPs to collaborate with community leaders to integrate culturally rooted practices such as folk art, music, and storytelling. These can facilitate emotional expression, alleviate stigma, and encourage collective recovery. This can be achieved through local volunteers from various NGOs, school teachers, and primary healthcare workers, who can amplify the reach and sustainability of interventions. This approach empowers them to see themselves as active agents in their recovery process and facilitates healing, establishing a foundation for long-term resilience and well-being.

5.2.3 Retailer-Level Interventions

Retailers, both public and private, play a critical frontline role in mitigating the anxiety-driven hoarding of essential goods. Key strategies include:

- Staggered time slots to the outlets (special time for the vulnerable groups, like the elderly)
- Prioritized and visible stocking of essential commodities to reinforce availability

- Implementation of purchase limits on high-demand items to promote equitable access
- Train staff to recognize anxiety among individuals by engaging them calmly
- Culturally tailored messages/hoardings/videos via social media using local languages by local leaders, influencers, and celebrities repeatedly in retail outlets

All these strategies can lessen the perceived anxiety, enhance trust by reducing uncertainty, and decrease irrational consumption behavior.

5.2.4 Nonspecific Community Interventions

There are several nonspecific community interventions that can help alleviate distress among disaster survivors. These include:

- Restoring daily activities
- Encouraging participation in relief work
- Reopening schools as soon as possible
- Promoting healthy habits, such as sleep hygiene techniques
- Educating individuals on the importance of avoiding substance use.

Although trauma-focused cognitive behavioral techniques and eye movement desensitization and reprocessing have been effective in preventing the development of post-traumatic stress disorder (PTSD) following a disaster in group settings, these have not been specifically evaluated or used for mass behaviors.

5.2.5 Use of Psychotropics

Post-disaster behaviors are often regarded as typical emotional responses from ordinary individual groups, which are generally self-limiting. Therefore, it is usually best to avoid the prophylactic use of psychotropic medications. Research does not indicate that these drugs are effective in reducing subsequent psychiatric comorbidities.

5.3 Tertiary Interventions

The primary area of focus of tertiary interventions is the restorative phase, focusing on the long-term rehabilitation, recovery, and prevention of chronic psychological states. It overlaps with the secondary interventions wherein the establishment of outreach camps and referral systems is assessed, and feedback mechanisms are in place to enhance the care. The capacity-building activities mentioned earlier need to be continued. Encouraging and engaging survivors in participation in religious, cultural, and spiritual practices through the local social networks fosters community resilience and strengthens collective consciousness (Kar, 2010; Math et al., 2015; Murthy, 2018).

It is crucial to recognize that disaster management involves not just mental health professionals but also various medical specialties and allied health practitioners as key stakeholders. Community members, including disaster survivors, teachers, and local religious leaders, play significant roles. For instance, the Kerala floods highlight this involvement, demonstrating community solidarity and resilience that extended beyond the initial heroic and honeymoon phase (Murthy, 2018). It is also important to note that those managing mass behaviors also deal with considerable stress while providing relief, and they too must be monitored for signs of burnout and trauma (Math et al., 2015).

The guidelines put forth by South Asian countries, like the National Disaster Management Training Module, Disaster Mental Health Services—Module 4 (India), have highlighted the need for and outlined the role of mental health services in the aftermath of a disaster and the preventive efforts required (Disaster Mental Health Services, 2023). Most of these guidelines are framed by the recommendations of the Inter Agency Steering Committee (IASC) on mental health and psychosocial support in emergency settings, 2007 (Carll, 2008).

In conclusion, the psychological impact of disasters extends far beyond the immediate aftermath, affecting individuals, communities, and societal structures. Effective management of mass behaviors and mental health consequences during disasters requires a multi-tiered approach, from prevention to long-term rehabilitation. Community integration is essential, as culturally anchored, participatory interventions foster resilience, reduce stigma, and promote sustained recovery. Embedding mental health support within broader disaster management frameworks mitigates distress and strengthens the social fabric, enabling communities to emerge stronger in the face of adversity (Kar, 2010; Murthy, 2018).

6 Conclusion

Disasters disrupt social systems, affect mental health, and influence collective human behavior. In a disaster-prone region like SA, understanding disaster patterns, their effects on mental health, and how communities respond is essential. This chapter explored the epidemiology of disasters, associated psychiatric outcomes, and mass behaviors that emerge in their aftermath. While communities often display positive behaviors such as altruism, mutual support, and resilience, disasters can also lead to adverse responses such as PB, violence, and looting when there are perceived insecurity, institutional mistrust, and unmet basic needs. Strengthening mental health support systems and incorporating behavioral insights into disaster planning can help address these issues. Sustainable, long-term solutions must focus on local contexts, capacity building, and be guided by evidence-based strategies. Policymakers should ensure timely communication, equitable resource distribution, and effective implementation of policies to strengthen disaster preparedness and support community recovery.

References

2014 Annual Report | Pages | WWF. (2014). World Wildlife Fund. https://www.worldwildlife.org/pages/2014-annual-report

Abbas, S., Abbas, H. S. M., & Zhang, Y. (2024). Psychological implications of man-made trauma and efficacy of "Teaching Recovery Techniques" on children and adolescents exposed to trauma. *European Journal of Trauma & Dissociation, 8*(2), 100397. https://doi.org/10.1016/j.ejtd.2024.100397

Adwi, M., Abdellatif, N., Sadek, I., & Elsheikh, M. (2025). Compassion satisfaction and fatigue in humanitarian aid workers. *Frontiers in Psychology*. https://doi.org/10.3389/fpsyg.2025.1522092

Ahmad, S., Feder, A., Lee, E. J., Wang, Y., Southwick, S. M., Schlackman, E., Buchholz, K., Alonso, A., & Charney, D. S. (2010). Earthquake impact in a remote South Asian population: Psychosocial factors and posttraumatic symptoms. *Journal of Traumatic Stress, 23*(3), 408–412. https://doi.org/10.1002/jts.20535

Ahsan, M. N., Takeuchi, K., Vink, K., & Warner, J. (2016). Factors affecting the evacuation decisions of coastal households during Cyclone Aila in Bangladesh. *Environmental Hazards, 15*(1), 16–42. https://doi.org/10.1080/17477891.2015.1114912

Aknin, L. B., & Whillans, A. V. (2021). Helping and happiness: A review and guide for public policy. *Social Issues and Policy Review, 15*(1), 3–34. https://doi.org/10.1111/sipr.12069

Alam, M. S., Chakraborty, T., Hossain, M. Z., & Rahaman, K. R. (2023). Evacuation dilemmas of coastal households during cyclone Amphan and amidst the COVID-19 pandemic: A study of the Southwestern region of Bangladesh. *Natural Hazards (Dordrecht, Netherlands), 115*(1), 507–537. https://doi.org/10.1007/s11069-022-05564-9

Ali, M., & Weltgesundheitsorganisation (Eds.). (2011). *Psychological first aid: Guide for field workers*. WHO.

Ali, M., Farooq, N., Bhatti, M. A., & Kuroiwa, C. (2012). Assessment of prevalence and determinants of posttraumatic stress disorder in survivors of earthquake in Pakistan using Davidson Trauma Scale. *Journal of Affective Disorders, 136*(3), 238–243. https://doi.org/10.1016/j.jad.2011.12.023

Alnabulsi, H., & Drury, J. (2014). Social identification moderates the effect of crowd density on safety at the Hajj. *Proceedings of the National Academy of Sciences of the United States of America, 111*(25), 9091–9096. https://doi.org/10.1073/pnas.1404953111

Aneelraj, D., Kumar, C. N., Somanathan, R., Chandran, D., Joshi, S., Paramita, P., Kasi, S., Bangalore, R. N., & Math, S. B. (2016). Uttarakhand disaster 2013: A report on psychosocial adversities experienced by children and adolescents. *Indian Journal of Pediatrics, 83*(4), 316–321. https://doi.org/10.1007/s12098-015-1921-1

Arafat, S. M. Y., & Kar, S. K. (2021). Prevention of panic buying during public health emergency. *Asia-Pacific Journal of Public Health, 33*(5), 685–686. https://doi.org/10.1177/10105395211014699

Arafat, S. M. Y., Hussain, F., Kar, S. K., Menon, V., & Yuen, K. F. (2020a). How far has panic buying been studied? *World Journal of Meta-Analysis, 8*(6), 447–461. https://doi.org/10.13105/wjma.v8.i6.447

Arafat, S. M. Y., Kar, S. K., Marthoenis, M., Sharma, P., Hoque Apu, E., & Kabir, R. (2020b). Psychological underpinning of panic buying during pandemic (COVID-19). *Psychiatry Research, 289*, 113061. https://doi.org/10.1016/j.psychres.2020.113061

Arafat, S. M. Y., Kar, S. K., Menon, V., Alradie-Mohamed, A., Mukherjee, S., Kaliamoorthy, C., & Kabir, R. (2020c). Responsible factors of panic buying: An observation from online media reports. *Frontiers in Public Health, 8*, 603894. https://doi.org/10.3389/fpubh.2020.603894

Arafat, S. M. Y., Kar, S. K., Menon, V., Kaliamoorthy, C., Mukherjee, S., Alradie-Mohamed, A., Sharma, P., Marthoenis, M., & Kabir, R. (2020d). Panic buying: An insight from the content analysis of media reports during COVID-19 pandemic. *Neurology, Psychiatry and Brain Research, 37*, 100–103. https://doi.org/10.1016/j.npbr.2020.07.002

Arafat, S. M. Y., Yuen, K. F., Menon, V., Shoib, S., & Ahmad, A. R. (2020e). Panic buying in Bangladesh: An exploration of media reports. *Frontiers in Psychiatry, 11*, 628393. https://doi.org/10.3389/fpsyt.2020.628393

Arafat, S. M. Y., Kar, S. K., & Kabir, R. (2021). Possible controlling measures of panic buying during COVID-19. *International Journal of Mental Health and Addiction, 19*(6), 2289–2291. https://doi.org/10.1007/s11469-020-00320-1

Arafat, S. M. Y., Kumar Kar, S., Singh, R., Menon, V., Sathian, B., & Kabir, R. (2022a). Panic buying research: A bibliometric review. *Nepal Journal of Epidemiology, 12*(3), 1224–1230. https://doi.org/10.3126/nje.v12i3.43436

Arafat, S. M. Y., Singh, R., Menon, V., & Yuen, K. F. (2022b). Prevention strategies of panic buying during disaster. In S. M. Y. Arafat, S. Kumar Kar, & R. Kabir (Eds.), *Panic buying and environmental disasters: management and mitigation approaches* (pp. 211–231). Springer International Publishing. https://doi.org/10.1007/978-3-031-10278-3_12

Arsenijević, J., Burtscher, D., Ponthieu, A., Severy, N., Contenta, A., Moissaing, S., Argenziano, S., Zamatto, F., Zachariah, R., Ali, E., & Venables, E. (2018). "I feel like I am less than other people": Health-related vulnerabilities of male migrants travelling alone on their journey to Europe. *Social Science & Medicine, 1982*(209), 86–94. https://doi.org/10.1016/j.socscimed.2018.05.038

Aseem, A., Chaudhry, N., & Hussain, M. E. (2022). Cranial electrostimulation improves slow wave sleep in collegiate population: A polysomnographic study. *Sleep Science (Sao Paulo, Brazil), 15*(1), 88–94. https://doi.org/10.5935/1984-0063.20220029

Asian Disaster Reduction Center (ADRC). (2023). https://www.adrc.asia/publications/databook/DB2023_e.php

Asim, M., Sathian, B., van Teijlingen, E., Mekkodathil, A. A., Babu, M. G. R., Rajesh, E., N, R. K., Simkhada, P., & Banerjee, I. (2022). A survey of post-traumatic stress disorder, anxiety and depression among flood affected populations in Kerala, India. *Nepal Journal of Epidemiology, 12*(2), 1203–1214. https://doi.org/10.3126/nje.v12i2.46334

Ayub, M., Poongan, I., Masood, K., Gul, H., Ali, M., Farrukh, A., Shaheen, A., Chaudhry, H. R., & Naeem, F. (2012). Psychological morbidity in children 18 months after Kashmir earthquake of 2005. *Child Psychiatry and Human Development, 43*(3), 323–336. https://doi.org/10.1007/s10578-011-0267-9

Ayub, M., Saeed, K., Kingdon, D., & Naeem, F. (2015). Rate and predictors of psychotic symptoms after Kashmir earthquake. *European Archives of Psychiatry and Clinical Neuroscience, 265*(6), 471–481. https://doi.org/10.1007/s00406-014-0561-1

Azad, M. A. K., & Khan, M. M. (2015). Post disasters social pathology in Bangladesh: A case study on AILA affected areas. *Sociology and Anthropology, 3*(2), 85–94. https://doi.org/10.13189/sa.2015.030203

Bandla, S., Nappinnai, N. R., & Gopalasamy, S. (2019). Psychiatric morbidity in December 2015 flood-affected population in Tamil Nadu, India. *The International Journal of Social Psychiatry, 65*(4), 338–344. https://doi.org/10.1177/0020764019846166

Bankoff, G., Frerks, G., & Hilhorst, D. (Eds.). (2013). *Mapping vulnerability: Disasters, development and people*. Routledge. https://doi.org/10.4324/9781849771924

Baral, I. A., & Bhagawati, K. C. (2019). Post-traumatic stress disorder and coping strategies among adult survivors of earthquake, Nepal. *BMC Psychiatry, 19*(1), 118. https://doi.org/10.1186/s12888-019-2090-y

Baytiyeh, H., & K. Naja, M. (2014). Can education reduce Middle Eastern fatalistic attitude regarding earthquake disasters? *Disaster Prevention And Management, 23*(4), 343–355. https://doi.org/10.1108/DPM-12-2013-0219

Beaglehole, B., Mulder, R. T., Frampton, C. M., Boden, J. M., Newton-Howes, G., & Bell, C. J. (2018). Psychological distress and psychiatric disorder after natural disasters: Systematic review and meta-analysis. *The British Journal of Psychiatry: the Journal of Mental Science, 213*(6), 716–722. https://doi.org/10.1192/bjp.2018.210

Benight, C. C. (2004). Collective efficacy following a series of natural disasters. *Anxiety, Stress & Coping, 17*(4), 401–420. https://doi.org/10.1080/10615800512331328768

Billore, S., & Anisimova, T. (2021). *Panic buying research: A systematic literature review and future research agenda* (SSRN Scholarly Paper 3808305). Social Science Research Network. https://papers.ssrn.com/abstract=3808305

Bonner, H. (1953). Mass behavior. In *Social psychology: An interdisciplinary approach* (pp. 378–403). American Book Company. https://doi.org/10.1037/13212-014

Bradshaw, S., & Fordham, M. (2013). *Women, girls and disasters: A review for DFID*. UK Department for International Development. https://www.gov.uk/research-for-development-outputs/women-girls-and-disasters-a-review-for-dfid

Braga, L. L., Fiks, J. P., Mari, J. J., & Mello, M. F. (2008). The importance of the concepts of disaster, catastrophe, violence, trauma and barbarism in defining posttraumatic stress disorder in clinical practice. *BMC Psychiatry, 8*(1), 68. https://doi.org/10.1186/1471-244X-8-68

Brindal, E., Kakoschke, N., Reeson, A., & Evans, D. (2022). Madness of the crowd: Understanding mass behaviors through a multidisciplinary lens. *Frontiers in Psychology, 13*, 924511.

Cantril, H. (1941). *The psychology of social movements*. Wiley.

Carey, R. M., & Markus, H. R. (2016). Understanding consumer psychology in working-class contexts. *Journal of Consumer Psychology, 26*(4), 568–582. https://doi.org/10.1016/j.jcps.2016.08.004

Carll, E. K. (2008). *IASC guidelines on mental health and psychosocial support in emergency settings* [Dataset]. https://doi.org/10.1037/e518422011-002

CBC News. (2007, June 29). Pakistani villagers hit by floods riot after little or no help arrives. *CBC News*. https://www.cbc.ca/news/world/pakistani-villagers-hit-by-floods-riot-after-little-or-no-help-arrives-1.635587

Centre for Excellence in Disaster Management and Humanitarian Assistance. (2024). https://www.cfe-dmha.org/LinkClick.aspx?fileticket=JcJqafHgiTU%3d&portalid=0

Centre for Research on the Epidemiology of Disasters (CRED). (2024). *2024 EMDAT report: The Human Cost of Disasters*. CRED, Université catholique de Louvain. https://files.emdat.be/reports/2024_EMDAT_report.pdf.

Chadda, R. K., Malhotra, A., Kaw, N., Singh, J., & Sethi, H. (2007). Mental health problems following the 2005 earthquake in Kashmir: Findings of community-run clinics. *Prehospital and Disaster Medicine, 22*(6), 541–545; discussion 546. https://doi.org/10.1017/s1049023x00005409

Chartoff, S. E., Kropp, A. M., & Roman, P. (2025). Disaster planning. In *StatPearls*. StatPearls Publishing. http://www.ncbi.nlm.nih.gov/books/NBK470570/

Chester, D. K., Duncan, A. M., & Dibben, C. J. L. (2008). The importance of religion in shaping volcanic risk perception in Italy, with special reference to Vesuvius and Etna. *Journal of Volcanology and Geothermal Research, 172*(3), 216–228. https://doi.org/10.1016/j.jvolgeores.2007.12.009

Christodoulou, N. (2024). Disaster psychiatry: An urgent field in psychiatry posing a pertinent question. *Psychiatrike = Psychiatriki, 35*(4), 265–268. https://doi.org/10.22365/jpsych.2024.022

Clarke, L. (2002). Panic: Myth or reality? *Contexts, 1*(3), 21–26.

CNN. (2010, August 18). Reports of looting, violence surface in flood-ravaged Pakistan. *CNN*. https://edition.cnn.com/2010/WORLD/asiapcf/08/17/pakistan.floods/index.html

Collins, J., Ersing, R., Polen, A., Saunders, M., & Senkbeil, J. (2018). The effects of social connections on evacuation decision making during Hurricane Irma. *Weather, Climate, and Society*. https://doi.org/10.1175/WCAS-D-17-0119.1

Cruz, R. V., Harasawa, H., Lal, M., Wu, S., Anokhin, Y., Punsalmaa, B., Honda, Y., Jafari, M., Li, C., & Huu Ninh, N. (2007). Asia. In M. L. Parry, O. F. Canziani, J. P. Palutikof, P. J. van der Linden, & C. E. Hanson (Eds.), *Climate change 2007: Impacts, adaptation and vulnerability. Contribution of Working Group II to the fourth assessment report of the Intergovernmental Panel on Climate Change* (pp. 469–506). Cambridge University Press.

Das, A., & Swain, P. K. (2024). Navigating the sea level rise: Exploring the interplay of climate change, sea level rise, and coastal communities in India. *Environmental Monitoring and Assessment, 196*(11), 1010. https://doi.org/10.1007/s10661-024-13191-z

Dehlin, M., & Lundh, L.-G. (2018). Compassion fatigue and compassion satisfaction among psychologists: Can supervision and a reflective stance be of help? *Journal for Person-Oriented Research, 4*(2), 95–107. https://doi.org/10.17505/jpor.2018.09

Disaster Anarchy—Mutual Aid and Radical Action. (2022). http://archive.org/details/oapen-20.500.12657-57974

Disaster Mental Health Services. (2023). *National disaster management training module-4*. National Institute of Disaster Management, Ministry of Home Affairs, Government of India.

Drury, J. (2020). Recent developments in the psychology of crowds and collective behaviour. *Current Opinion in Psychology, 35*, 12–16. https://doi.org/10.1016/j.copsyc.2020.02.005

Drury, J., Novelli, D., & Stott, C. (2013). Representing crowd behaviour in emergency planning guidance: 'Mass panic' or collective resilience? *Resilience, 1*(1), 18–37. https://doi.org/10.1080/21693293.2013.765740

Drury, J., Carter, H., Cocking, C., Ntontis, E., Tekin Guven, S., & Amlôt, R. (2019). Facilitating collective psychosocial resilience in the public in emergencies: Twelve recommendations based on the social identity approach. *Frontiers in Public Health, 7*, 141. https://doi.org/10.3389/fpubh.2019.00141

Dunn, E. W., Aknin, L. B., & Norton, M. I. (2008). Spending money on others promotes happiness. *Science, 319*(5870), 1687–1688. https://doi.org/10.1126/science.1150952

Dynes, R. R. (1994). *Situational altruism: Toward an explanation of pathologies in disaster assistance* (Preliminary Papers, pp. 1–15).

Ehring, T., Razik, S., & Emmelkamp, P. M. G. (2011). Prevalence and predictors of posttraumatic stress disorder, anxiety, depression, and burnout in Pakistani earthquake recovery workers. *Psychiatry Research, 185*(1–2), 161–166. https://doi.org/10.1016/j.psychres.2009.10.018

Ekanayake, S., Prince, M., Sumathipala, A., Siribaddana, S., & Morgan, C. (2013). "We lost all we had in a second": Coping with grief and loss after a natural disaster. *World Psychiatry, 12*(1), 69–75. https://doi.org/10.1002/wps.20018

Espinola, M. (2016). Fear-related behaviors in situations of mass threat. *Disaster Health, 3*, 102.

Figley, C. R. (1995). *Compassion fatigue: Coping with secondary traumatic stress disorder in those who treat the traumatized*. Brunner/Mazel. https://www.amazon.com/Compassion-Fatigue-Traumatic-Treated-Traumatized/dp/1556237553

Fitch, T., Villanueva, G., Quadir, M. M., Sagiraju, H. K. R., & Alamgir, H. (2015). The prevalence and risk factors of post-traumatic stress disorder among workers injured in Rana Plaza building collapse in Bangladesh. *American Journal of Industrial Medicine, 58*(7), 756–763. https://doi.org/10.1002/ajim.22471

Fletcher, H. W., & Aunger, R. (2024). Understanding mass panic. *Journal of Applied Social Science, 18*(2), 288–308. https://doi.org/10.1177/19367244241245702

Fletcher, S. M., Thiessen, J., Gero, A., Rumsey, M., Kuruppu, N., & Willetts, J. (2013). Traditional coping strategies and disaster response: Examples from the South Pacific region. *Journal of Environmental and Public Health, 2013*, 264503. https://doi.org/10.1155/2013/264503

Fowlkes, M. R., & Miller, P. Y. (1983). *Love canal: The social construction of disaster*. Federal Emergency Management Agency.

Freud, S. (1921). *Group psychology and the analysis of the ego*. Internationaler Psychoanalytischer Verlag. https://archive.org/details/grouppsychology00freu

Gaillard, J. C., & Texier, P. (2010). Religions, natural hazards, and disasters: An introduction. *Religion, 40*(2), 81–84. https://doi.org/10.1016/j.religion.2009.12.001

Gayathri, H., Gulhare, S., & Verma, A. (2020). Understanding crowd dynamics in processions during mass religious gatherings a case study of Shahi Snan in Kumbh Mela. *Collective Dynamics, 5*, 403–412. https://doi.org/10.17815/CD.2020.76

Gianisa, A., & Le De, L. (2018). The role of religious beliefs and practices in disaster. *Disaster Prevention and Management, 27*(1), 74–86. https://doi.org/10.1108/DPM-10-2017-0238

Global assessment report on disaster risk reduction (2009). | UNDRR. (2009, May 15). https://www.undrr.org/publication/global-assessment-report-disaster-risk-reduction-2009

Global Forum on Migration and Development (GFMD). (2024). *Bangladesh: Disaster Risk Reduction and Climate Resilience*. GFMD Platform for Partnerships. https://www.gfmd.org/pfp/ppd/19341

Global risks 2014: Ninth edition | PreventionWeb. (2014, January 17). https://www.preventionweb.net/publication/global-risks-2014-ninth-edition

Goodwin, J., Savage, E., & Horgan, A. (2016). Adolescents' and young adults' beliefs about mental health services and care: A systematic review. *Archives of Psychiatric Nursing, 30*(5), 636–644. https://doi.org/10.1016/j.apnu.2016.04.004

Government of India. (2005). *Disaster Management Act, 2005 (Act No. 53 of 2005)*. Ministry of Home Affairs. https://www.mha.gov.in/sites/default/files/The%20Disaster%20Management%20Act%2C%202005.pdf

Government of Nepal. (2017). *Disaster Risk Reduction and Management Act, 2074 (2017)*. Ministry of Home Affairs. https://bipad.gov.np/uploads/publication_pdf/DRRM_Act_and_Regulation_english.pdf

Government of the Islamic Republic of Pakistan. (2010). *National Disaster Management Act, 2010 (Act No. XXIV of 2010)*. National Assembly of Pakistan. https://pakistancode.gov.pk/pdffiles/administrator5b224d4541235a4a7d478cf039722c33.pdf

Government of the People's Republic of Bangladesh. (2012). *Disaster Management Act, 2012 (Act No. 34 of 2012)*. Legislative and Parliamentary Affairs Division, Ministry of Law, Justice and Parliamentary Affairs. https://legislativediv.portal.gov.bd/sites/default/files/files/legislativediv.portal.gov.bd/page/5a6bca14_6a2e_44e4_b155_c8147d1edd65/23.%20Disaster%20Management%20Act%2C%202012.pdf

Granovetter, M. (1978). Threshold models of collective behavior. *American Journal of Sociology, 83*(6), 1420–1443. https://doi.org/10.1086/226707

Gupta, A. (2014, September 2). Food riots in Bihar as hungry flood victims take to streets. *Down To Earth*. https://www.downtoearth.org.in/environment/food-riots-in-bihar-as-hungry-flood-victims-take-to-streets-46151

Gupta, M. K., Bhardwaj, P., Goel, A., Saurabh, S., & Misra, S. (2021). COVID-19 appropriate behavior in India: Time to invest for the benefits in future. *Journal of Family Medicine and Primary Care, 10*(5), 1818–1822. https://doi.org/10.4103/jfmpc.jfmpc_2382_20

Haghani, M., & Feliciani, C. (2024, July 3). Deadly crowd crush at Indian religious gathering shows how dangerous leaving an event can be. *The Conversation*. https://theconversation.com/deadly-crowd-crush-at-indian-religious-gathering-shows-how-dangerous-leaving-an-event-can-be-233864

Hanć, T., Gomula, A., Nowak-Szczepanska, N., Chakraborty, R., & Kozieł, S. (2022). Prenatal and early postnatal exposure to a natural disaster and attention-deficit/hyperactivity disorder symptoms in Indian children. *Scientific Reports, 12*(1), 16235. https://doi.org/10.1038/s41598-022-20609-6

Hatfield, E., Cacioppo, J. T., & Rapson, R. L. (1994). *Emotional contagion* (pp. vii, 240). Editions de la Maison des Sciences de l'Homme.

Hettiarachchi. (2024). *Disaster risk reduction in Sri Lanka*. Sambuz. https://www.sambuz.com/doc/disaster-risk-reduction-sri-lanka-ppt-presentation-515436

Hock, R., Rasul, G., Adler, C., Cáceres, B., Gruber, S., Hirabayashi, Y., Jackson, M., Kääb, A., Kang, S., Kutuzov, S., Milner, A., Molau, U., Morin, S., Orlove, B., Stetzler, H., Allen, S., Arenson, L., Banjeree, S., Barr, I., & Zhang, Y. (2019). *Chapter 2: High mountain areas* (p. 94).

Hoffman, S. M., & Oliver-Smith, A. (2002). *Catastrophe & culture: The anthropology of disaster*. School of American Research Press.

Hogg, M. A.. (2001). A social identity theory of leadership. https://journals.sagepub.com/doi/10.1207/S15327957PSPR0503_1

Hollifield, M., Hewage, C., Gunawardena, C. N., Kodituwakku, P., Bopagoda, K., & Weerarathnege, K. (2008). Symptoms and coping in Sri Lanka 20–21 months after the 2004 tsunami. *The British Journal of Psychiatry: the Journal of Mental Science, 192*(1), 39–44. https://doi.org/10.1192/bjp.bp.107.038422

Hui, C. H., Triandis, H. C., & Yee, C. (1991). Cultural differences in reward allocation: Is collectivism the explanation? *British Journal of Social Psychology, 30*(2), 145–157. https://doi.org/10.1111/j.2044-8309.1991.tb00931.x

Illiyas, F. T., Mani, S. K., Pradeepkumar, A. P., & Mohan, K. (2013). Human stampedes during religious festivals: A comparative review of mass gathering emergencies in India. *International Journal of Disaster Risk Reduction, 5*, 10–18. https://doi.org/10.1016/j.ijdrr.2013.09.003

Intergovernmental Panel on Climate Change. (2012). https://www.ipcc.ch/2012/

International Committee of the Red Cross (ICRC). (1994). *Code of conduct for the International Red Cross and Red Crescent Movement and NGOs in disaster relief*. ICRC. https://www.icrc.org/sites/default/files/external/doc/en/assets/files/other/icrc_002_1103.pdf

Ishikawa, M., Yamamoto, N., Yamanaka, G., Suwa, K., Nakajima, S., Hozo, R., Norboo, T., Okumiya, K., Matsubayashi, K., & Otsuka, K. (2013). Disaster-related psychiatric disorders among survivors of flooding in Ladakh, India. *The International Journal of Social Psychiatry, 59*(5), 468–473. https://doi.org/10.1177/0020764012440677

Ishiwatari, M. (2013). *Disaster risk management at the national level*. 448. https://www.adb.org/publications/disaster-risk-management-national-level

Islam, M. R. (2023). Introduction: Disaster, displacement and resilient livelihoods in South Asia. In M. R. Islam (Ed.), *Disaster, displacement and resilient livelihoods: Perspectives from South Asia* (pp. 1–15). Emerald Publishing. https://doi.org/10.1108/978-1-80455-448-720231001

John, P. B., Russell, S., & Russell, P. S. S. (2007). The prevalence of posttraumatic stress disorder among children and adolescents affected by tsunami disaster in Tamil Nadu. *Disaster Management & Response: DMR: An Official Publication of the Emergency Nurses Association, 5*(1), 3–7. https://doi.org/10.1016/j.dmr.2006.11.001

Jordan, J. J., Yoeli, E., & Rand, D. G. (2021). Don't get it or don't spread it: Comparing self-interested versus prosocial motivations for COVID-19 prevention behaviors. *Scientific Reports, 11*(1), 20222. https://doi.org/10.1038/s41598-021-97617-5

Joseph, J. K., Anand, D., Prajeesh, P., Zacharias, A., Varghese, A. G., Pradeepkumar, A. P., & Baiju, K. R. (2020). Community resilience mechanism in an unexpected extreme weather event: An analysis of the Kerala floods of 2018, India. *International Journal of Disaster Risk Reduction, 49*, 101741. https://doi.org/10.1016/j.ijdrr.2020.101741

Kane, J. C., Luitel, N. P., Jordans, M. J. D., Kohrt, B. A., Weissbecker, I., & Tol, W. A. (2018). Mental health and psychosocial problems in the aftermath of the Nepal earthquakes: Findings from a representative cluster sample survey. *Epidemiology and Psychiatric Sciences, 27*(3), 301–310. https://doi.org/10.1017/S2045796016001104

Kanta Kafle, S. (2017). Disaster risk management systems in South Asia: Natural hazards, vulnerability, disaster risk and legislative and institutional frameworks. *Journal of Geography & Natural Disasters, 7*(3). https://doi.org/10.4172/2167-0587.1000207

Kar, N. (2009). Psychological impact of disasters on children: Review of assessment and interventions. *World Journal of Pediatrics: WJP, 5*(1), 5–11. https://doi.org/10.1007/s12519-009-0001-x

Kar, N. (2010). Indian research on disaster and mental health. *Indian Journal of Psychiatry, 52*(Suppl1), S286–S290. https://doi.org/10.4103/0019-5545.69254

Kar, N., & Bastia, B. K. (2006). Post-traumatic stress disorder, depression and generalised anxiety disorder in adolescents after a natural disaster: A study of comorbidity. *Clinical Practice and Epidemiology in Mental Health: CP & EMH, 2*, 17. https://doi.org/10.1186/1745-0179-2-17

Kar, N., Krishnaraaj, R., & Rameshraj, K. (2014). Long-term mental health outcomes following the 2004 Asian tsunami disaster: A comparative study on direct and indirect exposure. *Disaster Health, 2*(1), 35–45. https://doi.org/10.4161/dish.24705

Kar, S. K., Menon, V., & Arafat, S. M. Y. (2020). Online group cognitive behavioral therapy for panic buying: Understanding the usefulness in COVID-19 context. *Indian Journal of Psychiatry, 62*(5), 607–609. https://doi.org/10.4103/psychiatry.IndianJPsychiatry_610_20

Kar, N., Samantaray, N. N., Kar, S., & Kar, B. (2022). Anxiety, depression, and post-traumatic stress a month after 2019 Cyclone Fani in Odisha, India. *Disaster Medicine and Public Health Preparedness, 16*(2), 670–677. https://doi.org/10.1017/dmp.2020.368

Keller, A. Z., & Al-Madhari, A. F. (1996). Risk management and disasters. *Disaster Prevention and Management: An International Journal, 5*(5), 19–22. https://doi.org/10.1108/09653569610131744

Khatri, G. K., Tran, T. D., Baral, S., & Fisher, J. (2018). Effect of the 2015 Nepal earthquakes on symptoms of common mental disorders among women who are pregnant. *Journal of Affective Disorders, 228*, 238–247. https://doi.org/10.1016/j.jad.2017.12.016

Kinateder, M. T., Kuligowski, E. D., Reneke, P. A., & Peacock, R. D. (2015). Risk perception in fire evacuation behavior revisited: Definitions, related concepts, and empirical evidence. *Fire Science Reviews, 4*(1), 1. https://doi.org/10.1186/s40038-014-0005-z

Kınık, K., Kuday, A. D., & Çalışkan, C. (2024). Psychological hardiness and compassion satisfaction among the Turkish Red Crescent: The case of 2023 Kahramanmaras earthquake. *Disaster Medicine and Public Health Preparedness, 18*, e58. https://doi.org/10.1017/dmp.2024.64

Kırseven, M. Y., & Işıklı, S. (2020). Investigation of the effects of violence experience during political demonstrations. *Europe's Journal of Psychology, 16*(3), 479–497. https://doi.org/10.5964/ejop.v16i3.1991

Kluckhohn, F. R., & Strodtbeck, F. L. (1961). *Variations in value orientations* (pp. xiv–450). Row, Peterson.

Krishnan, R., Shrestha, A. B., Ren, G., Rajbhandari, R., Saeed, S., Sanjay, J., Syed, M. A., Vellore, R., Xu, Y., You, Q., & Ren, Y. (2019). Unravelling climate change in the Hindu Kush Himalaya: Rapid warming in the mountains and increasing extremes. In P. Wester, A. Mishra, A. Mukherji, & A. B. Shrestha (Eds.), *The Hindu Kush Himalaya assessment: Mountains, climate change, sustainability and people* (pp. 57–97). Springer International Publishing. https://doi.org/10.1007/978-3-319-92288-1_3

Krüger, F., Bankoff, G., Cannon, T., Orlowski, B., & Schipper, E. L. F. (2015). *Cultures and disasters: Understanding cultural framings in disaster risk reduction*. Routledge. https://doi.org/10.4324/9781315797809

Kulatunga, U. (2010). Impact of Culture towards Disaster Risk Reduction. *International Journal of Strategic Property Management, 14*(4), 304–313. https://doi.org/10.3846/ijspm.2010.23

Kumar, M. S., Murhekar, M. V., Hutin, Y., Subramanian, T., Ramachandran, V., & Gupte, M. D. (2007). Prevalence of posttraumatic stress disorder in a coastal fishing village in Tamil Nadu, India, after the December 2004 tsunami. *American Journal of Public Health, 97*(1), 99–101. https://doi.org/10.2105/AJPH.2005.071167

Kumar, M., & Fonagy, P. (2013). Differential effects of exposure to social violence and natural disaster on children's mental health. *Journal of Traumatic Stress, 26*(6), 695–702. https://doi.org/10.1002/jts.21874

Kundu, K., Das, A., Kachhawaha, G., Jhajharia, S., Kaur, B., Mudgal, K., Sharma, C., Neupane, D., Khan, Z., Kant, R., Bairwa, M., Kumar, S., Routhu, B., Kumar, R., Singh, M., & Gupta, R. (2025). Mental health and sleep routines: Uttarkashi, India tunnel collapse workers' experience. *Sleep Medicine, 126*, 329–335. https://doi.org/10.1016/j.sleep.2024.12.017

Lavigne, F., De Coster, B., Juvin, N., Flohic, F., Gaillard, J.-C., Texier, P., Morin, J., & Sartohadi, J. (2008). People's behaviour in the face of volcanic hazards: Perspectives from Javanese communities, Indonesia. *Journal of Volcanology and Geothermal Research, 172*(3), 273–287. https://doi.org/10.1016/j.jvolgeores.2007.12.013

Le Bon, G. (1895). *The crowd: A study of the popular mind*. T. Fisher Unwin. https://www.files.ethz.ch/isn/125518/1414_LeBon.pdf

Leonard, R. (1985). Mass evacuation in disasters. *The Journal of Emergency Medicine, 2*(4), 279–286. https://doi.org/10.1016/0736-4679(85)90108-8

Li, Y., Zhang, X., & Wang, L. (2023). The effect of disasters on altruistic behavior and its mechanisms. *Journal of Disaster Psychology, 12*(3), 45–60.

Liu, W., & Aaker, J. (2008). The happiness of giving: The time-ask effect. *Journal of Consumer Research, 35*(3), 543–557. https://doi.org/10.1086/588699

Lommen, M. J. J., Sanders, A. J. M. L., Buck, N., & Arntz, A. (2009). Psychosocial predictors of chronic Post-Traumatic Stress Disorder in Sri Lankan tsunami survivors. *Behaviour Research and Therapy, 47*(1), 60–65. https://doi.org/10.1016/j.brat.2008.10.009

Mall, R. K., Srivastava, R. K., Banerjee, T., Mishra, O. P., Bhatt, D., & Sonkar, G. (2019). Disaster risk reduction including climate change adaptation over South Asia: Challenges and ways forward. *International Journal of Disaster Risk Science, 10*(1), 14–27. https://doi.org/10.1007/s13753-018-0210-9

Mamun, M. A., Safiq, M. B., Hosen, I., & al Mamun, F. (2021). Suicidal behavior and flood effects in Bangladesh: A two-site interview study. *Risk Management and Healthcare Policy, 14*, 129–142. https://doi.org/10.2147/RMHP.S282965

Manthorpe, J., Iliffe, S., Gillen, P., Moriarty, J., Mallett, J., Schroder, H., Currie, D., Ravalier, J., & McFadden, P. (2022). Clapping for carers in the Covid-19 crisis: Carers' reflections in a UK survey. *Health & Social Care in the Community, 30*(4), 1442–1449. https://doi.org/10.1111/hsc.13474

Math, S. B., Tandon, S., Girimaji, S. C., Benegal, V., Kumar, U., Hamza, A., Jangam, K., & Nagaraja, D. (2008). Psychological impact of the tsunami on children and adolescents from the Andaman and Nicobar islands. *Primary Care Companion to the Journal of Clinical Psychiatry, 10*(1), 31–37. https://doi.org/10.4088/pcc.v10n0106

Math, S. B., Nirmala, M. C., Moirangthem, S., & Kumar, N. C. (2015). Disaster management: Mental health perspective. *Indian Journal of Psychological Medicine, 37*(3), 261–271. https://doi.org/10.4103/0253-7176.162915

Mathew, G., Varghese, A. D., Sabu, A. M., & Joseph, A. (2021). Screening for post-traumatic stress disorder among adolescents following floods- a comparative study from private and public schools in Kerala, India. *BMC Pediatrics, 21*(1), 462. https://doi.org/10.1186/s12887-021-02933-4

Mathew, G., Varghese, A. D., Paulose, J., & Benjamin, A. I. (2024). Community-based screening for post-traumatic stress disorder among flood victims—A cross-sectional study from Kerala, India. *Indian Journal of Psychiatry, 66*(4), 367–372. https://doi.org/10.4103/indianjpsychiatry.indianjpsychiatry_749_22

Mawson, A. R. (2005). Understanding mass panic and other collective responses to threat and disaster. *Psychiatry, 68*(2), 95–113. https://doi.org/10.1521/psyc.2005.68.2.95

McPhail, C. (1989). Blumer's theory of collective behavior: The development of a non-symbolic interaction explanation. *The Sociological Quarterly, 30*(3), 401–423.

Memon, N. (2013). Disaster in South Asia. *Terre des Hommes.* https://www.tdh.de/fileadmin/user_upload/inhalte/04_Was_wir_tun/Themen/Humanitaere_Hilfe/Katastrophenhilfe/Disaster_in_South_Asia_-_Naseer_memon.pdf

Menon, V., & Varadharajan, N. (2021). Prevention of panic buying. In S. M. Y. Arafat, S. K. Kar, & R. Kabir (Eds.), *Panic buying: Perspectives and prevention* (pp. 103–113). Springer International Publishing. https://doi.org/10.1007/978-3-030-70726-2_8

Milsten, A. M., Kang, C. S., & Nemeth, I. (2024). Maladaptive behaviors in disasters: Case study evaluation of Hurricane Hugo, Hurricane Katrina and the Haiti Earthquake. *Frontiers in Public Health, 12*. https://doi.org/10.3389/fpubh.2024.1396517

Mohamed Shaluf, I. (2007). Disaster types. *Disaster Prevention and Management: An International Journal, 16*(5), 704–717. https://doi.org/10.1108/09653560710837019

Mostafizur Rahman, M., Alam Shobuj, I., Tanvir Hossain, M., & Tasnim, F. (2023). Impact of Disaster on mental health of women: A case study on 2022 flash flood in Bangladesh. *International Journal of Disaster Risk Reduction, 96*, 103935. https://doi.org/10.1016/j.ijdrr.2023.103935

Motamed-Jahromi, M., Meshkani, Z., Mosavi-Negad, S. M., Momenabadi, V., & Ahmadzadeh, M. S. (2021). Factors affecting panic buying during COVID-19 outbreak and strategies: A scoping review. *Iranian Journal of Public Health, 50*(12), 2473–2485. https://doi.org/10.18502/ijph.v50i12.7929

Murthy, R. S. (2014). Mental health of survivors of 1984 Bhopal disaster: A continuing challenge. *Industrial Psychiatry Journal, 23*(2), 86–93. https://doi.org/10.4103/0972-6748.151668

Murthy, R. S. (2018). Disaster mental health and social psychiatry: Challenges and opportunities. *Indian Journal of Social Psychiatry, 34*(4), 323. https://doi.org/10.4103/ijsp.ijsp_84_18

Arunotai, N. (2008). Saved by an old legend and a keen observation: The case of Moken sea nomads in Thailand. In R. Shaw, N. Uy, & J. Baumwoll (Eds.), *Indigenous knowledge for disaster risk reduction: Good practices and lessons learnt from the Asia Pacific region* (pp. 73–78). UNISDR Asia and Pacific.

Naeem, F., Ayub, M., Masood, K., Gul, H., Khalid, M., Farrukh, A., Shaheen, A., Waheed, W., & Chaudhry, H. R. (2011). Prevalence and psychosocial risk factors of PTSD: 18 months after Kashmir earthquake in Pakistan. *Journal of Affective Disorders, 130*(1–2), 268–274. https://doi.org/10.1016/j.jad.2010.10.035

Nagel, T. (with Internet Archive). (1978). *The possibility of altruism*. Princeton University Press. http://archive.org/details/possibilityofalt0000nage

National Disaster Management Authority (NDMA), M. (2025). *Disaster risk reduction strategy, Maldives 2024–2030*. National Disaster Management Authority. https://ndma.gov.mv/en/publications/disaster-risk-reduction-strategy-maldives-2024-2030-1

NDTV. (2015, April 29). Nepal earthquake: Riot police intervene as anger erupts among survivors. *NDTV*. https://www.ndtv.com/world-news/nepal-earthquake-riot-police-intervene-as-anger-erupts-among-survivors-759212

Nestrovski, A., & Seligmann-Silva, M. (2000). Catástrofe e representação. In *Catástrofe e representação* (pp. 264–264). https://pesquisa.bvsalud.org/portal/resource/pt/psa-108429

Neuner, F., Schauer, E., Catani, C., Ruf, M., & Elbert, T. (2006). Post-tsunami stress: A study of posttraumatic stress disorder in children living in three severely affected regions in Sri Lanka. *Journal of Traumatic Stress, 19*(3), 339–347. https://doi.org/10.1002/jts.20121

Nitzgen, D. (2022). Mass behaviour and mass psychosis: Robert Wälder: An amendment of Freud's 'Theory of Mass Psychology'. *Group Analysis, 55*(3), 342–352. https://doi.org/10.1177/05333164221120886

Noji, E. K. (2000). The public health consequences of disasters. *Prehospital and Disaster Medicine, 15*(4), 147–157.

O'Connell, E., Abbott, R. P., & White, R. S. (2017). Emotions and beliefs after a disaster: A comparative analysis of Haiti and Indonesia. *Disasters, 41*(4), 803–827. https://doi.org/10.1111/disa.12227

Oliver-Smith, A. (1996). Anthropological research on hazards and disasters. *Annual Review of Anthropology, 25*, 303–328.

Ovesen, P., & Heiselberg, S. (2016). *The humanitarian response to the 2015 Nepal earthquake*. United Nations. https://www.un.org/en/chronicle/article/humanitarian-response-2015-nepal-earthquake

Pan American Health Organization. (2000). Los desastres naturales y la protección de la salud. https://www.paho.org

Panthi, S., Bräuning, A., Zhou, Z.-K., & Fan, Z.-X. (2017). Tree rings reveal recent intensified spring drought in the central Himalaya, Nepal. *Global and Planetary Change, 157*, 26–34. https://doi.org/10.1016/j.gloplacha.2017.08.012

Parameswaran Kunjukrishnan, R., & Krishnakumariamma, S. (2024). Understanding crowd dynamics and disaster risks in Kerala temple festivals: Strategies for effective management. *International Journal of Disaster Risk Management, 6*(2), 265–277. https://doi.org/10.18485/ijdrm.2024.6.2.17

Parliament of the Democratic Socialist Republic of Sri Lanka. (2005). *Sri Lanka Disaster Management Act, No. 13 of 2005*. Department of Government Printing. https://www.dmc.gov.lk/images/DM_Act_English.pdf

Parliament of the Kingdom of Bhutan. (2013). *Disaster Management Act of Bhutan, 2013*. Office of the Attorney General. https://oag.gov.bt/wp-content/uploads/2010/05/Disaster%20Management%20Act%20of%20Bhutan%202013.pdf

Patwary, M. M., Bardhan, M., Haque, M. A., Moniruzzaman, S., Gustavsson, J., Khan, M. M. H., Koivisto, J., Salwa, M., Mashreky, S. R., Rahman, A. K. M. F., Tasnim, A., Islam, M. R., Alam, M. A., Hasan, M., Harun, M. A. Y. A., Nyberg, L., & Islam, M. A. (2024). Impact of extreme weather events on mental health in South and Southeast Asia: A two decades of systematic review of observational studies. *Environmental Research, 250*, 118436. https://doi.org/10.1016/j.envres.2024.118436

Pecio, M. (2025). Issues of crowd evacuation in panic conditions. *Urban Science, 9*(7), 7. https://doi.org/10.3390/urbansci9070258

Petersen, M. B. (2020). The evolutionary psychology of mass mobilization: How disinformation and demagogues coordinate rather than manipulate. *Current Opinion in Psychology, 35*, 71–75. https://doi.org/10.1016/j.copsyc.2020.02.003

Pillai, M. P. (2024). The long journey home: Viapolitics in the journey of migrant labourers during COVID-19 lockdown in India. *Mobilities, 19*(6), 1041–1053. https://doi.org/10.1080/17450101.2024.2356568

Ponnamperuma, T., Sumathipala, A., & Siribaddana, S. (2020). Posttraumatic stress and co-occurrence of mental health problems in Sri Lankan adolescents. *Asian Journal of Psychiatry, 54*, 102444. https://doi.org/10.1016/j.ajp.2020.102444

PTI. (2020). Chemist shops run out of hand sanitizers, face masks in several parts of Delhi-NCR. *The Economic Times*. https://economictimes.indiatimes.com/news/politics-and-nation/chemist-shops-run-out-of-hand-sanitizers-face-masks-in-several-parts-of-delhi-ncr/articleshow/74479308.cms

PTI. (2024, October 22). Cyclone Dana: Vegetable price soars in Odisha markets as people resort to panic buying. *CNBC-TV18*. https://www.cnbctv18.com/india/cyclone-dana-vegetable-price-soars-in-odisha-markets-as-people-resort-to-panic-buying-18123451.htm

Putri, A. M., Retsan, A., Andika, H., & Hendriana, E. (2021). Antecedents of panic buying behavior during the COVID-19 pandemic. *Management Science Letters*, 1821–1832. https://doi.org/10.5267/j.msl.2021.1.021

Pyari, T. T., Kutty, R. V., & Sarma, P. S. (2012). Risk factors of post-traumatic stress disorder in tsunami survivors of Kanyakumari District, Tamil Nadu, India. *Indian Journal of Psychiatry, 54*(1), 48–53. https://doi.org/10.4103/0019-5545.94645

Rahman, M. M., Shobuj, I. A., Hossain, M. T., Alam, E., Islam, M. K., & Hossain, M. K. (2025). Flood impact on men's mental health: Evidence from flood-prone areas of Bangladesh. *Frontiers in Public Health, 13*, 1529558. https://doi.org/10.3389/fpubh.2025.1529558

Rahmani, M., Muzwagi, A., & Pumariega, A. J. (2022). Cultural factors in disaster response among diverse children and youth around the world. *Current Psychiatry Reports, 24*(10), 481–491. https://doi.org/10.1007/s11920-022-01356-x

Rajkumar, R. P. (2021). A biopsychosocial approach to understanding panic buying: Integrating neurobiological, attachment-based, and social-anthropological perspectives. *Frontiers in Psychiatry, 12*, 652353. https://doi.org/10.3389/fpsyt.2021.652353

Rajkumar, A. P., Mohan, T. S., & Tharyan, P. (2015). Lessons from the 2004 Asian tsunami: Nature, prevalence and determinants of prolonged grief disorder among tsunami survivors in South Indian coastal villages. *The International Journal of Social Psychiatry, 61*(7), 645–652. https://doi.org/10.1177/0020764015570713

Ranasinghe, P. D., & Levy, B. R. (2007). Prevalence of and sex disparities in posttraumatic stress disorder in an internally displaced Sri Lankan population 6 months after the 2004 Tsunami. *Disaster Medicine and Public Health Preparedness, 1*(1), 34–41; discussion 41–43. https://doi.org/10.1097/DMP.0b013e318068fbb7

Ranasinghe, P. D., Zhang, X., Hwang, J., Ranasinghe, P. M., Karunathilake, I. M., & Everly, G. S. (2022). PTSD and depression 8 years after the 2004 Tsunami in Sri Lanka. *Disaster Medicine and Public Health Preparedness, 17*, e183. https://doi.org/10.1017/dmp.2022.73

Ravan, J. R., Panda, U. K., Pattnaik, J. I., Banerjee, S., Chaudhuri, T., Patil, S., & Das, R. C. (2024). The psychological impact of disaster on first responders in the aftermath of Bahanaga train tragedy: A mixed methods approach. *Indian Journal of Psychiatry, 66*(11), 1043–1049. https://doi.org/10.4103/indianjpsychiatry.indianjpsychiatry_231_24

Reicher, S., Stott, C., Cronin, P., & Adang, O. (2004). An integrated approach to crowd psychology and public order policing. *Policing An International Journal of Police Strategies &*

Management, 27, 558–572. References—Scientific Research Publishing. https://www.scirp.org/reference/referencespapers?referenceid=1248695

Reuters. (2007, August 14). Flood victims loot food in rain-ravaged South Asia. *ReliefWeb*. https://reliefweb.int/report/india/flood-victims-loot-food-rain-ravaged-south-asia

Rudd, M., Aaker, J., & Norton, M. I. (2014). Getting the most out of giving: Concretely framing a prosocial goal maximizes happiness. *Journal of Experimental Social Psychology, 54*, 11–24. https://doi.org/10.1016/j.jesp.2014.04.002

Sahoo, P. K., Biswal, S., Kumar, H., & Powell, M. (2022). Urban to rural COVID-19 progression in India: The role of massive migration and the challenge to India's traditional labour force policies. *The International Journal of Health Planning and Management, 37*(1), 528–535. https://doi.org/10.1002/hpm.3327

Sasaki, N., Watanabe, K., Kanamori, Y., Tabuchi, T., Fujiwara, T., & Nishi, D. (2024). Effects of expanded adverse childhood experiences including school bullying, childhood poverty, and natural disasters on mental health in adulthood. *Scientific Reports, 14*(1), 12015. https://doi.org/10.1038/s41598-024-62634-7

Schipper, E. L. F. (2010). *Religion as an integral part of determining and reducing climate change and disaster risk: An agenda for research* (ISS Working Paper No. 347). Institute of Social Studies. https://repub.eur.nl/pub/19163

Sendai Framework for Disaster Risk Reduction 2015–2030. (2015).

Sharan, A., & Gaillard, J. C. (2025). Re-gendering the Sendai framework for disaster risk reduction: Experiences of gender diverse groups from India and the Philippines. *International Journal of Disaster Risk Science, 16*(1), 92–102. https://doi.org/10.1007/s13753-024-00612-3

Sharma, J. P. (2020). As India exports hydroxychloroquine, Punjab faces acute shortage of the medicine due to panic buying. *Outlook India*. https://www.outlookindia.com/website/story/india-news-as-india-exports-hydroxychloroquine-punjab-faces-acute-shortage-of-the-medicine-due-to-panic-buying/350507

Sharma, A., & Kar, N. (2019). Posttraumatic stress, depression, and coping following the 2015 Nepal earthquake: A study on adolescents. *Disaster Medicine and Public Health Preparedness, 13*(2), 236–242. https://doi.org/10.1017/dmp.2018.37

Sheikhi, R. A., Javanbakhtian, R., & Heidari, M. (2025). Looting and antisocial behavior after disasters: A systematic review. *BMC Public Health, 25*, 309. https://doi.org/10.1186/s12889-025-21285-7

Shrivastava, P., Mitroff, I. I., Miller, D., & Miclani, A. (1988). Understanding industrial crises[1]. *Journal of Management Studies, 25*(4), 285–303. https://doi.org/10.1111/j.1467-6486.1988.tb00038.x

Silwal, S., Dybdahl, R., Chudal, R., Sourander, A., & Lien, L. (2018). Psychiatric symptoms experienced by adolescents in Nepal following the 2015 earthquakes. *Journal of Affective Disorders, 234*, 239–246. https://doi.org/10.1016/j.jad.2018.03.002

Silwal, S., Chudal, R., Dybdahl, R., Sillanmäki, L., Lien, L., & Sourander, A. (2022). Post-traumatic stress and depressive symptoms among adolescents after the 2015 earthquake in Nepal: A longitudinal study. *Child Psychiatry and Human Development, 53*(3), 430–439. https://doi.org/10.1007/s10578-021-01136-3

Sim, K., Chua, H. C., Vieta, E., & Fernandez, G. (2020). The anatomy of panic buying related to the current COVID-19 pandemic. *Psychiatry Research, 288*, 113015. https://doi.org/10.1016/j.psychres.2020.113015

Smelser, N. J. (with Internet Archive). (1962). *Theory of collective behavior*. Routledge and K. Paul. http://archive.org/details/theoryofcollecti0000smel

Srivastava, K. (2010). Disaster: Challenges and perspectives. *Industrial Psychiatry Journal, 19*(1), 1–4. https://doi.org/10.4103/0972-6748.77623

Stamm, B. H. (2010). The professional quality of life scale: Compassion satisfaction and compassion fatigue. In *The compassion fatigue workbook* (pp. 1–16). Sidran Press.

Suar, D., Das, S. S., & Alat, P. (2015). Bereavement, postdisaster trauma, and behavioral changes in tsunami survivors. *Death Studies, 39*(1–5), 226–233. https://doi.org/10.1080/07481187.2014.979957

Sutar, R., Majumdar, A., Amudhan, S., Satpathy, P., & Singh, V. (2022). Disaster and mental health preparedness in India: A scoping review. *Indian Journal of Community Health, 34*(2), 154–160. https://doi.org/10.47203/IJCH.2022.v34i02.004

Suwalowska, H., Amara, F., Roberts, N., & Kingori, P. (2021). Ethical and sociocultural challenges in managing dead bodies during epidemics and natural disasters. *BMJ Global Health, 6*(11), e006345. https://doi.org/10.1136/bmjgh-2021-006345

Tajfel Turner. (1979). *Tajfel Turner 1979 an integrative theory of intergroup conflict. PDF | PDF.* https://www.scribd.com/document/414283115/Tajfel-Turner-1979-An-Integrative-Theory-of-Intergroup-Conflict-pdf

Taub, A. (2016). American authoritarianism: The political science theory that explains Trump rally violence. *Vox*. https://www.vox.com/2016/3/14/11224216/authoritarianism-trump-rallies-violence

Telles, S., Singh, N., & Joshi, M. (2009). Risk of posttraumatic stress disorder and depression in survivors of the floods in Bihar, India. *Indian Journal of Medical Sciences, 63*(8), 330–334.

The human cost of disasters*: An overview of the last 20 years (2000–2019) | UNDRR*. (2020, October 12). https://www.undrr.org/publication/human-cost-disasters-overview-last-20-years-2000-2019

The News Minute. (2015, December 7). Chennai floods: Looting relief materials in a time of tragedy. *The News Minute*. https://www.thenewsminute.com/article/chennai-floods-looting-relief-materials-time-tragedy-36360

The Statesman News Service. (2024, October 14). TN cyclone warning: Panic buying and parking cars on flyovers. *The Statesman*. https://www.thestatesman.com/india/tn-cyclone-warning-panic-buying-1503240791.html

Thomas, J. J., B, P., Kulkarni, P., & Murthy M R, N. (2021). Exploring the psychiatric symptoms among people residing at flood affected areas of Kodagu district, Karnataka. *Clinical Epidemiology and Global Health, 9*, 245–250. https://doi.org/10.1016/j.cegh.2020.09.006

Thomas, P., Varghese, S. M., & Benjamin, A. I. (2023). People's response to disaster: A population based study of the victims of 2018 flood in Kerala, South India. *Indian Journal of Community Medicine: Official Publication of Indian Association of Preventive & Social Medicine, 48*(2), 310–315. https://doi.org/10.4103/ijcm.ijcm_309_22

Times News Network. (2025). Panic buying starts, prices also start rising. *Times of India*. https://timesofindia.indiatimes.com/city/ludhiana/panic-buying-starts-prices-also-start-rising/articleshow/120971610.cms

Tiwari, V. (2020, March 22). Watch: Clapping, beating utensils – How India thanked COVID-19 fighters. *NDTV*. https://www.ndtv.com/india-news/watch-clapping-beating-utensils-how-india-thanked-covid-19-fighters-2201476

Tran, T. T., Lee, J., Sleigh, A., & Banwell, C. (2019). Putting culture into prehospital emergency care: A systematic narrative review of literature from lower middle-income countries. *Prehospital and Disaster Medicine, 34*(5), 510–520. https://doi.org/10.1017/S1049023X19004709

Trieb, C.-A. (2015). *Vulnerability to natural hazards: A gender perspective in disasters* [Management Center Innsbruck]. https://doi.org/10.13140/RG.2.2.24270.87367

Turner, R. H., & Killian, L. M. (with Internet Archive). (1987). *Collective behavior*. Prentice-Hall. http://archive.org/details/collectivebehavi00turn

Turner, B. A., & Pidgeon, N. F. (1997). *Man-made disasters*. Butterworth-Heinemann. https://archive.org/details/manmadedisasters0000turn

Ultramari, C., & Szuchman, T. (2017). Natural disasters: Altruism, interests, and opportunities. *Ambiente & Sociedade, 20*(2), 1–18. https://doi.org/10.1590/1809-4422ASOC173R2V2022017

United Nations Environment Programme. (2004). *UNEP annual evaluation report 2003*. United Nations Environment Programme. https://wedocs.unep.org/bitstream/handle/20.500.11822/187/UNEP_Annual_Evaluation_Report_2003.pdf

United Nations International Strategy for Disaster Reduction. (2009). UNISDR terminology on disaster risk reduction. https://www.unisdr.org/files/7817_UNISDRTerminologyEnglish.pdf

United Nations International Strategy for Disaster Reduction (UNISDR). (2005). *United Nations International Strategy for Disaster Reduction (UNISDR)* (World Conference on Disaster Reduction, Kobe, Hyogo, Japan, 18–22 January 2005). United Nations. https://www.unisdr.org/2005/wcdr/intergover/official-doc/L-docs/Final-report-conference.pdf

United Nations Office for Disaster Risk Reduction. (2007, August 30). *Definition: Disaster*. https://www.undrr.org/terminology/disaster

Venkatesh, N. (2024). Social anarchism and the rejection of moral tyranny, by Jesse Spafford. *Mind*, fzae014. https://doi.org/10.1093/mind/fzae014

Vestergren, S., Uysal, M. S., & Tekin, S. (2022). Do disasters trigger protests? A conceptual view of the connection between disasters, injustice, and protests—The case of COVID-19. *Frontiers in Political Science, 4*. https://doi.org/10.3389/fpos.2022.836420

von Sivers, I., Templeton, A., Künzner, F., Köster, G., Drury, J., Philippides, A., Neckel, T., & Bungartz, H.-J. (2016). Modelling social identification and helping in evacuation simulation. *Safety Science, 89*, 288–300. https://doi.org/10.1016/j.ssci.2016.07.001

Weber, M. (1947). *Weber, Max. The theory of social and economic organization [1947]*. http://archive.org/details/weber-max.-the-theory-of-social-and-economic-organization-1947_202106

Weiss-Sidi, M., & Riemer, H. (2023). Help others—be happy? The effect of altruistic behavior on happiness across cultures. *Frontiers in Psychology, 14*, 1156661. https://doi.org/10.3389/fpsyg.2023.1156661

Wickrama, T., Wickrama, K. a. s., Banford, A., & Lambert, J. (2017). PTSD symptoms among tsunami exposed mothers in Sri Lanka: The role of disaster exposure, culturally specific coping strategies, and recovery efforts. *Anxiety, Stress, & Coping, 30*(4), 415–427. https://doi.org/10.1080/10615806.2016.1271121

Wind, T. R., Joshi, P. C., Kleber, R. J., & Komproe, I. H. (2013). The impact of recurrent disasters on mental health: A study on seasonal floods in northern India. *Prehospital and Disaster Medicine, 28*(3), 279–285. https://doi.org/10.1017/S1049023X13000290

Wlodarczyk, A., Basabe, N., Páez, D., Amutio, A., García, F. E., Reyes, C., & Villagrán, L. (2016a). Positive effects of communal coping in the aftermath of a collective trauma: The case of the 2010 Chilean earthquake. *European Journal of Education and Psychology, 9*(1), 9–19. https://doi.org/10.1016/j.ejeps.2015.08.001

Wlodarczyk, A., Basabe, N., Páez, D., Reyes, C., Villagrán, L., Madariaga, C., Palacio, J., & Martínez, F. (2016b). Communal coping and posttraumatic growth in a context of natural disasters in Spain, Chile, and Colombia. *Cross-Cultural Research, 50*(4), 325–355. https://doi.org/10.1177/1069397116663857

World Bank. (2023, October 17). *South Asia: Disaster risk management is key to durable development*. World Bank Blogs. https://blogs.worldbank.org/en/endpovertyinsouthasia/south-asia-disaster-risk-management-key-durable-development

World Disasters Report 2010: Focus on urban risk | IFRC. (2017, December 18). https://www.ifrc.org/document/world-disasters-report-2010-focus-urban-risk

World Health Organization. (2020, March 3). *Shortage of personal protective equipment endangering health workers world-wide*. World Health Organization. https://www.who.int/news/item/03-03-2020-shortage-of-personal-protective-equipment-endangering-health-workers-worldwide

World Health Organization & UNHCR. (2015). *mhGAP humanitarian intervention guide (mhGAP-HIG): Clinical management of mental, neurological and substance use conditions in humanitarian emergencies*. World Health Organization. https://iris.who.int/handle/10665/162960

Yasir Arafat, S. M., Kar, S. K., Menon, V., Marthoenis, M., Sharma, P., Alradie-Mohamed, A., Mukherjee, S., Kaliamoorthy, C., & Kabir, R. (2020). Media portrayal of panic buying: A content analysis of online news portals. *Global Psychiatry*. https://doi.org/10.2478/gp-2020-0022

Young, B. H., Ford, J. D., Ruzek, J. I., Friedman, M. J., & Gusman, F. D. (1998). *Disaster mental health services: A guidebook for clinicians and administrators*. National Center for Post-Traumatic Stress Disorder.

Yuen, K. F., Wang, X., Ma, F., & Li, K. X. (2020). The psychological causes of panic buying following a health crisis. *International Journal of Environmental Research and Public Health, 17*(10), 3513. https://doi.org/10.3390/ijerph17103513

Zagefka, H., & James, T. (2015). The psychology of charitable donations to disaster victims and beyond. *Social Issues and Policy Review, 9*(1), 155–192. https://doi.org/10.1111/sipr.12013

Zaidi, S., Kamal, A., & Baig-Ansari, N. (2010). Targeting vulnerability after the 2005 earthquake: Pakistan's livelihood support cash grants programme. *Disasters, 34*(2), 380–401. https://doi.org/10.1111/j.1467-7717.2009.01134.x

Zaki, J. (2020). Catastrophe compassion: Understanding and extending prosociality under crisis. *Trends in Cognitive Sciences, 24*(8), 587–589. https://doi.org/10.1016/j.tics.2020.05.006

Zaumseil, M., & Schwarz, S. (2014). Understandings of coping: A critical review of coping theories for disaster contexts. In M. Zaumseil, S. Schwarz, M. von Vacano, G. B. Sullivan, & J. E. Prawitasari-Hadiyono (Eds.), *Cultural psychology of coping with disasters: The case of an earthquake in Java, Indonesia* (pp. 45–83). Springer. https://doi.org/10.1007/978-1-4614-9354-9_2

Zeng, N., Li, Z., Ng, S., Chen, D., & Zhou, H. (2020). Epidemiology reveals mask wearing by the public is crucial for COVID-19 control. *Medicine in Microecology, 4*, 100015. https://doi.org/10.1016/j.medmic.2020.100015

Zhang, K., Zhang, N., Wang, J., Jiang, J., & Xu, S. (2022). Exploring the roles of fear and powerlessness in the relationship between perceived risk of the COVID-19 pandemic and information-avoidance behavior. *Frontiers in Psychology, 13*. https://doi.org/10.3389/fpsyg.2022.1005142

Zimbardo, P. G. (1969). The human choice: Individuation, reason, and order versus deindividuation, impulse, and chaos. *Nebraska Symposium on Motivation, 17*, 237–307.

Chapter 16
Disaster and Media Response

Ravi Philip Rajkumar

1 Introduction: Media, Behavior, and Health

The term *media* refers to "instruments which help people to disseminate, receive, and share information, experiences, or entertainment on a large scale among themselves" (Lee, 2014). Media can be broadly categorized into two types. *Mass media*, sometimes referred to as "conventional" or "traditional" media, designates those instruments and forms of communication that predate digital technologies and the Internet. These include books, magazines, newspapers, radio, television, and films. *Digital media* refers to those media that depend on the use of the Internet and digital technologies, such as computers, smartphones, tablets, blogs, podcasts, or specific online platforms. *Social media* is a subset of digital media used chiefly or exclusively for social purposes, whether personal or professional (Aichner et al., 2021).

The media are an integral part of modern society. They convey information about local, national, and current affairs, provide entertainment, and influence patterns of individual and social behavior. An average individual spends anywhere from 4 to 9 hours a day consuming or interacting with media (Twenge et al., 2019; Sharma & Gautam, 2023). Because of their broad reach and impact, the media have a key influence on individuals' health-related behaviors and practices. On the one hand, media can be invaluable in informing and educating the public about health and disease-related issues, and recommending adaptive behaviors such as dietary modification, exercise, immunization, or road safety practices. On the other hand, they can also promote maladaptive behaviors, such as substance misuse or unhealthy eating practices, and disseminate myths or misinformation about specific diseases or treatments (Li et al., 2021). The latter phenomenon has been worsened by the

R. P. Rajkumar (✉)
Department of Psychiatry, Jawaharlal Institute of Postgraduate Medical Education and Research (JIPMER), Puducherry, India

N. Kar et al. (eds.), *Climate Change, Disaster and Mental Health in South Asia*, South Asian Perspectives in Mental Health and Psychology,
https://doi.org/10.1007/978-981-95-3690-0_16

proliferation of digital media access and usage. This rapidly exposes users to large volumes of misleading, ambiguous, or inaccurate information without any form of expert review or "filter" (Moore et al., 2021).

The Janus-faced effect of media on health and well-being is particularly visible during a disaster or other public crisis. Disasters, whether of natural or of human origin, cause both immediate and ongoing threats to the safety and well-being of individuals and communities. Faced with a disaster, humans respond in varied ways, including both pro- and anti-social forms of behavior. Popular imagination tends to emphasize the latter, but behavioral and social scientists have found that the former predominates. Individuals tend to seek affiliation and companionship, protect members of their family or community, and offer help in the aftermath of a disaster. However, both individuals and groups are susceptible to waves of "panic," which reflect the evolutionarily ancient "fight or flight" response to threat. When it does occur, panic can accentuate the harm caused by a disaster and delay recovery efforts (Gantt & Gantt, 2012). In such a complex scenario, media can be either a help or a hindrance to disaster preparedness and recovery. They can be invaluable in providing early warnings, facilitating safety measures such as evacuation or relocation, providing communities with updates about disaster progression and relief, and in reuniting members of a family or community (Paek et al., 2010; Tan & Hao, 2022). On the other hand, they can exacerbate maladaptive or dissocial behavior, trigger or sustain panic, and hinder relief efforts by healthcare, law enforcement, or humanitarian workers in several ways (Box 16.1):

Box 16.1 Potential Harmful Effects of Media Coverage During a Disaster

- Exaggeration or underreporting of specific aspects of a disaster, due to a lack of training on the part of media personnel (de Ville de Goyet, 2007; Lowrey et al., 2007).
- Exaggerations of specific risks, leading to high levels of anxiety and outbreaks of panic, "mass psychogenic illness," or "mass hysteria" (LoVecchio et al., 2004; Vasterman et al., 2005).
- Biases of an ideological nature, leading to social polarization, conflict, or disengagement. This can hinder community recovery, reduce resilience, and interfere with the efforts of relief or healthcare workers (Ploughman, 1997; Carlé et al., 2004; Barnes et al., 2008; Tin & Ciottone, 2023).
- Exposure of affected populations to massive amounts of unverified information, including misleading or "fake" news, leading to an information epidemic or "infodemic." This is a particularly grave concern in relation to digital media (Houston et al., 2015; Pashaei Asl et al., 2022; Briand et al., 2023).

For this reason, public health experts have labeled media as both an "ally" and an "adversary" during disasters (Ball-Rokeach & Loges, 2000). Some have gone further, referring to the "disaster of misinformation" or "second disaster" that can accompany a natural or man-made disaster (Madianou, 2020; Muhammed & Mathew, 2022). Finding ways to maximize the beneficial potential of the media—while minimizing, or ideally preventing, this "second disaster"—is an essential component of disaster preparedness.

This chapter examines the "dual" role of the media in relation to disasters, with a particular focus on the South Asian context. Theoretical details of the links between media studies, psychology, and neurobiology will be outlined briefly, but the predominant focus will be on empirical data. The links between disasters, the media, and affected populations will be examined under three broad categories:

1. How does the media respond to disasters?
2. What are the negative aspects of this response, and how does this impact affected individuals and communities?
3. How can the media play a positive role in resilience and recovery from a disaster?

Finally, recommendations for how the media can best contribute to disaster preparedness and recovery will be outlined as part of a broader framework in which policymakers, professionals, media personnel, humanitarian workers, and affected populations are all key stakeholders (Lobb & Mock, 2007).

2 Theoretical Considerations

Media can be studied at least at three levels. The first, based on analysis of the contents or components of a medium, is the province of media or communication studies. The second, involving the psychological processes involved in perceiving and responding to media, is a branch of psychology. The third, which focuses on the neural correlates of information processing following media exposure, is relatively recent and belongs to the fields of social and cognitive neuroscience (Takeuchi et al., 2015). There has been little interdisciplinary research linking these three levels to date. Nevertheless, it is important for researchers to have at least a working knowledge of these three fields when studying the relationship between media and social events affecting entire communities or populations (Schmälzle & Huskey, 2023). To use a recent example, presentation of specific images in the media was hypothesized to trigger fear- or anxiety-related neural circuitry, leading to a specific maladaptive behavior—panic buying—during the COVID-19 pandemic (Alchin, 2020). To prevent this from happening, or at least to attenuate it, all three "levels" need to be understood: (a) the way in which specific media content, such as images, phrases, or sounds, trigger anxiety or panic, (b) the psychological processes, such as cognitive appraisals or negative affective responses, that influence a particular behavioral response to this content, and (c) the neurobiological substrate for these processes. Research on the third of these facets is still in its early stages.

Another concept that is heuristically useful in evaluating the effect of media on behavior during a disaster is Marshall McLuhan's classification of media into *hot* and *cold* (or cool). *Hot media*, such as the radio or photographs, engage a single sense at a high level, involving passive transfer of large amounts of data, and require little interaction or participation from the receiver. *Cool media*, such as television or telephonic conversations, provide less sensory data and require participation, interpretation, or even completion from the receiver (McLuhan, 1964). From a psychological perspective, a *hot* medium may be useful in providing specific information or instructions about disaster preparedness or relief. On the other hand, it might "overload" individuals with data or imagery, including distressing content. This could lead to responses such as anxiety, panic, or traumatic stress. A *cold* medium would bring into play an individual's diathesis. Responses to it would vary substantially depending on biological variables, psychological factors such as cognitive biases, and social and cultural norms.

Digital media, and especially social media, are unique in several ways (Box 16.2):

Box 16.2 The Unique Properties of Digital Media

- Digital media do not fit neatly into McLuhan's classificatory schema. For example, a social media post can combine photographs (a cool medium) and text that is open to interpretation and with which the user can interact (a hot medium).
- Digital content can be created by almost anyone: it is not under the direct control of government, media agencies, or other expert bodies.
- Digital media exposure tends to be far larger in volume and heterogenous in quality than mass media during a disaster.
- Digital media are not confined in their purpose to providing information or opinions: they are often used for entertainment, leisure, or social interaction.

For this reason, cognitive, emotional, and behavioral responses to digital media tend to be diverse and less predictable than those seen with mass media. Digital media are the major contributors to the "infodemic" phenomenon during a disaster (White et al., 2023). Moreover, some maladaptive behaviors related to digital media—such as sharing "fake news" on these—can occur simply due to users attempting to "pass time" or entertain themselves during a disaster (Balakrishnan et al., 2022).

When considering the impact of media coverage on a disaster-affected community, it is important to know what sort of media are generally used by its members. In a community with low digital literacy, where media such as radio or newspapers predominate, direct engagement of government and healthcare personnel with media agencies could facilitate favorable outcomes (Friedman, 1995). On the other hand, in a population with high levels of digital media usage, such a "public relations" approach may not suffice, and other strategies to mitigate against an "infodemic" should be considered (Briand et al., 2023). It is also important to remember that in most countries, individuals rely on both "old" and "new" media during disasters, and their emotional and behavioral responses to them may not align neatly with the predictions of theory (Xu et al., 2020; Güzel & Ergün, 2021).

3 Mass Media Response to Disasters: A Global Overview

Research into the way media respond to disasters, and how these responses affect health and behavior, can be traced back to the 1960s. A review of the medical literature can identify two broad categories of publications:

1. Those dealing with interactions between the healthcare system and the media.
2. Those addressing how disasters are covered in the media, and how this coverage affects individuals and communities.

As there is little overlap between these two publication types, especially in practice, they each will be reviewed separately.

3.1 Media Interactions with Healthcare Professionals and Systems During a Disaster

In the decades following the Second World War, a limited number of papers began to discuss the role of radio in communication by hospitals during disasters (Jenkins, 1962; Shoenfeld, 1965). A 1972 editorial in the *British Medical Journal* examined the role of radio and telephonic communication in ensuring coordination between hospitals and first responders (British Medical Journal, 1972). This early literature was mainly focused on how hospital staff could use media to communicate emergency needs. The importance of effective communication between healthcare professionals and the press during a disaster was emphasized by several authors, including O'Leary (1982), Allison (1984), and Friedman (1995). Horsfall (1985) described the potential danger of a media "invasion" at the site of a disaster, interfering with relief efforts. Partington and Savage (1985) were among the first to provide guidelines on how physicians should interact with mass media during disasters. Similar guidance on how medical experts could best communicate with the press during disasters was provided by De Marchi (1991), Kelly (1998), and Anzur (2000). The concerns addressed by these guidelines are outlined in Box 16.3.

Box 16.3 Key Concerns for Healthcare Professionals When Communicating with the Media During a Disaster

- Determining the type of information to be released at different time points
- The need to build trust between health and relief workers and the press
- Clear and succinct communication at regular intervals
- Protecting the privacy of victims and their families
- Organizing media interactions so that they do not interfere with victim safety and treatment

The year 1990 saw the beginning of the International Decade for Natural Disaster Reduction. In this context, Rattien (1990) emphasized the essential role played by mass media in disaster preparedness and response and called for greater collaboration between media personnel, disaster relief personnel, and researchers involved in disaster management. From a technical perspective, Yoho (1994) was one of the first to predict that advances in wireless communication could improve disaster response: he foresaw the importance that mobile phones and related devices would assume in such situations in the future. The need to restrict media access in particularly high-risk situations, such as terrorist attacks, was discussed by Christen et al. (1999). Nocera (2000) highlighted the need for "ethical journalism" during a disaster and how media personnel's failure to adhere to ethical principles could cause distress and lower the morale of victims, communities, and healthcare workers. These ethical principles are summarized in Box 16.4.

Box 16.4 Principles of Ethical Journalism When Covering Disasters

- Accurate reporting of disaster-related facts, without exaggeration, distortion, or suppression
- Presenting images and videos in an accurate manner, without distortion or selective editing
- Giving affected individuals the right to respond to critical or unfavorable media coverage
- Respect for victims' privacy and the grieving process
- Obtaining interviews and information in a transparent and fair manner
- Avoiding bias based on personal, ideological, or commercial considerations
- Disclosing conflicts of interest

(Nocera, 2000)

The need for better media use—in terms of both coverage and interactions with professionals and aid workers—has also been emphasized by professional groups in the field of disaster medicine (De Grace et al., 2001).

Laurie Garrett, a journalist who was awarded a Pulitzer Prize for her coverage of the Ebola epidemic in Zaire, provided a cogent, complementary response to the concerns raised by these guidelines. Her work highlighted the need for reciprocal understanding and cooperation between the media and other stakeholders during a disaster (Box 16.5):

Box 16.5 Journalists' Expectations When Interacting with Healthcare Professionals or Authorities During a Disaster

- Mutual respect between health experts and journalists, including the availability of a trained liaison officer
- Providing journalists with valid, easily accessible, and up-to-date information
- Avoiding the scapegoating or stigmatization of the media (for example, blaming them for cases of panic or antisocial behavior on the part of the public, or dismissing them as "sensationalistic")
- Empathy for the difficulties and pressures that media personnel operate under.
  (Garrett, 2001)

In other words, media responses during a disaster are not a "one-way street"—they also reflect and require the cooperation of governments, professionals, and the public. If healthcare professionals and media personnel work toward mutual understanding and cooperation, the media can be an asset not only in "general" disaster management, but in constructing helpful narratives about the mental health problems associated with disasters, and the remedies available for them (Newman & Shapiro, 2014).

3.2 *Media Depictions of Disasters, and Their Effects on Communities and Individuals*

3.2.1 Community Effects

The second line of research, addressing types of media coverage given to disasters, and their potential risks and benefits, began about 10 years later. In 1977, Claude de Ville de Goyet, an expert in disaster preparedness and relief, began to examine the role of the media in propagating misleading information after a disaster—more specifically, exaggerating the risk of infectious disease outbreaks after natural disasters, leading to public anxiety and unnecessary diversion of resources (de Ville de Goyet

Table 16.1 Disaster "myths" that often circulate in mass media

Myth	Actual observations
Foreign medical assistance is needed after a disaster.	Most countries and populations have qualified medical personnel to address health needs. External experts are needed only in selected cases.
Immediate help from the international community is needed after a disaster.	Most post-disaster needs are met by local communities, governments, or NGOs. Hasty international assistance can confuse and disorganize local disaster responses.
Infectious disease outbreaks are very common after disasters.	Such outbreaks are rare and can be prevented or controlled by improving local sanitation and educating the public.
Disasters cause antisocial behavior in affected individuals.	Antisocial behavior is the exception rather than the rule. Most individuals and communities behave in a prosocial manner after a disaster.
Disaster-affected populations suffer from "shock" and cannot look after their own needs independently.	Many disaster-affected individuals and populations exhibit resilience and resourcefulness.
Disasters can kill anyone "at random."	Socioeconomically vulnerable populations are usually the worst affected by disasters.
Temporary settlements are the best solution for people left homeless by disasters.	Such settlements are of limited efficacy. Obtaining materials and rebuilding local housing is a more permanent and viable solution.
Disaster victims require food, and/or are starving.	Food aid is required only if disasters cause crop loss or directly affect food supplies.
Disaster victims always require clothing.	Clothing is required only in selected cases.
After a disaster, conditions "return to normal" after a few weeks or months.	Disasters can have long-lasting impacts on physical and mental health and socioeconomic well-being.

et al., 1977). Subsequent work by this author and other experts working in disaster management identified eight "myths" that were commonly endorsed in mass media coverage of disasters. Though these myths did not necessarily originate from the media and were circulated by government officials and the public as well, the media were found to play a significant role in propagating them (Arnold, 2006; Alexander, 2007; Jacob et al., 2008; Milsten et al., 2024). These myths are enumerated in Table 16.1:

The need to avoid such myths when reporting on disasters was incorporated into guidelines drafted by the World Health Organization and other expert bodies (Lowrey et al., 2007). The media responded positively to this recommendation and have stopped endorsing at least some of them. For example, Morgan and de Ville de Goyet (2005) found that media coverage of the 2004 Indian Ocean tsunami provided largely accurate information about the risk of infectious disease outbreaks associated with dead bodies.

Some reports have attempted to examine the "double-edged" nature of media coverage following a disaster. Gist and Stolz (1982) described the usefulness of mass media in educating the public about mental health after a hotel collapse in Kansas City in 1981. McKay (1983) reviewed newspaper reports of a bushfire in

Australia. These reports emphasized individual acts of heroism, the helplessness of victims, and the extent of the devastation caused. While the information provided was accurate, there was little or no coverage of how to respond to such situations proactively. She concluded that while the reports were useful in sensitizing communities to the danger of such fires, they did not contribute to preparedness. Penelope Ploughman (1995) provided an elaborate description of how the media could shape narratives after disasters, such as emphasizing the role of natural factors and downplaying human errors or omissions. Similar observations were made a decade later by Boholm (2009) in relation to flooding and landslide risk in Sweden, and by Shrum (2014) in relation to Hurricane Katrina in the United States. Ploughman (1997) also examined how the media act as "gatekeepers" of public perception following a disaster, and how media narratives could be shaped by "vested interests." This effect was observed during the COVID-19 pandemic in South Korea, where media "framing" appeared to favor the interests of a particular political faction (Jo & Chang, 2020), and after floods in Australia, where media indulged in a "blame game" where failure in disaster preparedness or response is often assigned to current or previous governments or corporations, regardless of the underlying facts (Ewart & McLean, 2015). Such "gatekeeping" may also lead to reduced mass media coverage of vulnerable populations, such as internally displaced people, after a disaster (Aondover et al., 2025). Osterholm (1999) examined the role of the media in shaping perceptions of potential, rather than actual, disasters, using the case of bioterrorism. He concluded that though news coverage might exaggerate the risks and consequences of such a disaster, its consequences could be devastating, and preparedness was essential. Media could play a key role in preparing communities for future disasters, particularly where these have occurred in the past, such as recurrent flooding or earthquakes. On the other hand, a document prepared by the International Work Group on Death, Dying and Bereavement (2002) described how media "extend the range of disasters and bring them into the homes of people across long distances," raising concerns over vicarious traumatization. This concern was confirmed in subsequent research, as discussed below (Sect. 3.2.2). Stephenson and Jamieson (2009) highlighted the mixed nature of newspaper coverage of the avian influenza epidemic in Australia. While this coverage emphasized the need for preparedness, infrastructure, and public health measures, it also contained negative aspects, such as the depiction of a "threat" from Asia, a lack of explanation of the rationale for preventive measures, and minimal mention of the general public's opinions or perceptions.

Specific Concerns Related to Foreign or International Media Coverage

Thus far, we have considered the effects of local or national media coverage on community well-being after disasters, but most large disasters are also covered by media agencies from other countries or with an international scope. The involvement of international media in disaster coverage has often given rise to controversies, either inadvertently or by design. Olsen et al. (2003) pointed out how mass media sometimes provide greater coverage of some disasters than others, leading to inequalities in humanitarian concern and aid—for example, less coverage was given to civil wars in Sudan and Angola than to similar conflicts in Somalia and Yugoslavia. This concern was echoed by Lobb and Mock (2007), who also discussed the need for a "cooperative communication initiative" involving the media and other stakeholders, leading to better distribution of humanitarian aid and improved recovery after disasters. Following the Haiti earthquake, some observers documented the role of the media in "disaster medical tourism," where flattering portrayals of foreign aid workers were circulated even if their assistance to local populations was minimal or even counterproductive (Van Hoving et al., 2010).

Another concern is the distorted reporting of a disaster in one country by media from other countries: during the 2011 tsunami in Japan, foreign newspapers exaggerated the risks of nuclear contamination and fallout, while minimizing the suffering and human displacement caused by the tsunami itself. These media also used terms such as "panic buying" and "hoarding frenzy," even though such behavior was rare among affected Japanese people (McCartney, 2011). The opposite can also happen: during the COVID-19 pandemic, Western media portrayed South Korea's management of this health crisis in a largely positive light, ignoring the difficulties faced by the general population (Kang, 2020a). When a disaster affects individuals of different nationalities at the same time, media coverage can potentially exacerbate pre-existing political tensions between these nations: this concern was flagged during the 2015 Hajj pilgrimage stampede disaster (Khan & Noji, 2016). During the COVID-19 pandemic, mass media coverage sometimes contributed to racial discrimination or stigmatization—for example, by portraying Chinese or Asians in general as being sources of infection (Liu et al., 2023).

A survey of over 350 international media stories on disasters found that these often failed to follow good communication practices: while nearly 84% provided important information about the disaster itself, only 4–25% were found to express empathy, provide recommendations for action, or communicate risk accurately (Parmer et al., 2016). Nevertheless, it would be wrong to characterize the role of these media agencies in disaster coverage as universally negative. During the 2019–20 Australian bushfires, international media coverage was associated with increased financial donations for the support of victims (Chapman et al., 2023).

The theoretical or actual effects of mass media coverage of disasters at the collective level are summarized in Table 16.2.

3.2.2 Individual Effects

Adverse Psychological and Behavioral Effects

Post-traumatic stress disorder (PTSD) is the most frequently studied psychological outcome in individuals exposed to media coverage of disasters. Certain vulnerable groups, such as children and adolescents, may be more vulnerable to this outcome (Libow, 1992). Pfefferbaum et al. (1999, 2000, 2008) examined the relationship

Table 16.2 Effects of mass media coverage of disasters on affected communities or countries

Potentially beneficial effects	Potentially harmful effects
Local or national media	
Countering disaster myths Emphasis on individual or group heroic acts Highlighting community needs—physical and psychological Identifying potential dangers in the natural environment Community sensitization toward disaster preparedness	Propagating disaster myths Lack of specific advice on safety or preparedness measures Downplaying the role of human error in the genesis of disasters Reduced coverage of some vulnerable populations Political, social, or racial bias in media narratives Exaggeration of risks Vicarious traumatization (*see* Sect. 3.2.2)
International or foreign media	
Providing accurate information about the impact of a disaster Coordinating international aid efforts Promoting voluntary donations to relief work in the affected country	Inequal coverage of different international disasters Low coverage of local concerns "Disaster medical tourism" Racial or ideological biases in narrative, leading to discrimination, stigmatization, or worsening of prior inter-country tensions Exaggeration of risks Lack of empathy in reporting Lack of specific advice on safety or preparedness measures Propagation of some disaster myths (e.g., antisocial behavior)

between television coverage of the Oklahoma bomb attack and PTSD in adolescents. They found a positive association between the two, which persisted even 2 years after the incident, but decreased gradually at a 3-year follow-up. They also reported that traumatized adolescents might watch more disaster-focused coverage on television, underlining the complex two-way relationship between media and its receivers.

More evidence of a link between exposure to media coverage and psychological distress was seen in the aftermath of the September 11, 2011 ("9/11") terrorist attacks. Ahern et al. (2002) found that, in persons personally affected by these attacks, viewing television images of the attack was correlated with symptoms of PTSD and depression. Due to the cross-sectional nature of this study and the fact that all participants had suffered direct losses due to the disaster, it could not be concluded that media coverage was itself responsible for these symptoms. The same group also reported an association between viewing large amounts (>12 hours) of 9/11 "anniversary" news coverage and new-onset symptoms of PTSD in the general population in New York (Bernstein et al., 2007). An independent survey of individuals not directly affected by the same disaster also found an association between exposure to media coverage and psychological distress (Wayment, 2004), while another group studying the same disaster found a link between such exposure and new-onset or recurrent depression nearly 3 years later (Pfefferbaum et al., 2021). A similar study of mothers and children exposed to television coverage of 9/11 found that such exposure interacted with family discord to predict child psychological distress (Kennedy et al., 2004). Fairbrother et al. (2003) also reported elevated PTSD symptoms in children exposed to graphic images of 9/11 on television. Adults who viewed higher numbers of disaster-related images on television after this attack also had higher levels of traumatic stress symptoms, even after adjusting for confounding factors (Ahern et al., 2004).

Apart from PTSD, media reports exaggerating threats to one's life during a disaster can be associated with symptoms of anxiety and depression. Individuals who viewed coverage of Cyclone Yasi in Australia in 2011 (Woods et al., 2014) experienced feelings of panic and helplessness that were associated with the level of threats communicated in media reports. In the case of man-made disasters, such as terrorist or sniper attacks, viewing media coverage on television can be associated with depressive symptoms and a lower sense of safety (Fullerton et al., 2019). During the 2023 Turkey earthquakes, higher or repeated exposure to media coverage was associated with symptoms of PTSD, anxiety, and depression, suggesting that there could be a "dose-response" relationship for such effects (Oz & Cona, 2024). Certain demographic groups may be particularly vulnerable to the mental health effects of disaster coverage in mass media: during the COVID-19 pandemic, television viewing was associated with high levels of fear and anxiety in elderly Romanian adults (Sargu et al., 2023). Some viewers may experience continuous disaster coverage in media as being "addictive," leading to "fear of missing out" (FOMO), increased consumption, and heightened stress: this was observed in Israelis during the ongoing Israel-Hamas ("Iron Swords") war (Kaim & Bodas, 2024).

Direct links between exposure to disaster-related media and specific maladaptive behaviors are less clear. Increased media coverage of the avian flu outbreak was associated with increased stockpiling of the anti-viral medication oseltamivir (Tamiflu) in the general population in the United States, but a direct causal link was not examined (Gasink et al., 2009). Viewing television coverage of the Tohoku earthquake was also associated with maladaptive eating behaviors in individuals from other countries, though it is not clear if this relationship was causal (Rodgers et al., 2012). Exaggerated somatic concerns may also be related to media coverage of some types of disasters. Following the 9/11 attacks, fears of bioterrorism were widely circulated in the media: such coverage was associated with a large number of phone calls to a poison center. The authors of this report considered this behavior a form of "epidemic hysteria" that could be driven by media coverage (LoVecchio et al., 2004). Following an explosion disaster in the Netherlands, a temporal association between increased media attention and medically unexplained symptoms in victims was observed, but this study did not test directly for causality (Yzermans et al., 2005).

Cumulative exposure to media coverage of disasters may also "sensitize" individuals and lead to an accentuated stress response to a subsequent disaster (Garfin et al., 2015), and individuals who have experienced a particular disaster may be at risk of developing PTSD symptoms when viewing media reports of a similar disaster (Terui et al., 2024). Sometimes, media "memorials" of a disaster can also affect the well-being of disaster survivors, but these effects are not linear. In a survey of individuals interviewed 10 years after the Wenchuan earthquake in China, exposure to such reports showed a U-shaped relationship with sleep quality: those who had high and low exposure to such media reports had better sleep than those with intermediate exposure (Ma & Lin, 2020).

Media coverage of a disaster may also have a negative effect on the mental health of healthcare workers, including mental healthcare personnel. Exposure to media coverage of the 2011 Great East Japan (Tohoku) earthquake for more than 4 hours a day was associated with PTSD symptoms in medical rescue workers (Nishi et al., 2012). In a survey of Japanese workers involved in running suicide helplines during the COVID-19 pandemic, nearly 13% reported "excessive media coverage" as playing a role in their own psychological distress (Ujihara et al., 2023).

The mental health effects of media coverage can, in some instances, extend to countries not directly affected by a disaster: this is an example of "vicarious traumatization." A study of the general population in Hong Kong—a region not directly affected by the 2004 Asian tsunami—found that 30–45% of those exposed to tsunami-related news reports experienced symptoms of PTSD. These symptoms were correlated with measures of the content of these reports (Lau et al., 2006). After the outbreak of the war between Russia and Ukraine in 2022, German citizens exposed to media reports of the war experienced elevated levels of anxiety and general distress (Gottschick et al., 2023).

Inconsistencies in the Above Evidence

Not all researchers have found a significant association between exposure to media coverage of disasters and adverse mental health outcomes. A study of Greek children during the 1999 earthquake found much lower levels of PTSD and anxiety symptoms in those who were only exposed to media images than in those close to the epicenter, suggesting that media exposure alone did not produce high levels of trauma (Groome & Soureti, 2004). A study of individuals exposed to an airshow disaster in Ukraine found only a weak association between television coverage of the incident and mental health (Bromet et al., 2005). In a retrospective analysis of emergency psychiatry visits for disaster-related anxiety in the United States over the period 1995–2001, there was no relationship between the intensity of media coverage and the rates of such visits (Claassen et al., 2011). Public media exposure was also not associated with health anxiety in evacuees during the Fukushima nuclear disaster in Japan (Orui et al., 2020). In individuals vicariously exposed to coverage of the MH17 Ukraine air crash, personality variables predicted acute stress responses, but media exposure did not (Jeronimus et al., 2019). During the COVID-19 pandemic, exposure to media coverage was associated with increases in positive and negative emotions, but did not induce symptoms of anxiety or depression: this suggests that not all emotional responses to disaster-related media are pathological (Liu et al., 2022).

Positive Psychological and Behavioral Effects

Studies reporting predominantly positive outcomes of media coverage on health or well-being are fewer in number, though their results are encouraging. A survey of respondents affected by a terrorist bombing of the United States embassy in Nairobi, Kenya, found that 70% drew hope from media coverage of the attack and 90% felt that they should be allowed to continue (Njenga et al., 2003). A study of two independent disasters—the Nairobi bombing and floods in Venezuela—found that the mass media could be used to promote mental health awareness and recovery, and this was perceived to be helpful by local communities (Otero & Njenga, 2006). Similarly, a media campaign focusing on mental health following Hurricane Katrina was associated with increased help-seeking by affected people (Beaudoin, 2008). An analysis of newspaper reports following the 9/11 attack found that 47% discussed coping mechanisms for emotional distress, though only 6% provided details of mental health services that could be contacted if required (Renzulli et al., 2006). A retrospective examination of a severe storm in Australia found that the local radio station played a key role in providing information related to public health and disaster readiness (Cretikos et al., 2007, 2008), though television was considered less important. The importance of radio in disaster preparedness was also reported in a survey of the general population in Indonesia (Romo-Murphy et al., 2011).

In general, mass media exposure can have a positive impact on risk perception and intentions to adopt safety behavior in individuals facing a natural disaster (Zhao et al., 2019). News exposure was also associated with a higher likelihood of willingness to donate to disaster relief campaigns in general (Oosterhof et al., 2009) and in the specific situation of the 2010 Haiti earthquake (Lobb et al., 2012). In situations where there is good communication between public health authorities and the media, good-quality information about emerging disasters, such as disease outbreaks, can be disseminated through local television networks (Pribble et al., 2010). Likewise, media education was found to be an important component of "Project Liberty," a successful, large-scale mental health initiative launched in response to the 9/11 attacks (Sederer et al., 2011).

In adults exposed to Typhoon Hato in China, higher media usage was associated with an increased likelihood of recovery from disaster-induced PTSD symptoms: this led to the researchers' tentative suggestion that, in some cases, access to reliable media information could protect against mental ill-health after a disaster (Shi & Hall, 2023). A result that may reconcile this finding with those of earlier studies was observed in a study of the 2014 Sewol ferry disaster in South Korea. In this study, "approach-oriented" media use—in which individuals in the general population actively sought out disaster-related information—was associated with PTSD symptoms, but also with perceived personal growth. In contrast, individuals who avoided such media coverage experienced low levels of PTSD symptoms, but no perceived growth. Thus, the initial "traumagenic" effects of media may give way to resilience-promoting or "salutogenic" effects over time (Wong et al., 2024). Though this finding is of great interest when considering exposure to media coverage of disasters, it requires replication. Individual perceptions of media coverage and their reactions to it can also vary over time: in children affected by the Tohoku earthquake, post-traumatic growth was associated with a more positive attitude toward media coverage (Yoshida et al., 2016). In a study of tourists who survived the 2004 South Asian tsunami, attitudes toward the media were largely neutral or positive 6 years after their initial interactions with journalists (Englund et al., 2022).

Disaster Survivors and the Media

Interactions between disaster survivors and media personnel have received relatively less research attention. Immediately after a disaster, victims may experience media coverage and repeated requests for interviews as intrusive or distressing (North et al., 2022). In a qualitative analysis of interviews with train crash survivors in Sweden, respondents identified three types of interaction: harmful, inconsequential, and helpful. Their reactions to subsequent media coverage could also be categorized in this way. Such a typology, though requiring replication, could be useful in framing survivors' psychological responses to media attention after a disaster and in devising guidelines to maximize "helpful" communication between journalists and disaster victims (Englund et al., 2014). A similar typology was observed in Swedish tourists affected by the 2004 Indian Ocean tsunami: interactions with journalists were described by respondents as either professional, supportive, or "a strain" (Englund et al., 2022).

The psychological and behavioral effects of mass media coverage of disasters at the individual level are summarized in Table 16.3.

3.2.3 Journalists' Perspectives

Media personnel are themselves vulnerable to psychological distress when covering a disaster. A study of journalists who arrived early at the site of the 2004 Asian tsunami found that 25% screened positive for general psychological distress, and 75%

Table 16.3 Effects of mass media coverage of disasters on individuals

Potentially beneficial effects	Potentially harmful effects
Promotion of hope Increased mental health awareness and help-seeking Promotion of adaptive coping mechanisms Increased individual disaster awareness and preparedness Higher likelihood of adopting safety measures Possible protective effect of reliable information on PTSD Possible effect on post-traumatic growth and "salutogenesis"	Precipitation or exacerbation of PTSD symptoms Precipitation or exacerbation of depressive and anxiety symptoms Heightened feelings of helplessness and reduced security Increased health or somatic anxiety "Addiction" to media coverage and "FOMO" Stockpiling or hoarding of essential materials Heightened stress among relief workers Heightened stress among survivors or victims Possible sensitization to psychological distress during future disasters

Abbreviations: FOMO, fear of missing out; PTSD, post-traumatic stress disorder had moderate-to-severe PTSD symptoms. Such symptoms not only require evaluation and treatment but may also interfere with journalists' abilities to cover the disaster in an objective manner (Sin et al., 2005). This was confirmed in a survey of journalists reporting on the 2011 Tohoku earthquake, which showed that the negative emotions they experience can affect the way they interpret and respond to disaster-related media (Uchida et al., 2015). Some psychologists, based on newspaper report analysis, have speculated that journalists' coverage of disasters reflects their own psychological trauma and the use of unconscious defense mechanisms (Huss & Eichenberg, 2016). In other cases, despite possessing adequate knowledge or details about a particular disaster, journalists may resort to superficial, inaccurate, sensationalistic, or ideologically biased accounts and give little space to public health, safety-related information, or preparedness for future disasters. This may be due to pressures from news corporations or other vested interests, such as political parties or businesses (Ohmori, 2016; Bright, 2017; Chipidza et al., 2022; Straub, 2024).

3.2.4 Summary: Implications of Mass Media Responses to Disasters

Communication between governments, healthcare systems, relief workers, and conventional media remains crucial to disaster readiness and management even in the current era. The effects of media coverage on community well-being and individual mental health are heterogeneous and depend on the type of disaster, pre-existing individual or community vulnerabilities, the type of media, and the nature of the coverage.

It is likely that any mental health effects of disaster coverage in the media can be understood in terms of a stress-diathesis model, in which pre-disaster psychosocial vulnerability (the diathesis) interacts with both disaster-related variables and the various facets of its coverage in the media (the stressors). This was verified in a study of individuals from Florida exposed to Hurricane Irma. Individuals who rated themselves as being more likely to experience PTSD symptoms consumed more disaster-related media, and this in turn was associated with impaired psychological adjustment after the hurricane (Thompson et al., 2019). Independent studies have confirmed a circular relationship between exposure to disaster-related media and PTSD, with each increasing the likelihood of the other (Jung et al., 2019). Likewise, during the COVID-19 pandemic, pre-existing fears of death or contagion interacted with media exposure to determine symptoms of anxiety or depression (Mahat-Shamir et al., 2023). On the other hand, individuals with high levels of self-rated social support were less likely to experience psychological distress when exposed to media coverage of disasters, emphasizing the role of protective as well as risk factors in such a situation (Horiuchi et al., 2019). Vicarious traumatization of individuals unaffected by a disaster through media reports is also related to underlying vulnerabilities, such as demographic factors or personality traits (Huang et al., 2022).

Another point that merits consideration is that the different types of mass media may differ in their psychological effects on individuals. In a study of individuals

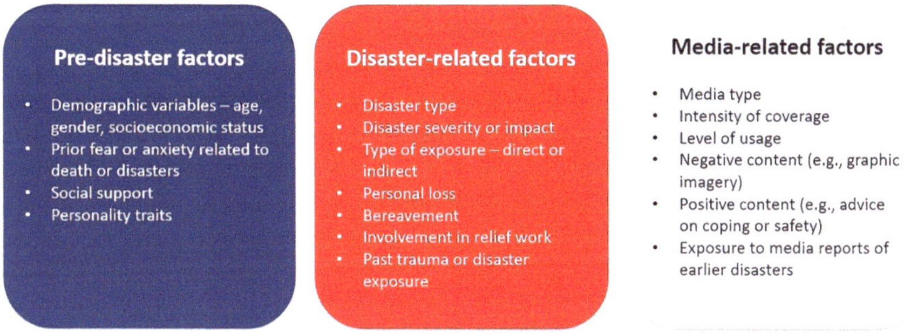

Fig. 16.1 Factors influencing individual psychological and behavioral responses to mass media coverage of disasters

exposed to the Tohoku earthquake and Fukushima nuclear disaster, coverage in local newspapers was associated with greater concern about the future, coverage in national newspapers was associated with less concern of this type, and radio coverage was associated with fears of social disruption (Sugimoto et al., 2013). The complex interaction between individual, disaster-related, and media variables in producing psychological and behavioral responses is summarized in Fig. 16.1.

In contrast to these often-discussed negative aspects, conventional media still play an important role in providing accurate information and early warnings, acting as a link between authorities and communities, and promoting prosocial and safety-oriented behaviors after a disaster. Their utility may be particularly high in communities where digital literacy is low. More recently, conventional media such as photographs have also been used to educate community members in disaster risk reduction strategies (Pickering et al., 2022).

It should be emphasized that the media alone is not responsible for psychological or social adverse outcomes in affected populations. This was underlined by an experiment conducted in healthy adults, some of whom were exposed to a simulated bioterrorism threat either with or without simulated media exposure. While the exposed groups had higher rates of psychogenic illness than the control group, there was no effect of media exposure per se (Broderick et al., 2011).

4 From Mass Media to Digital Media: New Opportunities and Challenges

Research on the response of digital media to disasters, and their downstream consequences, has grown rapidly in the past two decades, keeping pace with the widely increased usage of these media by all sectors of society (Farnham, 2006). It is not an exaggeration to state that these media have "redefined social interaction and communication" in much of the world (Leykin et al., 2016). A careful examination of the literature reveals that there are two sides to their usage and impact during a disaster.

4.1 Positive Effects on Well-Being and Disaster Readiness

James (2005) noted that text messages from mobile phones could be sent and received during a disaster even when "conventional" media were not functioning and suggested that this could be leveraged for disaster preparedness and management: such a scenario was observed during the 2016 Louisiana floods in the United States (Bosch, 2017). A similar advantage of social media over conventional means of disaster communication was reported by a flood-affected community in Ecuador (Tauzer et al., 2019). Digital media also offer advantages over mass media in terms of geographical reach: for example, international students seeking information about disasters in their home country usually have recourse to the Internet (Lu et al., 2007). During the 2008 Iowa floods, the Internet was the second most important source of information for affected households, ranking behind television (Murphy et al., 2010). When Taiwan was affected by a typhoon in 2009, online social networks and mobile devices were helpful in multiple facets of disaster management: providing information, recruiting volunteers, and distributing emergency supplies (Huang et al., 2010).

The Internet also serves as an important means of reporting damage and soliciting assistance: it was found to be useful in promoting donations for disaster relief after a landslide in Guatemala (Peltan, 2009). Likewise, social media were helpful in mobilizing donations for international aid after the 2010 Haiti earthquake (Keim & Noji, 2011) and may have had a more sustained effect on donations than conventional media (Lobb et al., 2012). For these reasons, some authors have referred to the current era of digital media and social networking as a "new age of opportunity" when dealing with disasters (Keim & Noji, 2011). Along similar lines, Crowe (2011) published a "social media manifesto" outlining the ways in which social media can be a particularly valuable resource in arranging and implementing disaster responses, while Wiederhold (2013) also emphasized its life-saving potential. Black et al. (2015) found that positive "tweets" about disaster preparedness were seven times more common than negative ones during the Tohoku earthquake, suggesting that social media could improve public health awareness in disaster situations. Yeager et al. (2015) conducted a detailed analysis of Twitter usage during the 2013 Hattiesburg tornado in the United States, and concluded that its unique features made it ideal to facilitate emergency and public health measures during disasters. During and after Typhoon Haiyan in the Philippines, the World Health Organization's regional office used Facebook, Twitter, and Instagram accounts to disseminate public health and preparedness messages, and these were followed by an increasing number of people as the content became more specific (Cool et al., 2015).

Social media activity can provide an estimate of the extent of structural or economic damage following a disaster, its overall severity, and the immediate needs of affected communities. This can facilitate the allocation of necessary resources or relief measures (Kryvasheyeu et al., 2016; Havas et al., 2017; Duan et al., 2020; Shoyama et al., 2021; Qu et al., 2023; Hou et al., 2024; Zou & Lv, 2025). In an infectious disease outbreak, it can also be used as an aid to traditional surveillance in identifying "waves" of new cases (Hossain et al., 2016) and in making tentative predictions of future case numbers (Kellner et al., 2023). Social media posts can also be used to monitor community mental health and plan appropriate care after a disaster (Kim et al., 2024): this was found to be feasible after the Sewol ferry disaster in South Korea (Woo et al., 2015) and the 2015 terrorist attack in Paris (Lin et al., 2017).

Positive use of digital media during a disaster is not confined to governments or relief agencies: "average people" often play an equal or even larger role in sharing useful information on social media, as was seen during five extreme weather events in the United States (Niles et al., 2019). Such usage can contribute to increased social cohesion, which can facilitate the efforts of local authorities and relief workers after a disaster (Fan et al., 2020) and contribute to post-traumatic growth (Levaot et al., 2021). The combined efforts of such users, referred to as "crowdsourcing," may also contribute to disaster preparedness and resilience (Clark et al., 2024). Social media use was found to improve adherence to infection control measures in Ethiopian citizens during the COVID-19 pandemic, suggesting that it could be an effective medium for the propagation of preventive health advice (Sadore et al., 2021).

Specific mobile phone applications ("apps") such as Zello, which emulate a conventional radio-based "walkie-talkie," have been suggested as alternatives to radio communication during extreme weather events (Chang et al., 2018). Dedicated social media pages or campaigns, such as the "All Right" initiative on Facebook to address mental health after the 2010–11 earthquakes in New Zealand, were rated as helpful by almost all users, and influenced behavior changes in 85% of those surveyed (Calder et al., 2020). Social media apps on smartphones can be used as a platform to provide psychological support during disasters, or to connect individuals to counseling services where direct contact is not feasible—for example, during the COVID-19 pandemic (Cheng et al., 2020; Ahmad et al., 2021). Though still largely an untapped resource in this regard, digital media can also be used to address needs such as spiritual support, which may not be a part of routine disaster relief measures or conventional media coverage (Papadopoulos et al., 2021; Nejati-Zarnaqi et al., 2024).

4.2 Negative Psychological and Social Effects

These beneficial effects of digital media should be contrasted with other, less desirable impacts or outcomes. Digital media coverage of disasters, whether through Internet news sites or social media, tends to have a low signal-to-noise ratio (Venegas-Vera et al., 2020). For example, in a survey of disaster-related reports from 119 websites, only 44% provided information that could guide individuals on how to act in the concerned situation (Tanner et al., 2009). In a similar examination of coverage of the Ebola epidemic on YouTube, it was found that death tolls and modes of transmission were mentioned, but issues such as the need for preparedness, funding, coordination, or health infrastructure were largely ignored (Basch et al., 2015). Social media can act as a rapid channel for the dissemination of misinformation ("fake news") and can sometimes affect the privacy of victims—for example, when a photograph of an affected individual is distributed online with a location tag (Keim & Noji, 2011). In a study of tweets during the initial phase of the COVID-19 pandemic, 22% were found to contain some form of false information about masking, vaccines, or other preventive measures (Trotochaud et al., 2023). A larger study of earthquake-related tweets in the period 2020–22 found that 19.5% contained misinformation, and 43.4% contained irrelevant or ambiguous information (Dallo et al., 2023). Social media may also propagate the "disaster myths" described in Table 16.1, leading to exaggerated fears of antisocial behavior and incorrect distribution of resources (Milsten et al., 2024). Internet-based media reports can also provide advice that is inaccurate or promote forms of aid that are counterproductive. For example, following a cyclone in Myanmar and an earthquake in China, Internet reports stated that stress could prevent breastfeeding and that infant formula was necessary to save children's lives. This could have had the unintended consequence of increasing donations of formula and discouraging breastfeeding, leading to increased infant morbidity (Gribble, 2013). During a mass shooting in Copenhagen, Denmark, misinformation and rumors on social media were found to impede the efforts of emergency medical responders (Hansen et al., 2023). Another concern related to digital media, with a potentially devastating impact on individual and community well-being, is the phenomenon of "digital terrorism," in which malicious actors—such as terrorist groups or their sympathizers—disseminate graphic or horrifying images of terrorist attacks using social media, with the aim of inducing panic and distress in their "target" population. A recent instance of such "digital terror" occurred during and after the October 7, 2023, attacks on Israel (Roe et al., 2025).

Social media effects on individual mental health and behavior may be positive or negative, depending on individual factors. During the Tohoku earthquake in Japan, Twitter usage was associated with feelings of both relief and stress in affected women, but only stress in affected men (Umihara & Nishikitani, 2013). Digital media may have deeper impacts on mental health than conventional media after a disaster: in a study of individuals affected by Typhoon Haiyan in the Philippines, YouTube use was associated with acute stress disorder, while Twitter use was associated with general distress. No such effect was seen for media such as television and newspapers. This has been attributed to "social contagion" of anxiety and stress through social media (Goodwin et al., 2015). Similarly, use of new media, but not traditional media, was associated with higher anxiety and stress during the COVID-19 pandemic in China (Chao et al., 2020). Because social media are more "democratic" in nature, accessible to any user with an Internet connection and account, the content tweeted by non-organizational or non-expert users varies widely in quality: it can not only contain messages of support but also propagate negative emotions or politically charged content with low informational value (David et al., 2016; Chipidza et al., 2022). At times, digital media may lead to exposure to graphic disaster-related images in an age-inappropriate manner, leading to emotional distress and behavioral problems in children and adolescents (Jones et al., 2016; Kurt et al., 2024). In a study of Chinese university students exposed to Typhoon Hato, exposure to either emotional reactions or information about drowning deaths was associated with the emergence of PTSD symptoms, suggesting that both the "social contagion" and "graphic imagery" components of social media can act as stressors (Hall et al., 2019). Exposure to online misinformation on the Internet can also be associated with increased mental distress in affected populations; this was observed during the Tohoku earthquake in Japan (Yumiya et al., 2019). Misinformation on social media can also contribute to antisocial behaviors such as food hoarding (Charilaou & Vijaykumar, 2021) and to the rejection of public health precautions, such as immunization (Wu et al., 2025). Higher use of social media during a disaster, sometimes colloquially referred to as "doomscrolling," can also be associated with depressive symptoms and increased stress (Zhao & Zhou, 2020; Taskin et al., 2024). Combined exposure to conventional and digital media coverage was linked to symptoms of acute stress disorder during the COVID-19 pandemic (Luo et al., 2021). Reliance on digital media was also associated with higher levels of health anxiety and risk perception during the Fukushima nuclear disaster in Japan (Nakayama et al., 2023). The stress caused by a prolonged disaster, such as the COVID-19 pandemic, may lead to excessive social media usage as a coping strategy, leading to social media addiction (Zhao & Zhou, 2021). As is the case with mass media, social media exposure can cause vicarious traumatization of individuals not directly exposed to a disaster: this was seen, for example, in Chinese youth exposed to social media coverage of an aircraft accident (Li et al., 2024).

The long-term effects of social media coverage of disasters, or the way in which such coverage evolves over time, remain to be explored fully (Ogie et al., 2022). In the case of a prolonged disaster, the beneficial impact of social media may give way to more ambiguous or negative effects. For example, during the COVID-19 pandemic in the United States, there was a high level of motivation and intent to adhere to safety measures in the early stages. Over time, this gave way to apathy, hostility, and the spread of misleading information about these measures (Mikal et al., 2021). Delayed negative effects of social media have also been documented: over 5 years after the Fukushima disaster in Japan, social networking site use—but not conventional news media exposure—was associated with higher anxiety (Fukasawa et al., 2021).

Certain limitations in the use of digital media during disasters, which can indirectly affect individual or community outcomes, should also be noted. Because of its dependence on technology, digital media may be "offline" in situations such as large power outages, and individuals may have to rely on conventional media in such cases (Burger et al., 2013). If authorities or healthcare professionals miss the opportunity to engage with social media or engage with it in a poorly organized manner, this can lead to heightened stress and distrust among the general population (Ng & Lean, 2012; Mendez et al., 2025). Likewise, if professionals or organizations are not familiar with the nuances of using specific types of social media or are hesitant to adapt to this "new" medium, this could also lead to missed chances for better

Table 16.4 Benefits and harms associated with digital media coverage of disasters

Potentially beneficial effects	Potentially harmful effects
May be accessible more easily and rapidly than mass media in some disasters Better geographical reach Rapid propagation of essential disaster-related information Improved disaster preparedness, public health awareness, and readiness to adopt safety measures Useful in recruiting volunteers and soliciting financial aid Rapid reporting of damage Can be used as a dynamic source of data on disaster scope and severity (e.g., property damage, new cases of infectious diseases) Can be used to monitor the mental health of affected communities Helpful in providing social and possibly spiritual support	Low "signal to noise" ratio—high levels of ambiguous or irrelevant information Propagation of "disaster myths" and erroneous advice about safety or health-related behaviors "Fake news" or disinformation, discouraging positive behavioral change (e.g., immunization), promoting mistrust and suspicion, and harming relief efforts "Digital terrorism" Possible interference with the privacy of victims Increased levels of stress, anxiety, and general psychological distress in frequent users or those engaged in "doomscrolling" Online "social contagion" of fear and anxiety Propagation of inflammatory content, causing social division or unrest Risk of exposure to graphic or violent imagery in child or adolescent users Vicarious traumatization Decrease in positive effects over time May be offline in certain types of disaster Lack of comfort among users (experts or community members) unfamiliar with digital media, and in those with low digital access or literacy

communication and interaction with volunteers or affected persons (Gurman & Ellenberger, 2015; Khan et al., 2019). Certain populations—for example, rural communities—may prefer other forms of communication once the acute phase of a disaster has passed. Attempting to engage with such groups chiefly through social media may lead to sub-optimal recovery from disasters (Lea & Beers, 2025) and may lead to increased stress (Gaffney et al., 2024).

The benefits and risks of digital media coverage of disasters are summarized in Table 16.4.

4.3 Summary: Implications of Digital Media Responses to Disasters

The potential for digital media to bridge the "disaster readiness gap" is substantial, though it is often overlooked (Gowan et al., 2015). Because of their unique properties, they can facilitate the dissemination of vital information and guide dynamic responses to disasters in "real time" (Callaghan, 2016; de Bruijn et al., 2019). It is important that these media are used in an ethical way by all stakeholders to minimize negative effects such as community distrust and individual psychological distress (Gehner & Oughton, 2016). Social media responses to a disaster are complex, consisting of both adaptive and maladaptive components, and disseminating information alongside opinions, rumors, and emotions. This leads to highly variable effects on psychological health and behavior, which are often dependent on pre-existing psychosocial vulnerabilities (Murthy & Gross, 2017; Liu et al., 2020): as one group of researchers has phrased it, digital media have "bright and dark sides" during disasters (Cato et al., 2021). Likewise, disaster-related information on social media often combines accurate and inaccurate or distorted data that can lead to maladaptive behavior. It is prudent, to quote one group of experts, to "trust, but verify" and not accept all information unconditionally (Mehta et al., 2017). Phenomena such as "fake news" on social media often reflect pre-existing biases, such as mistrust of governments or social fault lines, and cannot be solved through simply placing curbs on them (Balakrishnan et al., 2022; Giotakos, 2022; Yang et al., 2023).

It is likely that the best outcomes in terms of both disaster response and individual well-being can be achieved by making use of both conventional and digital media (Wolkin et al., 2019) and by using social media in a way that facilitates and synergizes with disaster relief efforts (Torpuş et al., 2025). Those involved in disaster relief should be aware that the timing of their engagement with digital media is crucial: early use of social media by authorities is more likely to have positive effects on public trust and disaster responses (Li et al., 2020). Apart from timing, the use of effective communication strategies adapted to the format of social media platforms is essential for favorable outcomes (Vera-Burgos & Griffin Padgett, 2020). Research in this field is growing rapidly, and it is important for those involved in using or managing social media during a disaster to keep abreast of it (Demiroz, 2020). A research priority for disaster experts is finding innovative ways of using digital and social media data to analyze past disasters and track current ones in a multidimensional way, monitoring disaster impacts, population needs, and physical and mental wellness. From the mass of information obtained in this way, it is necessary to filter out the "signal" from the mass of "noise" in order to create a knowledge base that will bridge the "disaster readiness gap," particularly in low- and middle-income countries where available resources need to be mobilized equitably and effectively (Chan & Purohit, 2020). Likewise, methods of disseminating essential advice and stemming the flow of misinformation should be investigated in depth. Preparedness efforts related to digital media should involve not just authorities or first responders, but the public—the "common man" or woman whose use of social media can contribute substantially to resilience and adaptive behavior during disasters (Chu & Yang, 2020). This could prevent newer media from becoming a "double-edged sword" during current and future disasters (Peyravi & Ahmadi Marzaleh, 2020). Certain specific techniques, such as the involvement of celebrity spokespersons, could aid local and global authorities in engaging more effectively with the public through online social networks (Malik et al., 2021). Those involved in providing "official" information, support, or guidance on social media during a disaster should plan their interventions in an organized manner, adapting their messaging to specific disaster or post-disaster situations, providing consistent messages, and keeping a channel open for feedback from affected individuals (Knox, 2023). These new media should be used not only to communicate with the public but to facilitate communication between the various actors and agencies involved in disaster recovery measures (Hu et al., 2023).

5 The South Asian Scenario

South Asia consists of eight countries—Afghanistan, Bangladesh, Bhutan, India, the Maldives, Nepal, Pakistan, and Sri Lanka—that together contain over 20% of the world's population, all of which are categorized as low- and middle-income. South Asian countries are at risk of a wide range of disasters, both natural and man-made (Mukherjee et al., 2022). According to some estimates, the frequency of extreme weather-related disasters may increase in South Asia in the coming decades, due to the effects of climate change (Mondal et al., 2021). Because of limitations in manpower, infrastructure, and expertise, disaster readiness and responses in South Asia are not always adequate (Khan & Mishra, 2022). The governments of these nations have recognized this, particularly in the wake of the COVID-19 pandemic, and many have taken active steps to improve their disaster readiness programs and policies (Jain et al., 2021). As is the case elsewhere in the world, the media are actively involved in covering disasters in South Asian countries. There are various facets to this coverage, which can either help or interfere with relief efforts, community resilience, and post-disaster recovery. These diverse aspects of media coverage, reviewed in Sects. 3 and 4, provide the necessary context for interpreting South Asian research on media responses to disasters. Indigenous research in this field is relatively young—dating back to 2001—but has already yielded several key findings that are of importance in improving South Asia's "disaster readiness gap." These may be conveniently classified into "positive" and "negative" dimensions, though some findings do not fit neatly into these categories, or combine aspects of both.

5.1 Beneficial or Adaptive Aspects of Media Response to Disasters in South Asia

5.1.1 Mass Media

Conventional media coverage of disasters in South Asia often highlights issues or concerns that are of vital importance to affected communities. This can facilitate the efficient dissemination of information, mobilization of resources, and manpower. After a 2004 fire at a school in Kumbakonam, India, authorities reported that they were able to communicate efficiency and promptly with local media. Among the parents of children affected by this disaster, 66% of mothers and 84% of fathers felt that media management during the tragedy had been appropriate (Satapathy & Walia, 2007). Local or national media often outperform international media in this regard: in a study of media coverage of the 2015 Nepal earthquake, "local" newspapers were superior to "foreign" media in addressing concerns related to infrastructure and finance (Dhakal, 2018). In a survey of Bangladeshi students during the COVID-19 pandemic, 82% agreed to the statement "The media played an effective role in making people aware about the coronavirus" (Ahmed et al., 2023). Local media can also provide key information about services such as telephone helplines for public assistance: this was observed in Nepal during the COVID-19 pandemic (Singh et al., 2022). In contrast, international media may provide extensive coverage during the early phases of a disaster, but be less attentive during the recovery and rebuilding process; this was observed in Pakistan during a 2005 earthquake (Cohen, 2006).

In conditions where access to other media is unavailable, conventional media can still be an essential component of disaster preparedness and recovery. During the 2005 Pakistan earthquake, FM radio played a multifaceted role in this process, allowing for communication between affected communities, relief workers, and the government. It also served as a source of positive or encouraging messages, allowing for a gradual return to "normal" life (Rahman et al., 2021). In an assessment of flood-prone regions in Bangladesh, two-thirds of those surveyed relied on television or radio messages for early warnings (Ansari et al., 2022). Similarly, where literacy poses a barrier to digital media usage, mass media are often the main source of disaster-related information. In a survey of adults without formal education in Pakistan, 75% relied on television for news about the COVID-19 pandemic (Salman et al., 2021).

Mass media may play a role in bringing to light the mental health burden of a disaster: during the 2022 flood in Pakistan, local newspapers highlighted the links between flood-related damage or economic loss and suicide, particularly in men (Mahesar et al., 2024). Likewise, they can be helpful in promoting prosocial behavior. In a study of news reports on panic buying from Bangladesh during the COVID-19 pandemic, the majority reported details accurately and provided advice on how to obtain goods without falling prey to panic or resorting to hoarding (Arafat et al., 2021).

Local media can also raise public awareness of controversies or shortcomings related to disaster relief, such as the government of Pakistan's attempts to obtain monetary compensation from the owners of the oil tanker *Tasman Spirit*, involved in a massive oil spill in Karachi in 2003. Media coverage of this issue highlighted not just the responsibilities of the concerned corporation in providing monetary support to affected populations, but the need for preparedness to ensure that future disasters of this sort are better handled by governments (Mian & Bennett, 2009). Likewise, the media played an important role in highlighting shortages of essential medical supplies in some parts of Tamil Nadu, India, during the COVID-19 pandemic (Sriram et al., 2025).

5.1.2 Digital Media

As noted in other countries, social media can be useful in identifying the concerns and emotions of the public when faced with a disaster. During a 2019 drought in Chennai, India, Twitter content not only revealed high levels of anxiety about water scarcity but also showed that users were discussing the causes of the drought and had a positive attitude toward sustainable solutions to the water crisis (Xiong et al., 2020). As the second wave of the COVID-19 pandemic affected India, analysis of Twitter content revealed that fear and surprise were the predominant emotions, while disease spread through crowds or political rallies, and disruption of education (e.g., cancellation of examinations) were commonly expressed concerns. Identifying such concerns facilitates the work of those involved in disaster management by helping them to engage more constructively with affected communities (Paul, 2022). Social media have also been used to study the time course of emotional responses to a disaster. During the 2015 floods in Chennai, India, analysis of Twitter content found that negative emotions peaked rapidly during the floods but reduced by over 50% over the next 2 months (Karmegam & Mappillairaju, 2020).

Social media can also be used for the rapid dissemination of warnings, instructions, or assistance: during the second wave of the COVID pandemic in Nepal, it proved useful in advertising a telephonic helpline run by a non-governmental organization to provide public health advice (Singh et al., 2022). Mobile applications such as WhatsApp can be useful in communicating relief workers' or volunteers' requirements for material and manpower: this was observed during the 2015 Nepal earthquake (Basu et al., 2017). Surveys of individuals affected by the 2007 and 2017 landslides in Bangladesh found that receiving early warnings through text or social media messages was considered an essential component of disaster preparedness (Alam & Islam, 2023). A survey of residents in a flood-prone region of the same country found that social media was perceived as valuable in providing early warnings, keeping in touch with other members of the community, and recruiting volunteers. Overall, it was considered to have significantly improved disaster readiness in this region (Alam et al., 2024).

Digital media can be equally valuable in promoting disaster readiness, particularly among youth who use it extensively. In a survey of high school students from Nepal, 83% of respondents obtained their information about disasters from the Internet. This information was associated with an improved awareness of disaster risk (Ghale et al., 2025). Among farmers in northeast India, 47% reported exposure to digital media. Those with such exposure had a greater awareness of possible future drought and modified their crop cultivation patterns accordingly, rendering them less economically vulnerable to such events (Kalita et al., 2024).

Analysis of social media content can also be used to identify misinformation or disinformation in its early stages: this was seen in an analysis of WhatsApp and Facebook content from Pakistani users during the COVID-19 pandemic (Ali et al., 2021a). Identifying such material can facilitate attempts to counter or correct misleading advice or narratives during a disaster.

5.2 *Maladaptive Aspects of Media Response to Disasters in South Asia*

5.2.1 Mass Media

Inaccurate information disseminated through mass media can contribute to anxiety and panic during a disaster. During the 2006 flood in Surat, India, media reports exaggerated the risk of an infectious disease outbreak, misattributed the cause of death of certain individuals whose cause of death was a pre-existing medical condition, and reported others as dead, though they were later found to be alive (Tripathi & Bansal, 2007). A similar phenomenon of misattribution of the cause of death was seen during the 2015 heat wave in Karachi, Pakistan: many media reports attributed death to the practice of fasting during Ramadan, though a subsequent review of death certificates found that this was not the case (Ghumman & Horney, 2016). The anxiety caused by media coverage can affect public engagement in profitable industries, such as tourism. Such a "tourism crisis" can last well beyond any actual disaster risk period, and has been documented in relation to media reporting on the 2004 tsunami in Sri Lanka (Robinson & Jarvie, 2008).

At times, mass media can exaggerate the physical damage caused by a disaster. During the 2004 Indian Ocean tsunami, mass media reported "catastrophic" damage to coral reefs in the Maldives, but a later examination by experts revealed lower levels of damage that varied in different regions (Goffredo et al., 2007). A related concern is exaggerated or inaccurate media reports about the risk of the recurrence of a disaster: during the 2015 Nepal earthquake, such reports were associated with higher levels of anxiety and with maladaptive coping strategies such as alcohol use (Hall et al., 2017).

Mass media can also have a negative effect on disaster relief or recovery efforts. Healthcare workers in Nepal reported that media personnel could interfere with the treatment of injured persons by entering hospital premises and taking unauthorized photographs: when reprimanded for the same, they were verbally aggressive to hospital staff (Singh et al., 2023). Fear of negative media coverage can negatively influence the interventions offered by healthcare workers. This was observed after the 2001 Gujarat earthquake, where surgeons reported that they opted for conservative management out of fear of media criticism of amputations: in many cases, amputation was eventually necessary (Roy et al., 2005). Exposure to graphic imagery in conventional media can also trigger or exacerbate symptoms of PTSD in relief workers. This was noted in a study of first responders to the 2023 Bahanaga train accident in India (Ravan et al., 2024).

The psychological effects of mass media coverage of disasters have not been studied systematically in South Asian populations. Uvais (2020) reported the case of a middle-aged woman who developed PTSD through exposure to television coverage of the 2019 flood in Kerala, India, without any direct exposure. It is unknown if such cases represent isolated incidents or if they are common and under-reported in disaster-affected communities.

As South Asian countries move toward alignment with the Sustainable Development Goals, an important issue is whether mass media provide sufficient coverage of ecological issues. A review of media coverage of disasters and related events in Nepal found that while there was adequate coverage of the human aspect of these incidents, issues such as animal or environmental health, or the links between environmental degradation and disasters, received little attention (Schwind et al., 2017). This may be because environment-themed programs are relatively unpopular among radio listeners in Nepal (Paudel et al., 2020).

5.2.2 Digital Media

Several researchers have drawn attention to the adverse mental health effects of digital media in South Asian communities during a disaster. A qualitative study of Indian citizens during the COVID-19 lockdown found that repeated searches for pandemic-related news on the Internet, as well as "doomscrolling," were associated with higher perceived anxiety and stress (Tudu, 2022). Another study of Indian adults during this period found that 65–84% felt they were being "overloaded" with COVID-19 news through social media. Exposure to misinformation on social media was associated with higher levels of stress in Bangladeshi students and professionals (Patwary et al., 2022a). In the same country, overall reliance on digital or social media for information during the COVID-19 pandemic was associated with higher levels of depression, anxiety, and stress in teachers (Hossain et al., 2022) and higher levels of anxiety and stress in the public (Patwary et al., 2021). Social media addiction has been reported as a complication of the COVID-19 pandemic in Bangladesh, particularly in those with high levels of anxiety. Those reporting such an addiction had lower self-reported health (Nur-A Yazdani et al., 2022). Exposure to graphic imagery of disasters through social media can also affect the mental health of rescue workers: this was noted in Indian first responders to a train accident (Ravan et al., 2024).

Levels of trust in digital media may be relatively low, as individuals grow more aware of the risks of misinformation. In a survey conducted in Pakistan during the COVID-19 pandemic, only 23% of respondents stated that they believed in social media information (Ali et al., 2021b). While social media do not "cause" misinformation or conspiracy theories, they can facilitate their rapid spread and amplify their social impact. In an examination of six specific rumors that arose during the COVID-19 pandemic in Pakistan, Ali (2022) found that these arose due to cultural, religious, or political factors, but traveled rapidly through social media and affected pandemic preparedness. However, he noted that such "narratives" could easily circulate by word of mouth or through conventional media as well.

5.3 *Other Specific Considerations*

The transition from conventional to digital media usage in South Asia has been uneven, with significant divisions along educational and economic lines. About half of healthcare workers, pharmacists, and students in Pakistan and Bangladesh reported relying on social media as their main source of information during the COVID-19 pandemic (Muhammad et al., 2022; Patwary et al., 2022b; Ahmed et al., 2023). On the other hand, rural respondents in Nepal reported difficulties in using digital media during the 2015 earthquake. Reasons for this included a lack of Internet connectivity, no formal education, low digital literacy, and unfamiliarity with the English language (Crane et al., 2017).

The difficulty in involving mass or digital media in specific preventive measures—such as crowd control—was highlighted by Burkle and Hsu (2011) in their retrospective analysis of the 2010 Ram Janki temple stampede in Uttar Pradesh, India. The need for effective communication between health authorities and the media was highlighted in a qualitative study of healthcare workers during the 2019 Nipah virus outbreak in Kerala, India. Respondents in this study noted that they were frequently asked for updates by the media and that, in some cases, individual journalists attempted to obtain information by posing as government authorities. Despite these challenges, they reported being able to disseminate accurate information and advice through a selected media route (Menon & George, 2021).

The mixed nature of messaging in relation to specific disaster-related issues was observed during the COVID-19 pandemic in India. In a survey of 500 Tweets, it was found that over 58% of users expressed negative attitudes toward the COVID-19 vaccine; however, several users also attempted to counter "myths" about the vaccine or to highlight issues such as vaccine shortages (Verma et al., 2023).

At times, attempts by the media to communicate useful information after a disaster may be misunderstood by South Indian populations. This may reflect a lack of health literacy, of clarity in media messaging, or both. For example, after the 2015 Nepal earthquake, some consumers of public health information disseminated through the media believed that chlorine tablets had to be ingested to prevent waterborne diseases (Hall et al., 2017).

There is little information on media-related vicarious traumatization of South Asian individuals exposed to coverage of disasters outside South Asia. In a study of Indian adolescents following the 9/11 terror attacks, adolescents who had witnessed the incidents on television reported higher levels of "shock and horror" than those who had read about them in newspapers (Ray & Malhi, 2005).

5.4 Summary: Conventional and Digital Media During Disasters in South Asia

The "double-edged" impact of media coverage of disasters in South Asia is similar to that seen in other geographical areas. Local mass media remain valuable in settings where there is low digital access or literacy: they can be used to raise awareness, provide early warnings, promote desirable behaviors, and highlight community concerns after a disaster. However, they may provide exaggerated or inaccurate estimates of disaster severity, leading to negative emotional responses and PTSD symptomatology. Interference with post-disaster healthcare or relief efforts, or with long-term recovery in certain industries, has also been documented. Digital media may have advantages over mass media in terms of speed and reach: they can help affected persons "stay connected" to each other if separated during a disaster and help in coordinating relief work and recruiting community volunteers. However, concerns related to possible "information overload," the spread of misinformation or disinformation, and negative mental health effects—including anxiety, depression, PTSD, and even social media addiction—have been identified in some South Asian communities affected by disasters. There is insufficient data on whether the benefits of either form of media outweigh their potential harms or on whether the frequency of specific outcomes (such as PTSD following digital media exposure) is different in South Asia when compared to the rest of the world.

From a practical point of view, these findings underline the need for good communication between authorities and mass media, for responsible reporting, and for the effective use of digital media in providing early warnings and safety recommendations. Digital media may be particularly useful in community engagement where there is a reasonable level of familiarity with technology. Some local experts have suggested ways in which digital media can be leveraged to identify key population concerns and monitor mental health after disasters. This could improve the utilization and uptake of disaster relief interventions by communities.

6 Recommendations

Media can contribute significantly to disaster relief, the reduction of human and economic costs, and the promotion of physical and mental health during and after disasters. However, not all media are equally effective in each disaster scenario, and both conventional and digital media have the potential to either aid or hinder recovery after a disaster (Lu et al., 2020). Social media, which combine the role of the mass media with social interaction and networking, provide a unique opportunity for individuals and communities, and not just experts or authorities, to play an active role in disaster preparedness and management (Sobowale et al., 2020).

Access to good-quality information through the media is a key determinant of mental well-being during a disaster. Both a lack of information and unreliable information are associated with depression and PTSD in affected individuals, and this, in turn, can lead to lowered public trust and a disconnect between authorities and communities (Kang, 2020b; Cal et al., 2024). In contrast, access to media that were perceived as trustworthy can protect against PTSD symptoms in individuals facing a disaster, and these beneficial effects are sustained over time (Estes et al., 2024).

A recent survey conducted by the United Nations Educational, Scientific and Cultural Organization (UNESCO) surveyed 60 media institutions, both private and public, across several geographic areas. It was found that 40% did not have a standard plan or procedure on how to respond to disasters, less than 50% provided emergency information or instructions on their online portals, and over 40% did not provide emergency updates on the evolution or progression of a disaster. Content uploaded by users of digital or social media was verified in less than 50% of cases, and only about 20–25% of personnel had participated in local disaster readiness programs. There was also evidence of poor integration between conventional and digital media (UNESCO, 2025). These findings place the evidence presented in this chapter in its real-world context and highlight the disaster readiness gap that exists at the level of the media.

However, there are also encouraging signs of change. The experience of the past five decades, and more specifically recent disasters such as the COVID pandemic, have taught us valuable lessons about how the media can best handle specific disaster scenarios. As a group of Spanish experts has stated, there is a need for "rapid, efficient, and truthful communication" during and after disasters, and the media is an integral part of such communication (González Del Castillo et al., 2022). Future disasters are likely to be accompanied by "infodemics," and it is essential to prepare for these in advance. This could include:

- The pre-emptive establishment of trusted conventional or social media sources to provide early warning or disaster communication
- The involvement of community leaders and other trusted voices or "gatekeepers"
- Community education or drills to train at-risk populations in identifying and verifying reliable information during a simulated disaster (Cuadra & Cotoron, 2025)

A clear media and social media policy is, therefore, an essential part of disaster preparedness, mitigation, and relief plans (Kasim & Oyerinde, 2024). Such a policy should incorporate the viewpoints of all concerned stakeholders, including media personnel themselves. The design and implementation of such a policy should be complemented by media guidelines that emphasize the constructive aspects of media coverage during a disaster. Such guidelines should be "trauma-informed," emphasizing the need to reduce sensationalism or graphic imagery that could increase traumatic stress in affected persons or relief workers (Ravan et al., 2024).

It is also important to take local culture into account when planning media-related interventions. Cross-national differences in cultural values can affect the extent to which individuals believe in information sources or adhere to specific behavioral recommendations regarding disaster preparedness or safety; they can also shape the way people experience and respond to disasters in their social media posts (Xu, 2023; Magaña et al., 2024). Media messaging, whether by governments or other aid agencies, should be tailored to local culture to ensure that it is heard and followed. Social media may prove particularly helpful in cases where there is mistrust of conventional media—for example, where these are perceived as biased or unreliable (Appleby-Arnold et al., 2021). Likewise, in countries where more than one language is spoken by different communities, it is essential that official communications—whether through mass or social media—be provided in a language that affected communities can understand, without undue use of jargon or technical terminology (Muruthi et al., 2025). These issues are particularly relevant in South India, where many countries have a multicultural social structure.

Research is also an essential component of improving media coverage during disasters. Such research would need to involve a wide range of stakeholders and should combine quantitative and qualitative measures. Details such as patterns of media usage, their demographic correlates, public engagement with and trust in different media sources, perceived benefits and risks, mental health consequences, and effects on behavioral change would need to be collected and analyzed in an interdisciplinary manner. Such research could be conducted at various levels—global, national, regional, and in vulnerable or special populations—to ensure that future disasters, whether limited or widespread in scope—could be handled more effectively by authorities, relief workers, the media, and the community, acting in concert (Généreux et al., 2021).

Finally, it should be remembered that the media is not the only driver of positive or negative emotions, behaviors, and community responses to the disaster: it is one of many "actors" involved in such a scenario and should not be used as a convenient scapegoat to "explain away" psychological distress, antisocial behavior, or inefficient relief efforts after a disaster. Poor preparedness, a lack of transparency or accountability on the part of authorities, and deficits in manpower and infrastructure contribute far more to negative outcomes after a disaster than either conventional or digital media (Galvez-Hernandez et al., 2025). Individuals' relationships with other community members and their attitudes toward governments and experts often shape their disaster-related behavior to a greater extent than media exposure (Shah & Wei, 2022). Likewise, when considering digital media, the role of users—who are themselves members of affected communities—in creating and disseminating specific types of content, or in using social media responsibly, cannot be overemphasized.

There may be a place for the development of guidelines on the responsible reporting of disasters by the media, along the lines of those that exist when reporting on suicide or crime. In recent years, such guidelines have been developed by UNESCO (UNESCO, 2025), the United Kingdom's Independent Press Standards Organisation (IPSO, 2004), and the United Nations Office for Disaster Risk Reduction (UNDRR, 2025). These guidelines address most of the ethical concerns raised in Boxes 16.3 and 16.4. However, they should be complemented by similar guidelines for authorities and relief workers and by community education and disaster readiness initiatives. Efforts should be made to actively engage local media agencies and their staff in disaster drills and other readiness initiatives. This would facilitate communication between these sectors, promote the efficient and rapid dissemination of warnings and advice, and ensure that accurate information reaches affected communities while warding off "infodemics." Ultimately, efficient engagement with and use of both types of media can contribute to post-disaster rebuilding, readiness, and resilience.

At a more global level, digital media could be leveraged to reduce cross-national inequalities in disaster preparedness (Ejem et al., 2025), and in a world that is increasingly interconnected, digital media may prove useful in building international or global disaster resilience in the future and in ensuring the most effective and humane allocation of foreign aid (Liu & Han, 2025).

7 Conclusion

Media respond in diverse ways to disasters. This diversity of responses leads to a diversity of outcomes for affected populations and individuals. Both digital and mass media can be invaluable in providing disaster-related information, warnings, and advice and in mobilizing local, national, and international resources. On the other hand, certain aspects of the media coverage of disasters can adversely affect individual mental health and the adoption of prosocial behavior or safety measures and interfere with relief efforts and community recovery. Media agencies often lack a specific policy or reference frame when reporting on disasters, leading to inefficient or inaccurate reporting. Digital media may offer solutions to some of these problems but carry their own risks in the form of disinformation, "infodemics," and harm to individual and community psychosocial health. The need for disaster preparedness on the part of the media has been highlighted both in expert opinion and in surveys of individual journalists or agencies. To maximize the beneficial effects of both media types, effective cooperation and communication between civil authorities, relief workers, media personnel, and at-risk or affected communities is essential. This is particularly the case in South Asia, where disasters may bring pre-existing social or political tensions into relief. In such a scenario, the media must walk a fine line between addressing local concerns and not contributing to psychological harm or social disruption. A key challenge for all stakeholders—both globally and in the South Asian region—is to ensure that the media contribute to disaster preparedness, relief, and reconstruction, while preventing or minimizing future infodemics.

References

Ahern, J., Galea, S., Resnick, H., Kilpatrick, D., Bucuvalas, M., Gold, J., & Vlahov, D. (2002). Television images and psychological symptoms after the September 11 terrorist attacks. *Psychiatry, 65*(4), 289–300. https://doi.org/10.1521/psyc.65.4.289.20240

Ahern, J., Galea, S., Resnick, H., & Vlahov, D. (2004). Television images and probable posttraumatic stress disorder after September 11: The role of background characteristics, event exposures, and perievent panic. *Journal of Nervous & Mental Disease, 192*(3), 217–226. https://doi.org/10.1097/01.nmd.0000116465.99830.ca

Ahmad, N. S., Hussain, Z., Abd Hamid, H. S., & Khairani, A. Z. (2021). Roles of social media and counselling support in reducing anxiety among Malaysian during Covid-19 pandemic. *International Journal of Disaster Risk Reduction: IJDRR, 63*, 102456. https://doi.org/10.1016/j.ijdrr.2021.102456

Ahmed, M. N. Q., Lalin, S. A. A., & Ahmad, S. (2023). Factors affecting knowledge, attitude, and practice of COVID-19: A study among undergraduate university students in Bangladesh. *Human Vaccines & Immunotherapeutics, 19*(1), 2172923. https://doi.org/10.1080/21645515.2023.2172923

Aichner, T., Grunfelder, M., Maurer, O., & Jegeni, D. (2021). Twenty-five years of social media: A review of social media applications and definitions from 1994 to 2019. *Cyberpsychology, Behavior, and Social Networking, 24*(4), 215–222. https://doi.org/10.1089/cyber.2020.0134

Alam, E., & Islam, M. K. (2023). Enhancing landslide risk reduction strategies in Southeast Bangladesh. *Jamba (Potchefstroom, South Africa), 15*(1), 1541. https://doi.org/10.4102/jamba.v15i1.1541

Alam, E., Collins, A. E., Islam, A. R. M. T., Paul, A., & Islam, M. K. (2024). Change in cyclone disaster vulnerability and response in coastal Bangladesh. *Disasters, 48*(2), e12608. https://doi.org/10.1111/disa.12608

Alchin, D. (2020). Gone with the wind. *Australasian Psychiatry, 28*, 636–638. https://doi.org/10.1177/1039856220936144

Alexander, D. E. (2007). Misconception as a barrier to teaching about disasters. *Prehospital and Disaster Medicine, 22*(2), 95–103. https://doi.org/10.1017/s1049023x00004441

Ali, I. (2022). Impacts of rumors and conspiracy theories surrounding COVID-19 on preparedness programs. *Disaster Medicine and Public Health Preparedness, 16*(1), 310–315. https://doi.org/10.1017/dmp.2020.325

Ali, I., Saddique, S., & Ali, S. (2021a). Local perceptions of COVID-19 in Pakistan's Sindh Province: "Political game", supernatural test, or western conspiracy? *Disaster Medicine and Public Health Preparedness*, 1–6. Advance online publication. https://doi.org/10.1017/dmp.2021.220

Ali, R., Jawed, S., Baig, M., Azam Malik, A., Syed, F., & Rehman, R. (2021b). General public perception of social media, impact of COVID-19 pandemic, and related misconceptions. *Disaster Medicine and Public Health Preparedness, 17*, e23. https://doi.org/10.1017/dmp.2021.229

Allison, E. J. (1984). Media relations at major response situations. *JEMS: A Journal of Emergency Medical Services, 9*(12), 39–42.

Ansari, M. S., Warner, J., Sukhwani, V., & Shaw, R. (2022). Protection motivation status and factors influencing risk reduction measures among the flood-prone households in Bangladesh. *International Journal of Environmental Research and Public Health, 19*(18), 11372. https://doi.org/10.3390/ijerph191811372

Anzur, T. (2000). How to talk to the media: Televised coverage of public health issues in a disaster. *Prehospital and Disaster Medicine, 15*(4), 196–198.

Aondover, E. M., Daushe, A. U., Ogunbola, O., & Aondover, P. O. (2025). Media coverage of internally displaced persons in two selected newspapers in Nigeria. *Journal of Migration and Health, 11*, 100301. https://doi.org/10.1016/j.jmh.2024.100301

Appleby-Arnold, S., Brockdorff, N., Jakovljev, I., & Zdravković, S. (2021). Disaster preparedness and cultural factors: A comparative study in Romania and Malta. *Disasters, 45*(3), 664–690. https://doi.org/10.1111/disa.12433

Arafat, S. M. Y., Yuen, K. F., Menon, V., Shoib, S., & Ahmad, A. R. (2021). Panic buying in Bangladesh: An exploration of media reports. *Frontiers in Psychiatry, 11*, 628393. https://doi.org/10.3389/fpsyt.2020.628393

Arnold, J. L. (2006). Disaster myths and hurricane Katrina 2005: Can public officials and the media learn to provide responsible crisis communication during disasters? *Prehospital and Disaster Medicine, 21*(1), 1–3. https://doi.org/10.1017/s1049023x00003241

Balakrishnan, V., Ng, W. Z., Soo, M. C., Han, G. J., & Lee, C. J. (2022). Infodemic and fake news – A comprehensive overview of its global magnitude during the COVID-19 pandemic in 2021: A scoping review. *International Journal of Disaster Risk Reduction: IJDRR, 78*, 103144. https://doi.org/10.1016/j.ijdrr.2022.103144

Ball-Rokeach, S. J., & Loges, W. E. (2000). Ally or adversary? Using media systems for public health. *Prehospital and Disaster Medicine, 15*(4), 188–195.

Barnes, M. D., Hanson, C. L., Novilla, L. M., Meacham, A. T., McIntyre, E., & Erickson, B. C. (2008). Analysis of media agenda setting during and after Hurricane Katrina: implications for emergencypreparedness, disaster response, and disaster policy. *American Journal of Public Health, 98*(4), 604–610. https://doi.org/10.2105/AJPH.2007.112235

Basch, C. H., Basch, C. E., Ruggles, K. V., & Hammond, R. (2015). Coverage of the Ebola virus disease epidemic on YouTube. *Disaster Medicine and Public Health Preparedness, 9*(5), 531–535. https://doi.org/10.1017/dmp.2015.77

Basu, M., Ghosh, S., Jana, A., Bandyopadhyay, S., & Singh, R. (2017). Medical requirements during a natural disaster: A case study on WhatsApp chats among medical personnel during the 2015 Nepal earthquake. *Disaster Medicine and Public Health Preparedness, 11*(6), 652–655. https://doi.org/10.1017/dmp.2017.8

Beaudoin, C. E. (2008). Assessment of a media campaign and related crisis help line following Hurricane Katrina. *Public Health Reports, 123*(5), 646–651. https://doi.org/10.1177/003335490812300515

Bernstein, K. T., Ahern, J., Tracy, M., Boscarino, J. A., Vlahov, D., & Galea, S. (2007). Television watching and the risk of incident probable posttraumatic stress disorder: A prospective evaluation. *The Journal of Nervous and Mental Disease, 195*(1), 41–47. https://doi.org/10.1097/01.nmd.0000244784.36745.a5

Black, D. R., Dietz, J. E., Stirratt, A. A., & Coster, D. C. (2015). Do social media have a place in public health emergency response? *Journal of Emergency Management (Weston, Mass.), 13*(3), 217–226. https://doi.org/10.5055/jem.2015.0235

Boholm, M. (2009). Risk and causality in newspaper reporting. *Risk Analysis: An Official Publication of the Society for Risk Analysis, 29*(11), 1566–1577. https://doi.org/10.1111/j.1539-6924.2009.01296.x

Bosch, D. (2017). Use of social media and e-government in disasters: 2016 Louisiana floods case study. *Journal of Emergency Management (Weston, Mass.), 15*(6), 391–405. https://doi.org/10.5055/jem.2017.0347

Briand, S., Hess, S., Nguyen, T., & Purnat, T. D. (2023). Chapter 1: Infodemic management in the twenty-first century. In T. D. Purnat, T. Nguyen, & S. Briand (Eds.), *Managing Infodemics in the 21st century: Addressing new public health challenges in the information ecosystem [internet]*. Springer. https://doi.org/10.1007/978-3-031-27789-4_1

Bright, C. F. (2017). Elections, news cycles, and attention to disasters. *Disaster Prevention and Management, 26*(4), 471–478. https://doi.org/10.1108/DPM-02-2017-0018

Broderick, J. E., Kaplan-Liss, E., & Bass, E. (2011). Experimental induction of psychogenic illness in the context of a medical event and media exposure. *American Journal of Disaster Medicine, 6*(3), 163–172.

Bromet, E. J., Havenaar, J. M., Gluzman, S. F., & Tintle, N. L. (2005). Psychological aftermath of the Lviv air show disaster: A prospective controlled study. *Acta Psychiatrica Scandinavica, 112*(3), 194–200. https://doi.org/10.1111/j.1600-0447.2005.00566.x

Burger, J., Gochfeld, M., Jeitner, C., Pittfield, T., & Donio, M. (2013). Trusted information sources used during and after Superstorm Sandy: TV and radio were used more often than social media. *Journal of Toxicology and Environmental Health, Part A, 76*(20), 1138–1150. https://doi.org/10.1080/15287394.2013.844087

Burkle, F. M., Jr., & Hsu, E. B. (2011). Ram Janki Temple: Understanding human stampedes. *The Lancet, 377*(9760), 106–107. https://doi.org/10.1016/S0140-6736(10)60442-4

Cal, A., Kabataş Yıldız, M., & Aydın Avci, İ. (2024). The effect of health-related media messages on fear and uncertainty about the COVID-19 pandemic. *Disaster Medicine and Public Health Preparedness, 18*, e129. https://doi.org/10.1017/dmp.2024.124

Calder, K., D'Aeth, L., Turner, S., Begg, A., Veer, E., Scott, J., & Fox, C. (2020). Evaluation of the all right? Campaign's Facebook intervention post-disaster in Canterbury, New Zealand. *Health Promotion International, 35*(1), 111–122. https://doi.org/10.1093/heapro/day106

Callaghan, C. W. (2016). Disaster management, crowdsourced R&D and probabilistic innovation theory: Toward real time disaster response capability. *International Journal of Disaster Risk Reduction: IJDRR, 17*, 238–250. https://doi.org/10.1016/j.ijdrr.2016.05.004

Carlé, B., Charron, S., Milochevitch, A., & Hardeman, F. (2004). An inquiry of the opinions of the French and Belgian populations as regards risk. *Journal of Hazardous Materials, 111*(1–3), 21–27. https://doi.org/10.1016/j.jhazmat.2004.02.004

Cato, S., Iida, T., Ishida, K., Ito, A., Katsumata, H., McElwain, K. M., & Shoji, M. (2021). The bright and dark sides of social media usage during the COVID-19 pandemic: Survey evidence from Japan. *International Journal of Disaster Risk Reduction: IJDRR, 54*, 102034. https://doi.org/10.1016/j.ijdrr.2020.102034

Chan, J. L., & Purohit, H. (2020). Challenges to transforming unconventional social media data into actionable knowledge for public health systems during disasters. *Disaster Medicine and Public Health Preparedness, 14*(3), 352–359. https://doi.org/10.1017/dmp.2019.92

Chang, A. H., Bega, R., & Hsu, E. B. (2018). Push-to-talk apps for disaster communications: Hurricane season brings technology adaptation. *American Journal of Disaster Medicine, 13*(3), 161–167. https://doi.org/10.5055/ajdm.2018.0297

Chao, M., Xue, D., Liu, T., Yang, H., & Hall, B. J. (2020). Media use and acute psychological outcomes during COVID-19 outbreak in China. *Journal of Anxiety Disorders, 74*, 102248. https://doi.org/10.1016/j.janxdis.2020.102248

Chapman, C. M., Hornsey, M. J., Fielding, K. S., & Gulliver, R. (2023). International media coverage promotes donations to a climate disaster. *Disasters, 47*(3), 725–744. https://doi.org/10.1111/disa.12557

Charilaou, L., & Vijaykumar, S. (2021). Influences of news and social media on food insecurity and hoarding behavior during the COVID-19 pandemic. *Disaster Medicine and Public Health Preparedness, 17*, e58. https://doi.org/10.1017/dmp.2021.315

Cheng, P., Xia, G., Pang, P., Wu, B., Jiang, W., Li, Y. T., Wang, M., Ling, Q., Chang, X., Wang, J., Dai, X., Lin, X., & Bi, X. (2020). COVID-19 epidemic peer support and crisis intervention via social media. *Community Mental Health Journal, 56*(5), 786–792. https://doi.org/10.1007/s10597-020-00624-5

Chipidza, W., Akbaripourdibazar, E., Gwanzura, T., & Gatto, N. M. (2022). Topic analysis of traditional and social media news coverage of the early COVID-19 pandemic and implications for public health communication. *Disaster Medicine and Public Health Preparedness, 16*(5), 1881–1888. https://doi.org/10.1017/dmp.2021.65

Christen, H. T., Denney, J. P., Maniscalco, P. M., & Rubin, D. L. (1999). Terrorism. Part III--Response procedures for terrorist/tactical violence incidents. *JEMS: A Journal of Emergency Medical Services, 24*(1), 58–66.

Chu, H., & Yang, J. Z. (2020). Building disaster resilience using social messaging networks: The WeChat community in Houston, Texas, during Hurricane Harvey. *Disasters, 44*(4), 726–752. https://doi.org/10.1111/disa.12388

Claassen, C., Kashner, T. M., Kashner, T. K., Xuan, L., & Larkin, G. L. (2011). Psychiatric emergency "surge capacity" following acts of terrorism and mass violence with high media impact: What is required? *General Hospital Psychiatry, 33*(3), 287–293. https://doi.org/10.1016/j.genhosppsych.2011.01.015

Clark, N., Boersma, K., Bonati, S., Fonio, C., Gehlhar, S., Habig, T., Larruina, R., Lüke, R., Morelli, S., Nielsen, A. B., Opromolla, A., Pazzi, V., & Raju, E. (2024). Exploring the impacts

of social media and crowdsourcing on disaster resilience. *Open Research Europe, 1*, 60. https://doi.org/10.12688/openreseurope.13721.3
Cohen, D. (2006). Rebuilding from the rubble. *BMJ (Clinical Research ed.), 332*(7532), 10. https://doi.org/10.1136/bmj.332.7532.10
Cool, C. T., Claravall, M. C., Hall, J. L., Taketani, K., Zepeda, J. P., Gehner, M., & Lawe-Davies, O. (2015). Social media as a risk communication tool following Typhoon Haiyan. *Western Pacific Surveillance and Response Journal: WPSAR, 6*(Suppl 1), 86–90. https://doi.org/10.5365/WPSAR.2015.6.2.HYN_013
Crane, O., Balen, J., Devkota, B., Ghimire, S., & Rushton, S. (2017). Use of information and communication technologies in the formal and informal health system responses to the 2015 Nepal earthquakes. *Health Policy and Planning, 32*(suppl_3), iii48–iii58. https://doi.org/10.1093/heapol/czx115
Cretikos, M. A., Merritt, T. D., Main, K., Eastwood, K., Winn, L., Moran, L., & Durrheim, D. N. (2007). Mitigating the health impacts of a natural disaster--the June 2007 long-weekend storm in the Hunter region of New South Wales. *The Medical Journal of Australia, 187*(11–12), 670–673. https://doi.org/10.5694/j.1326-5377.2007.tb01470.x
Cretikos, M., Eastwood, K., Dalton, C., Merritt, T., Tuyl, F., Winn, L., & Durrheim, D. (2008). Household disaster preparedness and information sources: Rapid cluster survey after a storm in New South Wales, Australia. *BMC Public Health, 8*, 195. https://doi.org/10.1186/1471-2458-8-195
Crowe, A. (2011). The social media manifesto: A comprehensive review of the impact of social media on emergency management. *Journal of Business Continuity & Emergency Planning, 5*(1), 409–420.
Cuadra, J. M., & Cotoron, V. N. (2025). Addressing false information through local capacity building in community-based disaster risk management. *Jamba (Potchefstroom, South Africa), 17*(1), 1836. https://doi.org/10.4102/jamba.v17i1.1836
Dallo, I., Elroy, O., Fallou, L., Komendantova, N., & Yosipof, A. (2023). Dynamics and characteristics of misinformation related to earthquake predictions on Twitter. *Scientific Reports, 13*(1), 13391. https://doi.org/10.1038/s41598-023-40399-9
David, C. C., Ong, J. C., & Legara, E. F. (2016). Tweeting supertyphoon Haiyan: Evolving functions of twitter during and after a disaster event. *PLoS One, 11*(3), e0150190. https://doi.org/10.1371/journal.pone.0150190
de Bruijn, J. A., de Moel, H., Jongman, B., de Ruiter, M. C., Wagemaker, J., & Aerts, J. C. J. H. (2019). A global database of historic and real-time flood events based on social media. *Scientific Data, 6*(1), 311. https://doi.org/10.1038/s41597-019-0326-9
De Grace, M., Ericson, D., Folz, H., Greene, W., Ho, K., & Pearce, L. (2001). Proceedings for the 5th Asia-Pacific Conference on Disaster Medicine: Creating an agenda for action. *Prehospital and Disaster Medicine, 16*(1), 18–21. https://doi.org/10.1017/s1049023x00025498
Demiroz, F. (2020). The use of social media during disasters: The development of the literature, its current topography, and future challenges. *Journal of Emergency Management (Weston, Mass.), 18*(3), 221–235. https://doi.org/10.5055/jem.2020.0468
de Ville de Goyet, C., Lechat, M. F., & Boucquey, C. (1977). Attitude face au risque d'épidémie lors de désastres soudains. *Revue d'épidémiologie et de santé publique, 25*(3), 185–194.
De Ville de Goyet C. (2007). Myths, the ultimate survivors in disasters. *Prehospital and Disaster Medicine, 22*(2), 104–105. https://doi.org/10.1017/s1049023x00004453
Dhakal, S. P. (2018). Analysing news media coverage of the 2015 Nepal earthquake using a community capitals lens: Implications for disaster resilience. *Disasters, 42*(2), 294–313. https://doi.org/10.1111/disa.12244
Duan, J., Zhai, W., & Cheng, C. (2020). Crowd detection in mass gatherings based on social media data: A case study of the 2014 Shanghai new year's eve stampede. *International Journal of Environmental Research and Public Health, 17*(22), 8640. https://doi.org/10.3390/ijerph17228640

Ejem, A. A., Okeke, S. V., Ojeka-John, R. O., & Adekeye, E. T. (2025). Social media and climate-related disaster management in Africa: A force-field analysis. *Jamba (Potchefstroom, South Africa), 17*(1), 1753. https://doi.org/10.4102/jamba.v17i1.1753

Englund, L., Forsberg, R., & Saveman, B. I. (2014). Survivors' experiences of media coverage after traumatic injury events. *International Emergency Nursing, 22*(1), 25–30. https://doi.org/10.1016/j.ienj.2013.03.010

Englund, L., Bergh Johannesson, K., & Arnberg, F. K. (2022). Media perception and trust among disaster survivors: Tsunami survivors' interaction with journalists, media exposure, and associations with trust in media and authorities. *Frontiers in Public Health, 10*, 943444. https://doi.org/10.3389/fpubh.2022.943444

Estes, K. D., Garfin, D. R., Holman, E. A., & Silver, R. C. (2024). Consuming hurricane-related media: The protective role of perceived trust. *Psychological Trauma: Theory, Research, Practice and Policy.*, Advance online publication. https://doi.org/10.1037/tra0001802

Ewart, J., & McLean, H. (2015). Ducking for cover in the 'blame game': News framing of the findings of two reports into the 2010-11 Queensland floods. *Disasters, 39*(1), 166–184. https://doi.org/10.1111/disa.12093

Fairbrother, G., Stuber, J., Galea, S., Fleischman, A. R., & Pfefferbaum, B. (2003). Posttraumatic stress reactions in new New York City children after the September 11, 2001, terrorist attacks. *Ambulatory Pediatrics: The Official Journal of the Ambulatory Pediatric Association, 3*(6), 304–311. https://doi.org/10.1367/1539-4409(2003)003<0304:psriny>2.0.co;2

Fan, C., Jiang, Y., & Mostafavi, A. (2020). Emergent social cohesion for coping with community disruptions in disasters. *Journal of the Royal Society, Interface, 17*(164), 20190778. https://doi.org/10.1098/rsif.2019.0778

Farnham, J. W. (2006). Disaster and emergency communications prior to computers/internet: A review. *Critical Care (London, England), 10*(1), 207. https://doi.org/10.1186/cc3944

Friedman, F. D. (1995). Public relations in disaster management and planning for emergency physicians. *The Journal of Emergency Medicine, 13*(5), 661–668. https://doi.org/10.1016/0736-4679(95)00075-1

Fukasawa, M., Kawakami, N., Nakayama, C., & Yasumura, S. (2021). Relationship between use of media and radiation anxiety among the residents of Fukushima 5.5 years after the nuclear power plant accident. *Disaster Medicine and Public Health Preparedness, 15*(1), 42–49. https://doi.org/10.1017/dmp.2019.132

Fullerton, C. S., Mash, H. B. H., Morganstein, J. C., & Ursano, R. J. (2019). Active shooter and terrorist event-related posttraumatic stress and depression: Television viewing and perceived safety. *Disaster Medicine and Public Health Preparedness, 13*(3), 570–576. https://doi.org/10.1017/dmp.2018.121

Gaffney, K. K., Duysen, E., Medcalf, S., & Wichman, C. (2024). Rural natural disaster stress: A survey of community resource use and effect. *Journal of Agromedicine, 29*(4), 688–700. https://doi.org/10.1080/1059924X.2024.2388862

Galvez-Hernandez, P., Dai, Y., & Muntaner, C. (2025). The DANA disaster: Unraveling the political and economic determinants for Valencia's floods devastation. *International Journal for Equity in Health, 24*(1), 64. https://doi.org/10.1186/s12939-025-02435-0

Gantt, P., & Gantt, R. (2012). Disaster psychology: Dispelling the myths of panic. *Professional Safety, 57*(8), 42–49.

Garfin, D. R., Holman, E. A., & Silver, R. C. (2015). Cumulative exposure to prior collective-trauma and acute stress responses to the Boston marathon bombings. *Psychological science, 26*(6), 675–683. https://doi.org/10.1177/0956797614561043

Garrett, L. (2001). Understanding media's response to epidemics. *Public Health Reports (Washington, D.C.: 1974), 116*(Suppl 2), 87–91. https://doi.org/10.1093/phr/116.S2.87

Gasink, L. B., Linkin, D. R., Fishman, N. O., Bilker, W. B., Weiner, M. G., & Lautenbach, E. (2009). Stockpiling drugs for an avian influenza outbreak: Examining the surge in oseltamivir prescriptions during heightened media coverage of the potential for a worldwide pandemic. *Infection Control and Hospital Epidemiology, 30*(4), 370–376. https://doi.org/10.1086/596609

Gehner, M., & Oughton, D. (2016). Ethical challenges in social media engagement and research: Considerations for code of engagement practices. *Journal of Radiological Protection: Official Journal of the Society for Radiological Protection, 36*(2), S187–S192. https://doi.org/10.1088/0952-4746/36/2/S187

Généreux, M., David, M. D., O'Sullivan, T., Carignan, M. È., Blouin-Genest, G., Champagne-Poirier, O., Champagne, É., Burlone, N., Qadar, Z., Herbosa, T., Hung, K., Ribeiro-Alves, G., Arruda, H., Michel, P., Law, R., Poirier, A., Murray, V., Chan, E., & Roy, M. (2021). Communication strategies and media discourses in the age of COVID-19: An urgent need for action. *Health Promotion International, 36*(4), 1178–1185. https://doi.org/10.1093/heapro/daaa136

Ghale, A., Jnawali, K., & Paneru, D. P. (2025). Knowledge on disaster risk reduction among secondary level students of public schools of Pokhara metropolitan city of Nepal. *BMC Public Health, 25*(1), 2058. https://doi.org/10.1186/s12889-025-23332-9

Ghumman, U., & Horney, J. (2016). Characterizing the impact of extreme heat on mortality, Karachi, Pakistan, June 2015. *Prehospital and Disaster Medicine, 31*(3), 263–266. https://doi.org/10.1017/S1049023X16000273

Giotakos, O. (2022). Fake news in the age of COVID-19: Evolutional and psychobiological considerations. *Psychiatrike = Psychiatriki, 33*(3), 183–186. https://doi.org/10.22365/jpsych.2022.087

Gist, R., & Stolz, S. B. (1982). Mental health promotion and the media. Community response to the Kansas City hotel disaster. *American Psychologist, 37*(10), 1136–1139. https://doi.org/10.1037/0003-066x.37.10.1136

Goffredo, S., Piccinetti, C., & Zaccanti, F. (2007). Tsunami survey expedition: Preliminary investigation of Maldivian coral reefs two weeks after the event. *Environmental Monitoring and Assessment, 131*(1–3), 95–105. https://doi.org/10.1007/s10661-006-9459-3

González Del Castillo, J., Martín-Delgado, M. C., Martín Sánchez, F. J., Martínez-Sellés, M., Molero García, J. M., Moreno Guillén, S., Rodríguez-Artalejo, F. J., Ruiz-Galiana, J., Cantón, R., De Lucas Ramos, P., García-Botella, A., García-Lledó, A., Hernández-Sampelayo, T., Gómez-Pavón, J., & Bouza, E. (2022). Lessons from COVID-19 for future disasters: An opinion paper. *Revista Española De Quimioterapia: Publicación Oficial De La Sociedad Española De Quimioterapia, 35*(5), 444–454. https://doi.org/10.37201/req/058.2022

Goodwin, R., Palgi, Y., Lavenda, O., Hamama-Raz, Y., & Ben-Ezra, M. (2015). Association between media use, acute stress disorder and psychological distress. *Psychotherapy and Psychosomatics, 84*(4), 253–254. https://doi.org/10.1159/000377706

Gottschick, C., Diexer, S., Massag, J., Klee, B., Broda, A., Purschke, O., Binder, M., Sedding, D., Frese, T., Girndt, M., Hoell, J. I., Michl, P., Gekle, M., & Mikolajczyk, R. (2023). Mental health in Germany in the first weeks of the Russo-Ukrainian war. *BJPsych Open, 9*(3), e66. https://doi.org/10.1192/bjo.2023.21

Gowan, M. E., Sloan, J. A., & Kirk, R. C. (2015). Prepared for what? Addressing the disaster readiness gap beyond preparedness for survival. *BMC Public Health, 15*, 1139. https://doi.org/10.1186/s12889-015-2440-8

Gribble, K. D. (2013). Media messages and the needs of infants and young children after Cyclone Nargis and the WenChuan earthquake. *Disasters, 37*(1), 80–100. https://doi.org/10.1111/j.1467-7717.2012.01289.x

Groome, D., & Soureti, A. (2004). Post-traumatic stress disorder and anxiety symptoms in children exposed to the 1999 Greek earthquake. *British Journal of Psychology (London, England: 1953), 95*(Pt 3), 387–397. https://doi.org/10.1348/0007126041528149

Gurman, T. A., & Ellenberger, N. (2015). Reaching the global community during disasters: Findings from a content analysis of the organizational use of Twitter after the 2010 Haiti earthquake. *Journal of Health Communication, 20*(6), 687–696. https://doi.org/10.1080/10810730.2015.1018566

Güzel, A., & Ergün, G. (2021). The mass media used by university students for becoming informed about disaster news and the effects of disaster news on quaternary victimization: The example

of Burdur Province in Turkey. *Social Work in Public Health, 36*(2), 246–258. https://doi.org/10.1080/19371918.2020.1864557
Hall, M. L., Lee, A. C., Cartwright, C., Marahatta, S., Karki, J., & Simkhada, P. (2017). The 2015 Nepal earthquake disaster: Lessons learned one year on. *Public Health, 145*, 39–44. https://doi.org/10.1016/j.puhe.2016.12.031
Hall, B. J., Xiong, Y. X., Yip, P. S. Y., Lao, C. K., Shi, W., Sou, E. K. L., Chang, K., Wang, L., & Lam, A. I. F. (2019). The association between disaster exposure and media use on post-traumatic stress disorder following typhoon Hato in Macao, China. *European Journal of Psychotraumatology, 10*(1), 1558709. https://doi.org/10.1080/20008198.2018.1558709
Hansen, P. M., Mikkelsen, S., Alstrøm, H., Damm-Hejmdal, A., Rehn, M., & Berlac, P. A.(2023). The Field's mass shooting: emergency medical services response. *Scandinavian Journal of Trauma, Resuscitation and Emergency Medicine, 31*(1), 71. https://doi.org/10.1186/s13049-023-01140-7
Havas, C., Resch, B., Francalanci, C., Pernici, B., Scalia, G., Fernandez-Marquez, J. L., Van Achte, T., Zeug, G., Mondardini, M. R. R., Grandoni, D., Kirsch, B., Kalas, M., Lorini, V., & Rüping, S. (2017). E2mC: Improving emergency management service practice through social media and crowdsourcing analysis in near real time. *Sensors (Basel, Switzerland), 17*(12), 2766. https://doi.org/10.3390/s17122766
Horiuchi, S., Ozaki, A., Inoue, M., Aida, J., & Yamaoka, K. (2019). Relation of high social capital to preferable emotional response to news media broadcasting of natural disasters: A nationwide cross-sectional study in Japan. *The Tohoku Journal of Experimental Medicine, 247*(2), 129–137. https://doi.org/10.1620/tjem.247.129
Horsfall, B. (1985). The Bradford disaster. Coping with a media invasion. *Health and Social Service Journal, 95*(4958), 934.
Hossain, L., Kam, D., Kong, F., Wigand, R. T., & Bossomaier, T. (2016). Social media in Ebola outbreak. *Epidemiology and Infection, 144*(10), 2136–2143. https://doi.org/10.1017/S095026881600039X
Hossain, M. T., Islam, M. A., Jahan, N., Nahar, M. T., Sarker, M. J. A., Rahman, M. M., Deeba, F., Hoque, K. E., Aktar, R., Islam, M. M., Hossain, M. Z., Siddiqua, L., Mahbub, Z., & Islam, M. N. (2022). Mental health status of teachers during the second wave of the COVID-19 pandemic: A web-based study in Bangladesh. *Frontiers in Psychiatry, 13*, 938230. https://doi.org/10.3389/fpsyt.2022.938230
Hou, H., Shen, L., Jia, J., & Xu, Z. (2024). An integrated framework for flood disaster information extraction and analysis leveraging social media data: A case study of the Shouguang flood in China. *The Science of the Total Environment, 949*, 174948. https://doi.org/10.1016/j.scitotenv.2024.174948
Houston, J. B., Hawthorne, J., Perreault, M. F., Park, E. H., Goldstein Hode, M., Halliwell,M. R., Turner McGowen, S. E., Davis, R., Vaid, S., McElderry, J. A., & Griffith, S. A. (2015). Social media anddisasters: a functional framework for social media use in disaster planning, response, and research. *Disasters, 39*(1), 1–22. https://doi.org/10.1111/disa.12092
Hu, Q., An, S., Kapucu, N., Sellnow, T., Yuksel, M., & Freihaut, R. (2023). Dynamics of inter-organisational emergency communication on Twitter: The case of Hurricane Irma. *Disasters, 47*(2), 267–297. https://doi.org/10.1111/disa.12547
Huang, C. M., Chan, E., & Hyder, A. A. (2010). Web 2.0 and internet social networking: a new tool for disaster management?--lessons from Taiwan. *BMC Medical Informatics and Decision Making, 10*, 57. https://doi.org/10.1186/1472-6947-10-57
Huang, X., Shi, Y., & Gao, G. (2022). Revealing personality triggers for media vicarious traumatization: A fuzzy-set qualitative comparative analysis. *Healthcare (Basel), 10*(10), 1850. https://doi.org/10.3390/healthcare10101850
Huss, J. H., & Eichenberg, C. (2016). Psychotraumatological Defence mechanisms in the print media coverage of 'September 11'. *Psychotherapie, Psychosomatik, Medizinische Psychologie, 66*(2), 74–81. https://doi.org/10.1055/s-0035-1569283

International Work Group on Death, Dying and Bereavement. (2002). Assumptions and principles about psychosocial aspects of disasters. *Death Studies, 26*(6), 449–462. https://doi.org/10.1080/074811802760138987
IPSO. (2004). *Guidance on reporting major incidents.* https://www.ipso.co.uk/resources/guidance-on-reporting-major-incidents/
Jacob, B., Mawson, A. R., Payton, M., & Guignard, J. C. (2008). Disaster mythology and fact:Hurricane Katrina and social attachment. *Public health reports (Washington, D.C. : 1974), 123*(5), 555–566. https://doi.org/10.1177/003335490812300505
Jain, P., Rakshit, B., Raina, B., & Bardhan, S. (2021). Regional integration and environmental sustainability during the COVID-19 pandemic: Evidence from South Asia. *International Social Science Journal.*, Advance online publication. https://doi.org/10.1111/issj.12291
James, J. S. (2005). Communication in a disaster: Success of text messages. *AIDS Treatment News, 414*, 4–5.
Jenkins, S. S. (1962). Is short-wave radio in your disaster plan? *Modern Hospital, 98*, 103–104.
Jeronimus, B. F., Snippe, E., Emerencia, A. C., de Jonge, P., & Bos, E. H. (2019). Acute stress responses after indirect exposure to the MH17 airplane crash. *British Journal of Psychology (London, England: 1953), 110*(4), 790–813. https://doi.org/10.1111/bjop.12358
Jo, W., & Chang, D. (2020). Political consequences of COVID-19 and media framing in South Korea. *Frontiers in Public Health, 8*, 425. https://doi.org/10.3389/fpubh.2020.00425
Jones, N. M., Garfin, D. R., Holman, E. A., & Silver, R. C. (2016). Media use and exposure to graphic content in the week following the Boston Marathon bombings. *American Journal of Community Psychology, 58*(1–2), 47–59. https://doi.org/10.1002/ajcp.12073
Jung, S. J., Winning, A., Roberts, A. L., Nishimi, K., Chen, Q., Gilsanz, P., Sumner, J. A., Fernandez, C. A., Rimm, E. B., Kubzansky, L. D., & Koenen, K. C. (2019). Posttraumatic stress disorder symptoms and television viewing patterns in the Nurses' Health Study II: A longitudinal analysis. *PLoS One, 14*(3), e0213441. https://doi.org/10.1371/journal.pone.0213441
Kaim, A., & Bodas, M. (2024). The impact of 24/7 news coverage on the mental health of Israelis in the 'Iron Swords' War: A cross-sectional analysis among television audience. *Stress and Health: Journal of the International Society for the Investigation of Stress, 40*(4), e3398. https://doi.org/10.1002/smi.3398
Kalita, B., Kumar, C. J., Hazarika, N., Baruah, K. K., & Borah, L. (2024). Exploring climate change adaptation practices and agricultural livelihoods among rice farmers of the Brahmaputra Valley in Northeast India. *Environmental Management, 73*, 1180–1200. https://doi.org/10.1007/s00267-024-01954-w
Kang, J. (2020a). The media spectacle of a Techno-City: COVID-19 and the South Korean experience of the state of emergency. *The Journal of Asian Studies, 79*(3), 589–598. https://doi.org/10.1017/S0021911820002302
Kang, E. (2020b). Association between psychological morbidities and information provision, reliability, and satisfaction among disaster victims: A cross-sectional study. *Journal of Psychiatric Research, 130*, 273–279. https://doi.org/10.1016/j.jpsychires.2020.08.010
Karmegam, D., & Mappillairaju, B. (2020). Spatio-temporal distribution of negative emotions on twitter during floods in Chennai, India, in 2015: A post hoc analysis. *International Journal of Health Geographics, 19*(1), 19. https://doi.org/10.1186/s12942-020-00214-4
Kasim, O. F., & Oyerinde, I. A. (2024). Social media and disaster management by the National Emergency Management in Nigeria: What it is and what it should be. *Journal of Emergency Management (Weston, Mass.), 22*(6), 597–610. https://doi.org/10.5055/jem.0839
Keim, M. E., & Noji, E. (2011). Emergent use of social media: A new age of opportunity for disaster resilience. *American Journal of Disaster Medicine, 6*(1), 47–54.
Kellner, D., Lowin, M., & Hinz, O. (2023). Improved healthcare disaster decision-making utilizing information extraction from complementary social media data during the COVID-19 pandemic. *Decision Support Systems*, 113983. Advance online publication. https://doi.org/10.1016/j.dss.2023.113983

Kelly, C. C. (1998). Dealing with the news media: Effective communication strategies for medical examiners. *The American Journal of Forensic Medicine and Pathology, 19*(2), 181–185. https://doi.org/10.1097/00000433-199806000-00017

Kennedy, C., Charlesworth, A., & Chen, J. L. (2004). Disaster at a distance: Impact of 9.11.01 televised news coverage on mothers' and children's health. *Journal of Pediatric Nursing, 19*(5), 329–339. https://doi.org/10.1016/j.pedn.2004.09.003

Khan, S., & Mishra, J. (2022). Critical gaps and implications of risk communication in the global agreements-SFDRR, SDGs, and UNFCCC: 3 select case studies from urban areas of tropics in South Asia. *Natural Hazards (Dordrecht, Netherlands), 111*(3), 2559–2577. https://doi.org/10.1007/s11069-021-05148-z

Khan, A. A., & Noji, E. K. (2016). Hajj stampede disaster, 2015: Reflections from the frontlines. *American Journal of Disaster Medicine, 11*(1), 59–68. https://doi.org/10.5055/ajdm.2016.0225

Khan, Y., Tracey, S., O'Sullivan, T., Gournis, E., & Johnson, I. (2019). Retiring the Flip Phones: Exploring social media use for managing public health incidents. *Disaster Medicine and Public Health Preparedness, 13*(5–6), 859–867. https://doi.org/10.1017/dmp.2018.147

Kim, J., Ki, M., Yang, J., Na, C., Kim, J., & Han, C. (2024). Feasibility of big data analytics in disaster psychiatry: Impact of Seoul Itaewon tragedy on sentiment distribution on Twitter. *Social Science & Medicine (1982), 359*, 117276. https://doi.org/10.1016/j.socscimed.2024.117276

Knox, C. C. (2023). Local emergency management's use of social media during disasters: A case study of Hurricane Irma. *Disasters, 47*(2), 247–266. https://doi.org/10.1111/disa.12544

Kryvasheyeu, Y., Chen, H., Obradovich, N., Moro, E., Van Hentenryck, P., Fowler, J., & Cebrian, M. (2016). Rapid assessment of disaster damage using social media activity. *Science Advances, 2*(3), e1500779. https://doi.org/10.1126/sciadv.1500779

Kurt, A., Topan, A., & Akkoç, B. (2024). The relationship between media exposure and mental health in children following Kahramanmaraş earthquakes in Turkey. *Journal of Pediatric Nursing, 78*, 7–13. https://doi.org/10.1016/j.pedn.2024.05.037

Lau, J. T., Lau, M., Kim, J. H., & Tsui, H. Y. (2006). Impacts of media coverage on the community stress level in Hong Kong after the tsunami on 26 December 2004. *Journal of Epidemiology and Community Health, 60*(8), 675–682. https://doi.org/10.1136/jech.2005.041897

Lea, C. S., & Beers, H. (2025). Communication preferences during the recovery phase of a hurricane disaster: Rural residents prefer face-to-face interaction. *Journal of Emergency Management (Weston, Mass.), 23*(1), 15–28. https://doi.org/10.5055/jem.0887

Lee, P. S. N. (2014). Mass media and quality of life. In A. C. Michalos (Ed.), *Encyclopedia of quality of life and Well-being research*. Springer. https://doi.org/10.1007/978-94-007-0753-5_1738

Levaot, Y., Greene, T., & Palgi, Y. (2021). Making and receiving offers of help on social media following disaster predict posttraumatic growth but not posttraumatic stress. *Disaster Medicine and Public Health Preparedness, 15*(4), 484–490. https://doi.org/10.1017/dmp.2020.43

Leykin, D., Aharonson-Daniel, L., & Lahad, M. (2016). Leveraging social computing for personalized crisis communication using social media. *PLoS Currents, 8*, ecurrents.dis.b2c5870adf1b7a77af82e7d5552aabe7. https://doi.org/10.1371/currents.dis.b2c5870adf1b7a77af82e7d5552aabe7

Li, S., Liu, Z., & Li, Y. (2020). Temporal and spatial evolution of online public sentiment on emergencies. *Information Processing & Management, 57*(2), 102177. https://doi.org/10.1016/j.ipm.2019.102177

Li, L., Novillo-Ortiz, D., Azzopardi-Muscat, N., & Kostkova, P. (2021). Digital data sources and their impact on people's health: A systematic review of systematic reviews. *Frontiers in Public Health, 9*, 645260. https://doi.org/10.3389/fpubh.2021.645260

Li, K., Li, J., & Li, Y. (2024). The effects of social media usage on vicarious traumatization and the mediation role of recommendation systems usage and peer communication in China after the aircraft flight accident. *European Journal of Psychotraumatology, 15*(1), 2337509. https://doi.org/10.1080/20008066.2024.2337509

Libow, J. A. (1992). Traumatized children and the news media: Clinical considerations. *The American Journal of Orthopsychiatry, 62*(3), 379–386. https://doi.org/10.1037/h0079350

Lin, Y. R., Margolin, D., & Wen, X. (2017). Tracking and analyzing individual distress following terrorist attacks using social media streams. *Risk Analysis: An Official Publication of the Society for Risk Analysis, 37*(8), 1580–1605. https://doi.org/10.1111/risa.12829

Liu, H., & Han, Z. (2025). Earthquake resilience and public engagement: A social media perspective. *Risk Analysis: An Official Publication of the Society for Risk Analysis.*, Advance online publication. https://doi.org/10.1111/risa.70041

Liu, T., Zhang, H., & Zhang, H. (2020). The impact of social media on risk communication of disasters-A comparative study based on *Sina* Weibo blogs related to Tianjin explosion and typhoon pigeon. *International Journal of Environmental Research and Public Health, 17*(3), 883. https://doi.org/10.3390/ijerph17030883

Liu, T., Zhang, S., & Zhang, H. (2022). Exposure to COVID-19-related media content and mental health during the initial outbreak of COVID-19 in China. *Scandinavian Journal of Psychology, 63*(4), 283–289. https://doi.org/10.1111/sjop.12805

Liu, L. S., Jia, X., Zhu, A., Ran, G. J., Siegert, R., French, N., & Johnston, D. (2023). Stigmatising and Racialising COVID-19: Asian People's experience in New Zealand. *Journal of Racial and Ethnic Health Disparities, 10*(6), 2704–2717. https://doi.org/10.1007/s40615-022-01448-7

Lobb, A., & Mock, N. (2007). Dialogue is destiny: Managing the message in humanitarian action. *Prehospital and Disaster Medicine, 22*(5), 423–428. https://doi.org/10.1017/s1049023x0000515x

Lobb, A., Mock, N., & Hutchinson, P. L. (2012). Traditional and social media coverage andcharitable giving following the 2010 earthquake in Haiti. *Prehospital and Disaster Medicine, 27*(4), 319–324. https://doi.org/10.1017/S1049023X12000908

LoVecchio, F., Katz, K., Watts, D., & Pitera, A. (2004). Media influence on Poison Center call volume after 11 September 2001. *Prehospital and Disaster Medicine, 19*(2), 185. https://doi.org/10.1017/s1049023x00001722

Lowrey, W., Evans, W., Gower, K. K., Robinson, J. A., Ginter, P. M., McCormick, L. C., & Abdolrasulnia, M. (2007). Effective media communication of disasters: Pressing problems and recommendations. *BMC Public Health, 7*, 97. https://doi.org/10.1186/1471-2458-7-97

Lu, H. Y., Case, D. O., Lustria, M. L., Kwon, N., Andrews, J. E., Cavendish, S. E., & Floyd, B. R. (2007). Predictors of online information seeking by international students when disaster strikes their countries. *Cyberpsychology & Behavior: The Impact of the Internet, Multimedia and Virtual Reality on Behavior and Society, 10*(5), 709–712. https://doi.org/10.1089/cpb.2007.9965

Lu, B., Zhang, X., & Wen, J. (2020). Real world effectiveness of information and communication technologies in disaster relief: A systematic review. *Iranian Journal of Public Health, 49*(10), 1813–1826. https://doi.org/10.18502/ijph.v49i10.4678

Luo, Y., He, X., Wang, S., Li, J., & Zhang, Y. (2021). Media exposure predicts acute stress and probable acute stress disorder during the early COVID-19 outbreak in China. *PeerJ, 9*, e11407. https://doi.org/10.7717/peerj.11407

Ma, Z., & Lin, Z. (2020). The impact of exposure to memorial reports on the 5.12 Wenchuan earthquake on sleep quality among adult survivors ten years after the disaster: Evidence for nonlinear associations. *Comprehensive Psychiatry, 97*, 152150. https://doi.org/10.1016/j.comppsych.2019.152150

Madianou, M. (2020). A second-order disaster? Digital technologies during the COVID-19 pandemic. *Social Media + Society, 6*(3), 2056305120948168. https://doi.org/10.1177/2056305120948168

Magaña, D., Durazo, A., Ramos, L., & Matlock, T. (2024). An analysis of metaphor in COVID-19 TV news in English and Spanish. *Journal of Communication in Healthcare, 17*(3), 254–264. https://doi.org/10.1080/17538068.2023.2255417

Mahat-Shamir, M., Pitcho-Prelorentzos, S., Kagan, M., Kestler-Peleg, M., & Lavenda, O. (2023). Adjustment disorder in the face of COVID-19 outbreak: The impact of death anxiety, media exposure, fear of contagion and hypochondriasis symptoms. *Omega, 87*(4), 1189–1206. https://doi.org/10.1177/00302228211034372

Mahesar, R. A., Khalil, H., Shaikh, S., Kalhoro, A., Rajar, A. B., Memon, M. A., & Mamun, M. A. (2024). Exploring suicidality in the aftermath of the 2022 flood in Pakistan: Insights from newspaper reports. *CNS Spectrums, 29*(1), 1–3. https://doi.org/10.1017/S1092852923002419

Malik, A., Khan, M. L., & Quan-Haase, A. (2021). Public health agencies outreach through Instagram during the COVID-19 pandemic: Crisis and emergency risk communication perspective. *International Journal of Disaster Risk Reduction: IJDRR, 61*, 102346. https://doi.org/10.1016/j.ijdrr.2021.102346

Marchi, B. D. (1991). Effective communication between the scientific community and the media. *Disasters, 15*(3), 237–243. https://doi.org/10.1111/j.1467-7717.1991.tb00457.x

McCartney, M. (2011). Medicine and the media. Panic about nuclear apocalypse overshadows Japan's real plight. *BMJ (Clinical Research ed.), 342*, d1845. https://doi.org/10.1136/bmj.d1845

McKay, J. M. (1983). Newspaper reporting of bush-fire disaster in south-eastern Australia-Ash Wednesday 1983. *Disasters, 7*(4), 283–290. https://doi.org/10.1111/j.1467-7717.1983.tb00836.x

McLuhan, M. (1964). *Understanding Media*. McGraw-Hill.

Mehta, A. M., Bruns, A., & Newton, J. (2017). Trust, but verify: Social media models for disaster management. *Disasters, 41*(3), 549–565. https://doi.org/10.1111/disa.12218

Mendez, S. R., Munoz-Najar, S., Emmons, K. M., & Viswanath, K. (2025). US state public health agencies' use of twitter from 2012 to 2022: Observational study. *Journal of Medical Internet Research, 27*, e59786. https://doi.org/10.2196/59786

Menon, V. B., & George, L. S. (2021). Response of the health system in Nipah outbreak in Ernakulam district: A qualitative analysis. *Journal of Family Medicine and Primary Care, 10*(9), 3355–3360. https://doi.org/10.4103/jfmpc.jfmpc_801_21

Mian, S., & Bennett, S. (2009). The Tasman Spirit oil spill: Implications for regulatory change in Pakistan. *Disasters, 33*(3), 390–411. https://doi.org/10.1111/j.1467-7717.2008.01080.x

Mikal, J. P., Wurtz, R., & Grande, S. W. (2021). Social media as a modern emergency broadcast system: A longitudinal qualitative study of social media during COVID-19 and its impacts on social connection and social distancing compliance. *Computers in Human Behavior Reports, 4*, 100137. https://doi.org/10.1016/j.chbr.2021.100137

Milsten, A. M., Kang, C. S., & Nemeth, I. (2024). Maladaptive behaviors in disasters: Case study evaluation of Hurricane Hugo, Hurricane Katrina and the Haiti earthquake. *Frontiers in Public Health, 12*, 1396517. https://doi.org/10.3389/fpubh.2024.1396517

Mondal, S. K., Huang, J., Wang, Y., Su, B., Zhai, J., Tao, H., Wang, G., Fischer, T., Wen, S., & Jiang, T. (2021). Doubling of the population exposed to drought over South Asia: CMIP6 multi-model-based analysis. *The Science of the Total Environment, 771*, 145186. https://doi.org/10.1016/j.scitotenv.2021.145186

Moore, J. B., Harris, J. K., & Hutti, E. T. (2021). 'Falsehood flies, and the truth comes limping after it': Social media and public health. *Current Opinion in Psychiatry, 34*(5), 485–490. https://doi.org/10.1097/YCO.0000000000000730

Morgan, O., & de Ville de Goyet, C. (2005). Dispelling disaster myths about dead bodies and disease: The role of scientific evidence and the media. *Pan American Journal of Public Health, 18*(1), 33–36. https://doi.org/10.1590/s1020-49892005000600006

Muhammad, K., Saqlain, M., Muhammad, G., Hamdard, A., Naveed, M., Butt, M. H., Khan, S., Ismael, N. S., Khan, Z., & Karatas, Y. (2022). Knowledge, attitude, and practices (KAPs) of community pharmacists regarding COVID-19: A cross-sectional survey in 2 provinces of Pakistan. *Disaster Medicine and Public Health Preparedness, 16*(5), 1864–1872. https://doi.org/10.1017/dmp.2021.54

Muhammed, T.,. S., & Mathew, S. K. (2022). The disaster of misinformation: A review of research in social media. *International Journal of Data Science and Analytics, 13*(4), 271–285. https://doi.org/10.1007/s41060-022-00311-6

Mukherjee, M., Wickramasinghe, D., Chowdhooree, I., Chimi, C., Poudel, S., Mishra, B., Ali, Z. F., & Shaw, R. (2022). Nature-based resilience: Experiences of five cities from South Asia.

International Journal of Environmental Research and Public Health, 19(19), 11846. https://doi.org/10.3390/ijerph191911846

Murphy, M. W., Iqbal, S., Sanchez, C. A., & Quinlisk, M. P. (2010). Postdisaster health communication and information sources: The Iowa flood scenario. *Disaster Medicine and Public Health Preparedness, 4*(2), 129–134. https://doi.org/10.1001/dmp.2010-v4n2-hre10009

Murthy, D., & Gross, A. J. (2017). Social media processes in disasters: Implications of emergent technology use. *Social Science Research, 63*, 356–370. https://doi.org/10.1016/j.ssresearch.2016.09.015

Muruthi, J. R., Raqueno-Angel, S., Di, Y., Muruthi, B. A., McRell, A. S., & McClure, H. H. (2025). Disaster communication and preparedness among middle-aged and older Latino migrants and seasonal farmworkers in western Oregon. *Journal of Communication in Healthcare*, 1–9. Advance online publication. https://doi.org/10.1080/17538068.2025.2514981

Nakayama, C., Iwasa, H., Moriyama, N., & Yasumura, S. (2023). Relationship between the effects of perceived damage caused by harmful rumors about Fukushima after the nuclear accident and information sources and media. *International Journal of Environmental Research and Public Health, 20*(3), 2077. https://doi.org/10.3390/ijerph20032077

Nejati-Zarnaqi, B., Khorasani-Zavareh, D., Sohrabizadeh, S., Ghaffari, M., Sabour, S., Nouri, F., & Mohammadi, R. (2024). Factors affecting the spiritual rehabilitation of people affected by natural disasters: A systematic review. *Journal of Injury and Violence Research, 16*(2) Advance online publication. https://doi.org/10.5249/jivr.v16i2.1877

Newman, E., & Shapiro, B. (2014). Clinicians and journalists responding to disasters. *Journal of Child and Adolescent Psychopharmacology, 24*(1), 32–38. https://doi.org/10.1089/cap.2013.0068

Ng, K. H., & Lean, M. L. (2012). The Fukushima nuclear crisis reemphasizes the need for improved risk communication and better use of social media. *Health Physics, 103*(3), 307–310. https://doi.org/10.1097/HP.0b013e318257cfcb

Niles, M. T., Emery, B. F., Reagan, A. J., Dodds, P. S., & Danforth, C. M. (2019). Social media usage patterns during natural hazards. *PLoS One, 14*(2), e0210484. https://doi.org/10.1371/journal.pone.0210484

Nishi, D., Koido, Y., Nakaya, N., Sone, T., Noguchi, H., Hamazaki, K., Hamazaki, T., & Matsuoka, Y. (2012). Peritraumatic distress, watching television, and posttraumatic stress symptoms among rescue workers after the Great East Japan earthquake. *PLoS One, 7*(4), e35248. https://doi.org/10.1371/journal.pone.0035248

Njenga, F. G., Nyamai, C., & Kigamwa, P. (2003). Terrorist bombing at the USA Embassy in Nairobi: The media response. *East African Medical Journal, 80*(3), 159–164. https://doi.org/10.4314/eamj.v80i3.8686

Nocera, A. (2000). Disasters, thc mcdia and doctors. *The Medical Journal of Australia, 172*(3), 137–139. https://doi.org/10.5694/j.1326-5377.2000.tb127942.x

North, C. S., Surís, A., McDonald, K., & Pollio, D. E. (2022). A qualitative longitudinal study of workplace issues, authorities and media, and relationships recounted by Oklahoma City bombing survivors after nearly a quarter century. *Journal of Occupational and Environmental Medicine, 64*(11), e722–e728. https://doi.org/10.1097/JOM.0000000000002681

Nur-A Yazdani, D. M., Abir, T., Qing, Y., Ahmad, J., Al Mamun, A., Zainol, N. R., Kakon, K., Agho, K. E., & Wang, S. (2022). Social media addiction and emotions during the disaster recovery period-the moderating role of post-COVID timing. *PLoS One, 17*(10), e0274898. https://doi.org/10.1371/journal.pone.0274898

O'Leary, D. S. (1982). When physicians meet the press. *The Hospital Medical Staff, 11*(10), 2–8.

Ogie, R., Moore, A., Wickramasuriya, R., Amirghasemi, M., James, S., & Dilworth, T. (2022). Twitter data from the 2019-20 Australian bushfires reveals participatory and temporal variations in social media use for disaster recovery. *Scientific Reports, 12*(1), 16914. https://doi.org/10.1038/s41598-022-21265-6

Ohmori, M. (2016). Looking back on media reports on the nuclear accident. *Annals of the ICRP, 45*(2_suppl), 33–36. https://doi.org/10.1177/0146645316666757

Olsen, G. R., Carstensen, N., & Høyen, K. (2003). Humanitarian crises: What determines the level of emergency assistance? Media coverage, donor interests and the aid business. *Disasters, 27*(2), 109–126. https://doi.org/10.1111/1467-7717.00223

Oosterhof, L., Heuvelman, A., & Peters, O. (2009). Donation to disaster relief campaigns: Underlying social cognitive factors exposed. *Evaluation and Program Planning, 32*(2), 148–157. https://doi.org/10.1016/j.evalprogplan.2008.10.006

Orui, M., Nakayama, C., Kuroda, Y., Moriyama, N., Iwasa, H., Horiuchi, T., Nakayama, T., Sugita, M., & Yasumura, S. (2020). The Association between Utilization of Media Information and Current HealthAnxiety Among the Fukushima Daiichi Nuclear Disaster Evacuees. *International Journal of Environmental Research and Public Health, 17*(11), 3921. https://doi.org/10.3390/ijerph17113921

Osterholm, M. T. (1999). The medical impact of a bioterrorist attack. Is it all media hype or clearly a potential nightmare? *Postgraduate Medicine, 106*(2), 121–130. https://doi.org/10.3810/pgm.1999.08.646

Otero, C. J., & Njenga, F. G. (2006). Lessons in posttraumatic stress disorder from the past: Venezuela floods and Nairobi bombing. *The Journal of Clinical Psychiatry, 67*(Suppl 2), 56–63.

Oz, I. T., & Cona, G. (2024). Impact of indirect trauma and disaster media exposure on psychological states and temporal processes: The Case of 2023 Turkey earthquakes. *Clinical Psychology and Psychotherapy, 31*(6), e70008. https://doi.org/10.1002/cpp.70008

Paek, H. J., Hilyard, K., Freimuth, V., Barge, J. K., & Mindlin, M. (2010). Theory-based approaches to understanding public emergency preparedness: Implications for effective health and risk communication. *Journal of Health Communication, 15*(4), 428–444. https://doi.org/10.1080/10810731003753083

Papadopoulos, I., Lazzarino, R., Wright, S., Ellis Logan, P., & Koulouglioti, C. (2021). Spiritual support during COVID-19 in England: A scoping study of online sources. *Journal of Religion and Health, 60*(4), 2209–2230. https://doi.org/10.1007/s10943-021-01254-1

Parmer, J., Baur, C., Eroglu, D., Lubell, K., Prue, C., Reynolds, B., & Weaver, J. (2016). Crisis and emergency risk messaging in mass media news stories: Is the public getting the information they need to protect their health? *Health Communication, 31*(10), 1215–1222. https://doi.org/10.1080/10410236.2015.1049728

Partington, A. J., & Savage, P. E. (1985). Disaster planning: Managing the media. *British Medical Journal (Clinical Research Ed.), 291*(6495), 590–592. https://doi.org/10.1136/bmj.291.6495.590

Pashaei Asl, Y., Dowlati, M., Babaie, J., & Seyedin, H. (2022). Integrated operations for natural disaster management: A systematic review. *Health Promotion Perspectives, 12*(3), 266–272. https://doi.org/10.34172/hpp.2022.33

Patwary, M. M., Bardhan, M., Browning, M. H. E. M., Disha, A. S., Haque, M. Z., Billah, S. M., Kabir, M. P., Hossain, M. R., Alam, M. A., Shuvo, F. K., & Salman, A. (2021). Association between perceived trusted of COVID-19 information sources and mental health during the early stage of the pandemic in Bangladesh. *Healthcare (Basel, Switzerland), 10*(1), 24. https://doi.org/10.3390/healthcare10010024

Patwary, M. M., Bardhan, M., Disha, A. S., Kabir, M. P., Hossain, M. R., Alam, M. A., Haque, M. Z., Billah, S. M., Browning, M. H. E. M., Kabir, R., Swed, S., & Shoib, S. (2022a). Mental health status of university students and working professionals during the early stage of COVID-19 in Bangladesh. *International Journal of Environmental Research and Public Health, 19*(11), 6834. https://doi.org/10.3390/ijerph19116834

Patwary, M. M., Hossain, M. R., Sultana, R., Dazhamyar, A. R., Parsa, A. D., Kabir, R., & Shoib, S. (2022b). Knowledge, attitudes and practices of healthcare professionals toward the novel coronavirus during the early stage of COVID-19 in a lower-and-middle income country, Bangladesh. *Frontiers in Public Health, 10*, 988063. https://doi.org/10.3389/fpubh.2022.988063

Paudel, P. K., Bastola, R., & Lopchan, P. T. (2020). The coverage of environmental issues in FM radios in Nepal: The current status and challenges. *Heliyon, 6*(7), e04354. https://doi.org/10.1016/j.heliyon.2020.e04354

Paul, S. (2022). Analyzing the attitude of Indian citizens during the second wave of COVID-19: A text analytics study. *International Journal of Disaster Risk Reduction: IJDRR, 79*, 103161. https://doi.org/10.1016/j.ijdrr.2022.103161

Peltan, I. D. (2009). Disaster relief and recovery after a landslide at a small, rural hospital in Guatemala. *Prehospital and Disaster Medicine, 24*(6), 542–548. https://doi.org/10.1017/s1049023x00007494

Peyravi, M., & Ahmadi Marzaleh, M. (2020). The double-edged sword of Iranian social media against COVID-19. *Prehospital and Disaster Medicine, 35*(4), 468–469. https://doi.org/10.1017/S1049023X20000722

Pfefferbaum, B., Nixon, S. J., Tucker, P. M., Tivis, R. D., Moore, V. L., Gurwitch, R. H., Pynoos, R. S., & Geis, H. K. (1999). Posttraumatic stress responses in bereaved children after the Oklahoma City bombing. *Journal of the American Academy of Child and Adolescent Psychiatry, 38*(11), 1372–1379. https://doi.org/10.1097/00004583-199911000-00011

Pfefferbaum, B., Seale, T. W., McDonald, N. B., Brandt, E. N., Jr., Rainwater, S. M., Maynard, B. T., Meierhoefer, B., & Miller, P. D. (2000). Posttraumatic stress two years after the Oklahoma City bombing in youths geographically distant from the explosion. *Psychiatry, 63*(4), 358–370. https://doi.org/10.1080/00332747.2000.11024929

Pfefferbaum, B., Jeon-Slaughter, H., Pfefferbaum, R. L., Houston, J. B., Rainwater, S. M., & Regens, J. L. (2008). Media coverage and children's reactions to disaster with implications for primary care and public health. *The Journal of the Oklahoma State Medical Association, 101*(12), 312–317.

Pfefferbaum, B., Palka, J. M., & North, C. S. (2021). Associations between news media coverage of the 11 September attacks and depression in employees of New York City area businesses. *Behavioral Sciences (Basel, Switzerland), 11*(3), 29. https://doi.org/10.3390/bs11030029

Pickering, C. J., Al-Baldawi, Z., McVean, L., Amany, R. A., Adan, M., Baker, L., Al-Baldawi, Z., & L O'Sullivan, T. (2022). "It's like youth are talking into a microphone that is not plugged in": Engaging youth in disaster risk reduction through Photovoice. *Qualitative Health Research, 32*(14), 2126–2146. https://doi.org/10.1177/10497323221136485

Planning for disaster. (1972). *British Medical Journal, 3*(5817), 3–4.

Ploughman, P. (1995). The American print news media 'construction' of five natural disasters. *Disasters, 19*(4), 308–326. https://doi.org/10.1111/j.1467-7717.1995.tb00352.x

Ploughman, P. (1997). Disasters, the media and social structures: A typology of credibility hierarchy persistence based on a newspaper coverage of the Love Canal and six other disasters. *Disasters, 21*(2), 118–137. https://doi.org/10.1111/1467-7717.00049

Pribble, J. M., Fowler, E. F., Kamat, S. V., Wilkerson, W. M., Goldstein, K. M., & Hargarten, S. W. (2010). Communicating emerging infectious disease outbreaks to the public through local television news: Public health officials as potential spokespeople. *Disaster Medicine and Public Health Preparedness, 4*(3), 220–225. https://doi.org/10.1001/dmp.2010.27

Qu, Z., Wang, J., & Zhang, M. (2023). Mining and analysis of public sentiment during disaster events: The extreme rainstorm disaster in megacities of China in 2021. *Heliyon, 9*(7), e18272. https://doi.org/10.1016/j.heliyon.2023.e18272

Rahman, S. I., Sial, N., & Moazzam, S. (2021). Role of frequency modulation radio in disaster communication: A case study of Pakistan earthquake. *Jamba (Potchefstroom, South Africa), 13*(1), 1047. https://doi.org/10.4102/jamba.v13i1.1047

Rattien, S. (1990). The role of the media in hazard mitigation and disaster management. *Disasters, 14*(1), 36–45. https://doi.org/10.1111/j.1467-7717.1990.tb00970.x

Ravan, J. R., Panda, U. K., Pattnaik, J. I., Banerjee, S., Chaudhuri, T., Patil, S., & Das, R. C. (2024). The psychological impact of disaster on first responders in the aftermath of Bahanaga train tragedy: A mixed methods approach. *Indian Journal of Psychiatry, 66*(11), 1043–1049. https://doi.org/10.4103/indianjpsychiatry.indianjpsychiatry_231_24

Ray, M., & Malhi, P. (2005). Reactions of Indian adolescents to the 9/11 terrorist attacks. *Indian Journal of Pediatrics, 72*(3), 217–221. https://doi.org/10.1007/BF02859259

Renzulli, D. R., Mebane, F., & Sieff, E. (2006). News coverage analyses of mental health services immediately after September 11, 2001. *Psychiatric Services (Washington, D.C.), 57*(9), 1339–1341. https://doi.org/10.1176/ps.2006.57.9.1339

Robinson, L., & Jarvie, J. K. (2008). Post-disaster community tourism recovery: The tsunami and Arugam Bay, Sri Lanka. *Disasters, 32*(4), 631–645. https://doi.org/10.1111/j.1467-7717.2008.01058.x

Rodgers, R. F., Franko, D. L., Brunet, A., Herbert, C. F., & Bui, E. (2012). Disordered eating following exposure to television and internet coverage of the March 2011 Japan earthquake. *The International Journal of Eating Disorders, 45*(7), 845–849. https://doi.org/10.1002/eat.22031

Roe, D., Gilboa-Schechtman, E., & Baumel, A. (2025). Digital terror: Its striking impact on public mental health. *Psychiatric Services (Washington, D.C.), 76*(1), 99–101. https://doi.org/10.1176/appi.ps.20240169

Romo-Murphy, E., James, R., & Adams, M. (2011). Facilitating disaster preparedness through local radio broadcasting. *Disasters, 35*(4), 801–815. https://doi.org/10.1111/j.1467-7717.2010.01234.x

Roy, N., Shah, H., Patel, V., & Bagalkote, H. (2005). Surgical and psychosocial outcomes in the rural injured--a follow-up study of the 2001 earthquake victims. *Injury, 36*(8), 927–934. https://doi.org/10.1016/j.injury.2005.02.017

Sadore, A. A., Handiso, D. W., Wontamo, T. E., Mekango, D. E., & Moges, S. (2021). Influence of social media use on practice of COVID-19 preventive measures among Ethiopian residents: An online cross-sectional study. *Disaster Medicine And Public Health Preparedness*, 1–6. Advance online publication. https://doi.org/10.1017/dmp.2021.184

Salman, M., Mustafa, Z. U., Asif, N., Shehzadi, N., Hussain, K., Khan, T. M., Mallhi, T. H., Khan, Y. H., Butt, M. H., Farrukh, M. J., & Saleem, F. (2021). Awareness of COVID-19 among illiterate population in Pakistan: A cross-sectional analysis. *Disaster Medicine and Public Health Preparedness, 17*, e31. https://doi.org/10.1017/dmp.2021.261

Sargu, L., Andrioni, F., Popp, L., Netedu, A., Bularca, M. C., Otovescu, A., Motoi, G., Negrilă, I., Goian, C., Coman, C., & Chirugu, G. (2023). The role of mass Media in Influencing the lifestyle of the elderly during the COVID-19 pandemic. *Healthcare (Basel, Switzerland), 11*(13), 1816. https://doi.org/10.3390/healthcare11131816

Satapathy, S., & Walia, A. (2007). Affected parents' and other stakeholders' perception of a fire disaster management in India: A situational analysis. *Disaster Management & Response: DMR: An Official Publication of the Emergency Nurses Association, 5*(4), 111–118. https://doi.org/10.1016/j.dmr.2007.08.002

Schmälzle, R., & Huskey, R. (2023). Integrating media content analysis, reception analysis, and media effects studies. *Frontiers in Neuroscience, 17*, 1155750. https://doi.org/10.3389/fnins.2023.1155750

Schwind, J. S., Norman, S. A., Karmacharya, D., Wolking, D. J., Dixit, S. M., Rajbhandari, R. M., Mekaru, S. R., & Brownstein, J. S. (2017). Online surveillance of media health event reporting in Nepal: Digital disease detection from a One Health perspective. *BMC International Health and Human Rights, 17*(1), 26. https://doi.org/10.1186/s12914-017-0134-2

Sederer, L. I., Lanzara, C. B., Essock, S. M., Donahue, S. A., Stone, J. L., & Galea, S. (2011). Lessons learned from the New York State mental health response to the September 11, 2001, attacks. *Psychiatric Services (Washington, D.C.), 62*(9), 1085–1089. https://doi.org/10.1176/ps.62.9.pss6209_1085

Shah, Z., & Wei, L. (2022). Interpersonal risk communication matters more than media risk communication in its impact on individuals' trust and preventive behaviors during COVID-19. *International Journal of Disaster Risk Reduction: IJDRR, 82*, 103369. https://doi.org/10.1016/j.ijdrr.2022.103369

Sharma, R., & Gautam, V. (2023). *New age digital media consumption: An exploratory study based in India. Working Paper*. Indian Institute of Management. https://www.iima.ac.in/publicationnew-age-digital-media-consumption-exploratory-study-based-india

Shi, W., & Hall, B. J. (2023). Trajectories of posttraumatic stress symptoms among young adults exposed to a typhoon: A three-wave longitudinal study. *International Journal of Public Health, 67*, 1605380. https://doi.org/10.3389/ijph.2022.1605380

Shoenfeld, H. (1965). Radio system helps in everyday business–but stands ready for disaster. *Hospitals, 39*, 82–85.

Shoyama, K., Cui, Q., Hanashima, M., Sano, H., & Usuda, Y. (2021). Emergency flood detection using multiple information sources: Integrated analysis of natural hazard monitoring and social media data. *The Science of the Total Environment, 767*, 144371. https://doi.org/10.1016/j.scitotenv.2020.144371

Shrum, W. (2014). What caused the flood? Controversy and closure in the Hurricane Katrina disaster. *Social Studies of Science, 44*(1), 3–33. https://doi.org/10.1177/0306312713498654

Sin, S. S., Chan, A., & Huak, C. Y. (2005). A pilot study of the impact of the Asian Tsunami ona group of Asian media workers. *International Journal of Emergency Mental Health, 7*(4), 299–305.

Singh, I., Bista, N. R., Maleku, K., Adhikari, P., Hyanmikha, A., Pradhan, S., & Kharel, R. (2022). Establishment of a rapid phone consultation service for COVID-19 public health support in Nepal. *Cureus, 14*(8), e27977. https://doi.org/10.7759/cureus.27977

Singh, P., Lamine, H., Sapkota, S., Bahattab, A., & Eriksson, A. (2023). Management of Mass-Casualty Incidents in Nepal: A qualitative case study of three district hospitals in Nepal. *Prehospital and Disaster Medicine, 38*(5), 606–611. https://doi.org/10.1017/S1049023X23006209

Sobowale, K., Hilliard, H., Ignaszewski, M. J., & Chokroverty, L. (2020). Real-time communication: Creating a path to COVID-19 public health activism in adolescents using social media. *Journal of Medical Internet Research, 22*(12), e21886. https://doi.org/10.2196/21886

Sriram, V., Vaidyanathan, G., Adithyan, G. S., Thakur, S. B., Kaur, S., Gl, H. N., Haque, S., & Muraleedharan, V. R. (2025). Capacity and crisis: Examining the state-level policy response to COVID-19 in Tamil Nadu, India. *Health Policy and Planning, 40*(2), 153–164. https://doi.org/10.1093/heapol/czae096

Stephenson, N., & Jamieson, M. (2009). Securitising health: Australian newspaper coverage of pandemic influenza. *Sociology of Health & Illness, 31*(4), 525–539. https://doi.org/10.1111/j.1467-9566.2009.01162.x

Straub, A. M. (2024). Post-tropical cyclone Fiona and Atlantic Canada: Media framing of hazard risk in the Anthropocene. *Disasters, 48*(4), e12641. https://doi.org/10.1111/disa.12641

Sugimoto, A., Nomura, S., Tsubokura, M., Matsumura, T., Muto, K., Sato, M., & Gilmour, S. (2013). The relationship between media consumption and health-related anxieties after the Fukushima Daiichi nuclear disaster. *PLoS One, 8*(8), e65331. https://doi.org/10.1371/journal.pone.0065331

Takeuchi, H., Taki, Y., Hashizume, H., Asano, K., Asano, M., Sassa, Y., Yokota, S., Kotozaki, Y., Nouchi, R., & Kawashima, R. (2015). The impact of television viewing on brain structures: Cross-sectional and longitudinal analyses. *Cerebral Cortex (New York, N.Y.: 1991), 25*(5), 1188–1197. https://doi.org/10.1093/cercor/bht315

Tan, H., & Hao, Y. (2022). Mapping the global evolution and research directions of information seeking, sharing and communication in disasters: A bibliometric study. *International Journal of Environmental Research and Public Health, 19*(22), 14878. https://doi.org/10.3390/ijerph192214878

Tanner, A., Friedman, D. B., Koskan, A., & Barr, D. (2009). Disaster communication on the internet: A focus on mobilizing information. *Journal of Health Communication, 14*(8), 741–755. https://doi.org/10.1080/10810730903295542

Taskin, S., Yildirim Kurtulus, H., Satici, S. A., & Deniz, M. E. (2024). Doomscrolling and mental well-being in social media users: A serial mediation through mindfulness and secondary

traumatic stress. *Journal of Community Psychology, 52*(3), 512–524. https://doi.org/10.1002/jcop.23111
Tauzer, E., Borbor-Cordova, M. J., Mendoza, J., De La Cuadra, T., Cunalata, J., & Stewart-Ibarra, A. M. (2019). A participatory community case study of periurban coastal flood vulnerability in southern Ecuador. *PLoS One, 14*(10), e0224171. https://doi.org/10.1371/journal.pone.0224171
Terui, T., Kunii, Y., Kawasaki, Y., Kakamu, T., Hidaka, T., Yabe, H., & Miura, I. (2024). Association between radiation risk perception related to the Fukushima nuclear disaster and traumatic stress symptoms induced by media reports of the Russian Invasion of Ukraine. *Disaster Medicine and Public Health Preparedness, 18*, e238. https://doi.org/10.1017/dmp.2024.255
Thompson, R. R., Holman, E. A., & Silver, R. C. (2019). Media coverage, forecasted posttraumatic stress symptoms, and psychological responses before and after an approaching hurricane. *JAMA Network Open, 2*(1), e186228. https://doi.org/10.1001/jamanetworkopen.2018.6228
Tin, D., & Ciottone, G. (2023). Unveiling the strengths and biases of media influence on disaster response. *Prehospital and Disaster Medicine, 38*(5), 683–684. https://doi.org/10.1017/S1049023X23006210
Torpuş, K., Usta, G., & Berkircan, E. (2025). Evaluation of the opinions of volunteers involved in disaster on the use of social media. *Disaster Medicine and Public Health Preparedness, 19*, e68. https://doi.org/10.1017/dmp.2025.65
Tripathi, V. S., & Bansal, R. K. (2007). Creating panic during disasters. *Indian Journal of Medical Ethics, 4*(2), 97. https://doi.org/10.20529/IJME.2007.038
Trotochaud, M., Smith, E., Hosangadi, D., & Sell, T. K. (2023). Analyzing social media messaging on masks and vaccines: A Case study on misinformation during the COVID-19 pandemic. *Disaster Medicine and Public Health Preparedness*, 1–9. Advance online publication. https://doi.org/10.1017/dmp.2023.16
Tudu, P. N. (2022). The danger in danger – A study on the psychological impact of COVID-19 lockdown on people in the Indian context. *International Journal of Disaster Risk Reduction: IJDRR, 77*, 103027. https://doi.org/10.1016/j.ijdrr.2022.103027
Twenge, J. M., Martin, G. N., & Spitzberg, B. H. (2019). Trends in U.S. Adolescents' media use, 1976–2016: The rise of digital media, the decline of TV, and the (near) demise of print. *Psychology of Popular Media Culture, 8*(4), 329–345. https://doi.org/10.1037/ppm0000203
Uchida, Y., Kanagawa, C., Takenishi, A., Harada, A., Okawa, K., & Yabuno, H. (2015). How did the media report on the Great East Japan earthquake? Objectivity and emotionality seeking in Japanese media coverage. *PLoS One, 10*(5), e0125966. https://doi.org/10.1371/journal.pone.0125966
Ujihara, M., Tachikawa, H., Takahashi, A., Gen, T., & Cho, Y. (2023). Factors related to psychological distress in suicide prevention supporters during the COVID-19 pandemic. *International Journal of Environmental Research and Public Health, 20*(6), 4991. https://doi.org/10.3390/ijerph20064991
Umihara, J., & Nishikitani, M. (2013). Emergent use of twitter in the 2011 Tohoku earthquake. *Prehospital and Disaster Medicine, 28*(5), 434–440. https://doi.org/10.1017/S1049023X13008704
UNDRR. (2025). *Reporting on disasters: Media resources*. https://www.preventionweb.net/collections/reporting-disasters-media-resources
UNESCO. (2025). *Media in the face of disasters*. https://www.unesco.org/en/articles/media-face-disasters
Uvais, N. A. (2020). Disaster-related media exposure and its impact on mental health. *Journal of Family Medicine and Primary Care, 9*(1), 448–449. https://doi.org/10.4103/jfmpc.jfmpc_981_19
Van Hoving, D. J., Wallis, L. A., Docrat, F., & De Vries, S. (2010). Haiti disaster tourism--a medical shame. *Prehospital and Disaster Medicine, 25*(3), 201–202. https://doi.org/10.1017/s1049023x00008001

Vasterman, P., Yzermans, C. J., & Dirkzwager, A. J. (2005). The role of the media and media hypes in the aftermath of disasters. *Epidemiologic Reviews, 27*, 107–114. https://doi.org/10.1093/epirev/mxi002

Venegas-Vera, A. V., Colbert, G. B., & Lerma, E. V. (2020). Positive and negative impact of social media in the COVID-19 era. *Reviews in Cardiovascular Medicine, 21*(4), 561–564. https://doi.org/10.31083/j.rcm.2020.04.195

Vera-Burgos, C. M., & Griffin Padgett, D. R. (2020). Using Twitter for crisis communications in a natural disaster: Hurricane Harvey. *Heliyon, 6*(9), e04804. https://doi.org/10.1016/j.heliyon.2020.e04804

Verma, M., Moudgil, N., Goel, G., Pardeshi, P., Joseph, J., Kumar, N., Singh, K., Singh, H., & Kodali, P. B. (2023). People's perceptions on COVID-19 vaccination: An analysis of twitter discourse from four countries. *Scientific Reports, 13*(1), 14281. https://doi.org/10.1038/s41598-023-41478-7

Wayment, H. A. (2004). It could have been me: Vicarious victims and disaster-focused distress. *Personality and Social Psychology Bulletin, 30*(4), 515–528. https://doi.org/10.1177/0146167203261892

White, B. K., Lavery, L., Ishizumi, A., Wright, A., Foley, T., Nguyen, T., Briand, S., Machiri, S., Hassan, N., Pastorino, A., & Purnat, T. D. (2023). Infodemic insights on trust in a health emergency: A narrative deep-dive. *Studies in Health Technology and Informatics, 305*, 46–47. https://doi.org/10.3233/SHTI230420

Wiederhold, B. K. (2013). In a disaster, social media has the power to save lives. *Cyberpsychology, Behavior and Social Networking, 16*(11), 781–782. https://doi.org/10.1089/cyber.2013.1532

Wolkin, A. F., Schnall, A. H., Nakata, N. K., & Ellis, E. M. (2019). Getting the message out: Social media and word-of-mouth as effective communication methods during emergencies. *Prehospital and Disaster Medicine, 34*(1), 89–94. https://doi.org/10.1017/S1049023X1800119X

Wong, A., Choi, Y. K., Lee, J. H., & Lee, H. S. (2024). A preliminary study of disaster media use as a coping mechanism and the psychological impact of the 2014 Sewol ferry disaster. *European Journal of Psychotraumatology, 15*(1), 2429268. https://doi.org/10.1080/20008066.2024.2429268

Woo, H., Cho, Y., Shim, E., Lee, K., & Song, G. (2015). Public trauma after the Sewol ferry disaster: The role of social media in understanding the public mood. *International Journal of Environmental Research and Public Health, 12*(9), 10974–10983. https://doi.org/10.3390/ijerph120910974

Woods, C., West, C., Buettner, P., & Usher, K. (2014). "Out of our control": Living through Cyclone Yasi. *International Journal of Qualitative Studies on Health and Well-Being, 9*, 19821. https://doi.org/10.3402/qhw.v9.19821

Wu, Q., Sano, Y., Takayasu, H., Havlin, S., & Takayasu, M. (2025). Twitter communities are associated with changing user's opinion towards COVID-19 vaccine in Japan. *Scientific Reports, 15*(1), 11716. https://doi.org/10.1038/s41598-025-95595-6

Xiong, J., Hswen, Y., & Naslund, J. A. (2020). Digital surveillance for monitoring environmental health threats: A case study capturing public opinion from twitter about the 2019 Chennai water crisis. *International Journal of Environmental Research and Public Health, 17*(14), 5077. https://doi.org/10.3390/ijerph17145077

Xu, Q. (2023). Comparing COVID-19 metaphors in Chinese and English social media with critical metaphor analysis. *Frontiers in Psychology, 14*, 1198265. https://doi.org/10.3389/fpsyg.2023.1198265

Xu, D., Zhuang, L., Deng, X., Qing, C., & Yong, Z. (2020). Media exposure, disaster experience, and risk perception of rural households in earthquake-stricken areas: Evidence from rural China. *International Journal of Environmental Research and Public Health, 17*(9), 3246. https://doi.org/10.3390/ijerph17093246

Yang, J. Z., Chu, H., & Liu, S. (2023). Official sources, news outlets, or search engines? Rumour validation on social media during Hurricanes Harvey and Irma. *Disasters, 47*(1), 163–180. https://doi.org/10.1111/disa.12519

Yeager, V., Cooper, G. P., Jr., Burkle, F. M., Jr., & Subbarao, I. (2015). Twitter as a potential disaster risk reduction tool. Part IV: Competency-based education and training guidelines to promote community resiliency. *PLoS Currents, 7*, ecurrents.dis.ce3fad537bd666770a649a076ee71ba4. https://doi.org/10.1371/currents.dis.ce3fad537bd666770a649a076ee71ba4

Yoho, D. R., Jr. (1994). Wireless communication technology applied to disaster response. *Aviation, Space, and Environmental Medicine, 65*(9), 839–845.

Yoshida, H., Kobayashi, N., Honda, N., Matsuoka, H., Yamaguchi, T., Homma, H., & Tomita, H. (2016). Post-traumatic growth of children affected by the Great East Japan earthquake and their attitudes to memorial services and media coverage. *Psychiatry and Clinical Neurosciences, 70*(5), 193–201. https://doi.org/10.1111/pcn.12379

Yumiya, Y., Murakami, M., Takebayashi, Y., Suzuki, S., & Ohira, T. (2019). Unreliable information as a risk factor for worse mental fatigue among residents in Fukushima after the nuclear power station accident. *The Tohoku Journal of Experimental Medicine, 248*(4), 261–272. https://doi.org/10.1620/tjem.248.261

Yzermans, C. J., Donker, G. A., Kerssens, J. J., Dirkzwager, A. J., Soeteman, R. J., & ten Veen, P. M. (2005). Health problems of victims before and after disaster: A longitudinal study in general practice. *International Journal of Epidemiology, 34*(4), 820–826. https://doi.org/10.1093/ije/dyi096

Zhao, N., & Zhou, G. (2020). Social media use and mental health during the COVID-19 pandemic: Moderator role of disaster stressor and mediator role of negative affect. *Applied Psychology: Health and Well-Being, 12*(4), 1019–1038. https://doi.org/10.1111/aphw.12226

Zhao, N., & Zhou, G. (2021). COVID-19 stress and addictive social media use (SMU): Mediating role of active use and social media flow. *Frontiers in Psychiatry, 12*, 635546. https://doi.org/10.3389/fpsyt.2021.635546

Zhao, M., Rosoff, H., & John, R. S. (2019). Media disaster reporting effects on public risk perception and response to escalating tornado warnings: A natural experiment. *Risk Analysis: An Official Publication of the Society for Risk Analysis, 39*(3), 535–552. https://doi.org/10.1111/risa.13205

Zou, X., & Lv, J. (2025). Analyzing the spatial-temporal dynamics of disaster risk based on social media data: A case study of Weibo during the Typhoon Yagi period. *Frontiers in Public Health, 13*, 1528199. https://doi.org/10.3389/fpubh.2025.1528199

Chapter 17
Mental Health and Disaster Management in South Asia

B. Sai Chaitanya Reddy, Dinakaran Damodharan, and Suresh Bada Math

1 Introduction

A disaster is defined as a serious disruption in the functioning of a society that causes human, material, economic, or environmental losses exceeding the affected community's ability to cope using its own resources (United Nations, 2004). Disasters are unpredictable and disrupt the social structure and functioning of society (Quarantelli, 1988). Classifying disasters solely as natural or human-induced is superficial and incomplete, as they often result from a combination of natural and social factors.

South Asia, home to over 2 billion people, remains one of the most disaster-prone regions in the world. According to the Centre for Research on Epidemiology of Disasters (2020), Asia experienced the highest number of disasters, with 3068 of the 7348 global disasters reported between 2000 and 2019. Some of the most devastating disasters in the region include the Indian Ocean Tsunami (2004), the Japan Tsunami and Earthquake (2011), the Pakistan Earthquake (2005), Cyclone Nargis in Myanmar (2008), and the Nepal Earthquake (2015)—each of which killed thousands (United Nations ESCAP, 2014). Bangladesh and north-eastern India face annual monsoon floods (e.g., 2017, 2019, 2020, 2021, 2022), which displace and kill millions of people. Flooding is the most frequent natural disaster in the region, occurring at least once a year in all South Asian countries (Rahman et al., 2025a; Shah et al., 2020).

B. S. C. Reddy · S. B. Math (✉)
Department of Psychiatry, National Institute of Mental Health and Neurosciences (NIMHANS), Bengaluru, Karnataka, India

D. Damodharan
Department of Psychosocial Support in Disaster Management (DPSSDM), National Institute of Mental Health and Neurosciences (NIMHANS), Bengaluru, India

N. Kar et al. (eds.), *Climate Change, Disaster and Mental Health in South Asia*, South Asian Perspectives in Mental Health and Psychology,
https://doi.org/10.1007/978-981-95-3690-0_17

The region's vulnerability to natural disasters stems from its geography. South Asia lies along the Eurasian and Indian tectonic plates, includes the Himalayas, and has melting glaciers and vast coastlines (South Asia, 2024). According to the India Meteorological Society, the frequency of floods has tripled since 2012 (Roxy et al., 2017). Moreover, South Asia contributes only about 8% of global CO_2 emissions, yet the region faces a disproportionately high impact from climate change due to emissions from more industrialized northern countries (UNICEF, 2022).

Human-induced disasters primarily result from environmental degradation, overpopulation, unplanned urbanization, and rapid industrialization. Incidents such as industrial accidents, armed conflict, terrorism, communal violence, and forced displacement have occurred frequently in the South Asian countries, and these have a profound, long-lasting impact on mental health. The Prevalence of Mental Health Issues is 2–3 times higher in the disaster-affected populations compared to the general population (Math et al., 2015). Beyond physical destruction and economic loss, disasters inflict profound psychological trauma, including post-traumatic stress disorder (PTSD), depression, anxiety, and suicidal ideation. Although several studies have reported these conditions, there is no comprehensive system to measure the psychological suffering of disaster survivors. Despite this, mental health (MH) continues to remain underrecognized in disaster response efforts (Heanoy & Brown, 2024; Makwana, 2019).

South Asia, which predominantly comprises low- to middle-income countries, faces unique challenges such as high population density, limited resources, inadequate infrastructure, low awareness of disaster-related mental health effects, and widespread stigma and neglect surrounding the mental health issues (Mudunna et al., 2025; Sagar et al., 2025). The region also suffers from a severe shortage of trained mental health professionals (psychiatrists, psychologists, psychiatric social workers, and psychiatric nurses) per 100,000 population when compared to European and Western countries, further exacerbating the mental health burden (World Health Organization, 2021). In this chapter, we examine the psychological impact of disasters in South Asia, evaluating the existing responses and outlining policy strategies based on the region's socioeconomic conditions and available human resources.

2 Mental Health and Disasters

A meta-analysis of 155 studies from Southeast Asian countries conducted between 1990 and 2023 reported the high burden of mental disorders (Majumder et al., 2023). The community's psychological responses after a disaster depend on a range of factors. These can be grouped into individual factors (such as coping skills, mental preparedness, and resilience), socio-cultural factors (like family support and community resources), and the severity of the disaster (including the death toll, property loss, and length of exposure).

After a disaster, survivors typically experience different emotional phases, including (a) the initial response phase (heroic phase): in the initial first few days or weeks, survivors in the community often show great courage and kindness toward their fellows. They may help rescue others, share food, offer shelter, and support each other emotionally. This phase may last from a day to several weeks, depending upon how severe the disaster is and how quickly help arrives. (b) The relief and hope phase: during this phase, relief agencies, the government, and NGOs begin providing aid through relief camps. Media attention peaks and survivors receive free medical aid, food, and shelter. VIPs' visits to the camps, administrations, and politicians express sympathy, often offering a lot of reassurances about rehabilitation. These events create an immense sense of relief and hope among survivors, who believe that their community will soon be restored and their losses compensated through monetary benefits. For this reason, this period is often referred to as the honeymoon phase, typically lasting 2–4 weeks.

As this period ends, relief materials and resources start to be distributed. VIP and politicians visit stops, media attention fades, and the involvement of administration, relief agencies, and NGOs begins to decline. Survivors then confront the harsh realities of post-disaster life. The complex process of rebuilding and rehabilitating starts to feel like a distant dream, obstructed by administrative hurdles, bureaucratic red tape, discrimination, injustice, and corruption. This sobering stage, known as the disillusionment phase, creates fertile ground for the emergence of mental health issues. This phase can last from 3 to 36 months before the community begins to return to a state of harmony. The role of mental health professionals becomes crucial during this period (Young et al., 1998; Math et al., 2015). Numerous studies have consistently reported high rates of depression, anxiety, PTSD symptoms, persistent fear, fear of recurrence, avoidance behavior, stress, social isolation, insomnia, somatic symptoms, suicidal thoughts and ideations, and substance misuse following both man-made and natural disasters.

3 Determinants and Risk Factors

The risk of developing mental health conditions like PTSD, depression, and anxiety after disasters is influenced by several factors. One of the strongest predictors is the intensity and severity of the disaster. Individuals who witness or experience extreme violence, explosions, or destruction are more likely to suffer from psychological trauma. The sudden or violent loss of loved ones can deeply affect mental well-being, often leading to prolonged grief or depressive symptoms. Physical injuries and forced displacement also increase the likelihood of mental distress, as they involve both physical and emotional suffering (Makwana, 2019). Marginalized groups, including ethnic and religious minorities, often face additional vulnerabilities due to systemic discrimination and exclusion from aid and healthcare services (Rahman et al., 2025c).

Social and economic factors further compound these risks. People with low income, poor education, or unstable jobs are particularly vulnerable. After a disaster, financial instability and inability to access essential services cause stress, anxiety, and a sense of hopelessness. Families struggling to meet basic needs often face immense psychological pressure, and children from these backgrounds are especially at risk of developing long-term mental health problems (Kirkbride et al., 2024). In summary, both the direct impact of the disaster and underlying socioeconomic disadvantages significantly shape mental health outcomes. Therefore, targeted support for groups is essential in designing effective disaster response and recovery plans.

4 Vulnerable Groups

Certain segments of society are disproportionately affected during and after a disaster due to their social, economic, and cultural vulnerabilities. Although all the population groups experience MH challenges after disasters, children appear to be especially vulnerable. Disaster memories tend to leave a lasting impact on children and may lead to long-term consequences. The American Psychological Association has stated that children are more susceptible to the psychological effects of disasters compared to adults. Children are often the first to suffer during disasters, facing heightened risks of sexual violence, exploitation, and displacement (Walinski et al., 2023). Refugees and internally displaced persons (IDPs) significantly increase their vulnerability to depression, PTSD, and chronic anxiety (Sukiasyan, 2024). Children who witness or endure violence may develop long-term emotional disturbances and behavioral problems (Coley, 2020). Adolescents may also struggle with feelings of uncertainty about their future, which can exacerbate anxiety and hopelessness. Risk factors such as female gender, low levels of education, poverty, physical injuries, and the loss of family members further increase vulnerability (Kar & Bastia, 2006). Peer support, group activities, daily routines, validation of their emotions, and mental health interventions tailored to this age group are essential for building resilience (Math et al., 2008a). Studies report PTSD and depression affecting around 30–50% of adults in these regions (Amin & Khan, 2009; Housen et al., 2019). Displaced survivors consistently exhibit higher levels of physical and psychological morbidity compared to non-displaced survivors in post-disaster contexts. Displacement not only disrupts access to shelter, health services, and social support networks but also amplifies exposure to secondary stressors such as overcrowding, uncertainty about the future, and economic hardship. A particularly distressing consequence is the loss of identity tied to one's area of residence, which often serves as a core component of individual and collective identity. Being uprooted from familiar geographies, cultural landmarks, and community ties erodes one's sense of belonging and continuity, leading to feelings of alienation, grief, and existential distress (Math et al., 2008b).

Elderly survivors are disproportionately affected in the aftermath of disasters, facing both heightened physical and psychological challenges. Age-related vulnerabilities, the presence of multiple comorbidities, disruption in continuity of care, and non-availability of essential medications for chronic illnesses significantly compromise their health outcomes. In addition, many elderly individuals experience survivor's guilt, especially when they outlive family members or community peers, further intensifying their psychological distress (Viswanath et al., 2012). Studies have consistently reported that women are more vulnerable than men during disasters. Reports from the 1991 and 2007 Bangladesh cyclones show that 80–90% of the fatalities were female. In the South Asian region, for every male death, four women die during disasters. The rates of injuries, mental health conditions, and disabilities are also significantly higher among women. Additionally, they face an increased risk of abuse and exploitation in the aftermath of disasters. The most commonly reported mental health conditions include depression, anxiety, and PTSD. The high fatality rates among women are attributed to several factors (Chowdhury et al., 2022; Fatema et al., 2021; Shamsuddoha et al., 2024). Social expectations require them to stay behind to take care of the household, often at the cost of their own lives. Moreover, cultural gender inequalities exclude them from the awareness training and disaster warnings, leaving them unprepared and more exposed.

Individuals with pre-existing mental illnesses may experience a worsening of symptoms due to stress, non-availability of psychotropics, stigma, and the loss of support systems (Math et al., 2008). Frontline workers, including healthcare personnel, soldiers, and relief workers, are exposed to repeated trauma, leading to moral injury, compassion fatigue, and burnout. Additionally, LGBTQ+ individuals and ethnic or religious minorities often face compounded discrimination during crises. This leads to increased social isolation and barriers in accessing psychological support (Moagi et al., 2021). These vulnerabilities are often intensified by poverty, displacement, gender inequality, and lack of education. Addressing the mental health needs of these groups requires trauma-informed, culturally sensitive, and accessible interventions that are fully integrated into broader disaster response and recovery frameworks.

5 Healthcare Access, Capacity, and Legal Frameworks

Mental health infrastructure remains weak across much of South Asia. In South Asia countries, primary care physicians are frequently undertrained in mental health care. According to the WHO, nearly 260 million people in the Southeast Asia region live with MH conditions, yet the treatment gap remains wide due to limited community mental health services and inadequate integration of mental health into primary care (World Health Organization, 2023). The specialist psychiatrist or mental health professional is usually limited to cities, and as per the World Health Organisation (WHO) 2021, World Mental Health Atlas 2020, the Southeast Asia region has 0.4 psychiatrists, 0.9 mental health nurses, 0.3 psychologists, and 0.1

social workers per every 100,000 population, which is far less than average global standards. As per the WHO, in 2025, Pakistan has only 0.19 psychiatrists per 100,000 population, worse than Southeast Asian countries. Considering the heavy population and given Mental health professionals (MHP) stats, the mental health gap is more than 80% for any mental health morbidity in South Asian countries. Integrating disaster mental health into primary and community healthcare systems is critical. Reducing stigma, building local capacity, and ensuring mental health interventions that are culturally appropriate will greatly improve outcomes.

Training primary care physicians in disaster mental health is urgently needed in South Asian countries. Better community preparedness and ongoing training programs are required as this area encounters floods almost every year. Identifying the local members forming teams, training them not only during the emergency states but also in the aftermath to deliver the psychosocial interventions will truly enrich the community capacity and can handle coordination gaps to a certain extent; reliance on local NGOs, training the NGOs enhances the preparedness for the disasters (Makwana, 2019). Moreover, ensuring the availability of appropriate social support and free access to healthcare, particularly for women, is essential in disaster-affected areas. All the South Asian countries notified the Disaster Management Act and designed their road maps to prevent and mitigate the effects of disasters (Kafle, 2017). Tailored, accessible, and inclusive mental health services must become a core component of all disaster preparedness and response frameworks.

6 Responses and Interventions

In South Asia, post-disaster responses often prioritize socioeconomic recovery, while psychosocial interventions tend to take a back seat. One of the most important things to remember is that medicalization or diagnosis with mental illness can follow a disaster. Disasters are extraordinary events, and people exposed may have more than normal or excessive emotional reactions, and they shall be given time to settle. Studies have shown that psychological first aid will reduce psychiatric morbidity. Psychological first aid can be delivered by community workers, and a psychiatrist or a qualified mental health professional can give short-term training to a large number of community workers in disaster-prone areas to deliver these services. Normalization of the routines (rebuilding the places, cooking and feeding the community, and informal schools) has been shown to facilitate early healing. A recent systematic review and meta-analysis of 27 studies has shown that psychotherapeutic interventions are effective for post-earthquake survivors and have been found to improve mental health. The location of research, type of disaster, and psychotherapeutic intervention all play a role in the effectiveness of psychotherapeutic interventions (Semerci & Uzun, 2023). All South Asian countries, for addressing mental health issues, formulated National Guidelines on Psychosocial Support and Mental Health Services, released in 2009, which focus on the psychosocial support and mental health services with emphasis on prevention, mitigation, preparedness, response, relief, and rehabilitation (Kafle, 2017).

In the aftermath of man-made disasters such as industrial or train accidents, timely training and the availability of responders play a crucial role in reducing physical injuries and mortality. Alongside immediate medical care, it is essential to screen survivors for mental health symptoms. This screening can be effectively carried out by disaster workers, volunteers, primary healthcare staff, and social workers who are already engaged in relief efforts. Individuals identified as having psychological distress should then receive primary and secondary levels of mental health support through psychiatric nurses, psychologists, occupational therapists, and psychiatrists. For the long-term rehabilitation of injured survivors, coordinated efforts by local governments, non-governmental organizations, and local health institutions are vital to ensure comprehensive recovery and reintegration (Kar, 2024; Swain et al., 2025).

However, there is a growing need to emphasize the importance of maintaining social relationships during and immediately after disasters, as well as preparing populations in disaster-prone areas for overall well-being during challenging times (Amatya & Khan, 2023). One effective approach is to implement awareness programs well in advance of a disaster in vulnerable regions. Planning and preparing strategies aimed at fostering resilience within communities can significantly reduce the psychological impact of disasters. Resilience can also be enhanced through individual traits, such as positive psychological adjustment, and through the community's collective ability to adapt to post-disaster challenges (Chandra et al., 2011; Ma et al., 2023).

7 Integration and Cooperation Among the South Asian Countries

Most countries in South Asia are still in the developing phase and tend to focus more on economic growth and sustainable livelihoods than on environmental protection.

(a) In 2015, a regional initiative, the **South Asian Annual Disaster Management Exercise (SAADMEx)**, focusing on enhanced disaster preparedness and response capabilities among the South Asian Association for Regional Cooperation (SAARC), was started, and the first meeting was held in Delhi. Delegates from India, Pakistan, Bangladesh, Sri Lanka, Nepal, Afghanistan, Bhutan, and the Maldives participated in the program. The main areas focused on include initial response, communication, coordination mechanisms, integration of exercises, public information and media coordination, and consular assistance. The first SAADMEx included a field training exercise simulating a chemical leakage due to an earthquake, including evacuation of affected people and analysis of capabilities.

(b) **SAARC Disaster Management Centre:** The organization aims to support disaster management and risk reduction in the SAARC region by formulating effective policies, strategies, and sustainable development frameworks. It promotes research to better understand meteorological phenomena, enhancing the early warning capabilities of National Meteorological Services, especially in India. The organization collects, documents, and shares data, case studies, indigenous knowledge, and good practices related to disaster risk reduction and sustainable development. It compiles vital regional weather information for forecasting and monitoring special weather events. Efforts are also made to strengthen regional response mechanisms to reduce casualties and ensure timely humanitarian aid during disasters. Furthermore, the organization fosters coordination among various stakeholders, including governments, international agencies, NGOs, and funding bodies, by facilitating interaction, knowledge exchange, and technology transfer. Regular training workshops, seminars, and conferences are organized to build capacity and share expertise on disaster management across Member States.

(c) **SAARC Agreement on Rapid Response to Natural Disasters (SARRND):** The main objective of this agreement is to provide effective regional mechanisms for rapid response to disasters to achieve a substantial reduction of disaster losses in lives and in social, environmental, and economic assets of the parties. Joint responses to disaster emergencies through concerted national efforts and intensified regional cooperation.

(d) **India Disaster Knowledge Network (IDKN)**: Governments should adopt the latest innovations and technologies, such as special satellites for disaster-related data, artificial intelligence, and geo-spatial systems. These tools can help monitor fast-changing situations and quickly share vital information with people living in disaster-prone areas. Disaster management and climate change issues shall be integrated into national programs, starting at the grassroots level. Each country should also appoint a dedicated apex body to track progress and ensure accountability. Strong regional cooperation is essential for South Asian countries to effectively respond to and reduce the impact of disasters that often cross national boundaries (Aviation & Defence Universe, 2015; SAARC Secretariat, 2011). Mental health must be positioned as a central pillar in disaster preparedness, climate change adaptation, and urban planning. This necessitates the training of first responders in psychological first aid, the integration of mental health services into primary care frameworks, and the scaling up of digital mental health infrastructure, such as Tele-MANAS in India. Furthermore, the implementation of telepsychiatry services offers a cost-effective and scalable solution to ensure continuity of care, especially in underserved and disaster-affected regions. These interventions are essential for mitigating the psychosocial consequences of climate change and disasters.

8 Conclusion

Mental health consequences of disasters in South Asia are profound and long-lasting. High prevalence of PTSD, depression, and anxiety, alongside socioeconomic and gendered vulnerabilities, highlights the need to prioritize mental health in disaster response. Existing responses, like community psychosocial support, have weaknesses in funding, coordination, training, and persistent stigma. To protect lives and livelihoods fully, governments must embed mental health into emergency preparedness, train Primary Care Physcians (PCPs), build community capacity, destigmatize mental illness, and ensure data-driven policies.

With these actions, South Asia can transform disaster resilience into holistic, inclusive health resilience. Quantitative evidence for the association between extreme weather events and mental health was limited primarily due to the absence of longitudinal data, exposure gradient, and comparison with an unaffected group and objective exposure measures. Variability in the tools used to express the common MH disorders may have influenced the results of this study. Another factor was the diverse time frames in which various studies have documented the prevalence of MH parameters following exposure to a traumatic event, thereby exhibiting a high degree of heterogeneity.

8.1 Recommendations: Mental Health Recommendations for Disaster Management in South Asia

1. Community Preparedness and Involvement
   - Strengthen community participation, as disaster frequency is increasing.
   - Conduct household surveys in affected areas to assess mental health needs after disasters.
   - Run periodic awareness programs on disaster-related mental health issues.
2. Relief and Immediate Response
   - Improve relief measures with the inclusion of mobile health units.
   - Enhance the training and preparedness of rescue teams and security forces.
   - Ensure proper referral systems for mental health care.
3. Availability of Mental Health Professionals
   - Ensure the availability of mental health professionals in disaster-affected regions.
   - Provide 2–3 years of long-term follow-up for survivors.

4. Capacity Building and Training
   - Train school teachers, college staff, and non-psychiatric doctors in disaster-related mental health care.
   - Conduct gatekeeper training in industries to enable early identification and referral.
   - Mobilize trained personnel quickly, especially in regions with limited mental health manpower.
5. Universal and Preventive Measures
   - Raise awareness among school and college students about the link between climate change, disasters, and mental health.
   - Promote efforts to reduce environmental causes contributing to natural disasters.

References

Amatya, B., & Khan, F. (2023). Disaster response and management: The integral role of rehabilitation. *Annals of Rehabilitation Medicine, 47*(4), 237–260. https://doi.org/10.5535/arm.23071

Amin, S., & Khan, A. W. (2009). Life in conflict: Characteristics of depression in Kashmir. *International Journal of Health Sciences, 3*(2), 213–223. https://pmc.ncbi.nlm.nih.gov/articles/PMC3068807/

Aviation & Defence Universe. (2015, November 24). *India hosts the first South Asian Annual Disaster Management Exercise*. https://www.aviation-defence-universe.com/india-hosts-the-first-south-asian-annual-disaster-management-exercise/

Centre for Research on the Epidemiology of Disasters. (2020). *Human cost of disasters: An overview of the last 20 years (2000–2019)*. United Nations Office for Disaster Risk Reduction (UNDRR). https://www.undrr.org/publication/human-cost-disasters-overview-last-20-years-2000-2019

Chandra, A., Acosta, J., Howard, S., Uscher-Pines, L., Williams, M., Yeung, D., Garnett, J., & Meredith, L. S. (2011). Building community resilience to disasters: A way forward to enhance national health security. *Rand Health Quarterly, 1*(1), 6.

Chowdhury, T. J., Arbon, P., Gebbie, K., Muller, R., Kako, M., & Steenkamp, M. (2022). Lived-experience of women's well-being in the cyclone shelters of coastal Bangladesh. *Prehospital and Disaster Medicine, 37*(4), 437–443. https://doi.org/10.1017/S1049023X2200070X

Coley, R. L. (2020). *Understanding the impacts of natural disasters on children*. Society for Research in Child Development. Available from Lindsay Turner Trammell, Director for Policy, Society for Research in Child Development https://www.srcd.org/research/understanding-impacts-natural-disasters-children

Fatema, S. R., East, L., Islam, M. S., & Usher, K. (2021). Health impact and risk factors affecting South and Southeast Asian women following natural disasters: A systematic review. *International Journal of Environmental Research and Public Health, 18*(21), 11068. https://doi.org/10.3390/ijerph182111068

Heanoy, E. Z., & Brown, N. R. (2024). Impact of natural disasters on mental health: Evidence and implications. *Healthcare (Basel), 12*(18), 1812. https://doi.org/10.3390/healthcare12181812

Housen, T., Lenglet, A., Shah, S., Henckaerts, L., Shah, H., Pintaldi, G., & Ventevogel, P. (2019). Trauma in the Kashmir Valley and the mediating effect of stressors of daily life on symptoms of posttraumatic stress disorder, depression and anxiety. *Conflict and Health, 13*, 58. https://doi.org/10.1186/s13031-019-0245-6

Kafle, S. K. (2017). Disaster risk management systems in South Asia: Natural hazards, vulnerability, disaster risk and legislative and institutional frameworks. *Journal of Geography and Natural Disasters, 7*, 207. https://doi.org/10.4172/2167-0587.1000207

Kar, N., & Bastia, B. K. (2006). Post-traumatic stress disorder, depression and generalised anxiety disorder in adolescents after a natural disaster: a study of comorbidity. *Clinical Practice and Epidemiology in Mental Health: CP & EMH, 2*, 17. https://doi.org/10.1186/1745-0179-2-17

Kar, N., Jagadisha, Sharma, P., Murali, N., & Mehrotra, S. (2004). Mental health consequences of the trauma of super-cyclone 1999 in Orissa. *Indian Journal of Psychiatry, 46*(3), 228–237. https://pubmed.ncbi.nlm.nih.gov/21224904/

Kirkbride, J. B., Anglin, D. M., Colman, I., Dykxhoorn, J., Jones, P. B., Patalay, P., Pitman, A., Soneson, E., Steare, T., Wright, T., & Griffiths, S. L. (2024). The social determinants of mental health and disorder: Evidence, prevention and recommendations. *World Psychiatry: Official Journal of the World Psychiatric Association (WPA), 23*(1), 58–90. https://doi.org/10.1002/wps.21160

Ma, C., Qirui, C., & Lv, Y. (2023). "One community at a time": Promoting community resilience in the face of natural hazards and public health challenges. *BMC Public Health, 23*, 2510. https://doi.org/10.1186/s12889-023-17458-x

Majumder, J., Saha, I., Saha, A., & Chakrabarti, A. (2023). Climate change, disasters, and mental health of adolescents in India. *Indian Journal of Psychological Medicine, 45*(3), 289–291. https://doi.org/10.1177/02537176231164649

Makwana, N. (2019). Disaster and its impact on mental health: A narrative review. *Journal of Family Medicine and Primary Care, 8*(10), 3090–3095. https://doi.org/10.4103/jfmpc.jfmpc_893_19

Math, S. B., John, J. P., Girimaji, S. C., Benegal, V., et al. (2008a). Comparative study of psychiatric morbidity among the displaced and non-displaced populations in the Andaman and Nicobar Islands following the tsunami. *Prehospital and Disaster Medicine, 23*(1), 29–34. https://doi.org/10.1017/s1049023x00005513

Math, S. B., Tandon, S., Girimaji, S. C., et al. (2008b). Psychological impact of the tsunami on children and adolescents from the Andaman and Nicobar Islands. *Primary Care Companion to the Journal of Clinical Psychiatry, 10*(1), 31. https://doi.org/10.4088/pcc.v10n0106

Math, S. B., Nirmala, M. C., Moirangthem, S., Kumar, N. C., et al. (2015). Disaster management: Mental health perspective. *Indian Journal of Psychological Medicine, 37*(3), 261–271. https://doi.org/10.4103/0253-7176.162915

Moagi, M. M., van Der Wath, A. E., Jiyane, P. M., & Rikhotso, R. S. (2021). Mental health challenges of lesbian, gay, bisexual and transgender people: An integrated literature review. *Health SA, 26*, 1487. https://doi.org/10.4102/hsag.v26i0.1487

Mudunna, C., Weerasinghe, M., Tran, T., Antoniades, J., Romero, L., Chandradasa, M., & Fisher, J. (2025). Nature, prevalence and determinants of mental health problems experienced by adolescents in south Asia: A systematic review. *The Lancet regional health. Southeast Asia, 33*, 100532. https://doi.org/10.1016/j.lansea.2025.100532

Quarantelli, E. L. (1988). Disaster crisis management: A summary of research findings. *Journal of Management Studies, 25*(4), 373–385. https://doi.org/10.1111/j.1467-6486.1988.tb00043.x

Rahman, M. M., Chaity, N. J., Hossain, T., & Alam, E. (2025a). Exploring factors affecting disaster risk perception in ethnic minority: A case study in Garo community, Bangladesh. *Progress in Disaster Science*. https://doi.org/10.1016/j.pdisas.2025.100424

Rahman, M. C., Sarkar, M., Kabir, M. J., & Kabir, M. H. (2025b). Vulnerability and adaptation in flood-prone ecosystems of Bangladesh: A case study of rice farming households. *Discover Sustainability, 6*(55). https://doi.org/10.1007/s43621-025-00848-z

Rahman, M. M., Shobuj, I. A., Hossain, M. T., Alam, E., Islam, M. K., & Hossain, M. K. (2025c). Flood impact on men's mental health: Evidence from flood-prone areas of Bangladesh. *Frontiers in Public Health, 13*, 1529558. https://doi.org/10.3389/fpubh.2025.1529558

Roxy, M. K., Ghosh, S., Pathak, A., Athulya, R., Mujumdar, M., Murtugudde, R., Terray, P., & Rajeevan, M. (2017). A threefold rise in widespread extreme rain events over central India. *Nature Communications, 8*, 708. https://doi.org/10.1038/s41467-017-00744-9

SAARC Secretariat. (2011). *SAARC agreement on rapid response to natural disasters (SARRND)*. https://saarc-sdmc.org/sarrnd

Sagar, R., Chatterjee, K., Thareja, S., Timothy, A., Yadav, A. S., Yadav, P., et al. (2025). NAMS task force report on mental stress. *Annals of the National Academy of Medical Sciences (India), 61*, 66–97. https://nams-annals.in/nams-task-force-report-on-mental-stress/

Semerci, M., & Uzun, S. (2023). The effectiveness of post-disaster psychotherapeutic interventions: A systematic review and meta-analysis study. *Asian Journal of Psychiatry, 85*, 103615. https://doi.org/10.1016/j.ajp.2023.103615

Shah, S. M. H., Mustaffa, Z., Teo, F. Y., Imam, M. A. H., Wan Yusof, K., & Al-Qadami, E. H. H. (2020). A review of the flood hazard and risk management in the south Asian region, particularly Pakistan. *Scientific African, 10*, e00651. https://doi.org/10.1016/j.sciaf.2020.e00651

Shamsuddoha, M., Jabed, M. A., Islam, M. S., Sultana, N., Imran, A., Rabbi, S. N. A., Jenat, T. U., Shams, S., & Sharif, M. M. (2024). Impacts of climate change-induced natural hazards on women and their human rights implications: A study in the southwest coast of Bangladesh. *Journal of Migration and Health, 9*, 100221. https://doi.org/10.1016/j.jmh.2024.100221

South Asia. (2024, June). *Wikipedia*. Retrieved July 2025, https://en.wikipedia.org/wiki/South_Asia

Sukiasyan, S. (2024). The mental health of refugees and forcibly displaced people: A narrative review. *Consortium Psychiatricum, 5*(4), 78–92. https://doi.org/10.17816/CP15552

Swain, S. P., Behura, S. S., Banerjee, S., Mahakul, S., & Kar, N. (2025). A qualitative mixed-method narrative study on psychotherapeutic support needs based on a series of 11 cases of survivors of the 2023 Odisha train accident. *Cureus, 17*(3), e81161. https://doi.org/10.7759/cureus.81161

UNICEF. (2022). *For every child, a liveable planet: Climate, environment, energy and disaster risk reduction advocacy brief.* UNICEF https://www.unicef.org/rosa/climate-change-and-environment

United Nations. (2004). *Living with risk: A global review of disaster reduction initiatives*. United Nations Publications. https://www.unisdr.org/files/7817_7819isdrterminology11.pdf

United Nations Economic and Social Commission for Asia and the Pacific. (2014). *Asia-Pacific disaster report 2014: Reducing vulnerability and exposure to disasters*. United Nations. https://news.un.org/en/story/2014/12/486682

Viswanath, B., Maroky, A. S., Math, S. B., et al. (2012). Psychological impact of the tsunami on elderly survivors. *The American Journal of Geriatric Psychiatry, 20*(5), 402–407. https://doi.org/10.1097/JGP.0b013e318246b7e9

Walinski, A., Sander, J., Gerlinger, G., Clemens, V., Meyer-Lindenberg, A., & Heinz, A. (2023). The effects of climate change on mental health. *Deutsches Arzteblatt International, 120*(8), 117–124. https://doi.org/10.3238/arztebl.m2022.0403

World Health Organization. (2021). *Mental health atlas 2020.* World Health Organization. https://iris.who.int/handle/10665/345946

World Health Organization. (2023, June 22). *Focus on expanding mental health services in the WHO South-East Asia Region*. https://www.who.int/southeastasia/news/detail/22-06-2023-focus-on-expanding-mental-health-services-in-the-who-south-east-asia-region

Young, B. H., Ford, J. D., Ruzek, J. I., Friedman, M., & Gusman, F. D. (1998). *Disaster mental health services: A guide for clinicians and administrators.* National Center for Post-Traumatic Stress Disorder. https://catalog.hathitrust.org/Record/005042397

Chapter 18
Psychological Interventions for Disaster and Trauma Survivors in South Asia: Bridging the Gap Between Need and Access

Saima Khan, Rizwana Amin, and Muhammad Alia Asadullah

1 Introduction

Disasters, sudden or gradual, leave behind more than just physical devastation; they disrupt the psychological state of individuals and communities (Heanoy & Brown, 2024). In many cases, the unseen mental health toll of these crises can persist long after visible wounds have healed. In regions with high population densities, socio-economic disparities, and a fragile health system, the psychosocial consequences of disaster exposure can be even more pronounced (Ramachandran et al., 2025). South Asia, a region shaped by its resilience and vulnerability, represents one landscape where the need for effective psychological intervention has never been more urgent.

South Asia, home to a quarter of the world's population, is one of the most disaster-prone regions globally. The region routinely experiences a range of natural disasters like cyclones, floods, earthquakes, landslides, as well as man-made crises, including political conflict, displacement, communal violence, and terrorism (Islam, 2023). The geographical position, rapid urbanization, environmental degradation, and socio-political complexities of South Asia increase the frequency and intensity of these events. Compounding the problem, large segments of the population live in poverty and lack access to basic services, rendering them especially vulnerable to the immediate and long-term impacts of disasters (Kafle, 2017).

S. Khan
Zayed University, Abu Dhabi Campus, United Arab Emirates

R. Amin (✉)
College of Humanities, Effat University, Jeddah, Saudi Arabia
e-mail: riamin@effatuniversity.edu.sa

M. A. Asadullah
College of Business Administration, University of Khorfakkan, Sharjah, United Arab Emirates

N. Kar et al. (eds.), *Climate Change, Disaster and Mental Health in South Asia*, South Asian Perspectives in Mental Health and Psychology,
https://doi.org/10.1007/978-981-95-3690-0_18

While efforts in disaster response typically prioritize physical survival and infrastructure rehabilitation, the emotional and psychological dimensions of recovery are often under-addressed. Exposure to disaster frequently results in psychological distress, trauma, loss of meaning, and disruption of social cohesion. Mental health is not a peripheral concern; it is central to long-term recovery, resilience-building, and the restoration of community function (Math et al., 2015). When left untreated, mental health issues such as depression, anxiety, post-traumatic stress disorder (PTSD), and prolonged grief can hinder both personal healing and societal rebuilding. Therefore, recognizing and addressing psychological well-being as a core component of disaster response is essential for sustainable recovery (Lowe et al., 2016).

Across countries like India, Nepal, Bangladesh, and Pakistan, psychological interventions have been delivered in the aftermath of major disasters ranging from the 2004 Indian Ocean tsunami to the 2015 Nepal earthquake, with varied levels of success. For instance, structured group therapies such as Problem Management Plus (PM+) in Nepal have shown promising outcomes in reducing anxiety and depression symptoms (Jordans et al., 2021), while teacher-led psychosocial support programs significantly improved mental health and hope among adolescents in earthquake-affected districts (Dhital et al., 2019). In India, community-based psychosocial support offered to tsunami-affected women facilitated emotional recovery through culturally grounded strategies (Becker, 2009). Despite these efforts, challenges persist. Financial constraints, stigma, shortage of trained professionals, weak mental health infrastructure, and the lack of culturally tailored therapies hamper the delivery and sustainability of psychological care (Rowe & Nadkarni, 2023;). Furthermore, interventions are often time-bound and externally funded, with little integration into existing health systems (Nahar et al., 2014). As disasters intensify due to climate change and political instability, South Asia urgently needs contextually adapted, community-based, and scalable psychological interventions embedded within primary care systems.

This chapter aims to bridge the gap between the significant psychological needs of disaster survivors in South Asia and the limited access to effective mental health care. It critically examines current intervention models, identifies key barriers such as financial constraints, workforce shortages, cultural mismatch, and systematic neglect, and highlights notable gaps in service provision. The chapter also explores promising practices that can be scaled in low-resource settings, emphasizing culturally grounded, community-based, and contextually adapted approaches. By offering evidence-based strategies and future directions, this work aims to support more inclusive and resilient mental health systems across the region, ensuring that psychological support is not a privilege afforded to a few but a right accessible to all and that no survivor is left without the care and dignity they deserve.

2 The Burden of Disasters in South Asia

Throughout South Asia's history, natural and man-made disasters have caused significant destruction and long-lasting damage. An analysis of the region's major disasters highlights how common and severe they are (Table 18.1, Kafle, 2017). India, Sri Lanka, and the Maldives were severely devastated by the 2004 Indian Ocean tsunami that hit off the coast of Sumatra. Hundreds of thousands of people died, and millions were displaced in the area as a result of the tsunami (Jang et al., 2021). A year after 2004, the Kashmir earthquake in northern India and Pakistan killed more than 80,000 people and left 3.5 million homeless. The disaster revealed the shortcomings in our emergency response procedures and infrastructure (Shah et al., 2022). In 2010, two provinces of Pakistan were completely submerged, obliterating everything that could be seen and leaving 20 million people without a place to live. A shortage of resources regarding social assistance and healthcare resulted from the substantial loss of livelihood caused by catastrophes in rural areas (Manzoor et al., 2022). The COVID-19 pandemic, which emerged as a worldwide health emergency in 2020, particularly affected South Asian countries, characterized by their dense populations. Because of the lockdowns, the healthcare system was overburdened (Babu et al., 2021), and the economy stagnated (Rasul et al., 2021). Resultantly, many people died, mental health conditions worsened (Hossain et al., 2020), and communities became socially fragmented.

Table 18.1 Major disasters in South Asia (2020–1943): lives lost and economic impact

Year	Disaster type	Country/region affected	Estimated lives lost	Estimated economic damage
2020	COVID-19 pandemic	Entire South Asia	1.5 million+*	Hundreds of billions USD*
2015	Nepal earthquake	Nepal	~9000	~$7 billion
2010	Pakistan floods	Pakistan (Sindh, Punjab, Khyber)	~1985	~$10 billion
2007	Cyclone Sidr	Bangladesh	~3447	~$2.3 billion
2005	Kashmir earthquake	Pakistan, India (Jammu & Kashmir)	~86,000	~$5.2 billion
2004	Indian Ocean tsunami	India, Sri Lanka, Maldives	~45,000 (in South Asia)	~$15 billion (regional share)
2001	Gujarat earthquake	India (Gujarat)	~20,000	~$5.5 billion
1998	Bangladesh floods	Bangladesh	~1100	~$2.8 billion
1993	Latur earthquake	India (Maharashtra)	~9748	~$260 million
1970	Bhola cyclone	East Pakistan (now Bangladesh)	~300,000–500,000	~$86 million (1970 USD)
1943	Bengal famine	India (Bengal)	~2.1 million	N/A

The emotional impact of such disasters is significant, yet mental health concerns are often overlooked after physical and structural damage is recognized. In South Asia, individuals who have survived disasters frequently experience persistent PTSD, anxiety, depression, substance use disorders, and difficulties in the grieving process (Suar et al., 2024). In the wake of the Kashmir earthquake and the 2010 flooding in Pakistan, it has been noted that PTSD and feelings of sadness affect many children and adolescents (Chung et al., 2014; Farooqui et al., 2017). Numerous survivors from Sri Lanka and India who endured the 2004 tsunami continue to confront trauma-related stress even years later (Kip et al., 2024). Among the mentioned categories, particularly, the COVID-19 pandemic has resulted in a notable increase in mental health issues, feelings of loneliness and fear, and suicides. The pandemic disrupts funeral ceremonies, leaving many families to handle unresolved feelings. It has been reported that some residents in disaster-impacted areas misuse alcohol and tranquilizers as a coping mechanism, which escalates the risk of family breakdown, child maltreatment, and domestic violence (Penninx et al., 2022).

In addition to psychological issues, disasters in South Asia significantly impact various aspects of social and personal life. Communities suffer from homelessness and displacement, and conflict over resources adds to their stress (Titz, 2021). Women and children are typically more vulnerable to human trafficking, exploitation (Dutta, 2021), and gender-based violence during and after catastrophes (Rezwana & Pain, 2021). Furthermore, individuals with mental health disorders often find it difficult to overcome their problems when they are ridiculed and receive inadequate, culturally incompetent psychological care. These societal implications create division within society, making many survivors feel isolated and unsupported.

Trauma causes psychological and social concerns often tied to the region's politics and ecology. High population density, poor urban design, poverty, unstable governance, and environmental deterioration make it vulnerable to repeated calamities (Kafle, 2017). Disasters are exacerbated by flood-prone settlements, forest degradation, inadequate infrastructure, and poor building code enforcement. Without corruption or political marginalization, aid to some groups may be disrupted. Political violence, natural disasters, and ongoing instability across the region contribute to widespread uncertainty, forced migration, and increased psychological stress. Disasters, droughts, rising sea levels, and extreme weather occurrences increased due to climate change, worsening poverty, and migration. Environmental and political forces slow rehabilitation and increase intergenerational trauma (Mitchell & Pizzi, 2021).

3 Current Literature for Psychological Support

3.1 Current Psychological Interventions

Across South Asia, psychological support in disaster settings has primarily been mobilized through non-governmental organizations (NGOs), international agencies, and national governments. Major disasters such as the 2004 Indian Ocean tsunami, the 2005 Pakistan earthquake, and the 2015 Nepal earthquake prompted the deployment of psychosocial support programs, including counseling, emotional first aid, and community-based interventions (ADPC, 2016). For instance, the Indian Red Cross Society and ActionAid implemented psychological counseling and emotional support through mobile health camps and trained local volunteers in Tamil Nadu and Andhra Pradesh (IRCS, 2025). In Nepal, following the 2015 earthquake, the government partnered with NGOs to deploy trained community psychosocial workers (CPSWs) who provided group sessions, stress management education, psychoeducation, and referrals (IASC, 2015). These efforts advanced mental health integration in disaster response, yet regional intervention structures and scopes warrant critical examination and evaluation.

3.2 Overview of Existing Psychosocial Support Programs

In response to major disasters, tsunamis, earthquakes, and forced displacement, South Asian countries have seen a range of psychosocial support initiatives led by NGOs, governments, and international agencies. Local and international NGOs have played a pivotal role in post-disaster mental health care. Following the 2004 tsunami, organizations like Sustainable Environment and Ecological Development Society (SEEDS) were established. India and ActionAid launched community-based programs using theater, storytelling, and women-led support groups to address trauma (Becker, 2009). Similarly, Basic Needs introduced a model in Pakistan combining psychiatric care with livelihood support following the 2005 earthquake (MHIN, 2025).

Governments have progressively expanded their involvement. In Nepal, the Ministry of Health, in partnership with TPO Nepal and WHO, deployed over 200 trained community psychosocial support workers (CPSWs) after the 2015 earthquake. These workers conducted home visits, facilitated group sessions, and provided referrals, effectively bridging access gaps and helping reduce distress (IASC, 2015).

International agencies have supported these initiatives by reinforcing national systems. WHO's Mental Health Gap Action Programme (mhGAP) has been implemented in Nepal and Bangladesh to train non-specialist health workers in the detection and management of depression and PTSD (Gómez-Carrillo et al., 2020). In Bangladesh's Cox's Bazar, UNICEF and Bangladesh Rural Advancement Committee (BRAC) collaborated to create women- and child-friendly spaces that offered structured therapy and emotional support for Rohingya refugees (Kubwalo, 2021).

However, despite the efforts, many of the programs have lacked long-term sustainability due to dependence on donor funding, limited integration into existing health infrastructure, and inadequate government follow-up. Services tend to be focused on urban centers or major camps, with rural and remote populations remaining underserved.

3.3 Use of Different Psychological Interventions

Following disasters and humanitarian crises in South Asia, a diverse range of psychological interventions have been deployed. While these approaches vary in theoretical foundations and delivery methods, they collectively aim to reduce psychological distress and support recovery.

Table 18.2 represents some therapies that are used in South Asia to mitigate the disaster impact.

Over the years, a wide range of psychological interventions have been used across South Asia in response to recurring natural disasters, with varying degrees of success and sustainability. Psychological first aid (PFA) has served as the most immediate and scalable method, used extensively after the 2004 Indian Ocean tsunami in Tamil Nadu and Sri Lanka, offering safety, emotional stabilization, and basic psychosocial support (Sim & Wang, 2021; Winders et al., 2021). Cognitive behavioral therapy (CBT), though more structured, was adapted in flood-affected regions of Pakistan and earthquake-hit Nepal using lay health workers and digital tools, showing measurable reductions in anxiety and depression when culturally tailored (Naeem et al., 2021; Khan, 2022). Group therapy approaches were widely accepted in collectivist societies such as Sri Lanka and the Andaman Islands,

Table 18.2 Evidence-based therapies for post-disaster mental health in South Asia

Evidence-based therapies	Description	Sustainability in South Asia
Psychological first aid (PFA) Sim and Wang (2021), Winders et al. (2021)	Immediate support on safety and stabilization	Highly feasible, adaptable to culture
Cognitive behavioral therapy (CBT) Naeem et al. (2021), Khan (2022), Contractor et al. (2023)	Structured therapy targeting thoughts and behaviors	Culturally tailored CBT is effective
Group therapy Husain et al. (2025)	Peer-based support and shared healing	Well, accepted in collectivistic settings
Narrative exposure therapy (NET) Priyadarshini and Sigroha (2025)	Trauma-focused storytelling approach	Promising for adults and adolescents
Mindfulness and yoga-based therapy Dossaji et al. (2025), Müller et al. (2024)	Stress regulation using traditional practices	High cultural fit and low cost
Expressive art therapy Ranasinha (2025), Hommel and Kaimal (2024)	Use of art, music, and drama for trauma processing	Effective for children and women
Telepsychiatry Kar (2024b), Batra and Erbas (2025), Swain et al. (2025)	Remote diagnosis and treatment via digital platforms	Growing potential with mHealth

providing shared spaces for grieving and support (Husain et al., 2025). In northern India and Nepal, narrative exposure therapy (NET) and expressive art therapies helped trauma survivors, especially women and children, to externalize distress through stories, drawing, and music (Priyadarshini & Sigroha, 2025). Mindfulness-based therapies and yoga, rooted in local traditions, were also applied in Indian and Nepalese disaster zones, showing promise in stress regulation and emotional resilience. Alongside these formal therapies, many communities continued to rely on indigenous healing practices, like spirit possession rituals in tribal Nepal or Ayurvedic treatments in post-tsunami Sri Lanka, which, while not evidence-based, offered cultural validation and spiritual relief. Though these traditional methods often lacked the tools to address trauma's psychological complexities, they resonated deeply within the local worldview and were perceived as effective by those who used them (Dossaji et al., 2025; Müller et al., 2024). Encouragingly, mental health responses in South Asia are slowly evolving, with increasing efforts to blend scientific interventions with culturally rooted practices, moving toward models that are both effective and respectful of local belief systems.

3.3.1 Psychological First Aid (PFA)

PFA is widely implemented in the immediate aftermath of disasters. Designed to stabilize emotions and promote safety, it is supported by the WHO and the International Federation of Red Cross and Red Crescent Societies (IFRC) as a foundational emergency intervention (Hermosilla et al., 2023). After the 2015 Nepal earthquake, community volunteers and psychosocial workers were trained using WHO's PFA guidelines to offer emotional support and facilitate referrals (IASC, 2015). Similarly, in India, post-tsunami, NGOs incorporated PFA into school-based and community-based responses. However, despite widespread uptake, empirical evidence of PFA's long-term efficacy remains limited.

3.3.2 Trauma-Focused Cognitive Behavioral Therapy (TF-CBT)

TF-CBT has been introduced to address trauma-related conditions such as PTSD, anxiety, and depression. It combines cognitive restructuring, exposure therapy, and skills training (de Arellano et al., 2014). Adapted versions, including WHO's Guided Self-Help Plus (GSH+), have been used among Rohingya refugees in Cox's Bazar, Bangladesh. This intervention delivered audio-based sessions via trained lay facilitators, leading to reported reductions in distress and improved functioning (Kubwalo, 2021). However, cultural and literacy barriers continue to affect the broader applicability of CBT in rural and low-resource settings, which often require contextual adaptation and simplification.

3.3.3 Modes of Psychotherapy Delivery in Post-Disaster Settings

In post-disaster contexts, the mode of delivering psychological support plays a critical role in accessibility and effectiveness, especially when infrastructure is compromised. Various formats, such as group sessions, telephonic counseling, online video consultations, and internet-based platforms, have been adapted to suit the needs of affected populations.

Group-based interventions, in particular, have proven beneficial for fostering collective coping and emotional resilience. These approaches allow for the expression of shared narratives, community-based problem-solving, and emotional processing within culturally familiar frameworks (Schwartze et al., 2019). In Sri Lanka, for example, following the civil war, internally displaced persons engaged in group sessions that integrated mindfulness practices and culturally relevant storytelling. Similarly, in tsunami-affected parts of India, community formats such as street theater and widow support circles enabled communal grieving and fostered social solidarity (UN.ESCAP, et al., 2009). While these methods have shown promise in reducing isolation and promoting collective recovery, formal evaluation of their long-term impact remains limited.

3.3.4 Psychoeducation

Psychoeducation serves as a foundational component of post-disaster mental health interventions. It involves informing survivors and communities about common psychological responses to trauma, coping mechanisms, and when to seek further help. Delivered through community workshops, printed materials, or digital media, psychoeducation helps normalize emotional reactions, reduce stigma, and empower individuals with practical tools to manage stress and anxiety. It is especially effective when tailored to local cultural and linguistic contexts, and can be implemented by trained community workers, teachers, or peer leaders (Phoenix, 2007).

3.3.5 Community-Based Approaches

Community-based psychosocial support is a widely utilized and sustainable strategy, especially in regions with limited access to clinical care. Programs often involve training local health workers or volunteers to deliver low-intensity psychological services and refer complex cases (Lindal, 2023). In Pakistan, the Basic Needs model integrated mental health care with livelihood and community mobilization following the 2005 earthquake. Primary health workers were trained to detect and manage mental health conditions at the grassroots level (MHIN, 2025). These approaches improve coverage and community ownership but require ongoing supervision and logistical support to ensure quality and consistency.

3.3.6 Indigenous Healing Practices

In many South Asian regions, traditional and religious healing practices remain a core component of mental health care. These may include consultations with religious leaders, faith healers, shamans, and religious rituals and ceremonies (Kar, 2006). In tribal regions of India and Nepal, mental illness is often attributed to spiritual causes like possession or curses. In Sri Lanka, Ayurvedic and Siddha medicine are often used for emotional recovery post-disaster. While these practices are culturally congruent and accessible, they are rarely integrated with formal mental health services and lack the tools needed to treat trauma-related cognitive and behavioral symptoms (Subudhi et al., 2024).

3.4 Critique: Gaps in Delivering Mental Health Support

Despite increased awareness, psychological interventions in disaster settings across South Asia suffer from several persistent challenges.

Scalability remains a major challenge as many operate as donor-funded pilot projects that do not transition into government-supported programs, further constrained by workforce shortages, limited national mental health budgets, and political instability across the region (Isaac, 2024). While the Basic Needs model demonstrated success in Pakistan and Nepal, it failed to expand nationally and diminished once funding ended. Similarly, WHO's mhGAP requires sustained investment and coordination, which many countries struggle to maintain independently (MHIN, 2025).

Programs are often reactive, focusing on immediate relief during the acute disaster phase. PFA and basic counseling are rapidly deployed in the early phases of a disaster but typically withdrawn within months, with little to no follow-up (Masood et al., 2021). For example, many services introduced after the 2015 Nepal earthquake ceased within a year, despite persistent psychological distress in affected communities, leaving survivors without support for long-term conditions like depression, psychosis, or substance use (IASC, 2015).

Cultural misalignment further limits effectiveness. Western-derived models like CBT often fail to resonate with local populations due to differences in beliefs about trauma, healing, and mental illness. In many rural areas, distress is interpreted through spiritual or supernatural frameworks (Sato, 2024). For example, in Sri Lanka, war-affected communities favored traditional rituals and collective healing ceremonies over formal therapy, which was viewed as alien and stigmatizing. Even when cultural adaptation is attempted, it is frequently superficial and limited to language translation (UN.ESCAP, et al., 2009).

4 Unmet Needs for Psychological Support

South Asia is one of the most disaster-prone regions globally, impacting millions. While physical relief is prioritized during emergencies, mental health support remains critically under-addressed.

4.1 Invisibility of Mental Health in Disaster Response

Disaster response frameworks across South Asian nations historically focus on immediate physical survival needs shelter, food security, and healthcare. Mental health, despite being a core component of holistic well-being, is often overlooked during both the relief and recovery phases (Math et al., 2015).

For instance, on December 26, 2004, the Indian Ocean tsunami struck the south-eastern coast of India, especially affecting Tamil Nadu's Nagapattinam and Cuddalore districts. Over 8000 people died in Tamil Nadu alone, tens of thousands lost homes and livelihoods, and massive infrastructure damage devastated fishing communities. In the aftermath, a multisectoral relief effort was mobilized rapidly. The Government of India, international agencies, and numerous local NGOs provided emergency shelter, food rations, water, sanitation facilities, and livelihood restoration programs. However, despite the profound psychosocial trauma, grief from massive family loss, displacement stress, and community disintegration, structured mental health interventions were minimal in the initial phases, it was limited to brief counseling by volunteers and basic psychosocial aid from local NGOs, with little to no coordination or long-term planning When mental health services were eventually introduced, they were fragmented, concentrated in urban areas, and not integrated into long-term recovery strategies (Gupta & Kumar, 2005).

In July 2010, unprecedented floods displaced over 14 million people in Pakistan, destroying 1.6 million homes. The Government of Pakistan, UN agencies, the Red Cross, and NGOs mobilized large-scale aid focused on food, shelter, healthcare, and infrastructure. However, psychosocial support was minimal, leaving many survivors with persistent anxiety, depressive symptoms, and unresolved grief, which impeded full recovery (Kirsch et al., 2012).

This exemplifies a persistent pattern in South Asia: mental health needs are invisible during disaster response, leaving psychological wounds unhealed even as physical reconstruction progresses. This neglect is compounded by cultural stigma; instead, symptoms like anxiety, grief, and trauma are commonly expressed through physical complaints that go unrecognized (WHO, 2017). Even when psychological needs are identified, limited mental health infrastructure, especially in rural and marginalized areas, means that few trained professionals are available to provide appropriate care. Funding constraints further restrict psychosocial support, as donors typically prioritize visible, tangible recovery efforts. Additionally, short-term relief programs rarely plan for sustained mental health care, leaving long-term psychological consequences unaddressed. Poor awareness among policymakers and a lack of mental health training for frontline responders, combined with weak coordination between disaster management and mental health systems, further deepens the gap in comprehensive care (Wainberg et al., 2017).

4.2 Lack of Trained Professionals and Mental Health Infrastructure in Rural and Remote Areas

A major barrier to providing effective psychological support in disaster-affected areas of South Asia is the acute shortage of trained mental health professionals and the limited availability of clinical infrastructure, particularly in rural and high-risk regions. According to the WHO, India had just 0.75 psychiatrists, 0.03 psychologists, and 0.07 social workers per 100,000 people, far below the global median. Similar or worse shortages are seen in Pakistan, Bangladesh, Nepal, and Sri Lanka. These shortages are more critical in rural areas, which are often hardest hit by disasters (Trivedi et al., 2007).

This gap stems from chronic underfunding, with mental health receiving under 1% of national health budgets. As a result, psychiatric training programs and psychology departments remained sparse. Furthermore, most mental health professionals are concentrated in cities. Over 70% of psychiatrists in India practice in urban areas, leaving rural communities with minimal access.

On the infrastructure side, mental health services are poorly integrated into primary care. Rural clinics and district hospitals rarely have dedicated mental health units. NGOs and international agencies often set up temporary psychosocial programs post-disaster, but these are short-lived due to limited donor funding and do not leave behind sustainable infrastructure (WHO, 2023).

This shortage forces survivors to rely on untrained community members, traditional healers, or religious leaders, sources that may be culturally acceptable but are often inadequate to address deep trauma, grief, or mental disorders triggered by disaster experiences. Without trained mental health workers, accurate diagnosis and effective treatment of disorders such as PTSD, depression, or anxiety are severely constrained (Shoib et al., 2021).

4.3 Addressing Diverse Psychotherapeutic Needs of Vulnerable Groups

Disasters disproportionately impact vulnerable groups, who face unique psychological needs that generic interventions often overlook. For instance:

Women are at higher risk of gender-based violence, sexual exploitation, and caregiving burdens after disasters. Supportive spaces such as women-only counseling groups and trauma-focused sessions can help women process abuse, rebuild emotional safety, and reduce long-term depression and anxiety. Addressing these issues is critical because untreated trauma in women often leads to social withdrawal, chronic mental health problems, and poor caregiving capacity, which affects entire families (IFRC, 2016).

Children experience disrupted schooling, separation from caregivers, and emotional distress. Following the 2015 Nepal earthquake, anxiety, nightmares, and behavioral problems surged among children in affected areas (UNICEF, 2015; Kar & Sharma, 2021; Sharma & Kar, 2019). Interventions like play therapy, art activities, and school-based counseling give children safe ways to express feelings and regain routine. These approaches are vital as they help prevent developmental delays, long-term anxiety, and learning difficulties, ensuring a smoother return to daily life (Schwartze et al., 2019).

Older adults face grief, isolation, and neglect, especially when they lose family or support networks. Many elderly people are left without assistance or companionship (Song et al., 2025). Community outreach and home-based counseling can reduce loneliness and depression in older adults, while peer support groups help restore a sense of purpose and connection. Without such interventions, older survivors are at risk of deepening isolation, cognitive decline, and deteriorating physical health (Rahman et al., 2025).

LGBTQ+ (Lesbian, Gay, Bisexual, Transgender, Queer+) individuals often face stigma and exclusion from relief services. During the 2018 Kerala floods, transgender persons reported discrimination in relief camps. Inclusive counseling and sensitization of aid workers can create safe spaces where LGBTQ+ survivors feel respected and supported. This is crucial to prevent retraumatization and isolation, and to promote mental well-being within marginalized groups often neglected in mainstream aid (HPN, 2022).

People with disabilities faced difficulties accessing shelters and essential services. Making psychosocial support accessible through sign language interpreters, mobility aids, and home visits can ensure they are not left behind. Accessible and disability-inclusive mental health services are essential to uphold their rights and ensure equity in post-disaster recovery. Inclusive interventions help prevent social isolation, neglect, and worsening of both mental and physical conditions (Ibn-Farid et al., 2024).

In sum, inclusive, targeted mental health care is essential, not just ethically, but for fair recovery and reintegration.

4.4 Case Vignettes from Disaster-Affected Communities

In South Asia, real stories from disaster-hit communities reveal the serious gaps in psychological support.

4.4.1 Case 01

In Nagapattinam, Tamil Nadu, India, after the 2004 Indian Ocean tsunami, a 35-year-old woman lost her husband and two children when waves destroyed her coastal village. While she quickly received food, shelter, and cash aid, no grief counseling or mental health support was provided in her area. Over time, she showed clear signs of depression—withdrawal, insomnia, and physical complaints but local services like the District Mental Health Program were rarely active in rural zones. Fear of stigma and lack of outreach left her isolated. Her emotional distress severely hampered her ability to work, rebuild her home, or reconnect socially. Her case illustrates how the absence of long-term, community-based mental health support deepens emotional suffering and obstructs functional recovery (Kumar, 2024).

4.4.2 Case 02

In Sindhupalchok, Nepal, after the 2015 earthquake, a 13-year-old boy lost close family members and his home. Aid agencies provided food, tents, and short-term child-friendly spaces for play and informal support. However, these spaces closed after a few months due to funding cuts. He began suffering from nightmares, fearfulness, and social withdrawal symptoms of post-traumatic stress but there was no local counseling available, and specialized care was hours away in Kathmandu. Within a year, he had dropped out of school and avoided social contact. His story highlights the urgent need for sustained, child-centered psychological care integrated within schools and communities to prevent long-term emotional and educational harm, but is often missing (Gautam et al., 2017).

Both examples demonstrate a clear lack of long-term, culturally appropriate psychological support essential for recovery.

5 Barriers to Access and Sustainability in Disaster Mental Health Care in South Asia

The provision of adequate mental health and psychosocial support in disaster situations, particularly in South Asia, is notably challenging due to intensified systemic weaknesses that exacerbate pre-existing barriers to access and sustainability. South Asia, represented by nations like Bangladesh, Nepal, Pakistan, Sri Lanka, and India, shares the interplay of constrained financial resources, lack of trained professionals, and pervasive stigma, which pose significant obstacles to achieving equitable and effective mental health outcomes in this region (Rowe & Nadkarni, 2023). The high rates of food insecurity (Azimi & Rahman, 2024), as well as displacement, ongoing violence, and unemployment (Audi et al., 2023), all negatively impact mental health (Debbarma et al., 2021). Furthermore, the frequent occurrence of natural disasters like earthquakes, cyclones, and floods puts these systems under continual stress (Heanoy & Brown, 2024). There are notable differences in disaster preparedness and response capabilities within the region. Kar et al. (2021) highlight the development of mental health integration in disaster relief within India's broader health policy, noting ongoing deficiencies in service delivery and a lack of coherence in responses to past disasters, such as the 1999 Odisha Cyclone and the 2004 Asian Tsunami. However, significant disparities may exist in the accessibility of psychiatric care between urban and rural regions, even within countries.

5.1 *Logistic and Financial Barriers*

In several South Asian nations, such as Nepal, Bangladesh, Pakistan, and India, access to and the sustainability of disaster mental health care are hampered by significant logistical and financial obstacles (Fatema et al., 2021). The 2015 earthquake in Nepal revealed critical deficiencies in mental health funding and infrastructure, with less than 1% of the national budget allocated to mental health services (Paudel et al., 2025; Shrestha et al., 2024). Bangladesh, susceptible to cyclones and flooding, struggles with resource scarcity, resulting in an emphasis on emergency response that prioritizes physical survival over psychological care (Khandoker et al., 2024). The ability of Pakistan to continuously ensure the necessary number of highly qualified mental health specialists are available at all times is hampered by the displacement and natural disasters that afflict people in Khyber Pakhtunkhwa and Balochistan (Shah et al., 2022).

Deteriorating infrastructure, overburdened health services, and a lack of coordination between disaster response and mental health initiatives are some of the major logistical obstacles facing India's National Mental Health Program's execution (Kar, 2025). Since Assam and Jammu and Kashmir are unreachable rural areas, providing psychosocial help during emergencies is difficult. Examples from certain countries show how efforts to address mental health concerns are hampered by logistical inefficiencies and financial constraints. National disaster management authorities in South Asia need to improve mental health services, make targeted investments in disaster-resilient infrastructure, and better integrate their policies to overcome these obstacles (Samad et al., 2025).

5.2 *Language and Cultural Discrepancies in Adopted Approaches*

Effective disaster mental health responses are severely hampered in South Asia by the lack of mental health guidelines, issues with the translation and implementation of written materials, and shortcomings at the policy and programmatic levels

(Samad et al., 2025). The distinctive values and beliefs that are common in South Asian communities are not taken into consideration by the many psychological interventions developed for disaster response that have their roots in the West. The social and spiritual perspectives prioritize the public needs of collectivistic societies, which are challenging for modern therapies that focus on an individual's particular problems to adapt (Port, 2024). Aside from that, the majority of these interventions are offered in English or other foreign languages, which makes them unintelligible to most individuals, particularly in rural areas and disaster areas (Wu & Chentsova-Dutton, 2025).

The perceived condescension from Western entities exacerbates the potential adaptation of these models. Since faith healers understand the urgent need for assistance within the theological or spiritual frameworks of their specific traditions and religions, people affected by disasters may seek their services rather than public health facilities (Ayub et al., 2024). Mental health support is often underutilized when there are no culturally relevant therapies or local language resources available.

5.3 *Inadequate Integration of Mental Health in Disaster Readiness*

At the policy level, there is a glaring absence of integration of mental health within the national framework for disaster planning and response (Kabir et al., 2024). Such as Bangladesh and Nepal's emergency planning or response teams in disaster management organizations rarely include mental health professionals (Sharma et al., 2024; Rahman et al., 2025). India and Pakistan possess mental health policies; however, there is often a lack of a clearly defined implementation strategy in times of disaster (Suar et al., 2024; Noorullah et al., 2024). This results in fragmented or inconsistent service delivery. Mental health is often overlooked in disaster risk reduction budgets, resulting in insufficient resources for long-term psychological recovery efforts (Cvetković, 2024).

5.4 *Lack of Follow-Up Services and Care Discontinuity*

Post-disaster Mental health care in South Asia is predominantly restricted to short interventions. Government and NGO-sponsored initiatives provide support in the initial post-disaster phases (Kar, 2006). Despite support, victims of cyclone Fani continued to suffer from anxiety, hopelessness, and PTSD (Kar et al., 2021); and the suffering of Asian tsunami survivors continued for years (Kar et al., 2014). There are hardly any structured follow-up arrangements for survivors with mental health problems in South Asian countries following natural disasters, human-made, or industrial disasters. However, the follow-up support is needed and feasible to organize (Kar, 2024a). Survivors are more susceptible to experiencing mental health issues if they lack adequate therapy following a disaster. The approach to mental health in developed nations markedly differs, emphasizing organized rehabilitation, peer support, continuous care, and universal access to primary healthcare services (Brooks et al., 2024).

6 Potential Actions: Enhancing Contextualized, Scalable, and Sustainable Interventions

Addressing these challenges involves deploying scalable, contextually pertinent solutions that efficiently utilize local resources. These resources encompass local expertise, indigenous knowledge, and community-based entities. Strategies must be formulated to meet the requirements and cultural contexts of the population, while promoting sustainable growth and community empowerment, by utilizing the pooled experience of regional knowledge networks and existing local institutions (Kangana et al., 2024).

6.1 Importance of Culturally Sensitive and Community-Based Interventions

In terms of the communities that were served by the interventions themselves, the treatments must be culturally relevant. Kar et al. (2014) suggest that community routines, religious values, and local customs should be taken into consideration for interventions to be successful. Interventions that involved community leaders and the use of contextual language discussing suffering, as was done in Odisha, were found to have more effective results than traditional psychotherapy.

It may be possible to increase the acceptance and effectiveness of intervention by using community members to foster peer support, storytelling, and participatory caretaking rituals for grief and recovery (Hommel & Kaimal, 2024). Traditional healers and spiritual leaders, who are often the only ones in charge, should not be forgotten but rather acknowledged as allies (Jayawickrama & Madhanagopal, 2025).

6.2 Disaster Preparedness and National Health Systems: Integrating Mental Health

Policies on national and regional disaster preparedness should give mental health top priority. It consists of creating psychological first aid procedures, making referrals, and ensuring that responders have past training. Kar (2024a) and Murthy et al.

(2025) contend that including mental health in disaster readiness drills and emergency plans is vital. Delivery of health should give mental health top priority. Pilot studies in South Asia show that including mental health components into main care models increases continuity and coverage for a greater population (Reist et al., 2022; Gurung et al., 2023).

6.3 Capacity Building: Engaging Community Health Workers, Educators, and Volunteers

Task-shifting approaches, such as training non-specialists to provide essential mental health support, can effectively mitigate the paucity of mental health practitioners. This approach to mental health care may be less costly than others because it uses volunteers, educators, and community health workers (Bolton et al., 2023). Following the catastrophic earthquake in Odisha, India, the region developed instructional resources for Anganwadi workers and ASHA (Accredited Social Health Activist) volunteers to aid in the identification, evaluation, and referral of traumatized persons (Suar et al., 2024).

Teacher-led school-based initiatives have been demonstrated to be particularly successful in aiding children and adolescents (Dodd et al., 2022). This population is especially vulnerable to mental health issues such as anxiety, PTSD, and suicidality (Kar, 2024b). Early educational support interventions must be implemented in schools in light of these vulnerabilities. These initiatives can markedly improve students' mental well-being, facilitating prompt intervention and assistance in familiar settings.

6.4 Remote Interventions with Technology and Mobile Health

Mobile health projects enable one to avoid problems resulting from restricted resources and distance. Self-help apps, telepsychiatry services, and SMS check-in systems are some digital solutions that can enable fast delivery of essential support during catastrophes and disasters (Batra & Erbas, 2025). Even among members of underprivileged groups, the general acceptance of mobile phones in South Asia emphasizes the possibilities of digital technologies in providing healthcare where physical infrastructure is scarce.

Kar (2024b) claims that digital interventions can significantly affect the way healthcare services are given. Designing these solutions calls for both digital literacy and cultural sensitivity to pay close attention. Lack of digital literacy might prevent many people in underprivileged areas from accessing essential healthcare treatments. Effective substitutes for more traditional means of conveying important healthcare information are local language and community radio-based projects, therefore enabling underprivileged individuals (Aldosari et al., 2023).

6.5 Local and International Stakeholders' Collaboration

Cooperation among several stakeholders guarantees that the preferences and viewpoints of the impacted populations will be very important in determining the approaches and activities applied during humanitarian operations (Corbett et al., 2022). For funders and NGOs, collaborating with the local community to create and carry out their strategies is a far more successful method than enforcing outside-produced plans that might not fit local requirements and resources (Maddock et al., 2021). Lack of cooperation during the 2004 tsunami crisis led to organizational issues that confused people and squandered resources. It showed that all the differences in humanitarian efforts would come from a more orderly approach (Suar et al., 2024).

This kind of coordination helps to ensure a more effective use of resources and the planning process. Involvement of those who went through the disaster, as well as the local community, guarantees projects are sensitive to the particular needs and culture of those impacted (Ngulube et al., 2024). Likewise, inspiring creative ideas and problem-solving calls for appreciating original ideas as well as supporting fresh styles of thinking. A plan is needed that welcomes other points of view, acknowledges the special insights of nearby communities, and lets them provide their expertise to the process (Jiao, 2025).

7 Future Directions and Policy Recommendations

7.1 Psychological Outcome Longitudinal Research

South Asian disaster survivors' long-term psychological well-being is still poorly understood due to a lack of longitudinal data on the subject. Few comprehensive studies have examined long-term effects spanning months or years, with much current research concentrating on acute stress reactions and rapid trauma that follow a disaster. Kar (2024b) emphasized the importance of longitudinal research and argued that they are necessary to develop effective policies and treatments. Through cohort analysis and multi-year follow-up studies, stakeholders can better understand how mental health changes over time in the wake of catastrophes, allowing them to tailor support networks and resources to the needs of impacted communities (Kohrt et al., 2025).

7.2 Embedding Mental Health in School-Based and Primary Care Systems

Regular mental health monitoring and care should be part of school and primary care center routines to protect the well-being of children and community members (Maddock et al., 2021). Throughout the academic year, the school consistently monitors and detects mental health difficulties in its students (Willmot et al., 2023). School counselors are uniquely qualified to respond first as health workers during student-related situations. Because of their specialization, they can recognize and manage all forms of mental health emergencies. Providing ongoing training and updates on new advances in mental health and intervention ensures that school counselors can provide excellent care to their children (Wines, 2023). It is critical to offer counselors a variety of training opportunities and resources to ensure they are prepared to address the requirements of their respective communities.

7.3 Developing Culturally Adapted Intervention Manuals and Toolkits

Customized manuals with an understanding of the languages, cultures, and economic situations of certain groups of people are the best way to help and get involved (Samad et al., 2025). These resources make sure that all the issues experts might have covered and all the answers given are complete. That way, more people in the community will be interested in the project because the rules will include useful ways to work together and share information.

In order to improve attempts to build communities, we need a set of rules that are specifically designed to meet the needs of each community. Each community's unique situation greatly affects the resources' possible benefits, which is why you should think about them. It is possible to help and guide people in the community by focusing on these parts. This will encourage them to be more dedicated and take part in activities that help them.

7.4 Program Design and Evaluation Using Survivor Voices

Programs should begin engaging survivors in ways that will empower them, rather than just being involved. This can be done by actively involving the community through focus groups, advisory boards with diverse perspectives, and narrative initiatives that honor individual experiences. By implementing these tactics, services can better align with the community's genuine needs, ensuring that survivors' viewpoints are not only heard but also have a significant influence on the development of new initiatives (Miller et al., 2021). The dignity of participants is upheld, and a sense of respect and ownership is cultivated. Ultimately, these strategies enhance program effectiveness and community involvement, leading to enduring, positive transformation.

8 Conclusion

As a vulnerable region, recovery teams in South Asia should closely attend to the psychological aspects and commit long-term to reflecting that reality. Although mental health is often neglected during disasters, grief and anguish can cause more stress than the physical damage. It is essential to change our approach to find sustainable and culturally appropriate actions instead of merely responding. Disaster relief must include long-term mental health treatments. Mental health services should be integrated into emergency plans, improved within regular health programs, and tailored to local languages and cultures. Generic methods from high-income nations are inappropriate for South Asian mental health therapy due to stigma, longstanding beliefs, and social inequalities.

Helping disaster victims emotionally requires legislation that prioritizes mental health, coordinated government care, and community involvement. Experts should consult communities and survivors throughout the preparation and implementation of interventions. Mental health professionals need to collaborate with communities, religious groups, and local organizations to ensure mental health support is accepted, accessible, and effective. Without this strategy, disaster victims may not receive psychiatric help, leaving them vulnerable to further decline. Integrating comprehensive, connected, and community-focused mental health care can help South Asia recover and prepare for future disasters.

References

Aldosari, N., Ahmed, S., McDermott, J., & Stanmore, E. (2023). The use of digital health by south asian communities: Scoping review. *Journal of Medical Internet Research, 25*, e40425. https://doi.org/10.2196/40425

Asian Disaster Preparedness Center. (2016, January 27). *Conference report: Bridging the gaps in mental health and psychosocial support in emergencies in Asia [Conference proceedings]*. Department of Public Health in Emergencies, Asian Disaster Preparedness Center. https://www.adpc.net/igo/category/ID1007/doc/2016-jNe5HU-ADPC-MHPSS_Report_I.pdf

Audi, M., Poulin, M., & Ali, A. (2023). Determinants of human wellbeing and its prospect under the role of financial inclusion in South Asian countries. *Journal of Applied Economic Sciences, 18*(4), 96–311. https://doi.org/0.5717jaes.V18.4(82)04

Ayub, B., Syed, A. A., & Zulfiqar, H. (2024). The pursuit of health through faith healing: An anthropological analysis of personalistic belief system. *Annals of Human and Social Sciences, 5*(2), 703–710.

Azımi, M. N., & Rahman, M. M. (2024). Food insecurity, environment, institutional quality, and health outcomes: evidence from South Asia. *Globalization and Health, 20*(1), 21. https://doi.org/10.1186/s12992-024-01022-2

Babu, G. R., Khetrapal, S., John, D. A., Deepa, R., & Narayan, K. M. V. (2021). Pandemic preparedness and response to COVID-19 in South Asian countries. *International Journal of Infectious Diseases, 104*, 169–174. https://doi.org/10.1016/j.ijid.2020.12.048

Batra, M., & Erbas, B. (2025). Extreme weather, vulnerable populations, and mental health: The timely role of AI interventions. *International Journal of Environmental Research and Public Health, 22*(4), 602. https://doi.org/10.3390/ijerph22040602

Becker, S. M. (2009). Psychosocial care for women survivors of the tsunami disaster in India. *American Journal of Public Health, 99*(4), 654–658. https://doi.org/10.2105/AJPH.2008.146571

Bolton, P., West, J., Whitney, C., Jordans, M. J. D., Bass, J., Thornicroft, G., Murray, L., Snider, L., Eaton, J., Collins, P. Y., Ventevogel, P., Smith, S., Stein, D. J., Petersen, I., Silove, D., Ugo, V., Mahoney, J., el Chammay, R., Contreras, C., … Raviola, G. (2023). Expanding mental health services in low- and middle-income countries: A task-shifting framework for delivery of comprehensive, collaborative, and community-based care. *Cambridge Prisms: Global Mental Health, 10*, e16. doi:https://doi.org/10.1017/gmh.2023.5.

Brooks, S. K., Rogers, M. B., Wessely, S., Patel, S. S., & Greenberg, N. (2024). Psychosocial impacts of post-disaster compensation processes: narrative systematic review. *BMC Psychology, 12*(1), 539. https://doi.org/10.1186/s40359-024-02025-9

Chung, M. C., Jalal, S., & Khan, N. U. (2014). Posttraumatic stress disorder and psychiatric comorbidity following the 2010 flood in Pakistan: Exposure characteristics, cognitive distortions, and emotional suppression. *Psychiatry: Interpersonal and Biological Processes, 77*(3), 289–304. https://doi.org/10.1521/psyc.2014.77.3.289

Contractor, A. A., Rafiuddin, H. S., Kaur, K., & Asnaani, A. (2023). Asian Indians in the United States and posttraumatic stress disorder interventions: A narrative literature review. *Trauma, Violence, & Abuse, 24*(4), 2395–2411. https://doi.org/10.1177/15248380221097435

Corbett, C. J., Pedraza-Martinez, A. J., & Van Wassenhove, L. N. (2022). Sustainable humanitarian operations: An integrated perspective. *Production and Operations Management, 31*(12), 4393–4406. https://doi.org/10.1111/poms.13848

Cvetković, V. M. (2024). *Disaster risk management.* Scientific-Professional Society for Disaster Risk Management.

de Arellano, M. A. R., Lyman, D. R., Jobe-Shields, L., George, P., Dougherty, R. H., Daniels, A. S., Ghose, S. S., Huang, L., & Delphin-Rittmon, M. E. (2014). Trauma-focused cognitive-behavioral therapy for children and adolescents: Assessing the evidence. *Psychiatric Services, 65*(5), 591–602. https://doi.org/10.1176/appi.ps.201300255

Debbarma, R., Majumdar, C. B., & Bhattacharjee, A. (2021). Internally displaced persons and mental health issues: A review analysis. *Indian Journal of Health and Wellbeing, 12*(2), 171–176.

Dhital, R., Shibanuma, A., Miyaguchi, M., Kiriya, J., & Jimba, M. (2019). Effect of psychosocial support by teachers on improving mental health and hope of adolescents in an earthquake-affected district in Nepal: A cluster randomized controlled trial. *PLoS One, 14*(10), e0223046. https://doi.org/10.1371/journal.pone.0223046

Dodd, S., Widnall, E., Russell, A. E., Curtin, E. L., Simmonds, R., Limmer, M., & Kidger, J. (2022). School-based peer education interventions to improve health: a global systematic review of effectiveness. *BMC Public Health, 22*(1), 2247. https://doi.org/10.1186/s12889-022-14688-3

Dossaji, A., Dickens, K. N., Leachman, K., & Deal, L. (2025). Yoga as a trauma-informed approach to working with clients. *COUNS-EDU. The International Journal of Counseling and Education, 10*(1), 1–11.

Dutta, M. (2021). Links between disaster and human trafficking. In *Disaster and human trafficking* (pp. 33–62). Springer. https://doi.org/10.1007/978-981-16-1630-3_2

Farooqui, M., Quadri, S. A., Suriya, S. S., Khan, M. A., Ovais, M., Sohail, Z., Shoaib, S., Tohid, H., & Hassan, M. (2017). Posttraumatic stress disorder: a serious post-earthquake complication. *Trends in Psychiatry and Psychotherapy, 39*(2), 135–143. https://doi.org/10.1590/2237-6089-2016-0029

Fatema, S. R., East, L., Islam, M. S., & Usher, K. (2021). Health impact and risk factors affecting South and Southeast Asian women following natural disasters: A systematic review. *International Journal of Environmental Research and Public Health, 18*(21), 11068. https://doi.org/10.3390/ijerph182111068

Gautam, K., Upadhyaya, S., Pant, S. B., Dhungana, S., Tulachan, P., Chapagai, M., & Ojha, S. P. (2017). Acute stress disorder in a ten year old child following a major earthquake. *Journal of Kathmandu Medical College, 5*(3), 98–100. https://doi.org/10.3126/jkmc.v5i3.18423

Gómez-Carrillo, A., Lencucha, R., Faregh, N., Veissière, S., & Kirmayer, L. J. (2020). Engaging culture and context in mhGAP implementation: fostering reflexive deliberation in practice. *BMJ Global Health, 5*(9), e002689. https://doi.org/10.1136/bmjgh-2020-002689

Gupta, V. K., & Kumar, A. (2005). Community-based disaster management: A case study from Tamil Nadu. In *Proceedings of the 42nd Indian Society of Earthquake Technology (ISET) Symposium.*

Gurung, D., Kohrt, B. A., Wahid, S. S., Bhattarai, K., Acharya, B., Askri, F., Ayele, B., Bakolis, I., Cherian, A., Daniel, M., Gautam, K., Girma, E., Gronholm, P. C., Hanlon, C., Kallakuri, S., Ketema, B., Lempp, H., Li, J., Loganathan, S., … Thornicroft, G. (2023). Adapting and piloting a social contact-based intervention to reduce mental health stigma among primary care providers: Protocol for a multi-site feasibility study. *SSM – Mental Health, 4*, 100253. doi:https://doi.org/10.1016/j.ssmmh.2023.100253.

Heanoy, E. Z., & Brown, N. R. (2024). Impact of natural disasters on mental health: Evidence and implications. *Healthcare, 12*(18), 1812. https://doi.org/10.3390/healthcare12181812

Hermosilla, S., Forthal, S., Sadowska, K., Magill, E. B., Watson, P., & Pike, K. M. (2023). We need to build the evidence: A systematic review of psychological first aid on mental health and well-being. *Journal of Traumatic Stress, 36*(1), 5–16. https://doi.org/10.1002/jts.22888

Hommel, S., & Kaimal, G. (2024). *Arts-based approaches to promote mental health and well-being: supporting children and families in conditions of adversity*. Routledge.

Hossain, M. M., Tasnim, S., Sultana, A., Faizah, F., Mazumder, H., Zou, L., McKyer, E. L. J., Ahmed, H. U., & Ma, P. (2020). Epidemiology of mental health problems in COVID-19: a review. *F1000Research, 9*, 636. https://doi.org/10.12688/f1000research.24457.1

HPN. (2022). *Making disaster risk reduction and relief programmes LGBTI-inclusive: examples from Nepal | Humanitarian Practice Network.*

Husain, N., Lovell, K., Chew-Graham, C. A., Lunat, F., Bee, P., Pierce, M., Atif, N., Aseem, S., Bhui, K., Bower, P., Brugha, T., Chaudhry, N., Ullah, A., Davies, L., Gire, N., Sharma, D., Miah, J., Ahmed, W., Kai, J., … Morriss, R. (2025). A group psychological intervention for postnatal depression in British mothers of South Asian origin – the ROSHNI-2 RCT. *Health Technology Assessment, 29*, 1–113. https://doi.org/10.3310/KKDS6622.

IASC. (2015). *Nepal earthquakes 2015: Desk review of existing information with relevance to mental health and psychosocial support*. Inter-Agency Standing Committe.

Ibn-Farid, Z., Islam, A. M., Roberts, P. S., & Glick, J. (2024). Disability inclusive disaster risk reduction (DiDRR) in South Asia: Status, prospects, and challenges. In L. M. Phipps & D. A. McEntire (Eds.), *Current and emerging trends in the management of international disasters*. Pressbooks; Mavs Open Press.

IFRC. (2016). *Unseen, unheard: Gender-based violence in disasters – Asia-Pacific case studies.* International Federation of Red Cross and Red Crescent Societies

IRCS. (2025). *Our programs and activities, Indian Red Cross Society.*

Isaac, M. (2024). Mental health services in South Asia: Past, present, and future. *South Asian Journal of Psychiatry, 2*, 1–8.

Islam, M. R. (2023). Introduction: Disaster, displacement and resilient livelihoods in South Asia. In *Disaster, displacement and resilient livelihoods: Perspectives from South Asia* (pp. 1–15). Emerald Publishing Limited. https://doi.org/10.1108/978-1-80455-448-720231001

Jang, S., Ekyalongo, Y., & Kim, H. (2021). Systematic review of displacement and health impact from natural disasters in Southeast Asia. *Disaster Medicine and Public Health Preparedness, 15*(1), 105–114. https://doi.org/10.1017/dmp.2019.125

Jayawickrama, J., & Madhanagopal, D. (2025). *Reintroducing nature into health and wellbeing*. Springer Nature Singapore. https://doi.org/10.1007/978-981-96-3090-5

Jiao, Y. (2025). Abstracts. *Psychological Reports, 128*(1_suppl), 12–227. https://doi.org/10.1177/00332941251315223

Jordans, M. J. D., Kohrt, B. A., Sangraula, M., Turner, E. L., Wang, X., Shrestha, P., Ghimire, R., Van't Hof E, Bryant, R. A., Dawson, K. S., Marahatta, K., Luitel, N. P., & van Ommeren, M. (2021). Effectiveness of Group Problem Management Plus, a brief psychological intervention for adults affected by humanitarian disasters in Nepal: A cluster randomized controlled trial. *PLoS Medicine, 18*(6), e1003621. https://doi.org/10.1371/journal.pmed.1003621

Kabir, R., Isigi, S. S., & Candussi, C. (2024). Public mental health and access to mental health services in South Asia. In *Access to mental health care in South Asia* (pp. 229–243). Springer Nature Singapore. https://doi.org/10.1007/978-981-99-9153-2_11

Kafle, S. K. (2017). Disaster risk management systems in South Asia: Natural hazards, vulnerability, disaster risk and legislative and institutional frameworks. *Journal of Geography & Natural Disasters, 7*(3). https://doi.org/10.4172/2167-0587.1000207

Kangana, N., Kankanamge, N., De Silva, C., Goonetilleke, A., Mahamood, R., & Ranasinghe, D. (2024). Bridging community engagement and technological innovation for creating smart and resilient cities: A systematic literature review. *Smart Cities, 7*(6), 3823–3852. https://doi.org/10.3390/smartcities7060147

Kar, N. (2006). Psychosocial issues following a natural disaster in a developing country: A qualitative longitudinal observational study. *International Journal of Disaster Medicine, 4*, 169–176.

Kar, N. (2024a). Anatomy of a catastrophe: Managing psychosocial consequence of the 2023 Odisha train accident. *Industrial Psychiatry Journal, 33*(2), 219–225. https://doi.org/10.4103/ipj.ipj_278_24

Kar, N. (2024b). Research, innovations, and ideas to facilitate mental healthcare delivery in South Asia. In *Access to Mental Health Care in South Asia* (pp. 197–227). Springer Nature Singapore. https://doi.org/10.1007/978-981-99-9153-2_10

Kar, N. (2025). Disaster mental health in India: A long journey ahead. In R. S. Murthy & N. Gupta (Eds.), *Leadership in Indian psychiatry: Converting thoughts into practice 1947–2025* (pp. 187–196). Swaroop Creative Agency.

Kar, N., & Sharma, A. (2021). Matching the symptom profile of adolescent disaster survivors with changing diagnostic criteria of posttraumatic stress disorder: Focus on ICD-11. *Indian Journal of Psychological Medicine, 43*(2), 100–105. https://doi.org/10.1177/0253717620926848

Kar, N., Krishnaraaj, R., & Rameshraj, K. (2014). Long-term mental health outcomes following the 2004 Asian tsunami disaster. *Disaster Health, 2*(1), 35–45. https://doi.org/10.4161/dish.24705

Kar, N., Samantaray, N., Kar, S., & Kar, B. (2021). Anxiety, depression, and post-traumatic stress a month after 2019 Cyclone Fani in Odisha, India. *Disaster Medicine and Public Health Preparedness, 16*, 670. https://doi.org/10.1017/dmp.2020.368

Khan, N. T. (2022). Cognitive behavioral therapy in Bangladesh. In *Cognitive behavioral therapy in a global context* (pp. 63–84). Springer International Publishing. https://doi.org/10.1007/978-3-030-82555-3_5

Khandoker, F., Uddin, J., Fariha, T., & Shumi, S. S. (2024). Importance of psychological well-being after disasters in Bangladesh: A narrative review. *International Journal of Scientific Research in Multidisciplinary Studies, 10*(10), 1–6.

Kip, A., Valencia, S., Glunz, E., Lowe, S. R., Tam, K.-P., & Morina, N. (2024). Prevalence of mental disorders in adult populations from the Global South following exposure to natural hazards: a meta-analysis. *Epidemiology and Psychiatric Sciences, 33*, e68. https://doi.org/10.1017/S2045796024000672

Kirsch, T. D., Wadhwani, C., Sauer, L., Doocy, S., & Catlett, C. (2012). Impact of the 2010 Pakistan floods on rural and urban populations at six months. *PLoS Currents*. https://doi.org/10.1371/4fdfb212d2432

Kohrt, B. A., Pedersen, G. A., Schafer, A., Carswell, K., Rupp, F., Jordans, M. J. D., West, E., Akellot, J., Collins, P. Y., Contreras, C., Galea, J. T., Gebrekristos, F., Mathai, M., Metz, K., Morina, N., Mwenge, M. M., Steen, F., Willhoite, A., van Ommeren, M., ... Yurtaev, A. (2025). Competency-based training and supervision: development of the WHO-UNICEF Ensuring Quality in Psychosocial and Mental Health Care (EQUIP) initiative. *The Lancet Psychiatry, 12*(1), 67–80. doi:https://doi.org/10.1016/S2215-0366(24)00183-4.

Kubwalo, K. N. (2021). *Rohingya refugee camps: Safe Spaces give women a fresh start in life*. UNICEF South Asia.

Kumar, M. (2024). *AP photos: The scars of a 9.1 earthquake and tsunami continue to haunt Indians for decades*. Associated Press.

Lindal, L. (2023). *Community-based mental health and psychosocial support: Volunteer manual*. International Federation of Red Cross and Red Crescent Societies, Reference Centre for Psychosocial Support. https://pscentre.org/wp-content/uploads/2023/03/Community-based-Mental-Health-and-Psychosocial-Support-Volunteer-Manual-.pdf

Lowe, S. R., Kwok, R. K., Payne, J., Engel, L. S., Galea, S., & Sandler, D. P. (2016). Why does disaster recovery work influence mental health?: Pathways through physical health and household income. *American Journal of Community Psychology, 58*(3–4), 354–364. https://doi.org/10.1002/ajcp.12091

Maddock, A., Blair, C., Ean, N., & Best, P. (2021). Psychological and social interventions for mental health issues and disorders in Southeast Asia: a systematic review. *International Journal of Mental Health Systems, 15*(1), 56. https://doi.org/10.1186/s13033-021-00482-y

Manzoor, Z., Ehsan, M., Khan, M. B., Manzoor, A., Akhter, M. M., Sohail, M. T., Hussain, A., Shafi, A., Abu-Alam, T., & Abioui, M. (2022). Floods and flood management and its socio-economic impact on Pakistan: A review of the empirical literature. *Frontiers in Environmental Science, 10*. https://doi.org/10.3389/fenvs.2022.1021862

Masood, Z., Moise, I. K., Spika, V., & Ramaprasad, J. (2021). Health interventions implemented in post-disaster South Asia: A scoping review. *International Journal of Disaster Risk Reduction, 63*, 102419. https://doi.org/10.1016/j.ijdrr.2021.102419

Math, S. B., Nirmala, M. C., Moirangthem, S., & Kumar, N. C. (2015). Disaster management: Mental health perspective. *Indian Journal of Psychological Medicine, 37*(3), 261–271. https://doi.org/10.4103/0253-7176.162915

MHIN. (2025). *Basic needs Pakistan*. https://www.mhinnovation.net/organisations/basicneeds-pakistan

Miller, A. B., Issa, O. M., Hahn, E., Agalab, N. Y., & Abdi, S. M. (2021). Developing advisory boards within community-based participatory approaches to improve mental health among refugee communities. *Progress in Community Health Partnerships: Research, Education, and Action, 15*(1), 107–116. https://doi.org/10.1353/cpr.2021.0010

Mitchell, S. M., & Pizzi, E. (2021). Natural disasters, forced migration, and conflict: The importance of government policy responses. *International Studies Review, 23*(3), 580–604. https://doi.org/10.1093/isr/viaa058

Müller, L., Rapoport, O., & Rahe, M. (2024). Mindfulness meditation improves mental health in flood survivors and disaster volunteers: A randomized wait-list controlled trial. *Mindfulness, 15*(11), 2750–2764. https://doi.org/10.1007/s12671-024-02467-7

Murthy, D., Kurz, S. E., Anand, T., Hornick, S., Lakuduva, N., & Sun, J. (2025). Examining hurricane–related social media topics longitudinally and at scale: A transformer-based approach. *PLoS One, 20*(1), e0316852. https://doi.org/10.1371/journal.pone.0316852

Naeem, F., Latif, M., Mukhtar, F., Kim, Y., Li, W., Butt, M. G., Kumar, N., & Ng, R. (2021). Transcultural adaptation of cognitive behavioral therapy (CBT) in Asia. *Asia-Pacific Psychiatry, 13*(1). https://doi.org/10.1111/appy.12442

Nahar, N., Blomstedt, Y., Wu, B., Kandarina, I., Trisnantoro, L., & Kinsman, J. (2014). Increasing the provision of mental health care for vulnerable, disaster-affected people in Bangladesh. *BMC Public Health, 14*, 708. https://doi.org/10.1186/1471-2458-14-708. PMID: 25011931; PMCID: PMC4099388.

Ngulube, N. K., Tatano, H., & Samaddar, S. (2024). Toward participatory participation: A community perspective on effective engagement in post-disaster recovery and reconstruction. *Community Development, 55*(6), 895–915. https://doi.org/10.1080/15575330.2024.2382169

Noorullah, A., Asad, N., Pirani, S., Iqbal, S., & Khan, M. M. (2024). Mental health care in Pakistan. In *Access to mental health care in South Asia* (pp. 113–135). Springer Nature Singapore. https://doi.org/10.1007/978-981-99-9153-2_7

Paudel, S., Chalise, A., Khatri, D., Poudel, S., & Khanal, A. (2025). Nepal's mental health system from public health perspective: a thematic synthesis based on health system building blocks. *The Lancet Regional Health – Southeast Asia, 36*, 100588. https://doi.org/10.1016/j.lansea.2025.100588

Penninx, B. W. J. H., Benros, M. E., Klein, R. S., & Vinkers, C. H. (2022). How COVID-19 shaped mental health: from infection to pandemic effects. *Nature Medicine, 28*(10), 2027–2037. https://doi.org/10.1038/s41591-022-02028-2

Phoenix, B. (2007). Psychoeducation for survivors of trauma. *Perspectives in Psychiatric Care, 43*, 123–131. https://doi.org/10.1111/j.1744-6163.2007.00121.x

Port, C. (2024). *Integrating the unconventional: Expanding the frames and practices of western psychotherapy*. Pacifica Graduate Institute.

Priyadarshini, A., & Sigroha, S. (2025). *Narratives for young readers on West Asia: War, trauma and resilience* (1st ed.). Routledge.

Rahman, M. M., Nasrin, J. A., Shobuj, I. A., Uddin, A., Mahmud, A., & Hossain, M. T. (2025). Cyclone-disaster preparedness in fishing community: A study on Shah Porir Dwip, Bangladesh. *International Journal of Disaster Risk Reduction, 116*, 105100. https://doi.org/10.1016/j.ijdrr.2024.105100

Ramachandran, A. K., Panneer, S., Rice, L., Rathnayake, U., & Kantamaneni, K. (2025). Addressing tropical cyclone risks: stratified for wellbeing and global policy coordination. *Natural Hazards, 121*(6), 6441–6466. https://doi.org/10.1007/s11069-024-07097-9

Ranasinha, R. (2025). *Exploring the impact of trauma-informed dramatherapy training on mental health practitioners in Myanmar: Perspectives on integration, effectiveness, and cultural adaptation*. https://doi.org/10.2139/ssrn.5139107.

Rasul, G., Nepal, A. K., Hussain, A., Maharjan, A., Joshi, S., Lama, A., Gurung, P., Ahmad, F., Mishra, A., & Sharma, E. (2021). Socio-economic implications of COVID-19 pandemic in South Asia: Emerging risks and growing challenges. *Frontiers in Sociology, 6*. https://doi.org/10.3389/fsoc.2021.629693

Reist, C., Petiwala, I., Latimer, J., Raffaelli, S. B., Chiang, M., Eisenberg, D., & Campbell, S. (2022). Collaborative mental health care: A narrative review. *Medicine, 101*(52), e32554. https://doi.org/10.1097/MD.0000000000032554

Rezwana, N., & Pain, R. (2021). Gender-based violence before, during, and after cyclones: slow violence and layered disasters. *Disasters, 45*(4), 741–761. https://doi.org/10.1111/disa.12441

Rowe, O., & Nadkarni, A. (2023). Barriers and facilitators to the implementation of mental health and psychosocial support programmes following natural disasters in developing countries: A systematic review. *Cambridge Prisms: Global Mental Health, 11*, e5. https://doi.org/10.1017/gmh.2023.91

Samad, M. A., Arifin, K., & Abas, A. (2025). A systematic literature review on the challenges of Southeast Asian countries in natural disaster management. *Cogent Social Sciences, 11*(1). https://doi.org/10.1080/23311886.2024.2435590

Sato, S. (2024). *Mental health stigmatization and access to care in South Asia: A study of India, Nepal, and Sri Lanka*. https://doi.org/10.22541/au.173016086.64721134/v1

Schwartze, D., Barkowski, S., Strauss, B., Knaevelsrud, C., & Rosendahl, J. (2019). Efficacy of group psychotherapy for posttraumatic stress disorder: Systematic review and meta-analysis of randomized controlled trials. *Psychotherapy Research, 29*(4), 415–431. https://doi.org/10.1080/10503307.2017.1405168

Shah, I., Mahmood, T., Khan, S. A., Elahi, N., Shahnawaz, M., Dogar, A. A., Subhan, F., & Begum, K. (2022). Inter-agency collaboration and disaster management: A case study of the 2005 earthquake disaster in Pakistan. *Jàmbá Journal of Disaster Risk Studies, 14*(1). https://doi.org/10.4102/jamba.v14i1.1088

Sharma, A., & Kar, N. (2019). Posttraumatic stress, depression, and coping following the 2015 Nepal Earthquake: A study on adolescents. *Disaster Medicine and Public Health Preparedness, 13*(2), 236–242. https://doi.org/10.1017/dmp.2018.37

Sharma, P., Gautam, K., & Marahatta, K. (2024). Access to mental health care in Nepal: Current status, potential challenges, and ways out. In *Access to mental health care in South Asia* (pp. 91–111). Springer Nature Singapore. https://doi.org/10.1007/978-981-99-9153-2_6

Shoib, S., Gupta, A. K., Ahmad, W., Joseph, S. J., & Bhandari, S. S. (2021). Mental health professionals as 'silent frontline healthcare workers': Perspectives from three South Asian

countries. *Open Journal of Psychiatry & Allied Sciences, 12*(2), 144–147. https://doi.org/10.5958/2394-2061.2021.00019.7
Shrestha, P., Limbu, A., Tiwari, K., & Chase, L. E. (2024). What matters for sustainable psychosocial interventions and who decides? Critical ethnography of a lay counselling program in Nepal. *SSM – Mental Health, 6*, 100359. https://doi.org/10.1016/j.ssmmh.2024.100359
Sim, T., & Wang, A. (2021). Contextualization of psychological first aid: An integrative literature review. *Journal of Nursing Scholarship, 53*(2), 189–197. https://doi.org/10.1111/jnu.12613
Song, C., Atun, F., Blanford, J. I., & Anthonj, C. (2025). Impact of flooding on the social and mental health of older adults- A scoping review. *Water Security*, 100190. https://doi.org/10.1016/j.wasec.2025.100190
Suar, D., Kar, N., & Panigrahi, G. S. (2024). Natural hazards, trauma, and its amelioration: Lessons learned from India. *International Journal of Disaster Risk Reduction, 108*, 104548. https://doi.org/10.1016/j.ijdrr.2024.104548
Subudhi, C., Paul, F. A., Moharana, K. C., & Saikia, P. (2024). Mental illness and health-seeking behavior: a systematic review of traditional healing practices in India. *Journal of Spirituality in Mental Health*, 1–16. https://doi.org/10.1080/19349637.2024.2434551
Swain, S. P., Behura, S. S., Banerjee, S., et al. (2025). A qualitative mixed-method narrative study on psychotherapeutic support needs based on a series of 11 cases of survivors of the 2023 Odisha Train Accident. *Cureus, 17*(3), e81161. https://doi.org/10.7759/cureus.81161
Titz, A. (2021). Geographies of doing nothing–internal displacement and practices of post-disaster recovery in urban areas of the Kathmandu Valley, Nepal. *Social Sciences, 10*(3), 110. https://doi.org/10.3390/socsci10030110
Trivedi, J. K., Goel, D., Kallivayalil, R. A., Isaac, M., Shrestha, D. M., & Gambheera, H. C. (2007). Regional cooperation in South Asia in the field of mental health. *World Psychiatry, 6*(1), 57–59.
UN.ESCAP, et al. (2009) *ICT for disaster risk reduction.* Retrieved from: https://hdl.handle.net/20.500.12870/5357
Unicef. (2015). *Nepal earthquakes: Looming crisis for children's emotional health.* United Nations International Children's Emergency Fund
Wainberg, M. L., Scorza, P., Shultz, J. M., Helpman, L., Mootz, J. J., Johnson, K. A., Neria, Y., Bradford, J.-M. E., Oquendo, M. A., & Arbuckle, M. R. (2017). Challenges and opportunities in global mental health: A research-to-practice perspective. *Current Psychiatry Reports, 19*(5), 28. https://doi.org/10.1007/s11920-017-0780-z
WHO. (2017). *Mental health is a critical component in disaster response and recovery | Regional Office for Africa.* https://www.afro.who.int/news/mental-health-critical-component-disaster-response-and-recovery
WHO. (2023). *Focus on expanding mental health services in the South-East Asia Region.* https://www.who.int/southeastasia/news/detail/22-06-2023-focus-on-expanding-mental-health-services-in-the-who-south-east-asia-region
Willmot, R. A., Sharp, R. A., Amir Kassim, A., & Parkinson, J. A. (2023). A scoping review of community-based mental health intervention for children and adolescents in South Asia. *Cambridge Prisms: Global Mental Health, 10*, e1. https://doi.org/10.1017/gmh.2022.49
Winders, W. T., Bustamante, N. D., Garbern, S. C., Bills, C., Coker, A., Trehan, I., Osei-Ampofo, M., & Levine, A. C. (2021). Establishing the effectiveness of interventions provided to first responders to prevent and/or treat mental health effects of response to a disaster: a systematic review. *Disaster Medicine and Public Health Preparedness, 15*(1), 115–126. https://doi.org/10.1017/dmp.2019.140
Wines, L. A. (2023). Student development and performance in academics, intrapersonal, and dispositions for school counselors-in-training to address mental health needs. In *Administrative leaders and school counselors* (pp. 85–120). Routledge. https://doi.org/10.4324/9781003219750-9
Wu, J., & Chentsova-Dutton, Y. (2025). Mind focus in western white cultures, behavior focus in East Asian cultures: An integrative review. https://doi.org/10.31234/osf.io/gs2q4_v1

Index

N. Kar et al. (eds.), *Climate Change, Disaster and Mental Health in South Asia*, South Asian Perspectives in Mental Health and Psychology,
https://doi.org/10.1007/978-981-95-3690-0

MIX
Papier aus verantwortungsvollen Quellen
Paper from responsible sources
FSC® C105338

If you have any concerns about our products,
you can contact us on
ProductSafety@springernature.com

In case Publisher is established outside the EU,
the EU authorized representative is:
Springer Nature Customer Service Center GmbH
Europaplatz 3, 69115 Heidelberg, Germany

Printed by Libri Plureos GmbH
in Hamburg, Germany